THE LIFE AND TIMES OF A
COLD WAR
SERVICEMAN

August 1928-30 November 1969

MAURICE F. MERCURE

Order this book online at www.trafford.com
or email orders@trafford.com

Most Trafford titles are also available at major online book retailers.

Printed in the United States of America.

ISBN: 978-1-4669-5386-4 (sc)
ISBN: 978-1-4669-5387-1 (e)

Library of Congress Control Number: 2012915509

Trafford rev. 11/14/2012

 www.trafford.com

North America & international
toll-free: 1 888 232 4444 (USA & Canada)
phone: 250 383 6864 ♦ fax: 812 355 4082

CONTENTS

INTRODUCTION

This book may be dry in parts, but it is exactly how a serviceman's life unfolds.

It may seem strange to some people, that your day to day existence (Daily Life) is dictated by pieces of paper. It is not like a civilian's that does not have a rigid routine, with military precision. In one sense, it gives you a feeling of security, knowing what is laid out for you. On the other hand, it gives you the feeling that someone else is pulling the strings for you to act.

As you retain copies of all these orders (paperwork) for your personal files, you have a running (chronological) history of your life. It covers all aspects—the good, the bad, and the ugly.

It may be hard for a civilian, non-military person, who has not had any exposure to military life, to understand all the paperwork in this book. While reading this book, take a moment to see how different a serviceman's life is compared to a civilian's.

As you will see, so many abbreviations are used in military written communications. This is necessary to cut down on the amount of paperwork and time consumed daily in the production of military orders. It is important to point out that extracts are used to shorten the size of paperwork issued to an individual.

I would like to summarize by saying discipline and control are very necessary to being a good serviceman. These methods are necessary for the military to perform its day to day mission, operations and its very existence, for its people must be able to react to any given situation without hesitation. If this were not so, the battle would be lost and lives wasted. This is why so many military people find it so hard to adjust to civilian life when they are discharged and/or retire from the military. It takes time to adjust to life without strict controls. It is why so many retirees seek jobs that require control, discipline, and continuity of daily life—such as policemen, firemen, teachers (in private and military schools), or they join the active reserves and National Guard Units, become bosses and CEO's, etc.

DEDICATION

This book is primarily dedicated to my wife, Margaret (Peggy), who definitely was the one behind the man and made him to be the best he could be; and to Frederick Banks (Peggy's father), who told me years ago that I should write a book about all the things that happened to us.

It is also dedicated to all the Cold War servicemen who lost their lives, and to their wives, their children and their parents.

THANK YOU

I wish to express my thanks, gratitude and total appreciation for the work done by Jane Bogatiuk; for an exceptional job of putting up with me; for her editing, correction of spelling, grammar, etc. Without her, this book would still be in its development stage.

Also, I would like to express my thanks to Jennifer Monaghan for her contributions to the "Incidents and Crises" section of this book.

AWARDS

A. Medals Awarded to the Author:

1. Bronze Star Medal
2. Army Good Conduct Medal
3. USAF Good Conduct Medal
4. World War II Victory Medal
5. National Defense Medal
6. US Vietnam Service Medal
7. Cold War Service Medal

B. Ribbons Awarded to the Author:

1. Bronze Star Ribbon
2. Army Good Conduct Ribbon, with four (4) bronze knots
3. USAF Good Conduct Ribbon, with two (2) silver knots
4. World War II Victory Ribbon
5. National Defense Ribbon
6. US Vietnam Service Ribbon
7. Air Force Longevity Service Ribbon
8. Air Force NCO Professional Education Service Ribbon
9. Air Force Small Arms Expert Ribbon
10. Cold War Service Ribbon

C. Foreign Awards:

1. Defense of Taiwan Medallion, presented by President Generalissimo Chiang Kai-shek.

INCIDENTS AND CRISES

During the Period
5 October 1946 through 30 November 1969

The following incidents and crises occurred during my term of service, from 5 October 1946 through 30 November 1969. Listed below are incidents and crises by date (approximate in some cases), and years (approximate years).

1946   <u>9 February 1946:</u> Stalin's Hostile Speech. He stated that the Communist world was not compatible with capitalism. Unofficial/official start of the Cold War.

   <u>5 March 1946:</u> Winston Churchill's Speech, "Sinews of Peace." An Iron Curtain has descended (fallen) on Eastern Europe, separating it from Western Europe.

   <u>10 March 1946:</u> Harry Truman's Speech. He demanded the Soviet Union withdraw from (leave) Iran.

   <u>1 July 1946:</u> Operation Crossroads A-Bomb Test. Public demonstration of an atomic bomb in America's arsenal.

   <u>25 July 1946:</u> America's Test Bravo, underwater explosion of an A-Bomb.

   <u>12 October 1946:</u> Austrian Food Crisis. New crisis in food feared by Austria.

1947   <u>12 March 1947:</u> President Truman establishes Truman Doctrine. Truman declared active role in Greek Civil War. Stated that U.S. would provide aid to countries whose governments are threatened with Communist take over.

1948   <u>25 February 1948:</u> Communist take over in Czechoslovakia.

<u>2 March 1948:</u> President Truman's Loyalty Program. Created to catch Cold War spies.

<u>14 March 1948:</u> Brussels Pact organized to protect Western Europe from communism.

<u>23 March 1948:</u> Austrian Pact talks snarled. The proposed Austrian Treaty members stating they were back to where they started. The whole premise, revolving around the Soviet Union economical demands on Austria.

<u>May 1948:</u> Israel declares its independence after being held down by the United Kingdom (British) and Arab assaults on it.

<u>14 May 1948:</u> Arab/Israeli War. Israel was victorious over the Arabs.

<u>29 June 1948:</u> Soviet Union seals off land routes to Berlin lasting eleven months.

<u>8 July 1948:</u> Berlin Crisis. Berlin blockade begins. West responds with massive airlift of provisions to the city.

1949   <u>1949:</u> Communist forces gain power in China. Nationalists forced to flee to Formosa (Taiwan).

<u>1949:</u> Soviet Union lifts Berlin blockade. Berlin airlift ends.

<u>29 August 1949:</u> The Soviet Union tests its first A-Bomb—thanks to Communist spies, Julius & Ethel Rosenberg.

<u>29 August 1949:</u> Soviet Union reported moving tanks up to the Yugoslavian border. No indication why this move was made.

<u>1949</u>: Communist Mao Zedong takes control of mainland China. Establishes the People's Republic of China.

<u>1 October 1949</u>: General Chang Kai Shek flees mainland China to Taiwan (Formosa) where he forms new Nationalist Government.

1950   <u>1950</u>: Austria's report card on new treaty during Hungarian Crisis. It is an enormous job for anyone.

<u>1950</u>: Communist forces occupy Tibet and form new government, forcing the Dalai Lama to flee.

<u>June 1950</u>: Polish workers revolt in Poznan, Poland. Rebellion put down by Soviet Army.

<u>25 June 1950</u>: Korean War begins. Stalin approved North Korean invasion of South Korea. North Korean Army equipped with Soviet weapons. U.S. and U.N. reply with military action. War lasted from 25 June 1950 through 27 July 1953.
　　During this war, the Chinese Army crossed the Yalu River in support of the North Koreans, who had been driven back across the 38th parallel to the Yalu River. Chinese forces drove the U.N. forces back across the 38th parallel.

1951   <u>1951</u>: North Korean offensive continues along with the Chinese to the 38th parallel. Truce negotiations fail.

<u>November 1951</u>: British (UK) and French forces invade the Suez Canal Zone to protect it. Egypt eventually takes control of the Suez Canal.

1952   <u>1952</u>: A-Bomb developed by Britain (UK) joining the U.S. and Soviet Union in the nuclear club.

<u>5 October 1952</u>: Crisis over the budget and food solved by Austrian cabinet resigning and reforming. This caused quite a stir in Western Alliance.

1953   <u>July 1953:</u> Korean Armistice signed. Korean War ends. No peace treaty signed.

<u>19 October 1953:</u> Trieste Crisis. Italy and Yugoslavia invited to a five-powered conference aimed at solving the explosive crisis over Trieste. The Big Three asked the Soviet Union to a no-strings-attached conference.

1954   <u>1954:</u> CIA intervenes in Guatemala and Iran helping to overthrow the government (unfriendly to the U.S.). It also helped to secure the government in Iran.

<u>1954:</u> Soviet Union rejects proposal to reunite Germany, so Berlin and East Germany continue to be separated from West Germany.

<u>July 1954:</u> Vietnam split at the 17th parallel resulting in North & South Vietnam; the Communist controlling North Vietnam.

1954-
1955   <u>1954-1955:</u> Taiwan Straits Crisis. U.S. and Republic of China (ROC—Taiwan) joined forces. Peoples Republic of China (PRC) was shelling Quemoy and Matso Islands every other day.

1955   <u>1955:</u> Warsaw Pact formed as a counter measure to NATO.

<u>1955:</u> World War II Allies signed treaty restoring Austria's independence. Austria was no longer a divided nation.

<u>15 May 1955:</u> Whereas Austria's negotiations with the former occupying powers, resolved in the treaty of 15 May 1955, peaceful coexistence of iron curtain. This is something that rarely happens.

1956   <u>1956:</u> Israel invades Sinai Peninsula.

<u>1956:</u> Fidel Castro begins revolution in Cuba which will result in Cuba becoming a Communist country.

29 June 1956: USSR sends tanks and troops into Poznan, Poland. The revolt will continue to smolder.

29 October 1956: Suez Canal Crisis begins with Israel's invasion of the Sinai Peninsula.

14 December 1956: President Eisenhower vows utmost aid during refugee crisis, managing refugees with food, clothing, housing and relocation as much as possible.

1957   1957: Egypt seizes Suez Canal. Britain (UK) and France respond with force. U.S. and Soviet Union negotiated cease fire.

1957: Israel withdraws from the Sinai Peninsula, thereby reducing tension in the Middle East.

1957: President Eisenhower announces "Eisenhower Doctrine," planning defense of Middle East against Communists.

15 January 1957: Politicians fear refugee crisis as there are 70,000 Hungarian refugees backed up in Austrian camps.

1958   1958: U.S. Marines intervene in Lebanon to bolster the legal government to prevent its overthrow. The Marines were to suffer severe casualties later on.

11 July 1958-15 October 1958: Lebanese Civil War. This caused a bit of concern in the Middle East.

November 1958: Khrushchev demands withdrawal of troops from Berlin, which was denied by the Big Three.

1959   January 1959: Cuba taken over by Fidel Castro. Tension begins to mount between Cuba and the U.S. The U.S. is waiting to see which way Cuba will turn.

1960 <u>1960:</u> U.S. relationship with Cuba deteriorates as Castro begins seizing U.S. assets. U.S. suspects Castro will enter the Soviet sphere.

<u>1960:</u> Cuba openly aligns itself with the Soviet Union and policies.

<u>May 19, 1960:</u> U-2 Incident. The Soviet Union Shoots down an American U-2 reconnaissance airplane over Soviet airspace. They capture the pilot, Francis Gary Powers, forcing the U.S. to admit to aerial spying. Powers, tells the Soviet everything.

1961 <u>13 August 1961:</u> Berlin border closed. U.S. expects the Soviet Union and East Germany (DDR) will take other action.

<u>April 1961:</u> Cuban exiles fail to invade Cuba and liberate it (Bay of Pigs). President Kennedy accepts responsibility. The British (UK) felt we should have denied responsibility.

<u>17 August 1961:</u> Soviets and East Germany build (erect) a wall around West Berlin dividing East and West Berlin.

1962 <u>1962:</u> The U. S. Establishes semi-permanent presence in Vietnam. The overall force would increase to 500,000.

<u>1962:</u> Erection of wall led to the Soviet Union ending blockade to Berlin. The wall did not stop East Berliners from attempting to cross into West Berlin.

<u>October 1962:</u> Cuban Missile Crisis. Soviet Missile buildup in Cuba revealed by satellite cameras in October 1962. President Kennedy requested their removal to no avail. He then ordered a naval blockade (calling it a "quarantine") of shipments of offensive military equipment to the island. Khrushchev agreed on October 29, 1962 to removal of Soviet missiles and equipment and end the crisis. Kennedy announced that missiles based in Cuba were being dismantled.

We also agreed to remove our missiles on the border of Turkey and the Soviet Union. This crisis was the closest to nuclear war between the U.S. and the Soviet Union.

1963   <u>20 November 1963:</u> John F. Kennedy was shot and fatally wounded in Dallas, Texas. Question at that time was, "Who shot the President?" This could develop into an international crisis. Vice-President Johnson assumed the office of President. The accused assassin, Lee Harvey Oswald, was shot and killed a short time later by Jack Ruby.

1964   <u>1964:</u> Investigating the Kennedy assassination, the Warren Commission determined that Oswald acted on his own in the killing of the President.

<u>1964:</u> Soviet leader Khrushchev falls from power and is ultimately replaced by Leonid Brezhnev.

<u>1964:</u> Turkey invades Cyprus. Greek army is no match for the Turkish forces. Turks took control of one-third (1/3) of the island. This action undermined NATO, as Turkey and Greece are part of the Alliance.

<u>1964:</u> U.S. military forces launch air attack on North Vietnam in response to alleged attack on a U.S. destroyer off the Vietnamese coast. Congress had passed the "Gulf of Tonkin" Resolution, which gave the President greater freedom to authorize combat action in Vietnam.

<u>August 1964:</u> Gulf of Tonkin Incident.

<u>18 December 1964:</u> Panama suspends relationship with the U.S. after riots. U.S. offered to renegotiate a new Panama Canal Treaty.

1965   <u>1965:</u> Fighting between Viet Cong, U.S. and South Vietnam. Presidents Kennedy, Johnson, and Nixon involved in support of South Vietnam.

April 1965: U.S. Marines sent to the Dominican Republic to fight Communist. These troops helped keep U.S. friendly government in control of the country.

July 1965: U.S. announces that it is dispatching 200,000 more troops to Vietnam; that this was needed to combat increased North Vietnamese and Viet Cong troop strength in South Vietnam.

1966 1966: U.S. B-52s bomb North Vietnam in support of the war in South Vietnam.

1967 1967: The U.S. Secretary of Defense, Robert McNamara, admits U.S. bombing strikes on North Vietnam failed to accomplish its mission.

1968 August 1968: Soviet Red Army crushes Czechoslovakian Revolt. Apparently the people of Czechoslovakia are unhappy with Communist control.

1968: North Korea captures USS Pueblo and its crew of 82.

December 1968: North Korea releases USS Pueblo and its crews of 82 men. This was after they examined all the secret material on board the ship. It is also likely the crew had destroyed some classified material before being boarded.

Civilians do not realize the stress, strain and turmoil that service members and their families go through during every incident and crisis. Because of the various teams service members are on, they are always awaiting team activation and being placed on alert. If the service member's wife and family accompany them overseas, it places a great stress, worry, and concern on them, wondering if and when the service member will have to leave home without warning and prior notification. In my case, my wife (as we had no children) always accompanied me overseas (except to Vietnam). While assigned to the strategic Air Command (SAC), I was always on an alert team, awaiting notification and moving out during an incident or crisis. As you can see by my book, I was mostly assigned to SAC while overseas. The rest of my overseas time was with Military Assistance Advisory Group (MAAG) and the Air Force

Communications Service (AFCS) while in the Air Force. During my time in the Army, I was assigned to the Signal Corps. We were always ready to move out at a moment's notice.

The mere fact that I was a cryptographer most of my service career (that is 19 out of 23 years) and NCOIC of all the crypto centers I worked in (all but 3 out of 12), it fell upon me, NCOIC, to decipher all incoming messages addressed to "For Eyes Only of the Commander." This put me in an unique position as the only person authorized to decipher this type of communication. So it fell upon me to notify the Commander (or his duly authorized representative in his absence). I was the first one to know of pending incidents or crises, having the responsibility to notify the Commander by personal contact, who in turn had me contact every one of the Control (Action) Team. Because of the requirement that only the NCOIC decipher "For Eyes Only of the Commander" messages, I had to keep the shift Supervisor of Communications advised of my whereabouts at all times. This put an additional strain (stress) on my wife and me, not knowing when I would be called upon to perform this duty. So it was nice when I retired from the military, not having to be subjected to recall to the Crypto Center and having to perform this duty.

In my absence from work, or leave, sick, or unaccountable, my assistant or designated person will take over my duties.

FOREWORD

I guess that I have always wanted to be a serviceman, since I was a little boy. This can be attributed to my being exposed to movies on the French Foreign Legion and the British Army in action, at the age of five (5) on. Such wonderful films as Beau Geste, Gunga Din, Four Feathers, the Lives of a Bengal Lancer, Charge of the Light Brigade, etc.

I wanted to see all the exotic places around the world. Well, I got my wish when I enlisted in the Armed Forces of the United States.

I was stationed in or visited the following countries: Austria, Azores, Belgium, Canada, France, Germany, Greece, Iceland, India, Iran, Ireland, Italy, Japan (Okinawa), Lebanon, Libya, Luxemburg, Morocco, Netherlands, Philippines, Portugal, Spain, Taiwan, Thailand, Turkey, United Kingdom and Vietnam.

It was also my pleasure to have visited the following major cities: Adana, Amsterdam, Ankara, Athens, Ayers, Bangkok, Beirut, Bilbao, Bonn, Bordeaux, Brussels, Cadiz, Casablanca, Dover, Dublin, Frankfurt (on Main), Gander, Innsbruck, Istanbul, Izmir, Kadena, Keflavik, Leghorn, Lisbon, London, Luxemburg City, Madrid, Marseille, Naples, New Delhi, Ostend, Oxford, Paris, Prestwick, Reykjavik, Saigon, Seville, Taiwan, Taipei, Teheran, and Tripoli, just to name a few.

My journeys also took me through thirty-five (35) of the fifty (50) states: Alabama, Arizona, California, Colorado, Connecticut, Delaware, Florida, Georgia, Hawaii, Illinois, Indiana, Kansas, Kentucky, Louisiana, Maine, Maryland, Massachusetts, Mississippi, Missouri, Nevada, New Hampshire, New Jersey, New Mexico, New York, North Carolina, Ohio, Oklahoma, Pennsylvania, Rhode Island, South Carolina, Tennessee, Texas, Vermont, Virginia, West Virginia, and also the District of Columbia (D.C.).

In my travels I also got to visit Newfoundland, Canada. It was like living a dream come true at times in all these places. Not everyone gets to live their boyhood dreams.

No one can contemplate what it is like to see and visit all these wonderful places. It was a delightful experience living amongst the people of a country that I was stationed in. You realize that it is so much more rewarding than just visiting a place for a short time. You get to experience the people, country, and their way of life. To sum it all up, it is something I shall never forget and will always remember and treasure all of my life.

It is important to point out that servicemen and their families are exposed to the following diseases while serving overseas: bubonic plague, chicken pox, dengue fever (breaking bone fever), diphtheria, hepatitis, influenza, malaria, measles, mumps, pulmonary plague, scarlet fever, small pox, various viruses and yellow fever.

During my career in the military, I had the honor and privilege to serve under the following listed officers:

Col. J. E. Glynn, USA

Lt. Col. John L. Fisher, USAF

Lt. Col. Frank G. Hinkle, USAF

Lt. Col. Dale N. Hoagland, USA

Lt. Col. Frederick H. Huebner, USA

Lt. Col. John B. Kelley, USAF

Lt. Col. Walter S. Reed, USAF

Lt. Col. Charles A. Wintermeyer, USAF

Maj. Nelson D. Courneyer, USAF

Maj. Leroy L. Saunders, USA

Maj. Robert D. Schicker, USA

Maj. Robert L. Schumacker, USAF

Maj. Robert Spiers, Jr. USAF

Capt. Robert O. Ball, Jr. USAF

Capt. Frederick M. Clement, USAF

Capt. Eugene C. McLaughlin, USAF

Capt. Joe S. Webb, USAF

1 Lt. Mark J. Chitwood, USA

1 Lt. George K. Loud, USAF

1 Lt. Richard D. Stevens, USAF

1 Lt. Bernard V. Vollrath, USA

CW3 Harry J. Markley, USA

Of these Officers, the following were outstanding, exceptional and extremely considerate:

Col. J. E. Glynn, USA

Lt. Col. John L. Fisher, USAF

Lt. Col. Dale Hoagland, USA

Lt. Col. John B. Kelly, USAF

Lt. Col. Charles A. Wintermeyer, USAF

However, of all these officers, Lt. Col. Hoagland was the best, outstanding and most considerate. His wife was the most friendly, kindest and amicable person I met in the service.

CHAPTER 1

AUGUST 1928 - 4 OCTOBER 1946
EARLY YEARS BEFORE SERVICE LIFE

<u>August 1928</u>: I was born at home, on Morris Street, Chicopee, Massachusetts, to August and Alice Fraichard. They had me baptized in Saint Anne's Roman Catholic Church, Chicopee, Massachusetts. My brother, Roger, was born in August 1929. The poor soul was born clubfooted. My mother used to take him, twice a week, to the Shriner's Hospital for Children, Springfield, Massachusetts, for treatment.

My brother Bob said that I was a cute baby with blonde curly hair, blue eyes, and very long eyelashes. Everyone just wanted to pick me up and make a fuss over me. This annoyed him to no end.

<u>May 1930</u>: We moved from Morris Street, to High Street, Holyoke, MA when I was one year and nine months old. On September 1, 1930, my brother Roger died. He was only one year and sixteen days old. My poor mother was heartbroken.

<u>November 1930</u>: My family moved from High Street, to Plymouth Place, Holyoke, MA. I guess that my mother wanted to get away from the house that reminded her of Roger. At that time I was only two years and three months old.

<u>April 1931</u>: When I was two years and eight months old, we moved from Plymouth Place to Hampden Street, Holyoke, MA. I do not know why we did.

<u>December 1931</u>: We moved from Hampden Street to Franklin Street, Holyoke, MA when I was three years and four months old.

At that time I had a tricycle, which I used to ride everywhere I could. If I could get out the gate, (when it was left unlocked), I would go onto the street. I would take off, only to be stopped by the beat cop, who used to bring me back home.

<u>March 1932</u>: I was three years and seven months old, when we moved from Franklin Street to Lyman Street, Holyoke, MA.

<u>May 1932</u>: We moved from Lyman Street to Maple Street, Holyoke, MA; at that time I was three years and nine months old.

<u>September 1932</u>: We moved from Maple Street to Westfield Road, Holyoke, MA; at the time I was four years and one month old. I used to play cowboys and Indians with my friends. Of course, I was always one of the Indians, and went barefooted. While dancing around the campfire one day, I stepped on a rusty nail. My mother immediately called the doctor, who came to the house to treat me. The wound was pretty bad; he had to put a drain in it and gave me a tetanus shot. He hurt me while putting in the drain, so I called him a "son-of-a-bitch." He laughed at me, thinking it was cute and funny, and gave me a dime. I don't know where I picked up that expression, but my mother was not pleased with me and washed my mouth out with soap and water.

When I was about five years old, I started a fire in one of the clothes closets in the house, destroying most of the clothes kept in it. The next day I asked my mother for a nickel, to buy a toy (lead) soldier. She told me that she needed all her nickels to buy and replace the clothes I had destroyed with the fire. I told her that if she did not give me a nickel, I would start another fire. Needless to say, this resulted in an immediate spanking from her. When my father came home from work that evening, she told him what I had said. He then proceeded to give me a spanking. I was becoming a very obnoxious and aggressive child. After this incident, when I did something wrong, I would receive a spanking from my father, using a razor strap (in use at the time to sharpen old-fashioned straight razors). The strap had been cut into nine strips (resulting in a cat-o-nine tails). Because of the fact that I was so stubborn, and had a very high pain threshold, I would just laugh at my father when he beat me. I would not give into him and/or cry. My mother told me that I was crazy because the more I laughed, the more he hit me. After beating me, he would send me to bed without my supper. My mother, who felt sorry for me, used to smuggle food in to me. She had to be careful because if he caught her, he would hit her too. My father finally figured out how to get to me, and make be behave. He gave root beer, cookies, and candy to my siblings, and nothing to me. I would cry and give in to him for some goodies too.

May 1933: I was four years and nine months old when we moved from Westfield Road to 403 Maple Street, Holyoke, MA. I am sure it was because of the fire I set in the closet. We did not have a lot of money that year to spend on Christmas presents (toys). I was pleasantly surprised when I received a large red metal fire truck from a girlfriend of my mother. It had rubber wheels, a steering wheel (that actually turned the front wheels), rubber hoses (that you could pump water through), wooden ladders, etc. We called my mother's friend "Aunt Bea." They had worked together in Skinner Silk Mills as young girls and had become very close friends before my mother got married. It was the nicest Christmas present that I received as a child. In fact it was the only Christmas present that I received that year.

July 24, 1933: My mother had twin girls on July 24, 1933—Elaine and Janice. It was the answer to her dreams, as she wanted a girl in the worst way. Elaine died the day after she was born. Janice lived for about ten months, dying on May 5, 1934. My mother was heartbroken. She wanted to bury Janice in the Roman Catholic cemetery, but was told by the parish priest, a Monsignor, that the child (as he put it) could not be buried in consecrated ground, as she had not been baptized. However, if she had three hundred dollars ($300.00), he could get a special dispensation from Rome for the child to be buried in consecrated ground. Because of the times and circumstances, my mother could not afford and/or raise that kind of money to give to the church. So Janice was buried somewhere else that did not require that the child be baptized. My mother was very disillusioned by the whole affair and left the church for good.

My mother had a pet dog (Pomeranian). She loved this dog who used to get up on her side of the bed. My father stated, "I hate the dog and his getting on the bed."

He further stated that he would do something about it if he found the dog on the bed again. Sure enough, when he came home from work, he found the dog on the bed. The next day he took the dog to Mountain Park (Amusement Center), where he was head gardener, and shot the dog. My mother never forgave him for this senseless act of cruelty.

One day while my mother was out shopping, my brother Gaston (who was six years older than I) was supposed to be looking after me (baby sitting). He did not do his job; instead, he was playing with his friends on the back porch. Since he was not paying any attention to me, I had managed to get into the kitchen pantry looking for root beer. I started sampling from all the bottles I could get my little hands on. Apparently I had sampled from a jug of cider, wine bottles, etc., and became drunk. When my mother came home, she found me sitting on the floor, with a bottle of wine between my legs, drunk as a skunk. She got very excited as to what to do, and she called to her next door neighbor, who told my mother not to let me fall asleep, as I would never wake up. She said my mother should walk me up and down the kitchen floor until I got sick and vomited. So my mother proceeded to walk me up and down the kitchen floor until I was ill and regurgitated. My brother Gaston really caught hell for his lack of supervision in seeing that I did not get into anything. He definitely received some type of punishment.

September 1934: We moved from 403 Maple Street to Newton Street, Holyoke, MA. At that time I was six years and one month old. I started going to school at the H. B. Lawrence Elementary School; it was a brand new building and an excellent school.

One day I came across a hobo. We got talking to each other, and he said that he had not eaten for a couple of days. So I took him home, asked my mother if she could help him, and she fed the poor man. This made me feel good, very happy, and pleased with myself.

While living on Newton Street, my mother used to take me to the movies, at least twice a week. We used to go to the Globe Theatre, most of the time. I guess that is why I am such a movie buff (fanatic) today. She never left me home alone—always had a grown up to look after me or took me with her.

When we were living on Newton Street, a fire broke out in the apartment block next door to us (not of my doing). It was a four-alarm fire. It took the fire department a long time to put it out. The whole family sat on the back porch and watched them fight the blaze. It is one of the few times I can remember my birth father and the whole family being together.

December 1936: My mother had enough of my father's cruelty to her and the family, so she left him, taking all the children with her. We moved from Newton Street (without my father) to 27 Bancroft Street, Springfield, MA. It seems my mother had been advised by a lawyer friend that she should leave my father one chair, one table, one bed, one dresser, one fork, one spoon, one knife, etc., when she left him. She did as he instructed her to do so that my father had something to sustain himself with.

April 1937: We moved from 27 Bancroft Street to Holyoke Street, Springfield, MA where I went to the Jefferson Street Elementary School. This was a tough school, in a bad neighborhood. The people there were not friendly at all. I did not like it there.

My father died in 1937. My mother made us all go to the funeral, since he was our father. What happened to my father was that he got drunk, fell down a flight of stairs and broke a rib, which punctured a lung. He passed out causing him to bleed to death before anyone found him. This happened when I was nine years old. My brother Gaston was so afraid to go to the funeral because he thought my father would get out of his coffin and beat him. I was not afraid nor scared of him, nor afraid to go to the funeral.

My mother remarried a divorcee, Elzear A. Mercure, in 1937, and they merged the two families together. There were five in my family and four in my stepfather's family, making a grand total of nine people in all.

I wanted a sailor suit so badly that I told my parents I would hang myself if I did not get one. They laughed at me and did not believe I would carry out my threat, so they said no. So I went into my bedroom, shut the door, stood on a chair, put a belt around my neck and hung it on a door hook. All someone had to do was open the door, knocking me off the chair and I would have been hung. My mother wondered why I was so quiet and what I was up to, so she sent one of my brothers out on the porch to look into my bedroom window to see what I was doing. He looked in the open window and saw what I was doing. He climbed through the open window and got me down from the door hook and chair. He removed the belt from around my neck, thus avoiding a terrible tragedy. My stepfather was so touched by my actions, that he bought me a sailor suit. He felt that if I was so determined about it and was so obsessed about getting a sailor suit, I should have it. My mother was not pleased with my actions and did not agree with my stepfather.

June 1937: The new combined family moved from Holyoke Street to Hartford Road, in Wilson, Connecticut, where I went to Wilson Elementary School. This was a typical country school house; it was quite nice. We lived in an old-fashioned farm house.

My brother Bob (Robert, four years older than I) ruptured his appendix while moving things into the house. My mother thought it was her fault for letting him carry things too heavy for him; he almost died, resulting in my mother babying him when he was better. She bought him a new bicycle so he could get about easier. This bike eventually passed from brother to brother over the years, finally ending up in my possession.

October 1937: The gipsy family (I dubbed the family this because we moved so much) moved from Hartford Road to Garden Street, Hartford, CT, where I attended Vine Street Elementary School. I really liked this school as everyone was so nice and friendly. I remember taking part in a school play where I played the part of a Mexican; I quite enjoyed it.

December 1937: We moved from Garden Street to Stockweather Street, Manchester, CT, where I attended Holister Elementary Street School. It was a nice school with friendly people. We lived in the same building as my grandmother.

While attending Holister Street Elementary School, my rich cousin, Richard Schaller, kept riding me day after day, calling me poor boy, saying that my clothes were terrible and my family was poor. This went on for weeks on end, until I could not take any more and I lost my cool. I exploded and proceeded to beat the stuffing out of him and tore his clothes. It took three teachers to pull me off of him, as I was enjoying it. All the kids in the school yard kept egging me on. Of course, I was in trouble with the principal, my grandmother, and my aunt Louise. I was called a little animal by them. Needless to say, he never bothered me again.

My half-sister Lorraine was born while we were living on Stockweather Street, in Manchester, CT. She was born on George Washington's birthday (February 22).

<u>July 1938</u>: The family moved again, from Stockweather Street to Essex Street, Springfield, MA. It may have been the results of my little set to with my cousin Richard which upset a lot of people as mentioned above.

I experienced my first major hurricane with my friend Eddie Banks (not realizing that I would go through many more in the future). We donned bathing suits and went out in the pouring rain. We did not realize the damage a storm like this could cause, and did cause. Once my mother saw what we were up to, she sent my stepbrother Alfred out to bring us indoors, out of the storm. Luckily for us, she did this, as that storm caused a terrific amount of damage in the area. As Springfield was built on an area full of underground springs, they backfired into the cellars, resulting in quite a mess. (*For a picture of Eddie Banks, my half-sister Lorraine, and me, see photograph A1.*)

While living on Essex Street, I attended Hooker Street Elementary School, which was located in a very tough neighborhood; however, this was an exceptionally efficient school with good teachers.

<u>August 1938</u>: We moved from Essex Street to 26 Allendale Street, Springfield, MA. I attended Lincoln Street Elementary School while living there. Lincoln Street Elementary School was located in a very nice quiet neighborhood, and it was relaxing going there.

I remember the German-American Bund holding rallies in downtown Springfield. I went along with a gang of boys (mostly Jewish) to downtown Springfield, where we threw eggs and tomatoes at the Nazis. We were chased by Brownshirts and the police.

Luckily they never caught us (the Allendale Aces) as we knew most of the back alleys and they did not. I was about eleven years old at the time this took place.

July 1941: Yes, we moved again in July 1941, from 26 Allendale Street to 406 Maple Street, Holyoke, MA. I was now back at my old school (H. B. Lawrence), the very first school that I had started in, and the school I would end up my school days in. It was like being home again, in a place I knew and belonged in.

Things were pretty good during the beginning of this period, until the Japanese bombed Pearl Harbor in Hawaii, on December 7, 1941, starting World War II for us (the USA).

The schools back then had scrap drives, where the school children scoured the city looking for scrap metal for the war effort. I can remember when Willard Rider and I found an old abandoned safe down by the Connecticut River. Somehow we managed to get it up on the road and up on its wheels. We then pushed it through the streets to the scrap pile in the H. B. Lawrence School yard (since we wanted our school to get the credit for it). The local newspaper found out about it and took a picture of us pushing the safe through the streets. They published the photo and a story about it. It was quite an achievement for two young boys. During this time, I took all my lead toy soldiers and broke them up with a hammer (so that no one could take them and use them), and placed them in a box on the scrap pile. Everyone at the time was doing what they could for the war effort.

My brother Bob enlisted in the Army Air Forces. Both my stepbrothers Alfred and Francis were drafted into the Army. Alfred became a Military Policeman (M.P.) and Francis became an infantryman. My brother Gaston was unable to pass the physical to enlist or to be drafted in any branch of the military, due to perforated eardrums. He took this very hard; however, he did enlist in the Massachusetts State Guard (the State Militia), created after the National Guard was federalized, and went off to war. He rose to the rank of Master Sergeant and served honorably until the end of the war. (*For a picture of my brother Gaston in Massachusetts State Guard uniform, see photograph A2.*)

I joined a Boy Scout Troop in the Second Congregational Church, and rose to the rank of Assistant Scout Master. Later I became a member of the church. Eventually I persuaded my family to join the church. The Reverend Albert J. Penner was the pastor at the time, and went on to be pastor in New York City and became famous.

When I was fourteen years old, my stepfather adopted me in August 1942. This took place in the U. S. District Courthouse in Springfield, MA. When the adoption took place, the court legally changed my name to Maurice Frank Mercure vice Maurice Frank Fraichard. It was changed on all legal documents, such as birth certificates, school records, etc. The only thing that was not changed was my baptism record in Saint Anne's Roman Catholic Church. It is the only way I can prove what my birth name was.

June 1944: I completed the 8th Grade, June 1944, with a passing grade of "C." However, I left school to go to work since my family needed the extra money. All my brothers and stepbrothers were in some branch of the service. Two of them were married, so they had to support their own families.

I went to work in the Press Products Division of Noma Electric Company in June 1944, until August, when I quit for a higher paying job. The Newton Paper Company hired me in August 1944, where I worked until joining the Army Air Forces in October 1946. I started out in the rag room and ended up as a backhand on a paper machine, making good money. As a matter of fact, I was making more money than my stepfather, who was working in the Press Products Division of Noma Electric Company.

December 1944: Yes, you guessed it, we moved from 406 Maple Street to 17 Morgan Street, Holyoke, MA. While residing there, my mother, who was crocheting, had to go to the bathroom, so she stuck the crocheting needle in the ball of yarn and put it on her chair. When she returned, she went to sit down in her chair, and accidently placed her hand on the ball of yarn, driving the crochet needle into the palm of her hand. I was sixteen at the time; I did not have a driver's license or have any available transportation. I was unable to take my mother to the hospital or to the doctor's office. In those days, we did not have the emergency 911 service available. So, I called our family doctor, Dr. Pindola. He told me that he had an emergency in his office and he could not come to the house right then. He told me what to do over the telephone. I was not to pull the needle out of her hand, because it would tear the ligaments and muscles and make the wound worse. I was to push the needle out the other side of her hand, cut off the hook (using a pair of pliers), then pull the rest of the needle out the way it had entered the hand. Then he said to apply pressure to the wound to stop the bleeding. When the bleeding stopped, I was to apply iodine to the wound, then bandage it, using gauze and adhesive tape. I proceeded to follow his instructions to the letter, and pushed the needle through to the other side of her hand. My mother was very good during the whole time this was going on, and did not complain about the pain or pass out on me. My half-sister Lorraine (ten years younger than I) was something else, screaming that her mother was going to die. I had to slap her face to shut her up. Everything went like clockwork, and I managed to get the job done. After finishing, I was to get my stepfather to take my mother to the doctor's office. When we arrived at his office, he commended me on a job well done—so did my parents.

May 1945: My brother Bob came home from the war in May 1945. I was about sixteen and eight months old at the time—about one year and four months before I enlisted in the Army Air Forces. We were residing at 17 Morgan Street at the time.

June 1945: We moved again, from 17 Morgan Street to 179 Beech Street, Holyoke, MA in June 1945. This was going to be my last civilian move for a long, long time. The war was winding down; the Germans had already surrendered. We just had the Japanese to take care of. My brother and stepbrothers were coming home. Two of them had been wounded. My brother Bob was wounded on a B-17 bombing raid over Germany and my stepbrother Francis had been wounded in the battle for St. Lo, France. Thank God all of them returned from the war.

August 1945: Ever since I was a little boy, I had always wanted to join the military, so when I was seventeen years old, I approached my parents and told them I wanted to enlist in the Army Air Forces. It seems I always wanted to see what was over the next hill. I wanted to travel the world and felt that the military would be the place for me to do so. However, my parents could not see it that way, and would not sign the papers giving me permission to enlist. My parents said that they needed me at home until all my brothers and stepbrothers were out of the service. They told me I could enlist when

I was eighteen, if I still wanted to—a promise that they did not intend to keep. They would try to talk me out of enlisting, arguing that they needed me more at home.

July 1946: During this period, my mother managed to get most of the family together for an outing to Hampden Ponds for a swim during July 1946. All her children and stepchildren were there, with the exception of my sister Lorretta and my stepbrother Alfred. (*For a picture of my stepsister Mildred, my mother, me, my nephew Bob, my half-sister Lorraine, my nephew Roger, my stepbrother Francis, and my brothers Bob and Gaston, see photograph A3.*)

October 2, 1946: The Newton Paper Company that I worked for had a policy of giving two weeks pay as a bonus when an employee enlisted in the military. When I advised them that I was enlisting in the Army Air Forces, they paid me the bonus along with my last week's salary. I left the two week's bonus on the kitchen table with a note for my mother saying that I was enlisting in the Army Air Forces. I kept one week's pay for myself to carry me over until I received my first pay from the USAAF, which would be at the end of October. The reason I did this (leaving my two week's bonus on the kitchen table, while my parents were away), was my parents could use the money. Also they did not want me to enlist in the military. We definitely would have had a big argument over it. They were away on a three-day vacation. It was impossible for them to stop me, since I was eighteen years old—the legal age to enlist without parents' permission.

October 4, 1946: I went to the recruiting station in Springfield, MA to enlist in the Army Air Forces instead of my home town. They administered the written test to me, which I passed. They then informed me that they were sending me to Albany, NY for my physical examination. They also informed me that I would be put up in a hotel until the physical was completed.

CHAPTER 2

4 OCTOBER 1946-15 MARCH 1947

USA ENLISTMENT, BASIC TRAINING, RADIO OPERATOR SCHOOL

A.	Fort Dix, NJ	6 Oct 1946-12 Oct 1946
B.	Lackland Army Air Field, TX	17 Oct 1946-29 Nov 1946
C.	Scott Army Air Field, IL	30 Nov 1946-15 Mar 1947

October 4, 1946: The Recruiting Station in Springfield, MA took all the particulars on me to enlist. After completing all the paperwork, they informed me that I would have to go to Albany, NY for my Enlistment Physical and if I passed, I would then be sworn in (administered the oath of allegiance to the United States and the Army Air Forces). They then provided me with train transportation to Albany, NY.

October 4, 1946: Arriving in Albany, I was put up in the New Kenmore Hotel. The next day, October 5, 1946, we would take our Enlistment Physical. That night some of the men awaiting their physical, filled condoms with water and dropped them out the windows on the people walking on the street below. When they hit the sidewalk, they burst, spewing water all over the place. Luckily no one was hit by these water missiles.

October 5, 1946: The National Guard Armory in Albany is where we took our Enlistment/ Induction Physicals—an all-day affair. There were literally hundreds of men there taking a physical examination—either as an enlistee or as inductee (draftee). During the examination, we were clad only in our undershorts. Toward the end of the examination line, something funny occurred. The person in front of me (approaching the final two doctors we had to see), was requested by the doctor to drop his undershorts, to bend over and spread his cheeks (for a rectal examination). The fool in front of me inserted his fingers in his mouth and bent over spreading his facial cheeks, saying aah! The psychiatrist who was the last doctor in the examination line (he was responsible for approving or disapproving examinees) immediately took that person's medical papers and stamped them "REJECTED." The whole Armory roared with laughter.

Upon completing and passing the Physical Examination, after numerous tests, pokes, and probes, I was administered the oath of allegiance to the United States of America, and sworn into the Army Air Forces.

October 6, 1946: The next day they sent us by train from Albany to Grand Central Station in New York City. From there they took us on the shuttle to Pennsylvania Station and we boarded a train for Fort Dix, Wrightstown, NJ.

Earlier, before enlisting in the Army Air Forces, I had a talk with my brother Bob (who I looked up to and believed everything he told me, as gospel) about joining the Army Air Forces, in which he had served during World War II. He informed me that I did not have to do anything until I had a uniform (which I foolishly believed). Boy, was he sadly mistaken.

While at Fort Dix (my first day) the following incident took place. A little Corporal came into the barracks and told me to fall out and drill with the other men. I informed him that I did not have a uniform, so that I did not have to do so. He stated "I am giving you a direct order to fall out and drill." I repeated my statement to him, and he left the barracks. He returned a few minutes later with the Company First Sergeant, who was about six feet three inches tall and weighing about 275 lbs. He stated, "Where is this smart-ass guard house lawyer son-of-a-bitch?" At that moment I knew that I was in big trouble. The Corporal immediately pointed me out to him. The First Sergeant grabbed me by the seat of my pants and the collar of my grey suit jacket. He literally carried me to the Mess Hall and threw me through the door. I landed at the feet of the Chief Mess Sergeant standing there. The First Sergeant informed him to give me the treatment, to wise me up so that I would realize the authority NCO's had, and that they should be obeyed at all times.

The Chief Mess Sergeant informed me, that I was not to remove my suit coat while working in the Mess Hall. He then proceeded to give me all the dirty jobs that he could find for me such as cleaning grease traps, garbage cans, etc. This went on for twelve hours a day for seven days. At the end of this period, I was ready to obey orders from an NCO without question.

The next thing I had to do was to go through a large warehouse with other recruits to receive our initial clothing allowance. We were instructed to strip down to our undershorts, removing our civilian clothes and placing them in a laundry bag provided for this. We were then told to send them home, as we would not have any need for them for a long, long time. I had no recourse but to throw away my dirty grey suit because it was completely covered in grease and was ruined. So in our undershorts we proceeded down the line of Supply Sergeants and Supply Personnel. The Supply Sergeants would guess at our clothing sizes, call them out, and the Supply Personnel would issue them to us. We were told that if they did not fit properly, we could exchange them at our next duty station, Lackland Army Air Field, where we would be issued the rest of our Basic Issue. The only thing they did right was to make sure our combat boots fit us, since an army travels on its feet. Upon receiving our clothing, we dressed. After dressing and putting our clothes in our duffle bags, we were marched to a waiting troop (passenger) train. The troop train consisted of ten troop cars and a troop mess (kitchen) car. The troop car was three bunks high instead of the normal two berths. The mess car was located at the head of the train, next to the locomotive. You had to walk through the mess car and as you did, food was placed on your mess kit. You then had to walk (return) to your troop car to eat your meal. The troop car next to the mess car got to eat first and the last troop car got to eat last.

We were transported from Fort Dix, NJ to our Basic Training Center at Lackland Army Air Field, San Antonio, Texas, by the slowest means and route available to us. It took five days to get to San Antonio, TX (Lackland Army Air Field). Since our train did not have a high enough priority, it was constantly being switched onto sidings, to let trains with a higher priority pass since they had the right of way over lower priority trains. We ran out of food after three days. Speculation was that the Mess Sergeant was selling food at the different stops we made along the way. It was apparent that a meat shortage existed at the time, making it very lucrative to sell it on the black market. If it had not been for the good, kind people living by the tracks, who found out about our situation and brought food to us, we would have been really hungry by the time we reached our final destination in Texas.

Upon arriving at Lackland Army Air Field, San Antonio, TX, we were assigned to Basic Training Flight 1342, for Basic Training. This is when I first met Larry Steffan; we became good friends. (*For a picture of me in Olive Drab (O.D.) uniform in the training area, see photograph A4 and for a picture of Larry see photograph A5.*)

During the first week of Basic Training, the entire flight was caught talking after lights out. We were ordered by our Drill Instructor (D.I.) to fall out in our combat boots, rain coats, and helmet liners. We were given close order drill for two hours in the pouring rain. This treatment cured us of talking after "lights out." Two people started talking the next night after "lights out" and were hit by flying combat boots. Things were real quiet after that. We did not have anymore night time close order drill sessions after that, right up to the end of Basic Training.

My favorite part of Basic Training was on the rifle range, where I did really good, number one in the flight. We took turns on the firing range, on the firing line, then in the target pits, marking the targets. In the target pits, you were responsible for marking the holes made by the person shooting at the target. We then would paste patches over the holes so the next shooter had a clean target to shoot at. Targets were pulled up and down to aid the shooter and the marker (paster) in the pit to perform their responsibility.

We went through the obstacle course once a week for eight weeks to improve our physical condition and aid us in being able to perform our combat mission. We did calisthenics every morning before breakfast to get us in shape. Between daily calisthenics and the weekly run on the obstacle course, we became lean, mean, fighting machines. If we had any baby fat, we lost it in the first week of Basic Training.

One interesting thing we did was to go through the gas chamber. Before doing this we were exposed to various smells to aid us in detecting and identifying gases. One such smell was new mown hay, for mustard gas, etc. We went into the gas chamber wearing our gas masks. Before leaving the gas chamber, we were ordered to take off our gas masks, AND TAKE A WHIFF (in the gas chamber, there was tear gas), long enough for it to take effect and really make us cry. Then we had to run out of the gas chamber into the fresh air.

One night on a forced march, we were split into two columns—one on either side of the road. They played a dirty trick on us, by passing an ambulance up the line of march, between the columns, releasing tear gas out the rear doors of the ambulance. Before anyone could get their gas mask out of its carrying case, and putting it on, it was too late. The gas had already began to take effect causing everyone to cry. This was done to teach us that you did not trust anyone.

One of the things drilled into us was that if we were under a gas attack, we do not take our gas mask off, even if we were sick—just lift one corner of the gas mask to let the vomit out. If it was just a little vomit, try swallowing it back to keep from being overcome by the gas.

One can really begin to hate their drill instructor (D.I.) from the very beginning of Basic Training. You finally realize that what he is doing is preparing you for combat.

Our Basic Training continued up to the day before Thanksgiving. We were given Thanksgiving Day off. The Mess Sergeants put on a very excellent dinner for us, in the Mess Hall. We could not have had a better meal than if we were at home with our families.

The meal was outstanding. We had a lot to be thankful for. *(For a copy of the menu for Thanksgiving Day, see attachment B1.)*

November 1946: Upon completing Basic Training in November 1946, we were administered a battery of tests (examinations) over a period of three days to determine which technical schools we qualified for, and should be assigned to. We started out with five hundred soldiers, and ended up with fifteen of us left who had passed all the tests. Everyone else had been eliminated. They needed five men for an IBM Repair Technician Training School Course. They took the top five scoring individuals for this school. Lawrence G. Steffan and I were in the remaining ten persons. They sent the rest of us to Radio Operator School at Scott Army Air Field, Belleville, IL.

Upon arriving at Scott Army Air Field, we were assigned to the Radio Operator School Training Group and reassigned to a Training Squadron. The school's motto was "Through These Gates Pass the Best Damned Radio Operators in the World."

In Radio Operator School, we were given instructions in Morse Code, Typing, Phonetic Alphabets, and Radio Equipment. We were taught Morse Code in the morning session and typing in the afternoon session. Also the use of the Phonetic Alphabets and Radio Equipment. All these instructions were given via ear phones (headsets). It was very tedious, and some of the students could not take the routine and cracked up and quit. They just jumped up and threw their typewriters onto the floor, and ripped off their headsets.

The typewriters we used had blank keyboards. There was a master chart of the keyboard on the wall in front of the class (with the home row keys highlighted). We were told to place our fingers on the home row keys. Then we were given finger exercises, such as j-u-j, space, f-r-f, space, until we had mastered the keyboard. The system really worked (if you had the temperament for it), and you were typing before you knew it. We were also given instructions in the Phonetic Alphabets used by the USAAF, Civilian Aviation Pilots, Control Tower Operators, NATO, etc. (*For copy of Phonetic Alphabets, see attachment B2.*)

We were marched from the barracks to the classrooms, mess hall and back to the barracks daily.

I learned Morse Code by association with other words and phrases with similar sounds such as DAH DAH DIT DAH (Pay Day Today), etc.

Student Squadrons were used to participate in parades in downtown St. Louis, Missouri.

Upon completing Radio Operator School, my friend Lawrence G. Steffan and I were assigned to the Air Proving Ground Command, at Eglin Army Air Field, Florida.

CHAPTER 3

15 MARCH 1947 - 27 NOVEMBER 1951

USA—EGLIN ARMY AIR FIELD— EGLIN AIR FORCE BASE, FLORIDA

A.	Eglin Army Air Field, FL	15 Mar 1947-17 Sep 1948
B.	Eglin Air Force Base, FL	18 Sep 1947-28 Nov 1951
C.	Lowry Air Force Base, CO (TDY)	10 Dec 1947-17 Jun 1948
D.	Fort Leavenworth, KS (TDY)	17 Jan 1949-19 Jan 1949
E.	Fort Benning, GA (TDY)	5 Feb 1949-6 Feb 1949
F.	Scott Air Force Base, IL (TDY)	8 Aug 1950-15 Oct 1950

March 1947: I arrived on Eglin Army Air Field, Florida, sometime in March 1947. The Army Air Field was the home of the Air Proving Ground Command, under the Command of Major General Kepner.

It was a huge Army Air Field, located on a very large Military Reservation. It consisted of the main Air Field (Eglin) and ten auxiliary Air Fields, with the Jackson Guard Forestry Preserve right in the middle of the reservation. Eglin Army Air Field was activated in 1935.

Two of the auxiliary Air Fields were being utilized by the United States Navy for training purposes. The nearest Naval Installation is Pensacola Naval Air Station, Pensacola, FL.

The Eglin Military Reservation is surrounded by the following cities and towns:

1.	Pensacola	7.	Mary Esther
2.	Crestview	8.	Niceville
3.	Defuniak Springs	9.	Portland
4.	Destin	10.	Rock Hill
5.	Fort Walton (now Fort Walton Beach)	11.	Shalimar
6.	Freeport	12.	Valpariso

State Roads and Highways Number 20, 53, 85, 87, 123, 285, 331, and 393 cut through the reservation at various locations. Highway No. 85 cuts through Eglin itself. Cars using this highway then were given a time dated pass (for use strictly between the East and West Gates). This Highway was patrolled by M.P.'s on motorcycles to make sure no one deviated from the highway; that they reached the gate they were heading for, within the time frame allocated; and to keep them from straying into "OFF LIMIT areas." As the transit vehicle entered, it had to obtain a through pass which had to be turned in at the gate as they exited. Nowadays, there is an Interstate Highway (No.10), which bypasses the reservation. There has always been a State Highway (No. 98) on the coastal route to Panama City, bypassing the reservation in the south. *(For a map of Eglin Military Reservation and surrounding area, see attachment B3.)*

I was assigned to Squadron D (Guard), 609th, upon arriving on the Air Field.

The barracks we lived in were made of wood, tar paper, and screen material. They (so I was informed) were originally built for Colonel Doolittle and his Tokyo Raiders. During the early part of World War II, Colonel James (Jimmy) Doolittle and his men trained on Eglin Army Air Field in conjunction with the United States Navy. The Navy was training them to take off from the Flight Deck of an Aircraft Carrier, with land based B-25 Medium Bombers, so they could bomb Japan—a feat never accomplished before in the history of Naval Aviation. Colonel Doolittle and his crews went on to successfully accomplish their mission on April 18, 1942, bombing Tokyo, Yokohama, Nagoya, Kobe and Osaka, Japan. The Aircraft Carrier used for this mission was the "Hornet," which President Roosevelt referred to as "Shangri-la," when he announced to the world about the raid. Living in these barracks gave one the feeling of great pride, knowing what these men had done.

One occupational hazard of living in these barracks next to the Squadron Armory, was when shifts (watches) changed and guards and M.P.'s were turning in, and/or drawing out weapons. It was not uncommon for a weapon to be accidentally discharged, during clearing of same. Bullet holes were a common sight in the walls of the barracks facing the armory. One evening while I was sitting up in bed (bunk) reading, I decided to lie down. Just after lying down, a bullet came through the wall where my head had been just a few minutes before. I can tell you it scared the living daylights out of me. I would not be here today, writing this book, if I had not lain down when I did. (*For a diagram of the area, see attachment B4.*)

The first enlisted man I came in contact with at Eglin was John (Big John) Mihajlovic, who introduced me to a novel way to flip for a Coke. He asked me if I would like to flip for a Coke. I said, "sure," expecting this to be where you flipped a coin to match the other person for a Coke—but not so. He immediately grabbed me by the ankles and proceeded to flip me upside down. Coins fell out of my pockets onto the ground. He yelled "I win, buy me a Coke." You could not argue with him, so you bought him a Coke. Later, when I thought about it, it really was amusing. He was a strange person indeed. One wondered how he got in the service in the first place.

He walked into my barracks one evening and started punching holes in the ceiling tiles, as he walked along. No one tried to stop him as they considered him to be crazy and dangerous.

He called home one day, asking for money. (I know because he took me along to pay for the call.) His father asked him, "John, are you coming home?" John replied, "No." His father replied, "Good, John, I will send you the money." Big John never paid me for the telephone call.

During Squadron Inspection, Big John was on latrine duty together with another Airman (believed to be the brains behind the scheme). They put tacks in the toilet seats, ran strings from one toilet seat to another, via tacks on the wall, all connecting to one major string at the entrance to the latrine. So, when the inspecting officer, Major Hudson, arrived with the First Sergeant, who yelled, "ATTENTION," Big John pulled the string causing all the toilet seats to rise, as if to attention. Boy did he catch hell for his actions since Major Hudson and the First Sergeant were not pleased at all. Everyone else thought it was very funny and laughed.

Another time, while on Guard Duty on the Flight Line, he literally chased the Sergeant of the Guard (who was in a Jeep), with a P-51 (Mustang) Fighter Plane. The Sergeant of the Guard managed to avoid being chopped up by the aircraft's propeller. The Mustang had been cannibalized for spare parts. It could, however, be turned over and started for taxying purposes. These aircraft were also used as targets on Range 51, by bombers and fighter aircraft, for testing purposes. There is no doubt that Big John scared the crap out of the Sergeant of the Guard. No one could believe that Big John did this on his own—that he just climbed into the aircraft cockpit and started the engine with his mentality.

Finally one night, while guarding the PX (Post Exchange) area, he broke into it and proceeded to rob it. When he was apprehended, it took the Sergeant of the Guard, two M.P.'s and the Duty Officer to subdue him. He was tried and convicted, sentenced to prison time and given a Dishonorable Discharge.

One of the Military Police Officers at the time was Captain Joe S. (Slaughter) Webb, who was a Golden Gloves Champion. As Duty Officer, he came to the aid of the Sergeant of the Guard and his men, and helped subdue Big John. Captain Webb was an outstanding Officer and was well liked by all the men under his command.

It is important to point out that, at this time, that the German Rocket Scientist, Dr. Werner Von Braun, and his associates were brought to the United States. They were assisting the Army Air Forces to develop a Rocket (Missile) Program of their own. As you know, Dr. Von Braun was responsible for the German V1, V2 and V3 Programs. I managed to see and meet Dr. Von Braun at Eglin Army Air Field. Some V2's and/or new designs were tested at Eglin.

The German Buzz Bombs (V1), were able to reach targets in England on their own and do quite a bit of damage. The V2, however, had a greater range and payload (of explosives) and were more successful in reaching England and destroying targets then the Buzz Bombs. One thing the V2's did not do was to make a lot of noise, like the Buzz Bomb did, and were harder to detect. The Buzz Bombs were much easier to detect because of the noise they made. The V3 was capable of reaching New York City, but had not been placed into production. The V1's and V2's kept hitting targets in England until the Allies destroyed their launching pads in Peenemunde.

The United States tested their new missiles at various locations in the U.S., such as White Sands, New Mexico, Vandenberg AAF, California and Eglin AAF, Florida, etc.

Our new Rocket Program was based on the German V1, V2, and V3 Rocket Program. The AAF test fired some of these rockets into Choctawhatchee Bay where they were recovered by the 609th Boat Squadron (later redesignated as the 3201st Boat Squadron). At that time, the Army Air Forces had all the necessary equipment to recover missiles from the Bay. The Boat Squadron at that time was responsible for Air/Sea Rescue Operations in that area—now in the capable hands of the United State Coast Guard.

I was promoted to Corporal in 1947 while serving in the 609th, D Squadron (Guard). (*For a picture of me in O.D. (Olive Drab) uniform, with Corporal Stripes, see photograph A6.*)

The unit I was in had the Security Responsibility of guarding and Internal Security Responsibility of the entire Air Proving Ground command.

The area we lived in was called "Skunk Hollow" (nickname). Most of the people living on the base lived up on the hill from Skunk Hollow. The hill was nicknamed "Polecat Hill." The barracks up on the hill were constructed of concrete, concrete blocks, glass (for the windows), wood for the porches and screen material to enclose them. They consisted of four-man rooms with their own bathrooms (consisting of showers, sinks and toilets, making them self-contained.) The barracks in Skunk Hollow were constructed of wood, glass, and screen material. They did not contain bathroom facilities. Bathrooms were contained in a centralized building, located in the middle of the barracks area.

The WAF Squadron was located in Skunk Hollow, and near the beach front in permanent buildings.

<u>Payroll Details</u>: Once a month, the Military Police/Air Police, mounted a payroll detail to pick up both the military and civilian payrolls for the base. The detail consisted of one half-truck armored car with a five-man crew of MPs/APs, with a 50 caliber machine gun on a swivel mount. There were also two jeeps, with one officer and three enlisted men in each vehicle. Each had a 30 caliber machine gun on a swivel pole. One jeep led the convoy with the second jeep bringing up the rear. There was also a helicopter (or light wing air craft) over the convoy at all times. A different route was used each month by the convoy. I had the privilege of being on this detail a couple of times.

Eglin Army Air Field/Eglin Air Force Base, was, at that time, the largest military installation in the United States. It had the largest climatic hanger in the world. They could make rain, snow, sand, wind, hail, heat, cold weather, and storms. It was so large, it could accommodate B-29s, B-36s, B-50s, bombers, and expose them to the elements for test purposes.

A major un-named hurricane hit the Panhandle in 1947, causing considerable damage to the area. All the Army Air Field's aircraft were evacuated (flown out) to Air Fields outside the storm's path. All doors and windows were boarded up. Blankets were nailed on the inside of windows to catch flying glass. We had a fairly large prison population, as I believe we were the regional prison for Alabama, Georgia, Louisiana, and Florida. The prisoners were evacuated in large trailer vans to prisons outside the path of the storm. One guard armed with a nightstick (billy club) was placed inside each van to maintain order and discipline. Prisoners were shackled in handcuffs and leg irons to prevent their escape. One jeep led the convoy, one jeep was between vans, and one jeep brought up the rear of the convoy. Each jeep had four guards in them with a 30- or 50-caliber machine gun, mounted on a pole. The size of the convoy depended on the number of prisoners being evacuated.

June 1, 1947: Assigned a new Military Occupational Specialty (MOS) of 055 (Clerk-non-typist), to work in the Pass & Registration Section of the Military Police Headquarters.

The first Provost Marshal I served under was Major Smith (commonly called "Bag-Em-Smith"). He got that nickname because of an incident requiring the placing of a corpse in a body bag. A body had been floating in the Choctawhatchee Bay for a few days, then washed ashore. It has been partially eaten by water creatures and birds, and was decomposing. No one would obey the Major's orders to place the body in a body bag because of its condition and smell. Major Smith waded out into the water, grabbed the body, and placed it into a body bag. Because the body was found on Eglin Military Reservation (and we did not know whether or not the body was a civilian or military member), it was our responsibility since it was in our jurisdiction. I was given the job of trying to fingerprint the body for identification. I could not do so, even with the use of paraffin and using all means available to me. So the coroner gave the job to the local FBI Office, who could get help from their laboratory in Washington, DC. I can still remember the incident, as the smell still lingers in my memory.

June 27, 1947: Assigned a new MOS of 405 (Clerk Typist), to work in the Pass & Registration Section of the Military Police Headquarters.

One morning I was awaken by the sounds of cats snarling and a snake's rattle and hissing. I jumped out of my bunk and looked out the window and I saw three cats and a diamond back rattlesnake engaged in a fight. Apparently the snake was trying to get one of the cat's kittens for a meal. The cats were holding their own and were keeping the snake at bay. They were really driving the snake crazy, with their spitting and darting to and fro. I drove the snake off by throwing rocks at it, as I did not have a weapon. After a few well-placed rocks, the snake slithered off. We had a lot of cats around to keep mice and rats away from the barracks and the Mess Hall.

We had a real wise guy from Brooklyn, NY, Nicholas Greico, working in the Pass & Registration Section of the Air Police Headquarters. He thought he was a real funny individual. He used to answer the telephone (when no one was around to reprimand him) in the following manner: "Rosie's Whorehouse. Rosie speaking." Also, "Joe's Poolroom. Eightball speaking." He did this until one day the telephone rang, and he answered with his usual "Joe's Poolroom. Eightball speaking." The voice on the other end of the telephone line said, "Do you know to whom you are speaking?" Nick replied, "No." The voice identified himself as "General Kepner." Greico replied do you know to whom you are talking to?" The General replied "No." Nick then said, "Good. It's for me to know and for you to find out," and then he hung up the telephone. About fifteen minutes later, a large Buick Staff car pulled up outside of Air Police Headquarters, Pass & Registration Section, and out jumped General Kepner. He rushed into the office demanding to know to whom he had been talking to before on the telephone. No one stepped forward to admit to the call. So the General had us all line up in a row. He then went down the line talking to each Airman, asking them their name, rank and serial number. When he got to Nick, he stated, "So you are the smart ass, son-of-a-bitch, that was just talking to me." He immediately had him arrested and informed the Provost Marshal that he wanted him court-martialed. Greico was tried and busted down to Airman Basic and fined $50.00 for his actions.

18 September 1947: President Harry S. Truman signed into law the Military Reorganizational Bill on September 18, 1947, creating the Department of Defense,

and the United States Air Force; changing the War Department to the Department of the Army; the Naval Department to the Department of the Navy; and redesignating the Army Air Forces to the Department of the Air Force (United States Air Force). The respective service branches would each have a Secretary over them under a Secretary of Defense. The bill also created the Chairman of the Joint Chiefs of Staff, who was over all the Chiefs of Staff of all the services. He reports directly to the Secretary of Defense. This bill put the Air Forces on an equal footing with the Army and Navy.

Squadron D (Guard), 609th became the 3201st Air Police Squadron; Military Policemen were now Air Police. The Squadron consisted of the following ranks for a grand total of 223 Officers and Enlisted Men:

1. 1 Lt. Col.
2. 3 Captains
3. 2 1st Lts.
4. 3 MSgts.
5. 4 TSgts.

6. 25 SSgts.
7. 42 Sgts.
8. 59 Cpls.
9. 50 PFCs
10. 34 Pvts.

Eglin Army Air Field was redesignated Eglin Air Force Base, and all existing units (with the exception of a few) were redesignated. (*For a list of all units on Eglin Air Force Base, see attachment B5.*)

<u>10 December 1947</u> Assigned to Lowry Air Force Base, Denver, Colorado, for the purpose of attending Stenographer School.

While at Lowry Air Force Base, I did something really foolish. As I was old enough to buy whiskey off the base, some young Airmen (wanting to celebrate graduation) asked me to buy them a couple of bottles of whiskey and bring it back on the base for them—which I did to my regret and sorrow. The young Airmen in question got drunk and literally picked up Cpl. Rosen's bunk with him in it. They threw the Second Floor Bay Chief and his bunk out of a second floor window, which was not open. Luckily there was snow on the ground and he was not seriously injured. During the investigation of this incident, many Airmen were interrogated. All refused to talk and blame anyone as to how they obtained the whiskey, with the exception of Airman Donald C. Puffer. He told the investigators that I had purchased and brought the whiskey onto the base. The Commanding Officer of the School Squadron had no choice but to have me court-martialed. I was brought before the Base Staff Judge Advocate, who advised me that I could remain silent and be given a special court-martial where I would appear before a board of officers, and, if found guilty as charged, could be reduced (busted) to Airman Basic and given a sentence of up to six months in the Guard House. Or, I could plead guilty and get a summary court-martial, be reduced to Airman Basic and serve up to three months in the Guard House. Of course, the latter sounded like the best deal to me. So I informed him that I was guilty and would take the summary court-martial. He said, "OK, Summary Court is now in session. I am the Judge, Prosecutor, Defense and the Jury. I find you guilty as charged and fine you $25.00. You will retain your rank." He told me that if he had to court-martial everyone guilty of bringing whiskey illegally onto the base and into the barracks, he wouldn't have time for anything else. I was grateful for my sentence and left a happy Airman. I was sure that I would catch hell when I returned to my Duty Station.

The City of Denver, Colorado, had a lot to offer to the personnel stationed on Lowry Air Force Base, in the way of entertainment—bowling alleys, roller skating rinks, ice skating rinks, dance halls, museums, theatres, movies, skiing, bob sledding, etc. The people there were very generous; we always had more than enough offers for the service men to go to homes for Thanksgiving, Christmas, etc., to participate in the holiday meals. The fire trucks were painted white and had large rotary colored lights on the front of them, making it easy to see them in the winter time against the snow. The trolley cars had a potbelly stove in the middle of them to heat the car in the winter time. The transportation service was excellent. Lowry Air Force Base was one of the best places to be, next to Eglin Air Force Base, Florida.

One day the Air Base Commander wanted to show the people of Denver how much the military spent in town. So, he made arrangements with the Base Finance Office to pay the Troops in silver dollars. To his delight, they showed up all over the Denver area showing local businesses and people the effect Lowry Air Fore Base was having on Denver's economy.

<u>26 April 1948</u>: The United States Air Force was the first Military Service to combine white and black units. This caused some major concerns and problems in the cities and towns located near the Air Bases in the South.

<u>30 April 1948</u>: General Hoyt S. Vandenberg was appointed Chief of Staff of the United States Air Force (USAF), this date.

<u>15 June 1948</u>: Graduated from Stenographer School on June 15, 1948. Upon Graduation, I returned to my Duty Station, Eglin Air Force Base, Florida. *(For copy of Graduation Program, see attachment B6. For picture of Graduating Class, see photograph A7. For copy of Graduation Photo Holder, see attachment B7. For copy of Certificate of Proficiency, see attachment B8.)*

<u>18 June 1948</u>: Upon returning to my Duty Station at Eglin, I was informed that the Provost Marshal wanted to see me. I reported to him as ordered. He told me, "Sit down, Cpl." He reviewed my records and informed me that he was glad that I had completed the Stenographer Course and that he would utilize me for all the cases that he felt the WAF Stenographers should not have to handle. After our conversation, when he was done explaining what he wanted me to do, he said, "That is all Cpl., you may go." During the interview, he never once mentioned what had transpired at Lowry AFB—what an understanding Commanding Officer, not to hold the incident against me.

<u>July/August 1948</u>: We had a prison break some time during July/August 1948. I had to pick up the Provost Marshal at his off-base home, outside the town of Fort Walton, on the road to Pensacola. I drove his Command Staff car, with the RED LIGHT flashing and SIREN blaring, to get him and bring him back to Eglin, so that he could take charge of the Recovery Effort. After picking up the Provost Marshal, we proceeded back to the base, picking up a local police escort. The escaped prisoners were apprehended by local Sheriff's Deputies off the reservation and returned to military control. Things then settled back to our normal routine.

<u>Hurricane Season 1948</u>: We had a major hurricane hit the Panhandle in 1948, causing considerable damage to the area. The same drill and procedures were followed as during the 1947 hurricane.

<u>30 September 1948</u>: Letter from Principal James Bower, Jr., H. B. Lawrence Junior High School, Holyoke, MA, stating that I had passed the 8th grade. *(For a copy of this letter, see attachment B9.)*

<u>25 December 1948</u>: The Mess Stewards outdid themselves with our Christmas Dinner, in the Mess (Dining) Hall, of the 3201st Air Police Squadron, 3201st Air Base Group, Eglin Air Force Base, FL. *(For a copy of the menu, see attachment B10.)*

<u>17 January 1949</u>: SPECIAL ORDERS NUMBER 11, HEADQUARTERS AIR PROVING GROUND, Eglin Air Force Base, Florida, dtd 17 Jan 49. <u>E X T R A C T</u> Paragraph 26. The fol Airmen (Guards) USAF 3201st Air Police Sq 3201st Air Base Gp Eglin AF Base Fla WP US Disciplinary Barracks Fort Leavenworth Kans o/a 17 Jan 49. On TDY not to exceed two (2) days purpose to transfer General Prisoner Ersel C. Smith AF 36XXXXXX to the CO thereat for which a signed receipt will be obtained upon compl of which will return to proper Sta Eglin AF Base, FL.

GUARDS

Cpl Maurice F. Mercure AF 12XXXXXX (NCOIC) Cpl Doyle E. Loverne AF 37XXXXXX Provost Marshal Eglin AF Base will comply w/AR 600-375. In accordance w/AR 35-4800 TO will determine and issue necessary number of Meal Tickets for guards en route and returning and for general prisoner en route to US Disciplinary Barracks Fort Leavenworth, Kans. TYPHOID. Tin. 2190425 90 1-16 P 431-02 S 99-999. Under Auth of AR 600-375. BY COMMAND OF MAJOR GENERAL KEPNER:

While passing through Nashville, Tennessee, Railroad Station, we were approached by some nuns, who wanted to know why we had the prisoner in leg irons and handcuffs. They wanted us to remove his leg irons to ease his well-being. I tried to explain to them that if we lost our prisoner, we would have to serve his sentence. They wouldn't listen to me and thought that we were insensitive and hard on him; that we were un-Christian in our approach; that we should stop treating him like an animal. They blessed the prisoner and said a prayer for him and our insensitive attitude. Having nothing more to discuss with them, we went on our way to the US Disciplinary Barracks, Fort Leavenworth, KS. We continued on our way, with the prisoner still in leg irons and handcuffs, without any further incidents. When we got to Fort Leavenworth and entered the big iron gates of the prison, it gave us goose bumps when they closed behind us. It is an eerie feeling to have them close behind you, cutting you off from the outside world. We were real pleased to leave the area and board the train for our return journey to Eglin AF Base, FL. I can tell you that we were very pleased to turn our general prisoner over to the Officer of the Day on duty, and obtain a receipt for him. We returned to Eglin AF Base, Florida, with haste, glad to leave Fort Leavenworth behind us. It was so nice to be on the outside of those walls.

25 January 1949: The United States Air Force adapted a new blue uniform for Air Force personnel in place of the Olive Drab (OD) uniform worn by Army personnel.

29 January 1949: The Air Research and Development Command (ARDC) (formerly the Air Proving Ground (APG), established at Kirtland Air Force Base, Albuquerque, New Mexico, on 29 Jan 1949.

3 February 1949: SPECIAL ORDERS NUMBER 24, HEADQUARTERS, AIR PROVING GROUND COMMAND Eglin Air Force Base, Florida, 3 February 1949. E X T R A C T Paragraph 6. The fol Airman (Guard) 3201st Air Police Squadron 3201st Air Base Gp Eglin AF Base Fla WP Fort Benning Ga o/a 5 Feb 49 on TDY not to exceed one (1) day purpose to deliver absentee to the CO thereof for disposition under the provisions of AR 615-300 upon compl of which will return to proper Sta Eglin AF Base Fla.

GUARDS

Cpl Maurice F. Mercure AF 12XXXXXX   Pfc Anthony J. Moraine AF
                                                                          13XXXXXX

ABSENTEE

Rct Raymond J. Thurber RA 12XXXXXX Co., "I" 101st Airborne Bn Camp Breckinridge, Kentucky.

Transportation O will determine and issue necessary number of Meal Tickets for Guards and Absentee in accordance w/AR 35-4800. Two (2) additional Meal Tickets are auth in case of unavoidable delays. In accordance W/Para 18 AR 615-300. The entire cost of transportation and subsistence will be charged against the absentee. TBMAA. TOMA. TOFNT. TIN 2190425 901-24 P 432-02 S 99-999. Under Auth of AFL 125-15 and AR 615-300. BY ORDER OF COLONEL WILSON:

Upon arriving at Fort Benning, Georgia, we turned our prisoner over to the Fort's Provost Marshal, and got a receipt for him. The first thing the Prison Guards at the Fort Benning Stockade did, was to take away his Airborne Jump Boots and then shave his head. They said they did this to all Airborne prisoners, because they were a disgrace to the 101st Airborne Division. We returned to our Duty Station Eglin on the first available train.

During one shift, I was assigned to Guard the Crypto Center in Johnson Hall, never realizing that one day, I would be working in the very same place. As I guarded the Crypto Center, I wondered what they did behind the Vault Door. I was soon to find out.

4 May 1949: The North Atlantic Treaty Organization (NATO) was created by the United States and its European Allies resulting in a major command of US Forces and all allied forces in Europe.

28 June 1949: SPECIAL ORDERS NUMBER 121, HEADQUARTERS, 3201ST AIR BASE Group, Eglin Air Force Base, Florida, dtd 28 Jun 49. Paragraph 9. The following named Airmen, Orgns indicated, are changed as shown below: NAME Maurice Mercure AFSN AF 12XXXXXX ORGNS 3201st Air Police Sq PRIMARY SSN CHANGED FROM 213SK TO 405SK. BY ORDER OF COLONEL FOSTER:

28 July 1949: SPECIAL ORDERS NUMBER 140, HEADQUARTERS 3201st AIR BASE GROUP Eglin Air Force Base, Florida, dtd 28 Jul 49. Paragraph 3. The fol named Airmen, orgns indicated, Eglin AFB, Fla, are promoted to grades indicated. Amended by APG Reg 35-16 dtd 7 Jul 49. Current Table of Distribution and 1st Ind Hqs APG Eglin AFB, Fla, dtd 27 Jul 49 to ltr fr Hqs 3201st AB Gp. SUBJ: "Promotion of Airman," to CG APG, Eglin AFB, Fla. TO BE SERGEANT Cpl (405) Maurice F. Mercure AF 12XXXXXX 3201st Air Police Sq. BY ORDER OF COLONEL FOSTER:

10 August 1949: The National Military Establishment was renamed the Department of Defense with a Secretary of Defense having command and control of the Army, Navy and the newly created United States Air Force (USAF).

15 August 1949: The United States Air Force in Europe (USAFE) was established as a Major Command, with all Air Force units in Europe in its Command (excluding major US Command units stationed in Europe). Headquarters, USAFE, was located in Germany, on Wiesbaden Air Base.

4 October 1949: SPECIAL ORDER NUMBER 193, HEADQUARTERS AIR PROVING GROUND, Eglin Air Force Base, Florida, dtd 4 Oct 49. E X T R A C T Paragraph 13. The fol amn asgd orgns ind Eglin AFB Fla will be discharged fr the mil sv eff 4 Oct 49. WD AGO Forms 53 & 55 (enlisted Record & Honorable Disch) will be given. EDCSA: 4 Oct 49. RANK MOS NAME AFSN COMP 3201st Air Police Sq 3201st AB Gp Sgt (405) Maurice F Mercure AFSN AF 12XXXXXX AUTH NO DAYS COMPENSATED FOR AR 615-360 Sixty (60) (ETS) TVL PAY TO: Holyoke (Hampden County) Mass. In accordance w/AFR 173-5 dtd 1 Jun 48 the FD will pay amn concerned in ad, as prescribed in para 37c(2) (a) AFR 67-18. USAF 5704500 060-211 P 539-02 03 S 99-999. BY COMMAND OF MAJOR GENERAL KEPNER:

5 October 1949: SPECIAL ORDERS NUMBER 194, HEADQUARTERS AIR PROVING GROUND, Eglin Air Force Base Florida dtd 5 Oct 49. E X T R A C T Paragraph 15. The fol amn having reenlisted at this sta in the gr as ind for a period

of three years unless otherwise ind for USAF unasgd under the prov of AFR 39-9 1949 a/o AFL 39-8 1949 are asgd to orgns ind and will rpt to the CO thereof for dy. No tvl involved. EDCSA: 5 Oct 49. 3201st Air Police Sq 3201st AB Gp Sgt (405) Maurice F. Mercure, AF 12XXXXXX. Amn enlisted for a period of six (6) years. BY COMMAND OF MAJOR GENERAL KEPNER:

21 November 1949: SPECIAL ORDERS NUMBER 217, HEADQUARTERS, 3201ST AIR BASE GROUP, Eglin Air Force Base, Florida, dtd 21 Nov 49. Paragraph 3. Sgt Maurice F. Mercure AF 12XXXXXX, 3201st Air Police Sq, Eglin AFB, Fla, is granted a reenlistment lv of absence for 11 days eff o/a 27 Dec 49. UP AR 600-115, par 5f. UP AFR 173-5, the Fin O will pay Airman in advance prescribed tvl allowance fr Eglin AFB, Fla to Holyoke, Mass, thence to Eglin AFB, Fla. Auth: 35-4810 5704500. 060-209 P 538-02-S 99-999. Address on lv: c/o Alice H. Mercure, 179 Beech St., Holyoke, Mass. BY COMMAND OF COLONEL FOSTER:

20 December 1949: SPECIAL ORDERS NUMBER 236, HEADQUARTERS 3201st AIR BASE GROUP, Eglin Air Force Base, Florida, dtd 20 Dec 49, Paragraph 1. SMOP 3 SO 217, this Hq as pertains to Sgt Maurice F. Mercure AF 12XXXXXX, 3201st Air Police Sq, as reads "is" granted a reenlistment lv of absence of 11 days eff o/a 27 Dec 49" is amended to read "is granted a reenlistment lv of absence for 16 days eff o/a 22 Dec 49." BY COMMAND OF COLONEL FOSTER:

22 December 1949: Drove home in a brand new 1949 Pontiac Chieftain, purchased with my reenlistment bonus of $360.00. Managed to drive home non-stop in 1½ days, using US Route 1. One of the Airmen I took to Boston was the son of Assistant Police Commissioner "Robert J. Fallon," who gave me his personal business card, signed by him, with a note on the back directing all Police Officers to render me assistance if needed.

While at home, I took my mother around the Holyoke area and she enjoyed it. We went to a French Bakery in South Holyoke and had the best jelly doughnuts that I have ever eaten.

My mother expected me to get out of the Air Force and live at home with her, in Holyoke. I had to tell her that I had just reenlisted for six more years. My girl friend, Katherine Miles, had also expected me to get out of the Air Force. But I had to tell her and disappoint her, too. The news that I had just reenlisted for six years was a big disappointment. She informed me that she did not want anything to do with me. She did not want a boy friend who was a career serviceman, nor did she want to marry one.

4 January 1950: On the way back to Eglin, I let someone else drive my car, while I slept in the back seat. I awoke to find that we had been stopped by the Sheriff's Department for speeding, somewhere in South Carolina. We were taken before a local Justice of the Peace, who fined us $25.00, a dollar for every mile over the speed limit. We managed to scrape up the fine between the five of us. If we had not raised the money for the fine, we would have been forced to work it off on the County Road Gang (Chain Gang). It was $25 or 25 days for all of us. That would have made us late reporting back to the base, where we would have had to face "Absence Without Leave (AWOL) charges. We continued on to the base, with me driving, without any further incidents.

28 January 1950: The Air Research and Development Command (formerly the Air Proving Ground Command APG), was established at Kirtland Air Force Base, New Mexico.

30 January 1950: ORDER NO. 3, 3201st Air Police Squadron, Eglin Air Force Base, Florida, dtd 30 Jan 50. Paragraph 1. The section to which assigned and Duty SSN on the following Airman of this organization is hereby made a matter of record: Sgt Mercure, Maurice F. AF 12XXXXXX, 405 (P-MOS) (405 DMOS SSN), Air Police Section. AUBREY F. JONES, CAPTAIN, USAF, COMMANDING:

29 February 1950: First B-50 Superfortress delivered to the Strategic Air Command (SAC) at Offutt Air Force Base, Nebraska. The B-50 was an improved version of the B-29.

<u>22 March 1950</u>: SPECIAL ORDERS NUMBER 56, HEADQUARTERS, AIR PROVING GROUND, Eglin Air Force Base Florida, dtd 22 Mar 50. <u>E X T R A C T</u> Paragraph 9. Under the provisions of AFL 35-704 as amended the fol Airman USAF org indicated Eglin AF Base, Fla are awarded the Prim AFS and Duty AFS. All SSN's will be retained during the interim period pending full implementation of the Career Program. Provisions of AFL 35-500 and AFL 35-704 as pertains to entries on official records and reporting will be complied with. Sgt Maurice F. Mercure AF 12XXXXXX, P MOS & AFS CONVERSION CLK TYPIST (405) APR CLK (70230) DUTY AFS APR CLK (70230). BY ORDER OF MAJOR GENERAL KEPNER:

<u>April 1950</u>: Joint Fire Power Demonstrations were held annually for the President, Joint Chiefs of Staff, and visiting allied dignitaries, in April of every year. President Harry S. Truman attended the demonstrations in April 1950. An Honor Guard was mounted for him. *(For picture of President Truman arriving at Eglin Air Force Base, on his Aircraft "Independence," and welcoming brass and Honor Guard, see photograph A8.)*

During the JFP Demonstrations, a glider, carrying Airborne Troops (without parachutes), broke in half, spilling troopers all over Range 51. These Gliders are made of plywood and belted together. This was a freak accident. The accident happened right in front of the President, Chiefs of Staff and visiting VIP's.

It is important to point out that President Truman, during his motorcade, made periodic stops to talk to some of the MP's guarding the route. He asked them how military life was, about living conditions, and their families. After all, he was the man who coined the phrase "The buck stops here."

During the basketball season, our Squadron was scheduled to play the Itawamba Junior College in Tupelo, Mississippi, the home of Elvis Presley (of course this was before he became famous). I used my car to take part of the basketball team to the game. While there, I ran out of money to buy gas. So I wired home, asking for a loan of $10.00. I never received an answer, one way or the other. I managed to scrape up enough money to buy gas for the return trip to Eglin. It was after this incident, that I got a job in the PX, as a short order cook, in the Snack Bar. I needed the extra money to buy gasoline for my car.

Later on I got a better job, ferrying films for the Base Cinema System. The Base had three Cinemas, but only received one set of movie films. To overcome this, the starting times for the three Cinemas were staggered—one starting at 5:00 PM, the second at 5:30 PM and the third and last one at 6:00 PM. This allowed the first reel, when it was finished, to be ferried to the second Cinema. After being shown at the second Cinema, it was ferried to the third Cinema, where it was shown, etc., until the entire movie was completed. You had to furnish your own transportation, but the salary was worth it. I worked four nights one week and three nights the next week. It was fun while it lasted, until I received my orders for England.

July 1950: We had a change of Command Ceremony, when Major General Kepner was replaced by Major General Boatner. The change of Command Ceremony was the largest review that I have ever seen or participated in, during my entire service career. I believe that every unit on Eglin must have participated. There must have been 3,500 troops passing in review. *(For a picture of the review, see photograph A9.)*

1950 Hurricane Season: We had a major hurricane hit the Panhandle in 1950, named "EASY." Boy was this a misnomer; in no way was this storm "EASY." The base managed to fly out all of its aircraft to air bases outside the storm's path. Considerable damage was done to buildings on the base. All necessary precautions and preparations were taken, but the storm was worse than anticipated. The base prison was completely evacuated to prisons outside the storm's path. This is one storm that I shall always remember.

8 August 1950: SPECIAL ORDERS NUMBER 152, HEADQUARTERS AIR PROVING GROUND, Eglin Air Force Base Florida, dtd 8 Aug 50. E X T R A C T Paragraph 7. The fol Airman USAF Sgt Maurice F. Mercure AF 12XXXXXX, 3201ˢᵗ Air Police Sq WP 3310ᵗʰ Tech Tng Gp 3310 Tech Tng Wg Scott AF Base I11 o/a 19 Aug 50 purpose attending Cryptographic Technician Course No 80500. BY COMMAND OF MAJOR GENERAL BOATNER: *(For a copy of this order, see attachment B11.)*

20 August 1950: SPECIAL ORDERS NUMBER 232, HEADQUARTERS, SCOTT AIR FORCE BASE AND 3310ᵀᴴ TECHNICAL TRAINING WING SCOTT AIR

FORCE BASE Illinois, dtd 20 Aug 50. E X T R A C T Paragraph 1. VOCO 20 Aug 50 CONFRD. Fol EM (W) (USAF) having rptd this B 19 Aug 50 fr Bs and per auth indicated are atchd (P/LSTU) 3312ᵀᴴ Tng Sq 3310ᵗʰ Tech Tng Gp 3310ᵗʰ Tech Tng Wg eff dt rptd on DS for aprx 8 wks for purpose of attending Crypto Tec Crse #80500 (SSN 805): (Par 7 SO 152 Hq APG Eglin AFB, Fla (APG) 8 Aug 50). Sgt Maurice F. Mercure AF 12XXXXXX. BY COMMAND OF BRIGADIER GENERAL MCBLAIN:

26 August 1950: SPECIAL ORDERS NUMBER 172, HEADQUARTERS 3310ᵀᴴ TECHNICAL TRAINING GROUP 3310ᵀᴴ TECHNICAL TRAINING WING Scott Air Force Base, Illinois, dtd 26 Aug 1950. E X T R A C T Paragraph 4. Sgt Maurice F. Mercure AF 12XXXXXX (W) (Air) (USAF) (P/L Pers) DS, 3201ˢᵗ Air Police SQ, Eglin AF Base, Fla., is reld fr atch 3312ᵗʰ Tng Sq and atchd 3314ᵗʰ Tng Sq w/n/c in dy pr MOS and will rpt to CO thereat 28 Aug 50. BY ORDER OF LIEUTENANT COLONEL KENDIG:

9 October 1950: SPECIAL ORDERS NUMBER 208, HEADQUARTERS 3310ᵀᴴ TECHNICAL TRAINING GROUP 3310ᵀᴴ TECHNICAL TRAINING WING Scott Air Force Base, Illinois, dtd 9 October 50. E X T R A C T Paragraph 26. The folg Amn (P/L Pers) orgn and Bs indicated grade Crypto Tec Crse are eff. upon dept reld fr atchd (Sq as shown) 3314ᵗʰ Tech Tng Gp 3310ᵗʰ Tech Tng Wg (ATRC) and WP on 16 Oct 50 fr Scott AF Base, Ill to their proper Bs in compliance w/ orders shown. Amn will rpt to Shipping & Recg O for processing at 0800 hrs 16 Oct 50. (For pers acctg only). Sgt Maurice F. Mercure AF 12XXXXXX, 3201ˢᵗ AP Sq, Eglin AFB, Fla. (Par 7 SO 152 Hqs, Air Proving Ground, Eglin AFB, Fla., 8 Aug 50). BY ORDER OF LIEUTENANT COLONEL KENDIG:

10 October 1950: HEADQUARTERS AIR TRAINING COMMAND STUDENT RECORD CARD—TECHNICAL TRAINING 213 955 Course Average 3.9 Above average student ACADEMIC EFFICIENCY Group I Superior. *(For copy of Student Record Card, see attachment B12.)*

10 October 1950: SPECIAL ORDERS NUMBER 209, HEADQUARTERS 3310ᵀᴴ TECHNICAL TRAINING GROUP 3310ᵀᴴ TECHNICAL TRAINING WING Scott

Air Force Base, Illinois. Dtd 10 October 1950. E X T R A C T Paragraph 1. Folg Amn (W) Pipeline DS, station as shown having completed Crypto Tec Crse (80500), Cl 08290 are awarded (MOS 805 as Prim and are converted to AFS Apr Crypto Opr; AFSC (29230) and are grad and reld fr dy as stus eff 13 Oct 50 and will remain atchd (Sq shown) pending f/o. 3314th Tng Sq Sgt Maurice F.

Mercure AF 12XXXXXX, DS Eglin AFB, Fla. BY ORDER OF LIEUTENANT COLONEL KENDIG:

13 October 1950: United States Air Force Training Command Certificate of Proficiency Cryptographic Technician. *(For a copy of this certificate, see attachment B13.)*

October 1950: (Undated Letter) HEADQUARTERS 3310TH TECHNICAL TRAINING GROUP, 3310TH TECHNICAL TRAINING WING Scott Air Force Base, Illinois. Letter of Congratulations, from Lt. Col. R. E. Kendig. *(For a copy of this letter, see attachment B14.)* During the Graduation Ceremony, I was presented with my Certificate of Proficiency by the Commander Air Training Command.

24 October 1950: SPECIAL ORDERS NUMBER NO 291, HEADQUARTERS 3201ST AIR BASE GROUP EGLIN AIR FORCE BASE, FLORIDA, dtd 24 October 1950. Paragraphs 2 & 3. 2. UP of par 511.1, AF Manual 35-1, 1 July 1948, as amended, the primary SSN of Sgt Maurice F. Mercure AF 12XXXXXX, 3201st Air Police Sq, 3201st AB Gp, is changed from 405 SK to 805 SSK. 3. UP of APG Reg 38-23, dtd 13 Sep, Sgt (805) Maurice F. Mercure AF 12XXXXXX, 3201st Air Police Sq, 3201st AB Gp, is reassigned to Hq & Hq Sq, 3201st AB Gp, EDCSA: 25 October 1950. BY ORDER OF LIEUTENANT COLONEL WRIGHT:

27 October 1950: HEADQUARTERS AIR PROVING GROUND Eglin Air Force Base, Florida Office of the Air Provost Marshal, dtd 27 Oct 50. Subj: Security Clearance Administrative Final Secret Clearance. *(For a copy of this letter, see attachment B15.)*

17 February 1951: SPECIAL ORDERS NUMBER 39, HEADQUARTERS 3201ST AIR BASE GROUP Eglin Air Force Base, Florida dtd 17 February 1951 E X T R A

<u>C T</u> Paragraph 1. UP of par 9c, APG Reg 35-10, dtd 14 Aug 50, and 1ˢᵗ Ind. dtd 16 Feb 51, file 220,01, Hqs APG, Eglin AF Base, Fla., to ltr hqs 3201ˢᵗ AB Gp Eglin AF Base, Fla., dtd 25 Jan 51, SUBJ: "Request for change in the classification of Airman," the fol named amn orgns indicated are awarded Primary AFSC's as indicated: Hq & Hq SQ, 3201ˢᵗ AB Gp <u>RANK</u> Sgt <u>NAME</u> Maurice F. Mercure <u>AFSN</u> AF 12XXXXXX <u>FROM AFSC TITLE</u> 29230 Apr Crypto Opr <u>TO AFSC TITLE</u> 29250 Sr Crypto Opr. BY ORDER OF COLONEL WRIGHT:

<u>18 February 1951</u>: SPECIAL ORDERS NUMBER 9, HEADQUARTERS & HEADQUARTERS SQUADRON 3201ˢᵀ AIR BASE GROUP Eglin Air Force Base, Florida dtd 18 February 1951. Paragraph 1. The duty asgmt on the following named Airman (Race W) is chgd as indicated. <u>RANK</u> Sgt <u>NAME</u> Mercure, Maurice F. <u>AFSN</u> AF 12XXXXXX <u>P-AFSC</u> 29250 <u>OLD Dy-AFSC</u> 29230 <u>NEW Dy-AFSC</u> 29250 <u>DY Sect</u> Comm JOHN A. MOXILY, MAJOR, USAF, COMMANDING:

<u>20 July 1951</u>: GENERAL ORDER NO 7 3201ˢᵀ AIR BASE GROUP 3201ˢᵀ AIR BASE WING Eglin Air Force Base, Florida dtd 20 July 1951. Paragraph—The fol named amn, 3201ˢᵗ AB Gp, 3201ˢᵗ AB Wg, Eglin AFB, Fla, orgns indicated are awarded the Good Conduct Medal a/o Clasp for period of service shown. Auth: 35-50, as amended: HQS 3201ˢᵀ AB GP <u>RANK</u> Sgt <u>NAME</u> Maurice F. Mercure <u>AFSN</u> AF 12XXXXXX <u>PERIOD OF SERVICE</u> 1 Jul 48-30 Jun 51. <u>MEDAL OR CLASP</u> Medal. BY ORDER OF MAJOR WRIGHT:

<u>8 August 1951</u>: SPECIAL ORDER NO 177 3201ˢᵀ AIR BASE GROUP 3201ˢᵀ AIR BASE WING Eglin Air Force Base, Florida. Dtd 8 August 1951. E X T R A C T Paragraph 7. UP of AF Ltr 39-7, 2 Jul 51 and Ltr Hqs APG Eglin AFB, Fla., dtd 31 Jul 51. File 220.2, the fol amn are promoted to grade indicated. AFUS temporary. Eff <u>8 August 1951</u>. <u>FROM SERGEANT TO STAFF SERGEANT</u>. Sgt 29250 Maurice F. Mercure AF 12XXXXXX HQS 3201ˢᵗ AB GP. BY ORDER OF COLONEL WRIGHT:

News of my promotion reached me in the Mess Hall, where I was pulling K.P. (Kitchen Police). I suddenly realized that I would never have to pull K.P. again, due to my new rank, because Staff Sergeant and above were excused from this duty.

<u>22 August 1951</u>: RECEIVED CERTIFICATE, FIRE PROTECTION AND CRASH RESCUE SECTION, INSTALLATION OFFICE Eglin Air Force Base, Florida dtd 22 Aug 51. *(For copy of picture of class participation, see photograph A10.)*

<u>28 August 1951</u>: SPECIAL ORDERS NUMBER 193, HEADQUARTERS 3201ST AIR BASE GROUP, Eglin Air Force Base, Florida, dtd 28 August 1951. Paragraph 4. The fol named Amn Hqs 3201st AB Gp, Eglin AF Base, Fla., are appointed the additional duty of Auxiliary Fire

Fighters, UP APG Reg 92-5. S SGT Maurice F. Mercure AF 12XXXXXX. BY ORDER OF COLONEL WRIGHT:

<u>11 September 1951</u>: USAFI FORM NO. A-10, UNITED STATES ARMED FORCES INSTITUTE, Madison, Wisconsin 11 September 1951. Military Test Report completed and passed, GED High School Level Test. *(For copy of this form, see attachment B16.)*

<u>20 September 1951</u>: USAFI FORM A-2, dtd 20 September 1951. U. S. Armed Forces Institute, Madison, Wisconsin dtd 20 Sept 51. Military Test Report completed and passed, GED High School Level Test. *(For copy of this form, see attachment B17.)*

<u>21 September 1951</u>: SPECIAL ORDER NO. 210, HEADQUARTERS 3201ST AIR BASE GROUP, Eglin Air Force Base, Florida, dtd 21 September 1951. E X T R A C T Paragraph 5. The fol amn Hq, 3201st AB Gp, Eglin AFB, Fla., are here by atchd to Hq Sq Sect, Hq 3201st AB Gp, for administration, in compliance with Ltr, Hq, APG, Eglin AFB, Fla, file 200.3, Subj: "Non-Compliance with Decimal Ltr File 322, dtd 2 Jul 51," dtd 17 Sep 51. SSgt Maurice F. Mercure. BY ORDER OF COLONEL WRIGHT:

<u>5 October 1951</u>: SPECIAL ORDERS NUMBER 230, HEADQUARTERS AIR PROVING GROUND Eglin Air Force Base, Florida, dtd 5 October 1951. E X T R A C T Paragraph 35. The folg amn are reld fr asmt & dy w/orgns ind (PP) (APG) this sta and asgd in gr to 2266th PPS (OsRepl) 2225th PPG (Con AC) Cp Kilmer NJ for subq

os asgmt on Project ETO 1112. Shipt identifier AP-A. Depns will not accompany nor join amn at AFORG. AFR 35-48 w/b complied with and all immunizations dird therein w/b accomplished im. Mailing address: Grade, Name, 12 XXX XXX, Cas Mail Directory APO 872 c/o PM NY NY. Fifteen (15) DDALVP. Tvl by mil coml acft, coml rail and/or bus is authd. TPA. If tvl is performed TPA 5 days tvl time authd. WP. PCS. PCA. TIN 5723500 248-341 P 533.5 02 03 05 07 S 909-999. Auth: Ltr AFPMP-2B-4 Hq USAF 21 Sep 51 Subj: Allocations and Withdrawals for FEAF and MATS-PAC Rotation. Rept to the CO AFORG NLT 12 Nov 51. EDCSA: 12 Nov 51. Hq 3201st AB Gp Ssgt Maurice F. Mercure AF 12XXXXXX (USAF) (W) (FSC O) (Db 14 Aug 28) (PAFSC 29250) (Shipping AFSC 29250) (DAFSC 29250) (TOE 6 yrs) (DOE 5 Oct 49) (DOS 4 Oct 55). BY COMMAND OF MAJOR GENERAL BOATNER:

9 October 1951: USAFI FORM A-66, UNITED STATES ARMED FORCES INSTITUTE, Madison, Wisconsin dtd 9 Oct 51. SUBJECT: Information on course completion, Test Results, and Accreditation Procedures. TO: SSgt Maurice F. Mercure 12 XXX XXX Hq, 3201st AB Gp, Eglin AFB, Florida. Official report of my High School Level GED was sent to my High School. *(For a copy of this form, see attachment B18.)*

10 October 1951: Home on leave, before going overseas.

30 October 1951: VA FORM FL-9-55, VETERANS ADMINISTRATION, WASHINGTON 24, D.C. dtd 30 Oct 51. Your application for Conversion of National Service Life Insurance approved.

20 November 1951: Restricted OUTGOING TRANSPORT USNS M. L. HERSEY SAILING o/a 28 Nov 51 STAGED AT CAMP KILMER, NEW JERSEY AB-B186A (a) 9th Increment Provisional Squadron 1689 APO 125 dtd 20 November 51 Reld Asgd 2266th Pers Processing Sq OR p/1 NAME 66. MERCURE, MAURICE F. DOB 14 Aug XX RANK SSgt AFSC-P 29250 SN AF 12XXXXXX AFSC-P 29250 TOE 6 Yrs. DROS DOS 4 Oct 55 COMP USAF RACE W FSC O page (3) AB-B186A(a) 9th Incr Prov Sq 1689 APO 125 o/a 28 Nov 51 PAGE 3 OF 12 Restricted. *(For a copy of this letter, see attachment B19.)*

<u>21 November 1951</u>: Restricted SPECIAL ORDERS NUMBER 234, HEADQUARTERS 2225TH PERSONNEL PROCESSING GROUP Camp Kilmer, New Jersey dtd 21 November 1951. <u>E X T R A C T</u> Paragraph 88. Per (POR quald) on atchd roster asgd 2266th Pers Processing Sq (OR) (p/1) (ConAC) this sta are dsgd shipt indicated, rsgd 7551st Pers Processing Sq (Repl) APO 125 c/o Postmaster New York, NY for fur asgmt & trans to orgns & stas indicated & WP NYPE Brooklyn, NY by rail, bus or govt mtr trans so as to rept o/a 28 Nov 51 to CG thereat for fur mv OCLUS. Depns, relatives, friends <u>&</u> pets will not accompany nor jn Pers at PE. TPA not auth. (EDCSA) between 2266th Pers Processing Sq (OR) (p/1) & 7551st Pers Processing Sq (Repl) w/b 8 Dec 51). <u>SHIPT</u> AB-B186-A(a) <u>INCR</u> 9TH <u>PROV SQ</u> 1689 RSGD ditto.

Shipt of privately owned automobile os auth IAW AFL 75-43 dtd 30 Apr 48 for Offs & Amn of the 1st three grades and Amn of the 4th gr w/7 yrs completed sv only. Provs AFR 35-48 dtd 4 Nov 49 (POR) w/b complied w/.

Marking & Handling of personal bag w/b accomplished IAW provs par 16 AFR 35-48.

Pers will advise correspondents by use of DD Form 415 (Notice of C of address) that mailing address w/b as indicated below. Pers will furn DD Form 413 to publishers: (RANK) (NAME) (12 XXX XXX) Prov Sq_____ APO 125 c/o Postmaster New York, NY.

Trans Off will furn trans to NYPE Brooklyn NY. TBGAA PCA PCS TIN 5723599 248-341 P 535.5-02 03 07 S99-999. (Auth: Restricted Ltr DAF Hq USAF Washington 25 D.C. File AFPMP-2B-3 subj: "Shipment Number (Unclassified)" dtd 21 Sep 51 & 23 Oct 51) (Re: MA Roster 183) BY ORDER OF COLONEL ROTH: Restricted. *(For a copy of S.O. No. 234, dtd 21 Nov 51, see attachment B20.)*

CHAPTER 4

28 NOVEMBER 1951 - 15 NOVEMBER 1954

ENGLAND—RAF STATION UPPER HEYFORD, OXON

A. Portsmouth, Eng		7 Dec 1951-7 Dec 1951
B. RAF Station Shaftsbury, Eng (TDY)		8 Dec 1951-11 Dec 1951
C. RAF Station Brize Norton, Eng (TDY)		11 Dec 1951-11 Dec 1951
D. RAF Station Upper Heyford, Eng		12 Dec 1951-15 Nov 1954
E. RAF Station Middleton Stoney, Eng		12 Dec 1951-19 Apr 1951
F. RAF Station So. Ruislip, Eng (TDY)		26 Jan 1952-26 Jan 1952
G. RAF Station Wyten, Eng (TDY)		29 Jan 1952-29 Jan 1952
H. RAF Station Burtonwood, Eng (TDY)		22 Apr 1952-23 Apr 1952
I. RAF Station Bicester, Eng (Visit)		1 Jul 1952-1 Jul 1952
J. RAF Station West Drayton, Eng (Tdy)		19 Jul 1953-15 Aug 1953
K. RAF Station Mildenhall, Eng (TDY)		Various times over the years
L. RAF Station Prestwick, Scotland, UK (TDY)		16 Nov 1953-17 Nov 1953
M. RAF Station High Wycombe, Eng (TDY)		Various times over the years

28 November 1951: On the high seas heading for the British Isles and Europe. What an ocean voyage this was going to be. It certainly was a real experience, one that I shall never forget.

Before sailing to the United States and picking up troops for the British Isles and Europe, the USNS (United States Naval Ship) General M. L. Hersey left Bremerhaven, Germany, loaded with White Russian Displaced Persons (D.P.'s). As she was leaving

Bremerhaven Harbor, she became involved in a collision with a freighter, causing damage to her bow. After temporary repairs in Bremerhaven, she continued on her way to the US. Reaching New York, she unloaded the D.P.'s. Instead of being dry docked and repaired, the US Navy, thinking she seemed fit, turned her around and sent her to the British Isles and Europe loaded with troops and their personal baggage. They were headed for the European Theatre of Operations (ETO). The ship had not been properly fumigated, causing problems for the troops. I can understand the military's urgent need to meet its new requirements and commitments; but, I thought that a delay was in order to repair and fumigate the General Hersey.

I was assigned to a compartment with seventeen other Airmen, one of whom was a cousin of the ship's Chief Baker. As I was friendly with his cousin, the Chief Baker had us assigned to the ship's bakery, where we baked bread for the ship's crew and the troops. The Chief Baker had us issued with white hats and dungarees, and gave us the run of the ship. We baked bread in the early hours of the morning, and at night, we showed movies to the officers, NCO's and their wives.

We passed out fresh bread to the Airmen in our compartment, next to the bakery. We did this to try to prevent them from becoming seasick, but to no avail, as the ship was experiencing severe weather. My friend and I did not get seasick, but the rest of the Airmen did. It got so bad that the ship's Captain ordered all the troops topside for fresh air. But most of them were so sick, that they could not do so. On orders from the ship's Captain, the ship's crew had to use fire hoses to drive them topside, so they could clean out their compartments. Poor souls were so sick that they were running from all ends simultaneously.

As we crossed the Atlantic Ocean, the ship began to take on some water through the temporary bow repairs. The water reached the cargo hold containing the troops' baggage. Some damage was done to some of the troops' baggage. My friend and I were lucky, as our baggage did not get wet. It seems that our baggage was at the top of the cargo hold. We did, however, have trouble with the pests left behind by the White Russian D.P.'s.

7 December 1951: We arrived in Portsmouth, England, and proceeded to disembark the troops, being assigned to England, from the ship. We were greeted on the dock by an RAF Sergeant and an RAF WAF, who gave us a cup of hot tea and a bullybeef

sandwich, and they said, "Welcome to the UK Yank." From Portsmouth, we were bused to RAF Station Shaftsbury, for processing and further assignment.

While at RAF Station Shaftsbury, I met an old friend of mine, Sgt. Lawrence (Larry) G. Steffan, who had been stationed with me at Lackland, Scott and Eglin Air Force Bases respectively. He informed me that he had married an English girl, from the Land Army. Over dinner, we reminisced about old times, and a good time was had by all.

7 December 1951: RESTRICTED. SPECIAL ORDERS NUMBER 127, 7551ST PERSONNEL PROCESSING SQUADRON APO 125, U. S. AIR FORCE dtd 7 December 1951.
E X T R A C T Paragraph 33. Folg named Amn (Inbound P/L) are reld fr asgmt w/this Orgn & reasgd to 7503rd Spt Wg, (3AF) (USAFE). APO 147, USAF. Amn WP o/a 11 Dec 51 by rail and/or Coml Trans to Brize Norton, Oxfordshire, England RUAT to CO, for dy. Tvl by coml rail, vessel and air auth. Tvl by mil acft or MSTS directed if avail and meets the requirements of the sv. PCS PCA TDN TCNT 5723500 280-361 P 533 (.7) 02-03-07-S99-999. Auth: AFR 35-59, 3rd AFR 11-1 & VOCG, 3rd Air Force. EDCSA: 21 Dec 51. NAME Mercure, Maurice F. AFSC-P 29250 RANK SSgt DROS 21 Dec 54 AFSN AF 12XXXXXX COMP USAF AFSC-S 29270 FSC O TOE 6 yrs DOS 4 Oct 55 RACE W BY ORDER OF LIEUTENANT COLONEL BATES: RESTRICTED.

11 December 1951: Departed RAF Station Shaftsbury by bus to RAF Station Brize Norton, for further processing and reassignment.

11 December 1951: RESTRICTED—SPECIAL ORDERS NUMBER 146, HEADQUARTERS 7503D AIR SUPPORT WING APO 147 US Air Force, 11 December 1951 E X T R A C T Paragraph 9. Folg named amn pres asgd Hq 7503d AS Wg are reld fr asgmt & resgd to 7509th AB Gp APO 147 USAF & w/p o/a 13 Dec 51. EDCSA: 26 Dec 51. S/R MPR & A/P W. accompany amn. PCA PCS TDN TBCAA 5723500 280-361 p 533 (.7)-02-03-07 S99-999. AUTH: AFR 35-59. RANK SSgt NAME Maurice F. Mercure AFSN AF 12XXXXXX DAFSC 29250. BY ORDER OF COLONEL BOOTH: RESTRICTED.

<u>11 December 1951</u>: We were transferred from RAF Station Brize Norton, to RAF Station Upper Heyford, Oxon, England, which was to be my new permanent Duty Station. I was billeted on RAF Station (Satellite of Upper Heyford) Middleton Stoney. Middleton Stoney was an old abandoned British Military Hospital of the World War II era. It was sadly in need of repairs. We lived in eight-man rooms, with a potbelly stove in the middle of the room. The stove kept us warm, as long as we did not let it go out. We used to cook canned whole chickens, and warmed up cans of soup, on the top of it. The bathrooms were a long way away, down a long windy corridor with broken windows. They had mostly bath tubs, instead of showers. Showers were at a premium, and sadly missed by all.

<u>14 December 1951</u>: SPECIAL ORDERS NUMBER 121, HEADQUARTERS, 7509TH AIR BASE GROUP APO 147, US AIR FORCE, dtd 14 December 1951. <u>C O N S O L I D A T E D</u>. Paragraph 4. Folg named amn having been asgd this orgn per par 9 SO 146 Hq 7503rd AS Wg APO 147 US Air Force are further asgd 7509th Opr Sq 7509th AB Gp APO 147 US Air Force & WP o/a 14 Dec 51. <u>EDCSA: 26 Dec 51</u>. PCA. No tvl involved. S/R & A/P w/accompany amn. AUTH: AFR 35-59. <u>RANK</u> SSgt <u>NAME</u> Maurice F. Mercure <u>AFSN</u> AF 12XXXXXX <u>DAFSC</u> 29250 BY ORDER OF COLONEL SNOWDEN:

<u>14 December 1951</u>: The Unit to which I was assigned was the 7509th Operations Squadron, 7509th Air Base Group, RAF Station Upper Heyford, England. I was placed in charge of the Base Crypto Center, as its NCOIC. The Base Crypto Center consisted of the following Personnel:

1. S Sgt Maurice F. Mercure, NCOIC
2. S Sgt Ivey L. Allbritton, Asst NCOIC
3. Sgt Robert L Richards
4. PFC Joe R. Herrick
5. PFC Joe W. Jacks
6. PFC Homer I. Moffitt

At Middleton Stoney, we had our own Mess Hall, and the Mess Sergeant was something else. When the menu called for "pork chops," and if you were the few lucky ones to eat first, you got pork chops. If you were not, you got "lamb chops." If the menu called for "hamburgers," again if you were the first to eat, you got "hamburgers." If not, you got "goatburgers." It appeared that the Mess Sergeant was selling our meat rations out the back door of the Mess Hall, to the locals, then served the troops whatever meat he could get on the local market—cheap. It must have been a very lucrative business because of rationing on the local economy and also with the shortage of good meat. I understand that he was caught by OSI and the local police, and was put out of business. When we moved into the new barracks on Upper Heyford, we did not have this problem.

10 January 1952: PERSONNEL ACTIONS MEMORANDUM NUMBER 2, HEADQUARTERS 7509TH AIR BASE GROUP APO 147 US AIR FORCE, dtd 10 January 1952. Paragraph 4. UP AFR 35-592 & USAFE Reg 50-2 folg named amn 7509th Operations Sq 7509th AB Gp APO 147 US Air Force are asgd duty in AFSC indicated. S Sgt Maurice F. Mercure AF 12XXXXXX PAFSC 29250 DAFSC 29250 BY ORDER OF LIEUTENANT COLONEL ROPER:

26 January 1952: RESTRICTED. SPECIAL ORDERS NUMBER 22, HEADQUARTERS 7509TH AIR BASE GROUP APO 147 US AIR FORCE, dtd 26 January 1952. C O N S O L I D A T E D Paragraph 1. Folg off & amn 7509th Opn Sq 7509th AB Gp APO 147 US Air Force are placed on TDY for a pd of one (1) day & WP o/a 26 January 52 to Hq 7th AD S. Ruislip, Middlesex, Eng for purpose of coordination of Crypto Matters & upon compl of TDY w/r proper orgn & sta WOD. FO making pmt on this o w/fwd cy of pd vou to Fisc O this sta. Funds chargeable to acctg clas TDN TPA is deemed more advantageous to the Govt 5723400 260-3009 P 458 (.6)-02 S61-708. AUTH: AFR 35-59 & TWX 7AD ODCA 536. 1ST LT ARTHUR M. BROWN AO 58XXXX S Sgt Maurice F. Mercure AF 12XXXXXX. BY ORDER OF COLONEL GILLEM II: RESTRICTED

31 January 1952: RESTRICTED. SPECIAL ORDERS NUMBER 4 HEADQUARTERS 3918TH AIR BASE GROUP APO 147 US AIR FORCE, dtd 31 January 1952. C O N

S O L I D A T E D Paragraph 12. Folg Off & amn 3918th Oprs Sq 3918th AB Gp APO 147 USAF are placed on TDY for a pd of one (1) day & WP o/a 29 Jan 52 to RAF Sta Wyton Eng for purpose of Cryptographic Matters & upon compl of TDY will rtn proper orgn & sta WOD. FO making pmt on this o w fwd cy of pd vou to Fisc O this sta. Funds chargeable to acctg clas TDN TPA it having been determined to be more advantageous to the Govt. tvl by privately owned veh is auth. 573400 267-9800 P 458 (6) 02 S61-708. AUTH: 7 AD Secret TWX ODG A334 DJM AFR 35-99. 1ST LT ARTHUR M. BROWN AO 58XXXX 3918TH Oprs Sq S Sgt Maurice F. Mercure AF 12XXXXXX 3918th Oprs Sq. BY ORDER OF COLONEL GILLEM II: RESTRICTED.

During this period the 7509th Air Base Group was redesignated the 3918th Air Base Group, consisting of the following units.

1. 3918th Air Base Group
2. Hq Sq Section, 3918th Air Base Group
3. 3918th Air Police Squadron
4. 3918th Food Service Squadron
5. 3918th Installation Squadron
6. 3918th Medical Squadron
7. 3918th Motor Vehicle Squadron
8. 3918th Operations Squadron
9. 3918th Supply Squadron

Attached Units:

1. 1st AFDS
2. 3rd Air Postal Squadron, Det. 6
3. 4th AAA Bn, Hq Btry
4. 4th AAA, Btry "D"
5. 44th Cml Smk Company
6. 1970-1 AACS Squadron
7. 3914th AB Squadron
8. 3930th AB Squadron

<u>March 1952</u>: A3C Herrick was accidently shot in the foot while on duty in the Base Crypto Center. Airmen were inspecting a Carbine (M1 A1). When I entered the Base Crypto Center, I told them to put it back in the rifle rack. Airman Herrick passed the weapon to another Airman, who was standing next to the rifle rack. Somehow, a live round had been chambered into the weapon. While taking the weapon from Airman Herrick, the other Airman's finger accidently got inside the trigger guard and the weapon was accidently discharged. The round struck Airman Herrick in the big toe. It was a good thing the weapon was not set on full automatic, but on semi-automatic. If it had been on full automatic, it would have been a disaster—no telling how many people could have been shot. Luckily the bullet passed between the bones in his big toe, and that he did not lose it. He recovered very nicely. This incident immediately caused a very big concern, and orders were issued stating weapons would only be removed from the weapons rack to defend the Base Crypto Center, and/or for cleaning purposes, under the supervision of an Officer and/or NCO.

<u>18 April 1952</u>: SPECIAL ORDERS NUMBER 63, HEADQUARTERS 3918TH AIR BASE GROUP APO 147 US AIR FORCE, dtd 18 April 1952. Paragraph 11. Folg amn 3918th Oprs Sq 3918th AB Gp APO 147 USAF are placed on TDY for a pd of four (4) days & WP o/a 22 Apr 52 to 6972d Comm Sec Flt, CIO, BURTONWOOD, Eng for Cryptographic Training & upon compl of TDY w/rtn proper orgn & sta WOD. FO making pmt on this o w/fwd cy of pd vou to Fisc O this sta. Funds chargeable to acctg clas TDN Rail TBGAA 5723400 267-9800 P 458 (.6)-02 S61-708. AUTH: TWX CIOAD-4-436 & AFR 35-59. S Sgt Maurice F. Mercure AF 12XXXXXX S Sgt Ivey L. Allbritton AF 38XXXXXX & A3C Joe R. Herrick AF 19XXXXXX BY ORDER OF COLONEL GILLEM II:

Went to Cinema one day in Oxford. Seeing all the lovely candy on the concession stand, I decided to have my fill. I told the young lady behind the counter what I wanted. She kept looking at me in amazement. When I asked her how much it was, she stated "May I have your Sweet Ration Coupons please?" I informed her that I did not have any Sweet Ration Coupons. She immediately took all the candy I had chosen back. Boy was I disappointed and embarrassed. I did not know at the time, that the British were still on rationing since World War II. I am pleased to say that a little while after this incident, candy came off rationing.

I used to go to the town of Bicester, just about every evening after work, and played "darts" with some of the local English chaps in the "Kings Head" (a local Pub). I managed to get high just about every night. At closing time, the Landlord used to say "Time, Ladies and Gentlemen, drink up and go home." A very nice Police Sergeant (Bobby) used to take me to the bus stop for Upper Heyford, and put me on the bus. Around this time, I felt the world owed me something, and I was rebelling against it. I remember starting a really big fight in the Pub one night. What happened, was some Scotsmen came into the Pub wearing kilts. The English chaps I was with dared me to see what they were wearing under their "kilts." Foolish me, three sheets to the wind, I tried to see what indeed they had on under their "kilts." They got excited when I tried to see; they hit me and pushed me away. The English chaps came to my aid and the fight began. The Bobbies (Police) came and broke up the fight. They took me to the bus stop for Upper Heyford (for my own protection) and put me on the bus. I was fast becoming a drunk.

19 April 1952: SPECIAL ORDERS NUMBER 64, HEADQUARTERS 3918TH AIR BASE GROUP APO 147 US AIR FORCE, dtd 19 April 1952. E X T R A C T Paragraph 11, SO 63 this Hq cs dtd 18 Apr 52 as pertains to TDY of amn to Burtonwood AFB for Cryptographic Trng is amndd to include: S Sgt Mercure S Sgt Allbritton & A3C Herrick are cleared for access of clasd mat up to & including Crypto. BY ORDER OF COLONEL GILLEM II:

30 April 1952: PERSONNEL ACTIONS MEMORANDUM NUMBER 29, HEADQUARTERS 3918TH AIR BASE GROUP APO 147 US AIR FORCE, dtd 30 April 1952. Paragraph 6. UP AFR 35-392 the DAFSC of the folg named amn asgd 3918th Oprs Sq is C as indicated. (Confirming—VOCO 18 Mar 52.) RANK S/ Sgt NAME Maurice F. Mercure AFSN AF 12XXXXXX NEW DAFSC 29250. BY ORDER OF COLONEL GILLEM II:

May 1952: I went to the Village of Bicester, with a friend of mine, Jack Gilley. As we were walking down the main road into the center of the town, we passed a Photographer's Shop. I noticed a picture of a young woman in RAF uniform in the window. I told Jack, "Now there is a young woman I wouldn't mind going out with."

He immediately informed me that she was a friend of his girl friend, June Molesworth, and that I could contact her through the switchboard at RAF Station Bicester, where she worked as a Telephone Operator. He further stated that her name was "Peggy Banks." (*For a copy of the picture I saw in the window, see photograph A11.*)

When I got back to Upper Heyford, I called RAF Station Bicester's switchboard from RAF Station Upper Heyford's switchboard, in the Communications Center, where I worked. I spoke to Peggy and made a double date with her, June Molesworth, and Jack Gilley. A girl friend told her, "You do not want to go out with him, because he drinks too much." She further stated, "His name, Mercure, rhymes with liqueur." Peg and I went to Mollies Restaurant, where the four of us had egg & chips (french fries). Then Peg and I went to the "Regal Cinema," where we saw "Mario Lanza" in the "Midnight Kiss." Mario sang "Be My Love" (very appropriate for the evening). It was an enjoyable meal, movie and evening, we had a really nice time. I continued to date Peggy, every night for a week. Her boss, Cpl Ron Camplin, did not like her going out with me (a yank), as he had been dating her. He told her she would have to work the weekend. So, she then asked him for a weekend pass to see her family. She did not tell him that she was going to take me home with her. She took me home with her to see her family at 36 Shakespeare Avenue, Hayes, Middlesex. Her mother and father made me welcome and put me at ease. They were a very nice couple. Likewise her sister Joan made me welcome and made me feel at home. Peg's mother put roses throughout the house for us—like she knew that I would propose to Peggy. On our seventh date, realizing she was the woman I had been looking for and the person that I wanted to spend the rest of my life with, I proposed to her and she accepted, making me a very happy individual. Now I realized that my life had changed; so, I gave up drinking and the Pub life. There was no question that I would be able to pursue my military career, as Peggy was a service brat, was in the service herself, and liked it. Also, the fact that her father was a retired Flight Lieutenant from the Royal Air Force, who served 29 ½ years in the military.

When we used to go to town, all the little children used to ask for gum. Their exact expression was, "Do you have any gum chum?" We would give them whatever we had on us at the time. One time, while out with Peggy, some of the kids continued to pester me, after I had given out all that I had. I remember one incident very well. A little girl was pestering me for gum. I told her that if she didn't leave me alone, I would kick her little fanny. Suddenly all the children began to laugh at this. Peggy immediately explained to me that "fanny" was not a word to use as it meant the opposite of what it meant to us (Americans). "Fanny" in England meant the front part of a female. To us it meant a persons rear end (backside). I understood immediately why they had laughed at what I had said. The English also could not understand why we sang the song "Hallelujah, I'm a bum," as "bum" meant "ass" to them. So they didn't understand why we called ourselves "asses."

Mr. Catlin, owner of Catlin's Taxicab Company, liked to think that he brought us together. Nothing could be farther from the truth. While using the men's room in Catlin's waiting room, the zipper on my trousers broke. I had to sit in the waiting room with my jacket over my fly. I managed not to expose myself and to get a taxicab and to get into it without causing any embarrassment. I am pleased to say I did not embarrass Peg or myself.

One spring day Peg and I went for a walk in the countryside. We decided to stop and sit down for a while. While sitting we started hugging and kissing each other, nothing else. It was a warm day, so I decided to take off my jacket. In the process of hugging and kissing, I got grass stains on my white shirt. So I had to wear my jacket to hide the grass stains. When we got back to Peg's house, I kept my jacket on, so not to embarrass us. Peg's mother thought that I was cold, so she lit the gas fire in the fireplace to keep me warm. It was so hot with my jacket on and the gas fire going, that I started sweating like a stuck pig. But I would not take my jacket off, and reveal the grass stains. When we finally left to go back to our respective stations, I was relieved to get away from the gas fire.

Peg and I started making plans with her family to get married. This entailed a lot of paperwork and physical effort on both our parts. Peg had to fill out and sign a letter of acquiescence—marriage. The United States Air Force, Office of Special Investigation (OSI) had to conduct a background investigation on Peg, because of my Crypto clearance and my job. Peg's father comments, "Who is going to investigate him?" (meaning me). We had to get physical examinations, to make sure everything was OK for us to get married. Peg had to fill out a Statement of Fiancee. I had to write to her Commanding Officer, RAF Station Bicester, for permission to marry her. I also had to submit an application for permission to marry her. It was also necessary for me to go to the Church of England's office in Westminster Abbey, London, to obtain a Special License to allow us to get married right away without posting Marriage Banns, as required by Church of England Canon Law. It cost £10 for this license, which in the end we did not need as we would have had sufficient time to Post the Banns.

1 July 1952: I was able to buy an engagement ring today, as it was payday, to confirm our engagement. Looking forward to getting married and spending the rest of my life with Peggy.

August 1952: Peg and I went to Battersea Park, London, to see the sights and ride some of the amusement rides. On our first ride, as I did not know the value and denomination of each coin as of yet, I held out my hand with a palm full of coins. Expecting the amusement attendant to take what the ride cost, instead, he took everything. I quickly learned the value and denomination of each coin, and this never occurred again. I talked Peg into taking an airplane ride, which she did not enjoy at all. I let her decide what she wanted to ride after that. I rode the switchback (roller coaster) by myself and quite enjoyed it. All in all, we had a grand time and enjoyed ourselves very much.

We had a photograph taken of us behind a Hawaiian man and a Hawaiian hula dancer. When Peggy's mother saw this picture she commented, "Peg, you have no top on." We explained to her that we just stood behind the photo prop and had our picture taken, and only our heads were showing.

August 1952: We set our wedding date for the 1st week of August 1952. Some stupid clerk in the squadron orderly room had promised me that the paperwork giving us permission to marry would be back by the first week in August. So, we set the wedding date based on his promise, in Saint Mary the Virgin Church, Hayes, Middlesex. The approval did not come in the first week in August as promised, so we had to cancel the wedding ceremony and the reception. Peg's father was furious and said that I did not want to get married. I assured him that I did. So we set a new date of October 5, 1952.

<u>22 August 1952</u>: Form UM-3M-7-52, UNIVERSITY OF MARYLAND, OFFICE OF THE REGISTRAR, College Park, Maryland. Report For Semester Ending August 28th 1952. Report of Mercure, Maurice Frank, Upper Heyford. Course History 5 Semester Hours 3 Grade B.

<u>22 September 1952</u>: We received permission to get married from Third Air Force, dtd 22 Sep 52. So, we went ahead with the final plans to get married on October 5, 1952.

<u>4 October 1952</u>: Traveled to London with A3C Joe W. Jacks (my Best Man), SSgt Richards and his wife, Delores. We stayed overnight in a hotel, so we could be ready in the morning for the wedding.

<u>5 October 1952</u>: We were supposed to be joined by A3C Moffitt. He failed to show up. So, A3C Jacks, SSgt Richards and his wife, Delores, made sure I got to the church early for my wedding.

<u>5 October 1952</u>: Peg's father took Joan (Peg's sister, who was the bridesmaid) to the church. While there he checked to see if I was there. He returned home and told Peg that I was at the church. She said, "Good. He is punctual for a change," as I was always late since punctuality was not one of my virtues. She was not going to the church unless I was there.

<u>5 October 1952</u>: We got married in St. Mary the Virgin Church, Hayes, Middlesex, by the Reverend Albert Hill, Rector of Hayes. I was standing at the altar, waiting for Peg to arrive, when suddenly she was there. She bumped me with her hip and said, "Frank, I am here." She looked so pure and beautiful in her white wedding gown. So the marriage ceremony began. Near the end of the marriage ceremony, the Reverend Hill tied our hands together with his stole. He then went on to say, "You are getting married not for the glory of the United Kingdom, nor for the Glory of the United States, but for the glory of GOD." It was a very moving and touching gesture on his part, and made the ceremony more meaningful. After the marriage ceremony, I had

to have the Reverend Hill sign the permission papers to show that he had married us. *(For a copy of the Permission Papers, see attachments B21A-B21I.)*

As we left the church, the bride and groom posed for a picture right outside the church. *(For a picture of the Bride and Groom, see photograph A12.)*

Little did we know or realize at the time that we were being observed by persons (unknown to us), that we would one day become involved with later on.

5 October 1952: A picture was taken of the bridal party just outside the entrance to the church. (*For a copy of the picture of the Bridesmaid, Groom, Bride and Best Man, see photograph A13.*)

5 October 1952: Peggy's mother and father had a picture taken with the Bridal Party on the lawn, just outside the wedding reception area. (*For a copy of this picture, see photograph A14.*)

5 October 1952: We then posed with everyone attending the wedding reception. *(For a copy of this picture, see photograph A15.)*

It was a very nice wedding reception; all Peg's relatives and friends attended. There was no one there from my side of the family in attendance. Only the Best Man, Joe W. Jacks, and two friends, Delores and Richard Richards, were there representing me. The wedding cake was magnificent and tasted really good. I believe that this was my first exposure to marzipan frosting. *(For a picture of Peg and me cutting the wedding cake, see photograph A16.)*

We left the wedding reception early by hired car, which took us to 36 Shakespeare Avenue, where we changed our clothes. We then took a bus to the Strand Palace Hotel, in downtown London, where we spent the night. *(For a copy of the picture of getting into the hired car and leaving the wedding reception, see photograph A17.)*

When we registered at the Strand Palace Hotel, I had to remind Peg that her name was now Mercure, not Banks.

Joe Jacks played the piano at the wedding reception to entertain the guests, with Aunt Cecile at his side to urge him on. There were twenty-four people attending the wedding reception and a grand time was had by all.

6 October 1952: My mother and step-father could not attend the wedding because of the large distance involved between Massachusetts USA, and Hayes, Middlesex, England. They loved going to wedding every chance they got. (For a copy of a picture of the author's mother and step-father, see photograph A18).

6 October 1952: We left the Strand Palace Hotel the next morning for Northholt Airport, where we would fly out to the Isle of Jersey, to spend a seven-day honeymoon. Peg's mother, father and her sister, Joan, met us at the airport to see us off.

We arrived on the Isle of Jersey from Northholt Airport and registered in the Royal Yacht Hotel, which was a very nice place. We went daily to this restaurant to have lunch, as we had breakfast and dinner in the Hotel. While having lunch in the restaurant the first day, we played the juke box. We found the song "Half as Much," sung by Rosemary Clooney, which we adopted as our song. We played it so much over the next five days, so many times, we drove the people crazy. In fact, the restaurant people had it removed from the juke box on the sixth day.

We spent seven wonderful days on the Island and had a good time walking around looking at all the sights. We found the Castle in the Sea very interesting. The only way into the Castle was by a causeway, which was under water most of the time. In the days of Knights, I am sure that it was a very good defense system. When we returned from our honeymoon on the Isle of Jersey, we spent a couple of days with Peg's family.

Upon returning to the Bicester/Upper Heyford area, we started apartment hunting, to find a place we could be together, instead of living apart on our respective duty stations. We looked at several places before selecting 55 Bernwood Road, Bicester, the home of Jim & Tina Meade. We had a bedroom, but had to share the kitchen, livingroom and bathroom. We realized after moving in, that we did not have much privacy. So we started looking for a new place to live which would give us the privacy that a newly wed couple deserved. We unfortunately lived at 55 Bernwood Road from October 1952 until April 1953.

Jim & Tina Meade had a little girl named Karen, who always used to peak at us when we were eating dinner. There was an archway between the livingroom and the kitchen. The Meade's had installed a curtain in the archway to separate the two rooms. Then they placed a sofa against the curtain in the livingroom area. Karen used to climb up on the sofa and peek through the curtain at us while we were eating our diner. She always seemed to have a runny nose, and invariably licked her upper lip causing us to feel sick to our stomachs and to lose our appetites. Because of this (a good excuse), we ate out as much as we could.

<u>24 October 1952</u>: SPECIAL ORDERS NUMBER 209, HEADQUARTERS 3918TH AIR BASE GROUP APO 194 US AIR FORCE, dtd 24 October 1952. Paragraph 11. VOCO's on dates indicated are confirmed. UP AFR 173-31 it having been determined that Govt qtrs and/or messing facilities were not available to the below listed EM, orgn & eff date indicated is authd sta qtrs & subs alws in lieu of Govt qtrs and/or messing facilities until terminated by competent auth dy sta is RAF Sta Upper Heyford, Oxon. S Sgt MAURICE F MERCURE AF 12XXXXXX 3918th Opr Sq 5 Oct 52. BY ORDER OF COLONEL GILLEM II:

We went home to 36 Shakespeare Avenue every chance we got and had a lot of fun doing things with Peg's family—such as going to Black Park, having picnics and going to Ruislip Lido, where we rode a miniature railway.

One day I brought home a bottle of Vodka and only had a couple of drinks from it. So one day, Peg said to me, "I am tired of having that bottle around the house, so you have to drink it up." She got a glass and started pouring Vodka for me to drink. We went through the whole bottle and boy was I drunk. She could not understand why I was so tipsy. She had to put me in my P.J.'s and get me into bed, as I was unable to do so myself. This never happened again, as I did not bring home any more bottles of spirits.

We were running late one day to catch the train to Princess Risbourgh Railway Station, where we changed trains for London. Tina said, "I know a shortcut to the Railway Station, across the fields in back of the house." We said, "OK, we will give it a try," so she led the way across the field. However, the field was extremely muddy and covered with cow manure, so our shoes got covered in mud and cow manure. As a matter of fact, one of Peg's shoes came off in the mud. We managed to retrieve it, and continued on our way. We looked like hell when we reached the Railway Station, as we had mud and cow manure all over our shoes, my trouser legs, and Peg's stockings. We caught the train on time and got on board with no trouble at all. The passengers on the train really looked at us in utter disgust, especially when the heat came on and dried the cow manure and mud, causing a big stink. So, they wondered what we had been up to. I can assure you that this never happened again, as we never used that shortcut to the station again.

We managed to find another apartment, 88 Sheep Street, Bicester, that would give us more privacy. The new apartment consisted of a bedroom, livingroom, and kitchen, but we had to share the bathroom with four other families. Our apartment was located on the third floor and the bathroom was located on the second floor.

Our move from 55 Bernwood Road to 88 Sheep Street was a very short journey. Peg remembers it well; she used a taxicab to make the move, as we had very little in the way of personal possessions at the time. She remembers sitting in the back seat of a taxicab, with a replica of the "Coronation Coach" (my toy) on her lap. The move went well and we were glad to have a place all to ourselves—except for the bathroom.

<u>12 November 1952</u>: SPECIAL ORDERS NUMBER 224, HEADQUARTERS 3918TH AIR BASE GROUP APO 194, US AIR FORCE, dtd 12 November 1952. Paragraph 8. VOCO's on dates indicated are confirmed. UP AFR 24-1 the folg named amn 3918th Opr Sq 3918th AB Gp 194 USAF is authd to rat sep. S Sgt MAURICE F MERCURE AF 12XXXXXX 5 Oct 52. BY ORDER OF COLONEL GILLEM II:

We had a murder on the Base, as follows: A Sergeant's wife had an argument with her husband about an affair he was supposed to be having with an English girl. She really got mad at him and hit him in the head with an axe (which was used to chop up wood for the fireplace) while he was lying in bed, killing him. She covered him up for the night. The next morning she went to the Base Chaplain's office, telling him she could not understand why her husband would not get out of bed for work. The Base Chaplain went to their quarters and found her husband in bed with an axe in his head—dead as a doornail. He immediately called the Air Police, who came and arrested her. They then turned her over to the British Police, as they had no jurisdiction over her—a civilian. She was tried in an English Court and found guilty—sentenced to 5 to10 years, as they had abolished the death penalty. A year later, she was pardoned by the Queen at Christmas time, which is a Royal Prerogative.

Right after this incident, they offered us these quarters, which we refused, due to the circumstances involved.

I was admitted to the Base Dispensary for a blood clot in my right leg. It came as quite a surprise to Peg, as they had failed to notify her (as I requested them to do) that they had taken me from work by ambulance to the Base Dispensary. The only way she found out, was from someone at work, when she called to find out where I was.

5 January 1953: SPECIAL ORDERS NUMBER 3, HEADQUARTERS 3918TH AIR BASE GROUP APO 194 US AIR FORCE, dtd 5 January 1953. E X T R A C T Paragraph 1. IAW SAC reg 55-16 folg amn orgn indicated is aptd to Control Team for 7 AD Opr 0 75-52: S/Sgt MAURICE F MERCURE AF 12XXXXXX Crypto Tech Crypto. BY ORDER OF LIEUTENANT COLONEL GOULD:

14 January 1953: PERSONNEL ACTIONS MEMORANDUM NUMBER 3, HEADQUARTERS 3918TH AIR BASE GROUP APO 194 UWS AIR FORCE dtd 14 January 1953. Paragraph 1. Folg named amn orgn indicated, this Gp, have their Prim AFSC upgraded as ind AFSC w/d as ind. AUTH: AFR 35-391 & AFR 35-392. RANK SSGT PAFSC 29250 NAME MAURICE F MERCURE AFSN AF 12XXXXXX NEW PAFSC 29270 AFSC W/D NONE ORGANIZATION 3918TH Oprs Sq BY ORDER OF LIEUTENANT COLONEL GOULD:

15 January 1953: 3918TH AIR BASE GROUP FORM 19, HEADQUARTERS 3918TH AIR BASE GROUP APO 194 US AIR FORCE dtd 15 January 1953. Communications Section 3918th Operations Squadron, Request for promotion to T/Sgt. *(For a copy of this form, see attachment B22.)*

16 January 1953: PERSONNEL ACTIONS MEMORANDUM NUMBER 5 HEADQUARTERS 3918TH AIR BASE GROUP APO 194 US AIR FORCE, dtd 16 January 1953. Paragraph 10. Folg named amn, 3918th Oprs Sq, this Gp, have their

Dy AFSC chgd as indicated. AUTH: 35-392. <u>RANK</u> SSGT <u>PAFSC</u> 29270 <u>NAME</u> MAURICE F MERCURE <u>AFSN</u> AF 12XXXXXX

NEW <u>DAFSC</u> 29270 <u>OLD DAFSC</u> 29250 BY ORDER OF LIEUTENANT COLONEL GOULD:

<u>1 February 1953</u>: Received telephone call from the Base Commander, to report to his office immediately. I reported to the Base Commander as requested. It seems that under the new Discrimination Regulations, A1C Robert L. Richards had made a complaint against me, stating that I was prejudice against Blacks—that I did not recommend him for promotion to Staff Sergeant because he was black. He claimed that he had asked me if I had put him in for Staff Sergeant and that I had said, "Yes," but in reality that I had not. Because after talking to me about it, he had gone into the Communications Office and asked Lt. Brown if I had indeed put him in for Staff Sergeant. He further stated that Lt. Brown informed him that I had not done so. He then went to the Base Commander's Office (instead of coming to me for confirmation) and logged a Discrimination Charge against me. Upon reporting to the Base Commander's Office, the Base Commander advised me of the charges made against me. I immediately informed the Commander that I had indeed recommended A1C Richards for promotion to Staff Sergeant and had proof of same. I asked the Commander for permission to be excused for a couple of minutes, so I could get the proof from my office down the hall. He excused me, and I obtained a copy of the memo I had sent to the Communications Office recommending A1C Richards for promotion to Staff Sergeant, for which I had obtained the initials of the NCOIC of Communications. I returned to the Base Commander's Office with said document and the CO read it, and then dropped all charges against me, and then excused me. He then called in Lt. Brown, to discuss the problem. I am so glad that I kept such good records of what I did, as this could have ruined my service career. A1C Richards went on to make Staff Sergeant and I went on to make Technical Sergeant as well.

<u>5 February 1953</u>: FORM UM-20M-8-52, dtd 5 Feb 1953. UNIVERSITY OF MARYLAND, OFFICE OF THE REGISTRAR, College Park, Maryland, report for

Semester Ending Feb 5, 1953, Report of Mercure, Maurice F. Upper Heyford. Course Psych 1, Semester hours 3, Grade X.

While taking the train to see Peg's family, I can still hear the Station Guard yelling "Come on, Yank, come on, Yank, the train has to go." I used to run up the stairs two at a time, crossing over the overhead bridge, down the stairs and jump on the train for Princess Risbourgh. *(For a picture of me at Bicester North Railway Station, see photograph A19.)*

14 February 1953: SPECIAL ORDERS NUMBER 36 HEADQUARTERS 3918TH AIR BASE GROUP APO 194 US AIR FORCE, dtd 14 February 1953. Paragraph 1. UP AFR 39-30 as amndd and AFL 39-7 as amndd the folg amn orgn ind are promoted to grade indicated (USAF-TEMP) w/date of rank 1 February 1953. TECHNICAL SERGEANT S/SGT MAURICE F. MERCURE AF 12XXXXXX 29270 3918th Oprs Sq BY ORDER OF COLONEL GILLEM II:

14 February 1953: I called SSgt Robert L. Richards into the Base Crypto Center, where I informed him that I did not want him working for me, as he did not trust me and I did not trust him. That HIS ACTIONS almost got me busted and would have ruined my service career. He agreed with me and requested immediate reassignment and transfer to another base.

While staying at 36 Shakespeare Avenue (Peg's parents' home), the chimney caught on fire. I ran to the nearest telephone call box across the street, and called 999 (Emergency Services) for the Fire Brigade. They came immediately and put the fire out. They informed us that they saw us get married in St. Mary the Virgin Church (as the Fire Station was right across the street from the church). They did something I had never seen American Firemen do. After they put the fire out, they came in with rags, mops and buckets and cleaned up. This was quite a pleasant surprise and experience I will never forget. Peg's mother was out playing Whist (a card game) in the local hall. So, Peg ran to the Whist Hall to tell her that the chimney caught on fire. Her mother said, "Did you call the Fire Brigade, and is the fire out?" Peg said, "Yes." So her mother said, "Good, there is no reason for me to go home then" and she continued playing cards.

Every chance we got, we went to the Fish & Chips Restaurant in Bicester, right across the street from us, next to the British Legion Club. It was something we both enjoyed very much.

28 March 1953: SPECIAL ORDERS NUMBER 64 HEADQUARTERS 3918TH AIR BASE GROUP APO 194 US AIR FORCE dtd 28 March 1953. Paragraph 7. IAW SAC REG 55-16 folg O & amn orgn indicated are aptd Control Team for 7AD Opr 0 75-52. CAPT EUGENE C. MCLAUGHLIN AO 66XXXX 3918th Opr Sq CRYPTO TSGT MAURICE F. MERCURE AF 12XXXXXX 3918th Opr Sq CRYPTO BY ORDER OF COLONEL GILLEM II:

We had to be able to defend RAF Station Upper Heyford against attack from enemy forces. We had periodic drills to aid us in defending the Air Base. The British Red Devils (Parachute Regiment) being the enemy force, would stage an attack on the airdrome. On one such attack they were breaking through our defensive positions on the flight line, when one of our firemen driving a Crash Rescue Fire Truck sprayed the attacking force with foam. He successfully halted the break through in that area. What a sticky, smelly mess; I felt sorry for the British Paratroopers, all covered in foam.

The paratroopers had been briefed, that in certain restricted areas Base Personnel had live ammunition and would respond with deadly force if attacked. One poor paratrooper landed between the blast wall and the Base Crypto Center. (The blast wall had been erected during World War II, to protect the people in the Headquarters Building.) Not realizing that he was in a restricted area, as the signs posting it as a restricted area were on the other side of the wall, he knocked on the window (painted over and with bars on it), and shouted, "You Yanks are my prisoners." This spooked and scared the Crypto Operator on duty, who's reaction was that someone was trying to break in. He seized a weapon and immediately opened fire through the glass window, knocking the paratrooper's helmet off and wounding him in the arm. The paratrooper called, "Don't shoot, I am unarmed." The Crypto Operator stopped shooting and, seeing that the man was wounded, called the Base Dispensary for an ambulance to take the trooper to the Base Dispensary for treatment. He was lucky that he did not get killed. This incident did cause quite a flap. The USAF had to insure the British that this would not happen again and that in the future, we would send people outside to escort any British Personnel landing inside the blast wall area, out of the area, and that we would not use deadly force to stop the incident.

<u>9 April 1953</u>: FORM UM-20M-8-52 UNIVERSITY OF MARYLAND, OFFICE OF THE REGISTRAR, College Park, Maryland dtd Apr 9, 1953. Report for semester ending Apr 9, 1953. Report of Mercure, Maurice F. Upper Heyford, COURSE His 6, Semester Hours 3, Grade B.

I used a closet on the side of the chimney in the bedroom for a darkroom. The door locked from the outside (and could only be opened from the outside). Peg used to open the door for me when I was finished developing the film. One morning while in the darkroom developing film, Peggy was supposed to open the door for me at 10:30 AM and let me out. However, she got to talking with the neighbors and forgot all about me. They went downstairs to the first floor, talking about womanly things. 10:30 AM came and went, but no Peggy to let me out. I started banging on the door and yelling, "Peg, let me out." Of course, she could not hear me down on the first floor. This went on for quite a while before one of them heard me, and Peg came to let me out. I can tell you that I was quite annoyed with her as it was very warm in the darkroom and I was wringing wet with perspiration when she opened the door. This never happened again as I had the landlord fix the lock so that it could be opened from the inside.

I used to ride as a passenger on SSgt Richard Richards motor scooter to the University of Maryland classes on Upper Heyford, from Bicester. We attended classes together.

Acting very foolishly one day, I set off a firecracker outside the window of a girl named Pat, forgetting about her being pregnant. Unfortunately I upset her very much. A week later my wife and her friend Rita decided that they would get even with me for what I did to Pat. So when I came home from work that evening, they would throw a firecracker into the hallway, hoping to scare me. They heard the hallway door go, then footsteps, thinking it was me. They threw a jumping firecracker into the hallway hoping to scare me. As it turned out, it was not me, but Joe Spillbush, whom they scared the living daylights out of.

While at 88 Sheep Street, I had to go into the Station Hospital at Middleton Stoney, to have a cyst removed from my tail bone (base of my spine) and to be circumcised, as

I was having trouble with both ends. Lt. Col. Serrinatti performed the circumcision, but left the cyst alone—why I do not know. Peg was so worked up, as this was the second time I was in the hospital since getting married. This time, however, she knew about my going in. Peg's mother stayed with her while I was in there. As a matter of fact, they walked from Bicester to Middleton Stoney to visit me. This was quite a feat for Peg's mother as she had bad feet. Poor Mum never once complained about her feet in all the time that I knew her. She loved to play cards, so I asked her to play and she joined me and two other patients. She thoroughly enjoyed herself.

They gave me a spinal shot for the surgery. I was awake during the whole time the operation was being performed. I watched part of the surgery until the blood began to flow profusely. They hung a plastic sheet in front of me to block my view.

We lived at 88 Sheep Street, Bicester, Oxon, England from April 1953 through November 1953.

We went to a Theatre in downtown London and saw the stage play "Guys & Dolls." It was an excellent performance, and we liked it very much. It was an enjoyable play and evening out on the town on our own.

10 June 1953: SPECIAL ORDERS NUMBER 117 HEADQUARTERS 3918TH AIR BASE GROUP APO 194 US AIR FORCE dtd 10 June 1953. E X T R A C T Paragraph 1. T SGT MAURICE F. MERCURE AF 12XXXXXX 3918TH Opr Sq 3918th AB Gp APO 194 USAF is hereby granted ord lv for a pd of twenty (20) days eff o/a 10 June 1953, w/permission to visit England and Holland while on lv. Address of amn on lv w/b: 36 Shakespeare Avenue, Hayes, Middlesex, Eng and c/o American Express, Amsterdam, Holland. Amn w/have in his possession sufficient dollar instru to defray all expenses incident to this lv. Amn w/have required documentation for entry into above country as set forth in USAFE Reg 30-10. Upon compl of lv amn w/rtn proper orgn & sta WOD. AUTH: AFR 35-22. BY ORDER OF COLONEL GILLEM II. (*For a copy of this order with immigration markings, see attachment B23*).

12 June 1953: We left the Port of Harwich, England, by Channel Ferry Boat for Hook von Holland, on an overnight journey.

<u>13 June 1953</u>: The next morning we arrived in the Port of Hook von Holland. We took a train to Amsterdam, and checked into our hotel. We toured the city of Amsterdam and surrounding countryside by Canal Boats, which was very exciting and interesting—seeing the fields of tulips, windmills, market places, and people dressed in native costumes (including wooden shoes).

While touring Amsterdam Harbor, we came across a ship bearing the name of "Bacchus." This ship reminded me, that this was Airman Moffitt's favorite "God" from Greek Mythology. So I took a picture of it for him. (*For a copy of this picture, see photograph A20.*)

We had a wonderful ten days in Holland, up to the day we left. One afternoon we went to the Cinema (Movies) and saw the "Queen Is Crowned," the Coronation of Queen Elizabeth.

When we went to check out, we were informed that American Express had only paid for half of our hotel bill. However, we had a receipt stating ten full days for two. So I told them to get their money from the American Express Agency. They agreed, based on our receipt. They asked us to contact our local American Express Office when we got back to Upper Heyford, and to inform them of what had transpired and ask them to correct the situation.

So we took the train to Hook-von-Holland, to catch the Channel Ferry Boat to Harwich, England. We had made arrangements for a compartment with sleeping accommodations for our return overnight journey. After boarding, we washed up, got into our night attire and into bed. Suddenly there was banging on our cabin door, and somebody was shouting "You have our cabin," which we did not. I got things settled with the ship's Purser and returned to bed without further interruptions.

<u>24 June 1953</u>: We arrived back in Harwich, England, and took a train to London and then on to Peg's family home in Hayes, Middlesex, where we spent the rest of our leave, talking about our vacation, and going out.

When we got back to Upper Heyford, we contacted the Base American Express Office and cleared up the matter about our hotel bill.

8 July 1953: ADJ 172 HEADQUARTERS 3918TH AIR BASE GROUP APO 194 US AIR FORCE dtd 8 July 1953. SUBJECT: Temporary Duty Travel To: See distribution. Paragraph 6. Folg named amn orgn indicated is placed on TDY for a pd of thirty (30) days & WP o/a 10 July 53 to 3911th Opr Sq 3911th AB Gp APO 197 USAF (West Drayton Middlesex, Eng) for purpose of attending Comd NCO Academy & upon compl of TDY w/rtn proper orgn & sta WOD. FO making pmt on this o w/fwd cy of pd vou to Fisc O this sta. Funds chargeable to acctg clas TDN Coml Rail and/or bus vessel air authd *indicates TPA authd 5743400 467-3100 P458-02 S61-708. TBGAA TBMAA is dir if aval & meets rqmts of the sv. Dependents will not accompany or join students. Housing & messing facilities are aval. AUTH: AFR 35-52 & Msg 7th Air Div PDMC 9470 dtd 18 Jun 53. *T/SGT MAURICE F. MERCURE AF 12XXXXXX 3918th Opr Sq. BY ORDER OF THE COMMANDER:

14 July 1953: ADJ 176 HEADQUARTERS 3918TH AIR BASE GROUP APO 194 US AIR FORCE dtd 14 July 1953. SUBJECT: Temporary Duty Travel To: See distribution. Paragraph 3. SMOP 6 LO this Hq cs ADJ 172 as reads "WP o/a 19 July 1953 to 3911th Opr Sq 3911th AB Gp APO 197 USAF (West Drayton, Middlesex, Eng)" is amndd to read "WP o/a 19 July 53 to 3911th Opr Sq 3911th AB Gp APO 197 USAF (West Drayton, Middlx, Eng) rptg to CO thereat NLT 1600 hrs 19 Jul 53." Pertains to TDY of amn to Comd NCO Academy. BY ORDER OF THE COMMANDER:

15 August 1953: CERTIFICATE, SEVENTH AIR DIVISION ACADEMY APO 197, U.S. AIR FORCE, dtd 15 Aug 53. This certificate was for completion of NCO Academy. (*For a copy of this certificate, see attachment B24.*)

Peg's father came to the Graduation Ceremony. I do not think that he was impressed with what he saw. He wanted to know why we ran (double time) off of the parade ground. I did not have an answer for him.

15 August 1953: Received diploma from 7th Air Division NCO Academy. (*For a copy of diploma, see attachment B25.*)

65

<u>Undated August 1953</u>: STUDENT EVALUATION SHEET, SEVENTH AIR DIVISION NCO ACADEMY, APO 197, US Air Force. Maurice F. Mercure, T/Sgt, AF 12XXXXXX, Class 53H. I believe that my rating was affected by Major James, as I had a run in with him, when he was CO of the 3918th Opr Sq at Upper Heyford. It is my opinion that he blamed me for his transfer to the 3911th Opr Sq. (*For a copy of this Student Evaluation Sheet, see attachment B26.*)

<u>18 August 1953</u>: Fish & Chips from the UK (Column), Air Force Times, European Edition, dtd 18 August 1953, by M/Sgt Robert B. McEnery.

Picture of NCO Academy Graduating Class 53H. (*For a copy of this picture, see Photograph A21.*)

<u>August 1953</u>: Bicester North Railway Station was the one we used the most, of the times we used the train, as it was the station that made connections with West Ruislip area. The Railway Station Guard there knew us very well. Peg used to get on the train while I bought the tickets. The Station Guard used to hold the train for me. After I bought the tickets, I would dash up the stairs two at a time, run across the bridge over the railway tracks, to the train on the other side, down the stairs and jump on the train. As soon as I got on board the train, the Station Guard would wave his green flag for the train to go.

We used Bicester Central Railway Station for trains going to Oxford, for trips for the day.

We went to a theatre in downtown London and saw the stage play "Call Me Madam." We really enjoyed this play very much. It was outstanding and well-acted. It was nice getting out of Bicester, into the big city. This was a real romantic time for us.

<u>September 1953</u>: The United States Air Force had a new Wing Communications Building built for the Strategic Air Command to replace our old (confining) Base Communications Centre. We moved into the new Crypto Centre in the new Communications Building, using our own Emergency Evacuation Plan. The whole operation went like clockwork, as everyone knew exactly what to do. The Base Air Provost Marshal and his Air Police cooperated fully with our instructions. They did

an outstanding job with perimeter security, and provided the security zone needed to accomplish the mission. Everyone involved, from the Motor Pool, Air Provost Marshal, Air Police, Fire Chief, Fire Department, Telephone Operators and especially the Crypto Operators, were to be highly commended for a job well done.

9 October 1953: LETTER, SUBJECT: Physical Condition of Mercure, Maurice T/Sgt AF 12XXXXXX, dtd 9 October 1953. 7515th Hospital Group APO 194 US AIR FORCE. (*For a copy of this letter, see attachment B27.*)

20 October 1953: PERSONNEL ACTIONS MEMORANDUM NUMBER 55 HEADQUARTERS 3918TH AIR BASE GROUP APO 194 US AIR FORCE dtd 20 October 1953. Paragraph 6. Cfmg VOCMDR 30 Sep 53. T/Sgt (29270) MAURICE F. MERCURE AF 12XXXXXX 3918th Oprs Sq this Gp, DAFSC chgd fr 29270 to 99015 (patient). AUTH: AFM 35-1, 7AD Reg 35-3, as amndd. BY ORDER OF THE COMMANDER:

November 1953: We found our third (and final) apartment at 92 Sheep Street, Bicester, which consisted of a livingroom and a kitchen on the first floor and a bedroom (with a fireplace) and a bathroom (which we shared with only one family) located on the second floor. All in all it was a much nicer place then 88 Sheep Street, where we shared the bathroom with four other families. We lived there from November 1953 until November 1954.

We had a radio at 92 Sheep Street, and I was unaware that you needed a license to play the same. Mr. Barden, the Assistant Postmaster (my landlord) asked me if I had a license for our radio. I replied "What do I need one for?" He quickly told me it was the law (money from the licenses was used to keep the BBC on the air, as they did not have commercials to pay for programming). He further informed me that I could get a license at the Post Office—which I did the next day, to keep things legal.

5 November 1953: The Rangecroft family lived next door to Peg's family. They had a little boy who was very inquisitive. He started talking to me, asking questions about the United States. He wanted to hear all about Halloween, and what the children did.

This was Guy Fawkes Night. He was a keen listener and asked many questions. On Guy Fawkes Night, the British have bonfires, fireworks, dress up in costumes and have a good time. The children love to make a "Guy," and carry it about in a wagon, and go around asking for a penny for the "Guy," to raise money for fireworks. This night is celebrated for the attempted blowing up of Parliament, with King James I in attendance, by "Guy Fawkes" in 1605, which failed. The Rangecroft family was baking potatoes (out in the garden) for the event. The little boy insisted that I be given one. His mother, after her son's insistence, gave me one. We all had an enjoyable evening.

17 November 1953: PERSONNEL ACTIONS MEMORANDUM NUMBER 58 HEADQUARTERS 3918TH AIR BASE GROUP APO 194 US AIR FORCE dtd 17 November 1953. Paragraph 12. T/SGT (29270) MAURICE F MERCURE AF 12XXXXXX 3918th Oprs Sq this Gp, DAFSC chgd fr 99015 (patient) to 29270, eff 24 Oct 53. AUTH; AFM 35-1. BY ORDER OF THE COMMANDER:

24 November 1953: SPECIAL ORDERS NUMBER 242 HEADQUARTERS 3918TH AIR BASE GROUP APO 194 US AIR FORCE dtd 24 November 1953. E X T R A C T Paragraph 15. Folg Offs & amn orgn ind this Gp are aptd mbrs of "SAC Control Tm" for purpose of conducting CPX exercises. AUTH: SAC Reg 55-16. CAPT EUGENE C. MCLAUGHLIN AO 66XXXX 3918th Opr Sq Comm Off TS CRYPTO 1ST LT MICHAEL K. HENRI AO 19XXXXX 3918th Opr Sq Asst Comm Off TS T/SGT MAURICE F. MERCURE AF 12XXXXXX 3918th Opr Sq Crypto Clk TS CRYPTO. BY ORDER OF THE COMMANDER:

22 February 1954: Public Law 513, 81st Congress, 2nd Session, dtd 22 February 1954. (*For a copy of this document, see attachment B28.*)

1 March 1954: Authorization and Consent Agreement, dtd 1 March 1954. (*For a copy of this agreement, see attachment B29.*)

We had a night on the town in London, where Peg and I saw the stage show "Paint Your Wagon." It was very interesting and we had a wonderful time out on the town, in the big city.

<u>25 March 1954</u>: FORM UM-20 M-8-52, UNIVERSITY OF MARYLAND OFFICE OF THE REGISTRAR, College Park, Maryland. Report for Semester ending March 25, 1954. Student Copy Report of MERCURE, Maurice Frank Upper Heyford COURSE Economics 31 Semester Hours 3, Grade C.

<u>27 April 1954</u>: AF FORM 295, CRYPTOGRAPHIC CLEARANCE CERTIFICATE, dtd 27 April 1954. MAURICE F. MERCURE, TSGT, AF 12XXXXXX.

<u>10 May 1954</u>: Letter, Subject: Security Clearance Notification (Mercure, Maurice F. T/Sgt AF 12XXXXXX) HEADQUARTERS 3918TH AIR BASE GROUP APO 194 US AIR FORCE dtd 10 May 1954 TO: Commander 3918th Operations Squadron ATTN: Unit Security Officer APO 194, US AIR FORCE. (*For a copy of this letter, see attachment B30.*)

<u>22 May 1954</u>: SPECIAL ORDERS NUMBER 28 HEADQUARTERS 3918TH OPERATIONS SQUADRON 3918TH AIR BASE GROUP APO 194 US AIR FORCE dtd 22 May 1954. Paragraph 1. T/SGT MAURICE F. MERCURE AF 12XXXXXX, this unit, is hereby granted thirty (30) days ord lv eff o/a 1 June 1954. Address on lv w/be Chine Court Hotel, Bournemouth and 92 Sheep St, Bicester, Oxon, and 36 Shakespeare Ave, Hayes, Middlesex. Amn w/have in his possession sufficient dollars instru to defray all expenses incident to this lv. Upon term of lv amn w/rtn this unit. AUTH: AFM 35-22. BY ORDER OF THE COMMANDER:

<u>5 August 1954</u>: Letter to American Embassy, VISA Section, 25 GROSVENORS Square, London, W1. Dtd 5 August 1954. (*For a copy of this letter, see attachment B31.*)

We went to the Regal Cinema at least two to three times a week, whenever they changed the films, so we could hold hands, hug and kiss in the dark. We always sat in the back row, and also watched the movie if it was interesting. The Manager of the Cinema used to bring us a cup of hot tea near the end of the movie.

<u>28 August 1954</u>: Letter To Whom It May Concern, dtd 28 August 1954. Subject: Margaret D. Banks Military Service. (*For a copy of this letter, see attachment B32.*) This letter was needed for her visa.

Went to the Eight Bells Pub, while living at 92 Sheep Street (which was practically next door), quite a lot on cold fall and winter nights, when we felt like cokes, potato crisp (chips), and/or a sandwich. I would put on a greatcoat (military overcoat), button it up to the top (as I did not wear my uniform jacket and/or shirt underneath). I was lucky that the Air Police never caught me and gave me a ticket for being out of uniform.

<u>23 September 1954</u>: My father-in-law, Flight Lieutenant Frederick Banks, was instrumental in my writing this book. He always told me I should write about all our experiences, because he thought a lot of it was funny and would be interesting to others. (*For a picture of him, see photograph A22.*)

<u>25 September 1954</u>: Request for promotion to M/Sgt, dtd 25 September 1954. BASE COMMUNICATIONS 3918TH OPERATIONS SQUADRON APO 194 US AIR FORCE T/SGT MAURICE F. MERCURE. (*For a copy of this request, see attachment B33.*)

<u>5 October 1954</u>: Peg and I decided to have a little celebration for our second Wedding Anniversary, at home by the fireside (in front of our fireplace in the livingroom). So sitting in our night attire, drinking champagne and eating potato chips (crisp) by the fireplace we listened to soft music on the radio, which put us in a really lovable mood. When who but our Landlady opens our livingroom door, and asks "Do you have a power failure, sitting in the dark, by candlelight?" Which we did not, and she knew it, as we were on the same power source (fuse) as she was. She was just being nosey, and her actions broke the romantic mood, that we were in. I could have killed her on the spot.

Real Love Changes Everything

<u>15 October 1954</u>: SPECIAL ORDERS NUMBER 217 HEADQUARTERS 3918TH AIR BASE GROUP (SAC) APO 194, NEW YORK, NEW YORK dtd 15 October

1954. E X T R A C T Paragraph 17. T SGT MAURICE F. MERCURE AF 12XXXXXX (UADSC-29270) is reld fr asgmt and dy 3918th Opr Sq this Gp APO 194 USAF (SAC) and is asgd Det 2 7551st Perp Sq (P/L) APO 202 USAF (Prestwick, Scotland) for further asgmt to 506th Strat Ftr Wg Dow Me (EIGHT AF) (SAC). 30 DDALV in ZI. Amn WP Det 2 7551st PerP Sq (P/L) APO 202 USAF RUAT to Comdr NLT between 0600 and 1000 hrs 15 Nov 54 for proc and trans to ZI. DEPN: MRS. MARGARET D. MERCURE (Wife age 29 yrs) UKPP 42XXXX (Visa No. 18XXX) is authd to tvl w/amn to dest in ZI at Govt expense. Bag alws on acft not to exceed 165 lbs. A/Pr for amn:18US-3D-2129-AF11/17. A/Pr for DEPN: 18US-3DE-2130-AF11/17. TPA PCS PCA TDN coml Rail and/or bus authd. TBGAA TBMAA 5753500 048-132 B531 (.9)-02-03-07 S99-999. EDCSA 15 Nov 54. AUTH: AFR 35-59 and Msg Hq 7ADiv PDMA 17185 dtd 11 Oct 54. Shpmt Hhld goods authd IAW JTR 22 Dec 50. BY ORDER OF THE COMMANDER

18 October 1954: SPECIAL ORDERS NUMBER 218 HEADQUARTERS 3918TH AIR BASE GROUP (SAC) APO 194, NEW YORK, NEW YORK dtd 18 October 1954. Paragraph 18. SMOP 17 SO 217 this hq as reads "furhter" is amndd to read: "further" and is further amndd to incl: Dow AFB Me." (Pertains to resgmt to ZI of T SGT MAURICE F. MERCURE AF 12XXXXXX 3918th Ops Sq). BY ORDER OF THE COMMANDER:

10 November 1954: Letter, Subject: Letter of Commendation T/Sgt M. F. Mercure AF 12XXXXXX, dtd 10 November 1954, BASE COMMUNICATIONS 3918TH OPERATIONS SQUADRON 3918TH AIR BASE GROUP APO 194 US AIR FORCE. TO: Whom It May Concern. *(For a copy of this letter, see attachment B34.)*

15 November 1954: SPECIAL ORDERS NUMBER 269 DETACHMENT 2 7551ST PERSONNEL PROCESSING SQUADRON (USAFE) APO 202, c/o Postmaster New York, New York dtd 15 November 1954. E X T R A C T Paragraph 1. FNA (P/L) are REL from ASG this ORG & are ASG to ORG & STA INDC. REPT DT W/B ESTAB by PAD. TPA within ZI with number of days OFL TVL time INDC. If POV is not used, TVL time W/B time of COMM CARR used. Concurrent TVL of DEPN AUTH. AMN WILL REPT, upon REC of these orders, to MATS Traffic Office, Booking

Hall, Prestwick APRT, for purpose of processing for MVMT by first AVAL ACFT to ZI. BAG ALWS for pers under the age of twelve (12) yrs will not EXC 65 pounds. BAG ALWS for pers twelve (12) yrs of age and over, will not EXC 100 pounds. ALL MIL PMT CERT W/B converted to US CURR and/or other negotiable INSTR prior to DEPT. MPR S/R & ALL A/P will ACMP AMN. Mail W/B ADD to show GR, name, AFSN & ZI DY ASG. CORR & PUB W/B notified of new ADD. SHIPMT of HHE & UNACMP BAG AUTH IAW CHAP 8, JTR & AFR 75-33. SHIPMT OF POV AUTH IAW 3D AFR 25-7. Air Priorities: as INDC. Thirty (30) DDALVP unless otherwise INDC. WP PCS TDN TBMAA 573500 048-132 P 531.9 02-03 S99-999. AUTH: AFR 35-59, AFR 35-13, AFM 30-3 & 3D AFR 11-1. <u>EDCSA: 6 DEC 54</u>. MIL PERS ARR Idelewild APRT, NY will REPT DET 1, 2225TH PERPGRU, Ft Hamilton, NY for purpose of processing of orders, RANK T/SGT NAME MAURICE F. MERCURE SN AF 12XXXXXX UAFSC 29270 OFL TVL TIME one (1) day DEPN (W) MARGARET D. Age 29 BR PP 42XXXX, VISA 18XXX Air Priority: 18US-3D-2129-AF11/17 & 18 US-3DE-2130-AF11/17 ASG 506TH STRATFWG. Dow AFB, Me (8TH AF) (SAC). BY ORDER OF THE COMMANDER:

Peg's mother, father, her sister Joan, Aunt Edie & Aunt Cecile came to the railway station to see us off to the USA, and to say "good-byes." They all came to see us off, as they did not know when they would ever see us again. After all our "good-byes," hugs, and kisses, we boarded the train for Prestwick, Scotland.

We arrived in Prestwick, (Ayers), Scotland, where we reported in, and where we processed for our flight to the United States. We were put up in a very nice Scottish couple's home for the night. They came for us early in the morning (after telephoning the Scottish couple that our flight was ready). They insisted on giving us breakfast and a snack to take with us. We corresponded and exchanged Christmas cards for a few years.

That morning we boarded the plane for the US. Crossing the Atlantic Ocean, our first stop was Gander, Newfoundland, Canada. From there we proceeded to McGuire Air Force Base, New Jersey.

CHAPTER 5

17 NOVEMBER 1954 - 5 OCTOBER 1955
USA—DOW AIR FORCE BASE, MAINE

A. Portsmouth Air Force Base, NH   24 Sep 1955-24 Sep 1955

<u>17 November 1954:</u> We arrived at McGuire Air Force Base, Wrightstown, New Jersey, on November 17, 1954. We were met at the airport by my family who had driven down from Holyoke, Massachusetts. Apparently they had expected Peggy to go back home with them. However, she wanted to stay with me as I processed through the various incoming military check points. The Air Force put us up for the night in a hotel near Fort Hamilton. My family returned to Holyoke, upset because Peggy would not go home with them. After all the incoming processing was completed, we took a train to Holyoke, where we spent a week with my family.

While at 200 Beech Street, I introduced Peggy to a good old-fashioned banana split at Friendly's Ice Cream Parlor, just across the corner from my mother's house. She really enjoyed it, even though she could not finish it. She thought at the time that it was too large. Later on she became used to the size and ate the <u>WHOLE THING</u>. We took (take out) banana splits back to the house for all my family.

My leave was drawing to a close, so we had to take a train to Dow AFB, Bangor, Maine. We sat on our suitcases on the train station platform, Holyoke, Massachusetts, and waited for the train to Boston where we would change trains for Bangor, Maine. A lady asked us where we were going. We told her, "Bangor, Maine." She said, "Maine is so beautiful; you will love and enjoy it there, especially in the fall." My stepfather accompanied us to the railroad station to see us off; he cried as we left.

We arrived in Bangor, Maine by train from Boston, Massachusetts. We took a taxi cab to Dow Air Force Base, where I reported in. Upon reporting in, they put us up in the base guest house until we could find and/or be assigned suitable living quarters. I checked in with the CO, 506th Strategic Fighter Wing, who in turn assigned me to the 506th Operations Squadron, 506th Air Base Group, (SAC). The CO of the 506th Operations Squadron, was Major John M. Benton. He assigned me to the Base Communications Center, under the Command of Major Linton J. Bassett. He in turn assigned me to the Base Crypto Center, under the Command of Captain Myron J. Gerdes, Crypto Security Officer.

We were assigned government quarters at 239 Elizabeth Avenue, Fairmont Terrace, (off-base housing), Bangor, Maine, and we moved in right away. This was off-base housing and was considered to be sub-standard by government standards. We thought they were super, compared to what we had been living in up to that time. The quarters were furnished by the Air Force with basic needs. So, we went out and bought a rug (for the living/dining room area), two red stuffed chairs, and a black & white television set from the New Central Furniture Store. It was glorious not having to share the bathroom with anyone else—so wonderful to be able to use it when we needed to, without anyone else being in there. The quarters consisted of two bedrooms, living/ dining room, kitchen, bathroom, and a large walk-in closet which was ideal for our needs. We only had to give up half of our Class "Q" (housing allowance) as monthly rent.

Our household goods from England were delivered to 239 Elizabeth Avenue by one man in a pickup truck. The person delivering them, just pushed the shipping crates off the back of the pickup truck onto the ground, resulting in most of our dishes (given to us as a wedding present by Peg's parents) being broken. Unfortunately, I had packed them myself, which prohibited us from filing a formal claim for reimbursement. We learned from this mistake to never pack our household goods (dishes) again—packed by owner (PBO). Because of this decision on our part, we never had a problem with packed by owner (PBO) again, as we let the movers (shipping company) pack everything, so that if anything was lost or broken, we would be able to make a formal claim for reimbursement—under packed by movers (PBM.)

The quarters were heated by a coal-fired furnace, which was located in the kitchen. The hot water heater (also located in the kitchen) was heated by natural gas. We had to light the gas ring when we needed hot water. We had a coal bunker on the outside of the house (kitchen). A coal chute connected the coal bunker to the kitchen. We had to open the coal chute and shovel coal from the bunker into the furnace. This arrangement did cause some problems, such as dust from the coal. Keeping the furnace banked, so that the fire did not go out at night, was quite a job. The second day we were in quarters, the fire in the furnace went out. Peg was afraid that the pipes would freeze, so she ran next door to ask our neighbor for help, as I was at work. Our next-door neighbor came right over, cleaned out the furnace and restarted it. He showed Peg how to bank the fire, so that it did not go out. After that incident, Peg did a wonderful job of banking it every night and keeping the furnace going.

We had our first TV (black & white screen). It was nice to just sit and watch "The Honeymooners," "I Love Lucy," "Father Knows Best," "Hawaiian Eye," etc., by ourselves. The Base Installations Squadron kept everything in shipshape and running order. If we had a problem with anything, all we did was call them, and they came right out to take care of it. We also had a telephone at the time which came in handy for calls from and to work. It also made calling Peg's family in England a lot easier—when we could afford it. The cost for a telephone call to England at that time was $4.00 per minute, and a ten minute call was $40.00. We managed to call Peg's family about two times a year. Then we had to limit our calls to ten minutes, as it was very steep (expensive) on my salary at the time.

Years later, after retiring from the service, we went back to Bangor and visited Fairmont Terrace Housing Area, only to find it had been torn down. All that remained was an open field, being used as a park. It was like a page had been torn out from our book of life.

It is important to point out that on 21 March 1946, the Strategic Air Command (SAC) was activated, under the command of General Curtis E. LeMay. This was to become the largest command in the United States Air Force. The Strategic Air Command (SAC) was the one command in which I would spend most of my Air Force career.

15 December 1954: AF FORM 1164, REQUEST FOR AND AUTHORIZATION OF LEAVE OF MILITARY PERSONNEL, dtd 15 Dec 54. TO: Commander 506th

Operations Squadron, Dow Air Force Base, Maine. Granted Ordinary Leave of 8 days EFF 30 Dec 54 MERCURE, MAURICE F. T/SGT AF 12XXXXXX BASE COMMUNICATIONS 506th Operations Squadron ADDRESS WHILE ON LEAVE: IN CARE OF Mrs. Alice H. Mercure, 200 Beech Street, Holyoke, Massachusetts AUTH: AFR 35-22 UPON COMPLETION WILL RETURN TO HIS PROPER ORGANIZATION Hq 506th ABGRU Dow AFB Maine dtd 17 Dec 54 ORDER NO ABG 555. BY ORDER OF THE COMMANDER:

<u>24 December 1954</u>: Our next door neighbor (who helped Peg with the furnace when it went out), invited us over to his house for a party on Christmas Eve. We had a smashing good time, as everyone was so friendly.

Spent New Year's Eve and day with my family in Holyoke, Massachusetts. We took a Greyhound Bus (round trip) to Holyoke and back to Bangor, Maine. Had a fairly good time seeing in the New Year. Peg didn't know about our custom of welcoming in the New Year with a kiss. So she was taken by surprise when my brother Gaston grabbed her and kissed her. She said, "What do you think you're doing?" and slapped his face. I explained to her about it, and she calmed down.

A disagreement took place between my mother and me. It seems my mother (once again) expected me to get out of the Air Force and live at home with her, for Peg to take care of the house, and for me to go to work and bring home my salary to her. My answer was "HELL, NO." No way was I going to be like my stepfather and Peg like my niece Elaine, to be a household slave. She also did not like it because Peggy talked about England most of the time. My mother forgot how all she talked about for years was France. How she left there when she was nine years old with her brother (my uncle Maurice), who was seven years old. But, she never forgot about it and talked about it. She sent care packages to France during the German Occupation and during World War II.

As we did not agree on things, and that I took Peg's side, it caused a lot of friction. So we left for Dow Air Force Base, Bangor, Maine, after telling my mother, that when she accepted us as we were, that we would consider visiting them again. Until then, we would remain in Bangor. In our haste to leave, I accidently left a grey suit behind. They didn't tell me about it until 1½ years later. It was quite apparent that someone had been wearing it, because of the wear and tear on it. Unfortunately we had a dry cleaner who used to come to the house and picked up our clothes for dry cleaning. Poor soul, I blamed him for losing my suit, and cancelled his service. He was emphatic about the fact that he had never picked up a grey suit from our house. But, I would not believe him, as the suit was missing. Till this day, I regret the fact that I did not believe him and that I did not continue with his dry cleaning service.

In Bangor, we used to go to the movies at least once a week, when the pictures changed. There were three movie theatres in Bangor at the time. Even though we had a TV set, the Cinema still had a place in our life style. We used to walk downtown, have a glass of lemonade in the summertime and a glass of orange soda in the wintertime, before going to the movies. After the movies, on our way home, we would get our groceries at the A & P Supermarket. Then we would take a taxi cab home, which in those days used to cost us about $.50.

We did not own a car during this period of our lives, but managed to get around by walking, taxi cab, bus, or taking rides from others with a car. I was lucky about getting to work as my assistant SSGT Francis L. McCarthy, who lived across the street from me, had a car and he took me to work.

Some of the people we knew were a bit weird, such as Sgt. Buster and his wife (especially her). They were very boring. He worked in the Base Finance Office. One day we spotted them walking down the road to our house, coming for a visit. We were just getting ready to go out; we did not want to spend a boring afternoon with them. So, we decided to avoid them (as they could be a pain in the ass, during discussions about anything). As we had no backdoor to the house, we decided to climb out the left rear window to escape them. They must have seen us leaving the side of the house. (Or, someone saw us and told them what we did.) He got even with us by stating that I had paid back an advance in pay (as he maintained my pay records), that I had gotten when we left England. That was not true, so for a couple of months after I had reenlisted (while we were at Westover Air Force Base), we received only $18.00 a month on payday. Luckily we had our Class "Q" allowance checks and some money we had saved to carry us over.

In the Crypto Center, I worked for Captain Myron Gerdes, who was the Crypto Security Officer. He was an avid stamp collector and used to bring his stamp album into the Crypto Center to work on it. One day when we were changing shifts and taking shift inventory (of classified documents), we found a Secret Crypto Document was missing. I immediately invoked a security lock down to find the missing Secret Crypto Document. All personnel, including myself, were searched. We found nothing. The Shift Supervisor and I came to the same conclusion, that Captain Gerdes had been working on his stamp album (at the position on the console, where the document which was missing was kept). The Captain had not yet left the building; he was in Captain Burda's office. Captain Burda was the Assistant Base Communications Officer/ Communications Security Officer. They were talking about work. I caught up with Captain Gerdes and requested that he return to the Crypto Center along with his stamp album, as we had had a security problem. So, he and Captain Burda accompanied me to the Crypto center. When Captain Gerdes had entered the Crypto Center, we requested permission to search his stamp album. We explained that we had a missing Secret Crypto Document and that he had been sitting at the console position where the document was missing from. He agreed to our searching his stamp album. We found the missing Secret Crypto Document in it, still in its sealed plastic container. The item had apparently gotten stuck between the pages of his stamp album. We did not have to report the incident to the Communications Security Officer, Captain Burda, as he was present during our search and us finding the document. He immediately issued a verbal order that no one could bring personal items into the Crypto Center. This was followed up by a written order. The only items to be allowed in were official packages, documents and/or official papers. Until this day, I like to think that Captains Burda and Gerdes were testing our Internal Security Procedures and that we passed with flying colors. After this incident, no one was allowed to bring anything into the Crypto Center of a personal nature.

When we first got married, we wanted children the worst way. We did not have any. So I blamed Peggy for us not having any. Poor Peggy went to the doctor and they told her there was nothing wrong with her and that I should be checked out to see if I had any problems. Being a so-called "macho" person, I did not believe that it could be me. But, after a while, I had no recourse but to go to the doctor to be tested. It turned out that I was the guilty party, who could not have children, because of my being exposed to radiation. I took it very hard; I did not feel like a man. Peggy was very good about it, and helped me through this difficult time. We explored many ways to have children. A couple were artificial insemination and adoption. We ruled out the idea of artificial insemination as the Archbishop of Canterbury (the head of the Church of England) was against it. We tried adopting, but we were never in one place long enough to get on the list to see it through to the end. We always got transferred somewhere else. So, we agreed that God did not intend for us to have any children and we accepted it. While in Bangor the second time, we tried once more to adopt a child. The Adoption Agency had a baby all picked out for us. However, we got orders to go overseas and the Adoption Agency said we could not have the baby, because we were leaving the country. It would have been different if we had had the baby for six months and then received orders to go overseas. They then would have let us take the baby with us when we left the country. We were very disappointed; we then gave up the idea of trying to adopt altogether.

We used to go for outings and picnics with Francis and Lynn McCarthy around the countryside, which we enjoyed immensely. The area around the base was very beautiful, especially in the fall. We have never forgotten these outings, as they were very special.

25 February 1955: SPECIAL ORDERS NUMBER 37 HEADQUARTERS 506TH AIR BASE GROUP (SAC) Dow Air Force Base Bangor, Maine dtd 25 February 1955. E X T R A C T Paragraph 5. The FNOA, 506th OPR SQ, 506th ABGRU (SAC) this STA is awarded the GCMDL and/or Bronze Clasp w/nr loops as indicated, for his DMST of HON, EFFCY, and FIDELITY during the PD INDC. AUTH: AFR 35-50. BRONZE CLASP W/2 LOOPS GR TECHNICAL SGT NAME MAURICE F. MERCURE AF 12XXXXXX INCL PD 20 JUL 51 TO 19 JUL 54. BY ORDER OF THE COMMANDER:

7 March 1955: SPECIAL ORDERS NUMBER 54 HEADQUARTERS 506TH STRATEGIC FIGHTER WING (SAC) Dow Air Force Base Bangor, Maine dtd 7 March 1955. E X T R A C T Paragraph 27. FNOA, are REL from ASGMT 506th OPR SQ, 506th ABGRU (SAC) this STA: ASG 4060th OPR SQ. 4060 ABGRU (SAC) this STA, REPT NLT 8 Mar 55. NTI. EDCSA: 8 Mar 55. AUTH: MSG HQ SAC DPLMA 17027, dtd 4 MAR 55. (*) INDC NEGROES GR TECHNICAL SGT NAME MAURICE F. MERCURE AFSN AF 12XXXXXX GR STAFF SGT ROBERT E. HARRISON AFSN AF 14XXXXXX GR STAFF SGT FRANCIS L. MCCARTHY AFSN AF 14XXXXXX. BY ORDER OF THE COMMANDER:

Listed below are a few of the units stationed on Dow before redesignation and after it:

1. 506th Strategic Fighter Wing (SAC)
2. Hq Sq, 506th Strategic Fighter Wing (SAC)
3. 506th Air Base Group (SAC)
4. Hq Sq, 506th Air Base Group (SAC)
5. 506th Air Police Squadron
6. 506th Air Refueling Squadron
7. 506th Field Maintenance Squadron.
8. 506th Food Service Squadron
9. 506th Installation Squadron
10. 506th Motor Vehicle Squadron
11. 506th Operations Squadron
12. 506th PD Maintenance Squadron
13. 506th Supply Squadron
14. 506th Tactical Hospital

Attached Units:

1. 33rd Crash Rescue Boat Flight (Southwest Harbor, Me.)
2. 71st Air Refueling Squadron.
3. 341st Air Refueling Squadron
4. 1974-2 AACS DET (MATS)

Redesignated Units and Attached Units

1. 4060th Air Refueling Wing (SAC)
2. Hq Sq, 4060th Air Refueling Wing (SAC)
3. 4060th Air Base Group (SAC)
4. Hq Sq, 4060th Air Base Group (SAC)
5. 4060th Air Police Squadron
6. 4060th Air Refueling Squadron
7. 4060th Field Maintenance Squadron

8. 4060th Food Service Squadron
9. 4060th Installation Squadron
10. 4060th Motor Vehicle Squadron
11. 4060th Operations Squadron
12. 4060th PD Maintenance Squadron
13. 4060th Supply Squadron
14. 4060th Tactical Hospital

Attached Units:

1. 33D Crash Rescue Boat Flight (Southwest Harbor, Me.)
2. 71st Air Refueling Squadron
3. 341st Air Refueling Squadron
4. 1974-2 AACS DET (MATS)

<u>June 1955</u>: It was not unusual for us to have a lot of snow in the wintertime in Maine. However, we did have a freak snowstorm in June 1955. It snowed for a couple of hours, with thunder and lightning, hail and then rain. The snow did not last long on the ground.

<u>16 August 1955</u>: LETTER, SUBJECT: RECOMMENDATION for NCO of the MONTH. OFFICE OF THE CRYPTO SECURITY OFFICER 4060TH OPERATIONS SQUADRON DOW AIR FORCE BASE BANGOR, MAINE MAURICE F. MERCURE TSGT AF 12XXXXXX dtd 16 August 1955. (*For a copy of this letter, see attachment B35.*)

<u>12 September 1955</u>: DD FORM 96, DISPOSITION FORM, dtd 12 Sept 1955. SUBJECT: Transfer of Non-Registered Material. TO: T/SGT M. F. MERCURE, 4060th Operations Squadron 4060th Air Base Group Dow Air Force Base Bangor, Maine. FROM: S/SGT F. L. McCarthy 4060th Operations Squadron 4060th Air Base Group Dow Air Force Base Bangor, Maine.

<u>23 September 1955</u>: AF FORM 1164, REQUEST FOR AND AUTHORIZATION OF LEAVE OF MILITARY PERSONNEL dtd 23 Sep 1955. TO: Commander 4060th

Operations Squadron Dow AFB, Bangor, Maine Ordinary 7 days leave EFF 27 Sept 1955. MERCURE, MAURICE F. T/SGT AF 12XXXXXX 4060th Operations Squadron Dow AFB, Bangor Maine. Crypto Section ADDRESS WHILE ABSENT IN CARE OF Mrs. Margaret D. Mercure 239 Elizabeth Ave Bangor, Maine REMARKS Amn due disch 4 Oct 55 AUTH: UP AFR 35-22 UPON COMPLETION WILL RETURN TO HIS PROPER ORGANIZATION Hq 4060th ABGRU, Dow AFB, Bangor, Me. DATE OF ORDER 26 Sep 55. ORDER NO. 470. BY ORDER OF THE COMMANDER:

Lynn McCarthy had a baby boy (little Stevie), in the Base Hospital at Dow AFB, Bangor, Maine. We attended little Stevie's Christening, along with Lynn, Francis, Lynn's friend, and S/Sgt Harrison. Lynn's friend and S/Sgt Harrison were surrogate godmother and godfather. (*For a copy of the picture of the Christening Party, see photograph A23.*)

September 1955: Used leave time to check out Portsmouth Air Force Base, New Hampshire. There was only one building on the base, belonging to the Air Base Squadron. No on-base housing existed; not yet built, under construction. Off-base housing cost an arm and a leg. Rental fees during off-tourist season were normal, tripled during tourist season. Base was so new, it only had a temporary Headquarters Building, housing the Air Base Squadron and Base Communications Center, as everything else was under construction. The cost of off-base housing was at a premium, as you had to compete with the construction workers, working on the Air Base, for rooms. So, we decided not to be stationed at Portsmouth Air Force Base, New Hampshire.

23 September 1955: SPECIAL ORDERS NUMBER 156 HEADQUARTERS 4060TH AIR REFUELING WING (SAC) Dow Air Force Base Bangor, Maine dtd 23 September 1955. E X T R A C T Paragraph 6. T SGT MAURICE F. MERCURE AF 12XXXXXX is REL from ASGMT 4060TH OPR SQ. 4060th ABGRU (SAC) this STA and DISCH EFF 4 Oct 55 under PROV AFR 39-19 ETS) and WP his HOR or place of acceptance for REL as he may elect. HOR: 179 Beech St, Holyoke, MASS. Future mailing address: 200 Beech St, Holyoke, MASS. PCS TDN. BY ORDER OF THE COMMANDER:

<u>26 September 1955</u>: SPECIAL ORDERS NUMBER 157 HEADQUARTERS 4060TH AIR REFUELING WING (SAC) Dow Air Force Base Bangor, Maine dtd 26 September 1955. <u>E X T R A C T</u> Paragraph 13. T SGT MAURICE F. MERCURE AF 12XXXXXX (UAFSC 29270) IS REL from ASGNT 4060th OPR SQ, 4060th ABGRU (SAC) this STA, ASG 4018th AB SQ (SAC) Portsmouth AFB, NH REPT NLT 7 Oct 55. TPA /1 Day TVL Time AUTH: If POV is not used, TVL time W/B that of CARR used. WP PCS TDN 5763500 067-5700 P531 (10)-02-03 S17-601. Dislocation ALW Other 5763500 P514-01 S99-999. EDCSA: 12 OCT 55. AUTH: AFM 35-11 and HQ USAF MSG AFPMP 851/54, 19 AUG 55 and COMABRON 4018 Portsmouth AFB MSG DP975, 8 SEP 55. BY ORDER OF THE COMMANDER:

<u>29 September 1955</u>: UNCLASSIFIED MESSAGE FM 4050TH AIR REL WG WESTOVER AFB, MASS TO COMDR DOW AFB, BANGOR, MAINE UNCLASSIFIED /BPER 926 ATTN: BASE REENL SECTION: REF IS MADE TO TEL CON YOUR OFFICE M SGT SHIFFRIN AND LT BASTEDO THIS HQS. VACANCY EXIST THIS STA FOR AFSC 29270 in GRADE OF T SGT: REQ AMN BE ASG TO 18TH COMMUNICATIONS SQ, 8TH AF THIS STA! AND THIS HQS ADVISED OF AMNS REPORTING DATE. BY 29/1911Z SEP RJEPO

<u>30 September 1955</u>: SPECIAL ORDERS NUMBER 161 HEADQUARTERS 4060TH AIR REFUELING WING (SAC) Dow Air Force Base Bangor, Maine dtd 30 September 1955. <u>E X T R A C T</u> Paragraphs 30 & 31. Paragraph 30. PARA 13 SC 157 this HQ CS PERT to T SGT MAURICE F. MERCURE AF 12XXXXXX (UAFSC 29270) REL from ASGMT 4060th OPR SQ, 4060th ABGRU (SAC) this STA: asg 4018th AB SQ (SAC) Portsmouth AFB NH W/EDCSA: 12 OCT 55 is REVO. Paragraph 31. T SGT MAURICE F. MERCURE AF 12XXXXXX (UAFSC 29270) is REL from ASGMT 4060th OPR SQ, 4060th ABGRU (SAC) this STA; ASG 18th COMM SQ (SAC) Westover AFB, MASS. REPT NLT 7 OCT 55. TBA W/2 days TVL time AUTH. If POV is not used, TVL time W/B that of CARR used. WP PCS TDN 5763500 067-5700 P531 (10)-02-03 S17-601. Dislocation ALW Other 5763500 048-246 P5 14-01 S99-999. EDCSA: 12 OCT 55. AUTH: AFM 35-11 and HQ USAF MSG AFPMP 851/54, 19 AUG 54 AND MSG from 4950th Air Refueling WG, BPER 926, Westover AFB, MASS, 19 SEP 55. BY ORDER OF THE COMMANDER:

<u>4 October 1955</u>: DD FORM 214 REPORT OF SEPARATION FROM THE ARMED FORCES OF THE UNITED STATES HONORABLE DISCHARGE AIR FORCE dtd 4 OCT 55. MAURICE F. MERCURE! AF 12XXXXXX! TSGT.

<u>5 October 1955</u>: DD FORM 4, ENLISTMENT RECORD-UNITED STATES AIR FORCE DEPARTMENT OF DEFENSE WASHINGTON D. C. MAURICE F. MERCURE, TSGT, AF 12XXXXXX dtd 5 October 1955.

<u>5 October 1955</u>: SPECIAL ORDERS NUMBER 164 HEADQUARTERS 4060TH AIR REFUELING WING (SAC) Dow Air Force Base Bangor, Maine dtd 5 October 1955. E X T R A C T Paragraph 1. S SGT MAURICE F. MERCURE AF 12XXXXXX having REENL in the REGAF for a PD of 6 yrs on 5 OCT 55. ASG 4060TH OPR SQ, 4060th AGRU (SAC) this STA, to fill own vacancy. EFF date of REENL AMN is PROM to GR of TSGT (TEMP) W/DR 1 FEB 53. PG S SGT W/DR 8 AUG 51. AUTH: AFM 39-9. BY ORDER OF THE COMMANDER.

<u>5 October 1955</u>: We left Bangor, Maine, by train for Chicopee Falls via Boston, for our new Unit, the 18th Communications Squadron, and new Base, Westover Air Force Base, Massachusetts.

CHAPTER **6**

6 OCTOBER 1955 - 10 SEPTEMBER 1956
USA—WESTOVER AIR FORCE BASE, MASSACHUSETTS

<u>6 October 1955</u>: We arrived in Chicopee Falls, Massachusetts area on 6 October 1955, by train from Bangor, Maine, via Boston, Massachusetts. Unfortunately our train did not have a baggage car, so our bags were put on a train with a baggage car. Our bags did not arrive until the next day. We were lucky that Peg had an overnight case with her, so we did have some night clothes with us. Since I did not have any clean underwear, I wore a pair of clean pajamas (PJs) under my uniform, hoping all the time that they would not show (stick out from the bottom of my trouser legs). It made for quite a day. I reported to the Commander 18th Communications Squadron and proceeded to process through the various base organizations and offices on the Incoming Checklist. We stayed in the base guest house until we found a place to live.

We found a place to live in South Hadley Falls, 49 Lyman Street, the home of Mrs. Brisbaugh. It was a self-contained apartment. There was one drawback, however—there was a connecting door between our apartment (kitchen door) and the landlady's living area. One of the main reasons we moved out in March was due to interruptions into our lives and living area. We had no privacy at all. 49 Lyman Street was just up the road from the cemetery where my father was buried. Our landlady was a very nosy person. She would always listen at the connecting door to our apartment, or ask if she could be of help to us.

It was nice being stationed on Westover Air Force Base. I was able to see the house I was born in since it was still standing on the Base. I did not get to go inside it, as I would have loved to do. Westover Air Force Base was built around my family's house on Morris

Street. It was also nice being able to look up old friends and/or run into them. One was Willard Ryder who I bumped into while he was working in the A & P Supermarket as Manager. There was, however, one big drawback; it was living so close to my mother.

18 October 1955: SPECIAL ORDERS NUMBER 121 HEADQUARTERS 4050TH AIR BASE GROUP (SAC) Westover Air Force Base, Mass. dtd 18 October 1955. Paragraph 4 VOCO date indc, fna, org indc (SAC) unless otherwise incd, this sta, is auth to mess sep from their org and auth mon alw in lieu of rat. GRADE TSGT NAME Maurice F. Mercure AFSN W22XXXXX and ORG 18th COMM SQ EFF DATE 7 Oct 55. AUTH: B Suppl Nr 1 to AFR 24-1. BY ORDER OF THE COMMANDER:

19 October 1955: MPO #189 18th Communications SQ (AF) Westover Air Force Base Massachusetts dtd 19 October 1955. BY ORDER OF THE COMMANDER:

31 October 1955: AF FORM 1256 DEPARTMENT OF THE AIR FORCE CERTIFICATE OF TRAINING, dtd 31 October 1955. This is to certify that T/Sgt Maurice F. Mercure, AF 12XXXXXX has completed the course in SAC Security Indoctrination Phase I. (*For copy of this form, see attachment B36.*)

Had to attend this course on SAC Security Indoctrination Phase I, which was necessary for me to perform my duties in the 18th Communications Squadron.

The 18th Communications Squadron's Communications Center was located in the old Norton Bomb Sight concrete block house. The Crypto Center was located in one of the vaults used to safeguard the bomb sights, during World War II. The concrete block house was capable of housing the complete Communications Operation.

We bought a brand new Chevrolet automobile to drive back and forth to work and other purposes. We had to dispose of it when we went to Turkey, as the company we had it financed with would not allow us to take cars out of the country.

Some of the units assigned to Westover Air Force Base are listed below:

1. 8th Air Force (SAC)
2. Hq Sq, 8th Air Force (SAC)
3. 8th Recon Technical Squadron

4. 5th Air Rescue Group (MATS)

5. Hq Sq, 5th Air Rescue Group (MATS)

6. 18th Communications Squadron (SAC) (AF)

7. 337th Fighter Interceptor Squadron (ADC)

8. 384th Air Refueling Squadron

9. 1917th AACS Squadron (MATS)

10. 3084th Avn Dep Gp (ADC)

11. 4050th Air Refueling Wing (SAC)

12. Hq Sq, 4050th Air Refueling Wing (SAC)

13. 4050th Air Base Group (SAC)

14. Hq Sq, 4050th Air Base Group (SAC)

15. 4050th Air Police Squadron

16. 4050th Field Maintenance Squadron

17. 4050th Food Service Squadron

18. 4050th Installation Squadron

19. 4050th Motor Vehicle Squadron

20. 4050th Operations Squadron

21. 4050th Supply Squadron

22. 4050th USAF Hospital

Peggy was beginning to feel homesick, and I didn't know when (or if) I would be assigned to England and/or Europe. So, I decided to send her home to see her family by using my State of Massachusetts World War II and Korean War Bonuses. I was able to book passage for her to England on the Dutch Ship SS Maasdam (out of Rotterdam, Netherlands), with return passage on the French Ship SS Liberte (Out of LeHavre, France), sailing from Southampton, England to New York City. She went home for five weeks and her mother, father and sister Joan were glad to see her. Boy did I miss her while she was gone. Life was boring and lonely without her. It was a good thing that I had my work to keep me occupied most of the time. While returning to the United States on the SS Liberte, the ship ran into a Noreaster (storm) along the east coast of the United States. I left South Hadley Falls a day earlier than when Peg's ship was due to arrive back in New York City. I had a shovel, salt, deicer, and sand in the trunk of the car. Driving down the Connecticut Turnpike, as I approached the

Connecticut/New York State Line, I was stopped by the State Police from both states. They advised me to get off the highway because of the storm. I explained to them that my wife was arriving the next day in New York City, on the French Liner the SS Liberte and I had to meet her. I told them she could not speak American (not a lie in the true sense of the word) and that she didn't have any money and would not know what to do if I did not meet her. After a brief consultation, and the fact she had no money, they agreed to let me go ahead since I had equipment in my trunk in case of emergencies, but said to take it easy and get there safely. I arrived in New York City without any problems. After a long wait on the docks, I managed to pick up Peg, who was very glad to see me. She had been worried about me out in the storm. We stayed overnight in a motel until the storm stopped. The next day we started back to South Hadley Falls and arrived home safely (God was with us). (*For a copy of a picture of Peg on the SS Maasdam, see photograph A24.*)

One day I was called to the Carswell Air Force Base Teletype Circuit by the Teletype Shift Supervisor, stating "Someone wishes to talk to you." Boy, was I surprised when it turned out to be S Sgt Ivey L. Allbritton, from my days in England (at RAF Station Upper Heyford). He called to inform me that he had reenlisted and was now stationed at Carswell Air Force Base, Texas. He had previously gotten out of the Air Force because his wife wanted him to. He didn't do well on the outside, so he reenlisted and wanted me to know that I was right and that he should have listened to me. I had previously told him, when he told me that he was getting out, that he would regret not reenlisting. He promptly told me "Hell no. No way. My wife would kill me." I told him to keep in touch with me and if he ran into anyone else from RAF Station Upper Heyford days, to tell them where I was stationed and to contact me.

April 1956: We found a new apartment at 119 Prospect Street, Willimansett, Massachusetts. It was a lovely apartment, self-contained, all to ourselves and located on the second floor. It was a lot closer to Westover AFB than 49 Lyman Street, making the trip back and forth from the base much easier.

While living at 119 Prospect Street, and using the front stairwell, I caught one of my heels on a carpet riser and fell down the flight of stairs on my back. This, I believe, was the beginning of my back problem.

<u>June 1956</u>: We had a terrible scare one day in June, as the base doctor told Peg she might have breast cancer, after an examination of her breast. They performed a breast biopsy in the base hospital. The doctor told Peg that if she had breast cancer, they would have to remove her breast. At that time, it was a total mastectomy (radical). The biopsy turned out to be benign, "HALLELUJAH, GOD BLESS." In the cold pouring rain, I managed to get to the Western Union Telegraph Office and sent a cable (wire) to Peg's parents, saying everything had turned out OK, that the mass was benign. Thank you God, Hallelujah!

<u>2 July 1956</u>: LETTER ORDER #650, HEADQUARTERS EIGHTH AIR FORCE (SAC) Westover Air Force Base Massachusetts SUBJECT: Permanent Change of Sation dtd 2 July 1956 TO: TECHNICAL SERGEANT MAURICE F. MERCURE AF 12XXXXXX (Utilization Air Force Specialty Code 29270) 18th Communications Squadron, Air Force (Strategic Air Command) Westover Air Force Base, Massachusetts. You are relieved from assignment 18th Communications Squadron, Air Force (Strategic Air Command) this station; assigned Detachment 1 2225th Personnel Processing Group, Air Force (Continental Air Command) Fort Hamilton, New York for further overseas assigned to 7250th Support Squadron (United Stated Air Forces in Europe) Air Post Office 206-A New York, New York on project June United States Air Forces in Europe-Turkey-0805. You will not depart this station prior to 12 August 1956. Transportation of dependent (Wife, Margaret D. Mercure—address 119 Prospect Street, Willimansett, Massachusetts) authorized concurrently with your movement in accordance with message Headquarters TUSLOG TPMP 28-F-3773-U dated 28 June 1956. Shipment of household effects (located at 119 Prospect Street, Willimansett, Massachusetts) authorized. Shipment of privately-owned vehicle authorized in accordance with Air Force Manual 75-1, as ammnded. If shipment of privately-owned vehicle is by other than Military Sea Transportation Service, it will be at no expense to the government. You and your dependent will be available for call of Port Commander, New York Port of Embarkation, Brooklyn, New York on or after 28 August 1956 at 119 Prospect Street, Willimansett, Massachusetts, for transportation to destination and will comply with all instructions contained in Port Call. If Port Call has not been received 10 days prior to the established availability date, you will contact the Commander, Logistic Control Group, New York Port of

Embarkation, Brooklyn, New York, preferably by wire, for further instructions. Application for passport for dependent will be submitted immediately to clerk of nearest State of Federal court in accordance with Air Force Regulation 34-61. Passport and Visa Division Military District of Washington, Room 1B874, The Pentagon, will be notified date and place application was submitted and furnished one copy of this order. Air Force Manual 35-6 will be complied with and immunizations in accordance with Air Force Regulation 160-102 will be accomplished immediately by you and your dependent. All mail will be addressed to show grade, name, Air Force Service Number, Casual Enlisted Section, Detachment 1 2225th Personnel Processing Group (Air Force), Fort Hamilton, New York. Baggage will be shipped in accordance with Air Force Regulation 75-33. 15 days delay en route authorized chargeable as ordinary leave provided it does not interfere with reporting on date specified and providing you have sufficient accrued leave. Address while on delay en route 119 Prospect Street, Willimansett, Massachusetts. Travel by privately-owned vehicle with 1 day travel time authorized. If privately-owned vehicle not used, travel time will be that of carrier used. Will proceed. Permanent Charge of station. Travel as directed is necessary in the military service. 5773500 048-132 P531.9-02 03 S99-999; dislocation allowance other: 577350 048-246 P514-01 S99-999. Effective date of change in strength accountability: 28 August 1956. Authority: Letter Headquarters United States Air Force AFPMP-2F dated 16 March 1956, Subject, withdrawal of Warrant Officers and Airman for June 1956 Personnel Processing Squadron Arrivals, and Strategic Air Command Regulation 35-19. BY ORDER OF THE COMMANDER: (*For a copy of this letter order with immigration markings, see attachment B37.*)

We used to go to a diner in Willimansett, where we used to get the freshest and best tasting milk we ever had.

We were frequent diners at Dunkin' Donuts, for the freshly made soups. They used to make their own soups everyday, not like the prepared soups (frozen) served there today. In fact, they do not serve soups there today at all. Back then, they used to give you free refills and a slice of bread & butter for 10¢. It was very nourishing and a filling meal in itself.

We used to go to a French Bakery in South Holyoke, where we got the best sugar coated jelly donuts in the country. My mother is the one who introduced us to that French Bakery.

My sister got married (the first time) while we were at Westover AFB. She insisted that I attend the wedding in a tuxedo, instead of my uniform, which I did to my regret. While attending the engagement party, two sailors crashed the party. My mother came to me to evict them, which I did. All the while I was in pain from a cyst on the base of my spine. By the way, the marriage did not last, and ended up in a divorce.

An Air Force doctor (an Hungarian refugee) in the Westover Air Force Base Hospital, lanced my cyst, so that it would drain, relieving the pain and pressure. It drained for a year, then closed, and has not given me any trouble since.

I went to work one day and to my surprise I ran into S Sgt Harrison, from Dow AFB, who was now working in the Communications Major Relay Station. It was nice meeting someone you knew from before, and we discussed old times.

11 July 1956: DD FORM 349 REQUEST FOR OVERSEAS MOVEMENT OF DEPENDENTS dtd 11 July 1956, Westover AFB, Massachusetts. MERCURE, MARGARET D. WIFE. 119 Prospect Street, Willimansett, Massachusetts. WIFE PREGNANT: NO. SHIPMENT OF HOUSEHOLD GOODS REQUESTED: YES. AIR TRANSPORTATION ACCEPTABLE: NO. EMERGENCY ADDRESS: Mr. & Mrs. FREDERICK BANKS, 36 Shakespeare Ave, Hayes MIDDLESEX, ENGLAND. I CERTIFY THAT THE INFORMATION CONTAINED HEREIN IS TRUE AND CORRECT AND THAT THE INDIVIDUALS LISTED ARE MY LEGAL DEPENDENTS AS DEFINED IN CHAPTER 7 JTR, EXCLUDING BLOOD AND/OR AFFINITIVE RELATIVE. I AGREE TO REMAIN IN THE OVERSEAS COMMAND ONE (1) YEAR AFTER ARRIVAL OF MY DEPENDENTS. FOR ARMY PERSONNEL ONLY: I WILL, WILL NOT ACCEPT TEMPORARY LIVING ACCOMMODATIONS (INTERIM HOUSING) WHICH MAY BE SCARCE, EXPENSIVE AND/OR SUBSTANDARD, AND MAY BE LOCATED A DISTANCE FROM MY DUTY STATION. I HAVE BEEN COUNSELED ON HOUSING CONDITIONS IN THE AREA OF MY ASSIGNMENT. REMARKS (include items requiring special accommodations, i.e., physical handicaps, health, etc.) Army enlisted personnel will furnish information required by SR 55-765S/AFR 75-26). Concurrent Travel Authorized IAW message, Headquartered TUSLOG TPMP 20-F-3775-U dated 28 June 1956 Principal and dependents w/b aval for Port Call at 119 Prospect Street,

Willimansett, Massachusetts Dependents applied for Naturalization on 3 July 1956. MAURICE F. MERCURE T/Sgt AF 12XXXXXX.

17 July 1956: We went to the US District Court House, Boston, Massachusetts, for Peg to become an American Citizen Petition No. 31XXXX. The Clerk interviewing her for citizenship asked her "Do you speak English?" Peg promptly replied, "I am English," no more needed to be said. She was administered the Oath of Citizenship and given Naturalization Certificate No. 76 XXXXX.

On our way to Boston on Interstate 90, we saw a sign which read "ICE COLD WATERMELON 10¢ A SLICE." We naturally stopped and had a slice, as Peggy just loves watermelon. The watermelon was ice cold and delicious.

4 September 1956: SPECIAL ORDER NUMBER 177 DETACHMENT #1 2225TH PERSONNEL PROCESSING GROUP (AIR FORCE) (CONAC) FORT HAMILTON BROOKLYN 9, NEW YORK dtd 4 September 1956. E X T R A C T Paragraphs 38 & 39. 38. T SGT MAURICE F. MERCURE AF 12XXXXXX (UAFSC 29270) REL frm ASG DET #1, this STA is designated SHIPMT #1—899 & is ASG 7250TH SUPRON APO 206A NYK. AMN WP W/DEPNS O/A 10 SEP 56 to NYPE Brooklyn, NY so as to REPT on same date to CG for further TRANS CCTTS aboard USNS UPSHUR. EDCSA: 4 OCT 56. PROV AFM 35-6 (POR) W/B complied with. AMN will advise correspondents & PUBL by use of AF Form 305 (NOTICE TO PUBL & C of address card) that mailing address will show rank, name, AF 12XXXXXX 7250TH SUPRON APO 296A NYK. PCS PCA TDN 5773500 048-132 P531.9-02 03 S99-999. (AUTH AFM 35-11.) 39. SMOLORD 650, 8TH AF WESTOVER AFB, MASS dtd 2 July 56 pertaining to RSG of T SGT MAURICE F. MERCURE AF 12XXXXXX 7250TH SUPRON APO 206A NYK as reads "15 days delay en route" 1ATR "DDALVAHP" BY ORDER OF THE COMMANDER:

Medic made me take a diphtheria shot even though I had just recently been given one. He said "I am the Medic and I say what you will have, and will not have." So he gave me the shot over my protest. It caused me to have a reaction, making me ill. I had a high fever, headache, and a cloud before my eyes, causing me to have blurred vision. We applied cold wet towels to my forehead, and I took aspirin. I was afraid that I would not make the shipment to Turkey, as everything had been completed to go. Managed to lower the fever, stop the headaches and got rid of the haze in front of my eyes, just in time to make the shipment.

9 September 1956: Fort Hamilton Form 0379(B) OVERSEAS PROCESSING SHEET dtd 9 September 1956. (*For a copy of this form, see attachment B38.*)

10 September 1956: LTR ORIENTATION FOR SURFACE TRAVEL ABOARD MILITARY SEA TRANSPORTATION SERVICE VESSEL, DTD 10 Sep 56. Baggage deadline and baggage handling. (*For a copy of this ltr, see attachment B39.*)

CHAPTER 7

10 SEPTEMBER 1956 - 11 NOVEMBER 1958
TURKEY—JUSMMAT/TUSLOG, ANKARA

A.	Casablanca, Morocco (Visit)	16 Sep 1956-16 Sep 1956
B.	Leghorn, Italy (Visit)	18 Sep 1956-18 Sep 1956
C.	Naples, Italy (Visit)	20 Sep 1956-20 Sep 1956
D.	Tripoli, Libya (Visit)	23 Sep 1956-23 Sep 1956
E.	Piraeus, Greece (Visit)	24 Sep 1956-24 Sep 1956
F.	Athens, Greece (Visit)	24 Sep 1956-24 Sep 1956
G.	Istanbul, Turkey (Visit)	27 Sep 1956-27 Sep 1956
H.	Ankara, Turkey	28 Sep 1956-11 Nov 1958
I.	Incirlik Air Base, Izmir, Turkey (TDY)	1 Mar 1957-14 Mar 1957
J.	Wheelus Air Base, Libya (Visit)	Various Dates
K.	Adana Air Base, Turkey (Visit)	13 May 1958-13 May 1958
L.	Wiesbaden Air Base, Wiesbaden, Germany (TDY)	2 Aug 1958-2 Sep 1958

10 September 1956: Upon boarding the USNS General Upshur, we were assigned different compartments—women in one and men in another. I became friendly with a Navy Chief Petty Officer (CPO). His wife was in the same compartment as my wife Peg. The Chief and I were sharing the same compartment with six other servicemen. The Chief was very friendly with the Ship's Purser, as they had sailed together before. So when we got to Casablanca, Morocco, a lot of people (passengers) got off the ship, especially from "A" Deck. The Purser, in conjunction with the Chief Stewart, got the Chief and I separate cabins on "A" Deck so that we were together with our wives, and

had them all to ourselves. They were really posh cabins with maid service. So from Casablanca to Istanbul we traveled in luxury, with A-1 treatment.

We had our meals in the Ship's Grand Diningroom, and they were excellent. Our meals were prepared by the Ship's Chief Stewart, Mr. Kenneth MacGregor. We ate our meals at a large round table, which accommodated eight people. Only a Colonel's wife did not dine with us, as she was seasick the entire voyage.

While on the ship, I had to pull Master at Arms Duty (Charge of Quarters (CQ)), one night. It was quite a stormy night and I was literally thrown up against a bulkhead (wall) and slid down a stairwell on my back, aggravating my previous back injury from the fall down a flight of steps. I went on Sick Call the next morning to see the Ship's Doctor, for examination and treatment. He told me "I do not want to clutter up the Ship's Dispensary, as this is my last run (as he was retiring from the Navy). In addition he stated, "Take some APC's (All Purpose Capsules, which he gave me) for pain, and get some bed rest." He also stated, "When you reach your final destination, see your Air Force Doctor." I managed to get around and do things, even with the pain in my back. Years later I had a disc removed from my spine.

<u>16 September 1956</u>: We had a Farewell Dinner for all the passengers going ashore in Casablanca, Morocco. It was a very enjoyable meal. (*For a copy of the menu, see attachment B40.*)

When we docked in Casablanca, a lot of Arab Longshoremen came on board. There was this German Shepherd (Alsatian) dog in a cage on the deck. He began to bark at the Longshoremen and got real excited. They (the Longshoremen) began to tease him by running sticks up and down the sides of the cage. Somehow, the cage door became unlocked and opened, letting the dog out of his cage onto the deck of the ship. All of a sudden, the Longshoremen began running for the side of the ship to get away from the dog. They literally dived head first off the ship, onto the deck below. I am sorry to say that this was very exciting and very humorous, at the time. The dog belonged to a Marine Major, who was the only one to get the dog under control and back into his cage. The Major informed me that the dog was a trained attack dog and did not respond to anyone else's commands, but his.

We went ashore to make a telephone call to Peg's family in Hayes, Middlesex, England. At that particular time in world events, the French Army was preparing to leave the country. They were slowly handing the city (of Casablanca) over to the Moroccan Army, section by section. The Central Post Office (containing the Telephone Exchange) was located in the section of the city that had been turned over to the Moroccans. It was completely surrounded by Moroccan Soldiers and Policemen. By the time we got past the sentries and into the building and tried to get a call through to London, it was time to return to the ship. We were later told by Peg's parents that the Moroccan Post Office had indeed managed to get through to them. But we had already started back to the ship. At least they knew that we had gotten as far as Casablanca and were OK.

On the way back to the ship, we passed a jewelry stall, and Peg saw a silver filagree bracelet that she liked. We stopped and asked how much it cost. The price was right, so she bought it. The merchant wrapped it up and gave it to Peg, after she had paid for it. When we got back to the ship, we found out that the merchant had switched the item that Peg liked for a worthless piece of junk. We could do nothing about it, as the ship was underway for Italy. It just goes to show and prove how the Moroccan merchant could use slight of hand to his advantage by switching a piece of worthless junk for the genuine piece of jewelry. I can assure you that Peggy was not pleased about it and wishes that she had worn the bracelet back to the ship instead of having it wrapped up.

From Casablanca we sailed to Leghorn (Livorno), Italy, our next port of call. Leghorn is located in Northern Italy and is a very nice, clean city. We went ashore and toured all the interesting sites that we could. We saw the Leaning Tower of Pisa and had our pictures taken in front of the tower. (*For a picture of us standing in front of the Tower, see photograph A25.*)

18 September 1956: We sailed from Leghorn (Livorno), Italy to our next port of call, Naples (Napoli), Italy. Going ashore, we stopped at a very nice restaurant and had a lovely spaghetti meal. Naples is located in the south of Italy and is not as clean and nice as Leghorn. We toured as much of the area as time would allow. In Naples we saw our first Eastern style toilet. It consisted of a porcelain base, with two footprints, and a hole for the waste material to go out. There was also a water tap (faucet) on the wall (at shin level) on the side of the toilet, for you to rinse your hands after going.

There was no soap or toilet paper provided. I can tell you it was quite an eye opener and experience, to see how the Eastern part of the world lives.

20 September 1956: We sailed from Naples (Napoli) to Tripoli, Libya, our next port of call.

22 September 1956: We arrived in Tripoli, Libya. The city looked nice from the ship with it's white walls—that is, the walls facing out to sea, towards the ship. It was quite a different story once you got inside the walls, into the city, and saw it for yourself. The city was quite dirty and full of flies and lots of beggars. A sight you cannot forget.

23 September 1956: We sailed from Tripoli, Libya, to our next port of call, Athens, Greece.

24 September 1956: We arrived in Piraeus, Greece, the port city for Athens. After docking and going ashore, we were bussed to Athens. In Athens we visited the Acropolis and toured the surrounding area. Peg ruined a pair of high heeled shoes there walking around the Acropolis on all those little pieces of stone and marble. High heeled shoes were not the kind of shoes to be worn while walking around the Acropolis. Flat-heeled shoes are the order of the day. Touring Athens and all of its sites was an adventure in itself.

25 September 1956: We sailed from Athens to Istanbul, Turkey, our next and final port of call. This was to be our last stop on our Mediterranean Cruise.

27 September 1956: We reached Istanbul, Turkey, and we proceeded to disembark. They then bussed us to the Istanbul Railway Station where we were met by an Army Transportation Officer (TO), and his staff from the Army Transportation Corps. They issued us train tickets for the journey to Ankara, on a Wagon-Lits-Cook Sleeping Car. We boarded a bus to take us to the train platform that the train was leaving from. Somehow, stupid me (being my usual unreliable, careless self) lost the train tickets on the bus. Peg proceeded to tell me I was a little child (that had not grown up) and could not be trusted with anything important. Luckily the Transportation Officer (TO) had

some extra tickets with him and he issued us replacements, which we had to pay for. He informed us that if the tickets were found and not used, we would be reimbursed. We were later told (in Ankara), that the tickets were indeed found and my records (pay records) were reimbursed. While waiting to board the train for Ankara, some slick person managed to open my bag and stole my pajama top, right under our noses.

We boarded the train for Ankara and were shown to our sleeping compartment where we washed up and got into our sleeping attire for bed. We got into our sleeping berths and fell asleep.

I awoke to find that the train had stopped in the middle of nowhere. The engineer began blowing the train's whistle like mad. Suddenly a band of horsemen came up over the hill overlooking the train tracks. They were heading right for the train. I suddenly thought that they were bandits attacking the train, to rob it, just like in the old movies. However, I was mistaken as it was a Turkish Auxiliary Cavalry Unit, used to patrol the tracks and guard the trains. I must say that they gave me quite a fright at first. We arrived in Ankara without any further incidents.

When we arrived in Ankara, we were given a booklet, advising us on what words we could not use in public. Such words as peach (which meant "bastard" in Turkish) and sick (one was not sick, but hasta). One went to the Hastani, not the hospital. We were at an outdoor market one day, when Peg said to me "Look at all those lovely peaches," and everyone turned and looked at us and gave us dirty looks. One had to be continuously on his guard as to what he or she were saying so as not to offend anyone.

While staying in a hotel, waiting to get a place to live, we had problems such as the city of Ankara turning off the water every day for a couple of hours to conserve it. I remember the first time it happened to us. Peg was in the shower, all lathered up, when it was turned off. We managed to get her rinsed off and dried. The conservation of water, gas, and electric, without warning, went on for the entire time we were in Turkey. It wasn't so bad once you had your own apartment, because you could use bottled water to rinse with. You had oil space heaters to heat the house. You could also use them to heat water to have an all over wash and also, to make tea and/or coffee. You did not have all these items in the hotel to cope with the outages.

In the American Snack Bar, the attendant asked you if you would like some "Fried Pot" (meaning French Fries of course and not marijuana) and "leemoan pie" (lemon pie), etc. We did manage to figure out what they meant. When we first arrived in Turkey, everything was an adventure.

September 1956: Our first apartment was at 2nd Street, #61, Bahceli Evler, Ankara, Turkey. It was a basement apartment, self-contained. It consisted of a living/dining room, kitchen and a bedroom. There was a potbelly stove in the bedroom to heat it in the wintertime. Little did we know that it would cause us a problem later on.

We periodically used the TUSLOG Shopping Center for procuring daily living items, water and recombined milk. (*For a copy of picture of author standing outside the entrance to the TUSLOG Shopping Center, see photograph A26.*)

Neighbors at our new apartment invited us out to dinner when we moved in. They took us to the Gar Casino Restaurant where we had a very good meal. When it came time for them to pay for the meal, they conveniently didn't have the money to pay for same. It fell upon us to pay for it. Luckily Peg and I, along with Betty & Bob (1st floor apartment), managed to scrape up the money to pay the bill. We wondered what would have happened if Betty, Bob, Peg and I did not raise the money to pay the bill. By the way, "Welcome to the neighborhood."

4 October 1956: PERSONNEL ACTIONS MEMORANDUM NUMBER 77 7250TH SUPPORT SQUADRON 7217TH SUPPORT GROUP (USAFE) APO 206-A, New York, NY dtd 4 October 1956 Paragraph 1. T/SGT MAURICE F. MERCURE AF 12XXXXXX, this orgn, this sta, is asgd PrimDy as Crypto Opr w/Comm El Op Sec, DAFSC 29250, UAFSC 29270, FUNCT ACCT 84020. Amn is asgd DEROS of Sep 58. Eff this dt. BY ORDER OF THE COMMANDER:

Went to work in the JUSMMAT Crypto Center, under the command of M/SGT ROCCO, as Day Shift Supervisor.

The American Military wanted some space to erect a Base Exchange, Base Commissary, and a Milk Recombining Plant. So they made a deal with the Turkish Government to furnish them an asphalt paving machine and spare parts to keep it running, in exchange for the City of Ankara's old bus garage and yard. Things went well for awhile, until the paving machine broke down and the Turks asked for spare parts to fix it. We did not have the spare parts available to fix it. The parts to keep it running had to be ordered through normal channels, from the Supply Depot in Germany. This did not sit well with the Turks as they had been promised spare parts immediately (if the paving machine broke down) to keep the machine running. The City of Ankara was in the process of a large repaving project, and it came to an immediate halt, as we did not keep our side of the agreement to furnish spare parts. They knew we had a spare asphalt paving machine in the Motor Pool Supply Yard, so they wanted to know why we could not just switch machines with them. The Turks were told, no way; we needed it for our own use, which made the Turks madder. So the Turks decided to take care of the matter in their own way. One night on a parallel track to the Motor Pool Supply Yard, they took action on the matter. A train pulled up with a crane car, picked up the new asphalt paving machine and loaded it on a flat car. They then off-loaded the broken asphalt paving machine into the Motor Pool Supply Yard (in place of the new machine). The Turks were now back in the paving business. Boy, were the Americans surprised the next day when they discovered the switch had been made. I don't know the final outcome of this situation, but I feel the Turks had won and proved their point.

The potbelly stove in our bedroom backfired one day, sending soot and smoke all over the place. This occurred because the coal we were burning was soft coal. This type of coal gives off a lot of soot. This built up in the stove pipe and blocked it, causing it to backfire. We proceeded to clean up the mess, anticipating a good cup of tea when we finished, in the dining room. So we placed and lit two oil space heaters in the dining room to make it nice and cozy and warm. To our dismay, when we had finished cleaning up the bedroom, we went into the dining room for our cup of tea only to find that one of the oil space heaters had backfired, filling the room with smoke and soot. We had to trim the wick on the heater that had backfired, and then clean up the room. We were both dead tired when we finished. We had our cup of tea, showered and went to bed. After this incident we made periodic checks of the stove pipe to make sure it was not blocked. We also trimmed the wicks of the oil space heaters, so that we did not have a repeat performance of this type.

A Turkish Army Draftee had to salute a regular Army Private, even if the draftee was an acting Corporal. Draftees, I was told, never got above the rank of acting Corporal. It was easy to recognize a regular Army Soldier from a draftee by their uniforms. A draftee wore a uniform made from course blanket material and the regular Soldier wore a uniform just like our own Army.

While working in the JUSMMAT Crypto Center, I became partial to hot sweet Turkish tea. We used to call down to the Turkish canteen and order hot tea, which they delivered hot right to the door of the Crypto Center. I was quite use to the hot sweet tea, over the coffee they used to serve. The coffee was a sweet paste, which I found very hard to swallow. Each to his own taste; the tea was a real picker upper.

A Colonel's son, who lived next door to us, used to throw rocks at us and our neighbors.

He was a little devil and a pain in the ass. I told him to stop throwing rocks at us. He replied, "My father is a Colonel and you are only a Sergeant, so I do not have to obey you." I went to his father and told him what his son was doing and said that I wanted it stopped before he hurt someone, and that if it did not stop, I would go to the General in charge of JUSMMAT and log a formal complaint. He immediately spoke to his son, who stopped throwing rocks at us.

8 March 1957: SPECIAL ORDERS NUMBER 30 7250TH SUPPORT SQUADRON 7217TH SUPPORT GROUP (USAFE) APO 254, NEW YORK, NY dtd 8 March 1958. Paragraph 3. T/SGT MAURICE F. MERCURE, AF 12XXXXXX, this sta is granted ord lv of absence for twenty-seven (27) days eff on or abt 15 Mar 57. Lv add: 36 Shakespeare Ave, Hayes, Middlesex, England. Amn's dependent wife (MRS. MAURICE F. MERCURE), auth to accompany amn. Air Travel on a space available basis is authorized to Paris, France UCAW this orgn this sta. AUTH: USAF Msg AFCVC 42176, as amended by USAF Msg AFCAV 32556 and USAF Msg AFCVC 40050. BY ORDER OF THE COMMANDER: (*For a copy of this S.O. with immigration stamps, see attachment B41.*)

11 March 1957: SPECIAL ORDERS NUMBER 31 7250TH SUPPORT SQUADRON 7217TH SUPPORT GROUP (USAFE) APO 254, NEW YORK, NY dtd 11 March 1957 Paragraph 5. SMOP 3, SO, CS, this orgn, this sta pertaining to ord lv of T/SGT MAURICE F. MERCURE AF 12XXXXXX, as reads: Amn's dependent wife (MRS. MAURICE F. MERCURE) auth to accompany amn. is amended to read: Amn's

dependent wife (MRS MARGARET D. MERCURE) US PASSPORT #22XXXX auth to accompany amn. BY ORDER OF THE COMMANDER:

Of all things, one day while out shopping, we bought a watermelon. We noticed that a local cinema was showing a film that we had wanted to see. Rather than giving up our watermelon, we took it into the cinema with us. No one objected, so we proceeded to do so. I believe that the ticket taker thought we were a bit loony, but made an exception for the crazy Americans.

We had to get our bottled drinking water from the Milk Recombining Plant at the Base Exchange. It was the only place that we could get sterilized drinking water. We had to take our own large water bottles (in wicker baskets) to the plant to get them filled. This was an excellent way to prevent us from getting sick from water bourne illnesses. It was useful for cooking and making hot and/or cold beverages, as we knew the water we were getting was sterilized and fit for human consumption. We also got recombined milk there, which was not like the real thing, but it would do in a pinch.

One cold winter evening, with ice on the ground, a Turkish man, driving a horse-drawn wagon, was going by the house. The horse was slipping and sliding all over the place. Poor horse was skinny, underfed, and was unable to cope with the loaded wagon under the prevailing weather conditions. The driver was using a whip on the horse to get it to pull the load. Peg wanted me to go outside and take the whip away from him, unharness the horse and bring it into the apartment and put it in our large bathroom out of the cold. I told her that this would cause an international incident and I would possibly go to jail, and/or be reduced in rank and also pay a fine for my actions. She thought that I was mean, insensitive and unsympathetic. I did nothing at all at the time, because I strongly believed my future was at stake.

The Army Doctor in the Base Dispensary in Ankara, after examining me, sent me by Air Evacuation Aircraft to the USAF Hospital at Incirlik Air Base, Izmir, Turkey, for my back. After two weeks bed rest there, they decided to send me back to Ankara.

My wife is something else. While I was in the Hospital in Izmir, she decided to go into downtown Ankara by herself during a demonstration over Cyprus. Luckily, even with her English accent, they did not bother her.

Peg decided to send a box of Turkish Delight candy (which she knew I liked) to me in the Hospital in Izmir, via the Turkish Postal System. Somehow, the package got split on one end, allowing cockroaches to get inside the package. When the package was delivered to me, out came those pesky creatures. Needless to say, we (my fellow patients and I) did not eat any of the candy, but threw it out.

During the Cyprus crisis, my wife stayed with some friends of ours, who worked in the American Embassy. We met them when we were staying in the hotel, when we first arrived in Turkey. (The Turkish Army invaded the Island of Cyprus on July 20, 1974 and occupied half of the island, with little or no resistance at all. They still hold half of the island today. The Greek Army and civilian population were no match for the Turkish Army. The Turks could have taken the whole island, but stopped after they had taken half of the island.)

March 1957: Sgt. Potter, who worked in the American Embassy (Ankara), on attache duty, stated (promised) to me that he would look after Peggy, while I was in the USAF Hospital (Izmir, Turkey). If anything occurred that required the evacuation of American citizens from Turkey because of a crisis, that he would see to it that Peggy would leave the country along with everyone else. That if it was necessary (if Peggy refused), he would physically put her on the aircraft. He informed Peggy that he would carry out his promise to me if necessary.

While in the Hospital in Izmir for my back problem, Peggy caught our friendly neighbor from the second floor stealing heating oil from our 55 gallon storage drum which we kept under the stairs, right outside our front door. Heating oil was rationed, and I made the mistake of not putting a padlock on it—a situation I rectified when I returned from the hospital and was informed by Peggy as to what had happened.

March 1957: During the Cyprus situation, the Turks posted a "NOTICE" on the apartment entrance that read "ENGLISH GO HOME." It was clear that they did not like the "ENGLISH," because of the crisis between them and Greece and the United Kingdom over the island.

14 March 1957: Going on leave, we left Esenboga Airport, Ankara, Turkey, on a space-available flight to Rhein-Main Air Base, Frankfurt, Germany. On our stopover in Athens, Greece, we were bumped from the flight by a Navy Captain and his wife. At that particular time in space—available flying, there was always the risk of being

bumped by someone of higher rank. Luckily, right after this incident, the United States Air Force issued a new regulation on space-available flying stating that once you were booked on a flight (manifested), you could not be bumped by anyone of higher rank, also on space-available status. It put space-available flying on a first-come, first-served basis. As we were bumped from our Frankfurt bound flight, we had to stay in a hotel in downtown Athens (checking daily for flight) for three days before we caught another flight to Rhein-Main Air Base, Frankfurt, Germany because we never knew when the next space-available flight might arrive. There was no regular schedule for flights of this type. While we were waiting for the next available flight, someone stole our 35 mm camera!

17 March 1957: We left Athens, Greece, and arrived at Rhein-Main Air Base and cleared through USAF Customs. One of the first things we did when we arrived at Rhein-Main, was to go to the terminal snack bar and have good large bananas and fresh milk. This was a treat since the bananas we got in Turkey were the small stringy African type and the milk was recombined, which was better than nothing. After having our fill, we took a taxi cab to the Frankfurt Railway Station where we caught a train to Ostend, Belgium.

18 March 1957: The train from Frankfurt arrived in Ostend on 18 March 1957 where we booked passage on the Channel Ferry Boat to Dover, England. That same day, we arrived safely in Dover, and proceeded by train to Peg's family home in Hayes, Middlesex, England. We spent a lovely eighteen-day vacation with them; we were sorry it was so short a time.

2 April 1957: PERSONNEL ACTIONS MEMORANDUM NUMBER 45 7250TH SUPPORT SQUADRON 7217TH SUPPORT GROUP (USAFE) APO 254, New York, NY dtd 2 April 1957. Paragraph 4. T/SGT MAURICE F. MERCURE, AF 12XXXXXX, this orgn, this sta, is rel fr PrimDy as Crypto w/Comm El Oper, DAFSC 29250, and asgd PrimDy as Crypto Supv w/Comm El Oper, DAFSC 29270. No chg in CAFSC or FUNCT ACCT. BY ORDER OF THE COMMANDER: (This PAM was issued while I was on leave.)

<u>5 April 1957</u>: We went to Dover by train and booked passage on the Channel Ferry Boat to Ostend, Belgium.

<u>6 April 1957</u>: We arrived safely in Ostend, Belgium, where we took a train to Frankfurt, Germany.

<u>6 April 1957</u>: We arrived in the Frankfurt Railway Station then took a taxi cab to Rhein-Main Air Base, Frankfurt, Germany.

<u>9 April 1957</u>: Clearing USAF Customs, Rhein-Main Air Base, Frankfurt, Germany, we boarded a plane for Turkey via Athens, Greece.

<u>11 April 1957</u>: We arrived at Esenboga Airport, Ankara, Turkey, safe and sound. We then took a taxi cab home. On our return home from leave, we ran into a really big problem there. When we first opened the front door to our apartment, a horrible smell greeted us. While we were away, the maid on the second floor apartment had accidently dropped a pair of woman's stockings into the commode. Instead of getting them out with something, she flushed them down the toilet. It appears that they went down the pipe to our basement apartment, where they plugged everything up so that everything flushed from the upstairs apartments ended up in our bathroom, on the floor. We called in a plumber to unplug the toilet and clean up the mess. I had to go to work, so I left the job to Peg. The plumber was successful in unplugging the system, however, during the job, Peg felt sorry for him, working in the bathroom with the heat and the stench, so she gave him a glass of bourbon (whiskey). She had to go out to the market to get some food. She felt she could trust him in the house by himself, so she went out. Peg had left the bottle of whiskey on the table instead of putting it away. While she was gone, he helped himself to some more whiskey. When she returned, she found him making flowers out of broken pieces of tile. He told her that he was drunk. She paid him for the work he had done and he left. When I got home from work, everything had been fixed and back to normal, except for the smell, which lingered for a couple of days.

I drove a pickup truck (a JUSMMAT vehicle) with my wife Peg in the front seat. She had to crouch down real low as we passed the Turkish Army Sentry on the gate.

We did this to go to the Turkish Army Cinema in the JUSMMAT Building. This was before they built the new American Cinema. While in the JUSMMAT Cinema one night, armed Turkish Soldiers, with fixed bayonets, came into the theatre chasing a stray dog through the movie section. What a scary experience this was for all the people there.

<u>18 June 1957</u>: PERSONNEL ACTIONS MEMORANDUM NUMBER 95 7250TH SUPPORT SQUADRON 7217TH SUPPORT GROUP (USAFE) APO 254, New York, NY dtd 18 June 1957. Paragraph 2. Dy Section and FUNCT of FNA, this orgn, this sta, are hereby ch as indc. T/SGT MAURICE F. MERCURE, AF 12XXXXXX, FROM <u>Dy Sec</u> CommElOpr FA 84020 TO <u>Dy Sec</u> Crypto Opn <u>FA</u> 84320. BY ORDER OF THE COMMANDER:

1st Lt Maurice B. Moore had me transfer some compatible Teletype Crypto equipment to a TUSLOG Detachment without authorization and approval from 17th Air Force. He told me to misplace the paperwork. Being a meticulous Crypto Accounting person, I kept a copy of the transfer report in a safe, to which I was the only one to have the combination. A copy of the combination was kept in a sealed envelope in another safe (just in case anything should happen to me). So when the Crypto Inspection Team showed up to inspect the Crypto Account, I was ready for them. They asked me where the transferred equipment was as it was listed on the Daily Inventory sheet, but unaccounted for. I informed the Major in charge of the Inspection Team that Lt. Moore had ordered me to transfer the equipment to a TUSLOG unit. He stated, "Your accounting records do not reflect this; besides, Lt. Moore denies that he ordered this transfer." I opened my controlled safe and produced the Transfer Report, with Lt. Moore's signature as Transferring Officer on it. The situation as far as I was concerned was now closed. It was now a matter between Lt. Moore and the Inspecting Officer. I can assure you that Lt. Moore was surprised by my actions, and that he was not happy with me, but could not do anything about it. Lt. Moore was relieved as Crypto Security Officer and as Crypto Custodian of the Crypto Account. 1st Lt. Richard P. Stevens was appointed to take his place.

We were in a Turkish taxi cab one day when the steering wheel came off in the driver's hands. He shouted "Hepsi-Tamum," and quickly managed to get it back on the steering column before losing control of his vehicle. This occurred in a Dolmus taxi cab and was a very scary situation. On another occasion a tire blew out and the driver yelled, "Choke Finel Elastic Hepsi-Tamum." The cab driver did not have a spare tire, so we transferred to another cab and went merrily on our way.

When the new American Cinema (theatre) was completed and opened, we went regularly to the movies. The theatre was built with several loges in it. We started sitting in one along with Captain Ernest B. Personeus and his wife. There were some young soldiers who used to save the loge for us by sitting in it until we or the Captain and his wife arrived. Everyone was so nice and friendly to each other. It was a pleasure going to the movies.

August 1957: Our second apartment was at 78th Street, Apt 6A1, Dichman Kopertifi, Ankara, Turkey. It was a basement apartment, consisting of a bedroom, livingroom with French doors, diningroom, kitchen, maid's room, and two bathrooms (one Western style and one Eastern style for Turkish domestics if we hired them). It was a very nice apartment, located in a very nice area of the city.

August 1957: Author's wife standing outside entrance to new apartment building. (*For a copy of this picture, see photograph A27.*)

August 1957: Picture of Turkish Military Policeman (M.P.) Just like the one who stands guard outside the entrance to our new apartment building. (*For a copy of this picture, see photograph A28.*)

August 1957: There was a new Turkish Cinema (Movie House), just around the corner from our apartment building, called "Renkli." We used it quite often. They served a soda called "Gasuz", which was just like 7 UP. (*For a picture of this cinema, see photograph A29.*)

In the new apartment building, we had a Turkish Army Military Policeman (MP) on guard duty when the Turkish Generals were in residence. He used to salute me as I entered or left the building. I must say it gave one the sense of security knowing that he was there.

The owners of the apartment block decided to have a central heating system installed in the building. A boiler was installed in the existing boiler room. Next workmen came to our apartment to install radiators. What a mess they made installing them. They could not speak English, nor could we speak Turkish. However, we both learned a few words and phrases from each other. The workmen did pickup the phrase, "What a mess," and repeated it. As Peg used to say to them every day that they worked in the apartment, "What a mess." When they were finished installing the radiators, to everyone's delight, they cleaned up most of the mess that they had made. Peg cleaned up the rest of it. On their way out of the apartment they said "Goodbye" in Turkish and a parting shot of "What a mess, what a mess," in English.

The karpigi (janitor) used to follow Peg to the local outdoor market to make sure she was not cheated on the weight of items and/or her change.

Our American neighbor, Tex (from Texas, of course), across the hall from us, had a saddle with blood on it. It was his badge of courage and he had to show it to everyone he came in contact with. Just like a Texan, who has cornered the world on bragging rights. He asked us if we had any extra blankets he could borrow for his children. We said we did and loaned them to him. We never took them back, as he had let his puppy sleep on them. We ended up (after they had been washed) giving them to the karpigi's family, as they needed them and would put them to good use. They lived in the boiler room area before the boiler was installed. We always called the karpigi's daughter "Red Dress," because all she ever wore was a red dress whenever we saw her. Her real name was "Iten."

Turkish merchants came to our front door selling things. One in particular was the "Egg Man," who used to yell "Eggies." Peg liked the Egg Man, because his eggs were always nice, big and fresh.

We woke up one morning to loud talking and noises just outside of our bedroom window. I got up and looked out of the window to see what was going on. To my amazement I saw an anti-aircraft gun right outside of our bedroom window, with a bunch of Turkish soldiers placing sandbags around it. Apparently the Turkish Army was on alert over something or other. The area we lived in was designated as an Air Defense Zone because of the Generals living in the building. It was nice to know that we would be defended in case of an air attack.

We used our local Post Office to make long distant telephone calls to Peg's family in Hayes, Middlesex, England. The Postmaster and his staff were very obliging, polite, and friendly to us. They were very accommodating, placing the calls through to England. They always provided a chair for Peg to sit down while waiting for her call to go through. The Postmaster would get out his stock of stamps for me to look at allowing me to select what I wanted for my stamp collection. Meanwhile, Peg made her call home. I acquired quite a nice collection of mint (unused) Turkish stamps while stationed in Ankara. It was a pleasant surprise to me to have this type of cooperation with the local Postmaster.

We went to the local Turkish cinema frequently, in the area where we lived. It was quite enjoyable as the sound track was in English, with Turkish sub-titles. We used to drink ice cold Gazus (which was like 7-Up soda). The cinema staff were very amicable.

We threw a party one night at our apartment for all the Crypto personnel who were off duty. We also invited some of the Teletype personnel, who were friendly with us. I remember one poor soul from Crypto, A2C Frank DeSantis, who got sick by drinking something he should not have. Peg was tending bar and mixing drinks when two Crypto Center persons told her what he liked to drink (as she wanted to know so she could fix him something he liked). They told her that he liked Bourbon whiskey, vodka, and gin in the same glass. So she mixed the drink in a tall glass for him. She did this not knowing that they were being mean to him. Frank was a very polite person, so when Peg gave him the drink, he proceeded to drink it. In a little while he began to get sick and rushed to the bathroom. We found him with his head in the toilet bowl and his backside in the douche bowl. His backside was getting wet from the warm water spray from the douche bowl. I told Peg not to listen to anyone about someone else's drink, but just to the individual. I informed her that she could have hurt Frank with that drink combination. Poor Frank—he had one hell of a hangover the next day.

During the party, Ssgt Donald Nauss lost his partial bridgework while singing "Good Old Mountain Dew." Don recovered his partial bridgework, rinsed them off and put them back in his mouth. Don and I became good friends. (Little did we realize that we would meet again in France, at Chateauroux Air Station.)

The Army doctor in the American dispensary decided that I should be Air Evac to the USAF Hospital at Wiesbaden Air Base, Wiesbaden, Germany for treatment of my back problem. The first stop we made was at Wheelus Air Base, Tripoli, Libya. I was taken to the base hospital where they looked at my medical records and examined me to see if they could help me. After consultation by the doctors, they decided to send me on to Wiesbaden Hospital. We stayed overnight and left the next morning for Germany. The plane landed at Ramstein Air Base, Germany and because of the lateness of the hour, they decided we should stay overnight at the 3rd Army General Hospital at Landsthul, which was right next door to the Air Base. We were taken by ambulance bus to the hospital. We were all wearing Air Evac tags, identifying the type of our illnesses. The Army Corpsman on duty, processing the patients into the hospital, apparently did not check my Air Evac tag, which stated that I should not lift or carry anything, as I had a bad back. However, the Corpsman gave me my medical records and told me to take them and my bag up the stairs to my designated ward on the second floor. When I reached my designated ward (after a great amount of labor) I reported to the ward nurse on duty. The nurse could see that I was in pain. She looked at my Air Evac tag and wanted to know why I was carrying my bag. I told her the Corpsman on duty at the incoming processing station told me to. She asked me how bad the pain was; I told her on a scale of 1-10, it was 8. The nurse immediately called the on-call duty doctor, and then had me get into PJs and into bed. The on-call duty doctor was furious at the Corpsman for making me carry my bag. He informed me that he would be disciplined. He then had the nurse give me an injection for the pain. The next morning the chief doctor in charge of the hospital came to se me. He checked me out and asked me how I felt. In informed him that the injection and bed rest had eased the pain. He wanted to know if I was going to make a formal complaint about how I was treated by the Corpsman. I assured him that I did not intend to. The doctor apologized for the actions of the Corpsman. He then made arrangements for me to be transported to the USAF Hospital at Wiesbaden, by ambulance. I was taken to the USAF Hospital at Wiesbaden in a Cadillac ambulance (not a square box type wagon, which we referred to as meat wagons). When I arrived at the emergency entrance to the hospital, everyone was surprised, because they expected a VIP and out came little ole me. I was admitted to the hospital where I stayed 30 days for treatment of my back problem which had been aggravated by my overnight stay at the 3rd Army General Hospital in Landsthul. I was assigned to a ward and examined by the neurosurgeon, who recommended I be given hydro-therapy as soon as possible. Two days later I was taken to the Hydro-Therapy Section for treatment. They immersed me into a large tank of warm water, placing me on a sling, so that my head was above the water. There was an attendant standing in the tank next to me. The attendant massaged my spine with a stream of hot water from a hose. When the treatment was over, I was taken back to my ward. This treatment completely drained me and made me weak as a kitten, to the point of almost passing out. The doctor ordered the treatment stopped and then ordered complete bed rest. After a couple of weeks bed rest and after consultation of the neurosurgeon and other doctors on the staff, they decided not to perform surgery on me. (*For a picture of the USAF Hospital at Wiesbaden Air Base, Germany and Clock Shop Building in the shape of a Cuckoo Clock, see photographs A30 and A31.*)

A week before being sent back to Ankara, I got food poisoning. It was determined after investigation that a German kitchen worker had left an aluminum bowl of salad out of the refrigerator in the sunlight and the mayonnaise had turned bad. The salad was then served to me and I got sick. After two days I was back to normal, so they gave me an afternoon pass to tour Wiesbaden. I was issued a necktie to identify me as a patient at the USAF Hospital. I decided that I would have something to eat and a glass of beer. I went to a little Gasthaus for a brockwurst on a roll and a glass of good German beer. I applied hot German mustard to my brockwurst roll and proceeded to eat it, impressing the German patrons in the bar who insisted on buying me a beer. We sang German drinking songs together and had a good time. Then I returned to the hospital after buying post cards and slides. Two days later, they sent me back to Turkey, having decided not to perform surgery on me.

On the way back to Ankara from Germany, we stopped over in Athens, Greece, where I sent a telegram to Peg telling her when I would arrive home. It seems that the Greeks and Turks hate each other so much, that they often do not exchange telegrams for 12 to 24 hours. So my telegram to Peg was held up for a few hours. I arrived home in Ankara a few hours before the telegram was delivered to Peg.

5 September 1957: AF FORM 47, CERTIFICATE OF CLEARANCE AND RECORD OF PERSONNEL SECURITY INVESTIGATION dtd 5 September 1957.

20 February 1958: SPECIAL ORDERS NUMBER 21 HEADQUARTERS THE UNITED STATES LOGISTIC GROUP APO 254, USAF. Paragraph 4. T/SGT MAURICE F. MERCURE, AF 12XXXXXX, Det 30, TUSLOG, APO 254, USAF is awarded permanent grade of TSGT with date of rank 1 Feb 53. FOR THE COMMANDER:

<u>10 March 1958</u>: PERSONNEL ACTION MEMORANDUM NUMBER 42, 7250th SUPPORT SQUADRON 7217th SUPPORT GROUP (USAFE) APO 254, N.Y., N.Y. dtd 10 March 1958. Paragraph 7. DEROS of T/SGT MERCURE, MAURICE F. AF 12XXXXXX, this organ, this sta, is chg fr 9 Sep 58 to 9 Dec 58. Auth: B/L fr T/Sgt Mercure, dtd 5 Mar 58. Subj: Req for Exten of O/S Tour, & 2nd Ind Hq TUSLOG, dtd 6 Mar 58. FOR THE COMMANDER:

<u>10 March 1958</u>: SPECIAL ORDERS NUMBER B107 7250TH SUPPORT SQUADRON 7217TH SUPPORT GROUP (USAFE) UNITED STATES AIR FORCE APO 254 NEW YORK, NY dtd 19 March 1958. Paragraph 1. Following named airman is attached 7217th SUPPORT GROUP (USAFE) for duty with Communications Section effective 20 March 1958. TSGT MAURICE F. MERCURE, AF 12XXXXXX, AFSC 29270. FOR THE COMMANDER:

<u>20 March 1958</u>: Personnel attached to the 7217TH SUPPORT GROUP (USAFE) APO 254, NEW YORK, NY CRYPTO CENTER

TSGT	MAURICE F. MERCURE, NCOIC	29270
SSGT	GORDON D. BENTLEY, ASST NCOIC	29250
SSGT	DONALD D. STANFIELD	29250
A1C	JOHN R. TRACY	29230
A2C	JOHN T. CHURCH	29250
A2C	FRANK J. DESANTIS	29230
A2C	WERNER G. FEIL	29230
A2C	JOE B. PEEL	29250
A2C	CHARLES E. VOGLER	29230
A2C	RENALDO CAMPUS	29230

<u>15 April 1958</u>: SPECIAL ORDERS NUMBER C-32. 7250TH SUPPORT SQUADRON 7217TH SUPPORT GROUP (USAFE) UNITED STATES AIR FORCE APO 254 NEW YORK, NY dtd 15 April 1958. Paragraph 1. TSGT MAURICE F. MERCURE, AF 12XXXXXX, this organization, this station is granted ordinary leave of absence for thirty days effective on or about 17 April 1958 for the purpose of visiting England.

Leave address: Mr. & Mrs. Frederick Banks, 36 Shakespeare Avenue, Hayes, Middlesex, England. Authority: AFR 35-22. FOR THE COMMANDER: (*For a copy of this SO with immigration markings, see attachment B42.*)

16 April 1958: LETTER, SUBJECT: TRANSPORTATION AUTHORIZATION NO. 9. 7250ᵀᴴ SUPPORT SQUADRON 7217ᵀᴴ SUPPORT GROUP (USAFE) UNITED STATES AIR FORCE APO 254, NEW YORK, NY dtd 16 April 1958. TO: MRS. MARGARET D. MERCURE, Dependent of TSGT MAURICE F. MERCURE, AF 12XXXXXX, Detachment 30, The United States Logistics Group APO 254 NEW YORK, NY. FOR THE COMMANDER: (*For a copy of this letter, see attachment B43.*)

17 April 1958: We left Esenboga Airport, Ankara, Turkey, on leave, for Paris, France, via Napoli, Italy.

18 April 1958: We arrived in Naples (Napoli), Italy. We left Naples, Italy for Marseilles, France.

18 April 1958: From the Airport in Naples, Italy, we caught a Space Available Flight to Marseilles, France.

18 April 1958: We arrived safe and sound at Marseilles Airport. We did not have any further chance of making a connecting Space Available Flight to Paris, so we took a taxi to the Marseilles Railway Station, where we caught a train to Paris.

19 April 1958: We boarded the train for Paris with a loaf of French bread, a stick of salami, cheese, and a bottle of wine. We rode in a Wagon-Lits-Cook Sleeping Car. Finding our compartment, which we shared with two other passengers, we ate our bread, salami, and cheese, and drank our wine. We enjoyed ourselves. I got a little high and proceeded to sing the French National Anthem at the top of my voice. The other passengers paid us no never mind and got undressed for bed right in front of us, and retired for the evening. We then did likewise and retired ourselves for the night.

<u>19 April 1958</u>: We arrived at the Paris Nord Railway Station where we caught a train for Boulogne, France. After arriving at the Boulogne Railway Station, we took a bus to the Channel Ferry Boat Terminal where we booked passage for Dover, England, and sailed the same day.

<u>20 April 1958</u>: We arrived safe and sound in Dover Channel Ferry Boat Terminal, where we proceeded to catch a train to Peg's family home.

<u>11 May 1958</u>: After spending 21 enjoyable vacation days with Peg's family, my leave was drawing to a close. We had to save some time for the return journey to Turkey.

We caught a train to the Dover Ferry Boat Terminal, Dover, England. After arriving, we proceeded to the Channel Ferry Boat Terminal and booked passage and sailed to Ostende, Belgium.

<u>12 May 1958</u>: We arrived at the Ostend Channel Boat Ferry Terminal in Ostend, Belgium, where we took a train to Frankfurt, Germany. After arriving at the Frankfurt Railway Station, we took a taxi to Rhein-Main Air Base, Frankfurt, Germany. Arriving at Rhein-Main Air Base, we boarded a Space Available Flight bound for Adana, Turkey.

<u>13 May 1958</u>: We arrived at Adana Air Base, Adana, Turkey, from Rhein-Main Air Base, Frankfurt, Germany.

As there were no immediate Space Available Flights to Esenboga Airport, Ankara, Turkey, and my leave was running out, we decided to take the overnight express (so called) to Ankara. The train car we would be traveling on was a Wagon-Lits-Cook Sleeper. As we had time to kill before the train left for Ankara, we decided to have a cold beer in a sidewalk café next to the Railway Station. So we ordered two cold beers. The waiter brought us the beers and opened them. He started to pour them into glasses. While he was pouring one of the beers, a wasp flew into the glass. We immediately brought it to the attention of the waiter. He just picked up the glass with the wasp in it and emptied it onto the grass. Then he continued to pour the remaining beer into the empty glass, as if nothing had happened. The waiter did not replace the beer in question with a new bottle. We still had to pay for the beer that the wasp flew into. Without further ado, we went to the Railway Station across the street to wait on the train for Ankara.

The sleeping car did not have air conditioning. It began to get hot in the car, so we opened a window to cool it off. Consequently, we also let a lot of soot into the compartment, since the train was being pulled by a steam engine which burned soft coal, which produces a lot of soot. So, early the next morning (before we arrived in Ankara) we closed the window to prevent a further influx of soot and began to remove our clothes in order to washup and put on clean clothes. For some reason unknown to us, the train stopped in the middle of nowhere. Stupid us had not pulled down the window shade. So, when another train stopped on the parallel track right outside our window, there we were, half naked, with a bunch of people in the train next to ours looking at us in awe. Boy were we caught with our pants down, causing us a great deal of embarrassment. We pulled down the window shade and got dressed in a hurry. Upon arriving in Ankara, later that day, we took a taxi home. Arriving home we found everything in apple pie order, with no surprises like we had on our last leave. We took a shower, put on clean clothes, had a cup of tea, listened to the radio, and then went to bed.

The Turkish people (especially the landlords) were after all the American furniture and appliances that they could get their hands on. We, in fact, sold our refrigerator to our landlord when we left the country.

Riding buses in Ankara was an experience you never forget. It was not something you would recommend to anyone. At the bus stations (stops), they used to have a bus employee to load the buses. He would shove people in (using his arms and knee to cram people in) and shut the doors. This would result in the bus being crammed with standing room only passengers, making it very difficult to get off at your stop.

Gypsies used to go through our trash cans looking for food. We threw out some oranges, which were going moldy (having green mold on them). They found them and ate them. They took whatever they wanted.

We had several sand storms, which came from Africa, crossing the Mediterranean Sea to Turkey. It made things quite uncomfortable, with grit (sand) getting up your nose, in your eyes, in your ears and in your mouth. We were always so glad when they were over.

We had a Military Stamp Club, which met once a month in members homes. It consisted of five (5) members. We used to have a great time swapping stamps and showing our newest acquisitions to fellow members.

We ate out a lot, in the American snack bars and NCO Clubs. The food was passable and not that expensive. However, the meals during the holidays were very good.

14 July 1958: We were alerted for possible shipment to Lebanon during the 1958 Lebanese crisis, as a member of a SAC Control Team. We were also alerted to a very heavy increase in Coded Traffic for the Crypto Center. I was on edge the whole time awaiting movement orders. Upon receipt of the alert notice I proceeded to the Crypto Center where I found only one Cryptographer on duty. He was swamped by the huge increase in Coded Traffic (Messages). I found out from the Operator on duty, that earlier, Lt. Moore had taken the Shift Supervisor and one Operator to the gym to play in a Basketball Tournament game. I immediately sent the Air Police to the gym, to bring back the Crypto Personnel. After dispatching the Air Police to bring back help, I pitched in to help the Operator on duty to decipher the messages that were piling up. Lt. Moore was very upset with me, because I had interrupted the basketball game. With arrival of the Chief of Communications, he soon realized that the mission was more important than his silly basketball game. We were ordered to stand down the next day on the Control Team movement.

One evening one of my men, A2C Renaldo Campus, threw a fifth of whiskey (bottle) through the windshield of a taxi during a heated argument over the fare. This occurred right in front of the NCO/Airmen's Club. It resulted in an immediate inter-country situation between the Turkish and American governments. The next morning after the incident, a Turkish Army Truck loaded with bricks and cement pulled up in front of the NCO/Airmen's Club. Turkish Army Soldiers began bricking in the front door to the club. We then had to use a side street entrance to the club, off the main street. The Turkish Army stationed an MP, the city of Ankara assigned a Policeman, and the USAF stationed an Air Policeman outside the new entrance to the club. This was to prevent any future incidents of this type from occurring again. Needless to say, disciplinary action was taken against A2C Campus. Restitution was made to the taxi driver for his windshield. A2C Campus was reduced to Airmen Basic (AB) and had his security clearance revoked. He was assigned to a less sensitive job until he was given a Bad Conduct Discharge.

14 August 1958: AF FORM 279 APPLICATION FOR IDENTIFICATION CARD dtd 14 August 1958. (*For a copy of this form, see attachment B44.*)

22 August 1958: SPECIAL ORDERS NUMBER A-217, TUSLOG DETACHMENT 30 APO 254 NEW YORK, NY dtd 22 August 1958. Paragraph 1. TSGT MAURICE F. MERCURE, AF 12XXXXXX, (Contro 29270). ASSIGNMENT: Relieved from assignment TUSLOG DETACHMENT 30 APO 254, NEW YORK, NY. Assigned to Special Weapons Center Kirtland AFB, NMex (ARDC), FOR THE COMMANDER: (*For a copy of this SO, see attachment B45.*)

9 October 1958: SPECIAL ORDERS NUMBER A-236 TUSLOG DETACHMENT 30 APO 254, NEW YORK, NY dtd 9 October 1958. Paragraph 1. So much of paragraph 1, SO A-217, this organization, this station dated 22 August 1958, pertains to assignment of TSGT MAURICE F. MERCURE, AF 12XXXXXX, is amended to include "PAPC 0800/0900, 10 November 1958. AMD PAR-WRI-3PC-4115-AF 11 PAR-WRI-3DA-4116-AF 11. And as reads "Airman will proceed on or about 28 October 1958," is amended to read "Airmen will proceed on or about 18 October 1958." FOR THE COMMANDER:

10 October 1958: LETTER, SUBJECT: COMMENDATION TO: Whom It May Concern, dtd 10 October 1958. TUSLOG DETACHMENT 30 APO 254, NEW YORK, NY. (*For a copy of this letter, see attachment B46.*)

14 October 1958: LETTER, SUBJECT: Letter of Appreciation DETACHMENT 18 TUSLOG APO 254, NEW YORK, NY. (*For a copy of this letter, see attachment B47.*)

18 October 1958: Copy of Special Order A-217 used in lieu of passport. (*For a copy of this SO, see attachment B48.*)

18 October 1958: The day we left Ankara, Turkey for the United States, the karpigi and his wife said good-bye to us, and kept bowing to us. The karpigi's wife was pregnant and their actions made us feel real uncomfortable, as we were not use to anyone bowing to us.

18 October 1958: When we were leaving for Esenboga International Airport, we were running late (my fault again). A Turkish General furnished us a sedan for the trip to the airport. I don't know what I would have done without Peg; she was my rock and anchor. The love that she possesses is unfathomable. We took the sedan to Esenboga International Airport. When we got to the airport, we were on the wrong side of the field that the aircraft was taking off from. We would not have made the plane on time by going around the field by road. To compensate for this, the airport director gave us a checkered flag, so we could cross the runway to the departure terminal and the waiting aircraft. So, Peg held the flag out the window of the sedan as we crossed the runway. We made it in time and boarded the aircraft for Istanbul. Imagine the passengers' surprise when a TSGT and his wife emerged from the sedan, instead of a VIP.

18 October 1958: We departed Esenboga International Airport on Turkish Airlines (Turk Hava Yolar) and arrived at Istanbul International Airport, where we made connections with a PANAM flight to Paris via Athens, Greece.

18 October 1958: We arrived at Paris International Airport (Orly Field), Paris, France. We took a train to the Channel Ferry Boat Terminal, Dieppe, France.

19 October 1958: We arrived at the Channel Ferry Boat Terminal Dieppe, France, where we booked passage and set sail for New Haven, England. Upon arrival in New Haven, we took a train to Peg's family home.

8 November 1958: My leave was drawing to a close after spending 21 fun-filled and happy days in Hayes, Middlesex, England, at Peg's family home. We took a train to Dover, England, to catch the Channel Ferry Boat to Ostend, Belgium. We landed at the Ferry Boat Terminal, Ostend, Belgium from where we took a train to Paris, France.

<u>9 November 1958</u>: Upon arriving at the Paris Railway Station, we took a local train to Paris International Airport (Orly Field).

<u>11 November 1958</u>: We left Orly Field bound for McGuire AFB, New Jersey, on a chartered aircraft. We arrived at McGuire Air Force Base and were processed through USAF ATCO, then took a train to my mother's house in Holyoke, Massachusetts.

Peg has been an absolute gem through all the moving, catching trains and planes, and dashing from one place to another. I don't know what I would have done without her love and her keeping me from goofing up.

CHAPTER 8

11 NOVEMBER 1958 - 19 NOVEMBER 1960

USA—KIRTLAND AIR FORCE BASE, NEW MEXICO

A. Sandia Base, NM   2 Apr 1959-19 Nov 1960

B. Nellis Air Force Base, NV (TDY)   12 May 1960-13 May 1960

C. Indian Springs Air Force Base, NV (TDY)   14 May 1960-15 May 1960
(Area 51)

<u>11 November 1958</u>: SPECIAL ORDERS NUMBER A-217 TUSLOG DETACHMENT #30 APO 254, NEW YORK, NEW YORK dtd 22 August 1958. Copy of Special Orders used to clear through ATCO McGuire AFB, N.J., 11 November 1958. (*For a copy of this Special Orders, see attachment B49.*)

After arriving at McGuire AFB, NJ and processing through the ATCO, we took a train to Holyoke, Massachusetts, to see my family.

When my leave was drawing to a close, we took a train to Boston, Mass. In the Boston Railway Station, we took a train to Grand Central Station, New York City, NY, where we booked a sleeper compartment to Chicago, Illinois. We boarded the train and traveled overnight to Chicago. We arrived in Chicago early in the morning, going across town to the railway station serving the Western part of the United States. We were now starting a new phase of our military career. Booking seats on a coach car to Albuquerque, New Mexico, we then boarded the Atchison, Topeka & Santa Fe Railroad, Super Chief. The trip was fantastic, seeing all the different parts of the country as we traveled through them.

We arrived in Albuquerque and took a cab to Kirtland Air Force Base. Upon arriving on base, I reported in to the Air Force Special Weapons Center, where I found out that I had been assigned to the 4900th Air Base Group. Reporting to the Commander 4900th ABGp, he informed me that I had been assigned to the Base Crypto Center, Base Communications. The Base Crypto Center was under the command of Major Robert Schumaker, to whom I reported for duty.

We stayed a couple of nights in the base guest house, while we looked for a place to live. Luckily we found a place at 1209 Grand Avenue (N.E.), Albuquerque. It was a nice apartment, consisting of a living/diningroom, bedroom, bathroom and a kitchenette. It suited our needs at the time.

25 November 1958: PERSONNEL ACTIONS MEMORANDUM A-249 HEADQUARTERS AIR FORCE SPECIAL WEAPONS CENTER Air Research and Development Command United States Air Force Kirtland Air Force Base, New Mexico dtd 25 November 1958. Paragraphs 14 & 15. 14. The PRIM CON & DY AFSC of T SGT MAURICE F. MERCURE, AF 12XXXXXX, 4900th AB GRU, this STA, is converted fr 29270 (Cryptographic Operations Supervisor) to 29071 (Cryptographic Operations Supervisor). Eff dt 31 AUG 58. AUTH: Change "L," 23 May 58, to AFM 35-11. 15. T SGT MAURICE F. MERCURE, AF 12XXXXXX, having been ASGD to 4900th ABGRU, this STA, per PARA 1, SO a-217, TUSLOG DET #30, APO 254, NYK, 22 AUG 58, & 1ST IND this HQ 23 SEP 58, this STA is ASGD DY AFSC 29151, CON AFSC 29171. DY SECT CRYPTO FUN ACCT Code 84320, DY Title Crypto Operator. No OJT. EDCSA: 1 NOV 58. AUTH: AFM 35-1, as amended. FOR THE COMMANDER:

28 November 1958: ARDC FORM 104 CERTIFICATE OF SECURITY CLEARANCE BRIEFING dtd 28 November 1958. (*For a copy of this certificate, see attachment B50.*)

Some of the personnel assigned to the Base Crypto Center, Kirtland Air Force Base, were:

1. MSGT Otis R. McCoy, NCOIC
2. TSGT Maurice F. Mercure, Asst NCOIC

3. SSGT Robert Chaves

4. SSGT Samuel A. Indillisano

5. SSGT Willard F. Marshal

6. A2C Stanley L. LeForge

7. A2C Robert R. Turner

8. 2 Civilian Operators

MSGT Stanley O. Christ was the NCOIC of Communications Operations. He had a nickname of SOCKS. He invited my wife and I to his house to meet his wife. Before we arrived at his house, MSGT Christ had accidently knocked over a lamp on the coffee table, causing a dent and a one inch scratch on it. His wife was furious with him (as she was a neat freak). We felt uncomfortable the whole time we were there. We sat on the edge of our seats until we left.

1 December 1958: LETTER, SUBJECT: Verification of Security Clearance TO: Commander Air Force Special Weapons Center ATTN: SWIM Kirtland Air Force Base, New Mexico dtd Dec 1, 1958. FOR THE COMMANDER: (*For a copy of this letter, see attachment B51.*)

4 December 1958: AF FORM 47 CERTIFICATE OF CLEARANCE AND RECORD OF PERSONNEL SECURITY INVESTIGATION HQ AFSWC Kirtland AFB, New Mexico dtd 4 Dec 58. (*For a copy of this form, see attachment B52.*)

24 December 1958: My brother Bob drove all the way from Covina, California, to spend the Christmas holidays with us. It was an enjoyable holiday time, as we had not spent the Christmas holiday together in years. It was a Christmas holiday that I shall never forget.

This is a sample of some of the units assigned to Kirtland Air Force Base:

1. AFSWC (AIR FORCE SPECIAL WEAPONS CENTER)

2. HQ AFSWC

3. NASWC (NAVAL AIR SPECIAL WEAPONS CENTER)

4. 93rd Fighter Interceptor Squadron
5. DET 462 USAF RCTS
6. 1090TH USAF SRW
7. HQ SQ 1090th USAF SRW
8. 1094TH Avn Dep Group
9. 587th Aircraft Control & Warning Squadron
10. 4900th Air Base Group
11. HQ SQ 4900th Air Base Group
12. 4900th CLM Squadron
13. 4900th Consolidated Maintenance Squadron
14. 4900th PM Squadron
15. 4900th Support Squadron
16. 4925th Test Group (Atomic)
17. 4925th Test Squadron (Sampling)
18. 4927th Test Squadron
19. 4928th Test Squadron
20. 4950th Test Group
21. 4952nd SUPRON
22. 6950th Special Activities Squadron

<u>2 April 1959</u>: SPECIAL ORDERS NUMBER 67 HEADQUARTERS SANDIA BASE ALBUQUERQUE, NEW MEXICO dtd 2 April 1959. Paragraph 8. Fol pers orgn indc are asg Pub Qtrs Nr indc this sta eff dates indc. NAME: MAURICE F. MERCURE GR TSGT & SN AF 12XXXXXX ORGN 4900th Air Base Gp Kirtland AFB N Mex QTRS NR 26 Perimeter DATE: 3 Apr 59. FOR THE COMMANDER:

We had a chair, which had been covered with material with Chess pieces printed on it. It was given to us by MSGT Telthorster before he shipped out for an overseas assignment. I used it for the Stamp Club meetings held in our house. We rotated the meetings in homes of club members who had one. Although there were six members, three did not have a home to hold the meetings in.

A 1st Lt (I can't remember his name) used to sit on that chair at the meetings. He stated he was always glad to leave when the meetings were over, as the chair had a very hard seat.

Sandia Base was located between Kirtland Air Force Base and Monsanto Base (operated by the USAF—It was a nuclear weapons storage facility, located in the foot hills of the Sandia Mountains.)

While living in the Albuquerque area, we were exposed to the following venomous wildlife:

1. black widow spiders—venomous bite
2. scorpions—poisonous bite
3. rattlesnakes—poisonous bite
4. tarantulas (spider)—painful sting, but not deadly
5. sidewinders (form of rattlesnake)—poisonous bite

Luckily air conditioning made it too cold for them and kept them out of our houses. Also, we did not have a cellar, where they could hide, since most houses were built without them. This did not give any of the wildlife mentioned above a place to live.

3 April 1959: We moved into public housing (government quarters) at 262 Perimeter Drive, Sandia Base (right next door to Kirtland AFB), from 1209 Grand Avenue, Albuquerque, NM. The apartment consisted of a kitchen, living/diningroom, two bedrooms, bathroom and garage. It was scheduled for renovation, under Sandia Base Renovation Plan.

The MPs (as Sandia Base was operated by the United States Army) used to close the gate to the housing area on Sandia Base at midnight every night. One night, as I was sitting up listening to the late news, a car approached the gate, speeding on the road from Kirtland AFB. He apparently did not see that the gate was closed until the last minute. He could not stop in time and hit the gate barrier, causing it to whiplash, go over the hood and smash the windshield. The driver, who I presumed was drunk, managed to get his car out from under the steel pipe barrier and flee the scene with the MPs in pursuit. The MPs had notified the Air Police on Kirtland AFB, that they were in pursuit of the car that had smashed into the gate barrier. To this day I do not know if they apprehended the vehicle in question or not.

After we moved into 262 Perimeter Drive, we needed transportation to get around to the Commissary, Base Exchange, theater, work, etc. So we purchased a secondhand 1950 Chrysler automobile. It was in excellent shape—no rust (due to the dry climate) and we only paid $200 for it. This vehicle lasted us until November 1962 when we sold it for $250 in Taipei, Taiwan. We lovingly called this car the "Green Hornet," because of its green color. (*For a picture of the "Green Hornet," see photograph A32.*)

In 1959 the Air Force decided to enlarge the Base Crypto Center by building a room on the side of the Crypto Vault and operations area. It doubled the size of the Crypto Center, and enhanced our overall operations capability. Our Crypto Accounting Clerk, Richard (Dick), was very pleased with the additional space, as it provided him room from the old part of the operations area for him to perform his accounting work without interference. It also allowed me to have my office space to myself.

May 1959: While residing at 262 Perimeter Drive, Sandia Base, Albuquerque, NM, my brother Bob packed in his job in Los Angeles, CA and showed up on our door step with baggage in hand, and informed us that he was moving in with us, without letting us know in advance. We had no idea that he had quit his job in California and wanted to move in with us. We had no recourse but to take him in. He immediately tried to get a job in our area paying him the same salary he had been getting in the Los Angeles area. After a month of trying, he gave up and decided to join the Air Force. My brother was not very practical. He wanted to join the Air Force expecting to get the rank of Sergeant (which he never held in the Army Air Forces). The highest he ever got was Corporal. He then expected an immediate Security Clearance and to go to work for me in the Crypto Center. I tried to tell him it didn't work that way; it took time to achieve this. He just couldn't tell the United States Air Force what he wanted and get it. So, he finally gave up the idea and decided to remain a civilian. He then decided to go back to California for a better paying job. Actually, we were glad to see him go, as he was upsetting our whole routine. It was putting a strain on our home life.

I had two civilians working for me in the Crypto Center. One was handling the Crypto Accounts paperwork and the other was working on shift work, as a Crypto Operator. I was continually having trouble with the one working on shift work, as he was a very heavy drinker. One night I received a telephone call at home from the

Teletype Shift Supervisor that the Crypto Operator on duty had locked himself out of the Crypto Center again. He had left his keys on a table when he went outside to pick up messages and the door locked behind him. So, consequently, he was locked out of the Crypto Center. This was not the first time he had done so. I immediately got dressed and my wife Peg, who was in her night attire, accompanied me to the Communications Center. She said she had a feeling that something was going to happen. Boy was she right! I was in such a hurry to get into the building and unlock the Crypto Center door that I did not look as I entered the door to the Communications Center. I bumped my head on a metal coatrack, splitting open my scalp. I unlocked the Crypto Center door and let the Crypto Operator in. I placed a handkerchief on the wound to keep the blood out of my eyes and off my face. We got in the car and I drove to the base dispensary. When I got there, they cleaned the wound and stitched it up. They gave me a shot for the pain and a tetanus shot in case the metal coatrack was rusty. They then told me to have my wife Peggy drive me home, and not to drive myself. I had to drive myself home as Peg could not drive. This incident was not the last time that this person locked himself out to the Crypto Center.

My wife and I used to like going out to the Albuquerque Airport and watch the planes landing and taking off, wishing that we were on them going to England. It was nice just sitting there and imagining that we were flying to some distant location.

My problem drinker one day decided to call Frank Sinatra on location in Rome, to tell him off. He got through to Mr. Sinatra and started badmouthing and cursing him. Mr. Sinatra just left the telephone off the hook and let our mutual friend run up a very large transatlantic telephone bill which he could not afford and nearly lost his telephone because of this.

I tried to have our civilian (the drinker) Crypto Operator relieved of his duties because of his actions, but the Civil Service Board would not approve of his dismissal. So I did some research to find a way to relieve the service of this burden. I came across a 205 (security) series regulation on security clearance, which states that you could have a person's security clearance revoked if they drank too much (in excess), so as to be a security hazzard. I requested our problem drinker's clearance be revoked by the Base Provost Marshal. Based on all the incidents he had been involved in, the Civil Service Board was advised of his clearance being revoked. They (the Civil Service Board) came back and said he may not be able to work in Crypto, but that he could work in the Teletype Section which did not require a security clearance. Therefore, he could not be dismissed. However, the service had the last laugh a little later when a security clearance was required to work in the Teletype Section, because of classified teletype circuits being installed therein. So, the service problem person was relieved from the communications sphere of operations.

We had a group of stamp collectors who used to meet at the various members' homes, once a month. It was a very interesting, worthwhile, and enjoyable group. I remember going to one member's home, where they had a pair of Siamese cats. These cats used to nip and scratch our legs while we were sitting around the table discussing and trading stamps. I had to end up telling the owner of the cats, and that I would not attend any further meetings at his home, unless he kept the cats locked up, so that they could not inflict any further scratches and bites on the members' legs. He complied with my wishes, and further meetings at his home went well.

25 June 1959: SWPM FORM 0-59 STATEMENT OF SERVICE dtd 25 June 1959. (*For a copy of this form, see attachment B53.*) As of 25 June 1959, I had 12 years and 8 months of active duty.

We took a vacation (leave) to Santa Fe, New Mexico for the Fiesta Festival. It was a very nice, enjoyable time, seeing all the locals in their native costumes. We took pictures of some little girls in their native dress.

29 June 1959: SPECIAL ORDERS NUMBER A-335 HEADQUARTERS AIR FORCE SPECIAL WEAPONS CENTER (ARDC) United States Air Force Kirtland Air Force Base, New Mexico dtd 29 June 1959. Paragraph. Each of the following named Airmen, 4900TH AB Gp, ARDC, this station, is awarded the Good Conduct Medal or Good Conduct Medal Clasp, as indicated, for his demonstration of exemplary behavior, efficiency, and fidelity during the period indicated. Authority: AFR 900-10. BRONZE CLASP WITH THREE LOOPS GRADE TSGT NAME MAURICE F. MERCURE AFSN AF 12XXXXXX FROM 1 JUN 54 TO 30 Jun 57. FOR THE COMMANDER:

9 July 1959: SPECIAL ORDERS NUMBER C-129 HEADQUARTERS AIR FORCE SPECIAL WEAPONS CENTER (ARDC) United States Air Force Kirtland Air Force

Base, New Mexico dtd 9 July 1959. Paragraph 11. TSGT MAURICE F. MERCURE, AF 12XXXXXX 4900th AB Gp, ARDC, this sta, DAFSC is changed from 29151 (Crypto Operator) to 29171 (Cryptographic Supervisor). AUTH: AFM 35-1 as amended. FOR THE COMMANDER:

23 July 1959: SPECIAL ORDERS NUMBER C-137 HEADQUARTERS AIR FORCE SPECIAL WEAPONS CENTER (ARDC) United States Air Force Kirtland Air Force Base, New Mexico, dtd 23 July 1959. Paragraph 6. The following named Airman, 4900th AB Gp, ARDC, this sta, having been administered the Airman Proficiency Test, on date indicated, for AFSC indicated, obtained score and qualification indicated. AUTH; AFM 35-8.

RANK	NAME	AFSN	TESTING	SCORE	QUALIFICATION	AFSC	DATE TESTED
SSGT	Samuel A. Indilisano	AF 33XXXXXX	29151	100	QUAL		-10 Jun 59
MSGT	Otis McCoy	AF 35XXXXXX	29171	102	QUAL		-10 Jun 59
TSGT	Maurice F. Mercure	AF 12XXXXXX	29171	128	QUAL		-10 Jun 59

FOR THE COMMANDER:

Kirtland AFB and Sandia Base Areas used to hold periodic Emergency Evacuation Drills from the housing areas. During the exercise, we were sent home to evacuate our families. I remember the rendezvous area, where we used to go to form up into convoys. We were instructed not to get out of our cars, because the area was littered with rattlesnakes and we could possibly be bitten. They used to instruct us to line up in convoys, by MPs wearing special boots because of the snakes. We were also given instructions as to where we were to proceed if threat (attack) was imminent. This was quite an experience in itself. It used to give us the feeling of possible danger and exposure to nuclear attack. We felt sorry for the civilian population who had no evacuation plan.

While at work one day we received a report concerning an Unidentified Flying Object (UFO), which was forwarded to the appropriate headquarters handling these types of reports. Handling of this type of report was limited to Supervisory Personnel. The report indicated that a woman was driving through Tijeras Canyon (outside of Albuquerque) at midnight when a large dark object flew over her car. She was driving at this time with her window open and her arm out of the window. She felt a prickly sensation, but thought nothing of it at the time until the next morning when she noticed that her arm and elbow were turning red as if burned. She went to the hospital to have it checked out. They informed her that the redness was a radiation burn and needed to be treated at once. The question remains how did she get radiation burns on her arm and elbow, driving through Tijeras Canyon at midnight. This I believe was listed as an unknown. This was not the only UFO report that we received and forwarded on to the appropriate headquarters authority.

I tried to teach Peg how to drive one day. So I drove out into the country side where I thought it would be safe to do so. The road we were on looked like a nice long flat road, which can be deceiving out in the dessert as they contain a lot of arroyos in the road, unseen by the naked eye. I found what I thought was a nice stretch of highway, and I began to show her how to drive. She was doing really well, until we passed a large flock of sheep on the lefthand side of the road. A large sheepdog was herding them and protecting them. He had a wide collar with spikes on it, to protect him from attacking wolves. The guard dog did not like the fact that we were so close to the flock, so he charged the car, scaring Peg, who let go of the steering wheel and stepped on the gas. Just at that time a large semi-trailer truck came up out of an arroyo, heading right for us. I am sorry to say that I said a couple of choice words (having the shit scared out of me). I grabbed the steering wheel and kept us and the truck from hitting each other. Peg never got over that experience and how I reacted and the wording I used. So she would not let me continue giving her anymore driving lessons. So, to this day, she does not know how to or want to drive.

24 November 1959: Statement of interview of my wife, by Lt. Col. Horton W. Strickland, Commander Headquarters Squadron Section, 4900th Air Base Group, Kirtland Air Force Base, NM, for application for Special Assignment. (*For a copy of this interview, see attachment B54.*)

<u>24 November 1959</u>: AF FORM 109 AIRMAN'S APPLICATION FOR SPECIAL ASSIGNMENT dtd 24 November 1959, with 3 attachments and 3 endorsements. ((*For a copy of picture taken for AF FORM 109 application for MAAG duty, see photograph A33.)*

<u>7 December 1959</u>: AF FORM 703, NOTIFICATION OF ACTION—WARRANT OFFICER AND AIRMAN SPECIAL ASSIGNMENT. HEADQUARTERS, USAF AFPMP-2D, Washington 25, DC.

Received acknowledgment from Headquarters USAF, on my Special Assignment Application with instructions for me to sit and await their decision.

<u>11 February 1960</u>: SPECIAL ORDERS NUMBER G-40 HEADQUARTER AIR FORCE SPECIAL WEAPONS CENTER (ARDC) United States Air Force Kirtland Air Force Base, NM. Dtd 11 February 1960. Paragraph 9. TSGT MAURICE F. MERCURE, AF 12XXXXXX, 4900th AB Gp (ARDC), this stn. DAFSC is changed from 29171 (Cryptographic Operations Supervisor) to 29180 (Communications Center Operations Superintendent). No change in PAFSC and CAFSC. No OJT. Authority: AFM 35-1, as amended. FOR THE COMMANDER:

<u>21 March 1960</u>: SPECIAL ORDERS NUMBER 60 HEADQUARTERS SANDIA BASE ALBUQUERQUE, New Mexico dtd 21 March 1960. Paragraphs 21 & 22. 21. FNE orgn indc this sta asg Pub Qtrs Nr indc this sta eff 22 Mar 60. 2102020 10-9620 P2763, 03, 07 S29-044 & 2102010 01-66 P1311-07 S99-999. TSGT MAURICE F MERCURE AF 12XXXXXX 4900th ABG KAFB. 22. Asg Pub Qtrs Nr indc this sta term for fol pers orgn indc this sta. TSGT MAURICE F MERCURE AF 12XXXXXX 4900th ABG KAFB 262 Perimeter. FOR THE COMMANDER:

7315 Bradshaw Avenue, Sandia Base. Sandia Base was in the process of remodeling Public Quarters, so when 7315 Bradshaw Avenue was completely renovated, we were moved from 262 Perimeter Drive (which was scheduled for renovation) into remodeled quarters at 7315 Bradshaw Avenue. They were fantastic. They had all new appliances in the kitchen and laundry room. New central heating and air conditioning units. New laundry room with storage cabinets and an in-the-wall ironing board. It had a self-contained entrance just off the kitchen's outside entrance. Peg liked this arrangement. There was also an in-the-ground garbage can, with a step-on lid opener. There was a garage with a large walk-in closet. The quarters consisted of two bedrooms, livingroom/diningroom, kitchen, bathroom, laundry room and a garage.

<u>31 March 1960</u>: AF FORM 1164 REQUEST FOR AND AUTHORIZATION OF LEAVE OF MILITARY PERSONNEL, dtd 31 March 1960. Request for 5 days ordinary leave. (*For a copy of this form, see attachment B55.*)

All the children in the neighborhood used to come to our house and sit on the front lawn with me, and I would tell them stories. Their mothers were not worried about them, as long as they knew where they were. I used to enjoy being with them and entertaining them. I remember one little girl coming to the house one day and knocking on the front door, and asking Peg if her Daddy could come out and play. I thought that this was very cute.

<u>12 May 1960</u>: AF FORM 626 REQUEST FOR AND AUTHORIZATION OF TEMPORARY DUTY TRAVEL ORDERS OF MILITARY PERSONNEL Hq 4900th ABGRU, Kirtland AFB, NM dtd 12 May 1960. (*For a copy of this form, see attachment B56.*)

Major ROBERT SCHUMAKER (COMMUNICATIONS OFFICER/CRYPTO SECURITY OFFICER) and I went TDY to Nellis Air Force Base and Indian Springs, Nevada. The reason for this trip was to coordinate message traffic handling between them and the Communications Center, Kirtland Air Force Base, Albuquerque, New Mexico. To our satisfaction, as we were the major players (also the Headquarters Unit) in this matter, all messages handled after this conference were processed without a hitch.

While there, we went into Las Vegas one night, where I won some money. Major Schumaker was not so lucky and dropped quite a few dollars at the Sands Casino.

Peg woke up one night while I was away and found a spider on her pillow. Believing that it was a black widow spider, she ran next door for help. Our next door neighbors went to the house with Peg and assured her that it was not a black widow spider. She was relieved and our next door neighbors returned to their home. All's well that ends well.

31 May 1960: AF FORM 1164 REQUEST FOR AND AUTHORIZATION OF LEAVE OF MILITARY PERSONNEL, HEDRONSEC, 4900th ABGRU, KAFB, NM dtd 31 May 1960. Request for 25 days ordinary leave. (*For a copy of this form, see attachment B57.*)

6 June 1960: We decided we would like to see the Grand Canyon—mostly my idea—taking a 25-day Ordinary Leave of Absence, beginning the 6th of June 1960. We started out on Interstate Highway Number 40 to Flagstaff, Arizona. On the way we saw the Painted Desert and the Petrified Forest. The Painted Desert was very beautiful and consisted of many colors. The Petrified Forest was an amazing place to see with all the fallen trees which had turned into stone over the ages. The drive was both very interesting and educational.

On our way to the Grand Canyon, we decided to sleep in our car for the night to save money. This was a very foolish thing to do as the Red Light Bandit was operating in the area at the time. He had caused a lot of scares, committing robberies and rapes during that period of time. We were lucky that we did not have an encounter with him—THANK GOD. The only mishap we had was when Peg closed the car door on my hand. I was holding in the door button, which turned on and off the internal overhead light to keep her from being illuminated, so that she would not be seen by cars coming in either direction, while she was relieving herself.

We reached the Grand Canyon without anything else occurring to us. While at the Grand Canyon, Peg was off doing something. On her return, she overheard some women saying, "Look at that crazy fool on the edge of the canyon. If he is not careful, he will fall in." Peg looked at the edge of the canyon and there I was laying down on the edge looking down into the canyon. She quickly got me away from the edge and chewed me out. The Grand Canyon was absolutely beautiful at sunset.

Peg's impression of the Grand Canyon was not the same as mine. She called it a big hole in the ground. I took some excellent pictures of the area. (*For a copies of a pictures of the Grand Canyon, see photograph A34 & A35.*)

In my haste to get to the bathroom, I twisted my ankle. The only ice we had available at the time was in a jug of lemonade, which we applied to my ankle, causing it to be sticky from the lemonade. Again I was acting irresponsible and childish, according to Peggy.

Our trip back to 7315 Bradshaw Avenue, Albuquerque, NM was very uneventful.

29 June 1960: SPECIAL ORDERS NUMBER A-308 HEADQUARTERS AIR FORCE SPECIAL WEAPONS CENTER (ARDC) United States Air Force, Kirtland Air Force Base, New Mexico dtd 29 June 1960. Paragraph 2. Each of the following named Airmen, Hq 4900th AB Gp, ARDC, this station, is awarded the Good Conduct Medal and/or Clasp as indicated for their demonstration of Exemplary Behavior, Efficiency and Honor during the period indicated. BRONZE CLASP WITH FOUR LOOPS TSGT MAURICE F MERCURE AF 12XXXXXX 30 Jun 57 to 29 Jun 60. FOR THE COMMANDER:

14 July 1960: SPECIAL ORDERS NUMBER A-335 HEADQUARTERS AIR FORCE SPECIAL WEAPONS CENTER (ARDC) United States Air Force Kirtland Air Force Base, New Mexico dtd 14 July 1960. Paragraphs 5 & 6. 5. So much of paragraph 2, SO A-308, 29 Jun 60, this Hq, this station, relating to the award of Good Conduct Medal and/or Clasp pertaining to the following named Airman, Hq 4900th AB Gp, ARDC, this station, is revoked. GRADE TSGT NAME MAURICE F. MERCURE AFSN AF 12XXXXXX. 6. Each of the following named Airmen, Hq 4900th AB Gp, ARDC, this station is awarded the Good Conduct Medal and/or Clasp as indicated for their demonstration of Exemplary Behavior, Efficiency and Honor during the periods indicated. Authority: AFR 900-10. GRADE TSGT NAME MAURICE F. MERCURE AFSN AF 12XXXXXX BRONZE CLASP WITH FOUR LOOPS FROM: 1 Jul 57 TO 30 Jun 60. FOR THE COMMANDER:

20 July 1960: SPECIAL ORDERS NUMBER G-203 HEADQUARTERS AIR FORCE SPECIAL WEAPONS CENTER Air Research and Development command Kirtland Air Force Base, New Mexico dtd 20 July 1960. Paragraph 14. TSGT MAURICE F. MERCURE, AF 12XXXXXX, 4900th AB Gp (ARDC), this station, DAFSC is changed from 29190 (Communications Center Operation Superintendent to 29171

(Cryptographic Operations Supervisor). No change in PAFSC, CAFSC, Duty Section, or Functional Account Code. No OJT. EDOA: 29 Feb 60. AUTHORITY: AFM 35-1, as amended. FOR THE COMMANDER:

A few houses down from us, a little girl was playing in the back yard. Her mother heard what she thought was a rattle. She wondered where her daughter found a rattle to play with. Looking out the kitchen window, she saw her daughter poking a stick at a coiled snake. She immediately called the Military Police (MPs). Upon arriving the MPs found the little girl poking a stick at a coiled up rattlesnake. They got the little girl away from the snake. Then the MPs immediately shot the snake (which went for them). It turned out to be a six-foot Diamond Back rattlesnake. They had a picture of it and the MPs in the Sandia Base Newspaper.

22 July 1960: SPECIAL ORDERS NUMBER G-206 HEADQUARTERS AIR FORCE SPECIAL WEAPONS CENTER Air Research and Development Command Kirtland Air Force Base, New Mexico dtd 22 July 1960. Paragraph 15. TSGT MAURICE F. MERCURE, AF 12XXXXXX 4900th AB Gp (ARDC), ths station DAFSC is converted from 29180 to 29190. No change in PAFSC or DAFSC. EDOA: 29 Feb 60. Authority: AFM 35-1, 1 Dec 59 FOR THE COMMANDER:

29 July 1960: AIR UNIVERSITY United States Air Force EXTENSION COURSE INSTITUTE Date 29 Jul 1960. Be it known M. F. MERCURE is a graduate of COMM CENTER SPECIALIST course in testimony whereof and by authority vested in us, this diploma is hereby conferred. Given at Gunter Air Force Base, Alabama, this day as dated above. ***** WILFRED W. WAGNER Lt Colonel, USAF Commandant WALTER E. TODD Lieutenant General, USAF Commander, Air University. FRANK D. HUTCHINS Colonel, USAF Air University Secretary.

2 August 1960: SPECIAL ORDERS NUMBER G-212 HEADQUARTERS AIR FORCE SPECIAL WEAPONS CENTER Air Research and Development Command United States Air Force Kirtland Air Force Base, New Mexico dtd 2 August 1960. Paragraph 3. The Assignment Limitation and Non-Eligibility for overseas Code, SC-4, of TSGT MAURICE F. MERCURE, AF 12XXXXXX, 4900TH AB Gp (ARDC),

this station, is changed from Code "M" (No deferment of any kind) to Code "Q" (Committed to an overseas assignment.) Authority: AFM 35-11, as amended: AFM 171-6, as amended; and Hq USAF (AFPMP-2D) Overseas Assignment Card No. 3161. FOR THE COMMANDER:

5 August 1960: LETTER, SUBJECT: Station Information AIR FORCE SECTION MILITARY ASSISTANCE ADVISORY GROUP, TAIWAN APO 63 SAN FRANCISCO, CALIFORNIA dtd 5 Aug 1960 From FRED M. DEAN Major General, USAF Chief. (*For a copy of this letter, see attachment B58.*)

5 August 1960: LETTER, SUBJECT: Station Information. 1170th USAF FOREIGN MISSION SQUADRON (MAP) 1170TH USAF FOREIGN MISSION GROUP (HQ COMD) APO 63 SAN FRANCISCO, CALIFORNIA dtd 5 Aug 1960. FROM WILLIAM L. CARTER CWO (W-2), USAF Commander. (*For a copy of this letter, see attachment B59.*)

14 September 1960: SPECIAL ORDERS NUMBER A-449 HEADQUARTERS AIR FORCE SPECIAL WEAPONS CENTER United States Air Force Kirtland Air Force Base, New Mexico dtd 14 September 1960. Paragraph 1. TSGT MAURICE F. MERCURE, AF 12XXXXXX, Control AFSC 29171. ASSIGNMENT: Relieved from assignment Hq 4900th AB Gp, ARDC, this station; assigned 1170th USAF Foreign Mission Sq, APO 63, San Francisco, California, 1170th USAF Foreign Mission Gp, Fort Myers, Arlington 8, Va, for duty with USAF Air Section, MAAG-Taiwan, on USAF Line Number 9914-Taiwan-29171-18 Nov (Rqn 614) 2-DELTA, REPORTING DATA: Seven (7) DDALVP. Leave address 1143 Los Robles Ave, Pasadena, Calif. Individual and dependent will report to MATS passenger service center, Travis AFB, California not earlier than 0400 hours, 19 Nov 60. Air Movement Designator for Airman: SUU-TPE-3PC-9038-AF. Air Movement Designator for Dependent: SUU-TPE-3DA-9038-AF. EDCSA: 24 Nov 60. GENERAL INSTRUCTIONS: AFM 75-4 will be complied with. All mail will be addressed to show grade, name, AFSN, 1170th USAF Foreign Mission Squadron, APO 63, San Francisco, California. Authority: Hq USAF (AFPMP-2D) Overseas Assignment Card Number 3161, 26 Jul 60. Airman possesses TOP SECRET Security Clearance. TRANSPORTATION: PCS.

TDN: 57-1111080.581161-6120 P414 S503700 0231 0232 0321 0390 (AP 1-484) CIC: 4A 161-1458 503700. Dislocation Allowance Other. Copies of all documents (orders, bills of lading, TR's, etc.) citing the above funding symbols will be forwarded to 1100 Support Group (CAF-3B), Bolling AFBN 25, D.C. Transportation of dependent (Margaret D. Mercure—Wife) is authorized concurrently with sponsor by message from CHMAAG, Taiwan, MGAG 5 980, 9 Aug 60, TPA with five (5) days travel time authorized. If POV is not used, travel time will be the time of the common carrier used. Travel by military aircraft, and/or vessel is authorized. Sixty-five (65) pounds plus thirty-five (35) pounds excess baggage authorized for air movement. FOR THE COMMANDER:

<u>31 October 1960</u>: Halloween Night, we gave out candy for treats, until we ran out. Never had so many children come to the house for Halloween Trick or Treats, resulting in us running out of candy. When we ran out of candy, we decided to turn off the outside light and the lights in the house and sit in the dark. It didn't do us any good, as one little boy came and knocked on our front door. He shouted, "Open up. I know that you are in there." We opened the door and proceeded to give him some fruit.

<u>Undated</u>: We had a National Guard Fighter Pilot, who accidently shot at a regular Air Force Plane (from the Strategic Air Command), causing serious damage to the plane and injuries to several crew members. National Guard Pilots used to make training passes at planes landing and taking off from the base. This pilot was going through the steps he would take to shoot down an enemy aircraft. During this stage he accidently hit the firing button, hitting a SAC aircraft coming in for a landing. The Regular Air Force personnel were so upset that they nearly broke regulations, and almost marched on the National Guard Squadron to seek revenge. This was a very tense and difficult time.

<u>1 November 1960</u>: SB FORM 27 HEADQUARTERS SANDIA BASE, Albuquerque, New Mexico. ASSIGNMENT OR TERMINATION OF PUBLIC QUARTERS Mercure, Maurice F. T/Sgt. (*For a copy of this form, see attachment B60.*)

<u>4 November 1960</u>: LETTER, SUBJECT: Extension of Enlistment, with two (2) endorsements. (*For a copy of this letter, see attachment B61.*)

<u>7 November 1960</u>: AF FORM 1411 EXTENSION OF ENLISTMENT IN THE REGULAR AIR FORCE MERCURE, MAURICE FRANK, dtd 7 November 1960. (*For a copy of this form, see attachment B62.*)

<u>9 November 1960</u>: SPECIAL ORDERS NUMBER G-303 HEADQUARTERS AIR FORCE SPECIAL WEAPONS CENTER Air Research and Development Command United States Air Force Kirtland Air Force Base, New Mexico, dtd 9 November 1960. Paragraph 1. The date of separation of TSGT MAURICE F. MERCURE, AF 12XXXXXX, 4900th AB Gp, ARDC, this station, is changed from 4 Oct 61 to 4 Dec 62. Enlistment extended for a period of fourteen (14) months. Authority: AFM 39-9 and 2d endorsement this Hq, SWPMR, to letter from TSgt Mercure, Subject: Extension of Enlistment, 4 Nov 60. FOR THE COMMANDER:

<u>November 1960</u>: On our way to Travis Air Force Base, California, we stopped in Flagstaff, AZ for gas and something to eat. While the gas station attendant was checking our car's oil for us, he informed us that our water pump was defective and needed replacing. As we didn't have any trouble with it so far, I was suspicious. So, we went and had breakfast at a nearby diner. While there I spoke to a local, who informed me of a good Indian (Native American) mechanic. He told me to tell the mechanic that he sent us. After having something to eat, we drove to the garage. I told him that he was recommended to us by the man in the diner. He checked out our water pump and informed us that there was nothing wrong with it. In fact that water pump lasted us up to the time we sold our car two years later. We continued on our way to my brother Bob's place in Pasadena, California.

<u>November 1960</u>: While proceeding to California on Interstate Highway #40, we had to drive through Topock, Arizona, to get to Needles, California. On the way to Topock, a car passed us, exceeding the speed limit. He was apprehended by an Arizona State Policeman (State Trooper), who pulled him over and gave him a ticket. As we approached the stopped State Police Car, the State Trooper motioned for me to pull over and stop. He told me he had been following us for a few miles and believed that I had wanted to speed. I take it he had noticed my uniform hanging up in the back of my car, so, he proceeded to give me a warning ticket. When we got back into the car

and proceeded to Topock, the State Trooper followed us to the state line. I guess he thought I would break the speed limit. I can only assume that he had a quota to fill and I was his victim, because I was in the military. When we were on the California side, I yelled back to him "Thank you, you son-of-a-bitch, for nothing." We went on to Needles, where we spent the night in a motel from out of the thirties. Just like Bates Motel, in the movie "Psycho." The next morning we proceeded to my brother Bob's place in Pasadena, California.

14 November 1960: We had seven days delay in route, so we stayed with Bob in Pasadena. He took us to Knotts Berry Farm where we had a good time. We also went to several nice restaurants and had very good meals. When our leave was over, we continued on our way to Travis Air Force Base, California, by car.

18 November 1960: We drove north to San Francisco, where we crossed the Golden Gate Bridge, on our way to Oakland. Arriving at the Oakland Army Terminal, we turned our car over to them for shipment to Taipei, Taiwan. We then took a bus to Travis Air Force Base.

18 November 1960: Arriving at Travis Air Force Base, we spent the night in the base guest house.

19 November 1960: We reported in to the MATS Passenger Service Counter, Travis Air Force Base at 7:00 AM. After processing through the MATS Passenger Service Counter, we boarded Flight P523, 10:00 AM for Taipei via Clark Air Base, Philippines.

CHAPTER 9

20 NOVEMBER 1960 - 19 DECEMBER 1962
TAIWAN MAAG/TAIWAN/ TAIPEI AIR STATION, TAIWAN

A. Tainan Air Station, Taiwan (TDY)   15 Jun 1962-17 Jun 1962
B. Taipei Air Station, Taipei   14 Dec 1961-10 Nov 1962

<u>20 November 1960</u>: We arrived at Hickam Air Force Base, Hawaii, then continued our flight to Clark Air Base, Philippines.

<u>21 November 1960</u>: We arrived at Clark Air Base, Philippines, where we spent the night in the base guest house. In the guest house, the rooms were separated by plywood walls, with the bottom two feet open and covered with screen material. One could hear and see something going on in the next rooms. A little girl in the next room to us kept bending down and peeking into our room through the screen material. It was very unnerving and uncomfortable. We just turned out the lights and went to bed, and ignored her.

<u>22 November 1960</u>: The next day we continued on our way to Taipei, Taiwan.

<u>23 November 1960</u>: We arrived in Taipei, Taiwan, on CAT (Chinese Civil Air Transport), from Clark AB, Philippines. Landing at Taipei International Airport, we stayed in a hotel, until we found an apartment. I used to ride a bus to work every day to the Sugar Building, which housed the MAAG Communications Center. The bus used to leave me off at the top of the road that the hotel was located on. Then I would walk the rest of the way to the hotel. As I walked to the hotel, I was propositioned by street

walkers. They would ask, "Do you want a long time?" I would answer, "No." Then they would ask, "Do you want a short time?" Again I would answer, "No." I told this to Peg, who would not believe me. So I told her, "Tonight when I come home, stand on the hotel balcony and watch the show." So that night she did as I requested and she saw and heard the whole show.

23 November 1960: SPECIAL ORDERS NUMBER C-49, 1170TH USAF FOREIGN MISSION SQUADRON (MAP) 1170TH USAF FOREIGN MISSION GROUP (HQ COMD) APO 63, SAN FRANCISCO, CALIFORNIA dtd 23 November 1960. Paragraph 12, TSGT MAURICE F. MERCURE, AF 12XXXXXX, this unit, Primary & Control AFSC 29171, is assigned duty with Dep C/S Comm & Elect, Hq MAAG, Taiwan in duty AFSC 29171. Trick Chief, effective 28 Nov 60. Functional Account 63000. Length of last overseas tour—D. DEROS established as 18 Nov 62.

December 1960: We moved into our 2nd floor apartment #15 (UP), Alley 27, Lane 18, Sec 4, Chung Shan N Rs, Taipei, Taiwan. The apartment consisted of a bedroom, a living/diningroom, kitchen, bathroom and a balcony. In order to have hot water for bathing, washing dishes, etc., we had to light a coal fire under the water tank. The hot water tank was located on the balcony. You got dirty lighting the coal fire under the hot water tank, so you were really ready to wash up when the water was hot. It was a necessary evil, but a pain in the ass.

December 1960: As we had our car (the Green Hornet) shipped to Taipei, Taiwan, we had to go to the Port City of Keelung to pick it up. We got to the Port of Keelung, to pick up the car, but it took a while to locate it. We had it gassed up, and it started OK. We drove it back to our apartment in Taipei and parked it in front of the building, without any problems. The next morning the car would not start; the battery was dead. So, we purchased a new battery at the PX that day and installed it in the car. The car performed very well after that. No trouble for two years, right up to the time we sold it to Wayne, our next door neighbor.

The area we lived in was called Gin Tan; it was a very nice area. It was located just down the hill from the Grand Hotel (owned by Madam Chiang Kai-shek). We used to go there once a month to eat. It was a fabulous place and the food and service was out of this world.

We met Alvin (Al) & Mary-Anne Dumont in the hotel when we first arrived in Taipei. Poor Al was very easily turned off of food, once we told him the sausages that he was about to eat had monkey brains in it (which they did not). So he refused to eat them. His wife Mary-Anne was just as bad as I was in turning him off of his food. Al was a very nice sensitive person, and we should have been ashamed of ourselves for telling him a lie about his food. Al was in the Air Force, stationed at Taipei Air Station, in the 2165th Communications Squadron. I did not know it at the time, but I would be stationed there with him later on.

We were introduced to June & Grady Smith by Alvin & Mary-Anne Dumont. The Smith's had an adorable little boy, whom they called Mr. Toot. He had big eyes and Peg thought he was loveable. We used to go to the Smith's for barbecue parties. They were such good hosts and put you at ease. We always had an enjoyable time at their home.

Undoubtedly, the most weird thing Peg and I ran into was on Taiwan. There was a lady who believed that she would turn black like a Negro if she drank coffee. She was an American and there was absolutely no way that we could convince her otherwise. She did not care, even if we had scientific proof to the contrary. Perhaps it had to do with the part of the States she came from or that she had been told that fairy tale when she was a little girl, to keep her from drinking coffee.

MAAG, Communications Center was responsible for providing communications personnel to the off-shore islands of Quemoy and Matsu. They sent people out to the Islands, especially if they did not agree with the establishment. I was always on edge that I would be shipped out to the Island, since I did not agree with the way things were done, but Major General Sanborn assured me that I would not be sent there.

January 1961: Chinese customs were pretty hard to understand at times. One was that if a car or train hit and killed a Chinese person in an accident, they would leave the body lie there at the scene of the accident, hoping that someone would come along and check the body to see if the person was still alive. The first person to touch the body was responsible for paying for the funeral. They hoped it was an American, so they could have a large funeral for the deceased.

Our Chaplains were Naval Officers; they were very good pastors. Their names were Chaplain Paul and Chaplain Ford.

We used to go to the Base Cinema (Theatre) every chance we got. Our favorite seats were in the back row. A sailor and his very large, fat wife kept coming to the cinema and sat in the back row. Because the woman was so large, the seats used to give way under her weight. The poor sailor (her husband) was very embarrassed. The theatre manager finally asked her not to come, as she was breaking so many seats—faster than they could get them repaired—and that the cinema could neither afford to fix them nor did it have the time to do so. He did not like having to tape the seats with a sign "Out of Service," until they could be fixed.

Peg and I used to go to the beach at Tam Sui. It was a Chinese military controlled beach with an MP on the gate and a snack bar. Americans didn't use this beach very often, as they preferred Camp McCalley, which was an American controlled and operated beach. We did not care for Camp McCalley, as it was always crowded and was a long way from our apartment. Tam Sui was much closer and convenient to us. We generally had the entire beach to ourselves, which we liked. Our drive back to our apartment from the beach was very enjoyable. Wearing our bathing suits and Chinese Coolie hats, it looked as though I had nothing on, but my coolie hat. We used to listen to Radio Free China, hosted by the Dragonman, and presented by Northwest Orient Airlines.

The restaurants in Taipei were very good and the food was excellent. The Grand Hotel's diningroom was the best on the Island. It was the place to go to have dinner—top notch meals, which were out of this world. They had the best Sweet and Sour Pork that we have every eaten. The January Restaurant was also a very good place to eat, but it could not compare with the Grand Hotel.

We used to go downtown to Haggles Alley to barter for goods, before the government tore it down to make way for new apartments and a shopping center. The store owners of Haggles Alley did not expect you to pay the price marked on the items. Instead, they expected you to haggle with them over the price. They used to say when we haggled over the price, that we were taking food from the mouths of their children and/or family. Of course this all came to an end when the Alley was demolished for progress. We missed the old Haggles Alley for its haggling and final prices. The new shops charged more because their overhead was higher, and prices were controlled by the government.

We had a local stamp club which met in the American Embassy which was attended by Chinese and Americans alike. I felt sorry for a Chinese collector who did not have a stamp catalogue. I had an extra one, so I gave it to him. The next day the Chinese Political Police called on me at work. They asked me if I had given a stamp catalogue to a Chinese member of the Stamp Club who was involved in an ongoing investigation. Apparently someone had noticed a picture of Mao Tse-tung on a postage stamp listed in the catalogue I gave to the Chinese member of the stamp club. They reported it to the police. Because the picture was not obliterated by a CHOP denouncing him as a bandit, he was accused of being a Communist. After much explaining and discussion with the Political Police, I was able to explain what had transpired—that I had given the stamp catalogue to the Chinese stamp club member, not realizing that Mao's picture was in the book without a CHOP obliterating it. They went through the stamp catalogue page by page to make sure there were no pictures of Mao. If there was, they would apply a CHOP to them. I finally convinced them that I was at fault and that the gentleman in question was not a communist, and that I did not know about the law that Mao's picture had to have a CHOP on it, obliterating same. All's well that ends well.

January 1961: We had three NCO Clubs that we could go to. Club 63, Shu Linkou and Taipei Air Station. Club 63 was by far the best club, and the one we used 90% of the time. It was the finest NCO Club, without exception, that we had come across in our service travels. Club 63 was just around the corner from where we lived. They had excellent arriving and leaving dinners every month. Also excellent holiday meals, such as Easter, Memorial Day, Labor Day, Thanksgiving and Christmas, etc. The Club also had a swimming pool, game room (with slot machines), stag bar, regular bars, barber shop, beauty parlor, etc. Club members in good standing could get free haircuts, shampoos, manicures, massages, etc. Club 63 was the Club used by MAAG personnel and anyone else who wished to be a member. Taipei Air Station NCO Club was on the other side of Taipei which was actually too far from our apartment to use. It was used by those persons who were stationed on the Air Station and/or who lived near it. Shu Linkou NCO Club was not as nice a club as Club 63 and/or Taipei Air Station NCO Club. Shu Linkou NCO Club was on the rough side and always very noisy. Shu Linkou was located close to the MAAG shopping and entertainment complex which included the chapel, cinema, post exchange, commissary, etc. Club 63 used to have 10¢ beer night (once a week), when they showed the television program "Markham," starring Ray Milland. It was a very enjoyable evening watching "Markham" and drinking ice cold beer. So, one had the choice as to which NCO Club they wished to be a member of. Membership in one allowed you to use the others.

10 January 1961: LETTER, SUBJECT: Request for Reassignment within MAAG (WORLDWIDE) and/or Transfer. TO: Commanding Officer 1170th USAF Foreign Mission Squadron APO 63 San Francisco, California. THRU: Officer in Charge MAAG Communications Center, APO 63, San Francisco, California. (*For a copy of this letter and attachment, see attachment B63.*)

12 January 1961: I went to see Major General Sanborn, Chief Air Force Section MAAG, about being sent to the off shore islands of Amoy (Quemoy) and Matsu, because I had a difference of opinion with the Officer in Charge of the MAAG Communications Center. When I first saw the General with his big bushy eyebrows and stern look, I thought that I had it and wondered why I had listened to my wife about seeing the General. But he turned out to be a very agreeable and understanding person, and listened to my complaint. After explaining the entire situation to the General's satisfaction, he asked me why I had not taken the matter to the Air Force Officer in the MAAG Communications Center. I informed him that we did not have an Air Force Officer in the MAAG Communications Center. The only Air Force Officer in the Sugar Building (home of the MAAG Communications Center) was in the Army STARCOMM Relay Station, next door to the MAAG COMM CTR. He thanked me for the information and stated "I will check it out." He also informed me not to worry about being sent to one of the off shore islands, as he would take care of that. He dismissed me and told me to return to work, as everything would be okay. I returned to the MAAG Communication Center to find that the attitude there had suddenly changed.

15 January 1961: Captain Schicker gave me the job of NCOIC of Crypto Accounting after my visit to General Sanborn's (who was taking over as Chief of MAAG) office. I believe that Captain Schicker and 1st Lt. Willis thought that I would fail to handle the Crypto Account (because of the difference in Air Force and Army Accounting

procedures) and they would have the last laugh. I immediately brought the Emergency Plans (Fire, Evacuation and Destruction) up to date. Then I proceeded to update the Standard Operating Procedures (SOP), as I had experience and exposure to Army Procedures & Policies, through correspondence courses and my JUSMMAT (in Turkey) tour of duty. I had no big problems with handling the Crypto Account. I read the Army Crypto Accounting Manual and took it from there. Shortly after bringing everything up to date, we had a Crypto Inspection by the Army Security Agency (ASA) and we passed with flying colors. This was the first inspection of the MAAG Crypto Account, without any discrepancies. The Army Inspecting Officer remarked, "How come it took an Air Force Sergeant to get this place in shape?" The Communications Officer, Crypto Security Officer, and the Assistant Chief of Staff of Communications & Electronics were all very pleased with the inspection results.

<u>15 February 1961</u>: FMSC FL-205. LETTER, SUBJECT: Certificate of Subcourse Completion, DEPARTMENT OF NONRESIDENT INSTRUCTION U.S. ARMY SIGNAL SCHOOL FORT MONMOUTH, NEW JERSEY dtd 15 February 1961. T/SGT MERCURE, Maurice F. AF 12XXXXXX, Box 13, Hqs MAAG (Dcsc & E) APO 63, San Francisco, California. (*For a copy of this letter, see attachment B64.*)

<u>March 1961</u>: We moved into our second apartment, located at #6 (UP), Alley 21, Lane 18, Sec 4, Chung Shan, N Rd, Taipei, Taiwan. This was also a second floor apartment (as we had been advised by other Americans to always get a second floor apartment due to flooding during a typhoon). The apartment consisted of a diningroom, livingroom, two bedrooms, bathroom, kitchen, and two balconies. We also had a roof top patio, which was nice for barbecues and parties when the weather was good. We had access to the roof top patio by a staircase in the livingroom. We were the only ones to have access to it. We lived in this apartment approximately 21 months.

We used pedicabs to move our possessions to our new apartment. The pedicab drivers were very good and friendly to us as we used them for a lot of things—like getting groceries at the commissary, and items at the base post exchange. They would see us walking and ask us if we wanted a ride. We would tell them no, because we wanted to walk. They would state "If no money, you our friend, we give you a ride for free."

We had our car washed once a week by a local boy who did not charge much and he did an excellent job. He could not pronounce my name properly but managed to call me "Fronk."

During a typhoon, I went downstairs to Bob's (my neighbor who lived under our apartment) on the first floor to help him put his electrical appliances and other items of value up out of the reach of the rising water, to keep them from being ruined by the flooding water. While there, I felt something go between my legs. Looking behind me, I saw that a snake had just swum between my legs. I told Bob, "That's it." Saying good-bye, I went back upstairs to get away from the rising water and whatever else might come in. We invited him and his wife up to our apartment to ride out the flood.

Sweetwater Canal (Binge Boo), was what we called the local canal (really an open air sewer). It was foul smelling and filthy. A fellow American Airman (Sgt. Van Ekovan), lost control of his car and drove it into the canal one night, while he was under the influence of alcohol. His car was removed from the canal; however, he could not get the smell out of it, so he sold it on the local Chinese Market. He was lucky that he did not drown, as he was in a very deep area of the canal. He had to throw away his civilian clothes that he was wearing the night this occurred.

I remember getting a flat tire on the Sweetwater Canal Road. I got out to replace it with the spare tire. An old man (Chinese Coolie) was walking by and decided to watch me change the tire, which I did in record time, with the old man saying, "Ding How, Ding How." He was quite impressed with the speed in which I accomplished the job.

The Chinese people used to watch Americans with dogs. When they thought the dogs were fat enough, and ready to be eaten (dog stew was a delicacy), they would steal the dogs to make stew out of them. This did not make them a big favorite of dog lovers and dog owners at all. A dog lover and/or dog owner had to keep their eyes on their pets at all times to prevent this from happening. This issue was a very thorny one between the Chinese and Americans.

18 May 1961: AF FORM 1164 REQUEST FOR AND AUTHORIZATION OF LEAVE OF MILITARY PERSONNEL dtd 18 May 1961. Granted five (5) days Ordinary Leave. TB 94 22 May 1961. MAURICE F. MERCURE, TSGT, AF 12XXXXXX, 1170th USAF Foreign Mission Squadron (MAP) APO 63, San Francisco, California. (*For a copy of this form, see attachment B65.*)

<u>23 May 1961</u>: Took five (5) days Ordinary Leave, effective this date.

<u>8 June 1961</u> AF FORM 1164. REQUEST FOR AND AUTHORIZATION OF LEAVE OF MILITARY PERSONNEL dtd 8 June 1961. MAURICE F. MERCURE, TSGT, AF 12XXXXXX, granted eighteen (18) days ordinary leave TB-122 12 June 1961. 1170 USAF Fgn Msn Sq APO 63 SFRAN, California. (*For a copy of this form, see attachment B66*)

<u>12 June 1961</u>: Took eighteen (18) days Ordinary Leave, effective this date.

We went with a sailor and his wife (Mickey) to get her a pair of made-to-order shoes. They welcomed us when we entered the shoe store, but when it came to making a pair of shoes for Mickey, they gasped in horror when they saw her feet. Chinese women generally have small feet, but Mickey's were so large. They just laughed amongst themselves and shook their heads in disbelief. Poor Mickey felt so bad about it, that she cried.

Norman Skelly was a 14-year-old boy who lived next door to us, and wanted to go out with us. His father did not mind him going with us, but he did not like the idea that Norman wanted to join the Air Force when he was eighteen, instead of joining the Navy like he did. We took Norman with us a couple of times, as he was a fine well-behaved boy, and was fun to be with. Of course, most of the time, we wanted to be on our own. (*For a picture of Norman, see photograph A36.*)

<u>4 July 1961</u>: On the fourth of July (Peg's birthday), Wayne (our next door neighbor) and I, while on the roof top patio of our apartment, were setting off fireworks (especially rockets). There was a school house just down the road from our apartment. We accidently launched a rocket, which went out of control and flew into an open window of the school house and exploded. The School Master (who lived in the school house) came out of the building madder than a wet hen. He saw a poor fireworks vendor selling fireworks and demonstrating his wares to buyers. At the time the School Master exited the school house, he assumed he was the one who sent the rocket through the open window into the building. He immediately started chasing the vendor down the road with a big stick. We thought the entire situation was funny. But just the same, we

hid behind the wall of the roof top patio so the School Master could not see us. Peg and Loeva (Wayne's wife) did not think it was funny and that we were mean laughing about it. So in essence we were in the dog house with our wives.

July 1961: While on duty in the MAAG HQ Bldg., as Charge of Quarters (CQ), I went to the Chinese operated snack bar and bought a hamburger. After eating the burger, I became ill (food poisoning). The Duty Officer on duty with me called the Naval Hospital for an ambulance. The Navy Ambulance arrived and the Navy Corpsman put me on a stretcher and started carrying me to the ambulance. They almost dropped me over the railing (on the second floor down the stairwell.) I arrived in the Naval Hospital and was assigned to a ward. They ran all kinds of tests on me to determine what was wrong with me. They pumped my stomach to get out the material that was causing me to be sick. They only fed me through the veins for a few days. One afternoon the nurse said I could go back on solids. She brought in a silver bowl with a cover on it. I was anticipating a good meal, but when she took off the lid it revealed a bowl of cracked ice. What a let down this was; I was mad as hell with her. She thought it was funny. At that time disposable needles had not been developed yet. Using a needle that had not been properly sterilized, they gave me an injection. The injection gave me hepatitis and a viral infection which almost killed me. I believe that the Naval Medical Service was using the hospital as a punishment center for doctors who had screwed up because so many complaints were made. Complaints had been made by patients against a large number of hospital staff including doctors and the hospital itself. The Army and Air Force Surgeons General made a surprise inspection of the facilities and personnel. Together they made an evaluation of all the complaints which were not favorable. The hospital's chief surgeon was always drunk and did horrible work. A young sailor was brought in for an appendectomy and instead of the regular little incision, he had a tremendous scar right across his belly. I was lucky the doctor who was treating me (Dr. Crockett) was a very good doctor. He did his absolute best in treating me. I was in the hospital for weeks. The Navy did not have or give convalescent leave (this I was told by Dr. Crockett) like the Army and Air Force did. So, he sent me home for thirty (30) days, carrying me on the hospital rolls all the time I was there. To this day I carry the hepatitis germ and cannot give blood. This was a time in my life that I tried to forget, but to no avail.

<u>July 1961</u>: While in the Naval Hospital some people were brought in from an automobile accident. They thought that they were all Americans; however, one turned out to be a Chinese (Taiwanese) citizen. They tried to get the Chinese Army Hospital up the road to take the injured person, but they refused since he was not in the Chinese Army. They tried civilian hospitals, but to no avail. The poor injured person was left out in the hallway on a stretcher where he died. We (the patients) could not understand why our Naval medical people did not help this human being.

We had a Navy nurse who made the patients take a nap in the afternoon. She came around checking to see that we were asleep. She lifted my eyelid to see if I was asleep or not. I told her, that if I had been sleeping, she would have woken me up by her actions.

<u>July 1961</u>: Major Schicker, the Army Signal Corps Officer in charge of the MAAG Communications Center, was kind enough to furnish my wife Peg with transportation (his personal jeep and driver), so she could visit me in the hospital. Sgt. John was the driver who drove her to the hospital most of the time. It was very good of Major Schicker to provide transportation for Peg since she did not drive and there was no bus transportation to the hospital. She really appreciated his kindness very much.

The town of Peitou, just outside of Taipei, was full of hotels that rented rooms by the hour and the day for purposes other than tourism. It turned out that the area was a haven for prostitutes, which we found out by accident when we tried to have a little vacation there away from Taipei. So we went to Peitou because of all the hotels there, but found out it was not for us, and we did not stay there. When trying to rent a room, they showed us one where the bed still had the sheets on it that were used by the people who used it last.

<u>10 October 1961</u>: On Double Ten Day (10 October), we went downtown to celebrate the birth of the Chinese Republic, founded by Dr. Sun Yat Sen. There was a very large and impressive parade. That night in the area where we lived, hundreds of little children paraded through the streets holding brown paper bags with candles in them. The candles were lit and produced an unusual effect. It was an amazing display for

the Republic of China. This is a major holiday for the Chinese and Taiwanese people, who always put on quite a show.

10 October 1961: We visited the Presidential Palace area in Taipei during the Double Ten Day Festivities.

23 October 1961: SPECIAL ORDERS NUMBER A-21 1170TH USAF FOREIGN MISSION SQUADRON (MAP) 1170TH USAF FOREIGN MISSION GROUP (HQ COMD) United States Air Force APO 63 San Francisco, California dtd 23 October 1961. Paragraphs 15 & 16. 15. TSGT MAURICE F. MERCURE, AF 12XXXXXX, is relieved from assignment 1170th USAF Fgn Msn Sq (AF Section MAAG-CHINA), (MAP) (HQ COMD), APO 63, and is honorably discharged effective 30 Oct. 61. Airman retained in service 26 days beyond FTS for convenience of the Government. DD Form 256AF will be furnished. Home of record: 200 Beech St., Holyoke, Mass. Cash settlement for sixty(60) days accrued leave is authorized in accordance with AFM 35-22. Authority: Para. 13b, AFR 39-10 (SDN-900). 16. TSGT MAURICE F. MERCURE, AF 12XXXXXX, having reenlisted in the Reg AF for a period of five (5) years on 31 Oct. 61 is assigned: 1170 USAF Foreign Mission Squadron (MAP) (HQCOMD), APO 63, SANFRAN, CALIF., w/duty AF Section MAAG, Republic of China. Date of Rank: 1 Feb. 53. Authority: AFM 39-9. FOR THE COMMANDER:

31 October 1961: Reenlisted in the Regular Air Force for a period of five (5) years, to fill my own vacancy.

8 November 1961: LETTER, SUBJECT: Reenlistment AIR FORCE SECTION MILITARY ASSISTANT GROUP, REPUBLIC OF CHINA APO 63, SAN FRANCISCO, CALIFORNIA dtd Nov 8, 1961. Maurice F. Mercure, AF 12XXXXXX. (*For a copy of this letter, see attachment B67.*)

20 November 1961: SPECIAL ORDERS A-28 1170TH USAF FOREIGN MISSION SQUADRON (MAP) 1170TH USAF FOREIGN MISSION GROUP (HQ COMD) APO 63, SAN FRANCISCO, CALIFORNIA dtd 20 November 1961. Paragraph 4. TSGT MAURICE F. MERCURE, AF 12XXXXXX CAFSC 29171 relieved from

assignment and duty 1170 USAF Fgn Msn Sq (AF Section) MAAG, CHINA (MAP) (HQCOMD) APO 63, SFRAN, CALIF. Assigned 2165 Communications Squadron (AFCS) APO 63, SFRAN, CALIF. (PAC Comm Line 122). EDCSA: 14 Oct 61. GENERAL INSTRUCTIONS: AUTH: AFM 35-11 & 2d Ind, Hq PAC Comm Area 16 Nov 61 to Ltr, 1170 USAF Fgn Msn Sq, APO 63, SFRAN, CALIF. SUBJ: Asgnmt of Amn. TRANSPORTATION: No travel involved.

12 December 1961: AF FORM 538, PERSONAL CLOTHING AND EQUIPMENT RECORD dtd 12 December 1961. MERCURE, MAURICE F. (*For a copy of this form, see attachment B68.*)

12 December 1961: We were issued new olive drab (OD) field jackets, field jacket liners, two (2) olive drab (OD) barracks bags and a radiation detector to replace our existing grey field jackets, etc. The Air Force was getting rid of all gray colored items of clothing and equipment (accessories) to bring us in line with the Army and Marine Corps.

14 December 1961: I was transferred to the 2165 Communications Squadron (AFCS), APO 63, SFRAN, CALIF, per my LETTER, SUBJECT: Request for reassignment within MAAG (WORLD WIDE) and/or transfer, dtd 10 January 1961. MERCURE, MAURICE F., AF 12XXXXXX. My new Commanding Officer was Major John B. Kelly, a man whom I grew to like and respect. I was very pleased to serve under him.

22 December 1961: SPECIAL ORDER P-90 2165 Communications Squadron AIR FORCE COMMUNICATIONS SERVICE UNITED STATES AIR FORCE APO 63, San Francisco, California dtd 22 December 1961. Paragraph 4. TSGT MAURICE F. MERCURE, AF 12XXXXXX, this Squadron (AFCS), this station is assigned duty as NCOIC Crypto Operations, AFSC 29171, Crypto Section, functional account 84320B effective 12 Dec 61 vice SSGT GERAND. T. SCHRADER, AF 13XXXXXX, relieved. Control AFSC 29171. DEROS: 18 Nov 62. Authority: AFR 35-1. FOR THE COMMANDER:

Ahbo was the all around handyman (repairman for the housing project). He used to deliver bottled water, bags of coal, etc. We had trouble with our bathroom sink; it was all plugged up. Ahbo fixed it by taking out the sink trap and pipe and replacing it with a straight plastic pipe, which did work. All we had to do to reach him was to shout "Ahbo" and he would appear.

There was this little boy named "Marty," who used to visit us every day. He would come to our front door, and yell "Piggy, Piggy (for Peggy), I want up." We would say OK and up he would come, up the stairs into our apartment. You would see his little hand just as he reached the top of the stairs. One of his pet sayings was "shit, shit." Peggy told him not to say "shit," but to say BIRD." So he started saying, "Shit, bird, shit, bird," instead. His mother asked him, "Where did you learn that?" He told her that Peggy had told him to say that. She asked Peggy about it and Peg told her how she tried to get him to say "bird" instead of saying "shit." But that he ended up saying, "Shit, bird, shit, bird," instead. He used to asked Peg for a paper lunch bag, then asked for a pickle, raisins, radishes, etc. We would then mix them altogether in the same bag and leave. I presumed that he ate them all at a later time. He had a friend named "Dennis" and would ask Peg for a bag for him. Then Marty would ask for a pickle, raisins, radishes. He would taste them all first, then put them in the bag for "Dennis." Marty used to like running along the ledge of the roof top patio, holding on to my hand (and I holding onto him to keep him from falling off the roof). He was absolutely fearless. He would climb up on the roof over the stairs (leading up to the roof top patio), and jump off into my arms. Peg thought that he was absolutely adorable. She would have loved to have had him as a son.

A little Chinese girl used to walk by our apartment just about every day and say "Ne ponsa." (You're fat.) Fat is good in Taiwan; it is a sign of being rich. So she must have thought that I was rich (wealthy). I used to counter with "Ne ponsa," (as she was plump). It was a little game played each time we saw each other.

Our other next door neighbor (to the right of our apartment—not Wayne, who lives to the left of us), was on his roof top patio with some friends. After the typhoon was over, and the water was beginning to recede, he told us that he did not have anything to eat. So Peg got some eggs from our kitchen, and threw them across to him. He caught the eggs one at a time in his white sailor's hat. They were at least able to have eggs for breakfast.

One day some American soldiers of Hawaiian decent threw a luau. They roasted some pigs under the ground on hot stones. The pigs were roasted to perfection and were delicious. We had heard of a luau before, but had never witnessed one. It is something you will always remember.

TSGT Robert (Bob) Paquet and I rescued a couple of Chinese boys who were drowning at Tam Sui Beach. According to Chinese customs, if you save someone's life, it belongs to you. We did not believe in this so we were not responsible for them. Bob received a medal from his Command (ADC), but I did not receive one from either AFCS or SAC. (*For a picture of Bob and me, see photograph A37.*)

11 January 1962: LETTER, SUBJECT: Letter of Appreciation MAAG COMMUNICATIONS CENTER ASSISTANT CHIEF OF STAFF, COMMUNICATIONS & ELECTRONICS APO 63 SAN FRANCISCO, CALIFORNIA, with 2 indorsements dtd as follows: Letter 11 January 1962, 1st ind. dtd 11 Jan 62 and 2nd ind. dtd 18 January 1962. TSGT Maurice F. Mercure, AF 12XXXXXX. (*For a copy of this letter and indorsements, see attachment B69.*)

15 June 1962: I was appointed Courier of Classified Crypto Material, as I had to Courier some TOP SECRET CRYPTO MATERIAL to Tainan Air Station, Tainan, Taiwan. The only available transportation at the time was an old Chinese Air Force C-46 aircraft, which had seen service over the Burma Hamp (according to a bronze plaque on the wall of the aircraft, next to the entrance door) when it was an American Army Air Force aircraft. It was the forerunner of the C-47 (Gooney Bird). Some C-47 aircraft are still being flown around the world today. My wife Peg accompanied me on the trip. When we arrived at Taipei International Airport, we were challenged by the Chinese, saying we could not board the aircraft carrying a sidearm (a .45 cal. pistol). I had to explain to them that I needed to be armed, as I was carrying classified material. Also to explain to the Chinese pilot and crew that I was no threat to them. They were afraid that someone might take the weapon from me and hijack the plane and fly it to the mainland. Finally, after a great length of time, I convinced them that I was not a threat to them and their aircraft and that no one was going to take my weapon away from me and use it on them. When the situation was settled, we were allowed to board the aircraft for our trip to Tainan. The flight engineer did not close the aircraft's door

until we were airborne. It was a very windy situation until the door was closed—also a bit scary. We proceeded to Tainan Air Station and landed without any further incident. It was quite an experience, which I hope never to encounter again. Major Kelly gave us three days to deliver the classified material that I was carrying to the appropriate office. We then were on our own to enjoy Tainan. We rented a hotel room for two nights and one day. The hotel room had a round bed in it, which we have never encountered since. While in Tainan, we visited various places one of which was the Temple of Yen-Ping, Chun Wang.

We had an enjoyable two nights in Tainan. We returned to Taipei International Airport on our friendly Chinese Air Force aircraft. I reported back to my duty station at Taipei Air Station.

<u>16 August 1962</u>: LETTER, SUBJECT: NCO of the Month (July) 2165 Communications Squadron (AFCS), Taipei Air Station, APO 63, SAN FRANCISCO, CALIFORNIA Box 27, dtd 16 August 1962 TSGT Maurice F. Mercure, AF 12XXXXXX. (*For a copy of this letter, see attachment B70.*)

<u>16 August 1962</u>: SPECIAL ORDER P-40 2165 Communications Squadron AIR FORCE COMMUNICATIONS SERVICE UNITED STATED AIR FORCE APO 63, San Francisco, California dtd 16 August 1962. Paragraph 2. The following named officers and airman, this sq (AFCS), this sta are appointed members of the Thrift Awareness (TAX) Board.

GRADE	NAME	POSITION
CAPT	DAVID J. PENNINGTON, 54XXXX	President
SMSGT	MILTON UNDERWOOD, AF 18XXXXXX	Member
TSGT	MILLER F. BARNES, AF14XXXXXX	Secretary
TSGT	BOBBIE M. DOWELL, AF 15XXXXXX	Member

TSGT	ALVIN DUMONT, AF 16XXXXXX	Member
TSGT	BILLIE L. GARDNER, AF18XXXXXX	Member
TSGT	MAURICE F. MERCURE, AF 12XXXXXX	Member
TSGT	DONALD A. SCHMIDT, AF 34XXXXXX	Member
A1C	JOHN A. KOSTELAC, AF 17XXXXXX	Member

FOR THE COMMANDER:

<u>September 1962</u>: The United States and the Soviet Union were at odds on West Berlin as the US had promised to defend the beleaguered city of West Berlin. The Americans were under severe pressure from the Russians. Earlier in the year, Khrushchev had threatened to take over West Berlin. He told Kennedy he was willing to bring the matter to a point of war. Khrushchev set a deadline of November 1962 for the resolution of the issue.

<u>September 1962</u>: President John Fitzgerald Kennedy warned the Soviet Union that the gravest issues would arise, should they place offensive weapons (a phrase widely understood to mean nuclear weapons) in Cuba.

<u>11 October 1962</u>: SPECIAL ORDER P-53 2165 Communications Squadron AIR FORCE COMMUNICATIONS SERVICE UNITED STATES AIR FORCE, APO 63 San Francisco, California dtd 11 October 1962. Paragraph 9. TSGT MAURICE F. MERCURE, AF 12XXXXXX, this sq (AFCS), this sta is asgd additional duty as Witnessing Official for routine accounting reports for COMSEC account 32314, eff 4 Oct 62. FOR THE COMMANDER:

<u>12 October 1962</u>: SPECIAL ORDER A-141 2165 Communications Squadron AIR FORCE COMMUNICATIONS SERVICE UNITED STATES AIR FORCE APO 63, San Francisco, California dtd 12 October 1962. Paragraph 1. TSGT MAURICE F.

MERCURE, AF 12XXXXXX, CONTROL AFSC 29171. ASSIGNMENT: Relieved from asgmt 2165 Comm Sq (AFCS), APO 63, San Francisco, Calif. Asgd 4038 Strategic Wing (SAC), Dow AFB, Me. EDCSA: 16 Dec 62. REPORTING DATA: DALVP. Leave address 293 Chestnut St., Holyoke, Mass. And c/o Mr. F. Banks, 36 Shakespeare Ave., Hayes, Middlesex, England. Sponsor and Dependent will report to MATS Passenger Service Counter, Taipei, Taiwan, NLT 0830 10 Nov 62, for scheduled departure on flight V85 departing at 1030 hrs. AMD: TPE-SUU-3PC-7825-AF-11 and TPE-SUU-3DA-7826-AF-11. Report to Comdr 4038 Strat Wg NLT 44 days after departure from CONUS POE. GENERAL INSTRUCTIONS: Authority: AFM 35-11 and Line Number DZ0448-USAF-Nov 62 returnee. "This is a Hq USAF directed move." Comply with AFM75-4. New mailing address is: GRADE, NAME, AF 12XXXXXX, 4038 Strategic Wing (SAC), Dow AFB, Maine. Medical clearance and immunization will be accomplished in accordance with AFR 160-102. TRANSPORTATION: PCS. TDN. 5733500 323 P537.02 S503725 2112 2122 1290 2290. CIC: 4 5 348 5376 503725. Dislocation allowance other. Transportation of dependent (wife—Margaret D.) is authorized concurrently with sponsor. Travel by mil acft authorized. Commercial air authorized when mil acft is not available. When traveling by acft a total of 66 pounds baggage authorized each individual. Upon arrival in the CONUS, TPA with 14 days travel time authorized. If POC is not used, travel time will be the time of the common carrier used. Shipment of household goods, hold baggage and POC authorized in accordance with JTR and AFM 75-4. In the event of Limited War or Mobilization, you will proceed as scheduled. In the event of general war or if the continental US is attacked by a foreign military force while you are en route to the port, you will report to the nearest active AF installation as soon as possible. FOR THE COMMANDER:

12 October 1962: I never in all my time in the military service felt so close to a major nuclear war, as I did when I received these orders, during the West Berlin Crisis and the Cuban situation. Especially the "In the event of general war or if the continental US is attacked by a foreign military force while you are en route to the port, you will report to the nearest active AF installation, as soon as possible."

Neither one of our apartments were ever robbed, like other Americans who were not so lucky. We believe the reason for this was the way we treated all the local Chinese, and were friendly with them. It is a fact that they (especially the pedicab drivers) looked after us and our goods. From the pedicab drivers, the boy who washed our car, Ahbo (the handyman), or weekly garbage collector, etc. The other Americans had dogs and guns to protect their property, and were still robbed.

14 October 1962: U.S. spy planes flying over Cuba spotted the first ballistic missiles on Cuba. The President was supplied with photographs showing nuclear missile bases under construction. The photos suggested preparation for two types of missiles: medium-range ballistic missiles (MRBM) able to travel about 1100 nautical miles (about 2000 km, or 1300 mi) and intermediate-range ballistic missiles (IRBM) able to reach targets at a distance of about 2200 nautical miles (about 4100 km or 2500 mi). These missiles placed most major U.S. cities—including Los Angeles, Chicago, and New York City—within range of nuclear attack. Kennedy also saw evidence of nuclear capable bombers.

The President stated if he ignored Soviet defiance of his pledge in September to oppose offensive weapons in Cuba, then all U. S. pledges might become suspect.

14 October 1962: I could now see why the war statement was inserted in Special Order A-141. The reason being the Berlin situation, the failed Bay of Pigs invasion, our missiles on the Turkish/Soviet border and possible trouble with the Soviet Union over Cuba. The Soviets were now allied with Cuba, since Fidel Castro declared Cuba a communist state.

16 October 1962: First day of the super heated Cuban Missile Crisis. The U. S. Government felt and agreed that a surprise air attack against Cuba—followed, perhaps, by a blockade and an invasion—was the only reasonable response.

18 October 1962: The US was to announce a quarantine zone around Cuba, within which US Naval forces would intercept and inspect ships to determine whether they were carrying weapons. Kennedy warned that if Khrushchev fired missiles from Cuba, the result would be "a full retaliatory response upon the Soviet Union."

<u>18 October 1962</u>: The President decided to go ahead with the quarantine. At the same time, the US military began moving soldiers and equipment into position for a possible invasion of Cuba.

<u>19 October 1962</u>: Peg and I were becoming tense over the situation and did not know one way or the other what was going to happen with our transfer and leave to England.

<u>19 October 1962</u>: The Joint Chiefs were for an air strike and an invasion, but Kennedy rejected their proposal, stating an invasion could escalate into a nuclear war.

<u>22 October 1962</u>: President Kennedy met with congressional leaders. The legislators' opinions mirrored those held by Kennedy and the majority of his advisors.

<u>22 October 1962</u>: The President announced by worldwide radio and television that the US had discovered Soviet missiles on Cuba. He demanded that Khrushchev withdraw them. He also said as a first step he was initiating a naval quarantine zone around Cuba. That US Naval Forces would intercept and inspect ships to determine if they were carrying weapons. The President again warned Khrushchev that if missiles were fired from Cuba, the result would be "a full retaliatory response upon the Soviet Union." Because international law defined a blockade as an act of war, Kennedy and his advisors decided to refer to the blockade as a quarantine. So the use of quarantine was to be used in place of blockade. The OAS (Organization of American States) agreed with the US.

<u>22 October 1962</u>: We were both feeling very uncomfortable and very tense about the situation—not knowing if we would continue on to Dow AFB and our vacation to England. This indeed was a very scary situation. The world was on the brink of a nuclear war, with terrible consequences, for both sides.

<u>26 October 1962</u>: Khrushchev sent an encrypted message to JFK offering to remove missiles from Cuba in return for a US pledge not to invade Cuba.

<u>28 October 1962</u>: Things began to improve when Khrushchev, in a worldwide radio broadcast, said he would pull "offensive" weapons from Cuba in return for a US pledge not to invade Cuba.

<u>28 October 1962</u>: We began to feel things were returning to normal and we would begin our journey to Dow AFB and take a much needed leave. Thanking God that the two leaders could reach an agreement and avoid the world's possible first nuclear war.

<u>6 November 1962</u>: We had a Semi-Annual Dining-In Ceremony in our NCO/EM Club Open Mess, on Taipei Air Station, Taipei, Taiwan. It was a very impressive ceremony attended by all ranks (officers, NCO's and enlisted men). A good time was had by all personnel attending it. We had a guest speaker, Brigadier General Gladwyn E. Pinkston, from Air Force Communications Service. The food was excellent and drinks were plentiful. This was one of the better Dining-Ins that I had ever attended. Lt. Col. Kelly was a keen believer in Dining-In Ceremonies. (*For a picture of the guest speaker, see photograph A38. For a picture of Crypto Personnel attending the Dining-In, see photograph A39. For a copy of the Dining-In Program, see attachment B71.*)

<u>10 November 1962</u>: Returning to the United States ZI (Zone of the Interior) on Flying Tiger Airlines (a charter company to take service personnel and their families back to the States). After completing a full tour of duty on Taiwan, we left Taipei International Airport, bound for Andersen Air Force Base, Guam. At that particular time, a large typhoon was just about to hit the island.

<u>10 November 1962</u>: Arriving over Guam, we landed at Andersen Air Force Base and took on passengers. We found out that the large typhoon was hitting Taiwan and was right behind us. While stretching my legs on the ground, I met a TSGT, who used to be stationed with me on Upper Heyford RAF Station, in England. At that time he was an A1C and was now a TSGT. He asked, "Are you still a TSGT?" I could have killed him at the time. We left Andersen Air Force Base for our next destination—Wake Island. Before we left, the Air Police informed us that, "the typhoon had just hit Taipei International Airport, causing considerable damage."

10 November 1962: Arriving at and landing on Wake Island, we took on some passengers. We learned that the large typhoon following us, had hit Andersen Air Force Base and caused a lot of damage. Wake Island is a very small island, just large enough to accommodate a large runway to handle jet aircraft. We took off from Wake Island bound for our next destination—Clark Air Base, Phillippines.

10 November 1962: We arrived at and landed on Clark Air Base, Philippines and took on some passengers. We processed thru Air Police Border Clearance Section. The local Air Police informed us that the large typhoon that was following us had hit Wake Island, causing some damage. We then took off for our next destination—Hickam Air Force Base, Hawaii. Upon getting airborne, everything seemed fine. About half way to Hickam Air Force Base, the radio went out and we had no contact with the mainland. Then we started losing oil (a leak) from one of our starboard engines. With the typhoon following behind us, our radio out, and a leaking engine, the trip to Hickam AFB was under a lot of stress. We were completely in the dark, as to what was going on.

11 November 1962: We finally made it to Hickam AFB, Hawaii, with no further problems. We took on some passengers and let a few off. Again we were informed that the large typhoon that had been following us since Taiwan, had hit Clark AB, causing some damage and playing itself out. It is quite apparent that we were in the hands of God, with the typhoon behind us, the radio being out, and an oil leak; He was looking out for us. With the typhoon played out and everything else under control, we could now relax. Our biggest fear was that the typhoon would overtake us and that would be that.

11 November 1962: We left Hickam AFB bound for our next destination—Travis Air Force Base, California. We all said, "Good-bye and farewell," to Flying Tiger Airlines and thanked God that we had made it to Hickam AFB. Everyone tried to get some much needed sleep, as we now felt a lot safer, with no problems facing us. We were now out of range of the typhoon, were on a USAF aircraft whose radio was working, and we had no oil leaks.

11 November 1962: Arrived and landed on Travis Air Force Base, California. We were advised that we were leaving the next day on a flight to McGuire Air Force Base, New

Jersey, staying overnight in the Base Guest House to rest up for our flight the next day.

12 November 1962: We boarded a USAF aircraft for our flight to McGuire AFB, New Jersey.

13 November 1962: Arriving over McGuire Air Force Base, New Jersey, we landed and disembarked. We then cleared through Immigration and US Customs. Then we checked with MATS Passenger Terminal Operations, to see if they had any Space Available Flights to Mildenhal RAF Station, England or Rhinemain Air Base, Germany. There were no Space Available Flights to either location at that time. We then took a bus to JFK International Airport, New York City. Upon arriving at JFK, we checked on flights to London, England. Finding the cheapest fare was with Icelandic Air Lines, we booked passage to London's Heathrow International Airport. After boarding the aircraft for Reykjavik, Iceland, for some reason or other, Peg became air sick all the way to Iceland. I do not know the reason she became air sick after all the flying (miles covered) she had just completed. The meals on the flight were excellent, and I ate both Peg's meals and my own. Upon landing at Reykjavik, Iceland, we deplaned. We then boarded an aircraft for London, via Luxemburg.

13 November 1962: Upon arriving at Luxemburg International Airport, we landed and left off and took on passengers. We then departed for Heathrow International Airport, London England, our next destination.

13 November 1962: Arriving and landing at Heathrow International Airport, London, England, we disembarked. We then took a bus to Hayes, Middlesex, location of Peg's family home where we stayed with Peg's family for about four weeks. We had a very enjoyable time, going around and doing and seeing places and things with her family. We went out to eat, went to the movies, Black Park, pubs, etc.

15 November 1962: I had my picture taken with Peg's family while visiting Hayes, Middlesex, England (*For a copy of this picture, see photo A40.*)

16 November 1962: While on leave in England, I had my picture taken with Jim, and my father-in-law, Frederick. (*For a copy of this picture, see A41.*)

11 December 1962: When our leave was up, we took a bus to Heathrow International Airport, for our return to the USA. We arrived at Heathrow the same day.

11 December 1962: We left Heathrow International Airport, London, England, for JFK International Airport, New York, USA.

12 December 1962: We arrived back in the USA, at JFK International Airport, New York City. After clearing through Customs and Immigration, we took a bus to Holyoke, Massachusetts, where we stayed with my family for a week.

19 December 1962: Our leave and travel time was drawing to a close, so we took a bus to Bangor, Maine (Dow Air Force Base).

CHAPTER 10

12 DECEMBER 1962 - 21 SEPTEMBER 1965
USA—DOW AIR FORCE BASE, MAINE

A. Griffiss Air Force Base, NY   16 Nov 1964-21 Nov 1964

December 1962: Upon arriving on Dow Air Force Base, I reported in to the Commander 4038th Strategic Wing (SAC), who informed me that I had been assigned to the Hq Sq 4038th Strat Wg (SAC), Base Communications Section, Base Crypto Center. Reporting to the Base Communications Section, I was interviewed by Major Reed, Base Communications Officer and Major Glass, Assistant Base Communications Officer. They asked me if I thought that I could run the combined Base Communications Section and the Base Crypto Center. My reply was, "Are you kidding? No problem at all." They were taken back by my answer and my quick reaction to their inquiry. I believe they thought that I was very conceited. Without a doubt, I went on to prove that I could run their little operation. After all the other jobs I had in the past, this was going to be a piece of cake. Major (later Lt. Col.) Wintermeyer, Director of Communications Electronics Division endorsed my Airman Performance Report, stating that I had done an outstanding and exceptional job. Major Wintermeyer backed me to the hilt, recommending me for promotion to Master Sergeant and for higher responsibilities.

December 1962: We were assigned to Base Housing at 24 Davis Road, Bangor, Maine. This was off Base Housing and was completely run by the military. We stayed in a local hotel for a couple of days and then in the base guest house for a few more days before moving into our newly assigned quarters. When we first moved into 24 Davis

163

Road, we had a major snow storm. We awoke to the sound of a snow blower. Looking out the hallway window, we saw this red hat bobbing up and down. We thought that it was a little boy, but it turned out to be our next door neighbor, Harvey, who was over six feet tall. He was plowing our side of the driveway (as we had dual garages and driveways) and he was also doing our sidewalk to the front door. I went outside to thank him and he said, "Welcome to the frozen north." Everyone in the Base Housing Area was very friendly, just like one big happy family.

December 1962: We resided in Government Quarters (24 Davis Road) from December 1962 through August 1965. The Quarters consisted of two bedrooms, living/diningroom, kitchen, bathroom, laundry room—with washer and dryer, a large walk-in closet—with a window, (so large, it could be used as a nursery), a garage and a basement. This was a two-story house, with the bedrooms and bathroom on the second floor.

4 January 1963: We bought a four-door green Plymouth Savoy and registered in the state of Maine.

January 1963: Listed below are some of the personnel assigned to the Teletype/Crypto Operations:

1. TSGT Maurice F. Mercure, NCOIC Communications Operations
2. TSGT Beverly C. Weir, NCOIC Teletype Section
3. SSGT John Donato, Teletype Section.
4. SSGT Hugh Pettigrew, Teletype Section
5. SSGT Maurice High, Teletype Section
6. SSGT Carl Lynn, Teletype Section
7. SSGT Paul Desjarlais, Crypto Operations
8. A1C Wentzel, Teletype Section
9. And many more, whose names I cannot remember.

I had some problems with some of the personnel assigned to the IBM circuit for awhile. Some operators were a little unclear as to what they were typing on the circuit.

So, I revised the SOP for the IBM operation and put a sign up over the circuit stating "Garbage in, Garbage out," which did the trick and operations improved 100%. I had no further trouble with this circuit after this.

16 January 1963: SPECIAL ORDER M-9 HEADQUARTERS 4038TH STRATEGIC WING (SAC) UNITED STATES AIR FORCE Dow Air Force Base, Maine dtd 16 Jan 63. Paragraph 1. TSGT MAURICE F. MERCURE, AF 12XXXXXX, and TSGT BEVERLEY C. WEIR, AF 14XXXXXX, Hq Sq 4038th Strat Wg., (SAC), this station, are appointed as Witnessing Officials for routine accounting reports as specified in AFCOMSEC 2. Auth: 94.1c. FOR THE COMMANDER:

31 January 1963: SPECIAL ORDER A-173 HEADQUARTERS 4038TH STRATEGIC WING (SAC) UNITED STATES AIR FORCE Dow Air Force Base, Maine dtd 31 January 1963. Paragraph. THE FOLLOWING NAMED AIRMEN ARE RELIEVED FROM ASSIGNMENT ORGANIZATION INDICATED (SAC), THIS STATION, AND ASSIGNED ORGANIZATION INDICATED (SAC), THIS STATION. NO CHANGE IN FUNCTIONAL CODE. NO CHANGE IN INDIVIDUAL PROFICIENCY TRAINING (OJT), IF APPLICABLE. EDCSA 1 February 1963. REPORTING DATE UNSPECIFIED. NO TRAVEL INVOLVED. RELIEVED FROM HQ SQ 4038TH STRAT WG. ASSIGNED HQ SQ 397TH BOMB WG TSGT MERCURE, MAURICE F. AF 12XXXXXX, TSGT WEIR, BEVERLEY C AF 14XXXXXX. SSGT DONATO, JOHN AF 12XXXXXX, SSGT PETTIGREW, HUGH P AF 15XXXXXX, A1C DESJARLAIS, PAUL A AF 11XXXXXX, A1C HIGH, MAURICE A AF 11XXXXXX. FOR THE COMMANDER:

January 1963: Below is a list of some of the units assigned to Dow Air Force Base, Maine, after reorganization:

1. 6th Air Division
2. Hq Sq 6th Air Division
3. Det 1, 8th Weather Squadron
4. 30th Air Defense Missile Squadron (BOMARC)
5. 71st Air Refueling Squadron

6. 75th Fighter Interceptor Squadron (ADC)

7. 216 A FTD (ATC)

8. 397th Bomb Wing (SAC)

9. Hq Sq 397th Bomb Wing (SAC)

10. 397th Combat Support Group (SAC)

11. Hq Sq 397th Combat Support Group (SAC)

12. 397th Airbourne Missile Maintenance Squadron

13. 397th Armament Electronic Maintenance Squadron

14. 397th Bomb Squadron

15. 397th Civil Engineer Squadron

16. 397th Combat Support Squadron

17. 397th Field Maintenance Squadron

18. 397th Food Service Squadron

19. 397th Installation Squadron

20. 397th Motor Vehicle Squadron

21. 397th Operations Squadron

22. 397th Organizational Maintenance Squadron

23. 397th Supply Squadron

24. 596th Bomb Squadron

25. 860th Medical Group (SAC)

8 May 1963: LETTER, SUBJECT: Letter of Appreciation 30th Air Defense Missile Squadron (BOMARC) UNITED STATES AIR FORCE Dow Air Force Base, Bangor, Maine dtd 8 May 1963. MAURICE F. MERCURE, TSGT, AF 12XXXXXX, with 1st Ind dtd 19 June 1963. (*For a copy of this letter, see attachment B72.*)

19 June 1963: Met an old friend of mine, SSGT Donald W. Lobbins, from the 2165th Communications Squadron, Taipei, Taiwan, now a member of the 30th Air Defense Missile Squadron (BOMARC). We discussed old friends and old times. I was very glad to help him with the 30th ADMS (BOMARC) Crypto Center problems.

19 September 1963: NAVMC 184-MCI (11-62). UNITED STATES MARINE CORPS this is to certify that TECHNICAL SERGEANT MAURICE F. MERCURE,

AF 12XXXXXX, USAF has completed the course prescribed by the Commandant of the Marine Corps for BASIC MESSAGE CENTERMAN, 25.8, given at Marine Corps Institute, Washington, D.C. this 19th day of September 1963. (*For a copy of this form, see attachment B73*)

I enjoyed taking the Communications Courses from the Marine Corps Institute. It gave me a real good knowledge and insight into how the other services handled Communications Operations.

23 September 1963: LETTER, UNITED STATES MARINE CORPS MARINE CORPS INSTITUTE, MARINE BARRACKS BOX 1775 WASHINGTON 13 D.C. FROM: Director TO: Commanding Officer SUBJ: Marine Corps Institute course completion of BASIC MESSAGE CENTERMAN 25.8 Rev: (a) MARCORPERSMAN, par 15112.5 Encl: (1) Certificate of Completion dtd Sep 19 1963. Paragraph 1. It is requested that enclosure (1) be presented to the student concerned and the required entry be made in his service record in accordance with reference (a), if applicable. 2. The student concerned has earned a course grade of B. A copy of this certificate has been forwarded to the appropriate headquarters for insertion in the student's official file. 3. Certain Marine Corps Institute Courses require material to be returned for use in the enrollment of other applicants. This may be ascertained by checking the course instruction sheet. If text return is required, a postage-free mailing bag was included with course materials for this purpose. J. A. LANE By direction.

October 1963: President John F. Kennedy stopped over on Dow Air Force Base when he was visiting the area, one month before he was assassinated in Dallas, Texas, on November 22, 1963. We took it very hard to hear about our Commander-in-Chief's death—after seeing him up close on Dow Air Force Base. He was accompanied by the White House Communications Staff. I knew a Sergeant on the team (cannot remember his last name), but his first name was William (Bill). I knew him when we were stationed together in England. The White House Communications Team took over operations of the Base Communications Center while President Kennedy was on the ground, in the area. I was approached by Bill and the senior member of the team, asking me if I would like to be a member of the team. It was a great honor, but I refused it, as they traveled so much. It was a good thing that I refused as the President was assassinated and the team changed for the new President. I was to meet Bill again in Spain with his wife Ann and their family. We were all given autographed photographs of the President and a P.T. 109 tie pin. We were all glad to see the White House Communications Team leave and things return to normal.

18 October 1963: AF FORM 1256 DEPARTMENT OF THE AIR FORCE CERTIFICATE OF TRAINING dtd 18 October 1963. This is to certify that MAURICE F MERCURE, AF 12XXXXXX, has satisfactorily completed the OJT SUPERVISOR COURSE, AJF 75000 (48 HOURS) given by 216A Field Training Detachment (ATC), DOW AIR FORCE BASE, MAINE on 18 OCTOBER 1963. (*For a copy of this form, see attachment B74.*)

Any additional information and training was very helpful in the pursuit of my duties. I am sure it would be of great help to me in the future.

28 October 1963: SPECIAL ORDER G-50 HEADQUARTERS 397ᵀᴴ BOMBARDMENT WING (H) (SAC) United States Air Force Dow Air Force Base, Maine dtd 28 Oct 63. Paragraph. The following named Airmen, Hq Sq 397 Bomb Wg, SAC, this station, are awarded the Air Force Good Conduct Medal, unless otherwise indicated, for the periods indicated. TSGT MAURICE F MERCURE, AF 12XXXXXX 1 Jul 60-30 Jun 63. FOR THE COMMANDER:

Receiving this medal was a good indication of how I was performing my duties. It was also nice to know that someone was pleased with my performance.

5 November 1963: IATDON FORM 13 LETTER, SUBJECT: Completion of Subcourse HEADQUARTERS US ASA TRAINING CENTER AND SCHOOL Fort Devens, Massachusetts dtd 5 November 1963. TO: T/SGT Maurice F. Mercure, AF 12XXXXXX, 24 Davis Road, Bangor, Maine 04401. Paragraph 1. You have successfully completed the following subcourse of the extension course program of the US ARMY SECURITY AGENCY SCHOOL. Subcourse Title 46—Safeguarding

Defense Information. Date Commenced 18 Sep 63. Date Completed 31 Oct 63. Rating attained Superior. (*For a copy of ths letter, see attachment B75.*)

This was a very informative look into how the Army handled Safeguarding Defense Information.

26 November 1963: IATIN FL 13 LETTER, SUBJECT: Completion of Subcourse HEADQUARTERS US AS A TRAINING CENTER AND SCHOOL Fort Devens, Massachusetts dtd 26 November 1963. TO: T/SGT Maurice F Mercure AF 12XXXXXX 24 Davis Road, Bangor, Maine 04401. Paragraph. You have successfully completed the following subcourse of the extension program of the US ARMY SECURITY AGENCY SCHOOL Fort Devens, Massachusetts. Subcourse and title 97—Composite I. Date Commenced 18 Sep 63. Date Completed 26 Nov 63. Rating attained Excellent. (*For a copy of this letter, see attachment B76.*)

27 November 1963: SCS FL 130 LETTER, SUBJECT: Completion of Army Extension Subcourse. DEPARTMENT OF NONRESIDENT INSTRUCTION U.S. ARMY SIGNAL SCHOOL FORT MONMOUTH, NEW JERSEY 07703 dtd 27 November 1963. TO: TSGT Maurice F Mercure AF 12XXXXXX 24 Davis Road, Bangor, Maine 04401. Paragraph 1. You have successfully completed Subcourse Number A18 titled Communications Center Operations. Date Commenced 28 Oct 63. Date Completed 18 Nov 63. Rating Superior. (*For a copy of this letter, see attachment B77.*)

28 January 1964: AF FORM 1227 REQUEST FOR TUITION ASSISTANCE-EDUCATION SERVICES PROGRAM dtd 28 Jan 64. Mercure, Maurice F TSGT AF 12XXXXXX 397 HQS. NAME OF SCHOOL UNIV OF MAINE ON BASE NAME OF COURSE FH 1 Freshman Composition I. (*For a copy of this form, see attachment B78.*)

12 February 1964: NAVMC 184-MCI (11-62) UNITED STATES MARINE CORPS. This is to certify that TECHNICAL SERGEANT MAURICE F. MERCURE AF 12XXXXXX USAF has completed the course prescribed by the Commandant of the Marine Corps for COMMUNICATIONS CENTER INSTALLATION AND

MANAGEMENT, 25.13 given at Marine Corps Institute, Washington, D.C. this 12ᵗʰ day of February 1964. The student concerned has earned a course grade of B.

March 1964: Of all the cars parked in front of the Base Communications Center building, why did one of the people working for me have to lose control of his vehicle and slide into my legally parked car? Luckily the person who hit my car was insured. The insurance company settled my claim to my satisfaction enabling me to buy a 1962 Renault, cream colored, 4-door Dauphine to replace my damaged vehicle. The poor Airman who hit my car was so terrified (completely ashen in color) when he came into my office to report that he had struck my parked car. Everything was settled, so we did not dwell on the fact of what had transpired.

9 March 1964: AF FORM 1710 LEAVE AUTHORIZATION—BALANCE RECORD dtd 9 Mar 64. To COMDT Hq Sq 397 BOMB WG MAURICE F MERCURE AF 12XXXXXX TSGT DCOCT-1 DUTY PHONE 2710 5 DAYS ORDINARY LEAVE EFFECTIVE 16 MAR 64 HQ 397 BOMBARDMENT WING (SAC) LEAVE IN CARE OF SELF—24 Davis Road, Bangor, Maine EMERGENCY PHONE 842-3343 LEAVE AUTHORIZATION NO. 05608 FOR THE COMMANDER:

I was able to purchase this car, thanks to the insurance company of the person who hit my parked car.

6 April 1964: AF FORM 75 USAF AIRMAN PERFORMANCE REPORT dtd 6 April 1964. MERCURE, MAURICE F. AF 12XXXXXX TSGT DATE OF GRADE 1 Feb 1953 Hq Sq 397 Bomb Wing (H) (SAC) Dow AFB, Maine. (*For a copy of this form, see attachment B79.*)

7 April 1964: STATE OF MAINE OFFICE OF SECRETARY OF STATE TEMPORARY OPERATOR'S LICENSE. The State of Maine was issuing temporary driver's licenses to military veterans. Maurice F. Mercure 24 Davis Road, Bangor, Maine.

13 April 1964: NAVMC 184-MCI (11-62) UNITED STATES MARINE CORPS this is to certify that TECHNICAL SERGEANT MAURICE F MERCURE AF 12XXXXXX

USAF has completed the course prescribed by the Commandant of the Marine Corps for BASIC WIRE COMMUNICATIONS, 25.1 given this 13th day of April 1964. The student concerned has earned a course grade of A.

13 April 1964: NAVMC 184-MCI (11-62) UNITED STATES MARINE CORPS. This is to certify that TECHNICAL SERGEANT MAURICE F MERCURE AF 12XXXXXX USAF has completed the course prescribed by the Commandant of the Marine Corps for TELETYPE OPERATOR, 25.11 given this 13th day of April 1964. The student concerned has earned a course grade of A.

17 April 1964: LETTER, SUBJECT: Letter of Appreciation 75TH FIGHTER INTERCEPTOR SQUADRON (ADC) United States Air Force Dow Air Force Base, Maine 04401 dtd 17 April 1964, 1st Ind dtd 22 Apr 64, 2nd Ind dtd 24 Apr 64, 3rd Ind dtd 18 May 1964, 4th Ind dtd 25 May 64, and 5th Ind dtd 30 May 1964. MAURICE F MERCURE, TSGT, AF 12XXXXXX. (*For a copy of this letter, see attachment B80.*)

Spring 1964: UNIVERSITY OF MAINE, AARON, MAINE GENERAL EXTENSION GRADE REPORT OFFICE OF THE REGISTRAR STUDENT'S COPY STUDENT'S NAME MERCURE, MAURICE F SPRING 1964 COURSE CONT EDU FH 1 FRESHMAN COMPOSITION HOURS 3 GRADE C EQUAL ITS 6.

25 May 1964: NAVMC 184-MCI (11-62) UNITED STATES MARINE CORPS. This is to certify that TECHNICAL SERGEANT MAURICE F MERCURE AF 12XXXXXX USAF has completed the course prescribed by the Commandant of the Marine Corps for BASIC RADIO AND VISUAL COMMUNICATION PROCEDURES, 25.3 given at Marine Corps Institute,

Washington, D.C. this 25th day of May 1964. The student concerned has earned a course grade of B.

8 June 1964: NAVMC 184-MCI (11-62) UNITED STATES MARINE CORPS. This is to certify that TECHNICAL SERGEANT MAURICE F MERCURE AF 12XXXXXX USAF has completed the course prescribed by the Commandant of the

Marine Corps for COMMUNICATIONS IN THE MARINE AIRCRAFT WING; 25.6, given at Marine Corps Institute, Washington D.C., this 8ᵗʰ day of June 1964. The student concerned has earned a course grade of A.

12 June 1964: AF FORM 1710 LEAVE AUTHORIZATION-BALANCE RECORD dtd 12 June 1964. To: Commandant Hq Sq 397 Bomb Wg Mercure, Maurice F AF 12XXXXXX TSgt OFFICE OR UNIT AND BASE ASSIGNED Hq Sq 397 Bomb Wg, Dow AFB, Me DUTY PHONE 2710 5 (five) days ordinary leave EFFECTIVE DATE 22 Jun 64 LEAVE IN CARE OF 24 Davis Road Bangor, Maine EMERGENCY PHONE 942-3343. LEAVE AUTHORIZATION NUMBER 07520.

This leave was for Rest and Recuperation from work and the strife of daily life.

Summer 1964: Base Commander's wife did not like the tulips that we had planted in front of Base Communications Center Building. So she had her husband order us to remove them and plant roses (or whatever she wanted). At that time I was wearing a cervical neck collar, due to an accident (whiplash). This made it quite difficult for me to help my men dig up the tulips and plant the new flowers. Needless to say, my men and I were quite furious with her interference in this matter. We managed to get the "tulips" removed and replant the area with new flowers which my men and I hoped would please the interfering b-g no end. It certainly did not make my men and I like her for all the trouble she caused by interfering with the way the Base Communications Center looked.

26 August 1964: NAVMC 184-MCI (11-62) UNITED STATES MARINE CORPS. This is to certify that TECHNICAL SERGEANT MAURICE F MERCURE AF 12XXXXXX USAF has completed the course prescribed by the Commandant of the Marine Corps for STAFF FUNCTIONS; COMBAT ORDERS, AND COMMUNICATION PLANS AND ORDERS,; 25.4, given at Marine Corps Institute, Washington D.C., this 26 day of August 1964. The student concerned has earned a course grade of A.

10 September 1964: AF FORM 1194 UNITED STATES AIR FORCE, SMALL ARMS MARKSMANSHIP CERTIFICATE OF ACHIEVEMENT IS PRESENTED TO TSGT MAURICE F MERCURE CAL. 30 M-1 CARBINE IN RECOGNITION

FOR QUALIFYING AS USAF SHARPSHOOTER. DATE AWARDED 10 Sept 64. RICHARD V. PELLERITI Major, USAF Commandant.

I loved going out on the rifle range where I always did outstanding shooting. It gave me the feeling of being combat ready, if the need arose.

16 September 1964: SPECIAL ORDER P-204 HEADQUARTERS 397TH BOMBARDMENT WING (H) (SAC) United States Air Force Dow Air Force Base, Maine dtd 16 September 1964. Paragraph 4. DOS of TSGT MAURICE F. MERCURE, AF 12XXXXXX, HQ 397 BOMB WG, (SAC), this sta, is changed from 21 Oct 66 to 21 Dec 67. Reason: To insure service retainability to complete overseas tour. AFM 39-9. TIN 907 FOR THE COMMANDER:

Undated 1964: We had a Base Commander (who did not have a Cryptographic Clearance) who thought that he could do anything. One afternoon he tried to get into the Crypto Center to inspect it. He was not on the access list of people cleared to enter the Crypto Center. He tried to push and force his way by me into the Crypto Center, causing much confusion and putting the area on alert. I had just told him that he could not go in the area, as he was not on the access list. It became necessary to draw my 45 cal. pistol and tell him that I would have to use deadly force to stop him. He became furious and upset, and yelled at me that he would have my stripes and stormed out of the building. He went to the Division Commander and logged a complaint against me. He informed the Division Commander that I had threatened to shoot him and had used bodily force to stop him from entering the Crypto Center. The Division Commander called me into his office and asked me what had transpired. I related to him that I had informed the Base Commander that he was not on the access list to enter the Crypto Center and that he (the Base Commander) had used force on me to get into the area in question. I explained how I had to use force to stop him, but to no avail. So, I had to draw my weapon and tell him that I would have to use deadly force if he continued to try to enter the area. I told him how he had become nasty and threatened to have my stripes. The Division Commander told the Base Commander that he was lucky. If it had been him, he would have shot him. There was no love lost between the Division Commander and the Base Commander. The Division Commander told me I did the right thing and not to worry about being busted. He then dismissed me and sent me on my way. The Base Commander was furious with the Division Commander's decision not to reduce me in grade for what I had done. But he could not do anything about it, as the Division Commander's decision was final.

9 November 1964: AF FORM 626 REQUEST AND AUTHORIZATION FOR TEMPORARY DUTY TRAVEL OF MILITARY PERSONNEL. TO: BASE DIRECTOR OF ADMINISTRATIVE SERVICES dtd 9 NOV 64. 1. REQUEST FOR AUTHORIZATION TO: Base Director of Administrative Services FROM: Hq 6 Air Div (DEXO), Dow AFB, Maine. 2. TEMPORARY DUTY TRAVEL ORDERS. 5. THE FOLLOWING INDIVIDUAL(S) WILL PROCEED AS INDICATED, UPON COMPLETION WILL RETURN TO PROPER STATION: *TSGT MAURICE F. MERCURE, AF 12XXXXXX (02-0200) Hq 397 Bomb Wg TOP SECRET 6. DEPARTING ON OR ABOUT 16 NOV 64. 7. APPROPRIATE NR. OF DAYS (INCLUDE TRAVEL TIME) 5. 8. DDALV 9. SPECIFIC PURPOSE OF TDY Staff assistance Visit in accordance with SACM 23-2. 10. ITINERARY FROM: Dow AFB, Maine TO: Griffiss AFB, NY RETURN TO: Dow AFB, Maine. TO: Griffiss AFB, NY RETURN TO: Dow AFB, Maine. 11. SPECIAL INSTRUCTIONS The requirement for utilization of government messing facilities will adversely effect the performance of the assigned mission. *With concurrence of Commanders concerned. 12. MODES OF TRAVEL B. TRAVEL TIME BY COMMON CARRIER IS 2 Days D. OTHER III AUTHORIZATION 13. AUTHORITY AFM 35-11 SAC 35-11 SAC and 8AF Supplements 14. DATE 12 Nov 64 15. SPECIAL ORDER NR. T-57 16. DESIGNATION AND LOCATION OF APPROVING HEADQUARTERS OR UNIT HEADQUARTERS 6TH AIR DIVISION (SAC) United States Air Force Dow Air Force Base, Maine. 17. APPROPRIATE ACCOUNTING SYMBOL 5753400 305 675 P458 213100 (896) 215100 (752 S661900D) 18. DISTRIBUTION 20.—DP 4-BDCRF 2-Each organization concerned 1—BDASPO 8—Individual(s) above 19. REQUEST FOR TDY IS APPROVED AND WILL BE PERFORMED. TDN. FOR THE COMMANDER:

16 November 1964: Went to Griffiss Air Force Base, New York, with the 6th Air Division Inspection Team to conduct an annual SAC Readiness Inspection Test. We were led by the 6th Air Division Commander. We flew to Griffiss AFB on an Air Force Air

Refueling Tanker Aircraft. This was an interesting experience in itself—to be shown how Mid-Air Refueling was accomplished and conducted. We did not participate in an actual Mid-Air Refueling, as most of the inspection team were not qualified nor had they been through the Compression Chamber. Refueling is conducted by the Refueling Boom Operator and is quite an art.

My job on the Inspection Team was to inspect the Communications Operations Section and the Crypto Center, to see that they were complying with United States Air Force Security Service, United States Air Force and Strategic Air Command Regulations, Letters and Manuals. Their Operation was good, but not quite up to the standards set at Dow AFB Communications Operations Section and Crypto Center. Several improvements were recommended to correct existing minor discrepancies. Our return trip to Dow AFB was uneventful.

1 December 1964: SPECIAL ORDER A-1418 HEADQUARTERS 397TH BOMBARDMENT WING (H) (SAC) United States Air Force Dow Air Force Base, Maine dtd 1 Dec 64. Paragraph 4. Following TSGT'S organizations indicated, SAC, this sta, are promoted to the permanent grade of MSGT, effective this date, with date of rank 1 Dec 64, unless otherwise indicated. Authority: AFR 39-29 and Ltr Hq 8AFOf 9 Sep 64. Instructions for the 1 Dec 64 Airman Promotion Cycle hq 397 Bomb Wg MAURICE F. MERCURE, AF 12XXXXXX. FOR THE COMMANDER:

Thank God! It had been a long time in coming. It had taken 11 years, from 1 Dec 53 to 1 Dec 64. Major Wintermeyer was the driving force behind my being promoted to Master Sergeant.

Undated 1964: DD FORM 528 ARMED FORCES OF THE UNITED STATES GENEVA CONVENTIONS IDENTIFICATION CARD Mercure, Maurice Frank MSGT USAF AF 12XXXXXX 14 Aug, issued to me right after I made MASTER SERGEANT on 1 December 1964. (*For a copy of this form, see attachment B81.*)

Undated 1964: We had a couple of civilian Telephone Operators working the midnight shift on the switchboard. As soon as they got on duty, they locked the door to the switchboard. They then would change into their night attire and bathrobes, for the night. One of their greatest joys was to remove the RED EMERGENCY TELEPHONE from its cradle on top of the switchboard. This would result in the Security Police scrambling on the Base Communications Center. After much persuasion, the use of the Civil Service Commission, and threats to fire them, they stopped using the RED EMERGENCY TELEPHONE to scramble the Security Forces, to see how long it would take them to arrive. The RED EMERGENCY TELEPHONE was only supposed to be used in case of a dire emergency and/or attack on the Base Communications Center. More than once I was on the carpet because of their actions. The Provost Marshal was very pleased that we finally got this situation under control.

Undated 1964: The Base Commander called the Base Switchboard complaining that he could not get through to Offutt Air Force Base. The operator informed him that all the lines were busy and had been for some time. He (the Base Commander) then ordered the operator to disconnect a call in progress and then connect him to Offutt. After a little hesitation, she complied with his wishes (order) and disconnected a call in progress. However, the line she broke the connection on was an incoming call from General Curtis LeMay, Commander in Chief, Strategic Air Command. General LeMay immediately called the NCOIC of the switchboard, demanding to speak to the Base Communications Officer. The NCOIC informed the General that the Base communications Officer was not in the building at the time. He then asked for the NCOIC of Base Communications Operation, and was connected to my telephone. General LeMay identified himself and proceeded to chew me out, reading the riot act to me. Meanwhile the Switchboard Operator and NCOIC had come into my office with all the particulars on this call. I proceeded to tell the General what had transpired. I explained to him that the civilian telephone operator involved had been ordered by the Base Commander to disconnect the call, and give him the line to Offutt. I was informed that no matter how much the Base Commander wanted a circuit to Offutt, his (General LeMay's) calls were never to be interrupted. He then demanded to be connected to the 6th Air Division Commander immediately. His call was instantly transferred to the Division Commander. The Division Commander, after listening to General LeMay's complaint, called me to his office along with the Base Commander. I immediately drove to 6th Air Division Headquarters and reported to the Division Commander. The

Base Commander was also ordered to report to the Division Commander—which he did. The Division Commander, a full Colonel (with date of rank over the Base Commander) and the Base Commander (who was also a full Colonel) had no love for each other. The Division Commander asked me what had transpired to make General LeMay so furious. I explained to him how the Base Commander had ordered a civilian telephone operator to disconnect a call in progress to Offutt and give him the line. The Division Commander informed the Base Commander that no one on earth orders the connection between General LeMay (Offutt) and the person he is talking to on Dow AFB to be disconnected. He further stated that as long as he was Division Commander, the Base Commander could forget about making General Officer. He then informed me that this should never happen again. And if it did, the Base Commander and I would be transferred to Alaska so fast, that we would not have time to pack our bags. He also told me to put in writing instructions to the Switchboard Operators, that at no time would they disconnect a call in progress between General LeMay and to whomever he was talking to and that if they did, he (the Division Commander) would personally destroy who did it. He then dismissed me from his office. I returned to the Base Communications Section and immediately issued written instructions as directed by the Division Commander.

January 1965: Peg and I decided to paint the livingroom at 24 Davis Road. Base Housing was kind enough to furnish us with the paint (color) we wanted. All went well until we started up the stairs to the second floor. We got halfway up the stairs when we ran out of paint. We could not get any more of the same color from Base Housing for us to finish the job. So, we had to leave it unfinished for the next family to take care of.

7 January 1965: UNCLASSIFIED MSG dtd 071700Z FM ATCO MCGUIRE AFB NJ TO TRANSPORTATION OFFICER DOW AFB MAINE BT UNCLAS DMPA AW 058-A/JAN 65. RECORDS THIS ATCO INDICATE THAT TSGT MERCURE, AF 12XXXXXX SCHEDULE TO DEPART MCGUIRE AFB ON FLIGHT 235/5 JAN 65 FAILED TO REPORT. TO ASSIST US IN DETERMINING IF INDIVIDUAL IS A BONA FIDE AWOL. REQUEST WE BE FURNISHED INFORMATION REQUIRED BY CHAPTER 2, PARA 3201 F(3) (E), AFM 75-4D NLT 8 JAN 1965. BT

McGuire AFB was furnished the information that I had made MSGT and the orders sending me to Trier AB, Germany, had been cancelled and that I was not AWOL.

22 January 1965: NAVMC 184-MCI (11-62) UNITED STATES MARINE CORPS This is to certify that MASTER SERGEANT MAURICE F. MERCURE, AF 12XXXXXX, USAF has completed the course prescribed by the Commandant of the Marine Corps for COMMUNICATIONS EMPLOYMENT—MARINE DIVISION, 25.10 given at Marine Corps Institute, Washington, D. C. this 25th day of January 1965. The student concerned has earned a course grade of B.

11 March 1965: LETTER, SUBJECT: AIRCOMNET Communications HEADQUARTERS STRATEGIC AIR COMMAND UNITED STATES AIR FORCE OFFUTT AIR FORCE BASE, NEBRASKA 68113, dtd 11 Mar 1965. TO: SAF (DOCEOT) Westover AFB, Mass 01022. With two (2) Ind. 1st Ind dtd 20 Mar 1965 and 2nd Ind dtd 22 March 1965. Member of the "TOP TEN CLUB" for January 1965. (*For a copy of this letter and endorsements, see attachment B82.*)

25 March 1965: NAVMC 184-MCI (11-62) UNITED STATES MARINE CORPS This is to certify that MASTER SERGEANT MAURICE F. MERCURE, AF 12XXXXXX, USAF has completed the course prescribed by the Commandant of the Marine Corps for THE MARINE NONCOMMISSIONED OFFICER, 03.3 given at Marine Corps Institute, Washington, D. C. this 25th day of March 1965. The student concerned has earned a course grade of B.

14 April 1965: UNCLASSIFIED MESSAGE. FM 3973STRATWG MORON AB SPAIN TO 397BOMBWG DOW AFB ME BT UNCLAS BDPMC1 04701 APR 65 YOUR BDPMC1 04561. 7 APR 65. PERTAINING TO MSGT MAURICE F. AF 12XXXXXX, CONCURRENT TVL IS APPROVED FOR GOVERNMENT QUARTERS UNDER MOVEMENT CONTROL NUMBER M-9-10. ESTIMATED PERIOD PRIVATE RENTAL WILL BE OCCUPIED PENDING ASSIGNMENT TO GOVERNMENT HOUSING IS THIRTY TO SIXTY DAYS. SHIPMENT OF HOUSEHOLD GOODS IS LIMITED TO 2,000 POUNDS PER PARA 5606, CHAP 6, AFM 75-4 AND ASGMT ORDERS MUST CITE THIS LIMITATION IN

ADDITION TO THE MOVEMENT CONTROL NUMBER INDICATED ABOVE. NONACCEPTANCE OF ANY CHANGE IN ASGMT OR REPT DATA SHOULD BE REPORTED TO THIS HQ IMMEDIATELY. FURNISH THIS HQ (BDPMC1) FIVE COPIES OF ALL ORDERS ISSUED BASED UPON THIS APPROVAL BT.

17 May 1965: SAC FORM 147 REQUEST FOR PERMANENT CHANGE OF STATION ORDERS OVERSEAS FROM BDPMC1 MSGT MAURICE F MERCURE AF12XXXXXX CONTROL 29170 ASSIGNMENT RELIEVED FROM ASSIGNMENT 397 BOMB Wg., SAC Dow AFB, Maine ASSIGNED TO 3973 STRAT Wg., SAC APO New York 09282 SAC PROJECT NUMBER OISK LINE NUMBER IS 7857 EDCSA 25 Sep 65 PROCEED DATE 31 July 65. SHIPMENT IDENTIFIER SAC-2EA-Spain-Sep AUTHORITY AFM 39-1, SAC Sup, SAC Ltr, (DPAMA) 23 Mar 65 Withdrawal of Airmen for foreign service assignment during Sep 65. LEAVE ADDRESS: American Express, New York Worlds Fair, NY, NY. DALP Yes DISLOCATION ALLOWANCE ENTITLEMENT INITIAL PCS THIS FISCAL YEAR COMPLIANCE WITH AFM 35-6 IS REQUIRED, MAIL WILL BE ADDRESSED TO SHOW NAME, GRADE AND SERVICE NUMBER SEE ABOVE TRAVEL OF DEPENDENT: AUTHORIZED CONCURRENT TRAVEL OF DEPENDENT IS AUTHORIZED YES AUTHORITY MSG, FROM 3973 Strat Wg. Moron AB, Spain, BDPMC1, 04701, 14 Apr 65. MARGARET D Wife FLIGHT RESERVATION FOR 1 Sep 65. TPA AUTHORIZED YES TRAVEL TIME 2 DAYS TRAVEL IS AUTHORIZED BY MILITARY AIR REMARKS Not auth pro pay Reporting time to APOE will be furnished at a later date. PERSONNEL OFFICER D. E. BERNARD, MSGT, USAF.

26 July 1965: AF FORM 899 PERMANENT CHANGE OF STATION ORDER—MILITARY MSGT MERCURE, MAURICE F. AF 12XXXXXX CAFSC 29170 RELIEVED Hq 397 Bomb Wg (SAC) Dow AFB, Maine 04401 ASSIGNED 3973 Strat Wg (SAC) APO New York 09282 DALVP YES EDCSA 25 Sep 65 LEAVE ADDRESS American Express, New York World's Fair, NY NY NEW MAILING ADDRESS Overseas organization assigned CONCURRENT TRAVEL MESSAGE BDPMC1, 94701, 1 Apr 65, From 3973 Strat Wg, Moron AB, Spain, TRAVEL TIME 2 DAYS 66 POUNDS BAGGAGE INCLUDING EXCESS IS AUTHORIZED

PER PERSON DISLOCATION ALLOWANCE CATEGORY Other MODES OF TRANSPORTATION AUTHORIZED FOR OVERSEAS TRAVEL MILITARY AIRCRAFT REPORT AT MATS PASSENGER SERVICE COUNTER MCGUIRE AFB FLIGHT NO. T-1281 WRI-TOJ-3PC-3DA-7645-6-F REPORTING TIME AND DATE FOR SCHEDULED DEPARTURE NET 2000, 20 Sep 65 NLT 2350, 20 Sep 65. REMARKS Authority: AFM 39-11, SAC Sup, SAC Ltr (DPAMA) 23 Mar 65, withdrawal of Airmen for foreign service assignment during Sep 65. SAC PROJECT Number OISK. Line Number IS7857. Shipment identifier SAC-2EA-Spain-Sep. AUTHORITY, AFM 35-11 AND SEE REMARKS DATE 26 Jul 65 SPECIAL ORDER NO. A-827. Hq 397TH BOMBARDMENT WING (SAC) Dow Air Force Base, Maine 04401. PCS EXPENSE CHARGEABLE TO 5763500 326 6757 P577.04 120000 (114) 216110 (34) 229900(40)229300(1016) 45667 212130(106) 212140(108) 66T900 TDN FOR THE COMMANDER:

26 July 1965: AF FORM 1710-3 LEAVE AUTHORIZATION-BALANCE RECORD 26 Jul 65 TO: HSC FROM MAURICE F. MERCURE, AF 12XXXXXX, E7 PHONE 2960 DCOCEO Dow AFB, MAINE 04401 5 Days ordinary leave 2 Aug 65 ON SEPARATE RATIONS LEAVE IN CARE OF SELF 24 Davis Road, Bangor, Maine EMERGENCY PHONE 945-6029 Hq 397 Bomb Wg (SAC) Dow AFB, Me. LEAVE AUTHORIZATION NUMBER 07246 DATE OF AUTHORIZATION 30 Jul 65. FOR THE COMMANDER:

30 August 1965: IBM M39238 TRANSCRIPT EXTENSION COURSE INSTITUTE USAF dtd 08-30-65. This certifies that the individual named hereon has satisfactorily completed the course indicated "Communications Officer 3008." MERCURE, MAURICE F AF 12XXXXXX MSG. (*For a copy of this form, see attachment B83.*)

August 1965: We moved to 533A Hammond Street, Bangor, Maine, 2nd floor apartment, after clearing Government Quarters (24 Davis Road). We lived there until we left for Spain (August 1965 through September 1965).

31 August 1965: AIR UNIVERSITY UNITED STATES AIR FORCE EXTENSION COURSE INSTITUTE, dtd 31 August 1965. Be it known MSGT M F Mercure AF

12XXXXXX is a graduate of COMMUNICATIONS OFFICER course 3008. (*For a copy of this diploma, see attachment B84.*)

13 September 1965: AF FORM 1466 CERTIFICATE OF MEDICAL CLEARANCE FOR DEPENDENT OVERSEAS TRAVEL. Mercure, Maurice F. MSGT AF 12XXXXXX OF MIL. TRAVEL Sep 65. 397 Bomb Wg, Dow AFB, Maine 04401 UNIT AND LOCATION OF OVERSEAS ASSIGNMENT 3973 Strat Wg, APO New York 09282 DEPENDENT Mercure, Margaret D. Wife. (*For a copy of this form, see attachment B85.*)

13 September 1965: AF FORM 246 RECORD OF EMERGENCY DATA, dtd 13 Sep 65 MERCURE, MAURICE FRANK AF 12XXXXXX MSGT SAC, 397th Bomb Wg, Dow AFB, Maine.

17 September 1965: AF FORM 911 SENIOR AIRMANS PERFORMANCE REPORT dtd 17 September 1965. Captain Frederick M. Clements replaced Major Walter S. Reed, Chief Operations Branch and Major Robert Spiers, Jr. replaced Lt. Col. Charles A. Wintermeyer, Chief Communications Electronic Division. These were two new reporting officials replacing officers I had worked under for 2 2/3 years. (*For a copy of this form, see attachment B86.*)

17 September 1965: We left Dow AFB and drove to Fort Hamilton, New York. Just outside of Portland, our car overheated; the water pump was defective. We had it repaired and continued on our way to Fort Hamilton.

17 September 1965: We arrived at Fort Hamilton and stayed in the Guest House for a few days. Using Fort Hamilton as a base of operations, we made daily trips to the New York World's Fair.

September 1965: Our trips to the New York World's Fair were very enjoyable and exciting. We took advantage of our time and spent it wisely on various rides and exhibits. We found the Republic of China's exhibit and went into it. It brought back memories of our time in Formosa and all the good times we had there. All-in-all we had a very good time at the New York World's Fair.

<u>19 September 1965</u>: We turned in our car at the Port for shipment to Spain and then took a bus to McGuire Air Force Base, New Jersey, to catch our flight to Spain.

<u>20 September 1965</u>: We reported in to the MATS Passenger Service Center, McGuire Air Force Base, as directed in my orders, before 2350 hours for flight number T-1281.

<u>20 September 1965</u>: We boarded the Aircraft. Our first destination was Andrews Air Force Base, Washington, D.C. Arriving at Andrews AFB, we took on additional passengers.

<u>20 September 1965</u>: We left Andrews AFB. Our next destination was Lages AB, Azores Islands.

<u>21 September 1965</u>: We arrived at Lages AB, and let off and took on passengers.

<u>21 September 1965</u>: We left Lages AB. Our next destination was Torrejon AB, Spain; we let off passengers. Then we took off for Moron AB, Spain—our final destination and the beginning of a new adventure.

CHAPTER 11

22 SEPTEMBER 1965 - 26 NOVEMBER 1966

SPAIN—MORON AIR BASE, SEVILLE

A. Frankfurt, Germany (TDY)   16 Apr 1966-18 Apr 1966

B. Chateauroux Air Station, France (Visit)   28 Apr 1966-29 Apr 1966

C. Torrejon Air Base, Madrid, Spain   Various visits

<u>22 September 1965</u>: We arrived on Moron Air Base, Spain, and were greeted by MSGT Brow. He (MSGT Brow, who was our sponsor) took my wife Peg and I to our newly assigned quarters. He and his wife had, earlier in the day, made up one bed and stocked the refrigerator with bacon, eggs, butter and a loaf of bread. The place was in a mess; it had just been fumigated and the furniture was piled up in the corner of each room. MSGT Brow then left us on our own, and was of no further help to us. I believe that MSGT Brow was upset over the fact that we were assigned to Officers Quarters and he was in Enlisted Quarters.

The quarters consisted of three bedrooms, livingroom, diningroom, bathroom, kitchen, maid's room, maid's bathroom and a veranda with swing. We also had a carport.

We decided to walk to downtown Seville to get something to eat. We returned to our newly assigned quarters after having something to eat. We then spent our first night therein.

<u>23 September 1965</u>: I reported to the CO, 3973D Strategic Wing (SAC). I was assigned to the 3973D Operations Squadron (SAC), for necessary "In Station Processing."

<u>23 September 1965</u>: SAC FORM 460 OFFICER AND AIRMAN BASE CLEARANCE dtd 23 September 1965. HEADQUARTERS 3973D STRATEGIC WING (SAC) APO NEW YORK 09282. MERCURE, MAURICE F AF 12XXXXXX, MSGT. (*For a copy of this form, see attachment B87.*)

<u>23 September 1965</u>: SPECIAL ORDER M-148 DEPARTMENT OF THE AIR FORCE HEADQUARTERS 3973D STRATEGIC WING (SAC) APO NEW YORK 09282 dtd 23 September 1965. Paragraph 1. MSGT MAURICE F MERCURE, AF 12XXXXXX, 3973 Ops Sq, SAC, this sta, is assigned public quarters I-14-A, Santa Clara Housing Area, New York, 09282, effective 23 Sep 65. Authority: AFR 30-5 FOR THE COMMANDER:

These Quarters were Officer Housing, as there were no Enlisted Quarters available at the time. As they had a surplus of Officers Housing, they assigned them to us. We would have to move out later when they needed them and Enlisted Quarters became available.

In the kitchen of our new quarters was a combination washer/dryer, the first I had ever seen. It wasn't until years later that I saw this type in the US.

<u>23 September 1965</u>: AF FORM 220 REQUEST, AUTHORIZATION AND PAY ORDER BASE SEPARATE RATIONS dtd 23 Sep 65 MPO NR 434. MERCURE, MAURICE MSGT AF 12XXXXXX 3973 Operations Squadron Moron Air Base, Spain MARRIED REQUEST AUTHORITY TO RATION SEPARATE FROM MY ORGANIZATION EFFECTIVE ON 22 September 1965 REASON FOR REQUEST AUTHORITY: AFM 177-105, Vol 1, AFM 35-54 Airman accompanied by his dependent and living on the economy. RECOMMENDED APPROVAL. PAUL R. HANDWERKER, Capt, USAF Commander, 3973 Operations Sq.

<u>25 September 1965</u>: STATEMENT IN ENGLISH AND SPANISH dtd 25 September 1965. Briefing on Security Regulations. (*For a copy of this statement, see attachment B88.*)

One day while in our quarters, a young boy on a bicycle entered the Santa Clara Housing Area. A Civil Guard Officer on a motor scooter came in behind the young boy, grabbed him by the hair and yanked him off of his bicycle. He then took him away to where I do not know. The Santa Clara Housing Area was guarded by the Spanish Civil Guard, resulting in our feeling very safe and secure.

4 October 1965: SCS FORM 1100 Certificate of Subcourse Completion, DEPARTMENT OF NON-RESIDENT INSTRUCTION U.S. ARMY SIGNAL CENTER AND SCHO8OL FORT MONMOUTH, N.J. 07703 MERCURE, MAURICE F. MSGT 3973 OPNS SQDN BX 7107. COMMUNICATION CENTER FUNDAMENTALS Rating SUPERIOR. (*For a copy of this certificate, see attachment B89.*)

6 October 1965: LETTER, SUBJECT: Forwarding of Certificate FM: DEPARTMENT OF THE ARMY HEADQUARTERS US ARMY SIGNAL CENTER AND SCHOOL FORT MONMOUTH, NEW JERSEY 07703. TO: Student Concerned. 1. The enclosed certificate is awarded for successful completion of correspondence work as indicated on certificate. 2. It is requested that you retain the original copy of certificate and forward second and third copies to the appropriate headquarters. FOR THE COMMANDER:

South of Seville there is a large Naval Base named Rota, at Cadiz, Spain, for submarines and other Naval vessels. It was the shipping and receiving point for personally owned automobiles. SSGT Herbert H. Smith and his wife drove Peg and me to Rota Naval Base, so we could pick up our car. The Smiths wanted us to go to Gibraltar for a visit with them, but we refused as our car had not been registered yet and did not have Spanish plates. Nor did we know what condition our car was in, based on our experience with our car that we picked up at Keelung when we were in Taipei, Taiwan. We drove to Seville without anything going wrong—to our relief. It was wonderful having our car again, instead of relying on someone else for transportation.

6 October 1965: SPECIAL ORDER P-200 DEPARTMENT OF THE AIR FORCE HEADQUARTERS 3973D STRATEGIC WING (SAC) APO NEW YORK 09282 dtd 6 Oct 65. Paragraph 7. MSGT MAURICE F. MERCURE, AF 12XXXXXX, 3973 Operations Sq, SAC, this stn, is assigned initial duty as Noncommissioned Officer in charge, Communications Center, Teletype/Crypto Operations Section, DAFSC 29170,

Functional Code 3144000, Program Element Identification Code 138, DEROS 19 Sep 1965, effective 23 Sep 1965. FOR THE COMMANDER:

13 October 1965: LETTER, SUBJECT: SHELTER MANAGER APPOINTMENT dtd 13 October 1965. Personnel Concerned. 1. The following named personnel, Organizations indicated, SAC, this station are appointed as alternate Shelter Managers for shelters indicated. Duties and responsibilities are outlined in Appendix 11, Annex J, Moron AB, 500 Plan. MSGT MAURICE F MERCURE, AF 12XXXXXX, 3973D OPS Sq SHELTER NR S-102. SSGT JAMES C. BOGGS, AF 15469293, 3973D OPS Sq SHELTER NR S-102. FOR THE COMMANDER:

20 October 1965: AF FORM 1193 UNITED STATES AIR FORCE SMALL ARMS MARKSMANSHIP CERTIFICATE OF ACHIEVEMENT is presented to MASTER SERGEANT MAURICE F. MERCURE IN RECOGNITION FOR QUALIFYING AS USAF EXPERT. (*For a copy of this certificate, see attachment B90.*)

Located at San Pablo, a satellite station of Moron Air Base, where a Chapel, NCO Club, Commissary, Base Exchange, Theatre (Cinema) and a Medical Detachment (Dispensary) of the 870th Med Gp. This was just up the road from the Santa Clara Housing Area. We went to the Chapel, just about every Sunday. These facilities were very convenient as it saved us a long trip to Moron AB—15 miles away.

22 October 1965: When we decided to take a leave and visit England, we asked Captain Tiffany for a 30-day leave. He stated all he would give us was 15 days. As this was not enough time (for our needs, as Peg's father was very ill), we went to see Major NELSON D. COURNOYER, Base Communications Officer (Captain Tiffany's superior). We explained to him why we needed and wanted 30-days leave. He approved our request and granted us a 30-day leave. This action did not endear me with Captain Tiffany and he had it in for me from thereon.

After being granted a 30-day leave, I went to the Civil Guard Station to request that they watch our house while we were on leave. I had a hard time conveying my message to them, as I could not speak much Spanish at the time, and they hardly spoke any English. I started out by touching my eyes and asking them to watch my CASA (house) while we were on leave. After a while, I finally got my message through to them. They in turn asked me for Kennedy Half Dollars, as he was a hero to them. Being the first Catholic President of the United States, they wanted a souvenir, showing Kennedy. I did happen to have a couple of them. So I gave them the coins; they were very pleased with them and grateful. They did watch our house while we were away on leave. Nothing happened to it while we were gone.

25 October 1965: CERTIFICADO CUARTEL GENERAL 3973 ALA ESTRATEGICA FUERZA AEREAS DE LOS EE. UU. BASE DE MORON, SEVILLA PARA QUE SURTA LOS DEBIDOS: Sr. D. en Maurice F Mercure, miembro de las Fuerzas Aereas de los EE. UU. En España, poseedor de un B-2, Carnet de Pasaje Numero 711/65 Cadiz y matricula de Madrid Numero M190-427, expedida por el Ministerio de Obras Publicas y por la Direccion General de Seguridad de JUSMG papa los siguientes tramites: 1. Sustituir una anterior matricula por la actual expedida a su nombre. 2. Proceder a la renovacion del anteriormente citado B-2. 3. Realizar la transferencia de 25 Octubre 65 a su nombre. 4. Obtener un B-2. DANIEL J. MOORE, Teniente, USAF Oficial de Seguridad.

25 October 1965: CUARTEL GENERAL 3973 ALA ESTRATEGICA FUERZA AEREAS DE LOS ESTADOS UNIDOS BASE AEREA DE MORON dtd 25 Octubre 65. A LAS AUTHORIDADES ESPAÑOLAS: Certifico por el presente que el Sr. D. en Maurice F Mercure, miembro de las Fuerzas Aereas de los EE. UU. En España, tiene todos sus documentos en tramite a traves de este Departamento de Seguridad para obtener un Permiso de Circulacion de la Jefatura Provincial de Trafico de Madrid, para el vehiculo matricula M-190-427 No. de motor: 1465329, No. de Chasis 48738. Y para que surta debidos efectos, como Permiso temporal, en tanto este Departamento reciba el citado Permiso de Circulacion, firmo el presente certificado en la Base Aerea Conjunta de Moron de la Ftra. (Sevilla, a 25 Octubre 65.) Dando gracias anticipadas, le saluda atentamente DANIEL J. MOORE, Teniente, USAF Oficial de Seguridad.

25 October 1965: AF FORM 1710-3 LEAVE AUTHORIZATION BALANCE RECORD dtd 25 October 1965. Comdr 3973 Ops Sq 55 DAYS ACCUMULATED AF

12XXXXXX Maurice F. Mercure MSGT 3973 Ops Sq (BDCO-CE) DUTY PHONE 2065 DAYS LEAVE GRANTED 30 Moron AB, Spain DAYS LEAVE REQUESTED 30 EFF O/A 29 Oct 65 DAY DEPARTED 30 October 1965 LEAVE IN CARE OF SELF 36 Shakespeare Ave Hayes Middlesex, Eng TEL: Hayes 5958 HQ 3973D STRAT WG, Moron AB, SP LEAVE NR 0933 FOR THE COMMANDER:

26 October 1965: SAC FORM 899 NOTICE OF SELECTION/NONSELECTION OF CAREER AIRMAN dtd 26 October 1965. MERCURE, MAURICE F. HSC CBPO 1. You have been selected for reenlistment in the Air Force. FRANK D. WILLIAMS Lieutenant Colonel, USAF Chief Military Personnel Division 4 Oct 65. 6. I understand that I have been selected and do desire to reenlist on my normal date of separation. NOTE: If I elect retirement I understand my application must be submitted to be effective not later than the month prior to my DOS.

Moron Air Base (Morón de la Frontiera) was 15 miles from our quarters in the Santa Clara Housing Area. It was quite a daily round trip, which took a lot out of you. The bus we rode on did not have a very good suspension system on it. However, it was nice to get home every night and put your feet up.

30 October 1965: We drove from Seville to Madrid on our way to London, England. We arrived in Madrid and drove on to Bilbao, where we spent the night in a pension.

31 October 1965: The next morning we set out for London, England through France, just across the border from Spain. We stopped in Boulogne, France, for a short rest and something to eat. Going to a hole-in-the-wall Bistro, we had a delicious sandwich. The sandwich consisted of freshly sliced ham on a baguette (roll) with mustard and an ice cold beer. After we rested for a while, we continued on our journey to Bordeaux.

31 October 1965: We arrived in Bordeaux and proceeded to the Channel Ferry Terminal. At the Ferry Terminal, we booked passage to Dover, England. We managed to get some sleep on the ferry boat.

<u>1 November 1965</u>: We arrived at the Ferry Terminal, Dover, England. We then proceeded to drive to Hayes, Middlesex. Arriving in Hayes, Middlesex, we stayed with Peg's family. As Peg's father was ill, we took him and Peg's mum out into the countryside. We stopped at various pubs to eat and drink. I tried to take them to places they had not been to in a very long time. My attempts were very successful and they enjoyed themselves. Some of the places we went to were Black Park, Ruislip Lido, and many more interesting places. We spent a most enjoyable three weeks with them. Peg's father had made arrangements to go to the hospital the first part of November for a complete physical examination.

Our leave time was drawing to a close, so we made preparations to drive back to Spain. Having had such a good time, we did not want to leave, but I had to. When we said good-bye to Peg's father, we didn't realize that this would be the last time we would see him alive.

<u>22 November 1965</u>: We drove to the Ferry Terminal, Dover, England. When we arrived at the Ferry Terminal, we booked passage for Bordeaux, France. This was an overnight voyage to the Ferry Terminal, Bordeaux, France.

<u>23 November 1965</u>: Arriving at the Ferry Terminal, Bordeaux, France, Peg called her father to see if he was OK. She had a nice chat with him and her mother. We stayed overnight in a hotel to rest up for the rest of our trip to Seville, Spain.

<u>24 November 1965</u>: Early in the morning, we set out for Seville. It was a very nice and peaceful trip through the countryside. We arrived at the French/Spanish border and crossed over into Spain. We then proceeded to Seville.

<u>25 November 1965</u>: We arrived in Seville in the wee hours of the morning. It was good to be back in our house, and to catch up on our sleep. We still had a couple days leave left, so we decided to rest and take it easy.

<u>27 November 1965</u>: Peg received very sad news that her father had passed away. She took it very hard and stated she should have stayed home with him and her mother.

Unfortunately her father passed away before he could make the hospital appointment at the end of the month. Peg didn't realize how ill he was and regretted not staying home in England with him. But we did have three lovely weeks and had a good time.

<u>31 December 1965</u>: MCS MCEC 839 EXTENSION SCHOOL MCEC. MARINE CORPS SCHOOLS, QUANTICO, VIRGINIA STUDENT PROGRESS REPORT dtd 31 Dec 65. MERCURE MF MSGT AF 12XXXXXX COURSE CODE DATE ENROLLED 09065 UNIT CODE USAF. (*For a copy of this form, see attachment B91.*)

<u>ACAD YR 1965-1966</u>: UME 18 UNIVERSITY OF MARYLAND EUROPEAN DIVISION OFFICE OF THE REGISTRAR undated FILE Copy for Army or Air Force Acad Yr 1965-1966. Moron/San Pablo Center COURSE Spanish 1 Semester Hours 3 GRADE C

<u>6 January 1966</u>: 12th Night (12 days after Christmas) The Day of the Three Kings, in downtown Seville. They had floats for the Three Kings (Magi-Wisemen) with people on them, who were throwing candy into the crowds. The night started out alright, but began to get foggy. It was a real pea soup fog after awhile. We decided to go home to Santa Clara. It was very hard driving in the fog, so we went real slow. On the way we picked up an Airman who was hitchhiking. After we picked him up and he was settled in the car, he informed us that it was too foggy for him to drive, so he parked his car and started hitchhiking. We managed to make it to Santa Clara without any incidents. The Airman was on his own when we got to Santa Clara, as he was going to San Pablo where he lived.

<u>14 January 1966</u>: NAVMC 184-MCI (11-62) UNITED STATES MARINE CORPS This is to certify that MASTER SERGEANT MAURICE F. MERCURE AF 12XXXXXX USAF has completed the course prescribed by the Commandant of the Marine Corps for RADIO RELAY FUNDAMENTALS AND OPERATIONS, 25.14 given at MARINE CORPS INSTITUTE, WASHINGTON, D.C. this 14th day of January 1966. The student concerned has earned a course grade of B.

<u>21 January 1966</u>: AF FORM 1227 REQUEST FOR TUITION-EDUCATION SERVICES PROGRAM dtd 21 January 1966. MERCURE, MAURICE F. MSgt AF 12XXXXXX 3973 Operations Sq, Box 7107, APO New York 09282 DUTY PHONE 2065 TYPE OF SCHOOL Univ of Maryland On Base TYPE OF STUDY College Undergraduate SPANISH 1—Elementary Spanish CREDIT HOURS 3 DAYS OF WEEK Daily HOURS OF MEETING 1200-1300 INCLUSIVE DATES 31 Jan-25 Mar 66. TUITION FEE PER HOUR SEMESTER $16.00 TUITION ASSISTANCE REQUESTED $36 TUITION COST TO STUDENT $12.00.

<u>9 February 1966</u>: Peg and I decided to have her mother come out to Spain and spend a few months with us—or as long as she liked—for a vacation. Her mother agreed to come out to us and stay as long as she wanted. She booked a flight to Madrid where we would pick her up and take her to Seville. Her daughter Joan gave her some bad advice about putting most of her money in an envelope and putting it in her luggage for safe keeping. After meeting her in Madrid, we checked into a hotel, to rest up for the trip back to Seville. Peg's mum opened her suitcase and discovered her money was missing. It seems an airline employee in London or Madrid had opened her suitcase and taken the money. Joan should have known better than to tell her to put her money in her suitcase. As everyone knows, airline employees are notorious for going through passengers baggage and taking things. Mum only had a little money left. We told her, "no sweat," because she didn't need any money while she was staying with us.

We proceeded the next day to Seville. On the highway to Seville, we had a flat tire. Peg's mum told Peg "Don't worry about it; Frank will take care if it." Her mother was absolutely wonderful during this incident. She had more faith and confidence in me than I had at the time. I went to get the spare tire (from the spare tire compartment), only to find that it was flat also. We were in the middle of nowhere; no place to telephone a garage. Not knowing what to do at the time, a Spanish family heading for Madrid stopped to assist us. The driver of the car had me get into his car with the two flat tires and drove me to the nearest garage, where I got the tires fixed. The driver of the car would not take anything for his service. They explained that it was Spanish law to stop and render assistance to a motorist having a problem. It was a decree handed down by General Franco that help would be rendered to all stranded motorists, breakdowns, and accident victims.

The garage the Spanish family took me to repaired the flat tires, then they drove me to my car. They then installed the repaired tire on the car. I paid them for their services and then we proceeded to Seville, without any further difficulties.

11 February 1966: SPECIAL ORDER G-4 DEPARTMENT OF THE AIR FORCE HEADQUARTERS 3973D STRATEGIC WING (SAC) APO NEW YORK 09282 dtd 11 February 1966. Paragraph 1. The following named individual is awarded the Small Arms EXPERT Ribbon. Authority: AFR 50-8. MSGT MAURICE F. MERCURE, AF 12XXXXXX DATE QUALIFIED 28 Jan 66. FOR THE COMMANDER:

23 February 1966: DA FORM 160 APPLICATION FOR ACTIVE DUTY dtd 23 February 1966. TO: Commanding General, US Army Area Command, ATTN: AENAG-PA, APO US FORCES, 09184. Mercure, Maurice F. 721A USAR 293 Chestnut Street Holyoke, Hampden County, Massachusetts 01040. 3973rd Operations Squadron Box 7107 APO, US Forces 09282. (*For a copy of this form, see attachment B92.*) Peg told me not to put in for Warrant Officer, that if I did, I would be sent to Vietnam. She turned out to be right.

While residing at I-14-A Santa Clara Housing Area, the furnace caught on fire. The furnace was located in the backyard, behind the house. We called the Fire Brigade (Bomberos) and they came and put out the fire. The fire was successfully put out and no major damage resulted from same. Base Housing checked out the furnace and with minor repairs, had it back in operation. It lasted us till we moved into our next set of quarters.

9 March 1966: DD FORM 98 ARMED FORCES SECURITY QUESTIONNAIRE dtd 9 March 1966. MAURICE FRANK MERCURE, AF 12XXXXXX, MSgt. (*For a copy of this form, see attachment B93.*)

11 March 1966: LETTER, SUBJECT; Request for Waiver. TO: Commanding General U.S. Army Area Command ATTN: AENAG-PA APO, US Forces 09184. FROM:

MAURICE F. MERCURE, AF 12XXXXXX, MSGT, USAF THRU: Commanding Officer 3873 Operations Squadron APO, US Forces, 09282. (*For a copy of this letter, see attachment B94.*)

11 March 1966: LETTER, SUBJECT: Request for Waiver. TO: Commanding General U.S. Army Area Command Attn: AENAG-PA APO. US Forces 09184 dtd 11 March 1966. FROM: EARNEST R. MEREDITH, FR54XXX Captain, USAF. (*For a copy of this letter, see attachment B95.*)

11 March 1966: LETTER SUBJECT: Transmittal of Application for Appointment. TO: U.S. Army Area Command ATTN: AENAG-PA APO, US Forces, 09184. Transmitted herewith is application for appointment pertaining to the undersigned MAURICE F. MERCURE, AF 12XXXXXX, MSGT, USAF.

15 March 1966: DD FORM 398 STATEMENT OF PERSONAL HISTORY dtd 15 March 1966. Maurice Frank Mercure MSgt (E-7) AF 12XXXXXX US Air Force Reg 3973D Opns Sq, Box 7107, APO NY 09282.

Peg's mother used to love going to the sidewalk cafés in downtown Seville. I used to get home feeling tired from the long bus ride. I could see that she wanted to go out, so I used to ask her if she would like to go to a sidewalk café. She was always happy to say "Yes, please." So we went downtown and it acted as a tonic for me. There was one particular sidewalk café where a waiter used to like waiting on us, especially when he found out that Mum was Peg's mother. The Spanish people liked families going out together as a group.

15 March 1966: LETTER, SUBJECT: Request for Educational Award. DEPARTMENT OF THE AIR FORCE HEADQUARTERS 3973D STRATEGIC WING (SAC) APO US FORCES

09282 dtd 15 March 1966. MSgt Maurice F. Mercure 3873 Operations Sq. (*For a copy of this letter, see attachment B96.*)

Every other Sunday, they had a Stamp Exchange and Bourse in downtown Seville. Peg and I would go there about once a month. We met a very nice old Spanish gentleman who used to interpret for us. One of his pet sayings was "more or less," when discussing the cost of trading stamps. The collectors there all wanted the John F. Kennedy commemorative stamp and/or the half dollar coin. I picked up a lot of nice material for my Spanish collection.

21 March 1966: STANDARD FORM 88 REPORT OF MEDICAL EXAMINATION dtd 21 March 1966 PURPOSE OF EXAMINATION Army Warrant Program. (*For a copy of this letter, see attachment B97.*)

23 March 1966: SAC FORM 133 STRATEGIC AIR COMMAND EDUCATIONAL ACHIEVEMENT CERTIFICATE dtd 23 March 1966. MAURICE F. MERCURE is awarded this Certificate in recognition of self-improvement gained through participation in the Strategic Air Command Aerospace Educational Program given at Offut Air Force Base, this 23rd day of March 1966. JOHN D. RYAN GENERAL. USAF COMMANDER IN CHIEF. (*For a copy of this form, see attachment B98.*)

28 March 1966: LETTER, SUBJECT: SAC Educational Achievement Award DEPARTMENT OF THE AIR FORCE HEADQUARTERS 3973D STRATEGIC WING (SAC) APO US FORCES 09282 TO: 3973 Operations Attached is a SAC Educational Achievement Award for an individual in your organization. Please present this award to him at your next Commander's Call. CORNELLO de KANTER, Civilian Education Services Officer. 1 Atch MSgt Mercure

11 April 1966: UNCLASSIFIED MESSAGE FR TANUS DIST FRANKFURT GER TO CO 3973D STRAT WING MORON AFB SPAIN BT UNCLAS AENFR-AB 4-4-51 SUBJ; WO EVAL BD 1. WO EVAL BD FOR MSGT MAURICE F. MERCURE AND SSGT WILBERT L. BAILEY WILL CONVENE ON MONDAY 18 APR 66 AT 0900 HRS, HQ TANUS DIST, ANNEX B, RM 1-M-27. 2. REQ FOR WAIVER ON MSGT MERCURE MUST BE SUBMITTED IN ACCORDANCE WITH PARA 6, AR 135-100. 3. REQ CONF, ATTN: AENFR-AB, THAT EM WILL APPEAR BEFORE SAID BD. BT.

13 April 1966: LETTER, SUBJECT: Request for Permissive TDY, dtd 13 April 1966. BDAS Request the following named individual be placed on permissive TDY for the purpose of meeting Warrant Officer Evaluation Board at Frankfurt, Germany. Orders should read for a period of 10 days with departure from this station on or about 14 April 1966. MSgt Maurice F. Mercure AF 12XXXXXX, Opns Sq SSgt Wilbert L. Bailey, AF 53XXXXXX, Ops Sq ERNEST R. MEREDITH, Capt. USAF Commander, 3973 Operations Squadron.

We were in Seville for the Annual Fair. It was a very colorful and exciting event. Lots of people were dressed up in authentic old Spanish costumes. We took a picture of a little girl in native dress. (*See photograph A42.*)

13 April 1966: SPECIAL ORDER TC-15 DEPARTMENT OF THE AIR FORCE HEADQUARTERS 3973D STRATEGIC WING (SAC) APO NEW YORK 09282 dtd 13 April 1966. Paragraph. The following named personnel, organization indicated, SAC, this stn, are authorized to proceed from this stn to Frankfurt, Germany on or about 14 April 1966, for approximately 10 days TDY for the purpose of meeting the Warrant Officer Evaluation Board at Frankfurt, Germany. Authority: AENFR-AB 4-4-51. MSGT MAURICE F MERCURE, AF 12XXXXXX 3973 Ops Sq SSGT WILBERT L. BAILEY, AF 53XXXXXX, Ops Sq FOR THE COMMANDER:

One night we awoke to the smell of cigarette smoke and the squeaking of our porch swing outside our bedroom window. I called out, "¿Qué pasa?" The reply was, "Pasa nada, Guarda Civil." (Civil Guard) They were sitting on our porch swing enjoying a leisurely smoke and break. We just rolled over and went back to sleep.

14 April 1966: USAFE FORM 80 LRA IDENTITY DOCUMENT FOR CROSSING BORDERS dtd 14 April 1966. MERCURE, Maurice F. AF 12XXXXXX Moron AB, Spain. (*For a copy of this form, see attachment B99.*)

15 April 1966: AF FORM 1098 PERSONNEL ACTION REQUEST dtd 15 Apr 66. 2188 Comm Sq Moron AB, Spain MERCURE, MAURICE F. MSGT AF

12XXXXXX. PERSONNEL ACTION NR 1253 dtd 15 Apr 66. (*For a copy of this form, see attachment B100.*)

The drainage pipe from the toilet bowl clogged up and backfired into the bathtub whenever we flushed the toilet. We called Base Housing and they sent a repair team. We were inconvenienced for a few days, but they fixed it and it worked wonderfully after that. We did have the maid's toilet that we could use if it became necessary.

15 April 1966: SPECIAL ORDER AA-189 DEPARTMENT OF THE AIR FORCE HEADQUARTERS 3973D STRATEGIC WING (SAC) APO NEW YORK 09282 dtd 14 April 1966. Paragraph. THE FOLLOWING NAMED PERSONNEL, ORGANIZATION PAS CODES INDICATED, SAC, THIS STN, ARE ASSIGNED 2188 COMMUNICATIONS SQ, AFSC, THIS STN, EDCSA 15 APR 66. AUTHORITY: AFM 35-11 AND LETTER, HQ SAC, TRANSFER OF OFFICERS, LTCOL AND BELOW, AND AIRMAN PERSONNEL, 11 APR 66. ALL AFSN'S ARE PREFIXED BY AF. PCA WITHOUT PCS. NO TRAVEL INVOLVED. MSGT MERCURE, MAURICE F. 29170 AF 12XXXXXX MVS DIP SSGT 29170 BAILEY, WILBERT L. AF 53XXXXXX FOR THE COMMANDER:

Listed below are some of the units assigned to Moron Air Base, Spain

1. 3973D Strategic Wing (SAC)
2. Hq Sq 3973D Strategic Wing (SAC)
3. 3973D Air Base Group
4. HGSG 3973 Air Base Group
5. 3973D Civil Engineer Squadron
6. 3973D Combat Defense Squadron
7. 3973D Consolidated Aircraft Maintenance Squadron
8. 3973D Food Service Squadron
9. 3973D Operations Squadron
10. 3973D Services Squadron
11. 3973D Supply Squadron
12. 3973D Support Squadron
13. 973D Transportation Squadron

14. 7473D Combat Support Group (USAFE)

15. 7473D Hq Sq Combat Support Group (USAFE)

16. 7473D Material Squadron

17. 7477ᵗʰ Petroleum Pipeline Squadron

18. DET 9, Atlantic Aerospace Rescue and Recovery Center, Mil Airlift. Comd.

19. DET14, 21ˢᵗ Weather Sq, Mil Airlift Comd

20. 840ᵗʰ USAR HOSPITAL

21. 2188ᵗʰ Communications Squadron (AFCS)

<u>16 April 1966</u>: SSgt Bailey and I caught a space available flight to Rhein Main Air Base, Frankfurt, Germany. We arrived at Rhein Main AB the same day and checked into Base Billeting. We did not have to go before the Warrant Officer Evaluation Selection Board until the 18ᵗʰ of April. We acquainted ourselves with the area, so we would not have any problems getting to the Selection Board on time.

<u>18 April 1966</u>: We went before the Warrant Officer Selection Board as scheduled. We were told when we have been before the Board, that we would be notified by message if selected.

<u>19 April 1966</u>: UNCLASSIFIED MESSAGE FR 2188 COMM SQ MORON AB SPAIN. TO: 7322 ABWG CHATEAUROUX AS FRANCE dtd 19 APR 66 BT UNCLAS BDCC-CE 08079 APR 66. FOR DIRECTOR OF ADMIN SERVICES. PLEASE PASS TO MSGT MAURICE F. MERCURE AND SSGT WILBERT L. BAILEY! TRAVELING ON PERMISSIVE TDY ORDER TC-15, 13 APRIL 1966. ISSUED BY THE 3973D STRATEGIC WING. SGT'S MERCURE AND BAILEY ARE AUTHORIZED FIVE DAYS LEAVE EFFECTIVE 20 APRIL 1966. PER 2188 COMM SQ LEAVE ORDER 1279 AND 1280 RESPECTIVELY. LEAVE ORDERS ARE DATED 19 APRIL 1966. BT.

<u>19 April 1966</u>: AF FORM 1710-3 LEAVE AUTHORIZATION BALANCE RECORD 2188 COMM SQ (CR) dtd 19 Apr 66 Maurice F. Mercure AF 12XXXXXX MSgt 2188 Comm Sq (OPNS) DUTY PHONE 2085. DAYS-LV-REQ 5 EFF O/A DATE 20 Apr 66 DAY-DEPART-LV 21 Apr 66. DAT-RETURN-LV 21 April 66 LEAVE IN

CARE OF SELF, 7322 ABWG, Chateauroux AB, FRANCE 2188 Comm Sq (AFCS), APO NEW YORK 09282 TYPE-MIL-LV Ord. MIL-LV-AUTH-NR 1279 DATE OF LV-AUTH 19 APR 66 FOR THE COMMANDER:

19 April 1966: SSGT Bailey and I stopped off at Chateauroux Air Station, France, where I met an old friend of mine from Det 30, TUSLOG (Turkey), TSGT Donald Nauss. Also met a SSGT that I was stationed with in Taipei, Taiwan. I do not recall his name, but we were to be stationed together at Trier AB, Germany until I made MSGT and my orders were cancelled. The reason we stopped over at Chateauroux Air Station, France, was because our Space Available Flight terminated there. We reminisced about old times until our new orders arrived, and we caught a flight to Moron Air Base, Spain.

20 April 1966: We departed Chateauroux AB and proceeded to Moron AB, Spain, arriving there the same day, wondering what the outcome of the Board would be.

25 April 1966: SPECIAL ORDER T-67 DEPARTMENT OF THE AIR FORCE HEADQUARTERS 870th USAF HOSPITAL (USAFE) APO NEW YORK 09282 dtd 25 April 1966. Paragraphs 4 & 5. 4. MSGT MAURICE F. MERCURE, AF 12XXXXXX, 2188 Comm Sq, AGCS, APO New York 09282, attached this unit, will proceed on or about 28 Apr 66 from Moron AB, Spain to 401st USAF Hosp, USAFE, Torrejon AB, Spain on TDY for approximately 2 days for the purpose of receiving further treatment. Upon completion return to Moron AB, Spain by mil acft is authorized. Transportation Officer will furnish necessary transportation. 66 lbs of baggage authorized when traveling by mil acft. TDN: 5763400 306 6749 P478 21339 S663700 ($7.99) Authority: AFM 36-11. 5. SO T-57 this Hq, dated 5 Apr 66 pertaining to TDY of MSGT MAURICE F. MERCURE is revoked. FOR THE COMMANDER:

28 April 1966: STANDARD FORM 513 CLINICAL RECORD CONSULTATION SHEET dtd 28 Apr 66 401st USAF HOSP, USAFE Torrejon AB, Spain. MERCURE, MAURICE F. MSGT AF 12XXXXXX 3973 Opns Sq. (*For a copy of this form, see attachment B101.*)

<u>11 May 1966</u>: AF FORM 911 SENIOR AIRMAN'S PERFORMANCE REPORT dtd 11 May 1966. Mercure, Maurice F. MSgt AF 12XXXXXX 3973 Operations Squadron Moron Air Base, Spain (SAC). (*For a copy of this form, see attachment B102.*)

<u>15 May 1966</u>: AF FORM 1227 REQUEST FOR TUITION ASSISTANCE— EDUCATION SERVICES PROGRAM dtd 16 May 1966. MERCURE, Maurice F. MSgt AF 12XXXXXX 2188 Communications, Box 7107, APO New York 09282. NAME OF SCHOOL Univ of Maryland LOCATION OF COURSE(S) On Base TYPE OF STUDY College undergraduate TITLE OF COURSE(S) AND NUMBER(S) SPEECH 1—Public Speaking CREDIT HOURS 3 DAYS OF WEEK MTWTh HOURS OF MEETING 1200-1315 INCLUSIVE DATES 6 Jun-23 Jul 66 TUITION FEE PER HOUR SEMESTER $16.00 TUITION ASSISTANCE $36.00 TUITION COST TO STUDENT $12.00.

<u>24 May 1966</u>: AF FORM 1098 PERSONNEL ACTION REQUEST 2188 Comm Sq Moron AB, Spain dtd 24 May 1966. MERCURE, MAURICE F. MSGT AF 12XXXXXX, PERSONNEL ACTION NR 1681. DUTY TITLE NCOIC Telecommunications Operations Sec. (*For a copy of this form, see attachment B103.*)

<u>June 1966</u>: We had an Annual Inspection by Air Force Communications Service, which we passed with flying colors. Picture of Air Force Communications Service (AFCS) Brigadier General Stone and the author inspecting the Base Switchboard, 2188 Communications Squadron (AFCS) Moron Air Base, Spain. (*For a copy of this picture, see photo A43.*)

<u>1 June 1966</u>: AF FORM 1297 TEMPORARY ISSUE RECEIPT dtd 1 June 1966. TO: (Responsible Officer) RICHARD A. LUND CAPT, MSC, USAF MSGT HARRY M. BAKER STOCK NO. 65455596105 EMERGENCY MEDICAL TREATMENT UNIT, PHASE 1EA QUANTITY ISSUED 1 COST $431.00. Serial No. Z22637 IN THE EVENT OF LEAVE, TDY, HOSPITALIZATION, ETC., THE CUSTODIAN IS RESPONSIBLE FOR INSURING THAT DAILY INSPECTIONS ARE ACCOMPLISHED. ANY CHANGE IN CUSTODIANS' DROS WILL BE REPORTED TO SUA2 USAF HOSP SAN PABLO AB. EXT 2182/2184 I

ACKNOWLEDGE RECEIPT AND RESPONSIBILITY FOR ITEM(S) SHOWN IN "QUANTITY ISSUED" COLUMN WHICH WILL BE RETURNED ON DATE SPECIFIED ABOVE. DATE 1 JUN 1966. TYPED OR PRINTED NAME, GRADE, AND ORGANIZATION MAURICE F. MERCURE MSGT 2188 Comm Sqdn Bldg 102 SIGNATURE DUTY PHONE 2298.

2 June 1966: AF FORM 1710-3 LEAVE AUTHORIZATION BALANCE RECORD dtd 2 June 1966. 2188 Comm Sq (CR) AF 12XXXXXX Maurice F. Mercure MSgt 2188 Comm Sq (TCO) DUTY PHONE 2085 DAYS-LV-GRANTED 5 DUTY LOCATION Moron AB, Spain DAYS-LV-REQ 5 EFF O/A DATE 9 Jun 66 DAY-DEPART-LV 9 Jun 66 LEAVE IN CARE OF Self, STREET ADDRESS Torrejon Hilton Hotel Madrid, Spain OFFICIAL DESIGNATION AND LOCATION OF APPROVING HEADQUARTERS 2188 Comm Sq (AFCS), APO New York 09282 TYPE MIL-LV Ord MIL-LV-AUTH-NR 2013 DATE-OF-LV-AUTH 2 Jun 66. FOR THE COMMANDER:

2 June 1966: SPECIAL ORDER P-15 DEPARTMENT OF THE AIR FORCE 2188 COMMUNICATIONS SQUADRON (AFCS) APO NEW YORK 09282 dtd 1 June 1966. Paragraph 2. The following named individuals are appointed as members of the COMSEC Monitoring Unit, with no change in DAFSC, Functional Account or Program Element Code, effective this date. Authority: Para 2c, AFR 205-7. MAJ NELSON COURNOYER, FV 30XXXXX, MSGT PAUL J BROW, AF 16XXXXXX, MSGT MAURICE F MERCURE, AF 12XXXXXX SSGT JAMES C BOGGS, AF 15XXXXXX. BY NELSON D. COURNOYER, Major, USAF Commander.

5 June 1966: During one of our trips downtown, we rode in a horse drawn carriage and had our picture taken. (*For a copies of these pictures, showing Peg, her mother and the author in a horse drawn carriage, in downtown Seville, see photo A44.*)

9 June 1966: We took Mum (Peg's mother) up to Madrid by car, so she could catch her flight to London. We stayed at the Torrejon Hilton Hotel, Madrid, Spain. I can say that we were sorry to see her go, as we had a lot of good times together. I know she had a good time with us and enjoyed the climate up to the time that she left. Her stay with us

was very relaxing for her, as she did not have a single asthmatic attack while staying with us. She was in the best condition since I have known her.

10 June 1966: SPECIAL ORDER M-49 DEPARTMENT OF THE AIR FORCE HEADQUARTERS 7473 COMBAT SUPPORT GROUP (USAFE) APO New York 09282 dtd 10 June 1966. Paragraph. The following named personnel, organizations indicated, this stn, are appointed as members of the Moron Classification Board for the purpose of classifying officers and airmen to the indicated career areas. The Board will be convened by the Commander and/or designated representative. The Senior Board member will act as the President and the Junior Member will be the Recorder. Authority: Para 8a and 10b, AFM 35-1 and AFR 11-1. GRADE, NAME ADSN, ORGANIZATION, AFSC CAREER AREAS: Communications Operations. SMSGT LESTER L MOORE, AF 14XXXXXX, 2188 Comm Sq, AFCS, 27290. MSGT PAUL J. BROW, AF 16XXXXXX, 2188 Comm Sq, ADCS, 29170. MSGT MAURICE F. MERCURE, AF 12XXXXXX, 2188 Comm Sq, AFCS, 29170. MSGT HERBERT D. SMITH, AF 14XXXXXX, 2188 Comm Sq, AFCS, 29370. FOR THE COMMANDER:

10 June 1966: SPECIAL ORDER M-50 DEPARTMENT OF THE AIR FORCE HEADQUARTERS 7473 COMBAT SUPPORT GROUP (USAFE) APO New York 09282 dtd 10 June 1966. Paragraph 3. MSGT MAURICE F. MERCURE, AF 12XXXXXX, 2188 Comm Sq, AFCS, this stn, is appointed as Phase I MMPNC Kit Custodian for building S-102, Moron AB, Spain. Authority: Para 25a (1), Chapter 15, Vol V. AFM 67-1. FOR THE COMMANDER:

14 June 1966: LETTER, SUBJECT: Change in Educational Level, dtd 10 June 1966. TO: Spanish Comm Rgn APO US Forces 09283. Request that the personal records of MSgt Maurice F. Mercure, AF 12XXXXXX, be changed to reflect 15 Semester hours of college. This change is based on 15 semester hours with the University of Maryland, effective 25 Mar 66. DARVILE E. LOVEWELL, SSgt USAF NCOIC, Base Education Office.

July 1966: RECOGNITION for the most outstanding Automatic Digital Network (AUTODIN) tributary station for April through June is presented to Maj. Nelson D.

Cournoyer, 2188th Communications Squadron commander, right, and MSgt Maurice F. Mercure, telecommunications operations NCOIC, center. Presentation of the plaque is made by Lt. Col. Joseph A. Novak, 2186th Communications Squadron Commander. This is the fourth consecutive quarter the telecommunications section of 2188th CS has won the award. (FRONTERA NEWS) (U.S. Air Force Photo). (*For a copy of this picture, see photograph A45.*)

11 July 1966: LETTER, SUBJECT: Letter of Transmittal FROM: MSgt MAURICE F. MERCURE. TO: Hq USAREUR (AFAAG-PM) APO New York 09403 dtd 11 July 1966. 1. Attached is a report of Medical Examination taken for the purpose of the Army Warrant Officer Program. 2. I was boarded by the TANUS District on 18 April 1966. My application was then forwarded to the Department of the Army for consideration, with a letter of transmittal to your office. 3. If additional information is desired, please notify me by message. MAURICE F. MERCURE, MSgt, USAF, NCOIC Telecommunications Operations. 1 Atcha/s.

20 July 1966: AF FORM 1098 PERSONNEL ACTION REQUEST 2188 Comm Sq (AFCS) Moron AB, Spain dtd 20 Jul 66 MERCURE, MAURICE F. MSGT AF 12XXXXXX PERSONNEL ACTION NR 2317 TO: Spanish Comm Rgn (CBPO), Torrejon AB, Spain FROM: 2188 Comm Sq (AFCS), Moron AB, Spain. (*For a copy of this form, see attachment B104.*)

25 July 1966: AF FORM 186 INDIVIDUAL RECORD—EDUCATIONAL SERVICES PROGRAM dtd 25 Jul 66 MERCURE, MAURICE F. MSgt AF 12XXXXXX 2188 Comm Sq, Moron AB, Spain. (*For a copy of this form, see attachment B105.*)

28 July 1966: AF FORM 911 SENIOR AIRMAN'S PERFORMANCE REPORT dtd 28 July 1966. MERCURE, MAURICE F. MSgt AF 12XXXXXX 2188 Comm Sq (AFCS) Moron AB, Spain. (*For a copy of this form, see attachment B106.*)

29 July 1966: SPECIAL ORDER G-25 DEPARTMENT OF THE AIR FORCE HEADQUARTERS SPANISH COMMUNICATIONS REGION (AFCS) APO NEW YORK 09283, MSgt Maurice F. Mercure, AF12XXXXXX is awarded the AF Good

Conduct Medal (1 OLC) for his demonstration of exemplary behavior, efficiency, and fidelity during the period 1 Jul 63 to 30 Jun 66. Authority: AFR 900-10. FOR THE COMMANDER:

1 August 1966: LETTER, SUBJECT: Letter of Transmittal FROM: TCO/MSgt Mercure TO: Hq USAREUR (AEAAG-PM), APO 09403. 1. Attached is a report of Medical Examination taken for the purpose of the Army Warrant Officer Program. 2. I was boarded by the TANUS District on 18 April 1966. My application was then forwarded to the Department of the Army for consideration, with a letter of transmittal to your office. 3. If additional information is required, please notify me by message. MAURICE F. MERCURE, MSgt, USAF NCOIC, Telecommunications Operations 1 Atcha/s.

1 August 1966: SPECIAL ORDER M-1 DEPARTMENT OF THE AIR FORCE 2188 COMMUNICATIONS SQUADRON (AFCS) APO NEW YORK 09282 dtd 1 August 1966 Paragraph. The following individual this unit, is assigned additional duty as indicated, with no change in DAFSC, Functional Account or PEC, effective this date, all previous orders in conflict are hereby rescinded. MSGT MAURICE F. MERCURE, AF 12XXXXXX, Unit Security NCO. NELSON D. COURNOYER, Major, USAF Commander.

1 August 1966: SPECIAL ORDER M-2 DEPARTMENT OF THE AIR FORCE 2188 COMMUNICATIONS SQUADRON (AFCS) APO NEW YORK 09282 dtd 1 August 1966. Paragraph 2. The following NCO, this unit, is appointed member of the 2188 Comm Sq NCO Advisory Council. In the absence of the designated chairman and/or recorder the senior member present will act as chairman and the junior member as recorder. All previous orders in conflict are hereby rescinded. Authority: AFR 11-1. MSGT MAURICE F. MERCURE, AF 12XXXXXX, member. NELSON D. COURNOYER, Major, USAF Commander.

5 August 1966: UNCLASSIFIED MESSAGE FM SPANISH COMM RGN TORREJON AB SPAIN TO 2188 COMM SQ MORON AB SPAIN BT UNCLAS CBPO-SA 05320. AUG 66. YOUR PR. SUBJECT: REENLISTMENTS DURING

OCTOBER 1966. MSGT MAURICE F. MERCURE, AF 12XXXXXX, IS ELIGIBLE TO REENLIST ON NORMAL ETS OF 30 OCT 66. REQUEST AF FORM 1411, CANCELLATION OF EXTENSION, OR DECLINATION STATEMENT BE FORWARDED TO ARRIVE THIS HEADQUARTERS NOT LATER THAN 29 AUG 66. BT.

11 August 1966: SPECIAL ORDER M-102 DEPARTMENT OF THE AIR FORCE HEADQUARTERS 7473 COMBAT SUPPORT GROUP (USAFE) APO New York 09282 dtd 11 August 1966. Paragraph. MSGT MAURICE F. MERCURE, AF 12XXXXXX, 2188 Communications Sq, this stn, will terminate public quarters I-14-A, Santa Clara Housing area APO New York 09284, and is assigned public quarters N-3-A, Santa Clara Housing area effective 15 Aug 66. Authority: AFR 30-6. This is a mandatory reassignment for the convenience of the Air Force and movement of household goods at the expense of the government is authorized, there will be no travel expenses for members and their dependents involved. 5773400 307 8022 P458 2293D S663700. FOR THE COMMANDER:

Our gardener, Mr. Gambria, did an exceptional job of taking care of our lawn and flowers. When we were told we had to move to Enlisted Quarters, he did not want to go there and take care of our lawn. After quite a friendly discussion, he agreed to go to our new quarters and take care of the lawn. We felt good about this as he would not do it for anyone else. He had a way with the lawn and flowers.

August 1966: Two at a time was the word in the 2188 Comm Sq recently, when they received both the Major Relay Award, held by SSgt Herbert Smith, Jr. (left) and the Manual Data Relay Award held by MSgt Maurice F. Mercure (center). Reading the citation which accompanied the two awards is Major Nelson D. Cournoyer, 2188 Commander. The Manual Data Relay Plaque represents the fifth consecutive quarter that 2188 Comm Sq has won the award.

11 August 1966: DD FORM 1299 APPLICATION FOR SHIPMENT OF HOUSEHOLD GOODS, MORON AIR BASE, SPAIN dtd 11 August 1966. MERCURE, MAURICE F. MSGT, AF 12XXXXXX. (*For a copy of this form, see attachment B107.*)

31 August 1966: SPECIAL ORDER M-3 DEPARTMENT OF THE AIR FORCE 2188 COMMUNICATIONS SQUADRON (AFCS) APO NEW YORK 09282 dtd 31 August 1966. Paragraph 1. The following individuals, this unit, are appointed members of the Unit Ground Safety Committee. In the absence of the designated Chairman and/or Recorder, the senior member present will act as Chairman and junior member as Recorder. SMSGT (P1) LESTER L. MOORE, AF 14XXXXXX Chairman, MSGT CHARLES R. RUSH, AF 13XXXXXX, Member, MSGT MAURICE F. MERCURE, AF 12XXXXXX Member, MSGT PAUL J. BROW, AF 16XXXXXX Member, TSGT (P1) LEO E. WASHER, AF 12XXXXXX Member, TSGT (P1)

EARLY L. LAND III, AF 14XXXXXX Member, A1C WILLIE S. COCKRELL, JR AF 16XXXXXX Recorder. NELSON D. COURNOYER, Major, USAF Commander.

1 September 1966: SPECIAL ORDER M-4 DEPARTMENT OF THE AIR FORCE 2188 COMMUNICATIONS SQUADRON (AFCS) APO NEW YORK 09282 dtd 1 September 1966. Paragraphs 2 & 3. 2. MSGT MAURICE F. MERCURE, AF 12XXXXXX, this unit, is appointed Alternate Cryptographic Custodian for Crypto Account Number 35XXX, effective this date. Vice MSGT PAUL J. BROW, AF 16XXXXXX, relieved. 3. The following named individuals are appointed as members of the COMSEC Monitoring Unit, effective this date. Authority: AFR 205-7. 1STLT JAMES T. BAKER, FV 31XXXXX, 1STLT THOMAS S. GRAYBILL, FV 31XXXXX. CWO-W4 TREVOR G. JAMES, FR 95XXXXX. MSGT MAURICE F. MERCURE, AF 12XXXXXX, TSGT (P1) PAUL G. WARNACK, AF 14XXXXXX. TSGT (P1) LEO E. WASHER, AF 12XXXXXX. SSGT JAMES C. BOGGS, AF 15XXXXXX. NELSON D. COURNOYER, Major USAF Commander.

12 September 1966: AF FORM 1710-3 LEAVE AUTHORIZATION BALANCE RECORD dtd 12 September 1966. 2188 Comm Sq (CR) AF 12XXXXXX Maurice F. Mercure MSGT 2188 Comm Sq (TCO) DUTY PHONE 2085 5 DAYS-LV-GRANTED 10 DUTY LOCATION Moron AB, SPAIN AB, SPAIN DAYS-LV-REQ 10 DAYS-LV 10 EFF O/A DATE 19 Sep 66 DAYS-DEPART-LV 21 Sep 66 LEAVE IN CARE OF American Embassy, Lisbon, Portugal 2188 Comm Sq (AFCS), APO N.Y. 09282

TYPE-MIL-LV Ord MIL-LV-AUTH-NR 2242 DATE-OF-LV-AUTH 15 Sep 66. FOR THE COMMANDER:

13 September 1966: SPECIAL ORDER M-5 DEPARTMENT OF THE AIR FORCE 2188 COMMUNICATIONS SQUADRON (AFCS) APO NEW YORK 09282 dtd 13 September 1966. Paragraphs 3 & 4. 3. So much of para 2, SO M-4, ths unit, 1 Sep 66, pertaining to the appointment of MSGT MAURICE F. MERCURE, AF 12XXXXXX, as Alternate Cryptographic Custodian for Crypto Account number 35XXX, as reads "effective this date" is amended to read "effective 31 Aug 66." 4. So much of para 3 SO M-4, this unit, 1 Sep 66, pertaining to the appointment of members of the COMSEC Monitoring Unit, as reads "effective this date" is amended to read "effective 31 Aug 66." NELSON D. COURNOYER, Major, USAF Commander.

23 September 1966: LETTER, SUBJECT: Appointment as a Reserve Warrant Officer of the Army under Title 10, United States Code, Section 591 and 597. DEPARTMENT OF THE ARMY OFFICE OF PERSONNEL OPERATIONS FORT BENJAMIN HARRISON INDIANAPOLIS, INDIANA 46249 dtd 23 September 1966 TO: WO (W-1) Maurice Frank Mercure AF 12XXXXXX 2188 Communications Squadron APO New York 09282 (Now serving as MSG, AFSN). (*For a copy of this letter, see attachment B108.*)

24 September 1966: We took a 10-day leave to Lisbon, Portugal, driving all the way from Seville, Spain. It was a very nice picturesque and enjoyable trip. We took an interesting and informative trip around Lisbon Harbor. When we toured the statue of Jesus, we met a very nice couple from Belgium, who decided they would accompany us on our sight seeing fun. The statue of Jesus overlooks Lisbon. It is just like the one in Rio de Janeiro, Brazil. The statue is located on a hill, just outside of Lisbon. You had to use an elevator to get up to the observation platform. The view from the observation platform was exceptionable and beautiful. You could see for miles in every direction, from the top of the statue.

On the way to Lisbon, Portugal, we had to cross a combination highway/railway bridge. The bridge was used by both cars and trains, but not at the same time. When the trains used the bridge, automobiles had to wait until the train had completely crossed the bridge. When the train had cleared the bridge, cars could then use it. It was a little difficult when you were on the bridge and a train came along.

When we left Lisbon to go back to Seville, we ran into a very large and heavy rain and thunder storm. Our windshield wipers broke down right in the middle of the storm, so we had to pull over and park until the storm was over. After the storm was over, we proceeded on our way to Seville. When we reached Seville, we had the windshield wipers repaired.

29 September 1966: LETTER, SUBJECT: Active Duty DEPARTMENT OF THE ARMY OFFICE OF PERSONNEL OPERATIONS FORT BENJAMIN HARRISON, INDIANA 46249 dtd 29 September 1966. FROM: RCPAP LETTER ORDER A-09-528 TO: Officer Concerned. (*For a copy of this letter, see attachment B109.*)

10 October 1966: LETTER, SUBJECT: Appointment and Concurrent Call to Active Duty. DEPARTMENT OF THE ARMY U. S. ARMY RESERVE COMPONENTS PERSONNEL CENTER FORT BENJAMIN HARRISON INDIANAPOLIS, INDIANA 46216 dtd 10 October 1966. THRU: USAF Military Personnel Center AFPMPKE Building 499C Randolph AFB, Texas 78148 TO: Commanding Officer 2188 Communications Squadron APO New York 09282. (*For a copy of this letter, see attachment B110.*)

12 October 1966: UNCLASSIFIED MESSAGE FM ASSTDCSPERSMILPERS USAF RANDOLPH AFB TEX TO RUTHHM/2188COMMSQ MORON AB SPAIN INFO RUCDAQ/AFCS RUFPBW/EAMECOMMAREA LINDSEY AS GERMANY RUTHBM/SPANISHCOMMRGN TORREJON AB SPAIN BT UNLAS AFPMAKE 16798 OCT 66 DA ADVISES MSGT MAURICE F. MERCURE! AF 12XXXXXX, SELECTED AND APPROVED FOR APPOINTMENT AND CONCURRENT CALL TO ACTIVE DUTY AS RESERVE WARRANT OFFICER (W-1) OF THE ARMY EFFECTIVE 25 NOV 1966. REPLY BY RETURN MESSAGE GIVING CAFSC

AND ADVISING WHETHER ANY COGENT MILITARY REASONS EXIST TO PRECLUDE DISCHARGE. BT.

TSGT O'Hara was assigned to replace me. He was told by SSGT Boggs that I was neglecting him by not showing him around the base and area. SSGT Boggs stated to TSGT O'Hara that when I arrived on Moron AB, MSGT Brow took Peg & I around the base and area, and that he helped Peg and I get settled in Public Housing. That of course was a big lie, as MSGT Brow just dropped Peg and I off at our quarters and left us to fend on our own. He got TSGT O'Hara so upset with his lies, that TSGT O'Hara tried to start a fight between him and me. SSGT Boggs wanted me to be disqualified from obtaining my Warrant Commission. I realized what was happening and did not let TSGT O'Hara provoke me into a fight. I am sure that it was a great disappointment to SSGT Boggs, as he wanted to get even with me for testifying against Captain Tiffany, his idol, as SSGT Boggs, TSGT Sheppard and Captain Tiffany were a clique and hung out together. They went out drinking and socializing together, and I refused to join them, since officer's and enlisted men were prohibited from socializing together.

13 October 1966: UNCLASSIFIED MESSAGE FM 2188 COMMSQ MORON AB SP TO RUWTFJ/ASSTRGSPERSMILPERS USAF RANDOLPH AFB TEX INFO RUCDAQ/AFCS RUFPBW/EAFECOMM AREA LINSEY AS GER RUTHBN/ SPANISHCOMMRGN TORREJON AB SP BT UNCLAS PR 00301 OCT 66 YOUR AFPMAKE 16798. 12 OCT 66. NO COGENT MILITARY REASON EXIST TO PRECLUDE DISCHARGE OF MSGT MAURICE F. MERCURE AF 12XXXXXX, FROM THE AF FOR THE PURPOSE OF ACCEPTING APPOINTMENT AND CONCURRENT CALL TO ACTIVE DUTY AS RESERVE WARRANT OFFICER (W-1) OF THE ARMY EFFECTIVE 25 NOV 66. BT.

14 October 1966: UNCLASSIFIED MESSAGE FM ASST DCS LNHS MIL PERS USAF RANDOLPH AFB TEX TO: 2188COMM SQ MORON AB SPAIN BT UNCLAS AFPMAKE 16005 OCT 66 FM AFPMAKE 16798. YOUR FR 00301 OCT 66 OMITTED CAFSC FOR MSGT MAURICE F. MERCURE, AF 12XXXXXX. ADVISE BY RETURN MESSAGE. BT

<u>14 October 1966</u>: LETTER, SUBJECT: Appointment and Concurrent Call to Active Duty FM USAFMPC (AFPMAKE) RANDOLPH AFB TEXAS 78148 TO: 2188 Comm Sq APO New York 09282 DEPARTMENT OF THE AIR FORCE HEADQUARTERS UNITED STATES AIR FORCE WASHINGTON, D. C. Dtd 14 October 1966. Paragraph 1. Comply with paragraph 2 of the attached letter from Department of the Army concerning Master Sergeant Maurice F. Mercure, AF 12XXXXXX. Authority for discharge will be paragraph 3-8a, AFM 39-10 and this letter. 2. Sergeant Mercure will be required to apply for discharge to be effective 24 November 1966, under the provisions of paragraph 3-8a, AFM 39-10, for the purpose of accepting appointment and concurrent call to active duty as a Warrant Officer of the Army. FOR THE CHIEF OF STAFF.

<u>15 October 1966</u>: I contacted Lt. Col. Wintermeyer at Wiesbaden AB, Germany, and asked him if he would get me an Army uniform to wear when I was sworn in. I gave him all my measurements including my hat size.

He did an exceptional job of getting me a complete Army Officer's uniform for me to wear as I was administered the oath of office.

Colonel Wintermeyer had expressed great pleasure with me making Warrant Officer, and being assigned to Frankfurt, Germany. He wanted me to visit him at Wiesbaden Air Base when I got to Germany and when I had the time. He was almost like a father to me.

I do not know what I would have done without his help. He was truly a great friend.

<u>24 October 1966</u>: LETTER SUBJECT: Request for discharge for purpose of accepting Warrant Officer appointment DEPARTMENT OF THE AIR FORCE 2188 Communications Squadron (AFCS) APO New York 09282 FM MSGT Maurice F. Mercure THRU: 2188 Comm Sq (CR) 1. In accordance with paragraph 3-8a, AFM 39-10 and Hq USAF Letter, Subject: Appointment and Concurrent Call to Active Duty, dtd 14 October 1966, request that I be discharged on the 24 November 1966. 2. The reason for this request is so that I can accept my Warrant appointment in the

Army Reserves on active duty. It is important that I be discharged the day before my appointment as U. S. Codes prohibit anyone from holding dual military service obligations. MAURICE F. MERCURE, MSGT, USAF NCOIC Telecommunications Operations. 1st Ind (CR) 2188 Comm Sq (AFCS), APO New York 09282 TO: 7473 Combat Support Gp (SPM) approved. Forwarded for action prescribed by paragraph 3-8a, AFM 39-10. NELSON D. COURNOYER, Major, USAF Commander. Cy to: Spanish Comm Rgn (CBPO-A) w/cy of RCPAP Ltr Order A-09-528, dtd 29 Sep 66. 2nd Ind (BPMC-4) 4 Mar 66 7473 Cmbt Gp (USAFE) APO New York 09282 TO: 2188 © Approved for discharge on 24 Nov 66. FOR THE COMMANDER BETTY P. LITTLE, Capt, USAF Chief Military Personnel Branch Personnel Division.

24 October 1966: LETTER, SUBJECT: Separation for the Convenience of the Government DEPARTMENT OF THE AIR FORCE 2188 COMMUNICATIONS SQUADRON (AFCS) APO New York 09282 dtd 24 Oct 66 TO: Spanish Comm Rgn (CBPO-SA). (*For a copy of this letter, see attachment B111.*)

4 November 1966: SPECIAL ORDER AA-513 DEPARTMENT OF THE AIR FORCE HEADQUARTERS 7473 COMBAT SUPPORT GROUP (USAFE) APO New York 09282 dtd 4 November 1966 Paragraph. MSGT MAURICE F. MERCURE, AF 12XXXXXX, 2188 Communications Sq, AFCS, this stn, DOB Aug 28, DOR: 1 Dec 64, PAFSC: 29170, is discharged from active duty and relieved from assignment 2188 Communications Sq, AFCS, this stn, and discharged under honorable conditions, effective 24 Nov 66. DD FORM 256 will be furnished. HOME OF RECORD AND FUTURE MAILING ADDRESS: 43 Newton Street, Holyoke, Massachusetts. Travel of dependents and Airman is authorized to the Zone of Interior up to one (1) year after date of Separation, in accordance with para 4175.6 Joint Travel Regulation. Travel by Military Air is authorized. Authority: Para 3-8a, AFM 39-10 and 1st Ind: 7473 Cmbt Spt Gp, Ltr, 4 Nov 66 to Ltr, 2188 Comm Sq, AFCS, 24 Oct 66. SDN 203 The following fund citation will apply: 2172010 01-431-432-433-434-435-436-437 P1411 S99-999. FOR THE COMMANDER:

9 November 1966: SPECIAL ORDERS NUMBER 209 HEADQUARTERS UNITED STATES ARMY EUROPE APO 09403 dtd 9 November 1966. EXTRACT

Paragraph 3. C 225 Fol rsg (diversion) dir. PCS (MDC): DA. WP TDN. 2172010 01-1111-1112-1113-1114-1115-1116-1117-P1411 S99-999. MERCURE, MAURICE F W22XXXXX WO1 SIGC USAR 721A HQ USAREUR APO 09403 Heidelberg Germany Rel fr asg (not jd): HQ USAREUR APO 09403 Asg to: 32d Sig Bn Corps APO 09757 Hoechst Germany Aloc: Feb-67-547 Aval date: 16 Dec 66 Auth: RCPAP LO A-09-528 DA OPO 29 Sep 66 Scty clnc: Clearance for access to clas info and mat to incl CRYPTO is rqr; resp commander will comply w AR 604-5. Lv data: NA EDCSA: 16 Dec 66. PPSC: NVAL ADC: OBV-3 yr BASD: NVAL BPED: NVAL ETS: NVAL Sp instr: Off wb atch to the USA Post, Paris, APO 09163 for pd 25 Nov 66 to 15 Dec 66 for rats, qtr, admin and nec proc for mov to new unit of asg. FOR THE COMMANDER IN CHIEF:

17 November 1966: LETTER, SUBJECT: Professional Books DEPARTMENT OF THE AIR FORCE 2188TH COMMUNICATIONS SQUADRON (AFCS) APO NEW YORK 09282 dtd 17 Nov 66. FM TCO/MSgt Mercure/2085 TO: Transportation Officer. (*For a copy of this letter, see attachment B112.*)

I had acquired a large lot of professional books, from all the correspondence courses I had completed. These books would come in handy and help me in the accomplishment of my duties—especially in my new career.

21 November 1966: SO-AA-5B DEPARTMENT OF THE AIR FORCE HEADQUARTERS 7473D COMBAT SUPPORT GROUP (USAFE) APO NEW YORK 09282, DTD 4 NOVEMBER 1966. Cleared Public Quarters N-3-H, Santa Clara Housing area, APO New York 09284, for our trip to Germany, via England. Submitted DD FORM 137 APPLICATION FOR BASIC ALLOWANCE FOR QUARTERS FOR MEMBER WITH DEPENDENT dtd 31 October 1966, for 21 November 1966. (*A copy of this form, see attachment B113.*)

We stayed in a hotel in downtown Seville, until we left the area on 25 November 1966, for our new assignment the 32d Signal Battalion, McNair Kasserne, Hoechst/ Frankfurt, Germany via England, where we stayed with Peg's family.

<u>24 November, 1966</u>: Our Renaud car broke down just before we transferred to Frankfurt, Germany. We managed to get a tow from SSGT Bailey to a garage, where they made temporary repairs, so we could use it. The car, after temporary repairs, could only go between 40 and 45 miles per hour, otherwise the car would stall out. We had quite a time with it, until we reached England, where we had it fully repaired.

<u>25 November 1966</u>: Major Nelson D. Cournoyer, Commanding Officer, 2188th Communications Squadron, Moron Air Base, Spain, administered the oath of office to me on 25 November 1966. I was now in the United States Army and was looking forward to my new career. (*For a copy of the picture of me being sworn in, see photo A46.*)

I had previously stated that the first person to salute me would receive five (5) dollars. After swearing me in, the Major told me to leave the building by the front door. Unknown to me at the time the 1st Sgt of the 2188th Comm Sq, was waiting for me so he would be the first one to salute me, so he could get the $5.00.

While staying in the hotel on the morning we left the area, I was in the elevator when it became stuck between floors. Peg got excited when she saw hotel employees with wrenches and wire cutters, because she thought they were going to cut the cable holding up the elevator car to get me out. I am glad to say that they did not cut the cable and they did manage to get me out. All's well that ends well. We proceeded to leave the area for our new adventure in life.

<u>25 November 1966</u>: We drove north to Madrid, which would be our first step on our way to England. We ran into a snow storm about an hour out of Madrid. Peg had to keep me awake by slapping my face, time and time again. It took us such a long time getting to Madrid because of the speed limitations. When we finally reached Madrid, we stayed overnight in a hotel, to rest up for the rest of the journey the following day.

<u>26 November 1966</u>: The next morning we set out for Bilbao, for the border crossing. While driving through the streets of Madrid, the car stalled out. As Peg could not drive, she had to get out and push the car until it started. The Spanish people on a

bus were shouting and cheering her on, as she pushed the car. We managed to get it started, and then proceeded on our way to the Spanish/French border. Luckily, we had no further problems.

26 November 1966: Reaching the Spanish/French border, we waited for the Air Force Representative, with our clearance papers (USAFE FORM 80) so we could cross the border into France. Then we could proceed on our way to Calais and the car ferry terminal for our trip to England.

While waiting for our clearance papers, I told the Spanish Border Guards that we were waiting for clearance papers. I also told the French Border Guards, what we were waiting on. It is quite apparent that both the Spanish and French Border Guards thought this was strange.

Finally an Air Force Representative showed up and informed us that we did not need clearance papers (USAFE FORM 80) as an agreement had been reached between the French government and the United States; that all we needed was our passports and/or special orders to cross. We then crossed over into France and proceeded north to Paris.

CHAPTER 12

26 NOVEMBER 1966 - 29 OCTOBER 1968

FRANCE—US ARMY POST, CAMP DELOGE, PARIS
GERMANY—MCNAIR KASSERNE, FRANKFURT/HOECHST

A. 14th Armed CAV, APO 09146 (TDY)   3 Apr 1967-4 Apr 1967

B. Wildflecken, Germany (TDY)   17 Apr 1967-18 Apr 1967

C. Giessen, Germany (TDY)   18 Apr 1967-19 Apr 1967

D. Darmstadt, Germany (TDY)   28 Apr 1967-25 Apr 1967

E. Darmstadt, Germany (TDY)   3 May 1967-4 May 1967

F. Darmstadt, Germany (TDY)   9 May 1967-10 May 1967

G. Heidelberg, Germany (TDY)   19 Jul 1967-21 Jul 1967

H. Landstuhl, Germany (TDY)   27 Jan 1968-2 Feb 1968

I. Garmish Recreational Area, Germany (TDY)   2 May 1968-3 May 1968

J. Kimbo Kasserne, Murnau, Germany (TDY)   21 Jul 1968-28 Jul 1968

K. Bremerhaven, Germany (TDY)   11 Oct 1968-13 Oct 1968

26 November 1966: We crossed over into France, and proceeded north to the US Army Post, Camp Deloge, Paris.

Reaching Paris, we proceeded to Camp Deloge, where I reported into the Officer-in-Charge. He in turn turned me over to the Personnel Section for processing.

A soldier kept saying, "Sir, Sir." (I did not think that he was talking to me, as I was so used to people saying, "Sarge, Sergeant," so I did not answer him.) Finally he said directly to my face, "Sir, I mean you." I then realized that he was talking to me, so I answered him. It came to my realization, that I was in a whole new phase in my career, as Warrant Officer, in the US Army.

They put us up in a hotel, until the processing was completed, and we could go on leave.

30 November 1966: They completed DA FORM 3054 ELECTION OF AMOUNT, BENEFICIARY DESIGNATION AND SETTLEMENT OPTIONS FOR SERVICEMEN'S GROUP LIFE INSURANCE dtd 30 November 1966. (*For a copy of this form, see attachment B114.*)

30 November 1966: The Personal Processing Center at Camp Deloge issued me the necessary papers to establish a 201 file on me, and all other paperwork, including pay records. I already had orders assigning me to the 32nd Signal Battalion, so when processing was complete, we went on leave to England.

We set out for the Calais Car Ferry Terminal, Calais, France. Reaching Calais, we booked passage on a Ferry to Dover and set sail for England. Arriving at Dover Car Ferry Terminal, we disembarked and drove north to Peg's mother's house in Hayes, Middlesex. We spent two weeks leave going around the countryside.

Our leave was drawing to a close, so we said our goodbyes and drove south to Dover to catch the car ferry to Ostend, Belgium. We boarded the ferry and set sail for Ostend. Arriving at Ostend, we drove west to Frankfurt, Germany, for my new duty station.

6 December 1966: DA FORM 1290 THE ARMY OF THE UNITED STATES OF AMERICA, DTD 6 December 1966. I was presented with this form by the Secretary of the Army, appointing me as a Reserve Warrant Officer, in the Army of the United States. (*For a copy of this form, see attachment B115.*)

15 December 1966: Arriving at McNair Kasserne, Hoechst/Frankfurt, I reported in to the Battalion Adjutant for necessary in processing. I was given a copy of AE FORM 3317 LEGAL STATUS OF US FORCES AGREEMENT, which I was to carry with me at all times. (*For a copy of this form, see attachment B116*).

We stayed in the Post Guest House until we were assigned Government Quarters.

17 December 1966: SPECIAL ORDERS NUMBER 266 HEADQUARTERS 32D SIGNAL BATTALION, APO 09757 dtd 17 December 1966. Paragraph 2. C 250. Fol indiv having been asg this sta/org are FUR ASG as indic. MERCURE, MAURICE F. W22XXXXX WO1 SIGC USAR 721A HQ USAREUR APO 09403 Fur asg: Co A (Comd Opns) 32D Sig Bn. Auth SO 209 para 3 C 225 HQ USAREUR APO 09403 ADC: OBV-3 yr BASD: NVAL BPED: NVAL ETS: NVAL PCS (MDC): DA Comp: USAR EDCS A: Eff 16 Dec 66 Sp Instr: NA FOR THE COMMANDER:

December 1966: Aerial view of McNair Kasserne—This is an excellent photograph of McNair Kasserne, showing the location of the 32D Signal Battalion. The Crypto Center's loading dock can be seen in the upper right hand corner of the quadrangle. Also various unit formations. Today there is a large steel fence all around the Kasserne area, which we saw when we visited the area in 1989. I do not know if it is still there, or even if the area is still used by the U.S. Army today. I don't know if the Kasserne is still in use and in existence today. (*For a copy of this picture, see photograph A47.*)

19 December 1966: Here is a picture of me in U. S. Army fatigues, after being processed through the 32D Signal Battalion. (*For a copy of this picture, see photograph A48.*)

19 December 1966: Assigned Government Quarters Number 2428-C-2 Hoechst, Frankfurt, Germany. The apartment consisted of three (3) bedrooms, livingroom, diningroom, kitchen and bathroom. It was located on the first floor of the building. It was nice being on the first floor and only having to go down one flight of stairs to the laundry room in the basement of the building.

22 December 1966: Lt. Col Hoagland (Battalion Commander) had a group of officers and their wives go to Wiesbaden Air Base Officers Club to see and hear Pearl Bailey perform and sing. We had a very great and enjoyable evening. The entertainment, food, and drinks were all good and everyone was happy that they went.

<u>23 December 1966</u>: SPECIAL ORDER NUMBER 278 HEADQUARTERS TANUS DISTRICT APO 09797 dtd 23 December 1966. Paragraph 9. TC 312. Bldg/Qtr asg indiv and depn as indic MERCURE, MAURICE F. W22XXXXX WO1 Co A 32d Sig Bn APO 09797 Asg bldg/qtr: 2428-C-2 Hoechst (Permanent) date: 19 Dec 66. FOR THE COMMANDER:

<u>25 December 1966</u>: We ate Christmas Dinner in the Battalion Mess Hall with the troops. It was a very enjoyable meal.

<u>27 December 1966</u>: DA FORM 10-233 HAND RECEIPT FOR EXPENDABLE OR NON-EXPENDABLE ITEMS dtd 27 Dec 66. MAURICE F. MERCURE, Co A 32 Sig Bn (Vault). (*For a copy of this form, see attachment B117.*)

I was issued a Pistol Automatic M-1911 A1, Cal 45, with one (1) each magazine, Cal 45. Serial Number (S.N.) #2340378, for use in the performance of my duties.

<u>31 December 1966</u>: SPECIAL ORDERS NUMBER 292, HEADQUARTERS V CORPS, APO 09079 dtd 31 December 1966. EXTRACT Paragraph 1. C 350. Fol indiv APPOINTED. MERCURE, MAURICE F W22XXXXX WO1 USA Co A, 32d Signal Battalion APO 09757 Apt to: (A) Alternate Crypto Custodian HHC V Corps Acct #3XXX. (B) Alternate Crypto Security Officer for HHC V Corps Acct #3XXX Eff date: 31 Dec 66 Pd: Indef Purpose: NA Scty clnc: Top Secret COSMIC Crypto Auth: Para 30 and 31, AR 380-40: Para 13, AR 380-41 Sp Instr: NA FOR THE COMMANDER:

<u>31 December 1966</u>: Appointed Alternate Crypto Custodian and Alternate Crypto Security Officer for HHC V Corps Account Number 3XXX. As Alternate Crypto Security Officer, I conducted Annual Command Crypto Inspections of the units assigned to V Corps. It was a job that I really liked and enjoyed it very much.

<u>18 January 67</u>: SPECIAL ORDERS NUMBER 14 HEADQUARTERS 32D SIGNAL BATTALION APO 09757 dtd 18 January 1967 Paragraph 1. TC 350. Fol indiv APPOINTED *HOAGLAND DALE N 08XXXX LTC SIGC Hq Co 32D Sig Bn

#THEAMAN FRANK J JR 01XXXXXX CPT SIGC Hq Co 32D Sig Bn %DAVIS MERRILL W 05XXXXXX 2Lt SIGC Co B (Fld Opns) 32D Sig Bn +MERCURE, MAURICE FRANK W22XXXXX WO1 SIGC Co A (Comd Opns) 32D Sig Bn Apt to: Bd of Off Eff date: 20 Jan 67 Pd: Approx 1 day Purpose: to intrw appl for apt to WO and USAR Auth: PAC AR 15-16 and AR 135-100 Sp Instr: Mbrs are apt w/conc of cdr concerned. * Indic President of Bd. # Indc mbr of bd % Indic recorder + Indic advisor w/o vote. FOR THE COMMANDER:

20 January 1967: Sat on Warrant Officer Selection Board and for United States Army Reserve Appointments. It went quite well and some of the applicants approved for and recommended for appointment. It was an opportunity to see how this type of board functioned, like the one that SSGT Bailey and I went before, for our selection to Warrant Officer.

24 January 1967: LETTER, SUBJECT: V 16XX XX XX XXXX-XXXF VETERANS ADMINISTRATION CENTER, WISSAHICKON AVE. AND MANHEIM ST, P. O. BOX 8979 PHILADELPHIA, PA 19101 dtd January 24, 1967. WO Maurice F. Mercure Co. A, 32nd Sig Bn. Corps APO New York, N.Y. 09797.

When I was assigned to the 32D Signal Battalion, I was presented with a beer stein with the V Corps, 32d Sig Bn and Hoechst AM emblems on it, and also my name and rank. It had an impression of a nude lady on the bottom of the stein. So, when you drank from it and were finished, you could make out the impression of the nude lady as you tipped it up to the light. Besides your name and rank, was the date your were assigned to the battalion. These beer steins were kept on shelves behind the bar. Once a month on 10¢ beer night, they would fill your stein with draft, for a dime. When you left the 32d Sig Bn, it was presented to you by the Battalion Commander, inscribed with the month and year you left. The Battalion Commander (Lt Col Dale C Hoagland), left the 32d Sig Bn before I did. So, unfortunately, the Adjutant (1st Lt Thomas C. Durenberger, who hated my guts) did not schedule a going away party for Peg and me, and did not have my beer stein inscribed with the month and year that I left the battalion. So my stein does not have this information on it. Somewhere else in this chapter, I indicated why the Adjutant did not like me. But I still treasure my beer stein always, as it reminds me of my good days in the 32d Sig Bn. After I had left the battalion for Vietnam, CWO Frank Rigalotto logged a formal complaint against the Adjutant with the Battalion commander, for not having a going away party for Peg and me. By the way, the Battalion Chaplain had the bottom of his stein painted blue.

McNair Kasserne area had its own chapel, theatre (cinema), gym, dispensary, dentist, NCO/EM Clubs, PX, and Officers Club. It was a little self-contained area in the town of Hoechst. If we wanted a larger PX or Commissary, all we had to do was go downtown to Frankfurt. The Post Exchange (PX) in downtown Frankfurt was huge. The Commissary was excellent; it supplied all the items one could use and/or think of for a good life.

Below is a list of personnel assigned to the Crypto Center of the 32d Signal Battalion.

1. CW2 Bruce R. Harbaugh
2. WO1 Maurice F. Mercure
3. WO1 Earl L. Simmons
4. SSG Harold W. Winnett
5. SP5 Edward L. Heil, Jr.
6. SP5 Charles R. Meredith
7. SP4 James J. Gustis
8. SP4 Allen T. Hardison

26 January 1967: DA FORM 669 GENERAL EDUCATIONAL DEVELOPMENT INDIVIDUAL RECORD (AR 621-5) dtd 25 January 1967. (For a copy of this form, see attachment B118).

15 February 1967: AE VGI-CI LETTER, SUBJECT: Travel and Assignment Restrictions TO: Commanding Officer 32D Signal Battalion APO 09757 HEADQUARTERS V CORPS APO 79, US Forces dtd 15 Feb 1967 Paragraph 1. In accordance with USAREUR Regulation 380-60 (clas), the following individual, designated Class II sensitive, is not eligible for assignment or travel (except as otherwise indicated) in prohibited areas listed in paragraph 5, cited directive:

Mercure, Maurice F. WO1 W22XXXXX
(Name, Grade, and Service Number)

2. These assignment and travel restrictions are effective until 1 September 1968, after which date the provisions of this letter do not apply. 3. This letter will remain in the individual's 201 file, until the date specified in paragraph 2, when this letter will be removed and destroyed. If the individual returns to the continental United States before the date specified in paragraph 2, this letter will be removed and destroyed before the departure. FOR THE COMMANDER:

I always wanted to visit and see West Berlin, but the letter (listed above) did not allow me to go through East Germany, to Berlin. So I never had the opportunity to do so. It was such a shame, as I always wanted to see West Berlin. It was just one of the things I had to live with.

The German Federal Post Office (Deuthes Bundes Post) conducted a guided tour of its Frankfurt Switchboard and Switching Center. Pictures were taken of this tour by the U.S. Army Signal Corps. (*For copy of this picture, see photograph A49.*)

This was a very interesting and informative tour of the German Federal Post Office Operations. We were treated very nicely by the German Federal Post Office's personnel.

6 March 1967: SPECIAL ORDERS NUMBER 57 HEADQUARTERS V CORPS APO 09079 dtd 6 March 1967. EXTRACT Paragraph 5. TC 350. Fol indiv APPOINTED. SIMMONDS, EARL L. W34XXXXX WO W1 USA Co A, 32d Sig Bn APO 09757. MERCURE, MAURICE F. W22XXXXX WO W1 USA Co A, 32d Sig Bn APO 09757 WINNETT, HAROLD W. RA17XXXXXX SSG E6 Co A, 32d Sig Bn APO 09757 MEREDITH CHARLES E. RA15XXXXXX SP5 E5 Co A, 32d Sig Bn APO 09757 HEIL, EDWARDS L. JR. RA13XXXXXX SP5 E5 Co A, 32d Sig Bn APO 09757 GUSTIS, JAMES J. RA16XXXXXX SP4 E4 Co A, 32d Sig Bn APO 09757 Ap To: Crypto Material Courier Eff date: 6 March 1967 Pd: Indef Purpose: To transport Crypto Material Auth: Para 43b (3), Ar 380-40 Sp instr: Auth to transport Crypto Material up to and including Secret. EM will familiarize themselves with AR 380-40, Sec VII before handling Crypto Material. FOR THE COMMANDER:

<u>28 March 1967</u>: LETTER ORDERS NUMBER 109 HEADQUARTERS 32D SIGNAL BATTALION APO 09757 dtd 28 March 1967 LETTER, SUBJECT: Temporary Duty TO: Indiv. Indic Paragraph TC 200. Indiv this sta placed on TDY as indic. PRSCTDY. TDN. Acct class: 2172020 89-1175 P20000-21 S91-530-GY MERCURE, MAURICE F. W22XXXXX WO1 USA Co A (Comd Opns) 32D Sig Bn SIMMONDS EARL L. JR W34XXXXX MEREDITH CHARLES E RA15XXXXXX SP5 E5 P2 Hq Co 32D Sig Bn TDY to: 14th Armd Cav, APO 09146 WP date: o/a 3 Apr 67 Pd: Approx 3 days Purpose: For Crypto Inspection Auth: VOCG V Corps Tvl data: Tvl by govt trans auth Sp instr: Within seven days subsequent to completion of TDY, indiv will submit necessary reimbursement voucher or a statement that no claim WB submitted to the Pers Off. FOR THE COMMANDER:

<u>29 March 1967</u>: LETTER ORDERS NUMBER 110 HEADQUARTERS 32D SIGNAL BATTALION APO 09757 dtd 29 March 1967. SUBJECT: Amendment of Orders TO: Indiv indic Paragraph TC 370. Fol orders AMENDED. SMO: LO 109 C 200 this HQ CS dtd 28 Mar 67 Pert To: TDY of MERCURE MAURICE F W22XXXXX WO1 USA ComA (Comd Opns) 32D Sig Bn, SIMMONDS EARL L JR W34XXXXX WO1 USA HQ Co 32D Sig Bn and MEREDITH CHARLES E RA15XXXXXX SP5 E5 P2 Hq Co 32D Sig Bn to 14th Armd Cav APO 09146 IATA: WINNETT HAROLD W RA 17XXXXXX SSG E6 SP P72B40 Co A (Comd Opns) 32D Sig Bn FOR THE COMMANDER:

Lt. Col. Hoagland was a great one for leaving parties. You could expect every month to attend one of these parties, for someone leaving the Battalion. These were nights when we wished the person(s) leaving God speed and good luck (especially if they were going to Vietnam).

Sometimes we used to go to the Crystal Officer's Club in downtown Frankfurt, located just behind the building housing V Corps. V Corps was located in the old I. G. Farben Building complex. After World War II, General Eisenhower used the building (I. G. Farben) for Supreme Allied Headquarters, during the occupation of Germany.

<u>3 April 1967</u>: The V Corps Command Crypto Inspection Team conducted the Annual V Corps Command Crypto Inspection of the 14th Armed Cav Crypto Center. All went

very well and the Inspection Team accomplished its mission. A written report was submitted to the V Corps Signal Officer Colonel J. E. Gwynn.

3 April 1967: We were assigned Permanent Quarters in Building No 6, 2429, Hoechst Housing Area effective 3 April 1967. The reason for the change in quarters was that they needed these larger quarters for a large family. These new quarters were not so good for location, like our first set, as they were located on the third floor and the laundry room was located in the basement. The quarters consisted of two (2) bedrooms, diningroom, livingroom, kitchen and bathroom.

10 April 1967: SPECIAL ORDERS NUMBER 80 HEADQUARTERS TANUS DISTRICT APO 09757, dtd 19 April 1967 EXTRACT Paragraph 4. TC 332. Bldg/ Qtr asg indiv and depn as indic. MERCURE, MAURICE F. W22XXXXX WO1 Co A 32d Sig Bn APO 09757 Asg bldg/qtr: 2429-B-6 Hoechst (perm) Eff date: 3 Apr 67 FOR THE COMMANDER:

11 April 1967: DA FORM 1506 STATEMENT OF SERVICE—FOR COMPUTATION OF LENGTH OF SERVICE FOR PAY PURPOSES dtd 11 Apr 67. MERCURE, MAURICE F. W22XXXXX. This record of service completed, was based on previous service in the United State Army Air Forces and the United State Air Force. All service time, no matter which branch of the service it was performed in, counts toward retirement. (*For a copy of this form, see attachment B119.*)

13 April 1967: DA FORM 31 REQUEST AND AUTHORITY FOR LEAVE dtd 13 April 1967. MERCURE, MAURICE F W22XXXXX, Co A 32d Signal Battalion APO 09757. OTHER (Specify) PASS 3 Days DATE FROM 0001 11 Apr 67 DATE (Inclusive) 2400 16 Apr 67. LEAVE ADDRESS B6 Building 2429 Hoechst Housing Area TEL: 315133 SIGNATURE Maurice F. Mercure In case of emergency telephone: 2315-676/865 Platoon Leader BA Places permitted to visit: Federal Republic of Germany DATE APPROVED: 13 Apr 67 NAME, GRADE & TITLE OF APPROVING AUTHORITY JOSEPH P. HAVILAND 1Lt., SigC., Adjutant. SIGNATURE OF APPROVING AUTHORITY Joseph P. Haviland.

<u>14 April 1967</u>: We were granted a three (3) day pass, so we could unpack and get our new quarters in shipshape condition. We drove down to Cologne, Germany, to tour the Cathedral which had been accidently hit by two bombs in World War II. Luckily they did little damage to the church. However, it was enough to annoy the German people.

<u>17 April 1967</u>: The V Corps Command Inspection Team had a nice trip to Wildflecken and Giessen, Germany. We conducted the Annual V Corps Command Crypto Inspection of these facilities. The inspection went well, and everyone concerned cooperated with the team. A written report of the inspection was submitted to the V Corps Signal Officer, Colonel J. E. Gwynn.

We had Peg's mother come out to us in Germany. Poor soul was ill with her asthma the whole time she was with us. It is apparent that the air from the chemical plants in Hoechst did not agree with her. The polluted air induced her bouts of asthma, which deteriorated and got worse. We had to take her to the Army Dispensary for treatment. The poor young Army Doctor who treated her was concerned for her, as he had never treated an older person before. He was so afraid that he would make a mistake in treating her. We decided it was best that she return to England rather than to continue to be sick. It was a shame, as we were looking forward to going out with her to the sidewalk cafes in Frankfurt/Hoechst area and driving her through the countryside.

We used to go to the Base Chapel almost every Sunday, in Hoechst Kasserne. The Chaplain, Major Peter Craig, was a very good pastor. We lived in the same building that he did. He and his family lived in C Stairwell on the second floor. We lived in B Stairwell on the third floor. We got on well with him and his family. In fact, young Danny Craig was a member of Peg's Cub Scout Den.

I had broken a pair of glasses (I always kept a spare pair) and went to the optician and obtained an order for a new pair of glasses. They always came by mail.

<u>24 April 1967</u>: The drive down to Darmstad, Germany, was a beautiful and relaxing trip. Upon arriving in Darmstad, I met my old friend SSGT Bailey, from the 2188th Communications Squadron, Moron Air Base, Spain. He was now a Warrant Officer in the United States Army and the area Cryptosecurity Officer. The V Corps Command

Annual Crypto Inspection went very well—without any problems, as I knew it would—since I trained Mr. Bailey when he was a SGT in the United States Air Force. A written report of the inspection was submitted to the V Corps Signal Officer, Colonel Gwynn.

25 April 1967: LETTER ORDERS NUMBER 142 HEADQUARTERS 32D SIGNAL BATTALION APO 09757 dtd 25 April 1967 LETTER, SUBJECT: Temporary Duty TO: Indiv indic Paragraph 200. Indiv this sta placed on TDY as indic. PRSCTDY. TDN. Acct Class: 217200 89-1175 P2000-21 S91-530-GY MERCURE, Maurice F. W22XXXXX WO1 USA Co A (Comd Opns) 32D Sig Bn HARDISON ALLEN JR RA14XXXXXX SP4 E4 HHC 32D Sig Bn TDY to: Wildflecken and Giessen, Germany WP date: o/a 17 Apr 67 Pd: Approx 2 days Purpose: For V Corps Command Crypto Inspection Auth: VOCO 32D Sig Bn Tvl data: Tvl by POV auth Sp instr: Within seven days subsequent to completion of TDY, indiv will submit necessary reimbursement voucher or statement that no claim WB submitted to the Pers Off. FOR THE COMMANDER:

The Officers and their wives went on various wine tasting trips. The food that the wineries served us and the wines they presented to us for tasting were excellent. Our Battalion Commander, Lt. Col. Hoagland, was very instrumental in arranging trips for the Officers and their wives to attend.

25 April 1967: We conducted our V Corps Annual Command Crypto Inspection and found the Darmstadt area in good shape. Some minor adjustments had to be made. Submitted written inspection report to the V Corps Signal Officer, Colonel Gwynn.

25 April 1967: LETTER ORDERS NUMBER 144 HEADQUARTERS 32D SIGNAL BATTALION APO 09757 dtd 25 April 1967 LETTER, SUBJECT: Temporary Duty TO: Indiv indic Paragraph TC 200. Indiv this sta placed on TDY as indic. RPSCTDY. Acct Class: 2172020 89-1175 P2000-21 S91-530-GY MERCURE, Maurice F W22XXXXX WO1 USA Co A (Comd Opns) 32D Sig Bn GUSTIS James J RA16XXXXXX SP4 E4 HHC 32D Sig Bn TDY to: Darmstadt, Germany WP date: o/a 24 Apr 67 Pd: Approx 1 day Purpose: For V Corps Command Crypto Inspection Auth VOCG V Corps tvl

data: Tvl by POV auth Sp Instr: Within seven days subsequent to completion of TDY, indiv will submit necessary reimbursement voucher or statement that no claim WB submitted to the Pers Off. FOR THE COMMANDER:

2 May 1967: LETTER ORDERS NUMBER 158 HEADQUARTERS 32D SIGNAL BATTALION APO 09757 dtd 2 May 1967 LETTER, SUBJECT: Temporary Duty. TO: Indiv indic Paragraph TC 200. Indiv this sta placed on TDY as indic. RPSCTDY. TDN. Acct Class: 2172020 89-1175 P2000-21 S91-530-GY MERCURE, Maurice F W22XXXXX WO1 USA Co A (Comd Opns) 32D Sig Bn GUSTIS James J RA16XXXXXX SP4 E4 HHC 32D Sig Bn TDY to: Darmstadt, Germany WP date: o/a 3 May 67 Pd: Approx 1 day Purpose: To conduct V Corps Command Crypto Inspection Auth: VOCG V Corps Tvl data: Tvl by POV auth Sp Instr: Within seven days subsequent to completion of TDY, indiv will submit necessary reimbursement voucher or statement that no claim WB submitted to the Pers Off. FOR THE COMMANDER:

3 May 1967: SP4 Gustis and I drove down to Darmstadt, Germany, to conduct the V Corps Command Crypto Inspection. As I indicated earlier on 24 April 1967, this was a very nice trip. The scenery was beautiful and relaxing. We conducted our inspection, finding some discrepancies, which we corrected on the spot, feeling that we had helped improve the security of the Crypto Center. A written report of the inspection and our findings was submitted to the V Corps Signal Officer, Colonel Gwynn.

9 May 1967: LETTER ORDERS NUMBER 171 HEADQUARTERS 32D SIGNAL BATTALION APO 09757 dtd 9 May 1967 LETTER, SUBJECT: Amendment of orders TO: indiv indic Paragraph TC 370. Fol Orders AMENDED. SMO: LO 144 TC 200 this HQ CS dtd 23 Apr 67 Pert to: TDY of MERCURE MAURICE F W22XXXXX WO1 USA Co A (Comd Opns) 32D Sig Bn and GUSTIS JAMES J RA16XXXXXX SP4 E4 HHC 32D Sig Bn to Darmstadt, Germany IATA: VOCO date ofm: 24 Apr 67 FOR THE COMMANDER:

9 May 1967: LETTER ORDERS NUMBER 172 HEADQUARTERS 32D SIGNAL BATTALION APO 09757 dtd 9 May 1967 LETTER, SUBJECT: Amendment of Orders

TO: Indiv indic Paragraph TC 370. Fol orders AMENDED. SMO LO 142 TC 200 this HQ CS dtd 25 Apr 67 Pert to: TDY of MERCURE MAURICE F W22XXXXX USA WO1 Co A (Comd Opns) 32D Sig Bn and HARDISON ALLEN JR RA14XXXXXX SP4 E4 HHC 32D Sig Bn to Wildflecken and Giessen, Germany IATA: VOCO date cfm: 17 Apr 67 FOR THE COMMANDER:

Because I knew how Air Force Salvage yards worked, I was to make periodic trips to the Salvage Yard at Wiesbaden Air Force Base. All I had to do was ask the Battalion Commander for a truck and a crew of two EM's to assist me in handling the items I was able to obtain. The Battalion Sergeant Major asked me the first time I went on a salvage run to try and get some hot water heaters for the barracks as they were experiencing some difficulties with the ones they had in the barracks. I was able to obtain four (4) brand new ones from the salvage yard. The SGT MAJ was so pleased that he wanted me to make more salvage runs. He would also tell me what he would like me to get if possible. I was able to procure a brand new electric grill for the NCO Club, as the one they had was on its last legs. Most of the items obtained were either surplus or discontinued items in the United States Air Force.

3 July 1967: SPECIAL ORDERS NUMBER 135 HEADQUARTERS 32D SIGNAL BATTALION APO 09757 dtd 3 July 1967. EXTRACT Paragraph 11. TC 350 Fol indiv this sta APPOINTED. MERCURE MAURICE F W22XXXXX WO1 USAR SIG 721A Co A (Comd Opns) 32D Sig Bn Apt to: Add dy as Custodian of NCO-EM Open Messes ECN-1637 Eff date: 3 Jul 67 Purpose: NA Auth: VOCO 32D Sig Bn Pd: Indef Sp instr: NA FOR THE COMMANDER:

3 July 1967: I was appointed as Custodian NCO-EM Open Messes ECN-1637. This was quite an interesting assignment in itself. The Joint Clubs were having monetary problems, and the Battalion Commander wanted someone he trusted to correct the situation. Upon appointment, I inventoried all the alcoholic beverages and placed them under lock and key (under my strict control). I was the only one who could issue them to the various bars. All bottles were marked by me (a line showing present contents), using a different color at the end of each day, showing consumption. That was how I caught a woman (civilian) bartender who was using her own alcoholic beverage instead

of the clubs. She then pocketed the money paid for the drinks. She was immediately fired and replaced. This tight inventory control system resulted in that bar making a profit. Slot machine keys were kept under my supervision and machines were only opened by me and the Duty Officer of the day to remove the money at the end of the day. This kept dishonest people from draining the money tube in the slot machines. It also provided a witness to the money removed, placed in a bag and sealed. Money was later counted by me and the bookkeeper. All slot machines began to make money for the club. The clubs began to make a profit and operate more efficiently. The Battalion Commander (Lt. Co. Hoagland) and the Battalion Sergeant Major were very pleased with the results. The club's cook in the NCO section became ill one day, and could not work. So Peg and I worked in the kitchen, doing the cooking. I must say that we did a good job and everyone was pleased with the food.

The Beer Company Michel Lobe, supplying the NCO-EM Clubs, agreed to furnish the clubs the material to build a walk-in cooler for beverages. A Sergeant from the Engineer Battalion, volunteered to erect (build) the walk-in cooler for the clubs. When he finished the job, we had a nice walk-in cooler for our beverages.

Diana Ross and the Supremes were singing in the NCO-EM Clubs for two days. The first night they were here, Diana had a problem, so she called me at home to straighten out the matter. I went to the club and took care of her problem and everything went fine after that.

18 July 1967: My trip to Heidelberg, Germany for the NCO-EM Clubs was a very interesting and productive trip. The club custodians selected performers to perform in the clubs, such as Diana Ross and the Supremes, Pearl Bailey, etc. Heidelberg is a very nice university city and is a beautiful place to see. We accomplished a lot for the clubs, entertainment wise, and daily operations of the clubs. It helped me in the running of the clubs.

19 July 1967: SPECIAL ORDERS NUMBER 307 HEADQUARTERS 32D SIGNAL BATTALION APO 09757 dtd 19 July 1967. SUBJECT: TEMPORARY DUTY TO: Indiv indic Paragraph TC 300. Indiv this sta placed on TDY as indic. RPSCTDY. MERCURE, MAURICE F W22XXXXX W01 Co A (Comd Opns) 32D Sig Bn TDY

To: USAREUR HQ Heidelberg, Germany WP date o/a 18 July 1967 Pd: Approx two days Purpose: Coordinate EM Club Activities Auth: VOCO 32D Sig Bn Tvl data: trans WB at no expense to the govt. Sp instr: None FOR THE COMMANDER:

<u>4 August 1967</u>: DD FORM 31 REQUEST AND AUTHORITY FOR LEAVE, dtd 4 Aug 67 MERCURE, MAURICE F. W22XXXXX WO1 Co A (Comd Opns), 32D Signal BN APO 09757 TYPE OF LEAVE OTHER (Specify) pass NO. OF DAYS 3 DATE FROM 8 Aug 67. DATE TO (inclusive) 10 Aug 67 LEAVE ADDRESS Frankfurt SIGNATURE Maurice F. Mercure DATE APPROVED 7 Aug 67 NAME, GRADE & TITLE OF APPROVING AUTHORITY JOSEPH E HAVILAND 1LT, SigC, Adjutant SIGNATURE OF APPROVING AUTHORITY Joseph E. Haviland.

<u>7 August 1967</u>: UNCLASSIFIED ROUTINE MSG TO COTANUS DIST FRANKFURT GER CMDR DOW AFB, BANGOR, MAINE UNCLAS AFZFR-SV-M 8-32 FOR TRA NCO. SUBJ: REQ STATUS FINANCIAL ACCOUNTABILITY W1 MAURICE MERCURE W22XXXXX. REQ STATUS OF FINANCIAL ACCOUNTABILITY HHG PPTY WO1 MAURICE F. MERCURE W22XXXXX, STORED AT FOX AND GINN WHSE, BRUNSWICK, ME. MBR CHANGED SERVICES FROM MSG E-7 AIR FORCE TO WO1 US ARMY. PPTY ORIGINALLY P/U 2 AUG 65 AND STORED UNDER SVC ORDER NO. (17-601) 66-27 BASIC AGREEMENT DSA 41111-31, LOT NO 603. REQ MSG CERTIFYING FINANCIAL RESPONSIBILITY HAS BEEN TRANSFERRED FROM THE USAF TO THE US ARMY.

<u>8 August 1967</u>: We were granted a three (3) day pass, so we could take it easy for a few days and get some rest. It was a nice quiet three days and we rested up.

<u>11 August 1967</u>: UNCLASSIFIED ROUTINE MSG FR 397BW DOW AFB ME TO TANUS DIST FRANKFURT GERMANY BT UNCLAS TSTM 17339 AUG 67. FOR TM. YOUR AEZFR-SV-M 8-32 7 AUG 67. FINANCIAL RESPONSIBILITY PPTY W1 MAURICE MERCURE, W22XXXXX HAS BEEN CHANGED FROM AIR FORCE TO ARMY. SUPPLEMENTAL SERVICE ORDER TO FOLLOW. BT

<u>12 August 1967</u>: SPECIAL ORDERS NUMBER 167 HEADQUARTERS 32D SIGNAL BATTALION APO 09757 dtd 12 August 1967 EXTRACT Paragraph 4 TC 253 Fol DY ASG/REL announced this sta. NTI McGUIRE JOHN S OF10XXXX 1Lt 02 Co A (Comd Opns) 32D Sig Bn DAVIS, MERRILL W 05XXXXX 1Lt 02 SigC Co A (Comd Opns) 32D Sig Bn SIMMONDS EARL L W34XXXXX WO1 USA Co A (Comd Opns) 32D Sig Bn MERCURE, MAURICE F W22XXXXX WO1 USA Co A (Comd Opns) 32D Sig Bn Apt to: Crypto Material Courier Eff date: 8 Aug 67 Pd: Indef Purpose: To transport Crypto Material Auth: para 42B (3), AR 380-40 Sp instr: Auth to transport Crypto Material up to and including Top Secret Crypto. Officers will familiarize themselves with AR 380-40, Sec VII before handling Crypto Material. FOR THE COMMANDER:

<u>14 August 1967</u>: ROUTINE UNCLASSIFIED MSG FM 397BW DOW AFB ME TO TANUS DIST FRANKFURT GERMANY BT UNCLAS TSTM 17340 AUG 67 FOR TRANSPORTATION OFFICER. REQUEST COPIES OF ASSIGNMENT ORDERS, YOUR STATION, TO EXTEND NON TEMPORARY STGE PERIOD OF HHGS PPTY OF WO1 MAURICE F MERCURE, W22XXXXX BT.

<u>24 August 1967</u>: Gave a speech to 92 American students and teachers, visiting Frankfurt, Germany, under the sponsorship of the "Seminar Fur Politik," on a Riverboat Restaurant. My speech was on the "Life of an American Soldier in Germany." This was an interesting experience and gave me some much needed exposure to public speaking.

I was requested by Frau Ulla Illing at the "Seminar Fur Politik," Frankfurt, Germany, to speak to the students and teachers from Wilmington, Delaware, U.S.A. A picture of me giving the speech was taken by the U. S. Army Signal Corps Photographic Sections. (*For a copy of this picture, see photograph A50.*)

<u>25 August 1967</u>: Received letter from "Seminar Fur Politik," in English and German, thanking me for giving a speech to a group of 92 American Students and teacher, in Frankfurt, on a riverboat restaurant. (*For a copy of this letter, see attachment B120.*)

<u>2 October 1967</u>: DA FORM 31 REQUEST AND AUTHORITY FOR LEAVE dtd 2 Oct 67 MERCURE, MAURICE WO1 W22XXXXX Co A 32D Sig Bn TYPE OF LEAVE ORDINARY NO. OF DAYS: 7. DATE FROM 5 Oct 67 DATE TO (INCLUSIVE) 11 OCT 67 LEAVE ADDRESS: FRANCE SIGNATURE: Maurice F Mercure HAS BEEN ISSUED CO, Co A JEH DATE EFFECTIVE: 3 OCT 67 NAME, GRADE & TITLE OF APPROVING AUTHORITY: JOSEPH E HAVILAND 1LT SigC, Adjutant SIGNATURE OF APPROVING AUTHORITY Joseph E Haviland.

We had a German Police General, from the Frankfurt District, address the officers and wives of the 32D Signal Battalion. It was an interesting and informative talk on Police Operations and the crime in the area. The photographic section of the Battalion took a picture of the occasion. (*For a copy of this picture, see photograph A51.*)

<u>3 October 1967</u>: SPECIAL ORDERS NUMBER 205 HEADQUARTERS 32D SIGNAL BATTALION APO 09757 dtd 3 October 1967 EXTRACT Paragraph 5. TC 372. Fol orders RESCINDED. SMO: SO 135 para 11, this HQ CS dtd 3 July 67 Per to: Add dy of MERCURE, MAURICE F W22XXXXX WO1 USAR SigC Co A 32d Sig Bn as Custodian of NCO-EM Open Messes ECN-1837 FOR THE COMMANDER:

<u>3 October 1967</u>: Relieved of Custodial Duties of the NCO-EM Clubs, now that they were making money. This was a very interesting and productive period, bringing the NCO-EM Open Messes back into paying for themselves and showing a profit. The Battalion Commander, Lt Col Dale Hoagland, and the Battalion Sergeant Major were very happy and pleased with what I had accomplished in the ninety days I was custodian. The policies and procedures I had put into place were written up for all the future custodians to comply with. I was glad when I was relieved of the duties of custodian of the NCO-EM Open Messes as it was a time-consuming job, especially being on call at night and also working nights as required by regulations. Peg & I could get back to doing things at a leisurely pace. We were able to get out and do the things we wanted and liked to do, such as going to the cinema (movies), going for rides through the countryside, eating out, etc., and not worrying about being called back to the clubs to take care of problems.

<u>5 October 1967</u>: We sent my mother tickets to come to Frankfurt, Germany, so we could take her to France where she was born (to see her hometown and house she was born in and lived in before coming to the USA). Our drive to France was very nice and enjoyable. With a little luck and perseverance (and the fact that my mother spoke fluent French), we managed to find the house. Her relatives welcomed us with open arms. After many hugs and kisses all around, we settled down to making friends with each other. My mother found that the toilets were still up the garden path, near a pig sty. My mother's relatives were very pleased to see her and meet Peg & me. They made us very welcome and were very good to us. We enjoyed our visit with them. They gave us something to eat and drink. They also informed my mother that she had a cousin in the next town. One of my mother's relatives was the Mayor of the town. He informed my mother that the town's records had been destroyed by fire, during the World War II German occupation. He also informed us that he had a flush toilet in his house. When we left my mother's relatives' house, the Mayor took us to his house to use the facilities. However, no matter how the ladies tried, they could not get the toilet seat to stay up. They would not use the toilet because of this and they did not want to sit on the toilet seat. They decided not to use the facilities. It seems that they were destined to use the great outdoors. On our way to the next town to see my mother's cousin, we found a deserted area to stop, where we could go to the toilet. I stopped the car and we got out in the total darkness to relieve ourselves. My mother, because of her dislocated hip, leaned on the rear of the car to support herself. When she did, the car started rolling forward. So, holding up my trousers with one hand, I chased after the car to stop it. It seems that I had neglected to set the emergency brake and had left the car in neutral. I caught up with the car and stopped it and applied the emergency brake. My poor mother fell over when the car started rolling. We helped her up and then we all finished relieving ourselves. We got back into the car and started on our way, when the ladies said they were cold; so I turned on the heater. In a little while, we detected a strong odor. Apparently my mother had fallen onto some of her stool. We managed to clean it off of her coat and proceeded on our way. We all had a good laugh about the incident.

We continued on to the next town, to see my mother's other cousins. Upon entering the town, we decided to seek directions. The very first person (a lady) we stopped to ask directions, said in French, "C'est Moi." ("It's me.") and got all excited. She took us to her house where we met her husband. They made us welcome, gave us something to eat and drink and gave us cigars. We had a long talk about things in general and the United States. When it came time to leave, my mother's cousin directed us to a relative who had a hotel. She gave us a note for him from her. We spent the night in the hotel, but did not get much sleep. The reason for this was my mother complained about her bed and wanted to change. So, Peg gave her bed to my mother. She didn't like that one either and wanted to change again. I gave her my bed, which she didn't like either. So she went back to her original bed. Another reason was the ladies had to go up the hallway to the toilet by themselves. As they were afraid of the dark, they would not go by themselves. They would also not stay in the room by themselves; so, I had to take them down the hall and wait outside for them. I was up and down all night long.

We had a wonderful breakfast of French coffee, cheese and crescent rolls. After breakfast, we proceeded to drive back to Frankfurt, Germany.

12 October 1967: SPECIAL ORDERS NUMBER 213 HEADQUARTERS 32D SIGNAL BATTALION APO 09757 dtd 12 October 1967 EXTRACT Paragraph 5. TC 350. Fol indiv this sta APPOINTED. MERCURE, MAURICE W22XXXXX WO1 USAR Co A (Comd Opns) 32d Sig Bn Apt to: Add dy as auditor of the Off Club Flower and Cup Fund Eff Date: 12 Oct 67 Purpose: To audit the Flower and Cup Fund of the Officers Club Auth: VOCO 32d Sig Bn Pd: Indef Sp Instr: NA FOR THE COMMANDER:

On the first floor of our building, there lived a German family (a Civil Servant), who had a little boy. When my mother was visiting us (she had a hard time getting up the stairs to our apartment because of a dislocated hip she had since birth. The little boy called her lazy because she did not like climbing up the stairs. We did our best to explain to him about her condition but to no avail. So we let it go at that.

On the second floor (under our apartment) lived a Warrant Officer and his family. He was a helicopter pilot. His son was a holy terror. One day while his mother was out on the balcony talking to neighbors (and he had just been disciplined by his mother), he locked her out on the balcony. He then proceeded to take her handbag, some money, and the keys to the apartment's front door. He then locked the front door with the keys in the lock on the inside of the door. As he was leaving the building, he called up to his mother and told her what he had done. Then he asked her what she was going to do about it, laughed and ran off. The neighbors called his father and told him what his son had done. The father came home, climbed up the balcony, broke a window pane in the balcony door, and got into the apartment. He was then able to unlock the front door. His was furious with his son, needless to say. When he caught up with him, he gave him a good hiding.

Lt. Col. Hoagland, Battalion Commander, used to assign each new 2ⁿᵈ Lt. to a Warrant Officer, for training purposes. The Lieutenant was instructed that he would do what ever the WO told him to do, until the Colonel was sure and satisfied that he was trained and could operate on his own. The Lieutenant did not like this, but did as the Battalion Commander ordered him to do. One Lieutenant asked me why I made more money then he. I told him that he got paid for what he did and I got paid for what I knew.

16 October 1967: C E R T I F I C A T E dtd 16 October 1967. This is to certify that WO1 Mercure, Maurice F. W22XXXXX) 15-XX-XXXX will return to CONUS or another overseas assignment on 31 August 1968. ROBERT C JACKSON WO1, USA, Custodian of Personnel Records.

4 November 1967: WO1 Maurice F. Mercure W22XXXXX Co A, 32d Signal Battalion Corps APO New York 09757 dtd 4 November 1967 Traffic Management Office 397th Bomb Wing (H) (SAC) Dow AFB, Maine 04401. ATTN Transportation Officer Dear Sir: Enclosed please find nine (9) copies of my orders assigning me to the 32d Sig Bn (Corps) APO New York 09757, also a statement of my DEROS. This is submitted in accordance with your message UNLLAS TSTM 17340 AUG 67. If there is anything else you need please let me know. Thank you very much for your cooperation in this matter. MAURICE F. MERCURE WO W1 USAR Incls: 1. 9 Copies of SO NO 209. 2. 32 Copies of statement of DEROS.

23 November 1967: We spent Thanksgiving Day dining with the troops in the Consolidated Mess of the 32d Signal Battalion, Frankfurt/Hoechst, Germany. We had a lovely meal with the Officers, their wives, and enlisted men of the 32d Signal Battalion. As usual the cooks (mess stewards) prepared and served an excellent meal.

Everyone enjoyed themselves and thanked "God" for our bountiful feast. (*For a copy of the menu, see attachment B121.*)

24 November 1967: DA FORM 31 REQUEST AND AUTHORITY FOR LEAVE dtd 24 November 1967. MERCURE, MAURICE F. WO1 W22XXXXX ORGANIZATION AND STATION Co A, 32d Signal Bn APO 09757 TYPE OF LEAVE ORDINARY NO OF DAYS 9 DATE FROM 20 Dec 1967 DATE TO (Inclusive) 28 Dec 67 I HAVE SUFFICIENT LEAVE ACCRUED TO COVER THIS ABSENCE LEAVE ADDRESS Fm—Hoechst, Germany London, England SIGNATURE Maurice F. Mercure DATE APPROVED 20 Nov 67 NAME, GRADE & TITLE OF APPROVING AUTHORITY DAVID T. KUHN 2LT., SigC, Asst Adjutant SIGNATURE David T. Kuhn

December 1967: The Battalion used to go on maneuvers once a year in northern Germany, near the Fulda Gap. I was assigned as Communications (Crypto Security) Officer for the rear area echelon. It was my responsibility to set up the Communications Center, and see that it was in working order (operational), as soon as we got to our designated area. I was accompanied by 2nd Lt. John Bell (who outranked me and was technically in charge of the Communications Center.) However, Lt. Col. Hoagland, Battalion Commander, had assigned 2nd Lt. Bell to me, so I could teach him the ropes. He had been instructed by the Battalion Commander to listen and observe so that on future maneuvers he could set up and run the Communications Center. But all he did was read comic books and/or just sit on his ass and not pay attention. When the Colonel called me into his office for a report on how Lt. Bell was doing, I said he was doing as the Colonel told him to do. Colonel Hoagland said, "Tell me the truth, as I have heard stories that I do not like." So, I told him the truth—that he just sat on his ass reading comic books. This made the Colonel very mad, and he stated the very next time we go out in the field, let him set up the Communications Center. So, the next time we went into the field, I instructed the NCOIC of the Communications Center that he was to take his orders from Lt. Bell. The Colonel had told Lt. Bell that he was now in charge, and he was responsible for the setting up and operation of the Communications Center. Consequently, the Communications Center was not set up and everything was in an uproar. The Battalion Commander got through to me on the radio-telephone and told me to take charge and bring the center on line. He had also called the Captain in charge of the area, and told him to relieve Lt. Bell. When we returned to the Kasserne, Lt. Col Hoagland called 2nd Lt. Bell into his office and told him that he would never make First Lieutenant (1st Lt.), as long as he (Col. Hoagland) was the Battalion Commander.

Every year in the winter time, we used to go on maneuvers to Northern Germany, in the Fulda Gap area. The site we went to was always covered in snow. I had the NCOIC of the Communications Center set up the men's tents first, then the Communications Center, and not to set up my tent, as I would spend the night in the Crypto van. It was so cold there that you had to break the ice on the water to shave. The field toilets (slit trench latrines) were so cold, that you had a hard time going. You always had a cold wind blowing up your bottom. So, you got in and out as soon as possible. The Captain in charge told my wife that I constantly complained about the weather and how cold it was. You can see that I did not like going to Northern Germany on maneuvers in the winter time. We used to drive to the Fulda Gap area with our windshields down, making it very cold. I used to like going on maneuvers when the weather was nice.

20 December 1967: We were granted a nine-day Ordinary Leave to visit London, England, so we could spend Christmas with Peg's mother and her sister, Joan.

20 December 1967: We drove from Frankfurt, Germany to Ostend, Belgium.

20 December 1967: Arriving at Ostend, Belgium, we went to the car ferry terminal, and boarded the ferry boat to Dover, England. We left Ostend, Belgium for Dover, England.

20 December 1967: We arrived at Dover, England Ferry Terminal and then drove to Hayes, Middlesex.

We had an enjoyable and lovely Christmas with Peg's family.

28 December 1967: We drove to Dover, England, where we took a ferry boat to Ostend, Belgium.

<u>28 December 1967</u>: Arriving at Ostend, Belgium, we drove to Frankfurt, Germany.

<u>29 December 1967</u>: We arrived in Frankfurt and drove to our apartment.

<u>24 January 1968</u>: LETTER ORDER NO DEPARTMENT OF THE ARMY HEADQUARTERS, US ARMY GENERAL HOSPITAL, FRANKFURT APO 09757 dtd 24 Jan 68 SUBJECT TRAVEL AUTHORIZATION TO: MERCURE, MAURICE F., WO1, W22XXXXX, Co A 32d Sig Bn, APO 09757 1. You are auth to tvl from, US Army General Hospital, Frankfurt, APO 09757, US FORCES, W/P o/a 27 Jan 68 to, US AGH LANDSTUHL, GERMANY, and rtn to US Army General Hospital, Frankfurt, as deemed necessary. 2. TDN. Military and/or commercial rail authorized. TBMAA. Trans chargeable to 2182020 06 904 P2460 S99999. TPA is authorized. Travel in fatigue or field uniform is authorized. 3. Authority: USAREUR Reg 40-353. 4. Date of disposition from this hospital is 27 Jan 68. FOR THE COMMANDER:

<u>26 January 1968</u>: LETTER ORDER NO. DEPARTMENT OF THE ARMY HEADQUARTERS, US ARMY GENERAL HOSPITAL. FRANKFURT APO 09757 SUBJECT: TRAVEL AUTHORIZATION TO: MERCURE, MAURICE F., WO1, W22XXXXX, CO A 32 SIG BN, APO 09757. 1. You are auth to tvl from US Army General Hospital, Frankfurt, APO 09757, US Forces, W/P ON/A <u>27 Jan 68</u> to <u>USAGH, Landstuhl</u>, and rtn to US Army General Hospital, Frankfurt as deemed necessary. 2. TDN Military and/or commercial rail authorized. TBMAA. Trans chargeable to 2182020 06 904 P2460 S9999. TPA is authorized. Travel in fatigue or field uniform is authorized. 3. AUTHORITY: USAREUR Reg 40-353. 4. Date of Disposition from this hospital is <u>27 Jan 68</u>. FOR THE COMMANDER NORMAN G. WALLACE, MAJ, MSC, ASST ADJUTANT.

<u>27 January 1968</u>: AE FORM 3099 CERTIFICATE OF HOSPITALIZATION (USAREUR CIR 40-340) dtd 27 January 1968 TO: MERCURE, MAURICE F. WO1 PATIENT'S IDENTIFICATION: 269370 MERCURE, MAURICE F. WO1 M 39 CAU USA P 21-0 1130 27 Jan 68 FROM 97TH General Hospital, APO 09757 DATE OF DISPOSITION 27 Jan 1968. I certify that the individual named on line one of the identification section above was admitted to this hospital on date indicated on

line four of the same section and was released from the hospital on the date indicated under the "Date of Disposition." TYPED NAME, GRADE, AND TITLE: NORMAN G. WALLACE MAJOR, MSC, Asst Registrant SIGNATURE: Norman G. Wallace.

27 January 1968: PATIENT EVACUATION MANIFEST FRANKFURT GERMANY dtd 27 Jan 68 MERCURE, MAURICE F., WO1, W22XXXXX Age-39 Wt-165 Med Class 11-B-E COMMANDING OFFICER Co A 32d Sig Bn, APO 09757 MERCURE, Margaret Age 38 Wt-120 NMA TO MERCURE, Maurice F. Commanding Officer Co A 32d Sig BN, APO 09757 USAFH FRANKFURT, GERMANY USAGH LANDSTUHL, GERMANY HOSPITAL TRAIN ROBERT C. KELLEY LTC, MSC Ass't Adjutant.

27 January 1968: I was taken by Medical Evacuation Train to US ARMY General Hospital, Landstuhl, Germany, from US ARMY General Hospital, Frankfurt, Germany. Peg was allowed to accompany me on the trip as a passenger on the Medical Evacuation Train. We had the whole train to ourselves. The train had just come from Landstuhl with a load of military patients to be airlifted to the United States. At US ARMY General Hospital, Landstuhl, Germany, I had orthopedic surgery—a lumbar laminectomy. A disc was removed from my spine.

We were very lucky, as they put Peg up in the Hospital Guest House for the entire time I stayed in the hospital.

I was very lucky that my Commanding Officer, Lt. Col. Hoagland, flew down from Frankfurt, to the US ARMY General Hospital, Landstuhl, to pin my new bars on me, because I was promoted to CWO 2, by SO No 25, DA HQS V CORPS APO 09757. He didn't have to do this as people in the hospital could be exempt from promotion until released from the hospital in a recovered condition. It was a Command Decision on his part, that he made. It was a gesture that I shall never forget.

When I was discharged from the hospital on convalescent leave, Lt. Col. Hoagland sent his personal staff car to the hospital to take Peg and me home. We gave a fellow patient a lift to Frankfurt where he had to arrange further transportation to his duty station. The Commander's driver took Peg to the Commissary so she could get groceries for us.

<u>27 January 1968</u>: DA FORM 8-275-2 CLINICAL RECORD COVER SHEET. (For Addressograph) (AR 40-400) (AR 40-2 for preparation of admitting Plate) dtd 27 Jan 68. (*For a copy of this form, see attachment B122.*)

<u>1 February 1968</u>: SPECIAL ORDERS NUMBER 25 DEPARTMENT OF THE ARMY HEADQUARTERS V CORPS APO 09079, dtd 1 February 1968. EXTRACT Paragraph 2. TC 303. By dir of SA fol WO PRM in AUS UP 10 USC 3449. Comdr will ntfy indiv. MERCURE, MAURICE F. W22XXXXX (015-XX-XXXX) SC Co A 32d Sig Bn APO 09757 WEINUM, CHARLES W31XXXXX (SSAN) 572-XX-XXXX AVN 350ᵗʰ Avn Co, 18ᵗʰ Avn Bn APO 09165 Gr (Fr-60): WO1 to CW2 DOR: 1 Feb 68 FOR THE COMMANDER:

<u>8 February 1968</u>: DA FORM 31 REQUEST AND AUTHORITY FOR LEAVE (AR 630-5) dtd 8 Feb 68 Mercure, Maurice WO2 W22XXXXX Atch to: MED US AGH LANDSTUHL APO 09180 TYPE OF LEAVE: X OTHER: (Specify) Conv lv to duty NO. OF DAYS: 30 DATE: FROM 0800 Hrs 9 Feb 68 DATE TO: (Inclusive) 0800 Hrs 9 Mar 68 LEAVE ADDRESS: Hoechst/Frankfurt SIGNATURE: Maurice F. Mercure IN COMP WITH PARA 18b USAREUR 40-3, INDIV WILL REPT TO LOCAL MEDICAL TREATMENT FACILITY FOR A MEDICAL EVALUATION FOR A RETURN TO DUTY STATUS. CONV LV IS NOT CHARGEABLE TO ACCRUED LV. THERE IS NO DAY OF GRACE ON CONV LV. DATE APPROVED: 8 Feb 68 NAME, GRADE & TITLE OF APPROVING AUTHORITY: TERRAL L. RODMAN, 1LT MSC, Commanding SIGNATURE: Terral L. Rodman.

<u>9 February 1968</u>: AE FORM 3099 CERTIFICATE OF HOSPITALIZATION (USAREUR Cir 40-340) MERCURE, MAURICE F. WO1 PATIENT'S IDENTIFICATION: 180633 MERCURE, MAURICE F. WO1 M 39 CAU USA P 21-3 1745 27 JAN 68 2D GENERAL HOSPITAL, APO 09180 DATE OF DISPOSITION: 9 FEB 68 TYPED NAME, GRADE, AND TITLE: TERRAL L. RODMAN, 1LT, MSC SIGNATURE: Terral L. Rodman.

<u>9 February 1968</u>: Granted a 30-day Convalescence Leave after surgery by MED USAGH, LANDSTUHL, GERMANY. We spent 30 days recuperating and resting.

We went to Garmish Recreation Center for a week and really relaxed. We went bike riding and to the movies, etc. I returned to duty when convalescence leave was up.

February 1968: I received a get-well card from the Officers of the 32d Signal Battalion. (*For a copy of this card, see attachment B123.*)

25 February 1968: LETTER AETVS1 DEPARTMENT OF THE ARMY HEADQUARTERS V CORPS APO 09079 Office of the Signal Officer TO: CW2 Maurice F. Mercure, Company A, 32d Signal Battalion APO 09757. Promotion congratulations and good health. (*For a copy of this letter, see attachment B124.*)

10 April 1968: COURT-MARTIAL APPOINTING ORDER NUMBER 11 DEPARTMENT OF THE ARMY HEADQUARTERS, 32D SIGNAL BATTALION APO 09757 dtd 10 April 1968. Paragraph 4. A special court-martial is hereby ordered to convene at Headquarters 32D Signal Battalion at 0900 hours, 17 April 1968 or as soon thereafter as practicable for trial of such persons that may be properly brought before it. The court will be constituted as follows: MEMBERS: MAJ LEMROY L. SAUNDERS 01 088XXX SigC HHC 32D Sig Bn; MAJ FRANK J. THEAMAN, JR. 01XXXXXX SigC HHC 32D Signal Bn; CPT FRANK M. PERRIN 097XXX Inf HHC Sig Bn; 1LT LEONARD C. GOBEIL 05XXXXXX SigC 32D Sig Bn; 1LT JON C. HASLEY 05XXXXXX SigC Co A 32D Sig Bn; 1LT WILLIAM T. KONDIK 05XXXXXX SigC Co B 32D Sig Bn; CW2 MAURICE F. MERCURE W22XXXXX USA Co A 32D Sig Bn COUNSEL; 1LT JACKSON E. SULLIVAN 05XXXXXX SigC Co B 32D Sig Bn TRIAL COUNSEL, not a lawyer in the sense of Article 27; 2LT GERARD P. WARING 05XXXXXX SigC Co A 32D Sig Bn ASST TRIAL COUNSEL, not a lawyer in the sense of Article 27. 1LT ROBERT S. CRANEY, JR 05XXXXXX SigC Co A 32D Sig Bn DEFENSE COUNSEL, not a lawyer in the sense of Article 27. 2LT KENT W. STERLING 05XXXXXX SigC HHC 32D Sig Bn ASST DEFENSE COUNSEL, not a lawyer in the sense of Article 27. BY ORDER OF LIEUTENANT COLONEL HOAGLAND:

12 April 1968: COURT-MARTIAL APPOINTMENT ORDER NUMBER 12 DEPARTMENT OF THE ARMY HEADQUARTERS, 32D SIGNAL BATTALION

APO 09757 dtd 12 April 1968. A special court-martial is hereby ordered to convene at Headquarters 32D Signal Battalion at 0900 hours, 22 April 1968 or as soon thereafter as practicable for trial of such persons that may be properly brought before it. The court will be constituted as follows: MEMBERS: MAJ LEMROY L. SAUNDERS 01XXXXXX SigC HHC 32D Sig Bn; MAJ FRANK J. THEAMAN, JR. 01XXXXXX SigC HHC 32D Sig Bn; CPT FRANK M. PERRIN 09XXXX Inf HHC 32D Sig Bn; 1LT DONALD E. JOSEPHS 05XXXXXX SigC HHC 32D Sig Bn; 1LT LEONARD C. GOBEIL 05XXXXXX SigC HHC 32D Sig Bn; 1LT JON C. HASLEY 05XXXXXX SigC Co A 32D Sig Bn; CW2 MAURICE F. MERCURE W22XXXXX USA Co A 32D Sig Bn COUNSEL; 1LT WILLIAM T. KONDIK 05XXXXXX SigC Co B 32D Sig Bn TRIAL COUNSEL, not a lawyer in the sense of Article 27. 2 LT LEE F. WOODWARD 05XXXXXX SigC HHC 32D Sig Bn ASST TRIAL COUNSEL, not a lawyer in the sense of article 27. 1LT WILSON S. GRAY 05XXXXXX SigC HHC 32D Sig Bn DEFENSE COUNCIL, not a lawyer in the sense of article 27. 1LT FRANK G. STUMP III 05XXXXXX SigC Co B 32D Sig Bn ASST DEFENSE COUNSEL, not a lawyer in the sense of article 27. BY ORDER OF LIEUTENANT COLONEL HOAGLAND:

17 April 1968: 17 April thru 29 May 1968, I sat on quite a few court-martials during this period—not my cup of tea—but it had to be done, as discipline had to be maintained and people punished for contravention of orders. Discipline is a must in maintaining morale to accomplish the mission.

17 April 1968: COURT-MARTIAL APPOINTING ORDER NUMBER 13 DEPARTMENT OF THE ARMY HEADQUARTERS, 32D SIGNAL BATTALION APO 09757 dtd 17 April 1968. Paragraph. A special court-martial is hereby ordered to convene at Headquarters 32D Signal Battalion at 0900 hours, 24 April 1968 or as soon thereafter as practicable for trial of such persons that may be properly brought before it. The court will be constituted as follows: MEMBERS: MAJ FRANK J. THEAMAN, JR. 01XXXXXX SigC HHC 32D Sig Bn; 1LT DONALD E. JOSEPHS 05XXXXXX SigC HHC 32D Sig Bn; 1LT WALTER C. WAHLEN 05XXXXXX SigC HHC 32D Sig Bn; 1LT LEONARD C. GOBEIL 05XXXXXX SigC HHC 32D Sig Bn; 1 LT JON C. HASLEY 05XXXXXX SigC HHC Co A 32D Sig Bn; CW2 MAURICE F. MERCURE W22XXXXX USA Co A 32D Sig Bn. COUNSEL: 1LT WILLIAM T.

KONDIK 05XXXXXX SigC Co B 32D Sig Bn, TRIAL COUNSEL, not a lawyer in the sense of Article 27. 2LT LEE F. WOODWARD 05XXXXXX SigC Co B 32D Sig Bn, ASST TRIAL COUNSEL, not a lawyer in the sense of article 27. 1LT WILSON S. GRAY 05XXXXXX SigC HHC 32D Sig Bn, DEFENSE COUNSEL, not a lawyer in the sense of article 27; 1LT FRANK G. STUMP III 05XXXXXX SigC Co B 32D Sig Bn, ASST DEFENSE COUNSEL, not a lawyer in the sense of article 27. BY ORDER OF LIEUTENANT COLONEL HOAGLAND:

18 April 1968: COURT-MARTIAL APPOINTMENT ORDER NUMBER 14 DEPARTMENT OF THE ARMY HEADQUARTERS, 32D SIGNAL BATTALION APO 09757 dtd 18 April 1968. Paragraph. A special court-martial is hereby ordered to convene at Headquarters 32D Signal Battalion at 0900 hours, 29 April 1968 or as soon thereafter as practicable for trial of such persons that may be properly brought before it. The court will be constituted as follows: MEMBERS: MAJ LEMROY L. SAUNDERS 01XXXXXX SigC HHC 32D Sig Bn; 1LT WALTER C. WAHLEN 05XXXXXX SigC HHC 32D Sig Bn; 1LT LOUIS P. KIERNAN 05XXXXXX SigC Co B 32D Sig Bn; 1LT DAVID C. JOHNSON 05XXXXXX SigC Co A 32D Sig Bn; 2LT PAUL M. SNOW 05XXXXXX SigC Co A 32D Sig Bn; CW2 FRANK A. REGALADO W32XXXXXX USA HHC 32D Sig Bn; COUNSEL: 1LT JACKSON E. SULLIVAN 05XXXXXX SigC Co B 32D Sig Bn, TRIAL COUNSEL, not a lawyer in the sense of Article 27. 2LT GERARD P. WARING 05XXXXXX SigC Co A 32D Sig Bn, ASST TRIAL COUNSEL, not a lawyer in the sense of Article 27. 1LT ROBERT S. CRANEY JR. 05XXXXXX SigC Co A 32D Sig Bn, DEFENSE COUNSEL, not a lawyer in the sense of Article 27. 2LT KENT W. STERLING 05XXXXXX SigC HHC 32D Sig Bn, ASST DEFENSE COUNSEL, not a lawyer in the sense of Article 27. BY ORDER OF LIEUTENANT COLONEL HOAGLAND:

18 April 1968: SPECIAL ORDERS NUMBER 83 DEPARTMENT OF THE ARMY HEADQUARTERS 32D SIGNAL BATTALION APO 09757 dtd 18 April 1968. Paragraph 1. TC 350. Fol indiv this sta APPOINTED. MERCURE, MAURICE F. W22XXXXX CW2 USA 721A Co A 32d Sig Bn APO 09757 APT TO: Inventory Off EFF DATE: 23 Apr 68 PD: Approx 1 day PURPOSE: To perform semi-annual inventory of McNair Theater #611 AUTH: USAREUR Reg 28-125 (Par 21b(1) SP INSTR:

Audit will be conducted prior to 25 Apr 68. Off will contact 1Lt Gray immediately upon completion of inventory as to the results. FOR THE COMMANDER:

I felt sorry for the Theatre (Cinema) manager who was accused by a young girl of molesting her. He was falsely accused by the young girl, because he would not let her in the Cinema (Theatre) free. He was cleared in that incident, but the stigma of the accusation never went away. It really ruined his chances for promotion and his career.

25 April 1968: LETTER, SUBJECT: Administrative leave FM Maurice F. Mercure W22XXXXX CW2, USA Co A, 32D Signal Bn APO 09757 TO: Commanding Officer 32D Signal Battalion APO 09757 dtd 25 Apr 68. Request administrative leave from 2 May 68 to 4 May 68. Purpose of this leave is to attend Scouting Annual Recognition Conference. MAURICE F. MERCURE W22XXXXX CW2, USA 1st Ind. TO: CW2 Maurice F. Mercure W22XXXXX Co A, 32D Sig Bn FROM: Co, 32D Sig Bn dtd 25 Apr 68 CMT #2 Recommend approval. FOR THE COMMANDER:

25 April 1968: COURT-MARTIAL APPOINTING ORDER NUMBER 16 DEPARTMENT OF THE ARMY HEADQUARTERS, 32D SIGNAL BATTALION APO 09757 dtd 25 April 1968 Paragraph 1. Court-Martial Appointing Order Number 14, this headquarters, dated 18 April 1968, is amended as follows: MEMBER DELETED: 1LT DAVID C. JOHNSON 05XXXXXX SigC Co A 32D Sig Bn. MEMBER ADDED: CW2 MAURICE F. MERCURE W22XXXXX USA Co A 32D Sig Bn. COUNSEL DELETED: 2LT GERARD P. WARING 05XXXXXX SigC Co A 32D Sig Bn. ASST TRIAL COUNSEL, not a lawyer in the sense of Article 27. 2LT KENT W. STERLING 05XXXXXX SigC HHC 32D Sig Bn ASST DEFENSE COUNSEL, not a lawyer in the sense of Article 27. COUNSEL ADDED: 2LT LEE P. WOODWARD 05XXXXXX SigC Co B 32D Sig Bn ASST TRIAL COUNSEL, not a lawyer in the sense of Article 27. 2LT JOHN M. KOZAK 05XXXXXX SigC Co A 32D Sig Bn ASST DEFENSE COUNSEL, not a lawyer in the sense of Article 27. BY ORDER OF LIEUTENANT COLONEL HOAGLAND:

26 April 1968: LETTER ORDER NUMBER 151 DEPARTMENT OF THE ARMY HEADQUARTERS 32D SIGNAL BATTALION APO 09757 dtd 26 April 1968

SUBJECT: Administrative Absence TO: Indiv indic Paragraph. C 346. ADMIN ABSENCE not chg as lv auth as indic. Upon compl will rtn proper unit/sta. MERCURE, MAURICE W22XXXXX (015-XX-XXXX) CW2 USA 721A Co A Eff Date: o/a 2 May 68 Pd: Approx three (3) days Purpose: To attend Scouting Annual Recognition Conference Auth to visit: Garmish Recreation Area. Auth: VOCO 32D Sig Bn Sp instr: NA FOR THE COMMANDER:

27 April 1968: COURT-MARTIAL APPOINTING ORDER NUMBER 17 DEPARTMENT OF THE ARMY HEADQUARTERS, 32D SIGNAL BATTALION 09757 dtd 27 April 68 Paragraph. Court-Martial Appointing Order Number 14, this headquarters, dated 11 April 1968 is amended as follows: MEMBER DELETED: MAJ LEMROY L. SAUNDERS 088XXX SigC HHC 32D Sig Bn; 1LT LOUIS P. KIERNAN 05XXXXXX SigC Co B 32D Sig Bn MEMBER ADDED: 1LT MERRILL W. DAVIS 05XXXXXX SigC HHC 32D Sig Bn; 1LT THOMAS G. DURENBERGER 05XXXXXX SigC HHC 32D Sig Bn BY ORDER OF LIEUTENANT COLONEL HOAGLAND:

1 May 1968: LETTER ORDERS NUMBER 205 DEPARTMENT OF THE ARMY HEADQUARTERS 32D SIGNAL BATTALION APO 09757 dtd 1 May 1968 SUBJECT: Amendment of Orders TO: Indiv indic Paragraph. TC 370. Fol orders AMENDED. SMO: LO 191 TC 346 this HQ CS dtd 26 Apr 68 Pert to: Admin Absence of MERCURE, MAURICE F. W22XXXXX (015-XX-XXXX) CW2, USA 721A As reads: Eff date o/a 2 May 68 Pd: Approx three (3) days IATA: Eff Date: O/A 1 May 68 Pd: Approx five (5) days FOR THE COMMANDER:

2 May 1968: Granted Administrative Absence of five (5) days to attend the Scouting Annual Recognition Conference at Garmish Recreation Area. My wife also attended as she was a Den Mother and I was the Assistant Cub Master. We had a wonderful time at the recognition dinner in the Casa Carioca.

The Casa Carioca, USAFEUR's most famous night club, in the Armed Forces Garmish Recreation area, located in Garmish—Partenkirchen, Germany, was a wonder to behold. The club in the shape (form) of a large horseshoe, with an ice rink in the center, where ice shows were performed. The dining area consisted of three tiers of tables surrounding the ice rink. This arrangement allowed the people entering dinner to observe the ice show without anyone blocking their view. The ice shows performed by Casa Carousel Skaters were out of this world, and never to be forgotten. Peg and I thoroughly enjoyed the meal and the nights's entertainment (performance).

Some of the Ice Shows put on by the Casa Caroca since 1950 up until we went there in 1968:

1. Alice in Wonderland
2. Yippie-Ice-Oh
3. Harum Scarum
4. Let's Do It!
5. Dolls for Sale
6. Stars and Stripes
7. Road to Garmish
8. Wine, Women & Song
9. Bottoms Up
10. Once in a Lifetime
11. Holiday in Garmish
12. Hello Again
13. States on Skates
14. Happy Birthday
15. Home Town—U.S.A.
16. Happy Holiday
17. Wonderful World
18. Hi Neighbor
19. Make a Wish
20. A Night at the Casa
21. Let's Celebrate
22. Go Go Going Places

19 May 1968: Joan (Peg's sister) called to let Peg know that their mother (Mum) was very ill and for her (Peg) to come home. As I could not get any leave at the time, Peg went home by herself. At least she was home with her mother during her illness.

23 May 1968: COURT-MARTIAL APPOINTING ORDER NUMBER 20 DEPARTMENT OF THE ARMY HEADQUARTERS 32D SIGNAL BATTALION APO 09757 dtd 23 May 1968 Paragraph. A special Court-Martial is hereby ordered to convene at headquarters 32D Signal Battalion at 0900 hours, 29 May or as soon there after as practicable for trial of such persons that may be properly brought before it. The court will be constituted as follows: MEMBERS: 1 LT MERRILL W. DAVIS 05XXXXXX SigC HHC 32D Sig Bn; 1LT WALTER C. WAHLEN 05XXXXXX SigC HHC 32D Sig Bn; 1LT THOMAS G. DURENBERGER 05XXXXXX SigC HHC 32D Sig Bn; 2LT ANSON S. RAMSEY OFXXXXXX SigC Co A 32D Sig Bn; CW2 FRANK A. REGALADO W32XXXXX USA HHC 32D Sig Bn; CW2 MAURICE F. MERCURE W22XXXXX USA Co A 32D Sig Bn COUNSEL; 1LT KENT W. STERLING 05XXXXXX SigC HHC 32D Sig Bn TRIAL COUNSEL, not a lawyer in the sense of Article 27. 2LT GERARD P. WARING 05XXXXXX SigC Co A 32D Sig Bn ASST TRIAL COUNSEL, not a lawyer in the sense of Article 27. 1LT LOUIS P. KIERNAN 05XXXXXX SigC Co A 32D Sig Bn DEFENSE COUNSEL, not a lawyer in the sense of Article 27; 2LT ELMER M. CASEY JR. OFXXXXXX SigC Co B 32D Sig Bn ASST DEFENSE COUNSEL, not a lawyer in the sense of Article 27. BY ORDER OF LIEUTENANT COLONEL HOAGLAND:

29 May 1968: Peg called me to tell me that her mother (Mum) had passed away. She had been very ill for days. I was very sorry to hear she had passed away, as I loved her more than my own mother. Mum treated me like I was her own son and had a tendency to spoil me. I will miss her very much.

3 June 1968: SPECIAL ORDERS NUMBER 119 DEPARTMENT OF THE ARMY HEADQUARTERS 32D SIGNAL BATTALION APO 09757 dtd 3 June 1968 Paragraph 1. TC 350. Fol indiv this sta APPOINTED. MERCURE, MAURICE F W22XXXXX CW2 USA 721A Co A 32D Sig Bn Apt to: Inventory Officer Eff date: 3 Jun 68 Pd: Approx 1 day Purpose: To perform a semi-annual inventory of McNair Theatre #611 Auth: USAREUR Reg 28-125 (Para 21b(1)) Sp Instr: Audit will be conducted prior to 8 Jun 68. Off will contact 1Lt Gray immediately upon completion of inventory as to the results. FOR THE COMMANDER:

<u>5 July 1968</u>: LETTER ORDERS NUMBER 318 DEPARTMENT OF THE ARMY HEADQUARTERS 32D SIGNAL BATTALION APO 09757 dtd 5 July 1968. Paragraph. TC 200. Indiv this sta placed on TDY to indic. RPSCTDY. TDN. Acct Class: 2192020 89-1145 P2100-21-213-219-220 S91589 BAA 2110.3000 MERCURE, MAURICE F W22XXXXX (015-XX-XXXX) CW2 Co A TDY to: USARCHEUR, Kimbo Kasserne, Murnau, Germany APO 09172 WP date: o/a 21 Jul 68 Pd: Approx seven (7) days Purpose: To attend USAREUR Crs NR 69-0 (Class #3) Auth: USARCHEUR Man 350-205 Scty Clas: TOP SECRET Crypto Tvl date: Tvl by POV auth Sp instr: Student meets all prerequisites of crs. Indiv will rept to the basement of bldg 120-C btwn the hrs of 0800 hrs and 1700 hrs on rept date indic. Indiv will have in his possession 15 cpys of these orders upon arrival at dest. Within seven (7) days subsequent to completion of TDY, indiv will submit nec reimbursement voucher or a statement that no claim will be submitted to the F&AO. This tvl is exempt from gold flow restrictions in accordance with USAREUR & 7A message SC 15092. FOR THE COMMANDER:

<u>18 July 1968</u>: DA FORM 31 REQUEST AND AUTHORITY FOR LEAVE (AR 630-5) DATE 18 July 1968 NAME, GRADE AND SERVICE NUMBER: MERCURE, MAURICE F. CWO2, W22XXXXX ORGANIZATION AND STATION Co A 32D Signal Battalion, APO 09757 TYPE OF LEAVE: X ORDINARY NO. OF DAYS: 30 DATE FROM: 3 Sep 68-0530 hrs DATE TO: 2 Oct 68-2400 hrs X I HAVE SUFFICIENT LEAVE ACCRUED TO COVER THIS ABSENCE LEAVE ADDRESS: 332 Kings Hill Ave. Middlesex, England SIGNATURE: Maurice F. Mercure REMARKS: CO DJK DATE APPROVED: 18 July 68 NAME, GRADE AND TITLE OF APPROVING AUTHORITY: JOHN S. MCGUIRE CPT, SigC, Adjutant SIGNATURE: John S. McGuire.

<u>30 July 1968</u>: SPECIAL ORDERS NUMBER 161 DEPARTMENT OF THE ARMY HEADQUARTERS 32D SIGNAL BATTALION APO 09757 dtd 30 July 1968 EXTRACT: Paragraph 8. TC 350 Fol indiv this sta APPOINTED. *MERCURE, MAURICE F W22XXXXX (015-XX-XXXX) CW2 USA 721A Co A 32D Sig Bn #COPELAND LELAND R RA17XXXXXX (559-XX-XXXX) SSG E6 Co A 32D Sig Bn Apt to: Add dy as inventory *Off #NCO Eff date: 1 Aug 68 Pd: Approx one (1)

day Purpose: To inventory the Officer Civilian Open Messes, NCO/EM Open Messes, McNair Kasserne, Hoechst, Germany. Auth: HQ 32D Sig Bn Ltr Subj: Monthly Inventory of McNair Off, EM/NCO Club dtd 13 Feb 68. Sp Instr: Indiv will be guided by USAREUR Reg 230-2 FOR THE COMMANDER:

7 August 1968: SPECIAL ORDERS NUMBER 168 DEPARTMENT OF THE ARMY HEADQUARTERS 32D SIGNAL BATTALION APO 09757 dtd 7 August 1968 Paragraph 7. TC 246. Fol rsg dir. WP. TDN. CIC 2 9 1 A 03 MERCURE, MAURICE F W22XXXXX (015-XX-XXXX) CW2 USAR 721A Co A, 32D Sig Bn Rept to: USA JATCO APCE Rhein/Main AFB Frankfurt, Germany Asg to: USARV TRANS DET APO SF 96384 for fur asg to be determined upon arrival in country Rept date: TBA HOR: 43 Newton St, Holyoke, Mass. AMD: TBA Mo OS (curr tour): 37 (N 36) Maj comd/agcy: HQ USAREUR Heidelberg, Germany Lv data: 13 DDALVAHP PCS (MDC): ZX Auth: DA Msg 869521 fr OPXR dtd 24 Jun 68 OBV: 3 Yrs BASD: 5 Oct 46 BPED: 5 Oct 46 EYS: 24 Nov 69 EDCSA: TBA Tvl data: TBA Aloc: OCT-M-195 Scty clnc: Top Secret Crypto Availability date: 30 Oct 68 Arr No OS: Sep 65 Temp adrs: 4505 Ellen Drive, Covina, California DOR: 1 Feb 68 Sp instr: Indiv auth 66 lbs bag allowance and additional 134 lbs excess baggage allowance. You will rept at the time and place indic in PC. Indiv will have complete and proper documentation, be in proper uniform and have only that quantity of bag auth. Indiv will obtain clearance papers seven working days prior to dprt. Indiv is credited with a full overseas tour of duty. Basic plague immunizations are required for all personnel traveling to or thru Vietnam or Thailand but tvl need not be delayed except for first two injections. Personnel will arrive at POE wearing appropriate seasonal uniform and will have in his possession only those items specified in App IV C 19, AR 700-8400-1. The introduction, purchase and possession of privately owned weapons is prohibited in the RVN. Shpmt of HHG, POV, and hold Bag auth. Indiv will clear orderly room and rept to the Pers Sec 24 hrs prior to dprt. Indiv will tvl to OS destination in unacc status. Indiv is directed to proceed to the USA Ret-Rsg Sta at McGuire AFB, NJ. Ft. Hamilton, NY; Charleston. AFB SC; or JFK International Airport, NY depending on POD. You will rept to the USAOSRPLST at Oakland, Calif for onward movement to RVN. Current FAA Regs require carry-baggage be limited to articles which can be stowed under passenger's seat not to exceed 21" X 16" X 8". Sp instr: (Cont) Depn

auth to reside at 332 Kings Hill Ave., Hayes Middlesex, England per CMP 4 DA Form 2496 fr DA, TAGO, Subj: Req for Auth for wife to live in England dtd 30 July 1968. Cncr tvl to England: MERCURE, MARGARET D (W) 4 Jul XX F51XXXX FOR THE COMMANDER:

10 August 1968: SPECIAL ORDERS NUMBER 171 DEPARTMENT OF THE ARMY HEADQUARTERS 32D SIGNAL BATTALION APO 09757 dtd 10 August 1968 Paragraph 3. TC 350. Fol indiv this sta APPOINTED. MERCURE, MAURICE F W22XXXXX CW2 (015-XX-XXXX) (721A) Co A, 32D Sig Bn Apt to: Add dy as Officers Club Custodian Eff date: 10 Aug 68 Pur: NA Auth: VOCO 32D Sig Bn Pd: Indef Sp instr: VICE 1Lt Gray as Officer Club Custodian FOR THE COMMANDER:

10 August 1968: I was appointed as Officers' Club Custodian over 1st Lt Thomas G. Durenberger, who was furious and held it against me.

Being Custodian of the Officers' Club was not half as demanding as Custodian of the NCO/EM Clubs. I had a Sgt. Wilson, who managed the Club, and he did an exceptional job of it. We worked well together as a team. I held this position until my departure for Vietnam.

One night we held a Game Night in the Club. I was running the black jack table and 1st Lt. Durenberger was running the poker table. He was losing money almost as fast as I was making it on the black jack table. I asked him to close it down as he was playing head to head with one person. But he refused to do so, so I spoke to Lt. Col. Hoagland and explained the situation to him. He ordered Lt. Durenberger to close down the poker table. He was absolutely livid and furious with me. He held this against me until I left the battalion. After the poker table was closed, the Club made a lot of money on the black jack table. The Battalion Commander was very pleased with the outcome.

14 August 1968: LETTER, DEPARTMENT OF THE ARMY HEADQUARTERS 32D SIGNAL BATTALION APO 09757 dtd 14 August 1968. TO: CWO Maurice F. Mercure Company "A" 32D Signal Battalion APO 09757 Dear Mr. Mercure: On

the occasion of the anniversary of your birth, 14 August 1968. I wish to extend my congratulations. May the coming years bless you and your family with health, wealth, and success. Yours sincerely DALE N. HOAGLAND LTC, SigC Commander.

31August 1968: DA FORM 10-102 ORGANIZATIONAL CLOTHING AND EQUIPMENT RECORD (AR 735-35) dtd 31 Aug 68. (*For a copy of this form, see attachment B125.*)

3 September 1968: SPECIAL ORDERS NUMBER 188 DEPARTMENT OF THE ARMY HEADQUARTERS Signal Battalion APO 09757 dtd 3 September 1968. Paragraph 7. TC 370. Fol orders AMENDED. SMO: SO #168 para 7 this HQ CS dtd 7 August 1968 Pert to: MERCURE MAURICE F W22XXXXX (015-XX-XXXX) CW2 USAR 721A Co A as reads: Rept date: TBA AMD: TBA EDCSA: TBA Tvl date: TBA IATR: Rept date: NLT 1500 hrs 16 Oct 68. AMD: FRF-WRI-3PU-5500-AZ-10 EDCSA: 27 Oct 68 TVL data: Air Trans to CONUS on flight Z-242 IATA: PC data (for next sta): Rept NLT 2400 hrs, 27 Oct to: Travis AFB, Fairfield, California 94535 for duty in Vietnam FOR THE COMMANDER:

3 September 1968: Granted a 30-Day Ordinary leave to visit 332 Kingshill Avenue, Hayes Middlesex, England. We drove to Ostend, Belgium.

3 September 1968: We arrived at Ostend, Belgium, where we boarded a ferry boat for Dover, England.

4 September 1968: Arriving at Dover, England, we drove to Peg's sister's house, where we spent an enjoyable visit. We all went to Weston-super-Mare and had a great time.

30 September 1968: Our leave was drawing to a close, so we drove to Dover to catch a ferry boat to Ostend, Belgium.

30 September 1968: We arrived at Ostend, Belgium Ferry Terminal and disembarked. We then drove to Frankfurt, Germany, and from there to our quarters in Hoechst, Germany.

<u>1 October 1968</u>: SPECIAL ORDERS NUMBER 211. DEPARTMENT OF THE ARMY HEADQUARTERS 32D Signal Battalion APO 09757 dtd 1 October 1968. Paragraph 9. TC 371. Fol orders REVOKED. SMO: SO # 191 this HQ CS dtd 6 Sep 68. Pert to: Board of Officers SMO: SO # 213 para 5 this HQ CS dtd 12 October 1967 Pert to: MERCURE MAURICE F W22XXXXX WO1 Co A (Comd Opns) 32D Sig Bn FOR THE COMMANDER:

<u>8 October 1968</u>: AETVS-P LETTER ORDERS NUMBER 539 SUBJECT: Administrative Absence DEPARTMENT OF THE ARMY Headquarters 32D Signal Battalion APO 09757 TO: Indiv indic Paragraph. TC 346. ADMIN ABSENCE not chg as lv auth as indic. Upon compl will rtn proper unit/sta. MERCURE MAURICE F W22XXXXX (015-XX-XXXX) CW2 USAR Co A, 32D Sig Bn Eff date: 11 October 1968 Auth to visit Bremerhaven, Germany No days: three (3) Purpose: To take POV to port. Auth: VOCO, 32D Sig Bn Sp instr: NA FOR THE COMMANDER:

<u>11 October 1968</u>: We drove to Bremerhaven, Germany and stayed overnight in the Guest House. The next day we turned our car into the Army Port Authorities for shipment to the USA. After turning our car over to APA, we took a train to Frankfurt.

<u>11 October 1968</u>: Arriving at the Frankfurt Railway Station, we took a taxi to our quarters in Hoechst.

<u>14 October 1968</u>: AE FORM 3086 MEDICAL STATEMENT FOR REDEPLOYMENT TO CONUS (USAREUR Reg 40-355) dtd 14/10/68 TO: WHOM IT MAY CONCERN FROM: Medical Installation) DISPENSARY 117TH ENG BN APO 09757, U.S. ARMY PATIENT'S NAME: MERCURE, MAURICE F. X 1. HAS BEEN INSPECTED AND MEDICALLY CLEARED FOR TRAVEL 4. NO KNOWN COMPLICATION(S) EXIST(S) THAT PRECLUDE TRAVEL BY WATER OR AIR. TYPED NAME AND GRADE OF EXAMINING PHYSICIAN S. M. OLKEN CPT MC SIGNATURE: S. M. Olken.

<u>14 October 1968</u>: AEZFR-H-H LETTER ORDERS DEPARTMENT OF THE ARMY HEADQUARTERS US FORCES SUPPORT DISTRICT HESSHI (PROV) APO 09757

Household Furniture Division. SUBJECT: Termination of Government Quarters TO: Individual concerned Paragraph. TC 333 BUILDING QUARTERS ASG/TERM for indiv and depn indic this sta. MERCURE, MAURICE F. W22XXXXX CW2 USAR Co A, 32d Sig Bn TERM: asg bldg/qtr: 2429-B-6 Hoechst Eff Date: 14 October 1968. FOR THE COMMANDER:

14 October 1968: QUARTERS CLEARANCE RECORD DATE: 14 10 68 NAME OF OCCUPANT: WO-1 MERCURE, M F NEW DUTY STATION: ZI QUARTERS A6: 2429-B-6 Hoechst ACCOUNT NUMBER: 5359 QUARTERS OF THE ABOVE HAVE BEEN CHECKED OUT. LOSS OR DAMAGES CHARGED WERE: $ NONE NAME OF QM OUTCHECKER: Mr. Schepper ACCOUNTABLE PROPERTY BOOK OFFICER: CHESTER M. WAGGONER 1LT. CHIEF, HHF DIVISION OCCUPANT SIGNATURE: Maurice F Mercure GRADE: CW2 SN/AGO NO: W22XXXXX ORGANIZATION CO A 32D SIG BN REMARKS: TELEPHONE BILL PAID MAURICE F MERCURE.

14 October 1968: DD FORM 1482 MATS TRANSPORTATION AUTHORIZATION NUMBER A-1586770 1. GRADE: CW2. 2. NAME (LAST, FIRST, MIDDLE INITIAL): MERCURE, MAURICE F. AND NO OTHERS. 3. AMD FRF-WRI-3PU-5500-AZ-10 4. SERVICE OR PASSPORT NO. W22XXXXX 6. BAGGAGE WEIGHT AUTHORIZED 200 lbs. SHIPPED 7. FISCAL DATA 2192010 01-3311-3313-3317 P1433 S99-999 CIC 2 9 1 A 03 8. ISSUED BY AND DATE: THOMAS G. DURENBERGER 1LT, SigC Adjutant 14 Oct 68 9. REPORT TO (APOE) USA JATCO APOE Rhein/Main a. NLT 1500 16 Oct 68 b. FOR FLIGHT NO. Z-242 c. DESTINATION (APOD) Wrightstown, New Jersey 10. SPECIAL INSTRUCTIONS: Pers and Med rec will acc indiv during tvl. 13 DDALVAHP auth in CONUS and destination is RVN 11. EMERGENCY ADDRESS DATA: Margaret D Mercure 332 Kingshill Ave Hayes, Middlesex, England.

16 October 1968: Lt. Durenberger (adjutant) scheduled me for OD (Officer of the Day) on the night of 16 October 1968, before leaving for the United States. I told him this was unfair, as I was leaving the next morning for the Zone of the Interior, and Peg was leaving at the same time for England. Which meant we would not have time

together before leaving. It would not have been so bad if we were both leaving for the states. He refused to change it.

Peg went to the Battalion Commander's wife, and explained the situation. The colonel's wife spoke to her husband, who got me off OD. Meanwhile, Chaplain Craig was going to get me off the detail if the Battalion Commander did not, so that Peg and I could have the night together before leaving the next morning for our separate destinations.

So, Lt. Durenberger did not get his way, to exercise his dislike for me. He failed to get even in his way of thinking.

16 October 1968: DA FORM 137 (AE) INSTALLATION CLEARANCE RECORD (AR 210-10) undated. (*For a copy of this form, see attachment B126.*)

16 October 1968: DA FORM 200 TRANSMITTAL RECORD (AR 330-10-1 or AR 330-15) dtd 16 Oct 68 TO: Commanding Officer USARV TRANS DET APO SF 93384 FROM: Commander Officer 32d Signal Battalion APO NY 09757 AS OF DATE: 16 Oct 68 DATE OF SHIPMENT: 16 Oct 68 TYPE OF ITEMS: HEALTH, DENTAL, FINANCE, 201 & DA Form 66 records. AUTHORITY FOR SHIPMENT VOCO 32d Sig Bn METHOD OF SHIPMENT: HAND CARRY. REMARKS: OFFICER WILL HAND CARRY ALL PERSONAL RECORDS TYPE NAME, GRADE, BRANCH AND TITLE: ROBERT C. JACKSON, CW2, USA PERS OFF SIGNATURE: Robert Lowe SP5

16 October 1968: AIRLINE PASSENGER TICKET: BAGGAGE CHECK AND MAC BOARDING PASS.

17 October 1968: We said our good-byes, hugs and kisses, then Peg got on her plane and left for London, England. It was a very sad time, as Peg and I would not see each other for a year.

17 October 1968: DD FORM 1580 MILITARY STANDBY AUTHORIZATION FOR COMMERCIAL AIR TRAVEL dtd 17 Oct 68. 1. LAST NAME—FIRST NAME—MI: MERCURE, MAURICE F 2. GRADE: CW2 3. SERVICE NUMBER: W22XXXXX

4. ORGANIZATION AND STATION CO A, 32D SIG BN APO N.Y. 09757 PERIOD OF AUTHORIZATION 5. DATE FROM: 17 Oct 68 6. DATE TO: 27 Oct 68 7. I CERTIFY THAT THE ABOVE NAMED PERSON IS TRAVELING AT HIS OWN EXPENSE DURING THE PERIOD STATED ABOVE ON: (CHECK ONE ONLY) C. AUTHORIZED LEAVE/FURLOUGH/PASS: CHECKED 8. ORGANIZATION: 438th W CTO P 9. STATION: MCGUIRE AFB, NJ 08641 10. CERTIFYING OFFICER'S NAME, GRADE & TITLE: ROBERT B. WINKLER GS-12 C 0XX 11. DATE: 17 Oct 68 12. SIGNATURE: Robert B. Winkler.

17 October 1968: AMERICAN AIRLINES PASSENGER'S COUPON NAME OF PASSENGER: M. F. MERCURE FROM/TO: BOS/LAX CARRIER: AA FARE CALCULATION: $76.00 AIRLINE 001 FORM 11 0 SERIAL NUMBER: 126:630 X10 FROM BOSTON FARE BASIS M CARRIER AA DATE M TIME 10 STATUS S/A TO LOS ANGELES FARE 76.00 TAX TF TOTAL 76.00 FORM OF PAYMENT MAC AM STAMPED 004 AMERICAN 004 AIRLINES Inc. Oct 17, 68 MCGUIRE AFB, NJ.

17 October 1968: I left Rhein-Main Air Base, Frankfurt, Germany, for McGuire Air Force Base, New Jersey, in the early hours of the morning.

17 October 1968: Arrived at McGuire AFB, NJ, October 17, 1968. My copy of SPECIAL ORDERS NUMBER 188, DEPARTMENT OF THE ARMY, Headquarters 32d Signal Battalion, APO 09757, dtd 3 September 1968, was stamped as follows: "ARRIVED & DEPARTED MCGUIRE AFB, NJ, OCT 17, 1968. By USAPERCEN ((14-1386-03) Returnee Reassignment Station, Ft. Hamilton, Bklyn, NY 11252.

17 October 1968: Left McGuire AFB by bus for Willimanset, Massachusetts, to see my family. Before leaving McGuire AFB, I purchased an American Airlines ticket from Boston, Massachusetts to Los Angels, California.

17 October 1968: Arrived at my half-sister's house in Willimanset. I spent an enjoyable time with my mother, half-sister, brother-in-law and their children. (*For a copy of picture of author in uniform, with his mother, nieces and nephew, see photograph A52.*)

<u>21 October 1968</u>: Having spent time with my family, it was time to leave them. I took a bus to Boston International Airport, Logan. Arriving at Logan International Airport, I caught a flight to Los Angeles International Airport. I flew on American Airlines. Upon boarding the flight to Los Angeles, the flight attendant asked me where I was going. I told her that I was on my to Vietnam. She immediately took me from the regular class section to first class telling me that since there was room in first class, I would be more comfortable there. I had a great time talking to the flight attendants, eating good food and having free drinks.

<u>21 October 1968</u>: Arriving at Los Angeles International Airport, I called my brother, Bob, who came and picked me up and took me to his apartment. We spent five wonderful days together. We ate out at good restaurants and visited Hayden Planetarium.

<u>26 October 1968</u>: My brother Bob took me to see his ex-wife, Betty, their children and his old house. Betty was a very nice person; the kids were cute and the house lovely. Betty decided that she and the children would see me off to Oakland by plane. While at the airport, we had something to eat and drink. (*For a picture of the author and Betty & Bob's children, see photograph A53.*)

During that time some "Hell's Angels" motorcycle gang members came into the restaurant. My brother, Bob, made some off-the wall remarks about them, which they overheard. They did not take it kindly and approached our table. They said, "Soldier, where are you going?" I told them that I was on my way to Vietnam. They said, "Keep well and return," but tell your big mouth friend to keep his remarks to himself or else. We were relieved to see them go back to their table. I believe that Bob thought that I could handle them in a fight, which was not true—no way—as I was a Signal Officer, not a Green Beret. I do believe that the Hell's Angels did not do anything, because I was on my way to Vietnam. When it came time to board the aircraft for Oakland, I was relieved.

<u>26 October 1968</u>: Flew to Oakland, California, from Los Angeles. Upon arriving, I took a bus to Travis Air Force Base. I spent the night in the Base Guest House. See statement of charges from Base Billeting Fund, receipt number 147896, dtd 27 Oct 68. The charges were $4.00. (*For a copy of this receipt, see attachment B127.*)

<u>27 October 1968</u>: DD FORM 1482 MAC TRANSPORTATION AUTHORIZATION NUMBER A-6491106, dtd 27 Oct 68. 1. GRADE: CW2 2. NAME (LAST, FIRST, MIDDLE INITIAL): MERCURE, MAURICE AND NO OTHER. 3. AMD SUU HOA 3 PUA 4. SERVICE OR PASSPORT NO. W22XXXXX 6. BAGGAGE WEIGHT AUTHORIZED: 200 SHIPPED 7. FISCAL DATA HQ 32D SIGNAL BATT SO 168 7 AUG 68 PCS MDC ZX 8. ISSUED BY AND DATE: MICHAEL P RILEY 1LT PCLO 27 Oct 68 9. REPORT TO: (APOE): TAFB a. ON (DATE/ TIME): 2200/27 Oct 68 b. FOR FLIGHT NO. T2B3/302 c. DESTINATION (APOD): HOA.

<u>28 October 1968</u>: Left Travis AFB for Kadena Air Base, Okinawa.

<u>29 October 1968</u>: Arrived Kadena Air Base, Okinawa.

<u>29 October 1968</u>: FORM NO OXF 11, OKINAWA REGIONAL EXCHANGE, dtd 29 Oct 68. Bought an AM/FM radio, for use in Vietnam. Paid $25.00 for same.

<u>29 October 1968</u>: Left Kadena Air Base for Bien Hoa Air Base, Vietnam.

CHAPTER 13

30 OCTOBER 1968 - 16 NOVEMBER 1969

VIETNAM—BIEN HOA AIR BASE, LONG BINH BASE, TAN SON NHUT AIR BASE, SAIGON

A. Bangkok, Thailand (R & R)   26 Apr 1969-30 Apr 1969

30 October 1968: Arrived on Bien Hoa Air Base, Vietnam, and after processing, I was bused to Long Binh Base, Vietnam.

30 October 1968: SPECIAL ORDERS NUMBER 304 DEPARTMENT OF THE ARMY HEADQUARTERS, USARV TRANSIENT DETACHMENT APO SAN FRANCISCO 96384 dtd 30 October 1968. EXTRACT Paragraph 147. TC 250. FOL INDIV HAVING BEEN ASG THIS ORG IS FURTHER ASG AS INDIC. PCS MDC N/A. MERCURE, MAURICE F W22XXXXX (015-XX-XXXX) CW2 SC 721A USARV TRANSIENT DET APO 96375 FUR ASG WIZR USA SPT CMD APO 96491 AUTH CG USARV EDCSA 5 11 68 SP INSTR THIS ORDER SUPPLEMENTS BASIC MSG ORDER AND PERSONNEL DATA PERTAINING TO ABOVE NAMED INDIVIDUAL. FOR THE COMMANDER:

30 October 1968: DA FORM 3161 REQUEST FOR ISSUE, dtd 30 October 1968. MERCURE, MAURICE F CW2 W22XXXXX. TO CIF, SUPCOMSGN APO 96491 (AT87FD) NOTE: CO, UNIT OF ASSIGNMENT: POS TO INDIVIDUAL CLOTHING AND EQUIPMENT RECORD. (*For a copy of this form, see attachment B128*).

4 November 1968: SPECIAL ORDERS NUMBER 303 DEPARTMENT OF THE ARMY US ARMY SUPPORT COMMAND SAIGON APO SAN FRANCISCO 96491, dtd 4 November 1968. EXTRACT Paragraph 62. TC 250. Fol indiv having been asg this sta/org are FUR ASG as indic. Rel fr: HQ USASUPCOM, SGN APO 96491 FUR asg: HHC, 29th GS Gp APO 96491 PCS (NDC): NA Auth: VOCG (MAJ KASTENBAUM) EDCSA: 5 Nov 68 SP instr: NA MERCURE, MAURICE F W22XXXXX (015-XX-XXXX) CW2 SC 721A FOR THE COMMANDER:

7 November 1968: SPECIAL ORDERS NUMBER 261 DEPARTMENT OF THE ARMY Headquarters, 29th Support Group APO San Francisco 96491 dtd 7 November 1968 EXTRACT Paragraph 1. TC 253. Fol DY ASG/REL announced this sta. NTI. MERCURE, MAURICE F. W22XXXXX (015-XX-XXXX) CW2 SC HHC, 28th Gen Spt Gp APO 96491 Dy asg: Pdy as Asst Adjutant (MOS 2110) Dy rel: fr: NA Eff date 5 Nov 68 VOCO date cfm FOR THE COMMANDER:

7 November 1968: S T A T E M E N T The residence indicated on FSA certificate (DD FORM 1561) dated 15 Oct 68, in which my dependents are residing, is subject to my management and control; further, I agree to notify my commanding officer promptly if I discontinue maintaining such residence or household while in receipt of Family Separation Allowance. (Member's Signature) Maurice F Mercure (DATE) 7 November 1968 Personnel or Certifying Officer W. G. Smith (DATE) 19 Nov 68.

7 November 1968: When I was assigned as Assistant Adjutant HHC 29th GS Gp one night I had Officer of the Day (OD) duty. I was being shown the ropes and location of all the Guard Posts, by the Adjutant. We were checking to see that the Guards were wide awake and not sleeping. I was sitting in the rear of the jeep, the Adjutant was sitting in the front. The Adjutant got out of the jeep to check a couple of Guard Posts and had me go on to check a Guard Post, and then return for him. I got into the front seat, and just as I got up to sit in the front seat of the jeep, a bullet pierced the rear right wheel well, right where I had just been sitting. It would have hit me in the right buttock and passed through the left buttock. God was with me at the time. I can assure you that it scared the hell out of me.

<u>9 November 1968</u>: LETTER, SUBJECT: Request for Reassignment, HHC 29th GS GP APO SF 96491 dtd 9 November 1968. (*For a copy of this letter, see attachment B129.*)

<u>10 November 1968</u>: One afternoon, I was crossing the Parade Ground, going to the P.X. On the way I met Major Lemroy L. Saunders (who was the Executive Officer of the 32nd Signal Battalion, when I was stationed in Germany.) He asked me how long I had been in country, and what unit I was assigned to. I told him I had only been in country a little over three weeks, and that I was assigned to the HHC, 29th GS GP, as assistant Adjutant. He stated, "What the HELL are you doing there?" as we have a shortage of Crypto Warrant Officers in the 160th Signal Group 1st Signal Brigade. Put in for a request for reassignment, and I will see that you are reassigned immediately. I thanked him for his advice and then we discussed our stay in Germany.

Getting back to my unit, I submitted a request for reassignment to the 160th Signal Group, 1st Signal Brigade.

<u>17 November 1968</u>: SPECIAL ORDERS NUMBER 322 DEPARTMENT OF THE ARMY Headquarters, US Army Support Command, Saigon APO US Forces 96491 dtd 17 November 1968 EXTRACT Paragraph 213. TC 254. RSG dir as indic. NTI. MERCURE, MAURICE F. W22XXXXX (015-XX-XXXX) CW2 SigC 721A HHC, 29th General Support Group APO 96491 Asg to: 160th Signal Group APO 96491 Rept date: 19 Nov 68 EDCSA: 19 Nov 68 Auth: Cmt #5, Request for RSG dtd 13 Nov 68 from CG, USARV Sp instr: None. FOR THE COMMANDER:

<u>17 November 1968</u>: I reported into the 160th Signal Group, and I was informed that the vacancy in their unit had just been filled and that I would have to be reassigned within the 160th Signal Group. I had visions of being assigned to a forward (field combat unit), but to my surprise, I was assigned to the 69th Signal Battalion, Saigon, which was located on Tan Son Nhut Air Base.

<u>18 November 1968</u>: SPECIAL ORDERS NUMBER 314 DEPARTMENT OF THE ARMY 160TH SIGNAL GROUP APO San Francisco 96941, dtd 18 November 1968. EXTRACT Paragraph 7. TC 254. RSG dir as indic this sta. NTI. MERCURE,

MAURICE F. W22XXXXX (015-XX-XXXX) CW2 SigC 721A HHC 19th Gen Spt Gp APO 96491 Asg to: HHC 69th Sig Bn APO 96307 Rept to: 19 Nov 68 Lv Data: N/A PCS (MDC): NZ09 EDCSA: 19 Nov 68 Sp instr: N/A FOR THE COMMANDER:

20 November 1968: SPECIAL ORDERS NUMBER 287 DEPARTMENT OF THE ARMY HEADQUARTERS 69TH SIGNAL BATTALION APO SAN FRANCISCO 96307 dtd 20 November 1968. EXTRACT Paragraph 7. TC 254. RSG DIR AS INDIC THIS STA. NTI. MERCURE, MAURICE F W22XXXXX (015-XX-XXXX) CW2 SC 721A HHC 69TH SIG BN APO 96307 ASG TO: CO A 69TH SIG BN APO 96307 LV DATA: NA RPT DATE 20 NOV 68 BPED/DEROS/ETS: NA EDCSA: 19 NOV 68 SP INSTR: OFF ASSIGNED TO (PARA 05 LINE 04 MTOE 11-098G DMOS 721A) DUTY OFFICER FOR THE COMMANDER:

26 November 1968: LETTER, SUBJECT: Battalion Staff Duty Officer Policy. MACV CommCenter SEE DISTRIBUTION OIC MACV CommCenter dtd 26 November 68 Paragraph 1. Effective immediately officers and warrant officers performing Battalion Staff Duty Officer will be authorized to take the morning off following the duty officer period. 2. Exception to this policy must be authorized by the OIC. FREDERICK H. HUEBNER, JR. LTC, SigC OIC MACV CommCenter.

December 1968: In the MACV Headquarters building is located the MACV Common User Communications Center, on Tan Son Nhut Air Base.

December 1968: In downtown Saigon you would see most people on bicycles, some on motor scooters and some in horse drawn vehicles.

January 1969: One night while going to work, I was getting into a 3/4 ton truck when I fell over a tire on the floor of the vehicle, causing a slight injury to my spine (back). This resulted in my having to go to physical therapy for three weeks.

One day while going to the hospital for physical therapy, a voice told me not to cross (cut across) a large open field next to the hospital—go around it. I was startled, but continued to start to cross the lot when again a voice said go around. Listening to the voice, I started going around the lot. It was a good thing that I had listened to the voice, as a Russian-made rocket landed in the middle of the field and exploded. I would have been somewhere in the middle of the large field and been killed or wounded by the missile.

7 February 1969: DA FORM 2496 DISPOSITION FORM SUBJECT: Appointment to: Personnel Concerned FROM: OIC MACV CommCenter dtd 7 February 1968. Destruction Officer of Classified Material. (*For a copy of this form, see attachment B130.*)

7 February 1969: LETTER, SUBJECT: Additional Duties FROM: MACV CommCenter TO: Personnel Concerned (FROM: Operations Officer) dtd 7 Feb 69 Paragraph 1. Effective immediately the following additional duties are assigned: a. CW2 Maurice F. Mercure—Promulgation of changes and revisions to the HQ USMACV Communications Center Standing Operating Procedures (SOP). b. CW2 Leopold K. Salzer III—Direction of the Awards Program for the Operations Division of the HQ USMACV Communications Center. 2. These additional duties should in no way effect the performance of the above named Warrant Officers' primary duty as HQ USMACV Duty Officers. HARRY J. MARKLEY CW3, USA Operations Officer.

7 February 1969: About three months after arriving in the MACV Communications Center, I was given the job of updating and revising the Station's Standing Operating Procedures (SOP), as a lot of changes had taken place. We were performing some duties on Verbal Orders of the OIC, such as, burn detail responsibilities for destroying Classified Material. It used to be the Duty Officer's responsibility to see that it was done, by overseeing its completion and clean up and policing the area to see that nothing was left unburned (not destroyed), so that person(s) unknown could use it for intelligence purposes. This was now the responsibility of the Non-Commissioned Officer in Charge (NCOIC) of the burn detail, per verbal order of Lt. Col. Huebner, Officer in Charge (OIC), of the Communications Center. So all these major changes had to be made.

11 February 1969: When the Crypto Security Officer (CW2 Breighthaup) inspected the Burn Area (Incinerator), he found material which had not been destroyed

(burned) completely. He reported the incident to the OIC MACV CommCenter, so an investigation was initiated.

<u>14 February 1969</u>: DA FORM 2820 STATEMENT BY ACCUSED OR SUSPECT PERSON dtd 14 February 1969. (*For a copy of this form, see attachment B131.*)

<u>20 February 1969</u>: SPECIAL ORDERS NUMBER 44 DEPARTMENT OF THE ARMY HEADQUARTERS 69TH SIGNAL BATTALION APO SAN FRANCISCO 96307 dtd 20 February 1969. EXTRACT Paragraph 2. TC 351 DAVIS, MERRILL W 05XXXXXX (003-XX-XXXX) CPT 593D SIG CO (SP) 69TH SIG BN APO 96307 MERCURE, MAURICE W22XXXXX (015-XX-XXXX) CW2 CO A 69TH SIG BN APO 96307 APT TO: SURPRISE CASH COUNT OFFICERS PURPOSE: TO CONDUCT SURPRISE CASH COUNT OF THE NCO/EM CLUB EFF DATE: 19 FEB 69 PD: MONTH OF FEBRUARY 1969 AUTH: USARV REG 230-60 SP INSTR: CASH COUNT OFFICERS WILL ENSURE THAT THE AMOUNT OF CASH COUNTED MUST COMPARE WITH THE AMOUNT OF CASH AS SHOWN IN THE BOOKS AND THAT ANY DIFFERENCE MUST BE INVESTIGATED. FOR THE COMMANDER:

<u>20 February 1969</u>: SPECIAL ORDERS NUMBER 44 DEPARTMENT OF THE ARMY HEADQUARTERS 69TH SIGNAL BATTALION APO SAN FRANCISCO 96307 dtd 20 February 1969. EXTRACT Paragraph 7. TC 351. FOL INDIV THIS STA APPOINTED: DAVIS, MERRILL W 05XXXXXX (003-XX-XXXX) CPT 593D SIG CO (SPT) 69TH SIG BN APO 96307 MERCURE, MAURICE W22XXXXX (015-XX-XXXX) CW2 CO A 69TH SIG BN APO 96307 APT TO: INVENTORY OFFICERS PURPOSE: TO INVENTORY CASH, STOCK OF THE NCO/EM CLUB EFF DATE: 19 FEB 69 PD: MONTH OF FEB 69 AUTH: USARV REG 230-60 SP INSTR: INVENTORY WB COMPLETED PRIOR TO OPENING OF BUSINESS ON THE 26 FEB 69. INVENTORY OFFICERS WILL CONTACT THE EXECUTIVE OFFICER FOR DETAILED INSTRUCTIONS. A COMPARISON WB MADE OF THE AMOUNT AS SHOWN ON THE STOCK RECORD CARDS. ANY DISCREPANCIES OF THIS COMPARISON WB INVESTIGATED BY THE INVENTORYING OFFICERS. FOR THE COMMANDER:

<u>1 March 1969</u>: LETTER, SUBJECT: Rebuttal to Conclusion of Investigating Officer FROM: MAURICE F. MERCURE, CW2 USA DEPARTMENT OF THE ARMY COMPANY A, 69TH SIGNAL BATTALION (ARMY) APO SAN FRANCISCO 96307 TO: Major Benny L. Lockett dtd 1 March 1969. (*For a copy of this letter, see attachment B132.*)

It is important to point out that CW3 Harry J Markley contacted Lt. Col. Huebner, in the hospital in Japan (as he was there with a broken back,) requesting him to send a message stating that he had indeed given a verbal order—that the NCOIC of the burn detail was responsible for the security of the detail and not the Duty Officer. Lt. Col. Huebner sent a message from Japan confirming that he did in fact give a verbal order, which caused the case against me to be dropped. I have CW3 Markley and Lt. Col. Huebner to thank for their actions in regards to this matter.

<u>1969</u>: While working my shift in the MACV Communications Center, a message came in marked "EYES ONLY FOR THE COMMANDER MACV, GENERAL ABRAMS." He was away in the Philippines at the time. We did, however, have authorization to deliver it to his Deputy, in General Abrams absence. I went to General Abrams office to deliver the message. They informed me that the General was in the Philippines and that his Deputy was authorized to sign for the messages. I, in good conscience, could not deliver the message to him as the message was all about him. So I returned to the Message Center with same. The Deputy Commander found out that I had tried to deliver the message to General Abrams, but was unable to deliver same, as he was away. He demanded the message from me at the Communications Center. I informed him that I could not release it to him. He left the area, only to return with the Provost Marshal and two MPs (Military Policemen). He demanded the message, but again I refused to give it to him. He then ordered the Provost Marshal and the two MPs to arrest me for insubordination. The MPs proceeded to place me under arrest. However, the trick Chief (former Green Beret) on duty (NCOIC) came out of the Communications Center with three of his men armed with .45 Cal. Sub-Machine Guns, and said, "You are not taking the Chief anywhere." He then escorted me back into the Communications Center where we stayed barricaded by MPs until General Abrams returned from the Philippines. Upon his return, he called me and told me to bring the message to him immediately. I did as he instructed (ordered).

I went to his office under escort and gave the General the message. I explained to him why I did not release the message to his Deputy. His Deputy immediately demanded my arrest for insubordination, and that I be relieved from my duties as Communications Center Duty Officer. General Abrams stated, "Hold on. Let me read the message first." After reading the message, he turned to me and said, "Chief, you did the right thing." He then turned to the Provost Marshal, and told him that the Deputy Commander was wrong. Turning to his Deputy, he stated, "Consider yourself under house arrest, pending investigation of the charges against you." He dismissed me and told me to return to my duty station. It is important to stress here that General Abrams went on to be Army Chief of Staff. However, I am sorry to say that he died of cancer.

<u>17 March 1969</u>: SPECIAL ORDERS NUMBER 67 DEPARTMENT OF THE ARMY HEADQUARTERS 69TH SIGNAL BATTALION APO SAN FRANCISCO 96307 dtd 17 March 1969. EXTRACT Paragraph 9. TC 350. FOL INDIV THIS STA APPOINTED. MERCURE, MAURICE F W22XXXXX (015-XX-XXXX) CW2 USA 721A CO A 69TH SIG BN APO 96307 APT TO: CLASS A AGENT TO FIN OFF 7TH FINS SEC APO 96309 EFF DATE: 30 MAR 69 PD: FOR MONTH OF MARCH 69 PURPOSE: TO PAY EM ASG OR ATCH TO CO A 69TH SIG BN APO 96307 AUTH: PARA 15-3 AR 37-103 SP INSTR: AGENT OFF W/FAMILIARIZE HIMSELF WITH THE CONTENTS OF FM 14-8. FUNDS W/NOT BE ENTRUSTED TO OTHERS FOR ANY REASON. PAYROLL TURN BACKS WB CLEARED WITH THE BN PERS OFF. PAYROLL WB TURNED BACK TO FIN NLT 5 DAYS AFTER PAYDAY. AFTER PAY ACTION IS COMPLETED PAY VOUCHERS WB PRESENTED TO PERS FOR SCREENING. FOR THE COMMANDER:

One part of the job of OIC of the Communications Center was handling all the casualty messages going to Washington, so someone could notify the family of the death of a loved one. We had so many of these messages. It was hard sending them. So many of them were for boys seventeen and eighteen. Very few seventeens—mostly servicemen eighteen or older.

<u>22 March 1969</u>: PERMISSIVE TRAVEL ORDERS NO 0365 FOR OUT-OF-COUNTRY R&R DEPARTMENT OF THE ARMY HEADQUARTERS, 69TH SIGNAL

BATTALION (ARMY) APO San Francisco 96307 dtd 22 Mar 69 MERCURE, MAURICE F. CW2 W22XXXXX (015-XX-XXXX) CO A 69TH Sig Bn (A).

March 1969: Received a beautiful picture of Peg, from her. I was very proud to display this picture on my bedside table and show it to everyone I could. (*For a copy of this picture, see photograph A54.*)

23 April 1969: SPECIAL ORDERS NUMBER 99, DEPARTMENT OF THE ARMY HEADQUARTERS 69TH SIGNAL BATTALION APO SAN FRANCISCO 96307 dtd 23 April 1969 EXTRACT Paragraph 9. TC 370. FOL ORDERS AMENDED. SMO: PARA 5 SO 96 THIS HQ CS. PERT TO: PAY OFFICERS AS READS: MERCURE, MAURICE F. W22XXXXX (015-XX-XXXX) CW2 CO A 69TH SIG BN APO 96307 IATR: GILMORE, CRAMER M II 05XXXXXX (176-XX-XXXX) 1LT SC CO A 69TH SIG BN APO 96307 FOR THE COMMANDER:

25 April 1969: SPECIAL ORDERS NUMBER 101 DEPARTMENT OF THE ARMY HEADQUARTERS 69TH SIGNAL BATTALION APO SAN FRANCISCO 96307 dtd 25 April 1969 EXTRACT PARAGRAPH 3. TC 350. FOL INDIV THIS STA APPOINTED. MERCURE, MAURICE F W22XXXXX (015-XX-XXXX) CW2 SC 721A HHC 69TH SIG BN APO 96307. APT TO: ALT COMSEC CUSTODIAN FOR ACCOUNT 5EV-XXX ALT COMSEC OFFICER FOR ACCOUNT 5EV-XXX EFF DATE: 24 APRIL 1969 AUTH: VOCO: OIC MACV COMCEN PD: INDEF SP INSTR: VICE MARKLEY, HARRY J W22XXXXX (185-XX-XXXX) CW3 CO A 69TH SIG BN FOR THE COMMANDER:

26 April 1969: Went on R&R to Bangkok, Thailand, by military aircraft. I had made arrangements with a Sgt. in the Communications Center that worked for me. He had a Thai wife living in Bangkok to assist Peg. He stated he would have his wife make hotel reservations for us and have her meet Peg at the Bangkok International Airport and take her to the hotel. The Sgt. informed me that his wife had made reservations for us at the NANA Hotel in Bangkok for our stay in Thailand. So, Peg set out from England to meet me in Bangkok for our R&R (Rest and Recuperation). Unfortunately the Sergeant's wife became ill and was unable to meet Peg at the airport. So, Peg arrived

at the airport with no one there to meet her. Luckily some very nice Thai gentleman at the airport called the NANA Hotel to confirm our reservations. After verifying this, he told Peg how much Thai money she would have to pay the taxi driver, who took her to the hotel. He then put her in a taxi cab and told the driver to take her to the NANA Hotel. She arrived at the NANA Hotel and registered. In the lobby of the hotel, she met an Army Signal Officer who managed to get a line through to my Officer's Quarters, and we talked for a while. The next day, I flew to Bangkok International Airport. Upon arriving at the airport, I took a taxi cab to the NANA Hotel and met Peg, who was so glad to see me. We took a tour of the Royal Palace and saw the King's large outdoor covered bed, which he used in the summertime. On the Palace grounds are a lot of statues of Buddha, including one made of jade.

We took a river boat tour of the Floating Market, which we found to be very interesting and enjoyable.

The next day we took a tour to see the Bridge over the River Kwai and the cemeteries of the soldiers who died building the railroad and the bridge. (*For a picture of the Bridge over the River Kwai, see photograph A55.*)

While in the hotel we went swimming in the hotel's pool. It was nice and warm and relaxing. Some young soldiers were also swimming in the pool. They thought that the scar on my back was the result of my being wounded in Vietnam. I informed them that it was from a disc operation in Germany.

We had a lovely spicy meal in a Thai Restaurant in Bangkok, Thailand. (*For a copy of picture of author and his wife in Thai Restaurant, see photograph A56.*)

Peg informed me, the day before our RNR was over, that she had gone to RNR station south ruislip's dispensary. For a check up, Ann to see what shots she would need for the trip to Bangkok. The doctor examined her, then gave her a pap test. It was discovered from the pap test, that she had large fibrod, which should be removed right away. She stated no way, I have to go to Bangkok, to spend and RNR with my husband. The doctor insisted she have it removed right away. Peg informed the doctor, that she would have it done when she returned from Bangkok. It was quite evident, that she was more concerned about me, and our RNR, the immediate surgery. So the doctor told her go to Bangkok and spend the RNR with your husband, and have a ball. I told her I hope the surgery goes well and then I would pray for her.

<u>30 April 1969</u>: While on R&R (rest and recuperation) in Thailand, we purchased two elephants for ourselves, and other items for our families.

Received telegram from RAF station south ruislip dispensary. Stating surgery was successful and Peg was doing fine. It also stated that the fibrod was not cancerous. (Nowadays, they do not do a historectomy for fibrods, as they are not cancerous. But back in 1969 they did not know.)

<u>9 May 1969</u>: LETTER, SUBJECT: Letter of Appreciation DEPARTMENT OF THE ARMY COMPANY A, 69TH SIGNAL BATTALION (ARMY) APO San Francisco 96307 dtd 9 May 1969 TO: CW2 Maurice F. Mercure W22XXXXX Company A, 69th Signal Battalion (ARMY) APO San Francisco 96307 dtd 9 May 1969 (*For a copy of this letter, see attachment B133.*)

<u>20 May 1969</u>: LETTER, SUBJECT: Pay Officers schedule DEPARTMENT OF THE ARMY COMPANY A, 69TH SIGNAL BATTALION (ARMY) APO San Francisco 96307 dtd 20 May 1969. MERCURE, Maurice F W22XXXXX CW2. (*For a copy of this letter, see attachment B134.*)

<u>10 June 1969</u>: DA FORM 1041 ELECTION OF OPTIONS UNDER RETIRED SERVICEMAN'S FAMILY PROTECTION PLAN dtd 10 June 1969 MERCURE, MAURICE FRANK W22XXXXX CW2 537 Chicopee Street Willimansett, Massachusetts 01013. (*For a copy of this form, see attachment B135.*)

<u>27 June 1969</u>: LETTER, SUBJECT: CAR INSURANCE FR CW2 Maurice F Mercure (015-XX-XXXX) Co A, 69th Signal Battalion (A) (MACV) APO San Francisco 96307 dtd 27 June 1969 TO: Government Employee Finance and Industrial Load Corporation 1206 N Hartford St., Arlington, Virginia 22201. (*For a copy of this letter, see attachment B136.*)

<u>June 1969</u>: Picture of 69th Signal Battalion Officers on patrol. 1Lt Bernard K. Vollrath, CW2 William C BreithaupT, CW3 Harry J. Markley and me. (*For a copy of this picture, see photograph A57.*)

<u>June 1969</u>: Picture of me in combat gear, in my room in the Battalion Officers Quarters, preparing to inspect Guard Post. (*For a copy of this picture, see photograph A58.*)

<u>June 1969</u>: Picture of CW3 Harry J. Markley, 1Lt Bernard K Vollrath and me in combat gear in the Battalion Officers Quarters, just before going on patrol in Saigon. (*For a copy of this picture, see photograph A59.*)

<u>18 July 1969</u>: LETTER, SUBJECT: Receipt of Retirement Application DEPARTMENT OF THE ARMY OFFICE OF THE ADJUTANT GENERAL WASHINGTON, D. C. dtd 18 July 1969 TO: Chief Warrant Officer W-2 Maurice F. Mercure 69th Signal Battalion APO San Francisco 96307. (*For a copy of this letter, see attachment B137.*)

<u>22 July 1969</u>: SPECIAL ORDERS NUMBER 178 DEPARTMENT OF THE ARMY HEADQUARTERS 69TH SIGNAL BATTALION APO SAN FRANCISCO 96307 dtd 28 JULY 1969 EXTRACT paragraph 2. TC 350. FOL INDIV THIS STA APPOINTED. HARWOOD, THOMAS W 562-XX-XXXX 1LT SC HHC 69 H SIG BN APO 96307 PURPOSE: TO PAY EM ASG OR ATCH TO HHC 69TH SIG BN APO 96307 MAXIE, EDDIE C 437-XX-XXXX 1LT SC HHC (SIG SPT) 69TH SIG BN APO 96306 PURPOSE: TO PAY EM ASG OR ATCH TO HHC (SIG SPT) 69TH SIG BN APO 96306 PURPOSE: TO PAY EM ASG OR ATCH TO HHC (SIG SPT) 69TH SIG BN APO 96307 LAURY, EDWARD P 273—XX-XXXX 1LT SC 593D SIG CO 69TH SIG BN APO 96307 PURPOSE: TO PAY EM ASG OR ATCH TO 593D SIG CO 69TH SIG BN APO 96307 MERCURE, MAURICE F (015-XX-XXXX) CW2 USA CO A 69TH SIG BN APO 96307 PURPOSE: TO PAY OFFICERS ASG OR ATCH TO HHC 69TH SIG BN APO 96307 APT TO: CLASS A AGENT TO FIN OFFICER 7TH FIN SEC (DISB) APO 96307 EFF DATE: 29 JUL 69 PD: 5 AUG 69 AUTH: PARA 15-3 AR 37-103 SP INSTR: AGENT OFFICER W/FAMILIARIZE HIMSELF WITH THE CONTENTS OF FM 14-8. FUNDS W/NOT BE ENTRUSTED TO OTHERS FOR ANY PURPOSE. PAYROLL TURN BACK WB CLEARED WITH THE BN PERS OFF. PAYROLL WB TURNED BACK TO FIN NLT 5 DAYS AFTER PAYDAY. AFTER PAY ACTION IS COMPLETED PAY VOU WB PRESENTED TO PERS FOR SCREENING. FOR THE COMMANDER:

<u>4 August 1969</u>: SPECIAL ORDERS NUMBER 190 DEPARTMENT OF THE ARMY HEADQUARTERS 69TH SIGNAL BATTALION APO SAN FRANCISCO 96307 dtd 4 AUGUST 1969. EXTRACT PARAGRAPH 4. TC 350. FOL INDIV THIS STA APPOINTED. MERCURE, MAURICE (015-XX-XXXX) CW2 CO A 69TH SIG BN APO 96307 APT. TO: PX INVENTORY OFFICER EFF DATE: 6 AUG 69 PD: MONTH OF AUG 69 PURPOSE: TO INVENTORY CASH & STOCK OF THE 69TH SIG BN PX. CAMP GAYLOR, RVN AUTH: VOCO 69TH SIG BN APO 96307 SP INSTR: INVENTORY WB COMPLETED PR TO OPENING OF BUSINESS ON 6 AUG 1969. INVENTORY OFFICER W/CONTACT THE ADJUTANT FOR DETAILED INSTR. FOR THE COMMANDER:

<u>9 August 1969</u>: DA FORM 11-78 PROJECTIONIST LICENSE (AR 1-8-30) dtd 9 Aug 69 Maurice F. Mercure (015-XX-XXXX) LICENSE NUMBER TSN-412. (*For a copy of this form, see attachment B138.*)

<u>15 August 1969</u>: UNIT ORDERS NUMBER 91 DEPARTMENT OF THE ARMY COMPANY A, 69TH SIGNAL BATTALION (ARMY) APO San Francisco 96307 dtd 15 August 1969 Paragraph 1. TC 350. Fol indiv this unit APPOINTED. MERCURE, MAURICE F. (015-XX-XXXX) CW2 SigC Co A 69th Sig Bn (A) APO 96307 Apt to: Maintenance Officer, Censorship Officer Eff date: 15 August 1969 Purpose: As stated Pd: Indef Auth: VOCO Sp instr: VICE HATCH, CHARLES A. 002-XX-XXXX CW2 SigC Co A 69th Sig Bn (A) APO SF 96307 CARLITS, ROBERT B. 183-XX-XXXX CW3 SigC Co A 68th SigBN (A) APO SF 96307 MERCURE, MAURICE F. (015-XX-XXXX) CW2 SigC Co A 69th Bn (A)APO SF 96307 Apt to: Destruction Officers & Witnessing Officers for the Destruction of Classified Material Eff date: 1 July 1969 VOCO date cfm: 1 July 1969 Purpose: As stated Pd: Indef Auth: VOCO Sp instr: VICE BREITHAUPT, WILLIAM C. 161-XX-XXXX CW2 SigC Co A 69th Sig Bn (A) APO SF 96307 VICE HATCH, CHARLES A. 002-XX-XXXX CW2 Sig C Co A 69th Sig Bn (A) APO SF 96307 WILLIAM D. HARRISON CPT, SigC Commanding.

<u>26 August 1969</u>: LETTER, SUBJECT: Command Information Classes for September DEPARTMENT OF THE ARMY COMPANY A, 69TH SIGNAL BATTALION

(ARMY) APO San Francisco 96307 dtd 26 August 1969 DATE 23-24 TOPIC: CIVIL AFFAIRS INSTRUCTOR CW2 Mercure, M. F. WILBUR D. HARRIS CPT, SigC Commanding.

4 September 1969: LETTER, SUBJECT: Weapons Inventory DEPARTMENT OF THE ARMY COMPANY A, 69TH SIGNAL BATTALION (ARMY) APO San Francisco 96307 dtd 4 Sep 69 The following officer is scheduled for weapons inventory on the date indicated below. The individual will report to the CO on their duty day. MERCURE, MAURICE F. CW2 20 Sep and 25 Oct 69 WILBUR D. HARRIS CPT, SigC COMMANDING.

16 September 1969: SPECIAL ORDERS NUMBER 226 DEPARTMENT OF THE ARMY HEADQUARTERS 69TH SIGNAL BATTALION APO SAN FRANCISCO 96307 dtd 16 September 1969 EXTRACT PARAGRAPH 1. TC 350. FOL INDIV THIS STA APPOINTED: MERCURE, MAURICE (015-XX-XXXX) CW2 SC CO A 69TH SIG BN APO 96307 APT TO: INVENTORY OFFICER PURPOSE: TO INVENTORY CASH, STOCK OF THE OFFICERS OPEN MESS EFF DATE: 25 SEP 69 PD: MONTH OF SEP 69 AUTH: USARV REG 230-60 SP INSTR: INVENTORY WB COMPL PR TO OPENING OF BUSINESS ON 26 SEP 69. INVENTORY OFF W/CONTACT THE XO FOR DETAILED INSTR. A COMPARISON WB MADE OF THE AMT SHOWN ON THE STOCK RECORD CARDS. ANY DISCREPANCIES OF THIS COMPARISON WB INVESTIGATED BY THE INVENTORY OFFICERS. FOR THE COMMANDER:

16 September 1969: UNCLASSIFIED MESSAGE FM TAG DA WASH DC TO: 69TH SIG BN TSN RVN BT UNCLAS AGPORO SUBJ: RETIREMENT A. YOUR MSG P 1301352 Sep 69 vol ret 1 DEC CW2 MAURICE F MERCURE (015-XX-XXXX) HAS BEEN APPR. HOWEVER FINAL PROCESSING HAS NOT BEEN COMPLETED. ORDERS WILL BE ISSUED ASAP. BT

19 September 1969: LETTER, SUBJECT: PAYCALL DEPARTMENT OF THE ARMY COMPANY A, 69TH SIGNAL BATTALION (ARMY) APO San Francisco 96307 dtd 19 Sep 69 The following officer is scheduled for APC Conversion Officer

(Payroll) on the date indicated below. The individual will report to the CO on his day of duty. MERCURE, MAURICE F. CW2 Oct WILBUR D. HARRIS, CPT, SigC Commanding.

23 September 1969: SPECIAL ORDERS NUMBER 183 HEADQUARTERS, DEPARTMENT OF THE ARMY, Washington, D. C., dtd 23 September 1969 E X T R A C T Paragraph 164. TC 433. CW2 MAURICE F. MERCURE (015-XX-XXXX) (CW2 SIGC-USAR eff 25 Nov 1969) upon his appl is ret from active svc under prov title 10 USC sec 1293 after more than 23 yrs active Fed svc. He is rel from asg and dy on EDCSA: 30 Nov 1969 and placed on AUS Ret List 1 Dec 1969 he is trf to USAR (Ret Res) and asg to USAR Cont Gp (Ret) USAAC, St. Louis, Mo. 63132. HOSTWOY. PCS. TDN. PPSIA. MDC 7BOO. SPN 77. Auth to ret: Oakland, CA. Req place of ret: Ft Devens, MA. BY ORDER OF THE SECRETARY OF THE ARMY: W. C. WESTMORELAND, General, United States Army, Chief of Staff OFFICIAL: KENNETH G. WICKHAM Major General, United States Army, The Adjutant General. A TRUE COPY ALBERT F. LAHAIR CW4, USA Asst. Adj Gen.

23 September 1969: UNCLASSIFIED MESSAGE FM TAG DA WASH DC TORHMSMVA/CO 69TH SIG BN TSN RVN INFO RHMLBHA/CO 160TH SIGNAL GP LONG BINH RVN RUEDGEA/CO USAG TRF PT FT DEVENS MASS BT UNCLAS AGPORD SUBJ: RETIREMENT CW2 MAURICE F. MERCURE (015-XX-XXXX) SIGC IS RET 1 DEC BY PARA 164 DASO 183 DTD 23 SEP AT FT DEVENS MASS IN ACD WITH DA MSG 892018 DTD 30 DEC 1968. RSG AND TRAVEL ORDERS WB ISSUED BY YOUR COMD UP PARA 5 OF DA MSG. BT

27 September 1969: SPECIAL ORDERS NUMBER 236 DEPARTMENT OF THE ARMY HEADQUARTERS 69TH SIGNAL BATTALION APO SAN FRANCISCO 96307 dtd 27 September 1969 EXTRACT PARAGRAPH 6. TC 371. FOL ORDERS REVOKED. SMO: PARA 1 SO 226 THIS HQ CS PERT TO: APT OF MAXIE, EDDIE C 437-XX-XXXX 1LT SC HHC (SIG SPT) 69TH SIG BN APO 96307 TO ADD DY AS INVENTORY OFF FOR OFF OPEN MESS APT OF MERCURE, MAURICE (015-XX-XXXX) CW2 SC CO A 69TH SIG BN APO 96307 TO ADD DY AS INVENTORY OFF FOR OFF OPEN MESS. FOR THE COMMANDER:

<u>29 September 1969</u>: SPECIAL ORDERS NUMBER 238 DEPARTMENT OF THE ARMY HEADQUARTERS 69TH SIGNAL BATTALION APO SAN FRANCISCO 96307 dtd 29 September 1969 EXTRACT PARAGRAPH 10, TC 274. FNI IS AUTH AND PERMITTED TO PROCEED TO A CONUS LOC OF PERSONAL CHOICE FOR PURPOSE OF RETIREMENT. (TRANSOCEANIC MOVEMENT OF MBR TO CONUS DEBARKATION AREA IS AUTH AND DIR TVL. MBR W/RPT AS DIR FOR TRANS TO CONUS DEBARKATION AREA. TDN.) OIC: 201401. MERCURE, MAURICE F (015-XX-XXXX) CW2 SC 721ACO A 69TH SIG BN APO 96307 ASG TO: USARV RTNE DET APO 96375 FOR FUR ASG TO FT DEVENS, MASS RPT DATE (TRANS): TO BE FURN AT A LATER DATE HOR: 196 CHESTNUT ST, HOLYOKE, MASS DATE RET: 1 DEC 69 AUTH PL OF RET: FT DEVENS, MASS REQ PL OF RET: FT DEVENS, MASS PL EAD: HOLYOKE, MASS PCS (MDC): 7800 LV DATA: 25 DDALVAHP MO OS (CURR TOUR): 12 (NT 12) MAJ COMD/ ACCY: USASTRATCOM-1ST SIG BDE AUTH: AR 635-100 AND PARA 164 DA SO #183 DTD 23 SEP 69 SPN: 77T COMP: USAR*V BPED: 5 OCT 46 DDUS: 28 OCT 68 DEROS: 27 OCT 69 EDCSA: (TO USARV RTNE DET APO 96375): 26 OCT 69 (TO FT DEVENS, MASS: 22 NOV 69 SP INSTR: PROVISIONS OF DA MSG 892018 DTD 30 DEC 69 W/APPLY PR TO DPRT OF MBR FR HIS DY STA. TVL OF MBR FR THE CONUS DEBARKATION AREA TO THE TRANSFER ACTIVITY AT THE CONUS LOCATION OF CHOICE IS BASED UPON MBR PERS REQ IS PERMISSIVE. MBR IS PRECLUDED FR REC ANY MONETARY SUM, GOV TRANS, OR A TRNS REQ FOR HIS TBL FR THE CONUS DEBARKATION AREA TO THE CONUS LOC OF CHOICE. MOVEMENT OF DEPENDENTS FR THE CONUS DEBARKATION AREA TO THE CONUS LOC OF MBR CHOICE AT GOVT EXP IS NOT AUTH. INDIV HOLD BAG MAY BE SHIPPED UPON REC OF THESE ORDERS THRU THE LOC TO. INDIV MUST HAVE HIS IMM RCD UP TO DATE PR TO DEPT FR HIS HOME STA. INDIV W/HANDCARRY HIS MPRJ. PERS MAIL W/NOT BE FWD TO US ARV RTNE DET. PSTL LOC CARDS W/INDIC UDT DEST AS FWD ADRS. INDIV W/HAVE SUF AMT OF MALARIA PRO TABS IN HIS POSS AND W/TAKE ONE TAB WKLY FOR 8 WKS. CUSTOM REG PROHIBI THE FOL ABOARD MIL ACFT IN PERS OR HOLD BAG: NARCOTICS, MARIJUANA, AMMO, FIREARMS, KNIVES, FIREWORKS, VN CURR IN EXCESS OF 500 PIASTERS, ITEMS PD IN COMMUNIST CHINA, N VN OR N KOREA; GOLD OR

SIL BULLION, OBSCENE OR PORNOGRAPHIC ART OR LIT, MORE THAN ONE BTL OF UNOPENED ALCOHOLIC BEV, ITEMS IN EX OF DMSY NEEDS, OR MORE THAN ONE CTN OF CIGARETTES. FOR THE COMMANDER:

10 October 1969: LETTER, SUBJECT: Promotion as a Reserve Warrant Officer of the Army (Para 20) THRU: Commanding Officer 69th Signal Battalion DEPARTMENT OF THE ARMY OFFICE OF PERSONNEL OPERATIONS FORT BENJAMIN HARRISON, INDIANA 46249 dtd 10 October 1969 MERCURE, MAURICE F. W22XXXXX USAR (SC) (*For a copy of this letter, see attachment B139.*)

11 October 1969: I was awarded the Bronze Star Medal by the President of the United States for meritorious service in connection with military operations against a hostile force in the Republic of Vietnam during the period 30 October 1968 to 1 October 1969. (*For a copy of this award, see attachment B140.*)

14 October 1969: SPECIAL ORDERS NUMBER 250 DEPARTMENT OF THE ARMY HEADQUARTERS 69TH SIGNAL BATTALION APO SAN FRANCISCO 96307 DTD 14 October 1969 EXTRACT PARAGRAPH 3. TC 350. FOL INDIV THIS STA APPOINTED. MERCURE, MAURICE (015-XX-XXXX) CW2 SC CO A 69TH SIG BN APO 96307 APT TO: SURPRISE CASH COUNT OFFICER PURPOSE: TO CONDUCT SURPRISE CASH COUNT OF THE OFFICER'S OPEN MESS, 69TH SIG BN APO 96307 EFF DATE: 20 Oct 69 PD: MONTH OF OCTOBER 1969 AUTH: USARV REG 230-60 SP INSTR: CASH COUNT OFFICER W/INSURE THAT THE AMOUNT OF CASH COUNTED MUST COMPARE WITH THE AMOUNT OF CASH AS SHOWN IN THE BOOKS AND THAT ANY DIFFERENCE IN THIS COMPARISON MUST BE INVESTIGATED AND RESOLVED. FOR THE COMMANDER:

18 October 1969: DA FORM 10-102 ORGANIZATIONAL CLOTHING AND EQUIPMENT RECORD (AR 735-35) dtd 18 Oct 69 MERCURE, MAURICE (015-XX-XXXX) (*For a copy of this form, see attachment B141.*)

18 October 1969: GENERAL ORDERS NUMBER 2619 DEPARTMENT OF THE ARMY HEADQUARTERS, 1st Signal Brigade (USASTRATCOM) APO San

Francisco 96384 dtd 18 October 1969 AWARD OF THE BRONZE STAR MEDAL Paragraph. Tc 320. The following AWARDS are announced. MERCURE, MAURICE F. (015-XX-XXXX) CHIEF WARRANT OFFICER TWO, COMPANY A 69TH SIGNAL BATTALION, APO 96307 30 OCTOBER 1968 TO 1 OCTOBER 1969 Awarded: Bronze Star Medal Date action: as indicated in standard name line theater: Republic of Vietnam Reason: For meritorious service in connection with military operations against a hostile force. Authority: By direction of the President under the provisions of Executive Order 11046, 24 Aug 62 & unclas msg 16695, Hq USARV, dtd 3 Jul 66 FOR THE COMMANDER:

One thing we really cherished and appreciated, where our daily letters to each other. We both kept them, for us to read and review after retirement.

In Vietnam, there were really only two seasons—the rainy (wet) season and the arid (dry) season. During the rainy season we had almost no let up in bad weather. During the arid (dry) season, you wished you could reach up and turn off the sun. We were fortunate that our Officer's quarters and MACV Headquarters were completely air conditioned. The poor troops out in the field did not have this luxury. All they had were tents and rain ponchos. They had so much to contend with, such as punji sticks, snakes, land mines, traps, etc, and of course the Viet Cong, NVA (North Vietnamese regulars).

18 October 1969: SPECIAL ORDERS NUMBER 254 DEPARTMENT OF THE ARMY HEADQUARTERS 69TH SIGNAL BATTALION APO SAN FRANCISCO 96307 dtd 18 October 1969 EXTRACT Paragraph 1. TC 370. FOL ORDERS AMENDED. SMO: PARA 10 SO 238 THIS HQ CS PERT TO: RET OF MERCURE, MAURICE F. (015-XX-XXXX) CW2 SC 721A CO A 69TH SIGNAL BATTALION APO 96307 AS READS: NA IATA: TVL DATA: OFF WILL RPT TO PERS. 69TH SIG BN 22 OCT FOR FINAL OUT-PROCESSING. INDIV W/HAVE VALID PASSPORT FOR INDIA, PAKISTAN AND SAUDI ARABIA. OFF W/HAVE SUFFICIENT FUNDS TO DEFRAY EXPENSES FR NEW DELHI, INDIA TO FRANKFURT, GERMANY. TVL FR NEW DELHI TO FRANKFURT WB ON A SPACE AVAILABLE BASIS. OFF AUTH CIRCUITOUS TVL HRV GERMANY TO CONUS WITH 30 DAY DELAY ENROUTE AUTH: INDIV AUTH TO VISIT GERMANY, FRANCE AND ENGLAND. DEP WIFE AUTH TVL FROM ENGLAND TO CONUS ON SPACE REQUIRED BASIS INDIV

W/RPT TO US ARMY ATCO! RHINE MAIN AFB TO ARRANGE ONWARD TVL TO CONUS. NOK: MARGARET DORIS MERCURE (WIFE) 332 KINGS HILL AVE, HAYES MIDDLESEX, ENGLAND. FOR THE COMMANDER:

19 October 1969: SPECIAL ORDERS NUMBER 255 DEPARTMENT OF THE ARMY HEADQUARTERS 69TH SIGNAL BATTALION APO SAN FRANCISCO 96307 dtd 19 October 1969 EXTRACT PARAGRAPH 1. TC 370. FOL ORDERS AMENDED. SMO: PARA 10 SO 238 THIS HQ CS. PERT TO: RET OF MERCURE, MAURICE F. (015-XX-XXXX) CW2 SC 721A CO A 69TH SIG BN APO 96307 AS READS: PCS (MDC): 7BOO IATR: PCS (MDC) 5DOO FOR THE COMMANDER:

19 October 1969: USAHAC FORM 258 S E R V I C E O R D E R S dtd 19 October 1969. You are authorized to provide service and/or material under Military Basic Tender 1. (RANK) CW2 (LAST NAME) MERCURE (INITIALS) M. F. (SERVICE) NUMBER (015-XX-XXXX) ADDRESS FOR PICK UP: 69TH SIG BN BOQ ROOM 25 TELEPHONE: MACV 3070 (OFFICE) (HOME) MACV 3772 3512 PROPERTY TO BE MEASURED ON: 21 OCT AT 0830 HOURS PROPERTY TO BE PACKED ON 22 OCT AT 0830 HOURS DESTINATION (STATE OR COUNTRY): MASS CONUS. (Signature of Ordering Officer) REMARKS: Personal Weapon Export Permit NO AIR Yes AFI SUR BRK MODE CEP X GSC IMP NO WAR TROPHY FIREARMS WILL BE SHIPPED IN UNACCOMPANIED BAGGAGE. PROHIBITED SHIPPING ITEMS: BATTERIES TOBACCO LIQUOR NARCOTICS MATCHES BUTANE PORNOGRAPHIC OR OBSCENE LITERATURE FIREARMS OR AMMUNITION ORGANIZATIONAL EQUIPMENT MEDICINE LIGHT BULBS WAR TROPHIES AEROSOL CANS LIQUIDS IN ANY FORM OF CONTAINER MOTORIZED VEHICLES REFERENCE: MACV DIRECTION 55-1 FAA REGULATION.

The commanding Officer, 69th Signal Battalion, presenting the author with a Vietnamese gong, as a retirement present. (*For a copy of this picture, see photograph A60.*)

20 October 1969: DA FORM 2962 SECURITY TERMINATION STATEMENT AND DEBRIEFING CERTIFICATE. (AR-380-5) DTD 20 OCT 69 FROM HHC, 69TH SIG

BN (A) APO 96307 MERCURE, MAURICE F CW2 015-XX-XXXX 14 AUG 28 CHICOPEE FAIRVIEW, MASS (*For a copy of this form, see attachment B142.*)

22 October 1969: DD FORM 619 STATEMENT OF ACCESSORIAL SERVICE PERFORMED HQ AREA COMMAND, RVN SGN dtd 20 October 1969. (*For a copy of this form, see attachment B143.*)

22 October 1969: COLUMBIA EXPORT PACKING, INC COLUMBIA STREET, TORRANCE, CALIFORNIA dtd 22 October 1969. (*For a copy of this form, see attachment B144.*)

23 October 1969: I left Tan Son Nhut Air Base, Saigon, Vietnam, for Bangkok, International Airport, Thailand, on a military aircraft to our next stop.

It was a wonderful feeling to say "good-bye" to Vietnam, and the danger of being killed or wounded. Certainly the Lord was with me and provided me with a Guardian Angel while in Vietnam.

23 October 1969: I arrived at Bangkok International Airport, Thailand, where I was informed that I had to leave the military aircraft, as it was going to Pakistan. The reason I had to get off was that I did not have a valid visa to visit Pakistan. So, I had to deplane and make arrangements with a civilian airline to go to London. I made flight arrangements with Pan American Airlines for my trip to London. I then boarded a Pan American Airlines aircraft for London, via Frankfurt, Germany. Our first stop was New Delhi, India.

23 October 1969: Arriving at the New Delhi International Airport, I got off the plane to stretch my legs and look around. Apparently I must have overstayed my time on the ground. I was paged by Pan American Airlines to return to the plane immediately, which I did, and the aircraft left for Tehran International Airport, Iran, our next stop.

23 October 1969: Arriving at Tehran International Airport, Iran, I did not leave the plane to look around. The aircraft left for our next stop, Beirut International Airport, Lebanon.

23 October 1969: We arrived at Beirut International Airport. Again, I did not get off the plane to look around. The aircraft departed Beirut International Airport for our next stop, Istanbul, Turkey.

24 October 1969: Arriving at Istanbul International Airport, I deplaned for a while to look around the airport terminal, and use my limited Turkish language. It was nice being in a familiar place and using my limited knowledge of the Turkish language (remembering my two year stay in Ankara, from 1958-1960). I got back on the aircraft and it took off for Athens, our next stop.

24 October 1969: Arriving at Athens International Airport, Greece, I did not leave the aircraft for a look around. We left for Frankfurt, Germany, our next stop.

24 October 1969: We arrived at Frankfurt International Airport, Germany. I had to deplane so I could catch an Air France flight for London, England, via Paris, France.

While on the ground, I sent a cable to Peg, asking her to meet me at Heathrow Airport, giving her my arrival time on British European Airways from Paris.

I also made arrangements with the Army on Rhein-Main Air Base for transportation for Peg and me to the United States. I arranged for us to leave from Mildenhall RAF Station for McGuire Air Force Base, New Jersey, USA, and for the Air Force to pick us up at Peg's sister's house and take us to Mildenhall, England. I boarded Air France flight for Paris and had some good snacks and excellent wine on the flight.

24 October 1969: I arrived at Paris International Airport (Orley), Paris, France. I left the flight to board British European Airways for London. We left Paris (Orley) International Airport for Heathrow International Airport, London, England, and to meet Peggy.

24 October 1969: Arriving at Heathrow International Airport, London, England, Peggy was not there to meet me. (The reason she was not there was because she did not get the cable I sent to her until after I had arrived at 332 Kingshill Ave., Hayes, Middlesex,

England.) After arriving at the airport, I took a bus to her sister's house to see what the problem was, and was relieved to find her there.

25 October 1969: We booked reservations at a hotel in Bournemouth, England, for two weeks from October 26 through November 8, 1969. Then we took a train to Bournemouth and upon arriving, we took a taxi to the hotel.

Our stay in Bournemouth was absolutely wonderful and relaxing, getting to know each other again. One day we took a walk along the beachfront, looking for the Chine Court Hotel, that we had stayed at in 1954. We fount it and it still looked the same as when we had stayed there. It was still in operation as a hotel.

8 November 1969: When our two weeks were up, we took a train to Hayes, Middlesex, and then a taxi to Peg's sister's house, where we stayed for nine days. We had an enjoyable time with them.

16 November 1969: A bus from RAF Station Mildenhall, picked us up at 332 Kingshill Avenue, Hayes, Middlesex, and transported us to the RAF Station.

16 November 1969: We arrived at RAF Station Mildenhall, and made arrangements for our flight to McGuire Air Force Base, New Jersey, USA.

We had a couple of days on our hands before our flight to McGuire Air Force Base, New Jersey, USA, so we stayed at the "Bird-in-Hand" Hotel, just outside RAF Station Mildenhall for a couple (two) nights.

While at the Bird-in-Hand Hotel, I had the largest piece of fish (for supper) that I have ever had in my entire life. I managed to eat it all with great relish, while Peg had a lovely and delicious steak and kidney pie dinner.

We had orders to report to RAF Station Mildenhall, early in the morning to catch our flight to McGuire AFB. We departed RAF Station Mildenhall on 19 November 1969 on a military aircraft for the USA.

CHAPTER 14

19 NOVEMBER 1969 - 1 DECEMBER 1969

USA—FORT DIX, NEW JERSEY

A. McGuire Air Force Base, NJ	19 Nov 1969-19 Nov 1969
B. Fort DIX, NJ	19 Nov 1969-19 Nov 1969
C. Fort Devens, MA	20 Nov 1969-30 Nov 1969

<u>19 November 1969</u>: We arrived at McGuire Air Force Base, New Jersey, and were met by U. S. Army Personnel, and taken through U. S. Customs by them. They then took us to the Returnee—Reassignment Station, U. S. Army Personnel Center, Fort Dix, New Jersey, for processing.

It is important to stress here, that I had literally flown around the world in just over a year. My journey began at Rhein-Main Air Base on 17 October 1968, by military aircraft for Gander Air Base, Newfoundland, Canada. Then I left Gander AB for McGuire Air Force Base, New Jersey, USA. I then flew from McGuire AB to Logan International Airport, Boston, Massachusetts. I left Logan International Airport on American Airlines for Los Angeles International Airport, California. Flying from Los Angeles International Airport (on commercial aircraft), I flew to San Francisco International Airport, California. Then I flew from Travis Air Force Base, California, to Kadena Air Base, Okinawa, Japan, by American Airlines. From Kadena AB, I flew to Bien Hoa Air Base, Vietnam, by military aircraft. On 23 October 1969, I left Tan Son Nhut Air Base, Saigon, Vietnam, for Bangkok, Thailand, by military aircraft. Then from Bangkok International Airport, Thailand, for New Delhi International Airport,

India, by Pan American Air Lines. I left New Delhi International Airport (by PanAm), for Tehran International Airport, Iran. Leaving Tehran International Airport, we flew to Beirut International Airport (by Pan Am), Lebanon. We left Beirut International Airport for Istanbul (by Pan Am), Turkey. From Istanbul, Turkey, we flew (by Pan Am) to Athens International Airport, Greece. I then flew from Athens, Greece to Frankfurt International Airport (by Pan Am), Germany. From Frankfurt International Airport, I flew to Paris International Airport (Orley), (by Air France), France. I then flew from Paris to Heathrow International Airport (by British European Airways), London, England, picking up my wife. We flew from Mildenhall RAF Station, (by Military aircraft) England, for McGuire Air Force Base, New Jersey, USA. My journey was over, literally flying around the world in just over a year.

This is something most people cannot claim to have done in their lifetime. It is something that will always be with me until I die.

After completing processing on Fort Dix, we boarded a bus for Fort Devens, Massachusetts.

20 November 1969: We arrived at Fort Devens. I reported to the Personnel Officer in Charge for in processing. After processing, the Officer in charge of the Personnel Center told me to take my wife and go home until the 29th of November, as there was nothing else for me to do—that I should return on the 29th for final processing and discharge (retirement).

20 November 1969: We boarded a bus for Willimansett, Massachusetts, and we stayed with my mother and my sister's family for eight days. My brother-in-law, Doug, had picked up our car at the Brooklyn Naval Yard (Brooklyn Army Depot) and kept it at his house for the year that I was in Vietnam. Upon retrieving our car, we proceeded to tour the surrounding countryside with my mother (who was living with my sister). We took her to the Log Cabin Restaurant for dinner (a place she and my step-father used to go). She thoroughly enjoyed it and also our trips to Mountain Park Amusement Center, Mt. Tom, and places we used to live at years ago.

29 November 1969: When it was time to leave, we drove to Fort Devens for final processing and discharge (retirement). We stayed in the Post Guest House for two nights.

<u>30 November 1969</u>: I completed the final phase of processing for discharge (retirement). I was presented with a Department of the Army Certificate of Appreciation from General W. C. Westmoreland, United States Army Chief of Staff. (*For a copy of this certificate, see attachment B145.*)

<u>30 November 1969</u>: So after 23 years, 1 month, three weeks and three days, it was time to say "good-bye" to the military, and hang up my uniform for civilian clothes. Most of my time in the military service was exceptionally good (especially my marriage to Peggy), except for one year in Vietnam, which was hell.

The only injuries I sustained were as follows:

1) While on Master at Arms (Charge of Quarters) duty on board the USNS Upshur (troopship) during a storm, I was thrown against a bulkhead and then down a flight of stairs, causing injury to my back (which later resulted in spinal surgery), resulting in back surgery in 1968.
2) While in Vietnam, one night while getting into the back of a 3/4 ton truck, I tripped over a tire on the floor of the vehicle, resulting in injury to my back (spinal surgery area), and my having to go to physical therapy for three weeks.
The Lord was with me during my years in the military and provided me with a Guardian Angel to look over me and keep me out of harms way.

<u>1 December 1969</u>: After receiving my Retirement Certificate (DD Form 363A) and final paperwork, we drove north to Portland, Maine, which was to be our new home in retirement. No more paperwork, no more special orders, no more verbal orders, and no more night work and duty, etc. (*For a copy of this form, see attachment B146.*)

In Portland, Maine, where we had decided to live in retirement, there was a small Coast Guard Station, with a small Ship Store (Naval Exchange) and a commissary. The nearest military installation was Brunswick Naval Air Station, which had a large Naval Exchange and a large commissary.

We would now spend a life free of military instructions, transfers, etc., being able to do all the things we wanted to do whenever we wanted to.

So a new Chapter in our lives was beginning and that is another story.

God Bless America.

Now at 84, as I finish writing this book, and have it published.

I am happy to announce that Peggy and I have been married for 60 (sixty) years next month with God's blessing. It is quite apparent that real love changes everything.

APPENDIX A

PHOTOGRAPHS

A1 Author, half-sister Lorraine & Eddie Banks

A2 Author's brother Gaston in Massachusetts State Guard uniform

A3 Step-sister Mildred (Emily), author's mother, author, nephew Bobby, half-sister Lorraine, nephew Roger, step-brother Francis, brothers Bob & Gaston

A4 Author in OD (Olive Drab) uniform in training area

A5 Author's friend Lawrence (Larry) Steffan

A6 Author in OD (Olive Drab) uniform with Corporal stripes

A7 Stenographer Graduating Class with class instructor, M. E. Wolfe

A8 Honor Guard for President Harry S. Truman

A9 Change of Command Ceremony, Flight Line, Eglin AFB, Fla.

A10 Class Participation, Auxiliary Fire Fighting School

A11 Author's wife, Peggy, in RAF uniform

A12 Bride & Groom outside side entrance of St. Mary's Church

A13 Bridal Party, just outside side entrance of St. Mary's Church

A14 Bridal Party with bride's mother & father

A15 Everyone attending the wedding reception, just outside of reception hall

A16 Bride & Groom cutting the wedding cake

A17 Bride & Groom leaving the wedding reception

A18 Author's mother & step-father

A19 Author outside Bicester North Railway Station

A20 Ship named "Bacchus" in Amsterdam Harbor

A21 7th Air Division NCO Academy—Graduating Class

A22   Author's wife's father in RAF uniform

A23   Christening party

A24   Author's wife, Peg, on the SS Maasdam, leaving for England

A25   Author & his wife standing in front of the Leaning Tower of Pisa

A26   Author, standing outside of the TUSLOG Shopping Center

A27   Author's wife standing outside of our 2nd Turkish apartment

A28   Turkish Military Policeman

A29   Renkli Cinema, Ankara, Turkey

A30   USAF Hospital, Wiesbaden AB, Germany

A31   Cuckoo Clock Building, Wiesbaden, Germany

A32   "Green Hornet"—our car

A33   Author and his wife

A34   Author's wife at the Grand Canyon

A35   Author at the Grand Canyon

A36   Norman Skelly

A37   Author & T/Sgt Robert (Bob) Paquet

A38   Guest Speaker at Dining-In, Taipei Air Station, Taipei, Taiwan

A39   Crypto Personnel Attending Dining-In

A40   Author and his wife with her family

A41   Author with his brother-in-law and father-in-law

A42   Little Spanish girl in native attire, Seville, Spain

A43   Brig. Gen. Stone and author, inspecting switchboard, Moron AB, Spain

A44   Author's wife, mother-in-law and author in horse-drawn carriage, Seville, Spain.

A45   Lt. Col. Novak, presenting Outstanding AUTODIN Award to Maj. Nelson D. Cournoyer and author

A46   Major Nelson D. Cournoyer, administering Oath of Office to author

A47   Aerial view of McNair Kassern, Frankfurt/Hoechst, Germany

A48   Author in U. S. Army fatigues, with Warrant Officer insignia

A49   Tour of Federal Germany Post Office (Bundes Post) Telecommunications Operations, Frankfurt, Germany

A50   Author addressing visiting U. S. Students on floating restaurant (river boat), Frankfurt, Germany

A51 German Police General addressing officers and their wives, in 32nd Signal Battalion Officers/Civilian open mess

A52 Author, his mother and half-sister's children

A53 Author and his brother Bob's children

A54 Picture of author's wife, sent to him from England to Vietnam

A55 Bridge over the River Kwai

A56 Author & wife, eating in Thai Restaurant, Bangkok, Thailand

A57 69th Signal Battalion Officers on patrol

A58 Author in combat gear, prior to inspecting Guard Post

A59 Author, CW3 Harry J. Markley, 1st Lt. Vollarth, in combat gear, prior to going on patrol

A60 69th Signal Battalion Commander presenting Author with going away present, just before leaving Vietnam

APPENDIX **B**

LIST OF ATTACHMENTS

B1	28 Nov 46	Thanksgiving Day Menu
B2	Undated	Phonetic Alphabets
B3	Undated	Map of Eglin Military Reservation
B4	Undated	Diagram of Police Squadron Area
B5	Undated	List of Units on Eglin AFB
B6	15 Jun 48	Graduation Program
B7	15 Jun 48	Graduation Photo Holder
B8	15 Jun 48	Certificate of Proficiency—Stenographer
B9	30 Sep 48	LTR, SUBJ: To Whom It May Concern
B10	25 Dec 48	Christmas Dinner Menu
B11	8 Aug 50	S. O. No. 152
B12	10 Oct 50	Student Record Card
B13	13 Oct 50	Certificate of Proficiency—Cryptographic
B14	Undated	LTR, SUBJ: Congratulations
B15	27 Oct 50	LTR, SUBJ: Security Clearance
B16	11 Sep 51	USAFI FORM No. A-10
B17	3 Oct 51	USAFI FORM A-2
B18	9 Oct 51	USAFI FORM A-66
B19	20 Nov 51	"Restricted" Outgoing Transport USNS GEN. M. L. HERSEY
B20	21 Nov 51	S.O. No. 234
B21A	24 Jun 52	Application for Permission to Marry, 1st Ind
B21B	3 Jul 52	Letter of Acquiescence—Marriage

B21C	9 Sep 52	LTR, SUBJ: Peggy Banks
B21D	18 Jul 52	LTR, SUBJ: Request for Security Investigation
B21E	26 Aug 52	CERTIFICATE
B21F	26 Aug 52	CERTIFICATE
B21G	Undated	Statement of Fiancé or Fiancee
B21H	26 Jun 52	LTR, SUBJ: Application for Permission to Marry
B21I	26 Jul 52	LTR, SUBJ: Request Permission to Marry
B22	15 Jan 53	Air Base Group Form 19
B23	10 Jun 53	S.O. No. 117
B24	15 Aug 53	Certificate—7th Air Division NCO Academy
B25	15 Aug 53	Diploma—7th Air Division NCO Academy
B26	Undated	Student Evaluation Sheet 7th Air Division, NCO Academy
B27	9 Oct 53	LTR, SUBJ: Physical Condition
B28	22 Feb 54	Public Law 513, 81st Congress, 2nd Session
B29	1 Mar 54	LTR, SUBJ: Authorization and Consent
B30	10 May 54	LTR, SUBJ: Security Clearance Notification
B31	5 Aug 54	LTR, SUBJ: VISA
B32	28 Aug 54	LTR, SUBJ: To Whom It May Concern
B33	25 Sep 54	LTR, SUBJ: Request for Promotion
B34	10 Nov 54	LTR, SUBJ: Letter of Commendation
B35	16 Aug 55	LTR, SUBJ: Recommendation for NCO of the Month
B36	31 Oct 55	AF Form 1256
B37	2 Jul 56	Letter Order #650
B38	9 Sep 56	Fort Hamilton Form 0379
B39	10 Sep 56	LTR, SUBJ: Orientation for Surface Travel Aboard Military Sea Transportation Service Vessels
B40	16 Sep 56	Farewell Dinner Menu
B41	8 Mar 57	S. O. No. 30
B42	15 Apr 58	S. O. No. C-32
B43	16 Apr 58	LTR, SUBJ: Transportation Authorization No. 9
B44	14 Aug 58	AF Form 279
B45	22 Aug 58	S. O. No. A-217
B46	10 Oct 58	LTR, SUBJ: Commendation

B47	14 Oct 58	LTR, SUBJ: Letter of Appreciation
B48	18 Oct 58	S. O. No. A-217
B49	11 Nov 58	S. O. No. A-217
B50	28 Nov 58	ARDC Form 104
B51	1 Dec 58	LTR, SUBJ: Verification of Security Clearance
B52	4 Dec 58	AF Form 47
B53	25 Jun 59	SWPM Form 0-59
B54	24 Nov 59	Statement of Interview
B55	31 Mar 60	AF Form 1164
B56	12 May 60	AF Form 626
B57	31 May 60	AF Form 1164
B58	5 Aug 60	LTR, SUBJ: Station Information
B59	5 Oct 60	LTR, SUBJ: Station Information
B60	1 Nov 60	SB Form 27
B61	4 Nov 60	LTR, SUBJ: Extension of Enlistment
B62	7 Nov 60	AF Form 1411
B63	10 Jan 61	LTR, SUBJ: Request for Reassignment
B64	15 Feb 61	FM SC FL-215
B65	18 May 61	AF Form 1164
B66	8 Jun 61	AF Form 1164
B67	8 Nov 61	LTR, SUBJ: Reenlistment
B68	12 Dec 61	AF Form 538
B69	11 Jan 62	LTR, SUBJ: Letter of Appreciation
B70	16 Aug 62	LTR, SUBJ: NCO of the Month (July)
B71	6 Nov 62	Dining-In Program
B72	8 May 63	LTR, SUBJ: Letter of Appreciation
B73	19 Sep 63	NAVMC 184-MCI (11-22) 25.8
B74	18 Oct 63	AF Form 1256
B75	5 Nov 63	IATDON Form 13
B76	26 Nov 63	IATIN FC 13
B77	27 Nov 63	SCS FL 130
B78	28 Jan 64	AF Form 1227
B79	6 Apr 64	AF Form 75

B80	17 Apr 64	LTR, SUBJ: Letter of Appreciation
B81	undated	DD form 528
B82	11 Mar 65	LTR, SUBJ: AIRCOMNET Communications
B83	30 APR 65	IBM M39238
B84	31 Aug 65	Air University, U. S. Air Force, Extension Course Institute Diploma
B85	13 Sep 65	AF Form 1466
B86	17 Sep 65	AF Form 911
B87	23 Sep 65	SAC Form 460
B88	25 Sep 65	Statement in English and Spanish
B89	4 Oct 65	SCS Form 1100
B90	20 Oct 65	AF Form 1193
B91	31 Dec 65	MCS MCEC 839
B92	23 Feb 66	DA Form 160
B93	9 Mar 66	DD Form 98
B94	11 Mar 66	LTR, SUBJ: Request for Waiver
B95	11 Mar 66	LTR, SUBJ: Request for Waiver
B96	15 Mar 66	LTR, SUBJ: Request for Educational Award
B97	23 Mar 66	Standard Form 88
B98	23 Mar 66	SAC Form 133
B99	14 Apr 66	USAFE Form 80 LRA
B100	15 Apr 66	AF Form 1098
B101	28 Apr 66	Standard Form 513
B102	11 May 66	AF Form 911
B103	24 May 66	AF Form 1098
B104	20 Jul 66	AF Form 1098
B105	25 Jul 66	AF Form 186
B106	28 Jul 66	AF Form 911
B107	11 Aug 66	DD Form 1299
B108	23 Sep 66	LTR, SUBJ: Appointment as a Reserve Warrant Officer of the Army
B109	29 Sep 66	LTR, SUBJ: Active Duty
B110	10 Oct 66	LTR, SUBJ: Appointment and Concurrent Call to Active Duty

B111	24 Oct 66	LTR, SUBJ: Separation for the Convenience of the Government
B112	17 Nov 66	LTR, SUBJ: Professional Books
B113	21 Nov 66	DD Form 137
B114	30 Nov 66	DA Form 3054
B115	5 Dec 66	DA Form 1290
B116	15 Dec 66	AE Form 3317
B117	27 Dec 66	DA Form 10-233
B118	26 Jan 67	DA Form 669
B119	11 Apr 67	DA Form 1506
B120	25 Aug 67	LTR, SUBJ: Seminar Fur Politik
B121	23 Nov 67	Thanksgiving Day Menu
B122	25 Jan 68	DA Form 8-275-2
B123	Feb 68	Get Well Card
B124	25 Feb 68	LTR, SUBJ: AETVSI
B125	31 Aug 68	DA Form 10-102
B126	16 Oct 68	DA Form 137 (AE)
B127	27 Oct 68	Base Billeting Fund
B128	30 Oct 68	DA Form 3161
B129	7 Nov 68	LTR, SUBJ: Request for Reassignment
B130	9 Nov 68	DA Form 2496
B131	14 Feb 69	DA Form 2820
B132	1 Mar 69	LTR, SUBJ: Rebuttal of Conclusion of Investigating Officer
B133	9 May 69	LTR, SUBJ: Letter of Appreciation
B134	20 May 69	LTR, SUBJ: Pay Officers Schedule
B135	10 Jun 69	DA Form 1041
B136	27 June 69	LTR, SUBJ: Car Insurance
B137	18 Jul 69	LTR, SUBJ: Receipt of Retirement Application
B138	7 Aug 69	DA Form 11-78
B139	10 Oct 69	LTR, SUBJ: Promotion as a Reserve Warrant Officer of the Army
B140	11 Oct 69	Bronze Star Medal Award
B141	18 Oct 69	DA Form 10-102
B142	20 Oct 69	DA Form 296

B143   20 Oct 69   DA Form 619
B144   22 Oct 69   Columbia Export Packers, Inc.
B145   30 Nov 69   Certificate of Appreciation
B146   1 Dec 69   DD form 363A

APPENDIX C

LIST OF ABBREVIATIONS

A	Army
AAA	Anti-Aircraft Artillery
AACS	Airways & Air Communications Service
AAF	Army Air Field
AAF	Army Air Forces
AAFTS	Army Air Forces Training Squadron
AB	Air Base
ABG	Air Base Group
ABGRU	Air Base Group
ABS	Absence
ABT	About
ABWG	Air Base Wing
ACC	Accompanied
ACCT	Accident
ACCT	Account
ACCTG	Accounting
ACCTS	Accounts
ACD	Accordance
ACFT	Aircraft
ACMP	Accompany
ACofS	Assistant Chief of Staff
ACP	Allied Communications Publication

AD	Active Duty
AD	Advance
AD	Air Division
ADC	Air Defense Command
ADD	Additional
ADD	Address
ADMN	Administrative
ADMIN	Administration
ADMS	Air Defense Missile Squadron
ADRS	Address
ADT	Adjutant
AE FORM	Army Europe Form
AEC	Army Extension Course
AEC	Atomic Energy Commission
AF	Air Force
AF FORM	Air Force Form
AFB	Air Force Base
AFCOMSEC	Air Force Communications Security
AFCOMSECM	Air Force Communications Security Manual
AFCS	Air Force Communications Service
AFCS FORM	Air Force Communications Service Form
AFGC	Air Force Good Conduct
AFGCMDL	Air Force Good Conduct Medal
AFL	Air Force Letter
AFLSA	Air Force Longevity Service Award
AFM	Air Force Manual
AFORG	Air Force Organization
AFR	Air Force Regulation
AFRES	Air Force Reserve
AFRTC	Air Force Reserve Training Center
AFS	Air Force Specialty
AFSC	Air Force Specialty Code
AFCS-S	Air Force Specialty Code—Shipping

AFSN	Air Force Serial Number
AFSWC	Air Force Special Weapons Center
AFUS	Air Force of the United States
AGCY	Agency
AGO	Adjutant General's Office
ALA	Alabama
ALOC	Allocation
ALT	Alternative
ALW	Allowance
ALWS	Allowances
AMC	Air Material Command
AMC	Air Movement Command
AMD	Amend
AMER	America
AMMO	Ammunition
AMDD	Amended
AMN	Airman
AMNS	Airman's
AMT	Amount
&	And
AO	Air Officer
A/O	and/or
AP	Air Police
A/P	Allied/Papers
APAL	Application
APG	Air Proving Ground
APG FORM	Air Proving Ground Form
APGC	Air Proving Ground Command
APLT	Applicant
APO	Aerial Post Office
APO	Air Post Office
APO	Army Post Office
APOE	Aerial Port of Embarkation
APP	Applicant

APPD	Approved
APPT	Applicant
APPL	Application
APPR	Apprentice
APPR	Approved
APPROX	Approximately
APR	Apprentice
APR	April
APR	Airman's Performance Report
APRT	Airport
APPX	Approximately
APT	Appoint
APTD	Appointed
ARMD	Armed
ARDC	Air Research and Development Command
ARDC FORM	Air Research and Development Command Form
ARM	Armored
ARR	Arriving
ARR	Arrival
ARV	Army Republic of Vietnam
ARV	Arrived
AS	Air Station
AS	Air Support
ASAP	As Soon As Possible
ASG	Assigned
ASG	Assignment
APT	Appointment
APT	Air Port
AR	Army Regulation
ARR	Arrived
ASGD	Assigned
ASGMT	Assignment
ASST	Assistant

A3C	Airman Third Class
ATC FORM	Air Training Command Form
ATCH	Attach
ATCHD	Attached
ATCO	Army Transportation Control Officer
ATRC	Air Training Command
ATTN	Attention
AUG	August
AUS	Army of the United States
AUTH	Authority
AUTH	Authorities
AUTHD	Authorized
AUTO DIN	Automatic Digital Network
AVAIL	Available
AVAL	Available
AVE	Avenue
AMN	Aviation
AWOL	Absent Without Leave
AW	Articles of War
B	Base
B & H	Bell & Howell
BAG	Baggage
BAS	Basic
BD	Board
BDE	Brigade
BEV	Beverage
BI	Background Investigation
BKLYN	Brooklyn
B/L	Basic Letter
BLDG	Building
BN	Battalion
BP	Base Pay

BR	Branch
BR	British
BS	Bases
BPER	Bureau of Personnel
BOMB	Bombardment
BOQ	Bachelor Officer Quarters
BSUPPL	Base Supplement
BTRY	Battery
BTL	Bottle
BTWN	Between
C	Change
C	Changed
C	Correspondence
CA	California
CAFSC	Control Air Force Specialty Code
CAL	Caliber
CALIF	California
C&E	Communications and Electronics
CAPT	Captain
CAR	Carrier
CARR	Carrier
CAS	Casual
CAS	Casualty
CAT	Category
CAU	Caucasian
CAV	Cavalry
CDR	Commander
CERT	Certificate
CERT	Certified
CFM	Confirm
CFM	Confirmed
CFMG	Confirming

CG	Commanding General
CHAP	Chapter
CHG	Change
CHG	Changed
CHGD	Changed
CHMAAG	Chief Military Assistance Advisory Group
CINCUSAEUR	Commander in Chief United States Army Europe
CIO	Command Issuing Office
CIV	Civilian
(CIV)	Civilian
CK	Clerk
CL	Class
CLAS	Class
CLASD	Classified
CLASN	Classification
CLER	Clerical
CLK	Clerk
CLNC	Clearance
CMBT	Combat
CMD	Command
CMSGT	Chief Master Sergeant
COMDR	Commander
CML	Chemical
CMT	Comment
CO	Commanding Officer
CO	Company
CO	Country
C/O	Care of
COA	Company Alpha
COB	Company Bravo
COL	Colonel
COLO	Colorado
COM	Command

COM	Commissioned
COMBRON	Commander Air Base Squadron
COMCEN	Communication Center
COMD	Command
COMDR	Commander
COMDT	Commandant
COML	Commercial
COMM	Common
COMM	Communications
COMM & ELECT	Communications & Electronics
COMP	Completed
COMP	Compliance
COMP	Component
COMPL	Completion
COMSEC	Communications Security
CON	Conference
CON	Continental
CON	Control
CON	Conversation
CONAC	Continental Air Command
CONCR	Concurrent
CONF	Confirmation
CONFRD	Confirmed
CONT	Continental
CONT	Continued
CONT	Control
CONUS	Continental United States
CONV	Convalescent
CONV	Convention
CORR	Correspondence
CP	Camp
CPL	Corporal
CPX	Communications Post Exercise

CPYS	Copies
CRS	Course
CRSE	Course
CRYPTO	Cryptographic
C/S	Chief of Staff
CSO	Crypto Security Officer
CTN	Carton
CURR	Currency
CURR	Current
CW	Chief Warrant
CW2	Chief Warrant 2nd Grade
CW3	Chief Warrant 3rd Grace
CW4	Chief Warrant 4th Grade
CWO	Chief Warrant Officer
CY	Copy
DA	Department of the Army
DA	Department of the Army Form
DAF	Department of the Air Force
DAFB	Dow Air Force Base
DAFSC	Duty Air Force Specialty Code
DASO	Department of the Army Special Order
DB	Date of Birth
DC	District of Columbia
DCO	Deputy Commander Operations
DCOCE	Deputy Chief of Operations Communications-Electronics
DCS	Deputy Chief of Staff
DD	Department of Defense
DD FORM	Department of Defense Form
DDALVP	Days Delay Authorized Leave Provided
DD FORM	Department of Defense Form
DDUS	Date Due in the United States
DEC	December

DEP	Deputy
DEPN	Dependent
DEPT	Department
DEPT	Departure
DEPTS	Dependents
DEROS	Date Estimated Return from Overseas
DEST	Destination
DEST	Destruction
DET	Detachment
DET 1	Detachment no. 1
DEV	Development
DFR	Dropped from the Rolls
DIR	Directed
DIR	Direction
DIR	Director
DIRD	Directed
DISB	Disbursement
DISCH	Discharge
DISCHD	Discharged
DIST	Distributed
DIST	District
DIV	Division
DMOS	Duty Military Occupational Specialty
DMST	Demonstration
DMST	Demonstrate
DMSTD	Demonstrated
DO	District Office
DOB	Date of Birth
DOD	Department of Defense
DOE	Date of Enlistment
DOE	Date of Expiration
DOR	Date of Reenlistment
DOR	Date of Rank

DOS	Date of Separation
DOSI	District Office of Special Investigation
DPRT	Departed
DPRT	Departure
DPS	Displaced Persons
DR	Drive
DR	Date of Rank
DR	Doctor
DROS	Date Return from Overseas
DS	Detached Service
DSGD	Designated
D-SSN	Duty-Service Specialty Number
DT	Date
DT	Duty
DTD	Dated
DTLD	Detailed
DV	Division
DY	Duty
DY-AFSC	Duty-Air Force Specialty Code
DYSECT	Duty Section
EAD	Extended Active Duty
EC	Electronics
ECI	Extension Course Institute
EDCSA	Effective Date Change Strength Accountability
EFF	Effective
EFFCY	Efficiency
8TH	Eighth Air Force
8TH	DISOSI Eighth District Office of Special Investigation
EL	Electronics
ELECT	Electrical
11TH	Eleventh
EM	Enlisted Men

EM	Enlistment
ENG	England
ENGR	Engineer
ENL	Enlistment
ENV	Envelope
EOS	Expiration of Service
ESTBL	Established
ETC	Et cetera
ETO	European Theatre of Operations
ETS	Expiration of Term of Service
EVAL	Evaluation
EVID	Evidence
EX	Examination
EX	Excess
EXC	Exceed
EXP	Expense
EXT	Extension
EXTEN	Extension
FAA	Federal Aeronautical Agency
F&AO	Finance & Accounting Officer
FBI	Federal Bureau of Investigation
FD	Finance Department
FD	Food
FEAF	Far East Air Force
FEB	February
FED	Federal
1ST	First
1Lt	First Lieutenant
1ST LT	First Lieutenant
FGN	Foreign
FILA	Familiarization
FIN	Finance
FINO	Finance Officer

FISCO	Fiscal Officer
FILAM	Familiarization
5TH	Fifth
FLU	Influenza
FLA	Florida
FLD	Field
FLT	Flight
FM	Field Manual
FM	From
FNA	Following Named Airmen
FNE	Following Named Enlisted Men
FNDL	Fundamental
FNI	Following Named Individual
FNOA	Following Named Officers and Airmen
FO	Finance Officer
FO	For
F/O	Fiscal Orders
F/O	Further Orders
FOJT	Formal On-the-Job Training
FOL	Following
FOLG	Following
FOLS	Follows
FR	From
FSA	Family Separation Allowance
FSC O	Fiscal Officer
F/S	Flying Status
FS	Flying Status
FSO	Fiscal Officer
FT	First
FT	Fort
FTD	Field Training Detachment
FTR	Fighter
FUN	Function

FUNC	Functional
FUNCT	Functional
FUR	Furnished
FURN	Furnish
FWD	Forwarding
FWD	Forwarded
GA Georgia	
GCMDL	Good Conduct Medal
GED	General Education Development
GEN	General
GER	Germany
GOVT	Government
GP	Group
GR	Grade
GRAD	Graduate
GRADS	Graduates
GS	General Support
H	Heavy
HEDRONSEC	Headquarters Squadron Section
HHC	Headquarters & Headquarters Company
HHE	Household
HHG	Household Goods
HHLD	Household
HHS	Headquarters & Headquarters Squadron
HIST	History
HLPR	Helper
HOLD	Holding
HON	Honor
HOR	Home of Record
HOSP	Hospital
HQ	Headquarters

HQ APG	Headquarters Air Proving Ground
HQ COMD	Headquarters Command
HQS	Headquarters
HQS & HQS	Headquarters & Headquarters
HRS	Hours
HS	High School
HTR	Haute
IATA	In Addition to Above
IATA	In Addition to Announced
IATR	Is Altered to Read
IAW	In Accordance with
ID	Identify
ID	Identification
IG	Inspector General
ILL	Illinois
ILO	In Lieu of
ILOT	In Lieu of Transportation
IMM	Immunization
IM	Immediately
IN BOUND P/L	Inbound Pipe Line
INC	Incorporated
INCL	Include
INCR	Increments
IND	Indicated
IND	Indorsement
INDC	Indicated
INDEF	Indefinite
INDEF	Indefinitely
INDIV	Individual
INDV	Individual
INFEC	Infectious
INFO	Information

IN/PAR	In Paragraph
INSTL	Installation
INSTLS	Installations
INSTR	Instructions
INSTRU	Instrument
INTVW	Interview
INV	Investigated
INV	Investigation
JAN	January
JATCO	Joint Army Traffic Control Officer
JFK	John F. Kennedy Airport
JFP	Joint Fire Power
JN	Join
JO	Joined
JR	Junior
JTR	Joint Travel Regulation
JUL	July
JUN	June
JUSMMAT	Joint U. S. Military Mission Aiding Turkey
KAFB	Kirtland Air Force Base
KANS	Kansas
K.P.	Kitchen Police
LAB	Laboratory
LACW	Loading Aircraft Women
LBS	Pounds
LDSP	Leadership
LIT	Literature
LO	Letter Order
LOC	Local
LOC	Location
LOC	Locator

LT	Lieutenant
LTC	Lieutenant
LT COL	Lieutenant Colonel
LTD	Limited
LTR	Letter
LV	Leave
M	No Deferment of any Kind
MA	Massachusetts
MA	Master
MAAG	Military Assistance Advisory Group
MAAG-TAIWAN	Military Assistance Advisory Group—Taiwan
MAC FORM	Military Airlift Command Form
MACV	Military Assistance Command Vietnam
MAJ	Major
MAN	Manual
MAP	Military Assistance Program
MAR	March
MARCORPERSMAN	Marine Corps Personnel Manual
MARY	Maryland
MAS	Massachusetts
MASS	Massachusetts
MAT	Material
MATS	Military Air Transport Service
MATS FORM	Military Air Transport Service Form
MATS-PAC	Military Air Transport Service—Pacific
MAX	Maximum
MBR	Member
MBRS	Members
MC	Medical Corps
MCI	Marine Corps Institute
MCM	Manual for Courts Martial
MCS	Marine Corps School

ME	Maine
MECH	Mechanical
MED	Medical
MGT	Management
MKM	Marksman
MIL	Military
MIL PMT CERT	Military Payment Certificates
MO	Missouri
MO	Monday
MO	Month
MO	Monetary
MON	Monday
MON	Monetary
MOP	Mustering Out Pay
MOS	Military Occupational Specialty
MOV	Movement
MP	Military Policeman
MPC	Military Payment Certificates
MPR	Military Pay Records
MPRJ	Military Pay Records Jacket
M.P.'S	Military Police
MSC	Medical Service Corps
MSG	Message
MSGT	Master Sergeant
MSN	Mission
MSTS	Military Sea Transport Service
MTOE	Military Table of Equipment
MTR	Motor
MV	Movement
MVMT	Movement
N	North
NA	Not Applicable

N/A	Not Applicable
NAVMC	Navy Marine Corps
NC	No Change
N/C	No Change
NCO	Non-Commissioned Officer
NCOAGR	Non-Commissioned Officer Academy Graduate
NCO/EM	Non-Commissioned Officer/Enlisted Men
NCOIC	Non-Commissioned Officer in Charge
NDAFSC	New Duty Air Force Specialty Code
NDSM	National Defense Service Medal
NE	Northeast
NEC	Necessary
NEV	Nevada
NH	New Hampshire
9TH	North
NJ	New Jersey
NKOREA	North Korea
NLT	No Later Than
NM	New Mexico
NMEX	New Mexico
NO	Number
NOK	Next of Kin
NON-COM	Non-Commissioned
NOS	Number
NOV	November
NOVN	North Vietnam
NR	Number
NSAT	Naval Support Activity
NSLI	National Service Life Insurance
NSTS	Naval Ship Transport Service
NTFY	Notify
NTI	No Travel Involved
NVA	North Vietnam

NVN	North Vietnam
NY	New York
NYK	New York City
NYNY	New York, New York
NYPE	New York Port of Embarkation
O	Office
O	Officer
O	Order
O/A	On or About
OBN	Obligation
OCS	Officer Candidate School
OCT	October
OD's	Olive Drab
ODAFSC	Old Duty Air Force Specialty Code
OFF	Officer
OFF'S	Officers
OFL	Official
OIC	Officer in Charge
OJT	On-the-Job Training
OLC's	Oak Leaf Clusters
(1 OLC)	One Oak Leaf Cluster
OP	Operations
OPN	Operation
OPNS	Operations
OPP	Operation
OPR	Operator
OPR	Operations
OPRS	Operations
ORD	Ordinary
ORG	Organization
ORGN	Organization
ORGNS	Organizations

OS	Overseas
O/S	Overseas
OSI	Office of Special Investigation
OS	REPL Overseas Replacement
OX	Oxfordshire
PAC	Pacific
PAC	Pacific Air command
PAC COM	Pacific Communications
PAD	Personnel Assignment Division
PAFS	Primary Air Force Specialty
PAFSC	Primary Air Force Specialty Code
PAFSN	Primary Air Force Serial Number
PAM	Personnel Actions Memorandum
PAPT	Passport
PAR	Paragraph
PARA	Paragraph
PBC	Packed by Carrier
PBO	Packed by Owner
PC	Permanent Change
PCA	Permanent Change Authority
PCS	Permanent Change of Station
PCTL	Percentile
PCR	Percentile
POV	Private Car Vehicle
PD	Paid
PD	Period
PD	Purchased
PDY	Primary Duty
PE	Pennsylvania
PE	Port of Embarkation
PER	Personnel
PERM	Permanent

PERP	Personnel Processing
PERPGRU	Personnel Processing Group
PERS	Personals
PERS ACCTG	Personnel Accounting
PERTS	Pertaining
PL	Public Law
PL	Publication
P/L-STU	Pile Line Student
PFC	Private First Class
PG	Permanent Grade
PL	Place
PL	Placed
PL	Public Law
P/L	Pipe Line
P/L PERS	Pipe Line Personnel
PM	Post Master
PM	Post Meridian
PM	Provost Marshal
P-MOS	Primary Military Occupational Specialty
PMT	Payment
POC	Privately Owned Car
POD	Point of Departure
POE	Point of Embarkation
POR	Previous Orders
POS	Position
POS	Protestant
POSS	Possession
POSTL	Postal
POV	Private Owned Vehicle
PP	Passport
PP	Permanent Party
(PP)	Permanent Party
PPG	Personnel Processing Group

PPS	Personnel Processing Squadron
PPTY	Property
PR	ay Records
PR	Primary
PR	Prior
PRES	Present
PRES	Presently
PREV	Preview
PRIM	Primary
PRIM-AFS	Primary Air Force Specialty
PRIMDY	rimary Duty
PRO	Protestant
PROC	Processing
PROGR	Program
PROM	Promoted
PROV	Provisions
PROVS	Provisions
PROV SQ	Provisional Squadron
P/S	Patient Service
PSTL	Postal
PSY	Psychology
PT	Port
P/U	Pick Up
PUB	Public
PUB	Publisher
PUBL	Publishers
PUBR	Publishers
PVT	Private
PX	Post Exchange
Q	Committed to an Overseas Assignment
QRS	Quarters
QTRS	Quarters

QUALD	Qualified
RA	Regular Army
(RACE W)	Race White
RAF	Royal Air Force
R&R	Rest & Recuperation
RAT	Rations
RCD	Received
RCT	Recruit
RECG	Receiving
RD	Road
RE	Record
RE	Relieved
RE	Reference
RE	Request
REASGD	Reassigned
REASGN	Reassign
REC	Receipt
REC	Record
RECG	Receiving
RECGO	Receiving Officer
REENL	Reenlisted
REENL	Reenlisting
REENL	Reenlistment
REF	Reference
REG	Regulation
REGAF	Regular Air Force
REGS	Regulations
REL	Relieved
REL	Relieving
RELD	Relieved
REPL	Replacement
REPT	Report

REPT	Reporting
REQ	Request
REQ	Requested
REQ	Required
REQMTS	Requirements
REQS	Requests
RES	Reserve
RESP	Respective
RET	Retired
RET	Return
RETD	Returned
RETS-RSG	Retention-Reassignment
REV	Revoked
REVO	Revoked
RFL	Refueling
RGN	Region
RM	Room
RPFD	Reporting for Duty
RPT	Report
RPTD	Reported
RPTG	Reporting
RQMTS	Requirements
RSG	Reassignment
RSGD	Reassigned
RSGMT	Reassignment
RTN	Return
RTN	Returned
RTNE	Returnee
RUAT	Report Upon Arrival to
RVN	Republic of Vietnam
RYRS	Ryukyu Islands
S	South

SA	Secretary of the Army
SAC	Strategic Air Command
SAC FORM	Strategic Air Command Form
SB	Should Be
SB	Sandia Base
SB FORM	Sandia Base Form
SC	Signal Corps
SC	South Carolina
SCH	School
SCTY	Security
SE	Southeast
SEC	Section
SEC	Security
2ND	Second
SECT	Section
SEP	September
SEP	Separate
SEP	Separation
SEP	Separately
SEP	September
7TH	Seventh
7AD	Seventh Air Division
SF	San Francisco
SFC	Sergeant First Class
SFRAN	San Francisco
SFW	Strategic Fighter Wing
SGN	Saigon
SGS	Sergeants
SGT	Sergeant
SHF	Super High Frequency
SHIPMT	Shipment
SHIPMT #1	Shipment Number One
SHIPT	Shipment

SIG	Signal
SIGC	Signal Corps
SIL	Silver
SK	Skilled
SMK	Smoke
SMO	So Much of
SMOLTRO	So Much of Letter Order
SMOP	So Much of Paragraph
SMSGT	Senior Master Sergeant
SN	Serial Number
SO	Special Orders
SOP	Standard Operating Procedure
SP	Special
SP	Specialist
SPECL	Specialist
SP4	Specialist Fourth Class
SPN	Spanish
SPT	Support
SQ	Squadron
SR	Senior
SR	Service
S RUISLIP	South Ruislip
S/R	Service Record
SSAN	Social Security Account Number
SSGT	Staff Sergeant
S/SGT	Staff Sergeant
SSK	Semi Skilled
SSN	Service Serial Number
ST	Street
ST	First
ST	Saint
STA	Station
STAS	Stations

STD	Standard
STEN	Stenographer
STGE	Storage
STN	Station
STRAT	Strategic
STUS	Students
SUP	Sufficient
SUBJ	Subject
SUBQ	Subsequent
SUBS	Subsistence
SUF	Sufficient
SUP	Supply
SUP RON	Support Squadron
SUPP	Support
SUPT	Superintendent
SUPV	Supervisor
SV	Service
SVC	Service
SWBCC	Special Weapons Branch Chief of Communications
T	Transportation
T	Tablet
TAB	Tablet
TAC	Tactical Air Command
TAC FORM	Tactical Air Command Form
TAG	The Adjutant General
TAGO	The Adjutant General's Office
TAGSCUSA	The Adjutant General School United States Army
TAX	Thrift Awareness Exercise
TBA	To Be Announced
TDN	Travel Days None
TDY	Temporary Duty
TEC	Technical

TEC	Technician
TECH	Technical
TEL	Teleconference
TEL	Telephone
TELECOMM	Telecommunications
TEMP	Temporary
TEMP USAF	Temporary United States Air Force
TERM	Terminate
TERM	Termination
3RD	Third Air Force
3RD	Third
39TH	Thirty Ninth
TM	Team
TM	Technical Manual
TM	Traffic Management
TNG	Training
TO	Transportation Officer
TO	Travel Orders
TOE	Term of Enlistment
TO'E	Table of Organization and Equipment
TO's	Travel Orders
TPA	Travel by Private Auto
TRAN	Transportation
TRANS	Transfer
TRANS	Transferred
TRANS	Transport
TRANS	Transportation
TRANS OFF	Transportation Officer
TRF	Transfer
TRF	Transferred
TRL	Travel
TRNG	Training
TR's	Transportation Request

TSGT	Technical Sergeant
T/SGT	Technical Sergeant
TSN	Tan Son Nhut
TUSLOG	The United States Logistics Group
TVL	Travel
TWX	Telegram/Wire/Cable
UAFSC	Utilization Air Force Code
UCWR	Upon Completion Will Return
UK	United Kingdom
UKPP	United Kingdom Passport
ULT	Ultimate
UM	University of Maryland
UNACC	Unaccompanied
UNACMP	Unaccompanied
UNACP	Unaccompanied
UNASG	Unassigned
UNASGD	Unassigned
UNCLAS	Unclassified
UNIV	University
UP	Under Provisions
US	United States
USA	United States Army
USA	United States of America
USAAC	United States Army Command
USAAC	United States Army Accounting Center
USAARV	United States Army—Army Republic of Vietnam
USA-ARVN	United States Army—Army of the Republic of Vietnam
USAEUR FORM	United States Army Europe Form
USAF	United States Air Force
USAFE	United States Air Force Europe
USAFE FORM	United States Air Force Europe Form
USAFERM	United States Air Force Europe Manual
USAFI	United States Armed Forces Institute

USAFI FORM	United States Armed Forces Institute Form
USAF-TEMP	United States Air Force Temporary
USAFSS FORM	United States Air Force Security Service Form
USAG	United States Army Group
USAGH	United States Army General Hospital
USAH	United States Army Hospital
USAOS RLSTA	United States Army Overseas Replacement Station
USAR	United States Army Reserve
USAREUR	United States Army Reserve Europe
USARV	United States Army Republic of Vietnam
USASCHEUR	United States Army School Europe
USA-STRAT COM	United States Army—Strategic Command
USA-STRAT COM	United States United States Army—Strategic Command 1st Signal 1st SIG BGDE Brigade
USA SUP COM	United States Army Support Command
USC	United States Code
USNS	United States Naval Ship
V	Fifth
V	Fifth Corps
V	Five
VA	Veterans Administration
VA	Veterans Affair
VA	Virginia
VEH	Vehicle
VHF	Very High Frequency
VIP'S	Very Important Persons
VN	Vietnam
VOC	Verbal Order Commander
VOCG	Verbal Order Commanding General
VOCMDR	Verbal Order of the Commander
VOCO	Verbal Order of the Commanding Officer
VOL	Volume

VOL	Voluntary
VOU	Voucher
W	Wife
W	With
W	White
(W)	White
W/Accompany	Will Accompany
WAF	Women's Air Force
WAFR	With Air Force Regulations
W/AMN	With Airmen
WASH	Washington
W/APPLY	Will Apply
W/AR	With Army Regulation
W/ARMY REG	With Army Regulations
W/B	Will Be
W/COMM	With Communications
W/CONC	With Concurrence
W/CONTACT	Will Contact
W/CONTROL	Will Control
WD	War Department
W/D	Withdrawn
WDAGO	War Department Adjutant General's Office
W/DATE	With Date
W/DEPNS	With Dependants
W/DR	With Date of Rank
W/DRAWN	Withdrawn
W/DUTY	With Duty
W/EDCSA	With Effective Date Change of Strength Accountability
W/FAMILIARIZE	Will Familiarize
W/FWD	Will Forward
WG	Wing
W/HAND CARRY	Will Hand Carry

WHSE	Warehouse
W/HAVE	Will Have
WILLPRO	Will Proceed
W/INDIC	Will Indicate
W/INSURE	Will Insure
WKLY	Weekly
WKS	Weeks
W/N/C	With No Change
W/NOT	Will Not
W/NR	With Number
W/O	Without
WO	Warrant Officer
WOD	Without Delay
WOJG	Warrant Officer Junior Grade
W/ONE	With One
W/OPERATORS	With Operators
W/OPERATIONS	With Operations
W/ORDERS	With Orders
W/ORGANS	With Organizations
WILL PRO	Will Proceed
W/P	Will Proceed
W/PAR	With Paragraph
W/PERMISSION	With Permission
W/PROFESSIONAL	With Professional
WRAF	Women's Royal Air Force
W/R	Will Return
W/REPORT	Will Report
W/RPT	Will Report
W/RTN	Will Return
W/TAKE	Will Take
W/THEM	With Them
W/THIS	With This
WT	Weight

WWIIVM	World War II Victory Medal
XO	Executive Officer
YOB	Year of Birth
YR	Year
YRS	Years
ZI	Zone of Interior

A1

A2

A3

A4

A5

A6

A7

A8

A9

A10

A11

A12

A13

A14

A15

A16

A17

A18

A19

A20

A21

A22

A23

A24

A25

A26

A27

A28

A29

A30

A31

A32

A33

A34

A35

A36

A37

A38

A39

A40

A41

A42

A43

A44

A45

A46

A47

A48

A49

A50

A51

A52

A53

A54

A55

A56

A57

A58

A59

A60

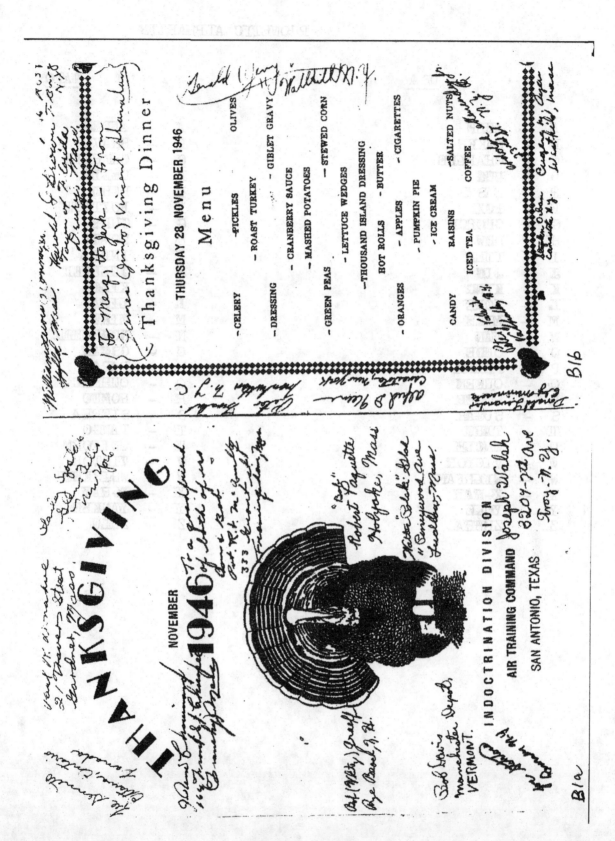

Thanksgiving Dinner

THURSDAY 28 NOVEMBER 1946

Menu

— CELERY — PICKLES — OLIVES

— DRESSING — ROAST TURKEY — GIBLET GRAVY

— CRANBERRY SAUCE — MASHED POTATOES

— GREEN PEAS — STEWED CORN

— LETTUCE WEDGES

—THOUSAND ISLAND DRESSING

HOT ROLLS — BUTTER

— ORANGES — APPLES — CIGARETTES

— PUMPKIN PIE

— ICE CREAM

CANDY RAISINS — SALTED NUTS

ICED TEA COFFEE

B1b

THANKSGIVING

NOVEMBER

1946

INDOCTRINATION DIVISION

AIR TRAINING COMMAND

SAN ANTONIO, TEXAS

B1a

PHONETIC ALPHABETS

USA			NATO		
A	–	ABLE	A	–	ALPHA
B	–	BAKER	B	–	BRAVO
C	–	CHARLIE	C	–	CHARLIE
D	–	DOG	D	–	DELTA
E	–	EASY	E	–	ECHO
F	–	FOX	F	–	FOXTROT
G	–	GEORGE	G	–	GULF
H	–	HOW	H	–	HOTEL
I	–	ITEM	I	–	INDIA
J	–	JIG	J	–	JULIET
K	–	KING	K	–	KILO
L	–	LOVE	L	–	LIMA
M	–	MIKE	M	–	MIKE
N	–	NAN	N	–	NOVEMBER
O	–	OBOE	O	–	OSCAR
P	–	PETER	P	–	PAPA
Q	–	QUEEN	Q	–	QUEBEC
R	–	ROGER	R	–	ROMEO
S	–	SUGAR	S	–	SIERRA
T	–	TARE	T	–	TANGO
U	–	UNCLE	U	–	UNIFORM
V	–	VICTOR	V	–	VICTOR
W	–	WILLIAM	W	–	WHISKEY
X	–	X-RAY	X	–	X-RAY
Y	–	YOKE	Y	–	YANKEE
Z	–	ZEBRA	Z	–	ZULU

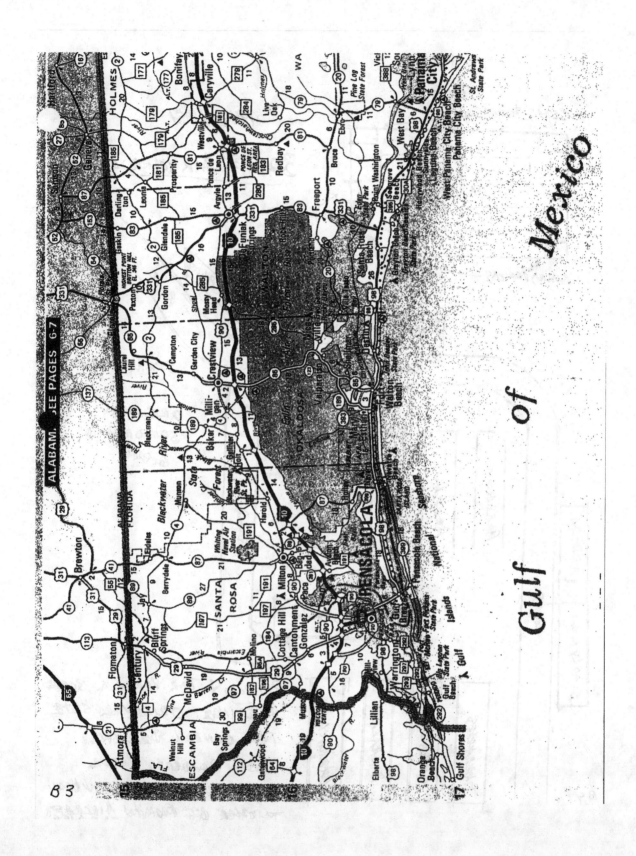

Gulf of Mexico

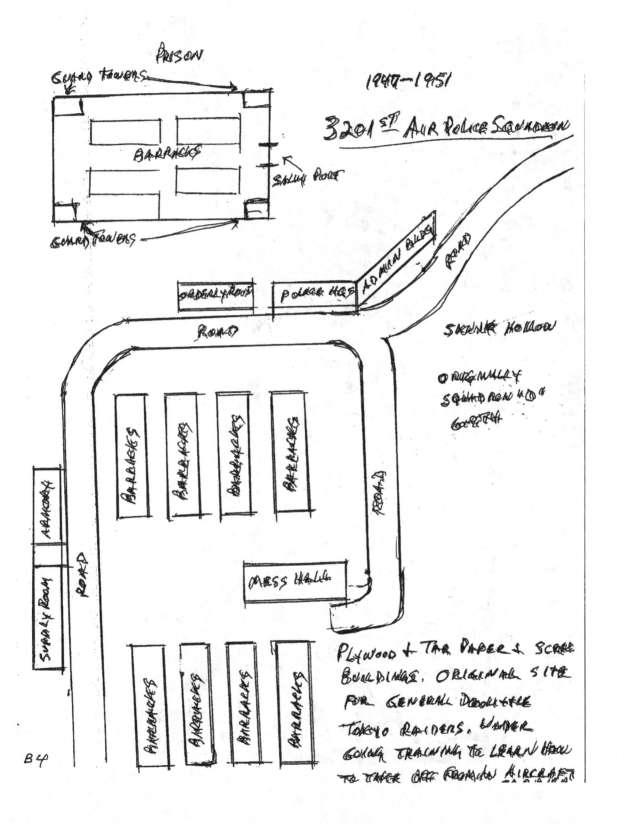

PRISON

GUARD TOWERS

BARRACKS

SALLY PORT

GUARD TOWERS

1947-1951

3201ST AIR POLICE SQUADRON

ORDERLY ROOM   POLICE HQS   ADMIN BLDG   ROAD

ROAD

SKUNK HOLLOW

ORIGINALLY
SQUADRON HQ &
ORDERLY

BARRACKS   BARRACKS   BARRACKS   BARRACKS

ROAD

ARMORY

ROAD

SUPPLY ROOM

MESS HALL

BARRACKS   BARRACKS   BARRACKS   BARRACKS

PLYWOOD + TAR PAPER + SCREEN
BUILDINGS. ORIGINAL SITE
FOR GENERAL DOOLITTLE
TOKYO RAIDERS. UNDER
GOING TRAINING TO LEARN HOW
TO TAKE OFF FROM AN AIRCRAFT

B4

Lowry Air Force Base

Denver, Colorado

Graduation Program

PROGRAM OF EXERCISES

BASE THEATER NUMBER 1

0930 Hours, 15 June 1948

Invocation	Chaplain Max T. Jank
Introduction	Captain Richard H. Cartwright
Guest Speaker	Colonel William J. Holzapfel Jr.
Presentation of Letters of Commendation	Colonel William J. Holzapfel Jr.
Presentation of Certificates of Graduation	
	Department of Transportation Training Captain John A. Keiper, Jr.
	Department of Armament Training Lt Colonel Robert T. Romine
	Department of Administrative Training Lt Colonel Oscar E. Lanctot
Benediction	Chaplain Max T. Jank

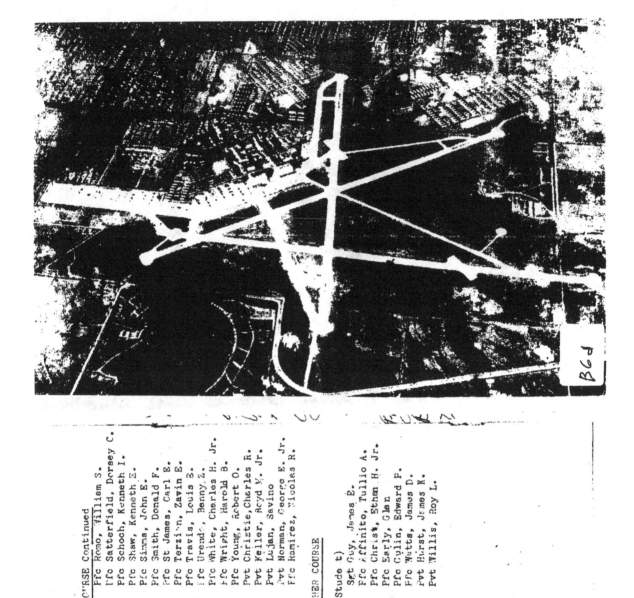

B6d

CLERK TYPIST COURSE Continued

Pfc Romero, Filemon M.
Pfc Saltz, John J.
Pfc Schichtel, Clarence T.
Pfc Scott, George J. Jr.
Pfc Shelton, Howard I.
Pfc Smith, Bobby R.
Pfc Staggs, James W.
Pfc Susso, John
Pfc Thompson, Carl C.
Pfc Truitt, Marion L.
Pfc Wall, Lester C.
Pfc Willis, Arthur R.
Pfc Wynne, Bennie H.
Pfc Zervis, Loren D.
Pvt Esquibel, Felix F.
Pvt Love, Robert L.
Pvt Mills, Billy J.
Pvt Ross, John N.
Pfc Roche, Robert F.

Pfc Romo, William S.
Pfc Satterfield, Dorsey C.
Pfc Schoch, Kenneth I.
Pfc Shaw, Kenneth E.
Pfc Simms, John E.
Pfc Smith, Donald F.
Pfc St James, Carl E.
Pfc Terzian, Zavin E.
Pfc Travis, Louis B.
Pfc Urendo, Benny Z.
Pfc White, Charles H. Jr.
Pfc Wright, Harold B.
Pfc Young, Robert O.
Pvt Christie, Charles R.
Pvt Keller, Boyd M. Jr.
Pvt Lujan, Savino
Pvt Norman, George E. Jr.
Pfc Ramirez, Nicolas R.

STENOGRAPHER COURSE

T/Sgt Pilcher, John W. (Honor Stude t)
Sgt Ducolon, Wayne P.
Cpl Mercure, Maurice F.
Pfc Andrews, Ira C.
Pfc Conrad, Clyde M.
Pfc Goudelock, James R.
Pfc Thompkins, Charles E.
Pvt Ashlock, Donald D.
Pvt Kaisersatt, Gerald J.

Sgt Guy, James E.
Pfc Affinito, Tullio A.
Pfc Christ, Ethan H. Jr.
Pfc Early, Glen
Pfc Gulin, Edward P.
Pfc Watts, James D.
Pvt Hurst, James K.
Pvt Willis, Roy L.

B6c

Photographed at

Lowry Air Force Base

Denver, Colorado

by the snowcapped Rockies

AUTOGRAPHS

United States Air Force

Air Training Command

Be it known that   Corporal Maurice F. Mercure, AF ████████

has satisfactorily completed the prescribed course of instruction of the

Air Training Command specializing in

Stenographer

In testimony whereof and by virtue of vested authority, we do confer upon

him this

═══ CERTIFICATE OF PROFICIENCY ═══

Given at Lowry Air Force Base, Colorado

on this Fifteenth   day of June

in the year of our Lord one thousand nine hundred and Forty-eight

Attest:
O. E. LANCTOT
Lt Col, USAF
Supervisor, Dept of Adm Tng

R. BEAM, Brigadier General, USAF

COMMANDANT

H. b. LAWRENCE JUNIOR HIGH SCHOOL

HOLYOKE, MASSACHUSETTS

JAMES BOWER, JR., PRINCIPAL

September 30, 1948

To Whom It May Concern:

Transcript of the record for Maurice Mercure
406 Maple St.
Holyoke, Mass.
Born - 1928-

English	C
French	C
Math.	C
Social Studies (History)	B
Manual Training	C +
Physical Training	A

Passing Grade   C

This student completed the eighth grade at the H.B. Lawrence Jr. High School, Holyoke, Mass., June 1944.

James Bower, Jr.
Principal

Christmas Greetings

1 9 4 8

3201st Air Base Group

Eglin Air Force Base, Florida

Christmas 1948

3201ST AIR BASE GROUP

EGLIN AIR FORCE BASE, FLORIDA

Roster

🎄 25 DECEMBER, 1948 🎄

3201ST AIR POLICE SQUADRON

★ ★

LT. COLONEL JOHN L. FISHER, Commanding Officer

Group Commander
JOSHUA H. FOSTER
Colonel, USAF

Executive Officer
WILLIAM C. HOOD, JR.
Lt. Colonel, USAF

CAPTAINS

Jarvis, Garland H.
Trimble, William W.
Webb, Joe S.

FIRST LIEUTENANTS

Erickson, Morris E.
Lemak, Steve

Hq. & Hq. Squadron
GUY EMERY
Captain, USAF

Boat Squadron
RALEIGH H. McQUEEN
Captain, USAF

Motor Vch. Squadron
OATTIS E. PARKS
Lt. Colonel, USAF

Air Police Squadron
JOHN L. FISHER
Lt. Colonel, USAF

MASTER SERGEANTS

Burgess, Vincent L.
Collins, Thomas
Wallace, Everette

Communications Squadron
HENRY J. HEUER
Lt. Colonel, USAF

WAF Squadron
BERTIE ROBERTS
1st Lt. USAF

TECHNICAL SERGEANTS

Heiny, William L.
Moore, Raymond J.
Skeen, Lee T.
Freeman, James A.

25th Weather Squadron
FRANCIS H. SMITH
Major, USAF

1920th AACS Squadron
GEORGE T. BOYD
Captain, USAF

STAFF SERGEANTS

Arredondo, Albert J.
Baker, Orvil R.
Beeta, Elmer R.
Bellflower, James H.
Brantley, Joe H.
Brewer, James P.
Burnett, Emmit R.
Burnett, Jewell C.
Campbell, Jack
Carr, Harold W., Jr.
Corbin, Robert D.
Culver, William H.
Dooley, Charles, Jr.

Dryer, John D.
Edwards, Lucein G.
Gilliland, Paul V.
Hamilton, Robert W.
Lambert, Benjamin F.
Latham, William J.
Pierce, Annie A.
Rezo, Manuel
Skipper, Johnnie F.
Teague, Paul N.
Tippett, Leonard J.
Truvinger, Ernest R.

584th AF Band
THOMAS G. KRONBERG
Major, USAF

SERGEANTS

Armitage, James C.
Balentine, Oswald P.
Bardsley, William R.
Buchanan, Raught J.
Christy, Johnny E.
DeHaven, Leon G.
Fontaine, Henry E.

Frazier, Harry E.
Goodwin, Billy M.
Grizzard, Carl L.
Hales, John D.
Harrison, Roy L.
Harvell, Verdyce V.
Hasch, Harold H.

MESS OFFICERS
1st Lt. Paul H. Iverson
1st Lt. M. E. Erickson
1st Lt. Richard E. Rhodes
1st Lt. Randolph C. Heard

MESS STEWARDS
M/Sgt. G. H. Sheppard
S/Sgt. J. P. Brewer
T/Sgt. J. H. Bivins
M/Sgt. W. C. Biggers

🎄 🎄 🎄 🎄 🎄 🎄

SERGEANTS (Continued)

Hiett, Olbert H.
Irwin, Merideth B.
Kean, Joseph C.
Larkins, Harold L.
Lester, William
Lucero, Elio P.
Martin, Cecil D.
McDougle, Lowell B.
Parker, Cecil B.
Phillips, Ray W.
Rea, Wayne C.
Rodgers, Willis A.
Ruppert, Sherman S.
Shields, Ernest G.
Simon, Stephen
Snyder, Jessie J.
Steele, Fred G., Jr.
Stubbs, Cecil R.
Thompson, Chester H. Jr.
Tuszle, Jack F.
Vaughan, Claude A.
Ward, Wendall S.
Wright, George E.
Yancey, George T.
Hazel, Eldon H.
Jackson, Ernest M.
Petty, Alton B.
Simmons, Lester J.

CORPORALS

Austin, Herbert R.
Booker, George H.
Bradley, George V.
Clotfelter, Delbert L.
Cly, John P.
Cook, Benjamin G.
Cruz, Herman, Jr.
Dukes, Arthur
Eurbin, Edward J.
Esposito, John V.
Fowler, Willie J.
Geer, Wilbert P.
Gerack, William H.
Gibson, Roland B.
Hibdon, Buster W.
Humphreys, Francis J.
Huxley, Walter G.
Jones, Frank
Lemelin, Joseph P.
Lovern, Doyle E.
McCormick, Charles L.
McGrath, John R.
Mercure, Maurice F.
Mika, John P.
Monz, Henry E.
Morris, Harvey L.
Murray, Frank J.
Oritway, William L.
Geisinger, Ronald K.
Pace, James G.
Pepper, Earnest B., Jr.
Perez, Manuel P.
Roberts, Lewis, Jr.
Romano, Panfilo J.
Self, Dale C.
Sellers, Acy V.
Shewhert, John P.
Smith, Ray C.
Stewart, Roy L.
Stern, Franklin, Jr.
Thorton, Vadrel L.
Valdez, Reuben B.
Vallejos, Arthur M.
Walters, George D.
Eiler, Horace D.
Winchell, Robert P.
Peter, Wolf, Jr.
Wyatt, Marion H.
Boothe, Cabhot
Breyman, Richard D.
Fincannon, E. C.
Harshberger, Edwin C.
Nunziella, Daniel F.
Owins, William B.
Pickren, Dan W.
Raines, Ralph B.
Shurtt, Curl H.
Vallejos, Octaviano F.
Zierle, John J.

PRIVATES FIRST CLASS

Anderson, Archie W.
Anderson, John J.
Atkinson, Edwin A.
Barr, Ernest E.
Barnes, Richard E.
Battisfore, Wesley R.
Baugh, George W.
Bertrand, Robert H.
Brown, Clifton
Bryan, Thomas E.

PRIVATES FIRST CLASS (Continued)

Bunch, James E.
Burke, Bobby L.
Buzbee, James W.
Carreiro, Ernest A.
Champion, Robert
Crook, Floyd C.
Cox, Joel E.
Danforth, Frank H.
Davidson, Eugene V.
Donaldson, Claude W., Jr.
Ernest, Floyd Jr.
Evans, Robert W.
Faison, Alan P.
Gainey, Thomas D.
Garner, Eugene H.
Gluska, Andrew
Grisecco, Nicholas R.
Ham, Eugene B.
Harris, George A., Jr.
Hart, Arlie A.
Hurley, Lloyd Jr.
Ivey, Charles R.
Jackson, LeRoy
Janik, Eugene J.
Johnson, Harold G.
Johnson, Walter E., Jr.
Jolly, Shields, Jr.
Kimmel, Robert V.
Langley, James E.
LeMaster, Floyd E.
Mahaffey, Charles H.
Marrs, Charles
Martin, Dexter N.
Matthews, Roy W.
Manning, James D.
Meacham, Don H.
Meyer, Richard C.
Midgette, Charles R.
Montavon, Joseph P.
Monte, Bruce I.
Mullins, William D.
Neukam, Elvis O.
Niederer, Richard A.
Notgrass, Billy G.
Parker, Eugene L.
Patton, Benny W.
Pratt, Clifford M., Jr.
Puety, Stanley E.
Reeves, Bobby R.
Rodgers, David J.
Santee, William P.
Sears, James A.
Shepard, Ralph L.
Stabe, Alvin G.
Stanley, Coy A.
Steffan, Laurence G.
Stipp, Edward E.
Szabo, Victor
Thompson, Jimmy T.
Treadway, Charles L.
Vissett, Ellis A.
Walker, Willie E.
Weaver, Clarence P.
White, Rubble A.
Whitchill, William O.
Whitehouse, Wallace W.
Wicks, Lawrence D.
Younge, James F.
Zimmorly, August F.

PRIVATES

Adams, William R.
Batista, Israel C.
Boyde, Herbert C.
Cobb, John D.
Cremer, Donald H., Jr.
Davis, Acue
Douglas, Lee R.
Fae, Walter G.
Frost, Norman F.
Giardino, Nicholas L.
Helton, George E.
Holdridge, Robert D.
Laramore, Harry A.
Jerkins, James F.
Fields, Gilbert E.
Gibson, George E.
Hart, James D.
Hughes, Louie R.
Kilgore, Reginald H.
McCoy, Bobby N.
McMahon, Leland H.
McMillen, Earl J.
Moreno, Plutarco C.
Myers, Charlie F.
Mowrey, Fred T., Jr.
Nealy, Charles M.
Perry, Paul F.
Porter, Robert H.
Potazo, George, Jr.
Fryor, Charles A.
Sorrels, William L., Jr.
Hawkins, Alfred J.
Overall, David M.
Wuldschlager, John J.

Merry Christmas

AND

A Happy New Year

1948

CHRISTMAS DINNER

MENU

SPICED TOMATO JUICE COCKTAIL

CELERY HEARTS   GREEN OLIVES   SWEET PICKLES

Roast Turkey with Oyster Dressing

GIBLET GRAVY   CRANBERRY SAUCE

SNOWFLAKE POTATOES   CANDIED SWEET POTATOES

BUTTERED GREEN BEANS

BUTTERED WHOLE KERNEL CORN

JELLIED CARROT AND PINEAPPLE SALAD

PARKER HOUSE ROLLS   BUTTER

MINCEMEAT PIE   FRUIT CAKE

COFFEE

FRESH FRUITS AND HARD CANDY

B109

B108

SYMBOLS: For other abbreviations see AFR 11-11 and TM 12-256A
   TCFNT: Transportat   officer will furnish necessar ransportation
   IGF: It being impracticable for the govt to furnis

HEADQUARTERS
AIR PROVING GROUND
Eglin Air Force Base Florida

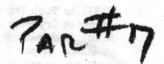

SPECIAL ORDERS
NUMBER   152   E X T R A C T   8 Aug 50

4. CAPT JEAN W LANPHERE ~~█████~~ USAF Hq & Hq Sq APG Eglin AF Base Fla
WP Mitchel AF Base NY o/a 9 Aug 50 on TDY not to exceed (14) days purpose
Represent APG as Personnel Liaison Officer to the Continental Air Command upon
compl of which will ret to proper sta Eglin AF Base Fla. Finance O making
payment on this order will forward a copy of the pd voucher to the Budget and
Fiscal O sta indicated. Tvl by mil acft is dir. TDN. 5714400 169-4000
P 468.9 (51) -02 03 S 08-894. Under auth of AFR 35-59.

5. VOCG APG on 7 Aug 50 granting Squadron Leader FRANCIS W DAVISON
59510 RAF Hq & Hq Sq APG Eglin AF Base Fla leave of absence for (7) days is
hereby confirmed.

6. The fol officers Hq & Hq Sq 3204th Med Gp Eglin AF Base Fla WP
Sternberg Auditorium Army Medical Department Research and Graduate School
Army Medical Center Wash DC o/a 16 Sept 50 on TDY not to exceed (10) days
purpose to attend Indoctrination Course on Medical Aspects of Nuclear Energy
reporting not later than 0800 hours 18 Sept 50 upon compl of TDY if not sooner
reld officer will ret to proper sta Eglin AF Base Fla:

MAJ SOLOMON E LIFTON ~~████~~ MC   CAPT EMMETT A HERNEL   AO~~████~~ MSC

Finance O making payment on this order will forward a copy of the pd voucher
to the Budget and Fiscal O sta indicated. TBMAA. TCFNT. TDN. 5714400
169-4000 P 478.9 (1) 02 03 S 08-894. Under auth of Ltr fr Hq USAF File
AFPMP-1 Subj: Indoctrination Courses on Medical Aspects of Nuclear Energy
dtd 2 Mar 50 and AFR 35-59.

7. The fol airmen USAF orgn indicated Eglin AF Base Fla WP Technical
Schools indicated o/a dates shown on DS purpose as specified upon compl of
DS if not sooner reld airmen will ret to proper sta Eglin AF Base Fla:

WP 3415th Tech Tng Gp 3415th Tech Tng Wg Lowry AF Base Colo o/a date shown
purpose as specified:

   WP o/a 24 Aug 50 purpose to attend Career Guidance course No 73100
   reporting not later than 26 Aug 50 for class commencing 29 Aug 50

T Sgt Melvin H Hoffman   AF~~████~~   Hq & Hq Sq 550th GM Wg

   WP o/a 28 Sept 50 purpose to attend Photo Interpretation Tech course
   No 94600 reporting not later than 30 Sept 50 for class commencing 3
   Oct 50 airman granted clearance as the result of a complete background
   investigation per par 5a (1) AFR 205-6

T Sgt Richard D Merkert   AF~~████~~   3200th Drone Sq

EXTRACT Pars 4 thru 7 SO 152 Hq APG Eglin AF Base Fla dated 8 Aug 50 (Cont'd).

EXTRACT Pars 4 thru 7 SO 152 Hq APG Eglin AF Base Fla dated 8 Aug 50 (Cont'd).

WP 3310th Tech Tng Gp 3310th Tech Tng Wg Scott AF Base Ill o/a 19 Aug 50 purpose attending Cryptographic Technician Course No 80500 reporting not later than 20 Aug 50 class commencing 23 Aug 50: Student meets the selection criteria contained in par 7a AFR 100-34 and has been granted a temporary cryptographic clearance based on favorable results of a National Agency Check in accordance w/ par 7a AFR 205-6 pending compl of required background investigation

Sgt Maurice F Maroure   AF▓▓▓▓▓   3201st Air Police Sq

Finance O making payment on this order will forward a copy of the pd voucher to the Budget and Fiscal O sta indicated. In accordance w/AFR 173-5 the FD will pay airmen concerned upon compl of DS the prescribed monetary alws in lieu of rat and qrs for tvl performed other than by air and period of TDY when govt qrs and ration in kind are not furnished while not in an air tvl status. TBMAA. TOFNT and required number of meal tickets. TDN. 5714400 169-4000 P 443.02 03 S 08-094. Under auth of Ltr fr Hq ATRC file 353 Subj: Allotment of quotas for Tech Courses dtd 19 Jul 50 - Ltr Hq USAF File AFPMP-2B-3 Subj: Allotment of Quotas for Cryptographic Tech Courses No 80500 dtd 24 Jul 50 and AFR 35-59.

   8. The fol airmen USAF 3201st Boat Sq 3201st Air Base Gp Eglin AF Base Fla WP Mobile Ala o/a 8 Aug 50 on TDY not to exceed (4) days purpose additional crewman to operate tug towing loaded barges upon compl of which will ret to proper sta Eglin AF Base Fla:

T Sgt Walter Jaworski   A▓▓▓▓▓   Sgt Ned H Weathers   AF
              Cpl Lowell M Poston   A▓▓▓▓▓

Finance O making payment on this order will forward a copy of the pd voucher to the Budget and Fiscal O sta indicated. In accordance w/AFR 173-5 the FD will pay airmen concerned in advance a/o upon compl of TDY the prescribed monetary alws in lieu of rat for (4) days and qrs for (3) days. TBMAA. Tvl by govt tugboat auth. TDN. 5714400 169-4000 P 468.9 (51) -02 03 S 08-094. Under auth of AFR 35-59.

          BY COMMAND OF MAJOR GENERAL BOATNER:

                                      M C WOODBURY
                                      Col USAF
                                      Deputy Commander

DISTRIBUTION:
   CO each orgn concerned   (2)
   Each officer concerned   (3)
   Each airman concerned   (3)
   Stat Services   (2)
   Comptroller   (5)
   3310th Tech Tng Wg Scott AF Base Ill   (5)
   3415th Tech Tng Wg Lowry AF Base Colo   (5)
   Sternberg Auditorium Army Medical Dept Research and Graduate School Army
   Med Center Wash DC   (5)

   EXTRACT Pars 4 thru 8 SO 152 Hq APG Eglin AF Base Fla dated 8 Aug 50.

1. Last Name	First Name	Initial	2. SN	3. Grade	4. SSN	5. Enlistment Status	6. Assigned Station & AF or Command
Marcus	Maurice	B.	■	Ret	405	D/S 6 yrs	Eglin Fla.

8. Age	9. Grade School (Years Attended)	10. High School (Years Attended)	11. College (Years Attended)	12. Date of Birth	13. Active Duty	14.	16. Race
32	8	None	None	14 Aug ■	a. Date Entered 5 Oct 49	Basic Training	White
					b. Total Service (yrs)	a. Date Completed: Brize Nel	N
						b. Length (weeks)	O

15. M C O

17. Previous Service School Courses

Stenographer Sch Lowry AFB 6 Mos. Grad June 48

16. Experience: Laborer — 12 (months)

Test Scores

Test	St Score	Test	St Score
OJT	2300	TC 7a	125
I - RV		TC 3c	90
II - AC		TC 4c	90
III - AR			125
IV - PA			
ARC-1			
MA	92	Instr. Sirm	123

20. 1st Choice of Course
30,500
Crypto Tech

21. 2d Choice of Course

22. 3d Choice of Course

23. Date Entered Course: 29 Aug 49

24.
1. Course Enrolled in Stenography AFSC 3121 Crypto Tech Cres.
2. Station Scott AFB
3. Graduating SSN
4. (a) OJT
(b) Formal Course

25. Class Number and Shift
03490

26. Symbol	27. Phase	28. Hours	29. Weighted Grade	30. Remarks
		54	3.7	O/A None
		70	3.9	
		58	3.9	
		58	3.8	Above average student
		59	4.0	
		60	4.0	

GRAD

31. Disposition
Grad.
Elim. Reason for Elim. or Holdover
Holdover

32. Certificate

34. Total or Average: 299 / 3.9

35. ACADEMIC EFFICIENCY
Group I Superior

1st Lt, USAF

33. Repeat cases
a. No Phases Repeated _____ b. Average grade based on orig phases only _____

B12a

AFTRC FORM NO. 9-3

STUDENT RECORD CARD

PERSONNEL RECORD

36.

Action		Per Par No.	T & O Order	Date	Reason
Asgd. to Class No. GS290		24	SO 174	29 Aug 44	GRDT
GRAD GRYPTO TECH	Par 1		SO 249	10 Oct 44	

37.

REMARKS

Reported	from														S. O. No.	152
19 Aug 44	Lwln AAB Fla							per par. no. 7						P. M. No.	22
	station							AAB 1							

1. Final Rating is a word of the student's ability.
   SUPERIOR, EXCELLENT, VERY SATISFACTORY, SATISFACTORY, UNSATISFACTORY.

2. Definition of numerical grading is as follows:

SCALE VALUE	DEFINITION
5	Completes work quickly and efficiently and understands basic principles thoroughly.
4	Completes work with little hesitancy; understands underlying principles better than average.
3	Has general idea of work to be done and performs job with some repetition and minor errors but indicates adequate knowledge of subject material.
2	Is able to complete part of work but does not understand underlying principles of subject material.
1	Cannot complete work satisfactory and has little knowledge of subject material.

3. In order to determine degree (S, S-Sk) attention is invited to pars 506.2 through 506, Sec V, af Manual No. 35-0-1, 3 April 1944 (as rev)

B12b

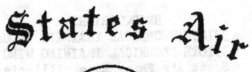

United States Air Force

Air Training Command

Be it known that Sgt Maurice F. Mercure, ████████

has satisfactorily completed the prescribed course of instruction of the

Air Training Command specializing in

CRYPTOGRAPHIC TECHNICIAN

In testimony whereof and by virtue of vested authority we do confer upon

him this

━━ CERTIFICATE OF PROFICIENCY ━━

Given at Scott Air Force Base, Illinois

on this   thirteenth   day of October

in the year of our Lord one thousand nine hundred and fifty

Attest:

Abraham McBride
1st Lt., USAF
SECRETARY

A. B. Ogden Jr.
Colonel, USAF
COMMANDANT

30-47-TC/Scott AFB, Ill./12 Jan 50/15M

HEADQUARTERS
3310TH TECHNICAL TRAINING GROUP
3310TH TECHNICAL TRAINING WING
Scott Air Force Base, Illinois

TO: Sgt Maurice F. Mercure, ▬▬▬▬▬

        I wish to congratulate you upon your successful completion of this
phase of your formal training and to express my appreciation for the exemplary manner in which you have conducted yourself. I also wish to
express my thanks for the splendid cooperation which you have given your
supervisors, instructors and other faculty members. As a student, your
task has not been easy and you have had to perform many duties which
have not been pleasant. However, whether in the service or civilian
life, we encounter the unpleasant things of life and have to learn to
take them in our stride as you have done. It is hoped that the education, information and material which you have gathered here will prove
of great benefit in your future job assignment and that you will find
the assignment pleasant and to your liking.

        Upon your departure from Scott Air Force Base, you will be assigned
to various organizations of the Air Forces where you will be confronted
with numerous problems pertaining to communications which were not
covered in your course of instruction. It is hoped that your education
has been such that it will enable you to successfully deal with the
majority of these problems.

        We are all interested in our Air Forces being the best trained in
the world in order to meet any emergencies which may arise. This can
be attained only so long as we all work together in assisting one
another in building up our training program. With this in mind, your
cooperation is solicited in completing the attached questionnaire after
you have completed approximately six months duty with your permanently
assigned organization. After completion of this questionnaire, it should
be mailed to the "Office of the School Secretary, 3310th Technical Trainin
Group, Scott Air Force Base, Illinois."

        The members of the Staff of the Communications School and I wish you
every success in your field of endeavor.

                                        R. E. KENDIG
                                        Lt Colonel, USAF
                                        Commanding

HEADQUARTERS
AIR PROVING GROUND
Eglin Air Force Base, Florida
Office of the Air Provost Marshal

Date **27 October 1950**

SUBJECT: Security Clearance

TO: **Commanding Officer
Hq. & Hq. Sq. 3201st
Eglin AFB, Florida
ATTN: Security Officer**

1.   Request the following entry be made in Form 66,
Service Record or 201 file (Civ) of:

Marcure, Maurice F., Sgt, ▮▮▮▮▮▮▮▮▮

"Administrative Final Secret Clearance granted
    25 Oct 50   .   Report of National Agency
check dated   **12 May 50**   conducted by OSI,
filed 8th OSI District Office, Maxwell Air Force Base,
Alabama."

2.   Any prior entries pertaining to security clearances
will be deleted or removed from the record.

3.   Clearance granted herewith constitutes an administrative determination affecting the loyalty and character fitness
of the person and does not of itself authorize disclosure of
any classified information to such person.

4.   Request reply by indorsement as to action taken by
Unit Security Officer.

DOUGLAS F. BELFIELD
Major, USAF
Security Officer

UNITED STATES ARMED FORCES INSTITUTE
MADISON 3, WISCONSIN

Test Completed   11 September 1951

*   *   *

This is to certify that

Maurice F. Mercure

has taken the USAFI General Educational
Development Test, high school level
Form   Z

Test No.	I Standard Score made by Examinee	II *Percentile for U. S.
1. Correctness and Effectiveness of Expression	41	18
2. Interpretation of Reading Materials in the Social Studies	63	90
3. Interpretation of Reading Materials in the Natural Sciences	59	82
4. Interpretation of Literary Materials	56	73
5. General Mathematical Ability	40	16

*To interpret percentile, read explanation on the reverse side of this form.

Glenn L. McConagha (signature)
GLENN L. McCONAGHA
Director

The official seal of the United States Armed Forces Institute is affixed only to
test reports sent to educational institutions or employers.

USAFI Form No. A-10
Rev 12-50.

UNITED STATES ARMED FORCES INSTITUTE
MADISON 3, WISCONSIN

BC

IN REPLY REFER TO: AFIE–U 352.12
SUBJECT: USAFI MILITARY TEST REPORT

3 OCT 1951

Commanding Officer
3201st AB Gp
Eglin AFB, Fla.

TO:

COPY SENT TO: Commanding Officer
Eglin AFB, Fla.
Attn: AI&E Officer

COPY SENT TO: (EXAMINEE)
S Sgt Maurice F. Mercure, ▮▮▮▮▮▮
3201st AB Gp
Eglin AFB, Fla.

1. This is a report of the record of educational achievement completed through the United States Armed Forces Institute by the examinee indicated above.

2. It is requested that this report be forwarded to the personnel office where the examinee's official military record is filed in order that permanent information may be transcribed on the record in accordance with the appropriate directive relating to educational work completed under the Armed Forces Education Program.

3. Your interest in the opportunities available to service personnel through USAFI is appreciated.

GLENN L. McCONAGHA
DIRECTOR

MILITARY TEST REPORT

DATE TEST COMPLETED	NAME OF USAFI TEST TAKEN	TEST RESULTS									
		TEST #1		TEST #2		TEST #3		TEST #4		TEST #5	
		STD. SCORE	U. S. PCT'L	STD. SCORE	U. S. PCT'L	STD. SCORE	U. S. PCT'L	STD. SCORE	U. S. PCT'L	STD. SCORE	U. S. PCT'L
11 Sep 1951	G E D HIGH SCHOOL LEVEL TEST	41	18	63	90	59	82	56	73	40	16
		(x) PASSED *		( ) FAILED				INCOMPLETE BATTERY			

		TEST #1		TEST #2		TEST #3		TEST #4		INCOMPLETE BATTERY
		STD. SCORE	U. S. PCT'L	STD. SCORE	U. S. PCT'L	STD. SCORE	U. S. PCT'L	STD. SCORE	U. S. PCT'L	TESTS *PASSED: TESTS FAILED: ☐
	G E D COLLEGE LEVEL TEST									

		TEST TITLE AND NUMBER	PROFICIENCY RATING
	END OF COURSE TEST		

		TEST TITLE AND NUMBER	LEVEL	PROFICIENCY RATING
	SUBJECT EXAMINATION			

	EDUCATIONAL QUALIFICATION TEST 2 CX	( ) PASSED *	( ) FAILED

		TEST #1	TEST #2	TEST #3	TEST #4	
	BASIC AND INTERMEDIATE ACHIEVEMENT TESTS GRADE LEVELS COMPLETED →					

▮ 017

* PASSED IN ACCORDANCE WITH MILITARY STANDARDS

USAFI FORM A–1

MC/es

U. __ED STATES ARMED FORCES INSTITU__
MADISON 3, WISCONSIN

9 OCT 1951

SUBJECT: Information on Course Completions, Test Results, and Accreditation
Procedure

TO: S Sgt Maurice F. Mercure, ███████████
        Hq, 3201st AB Gp
        Eglin AFB, Florida

PARAGRAPHS WITH ENCIRCLED NUMBERS APPLY PARTICULARLY TO YOUR CASE.

(1).   An official report of your high school level GED test results is this
date being forwarded to the Principal, Holyoke High School, Holyoke, Massachusetts.

2.   A military test report

(3)   All questions concerning the amount of credit which your school grants
for military training, for USAFI correspondence courses, or for the results of
USAFI tests should be addressed direct to that institution. USAFI is not
authorized to grant nor recommend the granting of credit since this is the
prerogative of civilian educational institutions.

4.   USAFI, Madison, is the only agency authorized to issue official reports
of USAFI test results to schools, employers, or other civilian agencies. Official reports cannot be issued to military personnel.

5.   When you have successfully completed a USAFI course or test, USAFI will
report the result of your work to a civilian educational institution or agency
at your request (provided such action is possible in conformance with established
policy), or upon request of the civilian educational institution or agency concerned. When making your request, include your date of birth; your date of first
entry into service; the name and address of the civilian educational institution
or agency to which the report is to be sent; and the approximate date test was
taken.

6.   If you wish to have USAFI course completion(s) or test results
forwarded for military purposes, it will be necessary that you submit the complete military address to which you wish the report(s) sent.

7.   A USAFI Certificate of Completion for course   was forwarded
to you on   in care of your commanding officer.

USAFI Form A-66
Rev 5-51

(over)

8. Inclosed are duplicate Certificate(s) of Completion and test report(s).

9. It is suggested that you inquire of your Personnel Officer as to whether a record of your completion of course   has been entered on your service records.

10. If you wish to have your in-service training evaluated, it is suggested that you complete the inclosed DD Form 295, "Application for the Evaluation of Educational Experiences During Military Service," in accordance with the instructions attached thereto. Page 2 of the application must be completed, approved, and signed by a commissioned officer who has access to your service records. The completed application, together with DD Form 296, signed by your Information and Education Officer, should then be forwarded to the school or employer for evaluation.

11. Write to your high school or college for specific course recommendations for which academic credit will be granted. Your school will notify you concerning the amount of credit granted and any recommendations for further study.

12. DD Form 305, "Application for Correspondence or Self-Teaching Course," must be submitted when applying for a USAFI course. (See inclosed USAFI Catalog for enrollment procedure.)

13. This installation has no record of your having submitted an accreditation application. (See paragraph 10 above.)

14. Attention is invited to the paragraphs indicated on the inclosed USAFI Accreditation Memorandum for the procedure to be followed by veterans desiring credit for in-service training.

GLENN L. McCONAGHA
Director

ARMY StL AGPC 75-71

OUTGOING TRANSPORT ___USNS GEN V. L. HERSEY___   SAILING o/a 28 Nov 51

STAGED AT ___CAMP KILMER, NEW JERSEY___   TROOP CLASS ___1___

AB-B186A(a)
9th Increment
Provisional Squadron 1689
APO 125   20 Nov 51

Reld Asgd 2266th Pers Processing Sq OR p/1

NAME	RANK	SN	AFSC-S	TOE	DCS	RACE
DOB	AFSC-P			DROS	COMP	FSC
51. CULLIGAN WILLIAM P	S SGT	AF11018622	95170	Indef	Indef	W
5 Aug 17	95170			Jun 51	USAF	41
52. CUMMINGS LEO P	S SGT	AF20646083	64150	6Yr	22 Oct 57	W
16 Jan 22	64150			Jul 48	USAF	0
53. DEAN FRANCIS F	S SGT	AF6831842	53250	6Yr	21 Dec 55	W
17 Jan 15	53250			May 48	USAF	57
54. DOWNS GLENN M	S SGT	AF18095635	95150	3Yr	11 Apr 52	W
29 Feb 28	95150				USAF	0
55. DUNMIRE BILLY E	S SGT	AF18099616	43151H	4Yr	15 Nov 52	W
8 Oct 27	43151H			Jan 50	USAF	4
56. FREE CLIFFORD H	S SGT	AF13241396	70250	6Yr	13 Jul 54	W
19 Feb 26	70250			Jun 46	USAF	0
57. GAUDETTE LEROY J	S SGT	AF37556403	64173	6Yr	2 May 56	W
24 Jan 24	64173			Jan 46	USAF	0
58. HARTLEY JAMES E	S SGT	AF14266397	90570	3Yr	29 Jun 52	W
27 Feb 28	90570			Sep 47	USAF	7
59. JENSEN DARRELL E	S SGT	AF37665804	73250	6Yr	12 Jan 57	W
4 Mar 24	73250			Sep 45	USAF	10
60. KANE JAMES P	S SGT	AF17273548	81250	4Yr	15 Dec 53	W
5 Sep 27	82150			Dec 49	USAF	19
61. KEFFER JAMES R	S SGT	AF13161088	60351	6Yr	21 Jul 56	W
17 Jul 30	60351				USAF	0
62. KRUPA THOMAS J	S SGT	AF13285062	20450	3Yr	7 Oct 54	W
16 Aug 30	20450				USAF	0
63. KUBES ALFRED F	S SGT	AF17250059	64152	3Yr	30 Dec 52	W
20 Mar 29	64152				USAF	0
64. MALCHUK JOHN J	S SGT	AF42153849	64150	4Yr	2 Jan 53	W
23 Apr 26	64150			Sep 49	USAF	21
65. MC HALE CHARLES P	S SGT	AF12263734	70270	3Yr	1 Oct 52	W
27 Jun 29	70270				USAF	0
66. MERCURE MAURICE R	S SGT	▮▮▮▮▮	29250	6Yr	4 Oct 55	W
14 Aug	29250				USAF	0
67. MOURING HAROLD E	S SGT	AF33428917	70130	6Yr	29 Jan 57	W
16 Jun 23	70130			Nov 48	USAF	60
68. OLAH JULIUS	S SGT	AF32783219	23351	6Yr	29 Dec 55	W
4 Feb 24	77251			Mar 45	USAF	22
69. PLEFFNER LEONARD J	S SGT	AF12159825	81250	4Yr	19 Nov 52	W
1 Jan 23	81250			Jun 45	USAF	20
70. PRICE WILLIAM R	S SGT	AF13014744	70130	6Yr	9 Jul 56	W
2 Oct 20	70130			Jun 45	USAF	26
71. PRUITT ARRIE	S SGT	AF34109110	96150	6Yr	9 Dec 55	W
22 Feb 19	96150			Jan 49	USAF	19
72. RICHARDS ROBERT A	S SGT	AF11144926	64150	3Yr	20 Jul 54	W
4 May 31	64150			Jun 49	USAF	10
73. SCHENDEL RAYMOND A	S SGT	AF20657296	53250	Indef	Indef	W
30 Aug 18	53250			Dec 46	USAF	52
74. SEWELL CURTIS M	S SGT	AF14247425	83150	6Yr	14 Jun 56	W
1 Nov 29	83150			May 50	USAF	0
75. SEGLER ARTHUR R	S SGT	AF14001316	47151	Indef	Indef	W
26 Aug 21	47151			UNK	USAF	17

PAGE (3)

AB-B186A(a) 9th Incr Prov Sq 1689 APO 125
o/a 28 Nov 51

Restricted

Restricted

WAP/mac

HEADQUARTERS 2225TH PERSONNEL PROCESSING GROUP
Camp Kilmer, New Jersey
21 November 1951

E-X-T-R-A-C-T

* * * * * * * * * * * * *

88. Pers (POR quald) on atchd rosters asgd 2266th Pers Processing Sq (OR) (p/1)(ConAC) this sta are dsgd shipt indicated, rsgd 7551st Pers Processing Sq (Repl) APO 125 c/o Postmaster New York NY for fur asgmt & trans to orgns & stas indicated & WP NYPE Brooklyn NY by rail, bus or govt mtr trans so as to rept o/a 28 Nov 51 to CG thereat for fur mv OGLES. Depns, relatives, friends & pets will not accompany nor jn Pers at PE. TPA not auth. (EDCSA between 2266th Pers Processing Sq (OR)(p/1) & 7551st Pers Processing Sq (Repl) w/b 8 Dec 51)

SHIPT	INCR.	FROM SQ	RSGD
AB-B186-B(a)	1st	1684	*Third AF
AB-A186-B(a)	5th	1685	ditto
AB-A186-A(a)	39th	1688	ditto
AB-B186-A(a)	9th	1689	ditto
AB-B186-A(a)	10th	1690	ditto
AB-B186-A(a)	11th	1691	ditto
AB-B186-B(a)	2d	1694	#928th Engr Avn Gp (USAFE) (FF) APO 125 c/o Postmaster New York NY

Shipt of privately owned automobiles os auth IAW AFL 75-43 dtd 30 Apr 48 for Offs & Amn of the 1st three grades & Amn of the 4th gr w/7 yrs completed sv only.

Provs AFR 35-48 dtd 4 Nov 49 (POR) w/b complied w/.

Marking & Banding of personal bag w/b accomplished IAW provs par 16 AFR 35-48.

Pers will advise correspondents by use of DD Form 415 (Notice of C of address) that mailing address w/b as indicated below. Pers will furn DD Form 413 to publishers:

(RANK)	(NAME)	(AFSN)	(RANK)	(NAME)	(AFSN)
*Prov Sq			#928th Engr Avn Gp		
APO 125 c/o Postmaster New York NY			APO 125 c/o Postmaster New York NY		

Trans Off will furn trans to NYPE Brooklyn NY. TBGAA PCA PCS TDN 5723500 248-341 P 533.5-02 03 07 S99-999. (Auth: Restricted Ltr DAF Hq USAF Washington 25 DC file AFPMP-2-E & AFPMP-2B-3 subj: "Shipment Numbers (Unclassified)" dtd 21 Sep 51 & 23 Oct 51)(Re: MA Roster 183)

* * * * * * * * * * * * *

BY ORDER OF COLONEL ROTH:

OFFICIAL:

WILLIAM A PARKER
2nd Lt, USAF
Asst Adj

[signature: William A Parker]

WILLIAM A PARKER
2nd Lt, USAF
Asst Adj

DISTRIBUTION:
1 — Adj
1 — Stat Control Br
1 — Locator
10 — SO Section
1 — Gp Mail Room
30 — Shipt Control Br

1.

Restricted

B/L fr S/Sgt Maurice F. Mercure, AF ████████, 3918th Operations Squadron, 3918th Air Base Group, APO 194, USAF, Subj: Application for permission to marry, dated 26 June 1952.

OS   1st Ind

3918TH OPERATIONS SQUADRON, 3918th Air Base Group, APO 194, US Air Force
    19 Sep 52

TO: Commanding Officer, 3918th Air Base Group, APO 194, US Air Force

    1. Recommend approval.

    2. From the official records in my custody and other information available to me, it appears that the applicant is not married. The proposed marrage will not bring discredit to the Air Force.

                              HERMAN L. SMITH
                              Major,   USAF
                              Commanding

5 Incls:
  1-Ltr of Acquiescence
  2-Background Investigation
  3-Cert of Phys (Mercure & Banks)
  4-Statement of Fiance of Fiancee
  5-Ltr of Permission (Mercure)

LETTER OF ACQUIESCENCE - MARRIAGE

.....ester RAF Station, Oxon, Eng
(Place)

3 July 1952
(Date)

1. The undersigned desires to marry **Maurice F. Mercure**
(NAME)

S/Sgt.   AF ▇▇▇▇▇▇   **3918th Operations Squadron**
(Grade)   (AFSN)   (Organization)

2. I have read and fully understand the provisions of 3AD Regulation 30-1.

a. My place of birth and date of birth is **Mustipha Barracks,**
Alexandria, Egypt

b. My legal residence or domicile is **36 Shakespear Ave., Hayes,**
Middlesex, England

c. My present address and occupation is **LACW Margaret D. Banks,**
2811893, Signal Section, RAF Station, Bicester, Oxon, England   WRAF Telephone
Operator
d. My religious preference is **Protestant**

e. I (~~have~~)(have not) been previously married. If so
(1) That marriage was terminated on ___**N.A.**___
(Date)

by (death).(divorce), and a certified copy of the (death
certificate) (divorce decree) is submitted herewith.

f. Number and ages of children, if any   **N.A.**

_____

(1) Name of father (mother) of such children   **N.A.**

_____

g. In event the undersigned is now divorced and has a child or
children by that prior marriage, and is desirous of transporting such child
or children to the United States, it will be necessary to submit, in connection with this letter, the written consent of the other parent, authorizing
the removal of such child or children from the United Kingdom, along with a
Court Order to the same effect.
h. Submitted herewith (if applicable) is a statement from the Visa
Section of the U.S. Embassy, to the effect that the (child) (children) of the
undersigned have met the physical requirements of the U.S. Immigration Laws.

M. Banks (Margaret Doris Banks
(Signature)

incl # 2 to 3AD Regulation 30-1   **MARGARET DORIS BANKS**
2318-50   (Name Typed or Printed)

HEADQUARTERS
UNITED STATES AIR FORCES IN EUROPE
Inspector General
Office of Special Investigations

UK District, OSI
US Navy 100
Fleet Post Office
New York, New York

44-4831   9 September 1952

SUBJECT: PEGGY BANKS

     TO: Commanding Officer
             3918th Operations Squadron
             3918th Air Base Group
             APO 147, USAF

     1. Reference is made to your letter dated 18 July 1952
File No.   , regarding the above named
SUBJECT who is the fiancee of

     2. In accordance with your request, appropriate back-
ground investigation has been conducted and no derogatory
information of a subversive nature has been revealed.

     FOR THE DISTRICT COMMANDER:

                         DONALD B. JAYNES
                         Major, USAF
                   Chief, Counter Intelligence Division
                         UK District, OSI

3918TH OPERATIONS SQUADRON
3918TH AIR BASE GROUP
APO 147, US Air Force

18 July 1952

SUBJECT: Request for Security Investigation

TO: Detachment Commander
             Brize Norton Detachment
             UK District OSI
             APO 147, US Air Force

     1. Request a security investigation be accomplished on Miss
Peggy Banks in accordance with 3 AD Regulation 30-1.

     2. Premarital check list enclosed.

          FOR THE COMMANDING OFFICER:

1 Incl   EDWARD E. ROED
     3 cys Premarital Check List   Capt, USAF
                                    Adjutant

OFFICE OF THE FLIGHT SURGEON
US Air Force Infirmary
3918th Air Base Group
APO 147, US Air Force

Date_ **26 August 1952**

C E R T I F I C A T E

This is to certify that <u>BANKS, Margaret Poris   Civilian</u>
                        (Name)   (Rank)   (AFSC)

Fiancee of S/Sgt Mccure, Maurice F. has been examined this date under the pro-
    (Organization)
visions of Par 4-1p 3rd AF Reg 30-1 dtd 19 Oct 1950 as amended and has been found
free of communicable diseases, confirmed by normal chest X-Ray and negative sero-
logical test for syphillis.

HERSCHEL L COPELAN

CAPT USAF (MC) AME

OFFICE OF THE FLIGHT SURGEON
US Air Force Infirmary
3918th Air Base Group
APO 147, US Air Force

Date **26 August 1952**

C E R T I F I C A T E

This is to certify that   **Mercure, Maurice F.**   **S/Sgt**   **AF**▬▬▬▬
                             (Name)   (Rank)   (AFSC)

3918th Operations Squadron   has been examined this date under the pro-
    (Organization)
visions of Par 4-1p 3rd AF Reg 30-1 dtd 19 Oct 1950 as amended and has been found
free of communicable diseases, confirmed by normal chest X-Ray and negative sero-
logical test for syphillis.

Herschel L. Copela...

HERSCHEL L COPELAND
CAPT USAF (MC) AME

STATEMENT OF FIANCE OR FIANCEE

SURNAME BANKS

(State name at birth if different
or if known by any other name) ___N.A.___

Full Christian name MARGARET DORIS

Date and Place of Birth MUSTIFIA BARRACKS, ALEXANDRIA, EGYPT

Nationality ENGLISH

Nationality at Birth
(If different from above) ___N.A.___

Full Name and   (FATHER) FREDRICK BANKS   ENGLISH

nationality at   (MOTHER) MAUD DOROTHY (KANE) BANKS   ENGLISH

birth -   (HUSBAND) N.A.
                    (OF WIFE) NA.

Private address and
telephone number (if any) 36 Shakespear Ave., Hayes, Middlesex, England

Permanent Address Same as above

Former Residences Father in RAF moved around continuously

National Registration No. BVAV 150-2

Pre-Marriage Check None

Particulars of Previous Employment including:

(1) Name of present or last
employer and length of service RAF   L. Lambert & Co LTD, Colne Works, High St.,
                                              Uxbridge, Middlesex, Eng.

(2) Present or last salary L 2 10s   L 4 15S

(3) Duties performed Telephone Operator   Labaratory Asst.

Incl # 3 to 3AD Regulation 30-1   2318-50

INSTRUCTIONS: Application is to be completed in triplicate, by typewriter or
print d in ink. Strike out words n applicable.

26 June 1952
(Date)

3918th Opns Sqdn. Upper Heyford Oxon, E
(Place)

SUBJECT: Application for permission to marry

TO   : Commanding Officer
        3918th Operations Squadron,
        APO 147, US AIR FORCE

    1. Under the provisions of 3AD Regulation 30-1, the undersigned
requests permission to marry Margaret Doris Banks
LACW Margaret D Banks 2811893
Signal Section. RAF Station. Bicester, Oxon   English
          (Address)   (Nationality)

        a. The prospective (husband)(wife) above named (has)(has not) been
previously married.

        b. If previously married, that marriage was terminated on N.A.
_____ by (death)(divorce), and a certified copy of the
(death certificate)(divorce decree) is submitted herewith.

        c. The above named person has N.A. children, and other persons
dependent upon (him)(her) for support.

        d. The prospective (husband)(wife) is 26 years of age. (If under
the age of 21, applicant must submit herewith written consent of parents or
guardian of the prospective husband or wife).

        e. A statement from the prospective (husband)(wife) is inclosed
herewith in compliance with par 1a (1) (f) of 3AD Regulation 30-1.

        f. If request is granted, marriage will be performed on or about
4 October 1952   and in   England
        (Date)   (Country)

    2. Applicant's full name, address and nationality is as follows:
Maurice Frank Mercure, AF ███████████, 3918th Opns Sqdn. APO 147   American

        a. Applicant (has)(has not) been previously married.

        b. If previously married, that marriage was terminated on N.A.
_____ by (death)(divorce) and a certified copy of the (divorce
decree)(death certificate) is submitted herewith.

        c. Applicant has N.A. children, and N.A. other persons
dependent upon (him)(her) for support.

        d. Applicant's religious preference is   Protestant

        e. Place and date of birth of the applicant is as follows: Aug 28
                                                                     (Date)
(City) Chicoppee   (State) Massachusetts

If applicant is under the age of 21, written consent of parents or guardian to the proposed marriage will be submitted as a part of the application.

f. My legal residence or domicile is 179 Beech Street, Holyoke, Massachusett s
(City)   (State)

g. Number and ages of children, if any ___N.A.___

h. Name of (mother)(father) of such children ___N.A.___

i. Date thirty-six (36) Foreign Service Credits on Current Overseas Tour are completed or approximate date of applicant's return to Zone of Interior ___29 November 1954___

j. Date of expiration of enlistment ___4 October 1955___

k. Date eligible for return to Zone of Interior ___28 November 1954___

3. By submission of this application and the signature affixed hereto, the applicant certifies that:

a. He has read and fully understands the provisions of 3AD Reg 30-1.

b. He has read and fully understands that any child or children of the prospective (husband)(wife) born of a previous marriage or out of wedlock, to which the applicant is not the father or mother, will receive no benefits under any preferential clauses in the immigration laws, and that restrictions as to quota, physical and mental conditions, and other disabilities, apply to these children.

c. He is advised and fully understands the War Department policy on housing of dependents and assignment of public quarters in overseas commands.

d. He has currently and will have at time of shipment, sufficient funds in his or her personal possession to defray all expenses of marriage and travel to place of residence in the Zone of Interior, and in connection therewith, has read and fully understands the provisions of 3AD Regulation 35-11.

Maurice F. Mercure
(Signature)

MAURICE F. MERCURE
(Name typed or printed)

SSGT ████████   3918th Opns Sqdd.
(Grade)(AFSN)   (Organization)

- 2 -

HEADQUARTERS
3918th OPERATIONS SQUADRON
APO 147, US AIR FORCE

26 July 1952

SUBJECT: Request Permission to Marry

TO   : Commanding Officer
           Bicester RAF Station
           Oxon, England

     The undersigned request permission to marry LACW Margaret Doris Banks,
2811893, Signal Section your station. We are planning to be married
4 October 1952. The necessary paper work has been initiated by my organization to make it possible for us to marry at this time. Thanking you for any
cooperation you may be able to give this matter, I am Yours Sincerely,

                                   MAURICE F. MERCURE
                                   SS6   USAF
                                   AF ▨▨▨▨▨▨▨▨

COMMUNICATIONS SECTION
~~3918th Operations Squadron~~
(Section)

(Date) ~~15 Jan 1953~~

TO: CO, ~~3918th Operations Squadron, APO 194, US Air Force~~

Request ~~S/Sgt Maurice R. Mercure, AF████████~~ be considered for
promotion to the grade of ~~Technical Sgt.~~ This recommendation is based on the
following ratings:

(Circle appropriate figure)

Promptness and attention to duty: 1 2 ③

Ability to supervise and lead subordinates: 1 2 3 4 5 ⑥ 7

Knowledge of specialty: 1 2 3 4 5 6 ⑦

Ability to cope with unique problems: 1 ②

Ability to understand instructions and complete
   an assignment: 1 2 ③

Initiative and cooperation: 1 2 3 ④

Attitude toward completing an assignment which
   may require overtime work:
   (Devotion to duty) 1 ② 3

RATING: (Obtain this by totaling circled figures) 28

Word picture enumerating on the above six (6) items:

   1. Since his initial assignment at this station approximately eleven
(11) months ago, S/Sgt Mercure has been performing the duty of NCOIC of the
Cryptographic Section.

   2. In consideration of the high skill level which must be maintained by
a Cryptographic Supervisor, the quantities of experience which must be held,
and the technical training and initiative necessary to hold this position, it
is pointed out that S/Sgt Mercure has consistently achieved this criteria and
has, since its origination, promoted the superlative standards of work which
are so essential to the efficient operation of a section of this kind. Three
(3) Cryptographic Command Inspections have brought forth the excellent report
that must be consistently maintained in a field in which security systems and
methods must be of prior importance in every case.

3918th Air Base Group From 19. Previous editions of this form are obsolete.
12 Nov 1952

EUGENE C. McLAUGHLIN
Capt   USAF
Communications Officer

Incl 1 to 3918th AB Gp Reg 39-1

B22

HEADQUARTERS
3918TH AIR BASE GROUP
APO 194 US AIR FORCE

SPECIAL ORDERS   10 June 1953
NUMBER   117

E-X-T-R-A-C-T

1. T SGT MAURICE F. MERCURE AF ████████ 3918th Ops Sq 3918th
AB Gp APO 194 USAF is hereby granted ord lv for a pd of twenty (20)
days eff o/a 10 June 1953 w/permission to visit England and Holland
while on lv. Address of amn on lv w/b: 36 Shakespeare Ave, Hayes,
Middlesex, Eng and % Amer Express, Amsterdam, Holland. Amn w/have
in his possession sufficient dollar instru to defray all expenses
incident to this lv. Amn w/have required documentation for entry
into above country as set forth in USAFE Reg 30-10. Upon compl of
lv amn w/rtn proper orgn & sta WOD. AUTH: AFR 35-22.

BY ORDER OF COLONEL GILLEM II:

OFFICIAL: JOHN W. GOOTEE
                                               Major, USAF
                                               Adjutant

JOHN W. GOOTEE
Major, USAF
Adjutant

DISTRIBUTION: "A"

SEVENTH AIR DIVISION
NCO ACADEMY
APO 197, US AIR FORCE

C E R T I F I C A T E

This is to certify that__T/Sgt Maurice F Mercure_____

completed the Seventh Air Division NCO Academy on___15 Aug 53_____.

Length of this course was four (4) weeks.

The above course of instruction consisted of the following subjects:

Personnel Management	40 hours
Leadership	16 hours
Drill & Command	24 hours
Organization of the Air Force	4 hours
Speech	16 hours
Military Law	6 hours
Supply	4 hours
Ground Safety	2 hours

ARTHUR H JAMES
Major   USAF
Commandant

DISTRIBUTION:

Original copy to Airman
Duplicate copy to Amn 201 file

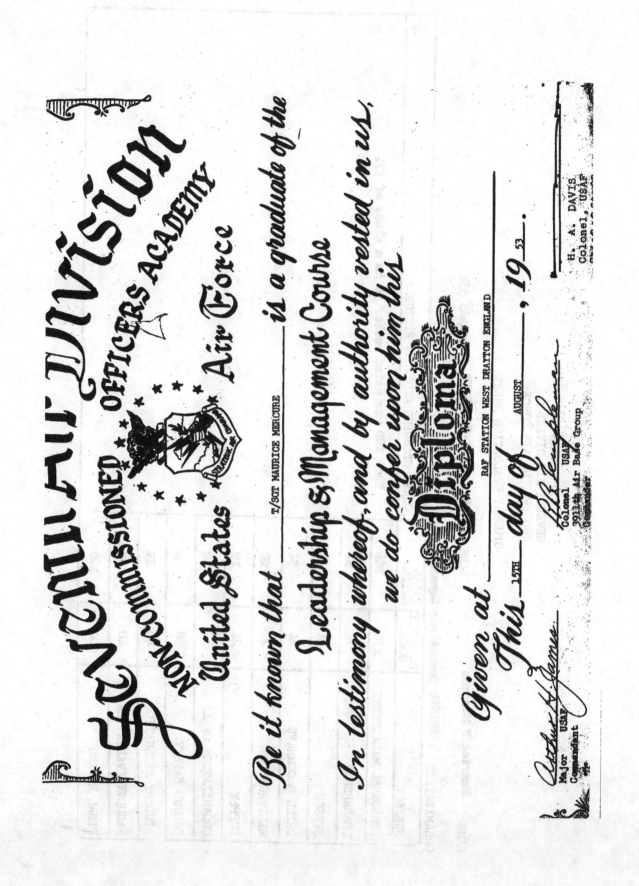

SAC in Miniature

Non-Commissioned Officers Academy

United States Air Force

Be it known that T/SGT MAURICE MERCURE is a graduate of the

Leadership & Management Course

In testimony whereof, and by authority rested in us,
we do confer upon him this

Diploma

RAF STATION WEST DRAYTON ENGLAND

Given at
This 15TH day of AUGUST , 19 53 .

Arthur A. James
Major   USAF
Commandant

P.K. Humphreys
Colonel   USAF
3911th Air Base Group
Commander

H. A. DAVIS
Colonel, USAF

NCO ACADEMY
SEVENTH AIR DIVISION
APO 197, US AIR FORCE

STUDENT EVALUATION SHEET

NAME Maurice P Herbers   RANK T/Sgt   AFSN ▬▬▬ .   CLASS 53H

ORGANIZATION 7918th Operations Squadron

SUBJECT	POSSIBLE SCORE	FINAL RATING	CLASS STANDING AND WORD PICTURES
PERSONNEL MANAGEMENT	130	106	This NCO was rated number 56 in a class of 57.
LEADERSHIP	74	57	
SPEECH	74	46	
DRILL & COMMAND	74	54	
MILITARY LAW	24	20	
SUPPLY	24	19	
ORGANIZATION OF AF	12	10	
GROUND SAFETY	8	8	
STUDENT EVALUATION	40	25	
FACULTY EVALUATION	40	35	
FINAL RATING	500	380	

7515th Hospital Group
APO 194, US Air Force

Date 9 October 1953

SUBJECT: Physical Condition of Mercure, Maurice T/Sgt AF ████
(Name, Grade, and Service No.)

TO: Commanding Officer 3918th Operation Squadron Upper Heyford
(Unit or Installation)

1. Profile serial.

	P	U	L	H	E	S	Suffix	Brief nontechnical Diagnosis (if applicable) is:
Previous Profile								
Revised Profile	1	1	1	1	1	1		

2. The above-named individual is being returned to your unit this date.

    a. He is considered *fit ~~unfit~~ for return to full duty.

    *b. The defect previously noted has been removed (state briefly additional duty he may now perform).

    *c. He has the following defects which require special consideration in his assignment:

    *d. In view of the above, he is considered unfit for the following types of duty (state briefly in nontechnical language the type of activity for which he is not fitted).

3. Any limitations mentioned above are considered *permanent *temporary. If temporary *the limitation will be automatically released ____NA____ *the individual should report
(date)
to ____NA____ for evaluation of his physical
(Medical Facility) (date)
capacity.

R.W. Zimmerman

R.W. ZIMMERMAN, 1st Lt., USAF (MC)
(Signature of medical officer)

*Strike out inapplicable words or subparagraphs.

000010

PUBLIC LAW 513, 81ST CONGRESS, 2D SESSION

TO ENHANCE FURTHER THE SECURITY OF THE UNITED STATES BY PREVENTING DIS-
CLOSURES OF INFORMATION CONCERNING THE CRYPTOGRAPHIC SYSTEMS AND THE
COMMUNICATION INTELLIGENCE ACTIVITIES OF THE UNITED STATES.

BE IT ENACTED BY THE SENATE AND HOUSE OF REPRESENTATIVES OF THE
UNITED STATES OF AMERICA IN CONGRESS ASSEMBLED, THAT WHOEVER SHALL KNOWINGLY
AND WILLFULLY COMMUNICATE, FURNISH, TRANSMIT, OR OTHERWISE MAKE AVAILABLE
TO AN UNAUTHORIZED PERSON, OR PUBLISH, OR USE IN ANY MANNER PREJUDICIAL TO
THE SAFETY OR INTEREST OF THE UNITED STATES OR FOR THE BENEFIT OF ANY
FOREIGN GOVERNMENT, TO THE DETRIMENT OF THE UNITED STATES ANY CLASSIFIED
INFORMATION (1) CONCERNING THE NATURE, PREPARATION, OR USE OF ANY CODE,
CIPHER, OR CRYPTOGRAPHIC SYSTEM OF THE UNITED STATES, OR ANY FOREIGN GOV-
ERNMENT; OR (2) CONCERNING THE DESIGN, CONSTRUCTION, USE, MAINTENANCE OR
REPAIR OF ANY DEVICE, APPARATUS, OR APPLIANCE USED OR PREPARED OR PLANNED
FOR USE BY THE UNITED STATES OR ANY FOREIGN GOVERNMENT FOR CRYPTOGRAPHIC
OR COMMUNICATION INTELLIGENCE PURPOSES; OR (3) CONCERNING THE COMMUNICATION
INTELLIGENCE ACTIVITIES OF THE UNITED STATES OR ANY FOREIGN GOVERNMENT; OR
(4) OBTAINED BY THE PROCESSES OF COMMUNICATION INTELLIGENCE FROM THE COMM-
UNICATIONS OF ANY FOREIGN GOVERNMENT KNOWING THE SAME TO HAVE BEEN OBTAINED
BY SUCH PROCESSES, SHALL BE FINED NOT MORE THAN $10,000.00 OR IMPRISONED
NOT MORE THAN TEN (10) YEARS, OR BOTH.

SECTION II

(A) THE TERM "CLASSIFIED INFORMATION" AS USED HEREIN SHALL BE CONSTRUED
TO MEAN INFORMATION WHICH, AT THE TIME OF A VIOLATION UNDER THIS ACT, IS FOR
REASONS OF NATIONAL SECURITY, SPECIFICALLY DESIGNED BY THE UNITED STATES
GOVERNMENT AGENCY FOR LIMITED OR RESTRICTED DISSEMINATION OR DISTRIBUTION.

(B) THE TERMS "CODE", "CIPHER", AND "CRYPTOGRAPHIC SYSTEM" AS USED
HEREIN SHALL BE CONSTRUED TO INCLUDE IN THEIR MEANINGS, IN ADDITION TO
THEIR USUAL MEANINGS, ANY METHOD OF SECRET WRITING AND ANY MECHANICAL OR
ELECTRICAL DEVICE OR METHOD USED FOR THE PURPOSE OF DISGUISING OR CONCEAL-
ING THE CONTENTS, OR SIGNIFICANCE, OR MEANING OF COMMUNICATIONS.

(C) THE TERM "FOREIGN GOVERNMENT" AS USED HEREIN SHALL BE CONSTRUED
TO INCLUDE IN ITS MEANING ANY PERSON OR PERSONS ACTING OR PURPORTING TO
ACT FOR OR ON BEHALF OF ANY FACTION, PARTY, DEPARTMENT, AGENCY, BUREAU, OR
MILITARY FORCE OR WITHIN A FOREIGN COUNTRY, OR FOR OR ON BEHALF OF ANY
GOVERNMENT OR ANY PERSON OR PERSONS PURPORTING TO ACT AS A GOVERNMENT
WITHIN A FOREIGN COUNTRY, WHETHER OR NOT SUCH GOVERNMENT IS RECOGNIZED
BY THE UNITED STATES.

(D) THE TERM "COMMUNICATION INTELLIGENCE" AS USED HEREIN SHALL BE
CONSTRUED TO MEAN ALL PROCEDURES AND METHODS USED IN THE INTERCEPTION OF
COMMUNICATIONS AND THE OBTAINING OF INFORMATION FROM SUCH COMMUNICATIONS
BY OTHER THAN THE INTENDED RECIPIENTS.

(B) THE TERM "UNAUTHORIZED PERSON" AS USED HEREIN SHALL BE CONSTRUED TO MEAN ANY PERSON WHO, OR AGENCY WHICH, IS NOT AUTHORIZED TO RECEIVE INFORMATION OF THE CATEGORIES SET FORTH IN SECTION 1 OF THIS ACT, BY THE PRESIDENT, OR BY THE HEAD OF A DEPARTMENT OR AGENCY OF THE UNITED STATES GOVERNMENT, WHICH IS EXPRESSLY DESIGNATED BY THE PRESIDENT TO ENGAGE IN COMMUNICATION INTELLIGENCE ACTIVITIES FOR THE UNITED STATES.

NOTHING IN THIS ACT SHALL PROHIBIT THE FURNISHING, UPON LAWFUL DEMAND, OF INFORMATION TO ANY REGULARLY CONSTITUTED COMMITTEE OF THE SENATE OR HOUSE OF REPRESENTIVES OF THE UNITED STATES OF AMERICA, OR JOINT COMMITTEE THEREOF.

I CERTIFY I HAVE READ THE ABOVE PERTINENT SECTIONS OF PUBLIC LAW 513, 81ST CONGRESS, 2D SESSION CONCERNING THE DISCLOSURE OF INFOR-MATION RELATIVE TO CRYPTOGRAPHIC SYSTEMS AND COMMUNICATION ACTIVITIES OF THE UNITED STATES: SIGNED BY PRESIDENT TRUMAN 13 MAY 1950.

NAME _Maurice F. McEnnee_

DATE _22 FEB 1954_

<u>AUTHORIZATION AND CONSENT AGREEMENT</u>

ORGANIZATION AND STATION
0918TH OPNS SQ UPPER HEYFORD

DATE   1 MARCH 1954

SERVICE NUMBER   AF ████████

NAME OF SERVICE MEMBER   USAF

DEPENDENT WIFE   MARGARTE DORIS

DEPENDENT CHILDREN   NONE
OR OTHER DEPENDENTS

   I, the undersigned, hereby authorize funds necessary for the proper care, subsistence, and well-being of my above-named dependents to be advanced to <u>MARGARET DORIS MERCURE</u>   in the event of an emergency declared by proper authority. I further authorize that funds so advanced shall be charged against any items of pay or allowances due, or to become due me subsequent to date of payment.

   Signature of my dependent appears below.

Maurice F. Mercure
Signature and Service No. of Service Mem
MAURICE F. MERCURE AF ████████ US

M. Mercure
Signature of Member's Dependent

HEADQUARTERS
3918TH AIR BASE GROUP
APO 194 US AIR FORCE

PM

10 May 1954

SUBJECT: Security Clearance Notification
           (Mercure, Maurice F. T/Sgt AF▮▮▮▮▮▮▮

TO: Commander
           3918th Operations Squadron
           ATTN: Unit Security Officer
           APO 194, US Air Force

1. The following individual, having met the appropriate requirements of AFR 205-6, 1 September 1950, is granted access to classified information and material as may be required in the performance of his official governmental duties as indicated.

Maurice F. Mercure - FINAL CRYPTOGRAPHIC - 6 May 1954

2. As required by paragraph 13a, AFR 205-6, the below quoted entry will be placed and maintained on the ▮▮▮▮▮▮▮▮▮▮▮▮▮▮▮▮▮▮▮▮▮ (airman's service) record provided the entry has not previously been made.

BI completed 17 August 1950 by 8th Dist OSI, Final Cryptographic Clearance granted 6 May 1954.

3. If the above named individual is an airman holding a commission in the reserve force, you will notify the appropriate number Air Force in order that notation may be made on the airman's master personnel records, as directed in the Air Force Regulation cited in par 2 above.

4. Your attention is directed to AFR 205-29, 5 October 1950.

BY ORDER OF THE COMMANDER:

ALVA V. MURRAY
Captain, USAF
Provost Marshal

92 SHEEP STREET
BICESTER, OXON
5 AUGUST 1954

AMERICAN EMBASSY
VISA SECTION
25 GROSVENORS SQUARE
LONDON, W 1

DEAR S IR:
                                                            LIKE
    I AM WRITING THIS LETTER TO INFORM YOU THAT I WOULD/TO
HAVE YOUR AGENCY SEND ME THE NECESSARY PARTICULARS IN ORDER
TO APPLY AN OBTAIN A VISA FOR TRAVEL TO THE U.S.A. WITH MY
HUSBAND T/SGT MAURICE F. MERCURE, AF ████████, 3918TH
OPERATIONS SQUADRON, 3918TH AIR BASE GROUP, APO 194, US AIR
FORC E.

    I ALREADY HAVE MY ENGLISH PASS PORT. HOPING TO HEAR
FOR YOU IN THE NEAR FUTURE I REMAIN YOURS SINCERELY.

                              MRS. MARGARTE D. MERCURE
                              92 SHEEP STREET
                              BICESTER, OXON

Royal Air Force,
Bicester,
Oxon

28th August, 1954

To Whom it may concern,

Mrs. M.D. Mercure formerly
No. ███████ L.A.C.W. Mercure, M.D

This is to certify that the above named
served in the Womens' Royal Air Force from 22nd September,
1949 until 31st October, 1952. Her trade during her
service with the W.R.A.F. was Telephonist II and her
assessments are as follows :-

Conduct -   Exemplary

Ability as
tradeswoman   Very Good

Personal qualities :-

Leadership   - Good

Co-operation - Good

Bearing   - Smart

2.   The above named was discharged from the W.R.A.F
under Q.R. para 652 clause W.26 ' At own request on marriage '
and has no liability to serve on the Reserve Forces.

3.   The following is a description of her duties as Telephonist II.

   " Operates telephone switchboards for private branch and service
     exchanges, maintains traffic records. Installs simple field
     telephone systems. "

4.   The following information is given by her Commanding Officer,
Squadron Leader H.M. Sanderson on her discharge.

   " L.A.C.W. Mercure's services are recommended to any employer
     to whom ability to learn, work well and good conduct are assets.

(B. M. RECHI)
Flight Lieutenant,
For   Officer Commanding,
       Royal Air Force Bicester.

Sgt Mercure (signature)

25 September 1954

3918th Operations Squadron

Master Sergeant //////

Maurice E. Mercure   T/Sgt   AF▮▮▮▮▮▮   29270

1. Since his initial assignment at this station approximately thirty-three (33) months ago, T/Sgt Mercure has been performing the duty of NCOIC of the Cryptographic Section. T/Sgt Mercure was instrumental in the designing and construction of the new Cryptographic Section in building 172. He helped to build new Cryptographic Section in building 172. He helped to play a vital part in the movement of the Cryptographic Section from Base Headquarters to the new Wing Operations Building which required the utmost security and caution.

2. In consideration of the high skill level which must be maintained by a Cryptographic Supervisor, the quantities of experience which must be held, and the technical training and initiative necessary to hold this position, it is pointed out that T/Sgt Mercure has consistently achieved this criteria and has, since its origination, promoted the superlative standards of work which are so essential to the efficient operation of a section of this kind. Nine (9) Cryptographic Command Inspections have brought forth the excellent report that must be consistently maintained in a field in which security systems and methods must be of prior importance in every case.

3. It is the opinion of this officer that favorable consideration, for promotion to Master Sergeant, would be to the best interest of the USAF

///////

//////

ROBERT O. BALL JR, Captain, USAF
Crypto Security Officer

B33

BASE COMMUNICATIONS
3918TH OPERATIONS SQUADRON
3918TH AIR BASE GROUP
APO 194 US AIR FORCE

COM   10 November 1954

SUBJECT: Letter of Commendation: T/Sgt M. F. Mercure, AF ██████████

TO: Whom It May Concern

    1. T/Sgt Maurice F. Mercure, AF ██████████, has been under my
direct supervision for the past fourteen (14) months. During that time,
he has displayed initiative and leadership; qualities which have made
him a real asset to the operation of the Base Crypto Section.

    2. T/Sgt Mercure, as NCOIC of the Base Crypto Center, from December
1951 to date, has turned in a record of efficient operation unexcelled by
any other section of like activity in the 7th Air Division. Numerous
Cryptographic Inspection Reports have brought this fact to attention of
Command cryptographic personnel. I feel that the special effort of T/Sgt
Mercure has made this situation possible.

    3. In smartness of appearance, honesty, devotion to duty and ability
to do the job without unnecessary supervision, T/Sgt Mercure is outstanding
and is truly a key NCO.

                                     Robert O Ball Jr
                                     ROBERT O. BALL JR.
                                     Captain, USAF
                                     Communications Officer

16 August 1955

SUBJECT: Recommendation for NCO of the Month

THRU: Base Communications Officer
          4060th Operations Squadron
          Dow AFB, Maine

TO: Commander
          4060th Operations Squadron
          Dow AFB, Maine

1. T/Sgt Maurice F. Mercure, AF ████████████, is assigned to the Base Cryptographic Center as Cryptographic Operations Supervisor (29270). He is responsible for managing cryptographic operations activity, plans and schedules workloads and duty assignments of cryptographic operators. Reviews and evaluates reports of violations of cryptographic security and procedures. Prepares routine or special reports concerning all phases of cryptographic operations. Instructs operators in cryptographic operations. Plans and conducts conferences. Resolves technical problems encountered in cryptographic operations. Inspects and evaluates cryptographic operations activity.

2. Since his initial assignment at this station approximately eight (8) months ago, T/Sgt Mercure has been performing the duty of NCOIC of the Base Cryptographic Section. T/Sgt Mercure was instrumental in the designing and construction of the crypto center operating console.

3. In consideration of the high skill level which must be maintained by a Cryptographic Supervisor, the quantities of experience which must be held, and the technical training and initiative necessary to hold this position, it is pointed out that T/Sgt Mercure has consistently achieved this criteria and has promoted the superlative standards of work which are so essential to the efficient operation of a section of this kind. A recent USAF Security Service survey has brought forth the excellent report that must be consistently maintained in a field in which security systems and methods are of paramount importance in every case. T/Sgt Mercure is the first person to obtain an excellent report since the activation of the Base Cryptographic Section.

(Crypto Subj: Recommendation for NCO of the Month)

4. T/Sgt Mercure performs his duties in an outstanding manner, setting a superior example for the personnel working with him and for him. He is always prompt for duty and appointments and is always neat in his personal appearance and habits. T/Sgt Mercure is truly a key NCO.

MYRON J. GERDES
Captain, USA
Cryptosecurity Officer

836

Department of the Air Force

CERTIFICATE OF TRAINING

This is to certify that

T/Sgt Maurice F. Mercure, AF

has satisfactorily completed the

course in SAC Security Indoctrination Phase I

Given by

18th Communications Squadron, Air Force, Westover Air Force Base, Massachusetts

31 Oct 55   Score: 100

GERALD P. WEISMAN
Capt, USAF
Training Officer

FORM 1256, 1 JAN 55

GPO:1955 O - 332252

HEADQUARTERS
EIGHTH AIR FORCE (SAC)
Westover Air Force Base
Massachusetts

LETTER ORDER #650   2 July 1956

SUBJECT: Permanent Change of Station

TO: TECHNICAL SERGEANT MAURICE F MERCURE AF ████████ (Utilization Air Force
           Specialty Code 29270)
           18th Communications Squadron, Air Force (Strategic Air Command)
           Westover Air Force Base, Massachusetts

        You are relieved from assignment 18th Communications Squadron, Air Force
(Strategic Air Command) this station; assigned Detachment 1 2225th Personnel
Processing Group, Air Force (Continental Air Command) Fort Hamilton, New York
for further overseas assignment to 7250th Support Squadron (United States Air
Forces in Europe) Air Post Office 206-A New York, New York on project June-
United States Air Forces in Europe-Turkey-C805. You will not depart this station
prior to 12 August 1956. Transportation of dependent (Wife, Margaret D Mercure —
address 119 Prospect Street Willimansett Massachusetts) authorized concurrently
with your movement in accordance with message Headquarters TUSLOG TPMP 28-F-
3773-U dated 28 June 1956. Shipment of household effects (located at 119 Prospect
Street Willimansett Massachusetts) authorized. Shipment of privately-owned
vehicle authorized in accordance with Air Force Manual 75-1, as amended. If
shipment of privately-owned vehicle is by other than Military Sea Transportation
Service, it will be at no expense to the Government. You and your dependent will
be available for call of Port Commander, New York Port of Embarkation, Brooklyn,
New York on or after 28 August 1956 at 119 Prospect Street Willimansett
Massachusetts for transportation to destination and will comply with all instructions contained in Port Call. If Port Call has not been received 10 days prior to
the established availability date, you will contact the Commander, Logistic
Control Group, New York Port of Embarkation, Brooklyn, New York, preferably by
wire, for further instructions. Application for passport for dependent will be
submitted immediately to clerk of nearest State or Federal court in accordance
with Air Force Regulation 34-61. Passport and Visa Division Military District of
Washington, Room 1B874, The Pentagon, will be notified date and place application
was submitted and furnished one copy of this order. Air Force Manual 35-6 will
be complied with and immunizations in accordance with Air Force Regulation 160-102
will be accomplished immediately by you and your dependent. All mail will be
addressed to show grade, name, Air Force Service Number, Casual Enlisted Section,
Detachment 1 2225th Personnel Processing Group (Air Force), Fort Hamilton, New
York. Baggage will be shipped in accordance with Air Force Regulation 75-33.
15 days delay enroute authorized chargeable as ordinary leave provided it does
not interfere with reporting on date specified and providing you have sufficient
accrued leave. Address while on delay enroute: 119 Prospect Street Willimansett
Massachusetts. Travel by privately-owned vehicle with 1 day travel time authorized.
If privately-owned vehicle not used, travel time will be that of carrier used.
Will proceed. Permanent change of station. Travel as directed is necessary in the
military service. 5773500 048-132 P531.9-02 03 S99-999; dislocation allowance
other: 5773500 048-246 P514-01 S99-999. Effective date of change in strength

LO #650, Hq Eighth AF (SAC) Westover AFB MASS dated 2 JUL 56 (CONT)

accountability: 28 August 1956. Authority: Letter Headquarters United States
Air Force AFPMP-2F dated 16 March 1956, Subject, Withdrawal of Warrant Officers
and Airmen for June 1956 Personnel Processing Squadron Arrivals, and Strategic
Air Command Regulation 35-19.

BY ORDER OF THE COMMANDER:

C. W. SUMMERS
CWO, W-3, USAF
ASTADJ

DISTRIBUTION:
60 AMN concerned
 5 COMDR 18th COSMRON AF
 5 COMDR DET 1 2225th PERPGRU FT Hamilton NY
 3 PSTLO DET 1 2225th PERPGRU FT Hamilton NY
 3 PSTLO POE FT Hamilton NY
 3 Port COMDR NYPE Brooklyn NY
 3 SACLO FT Hamilton NY
 2 Passport and Visa DIV, MIW, Room 1D874, The Pentagon, Washington DC
 1 OSR

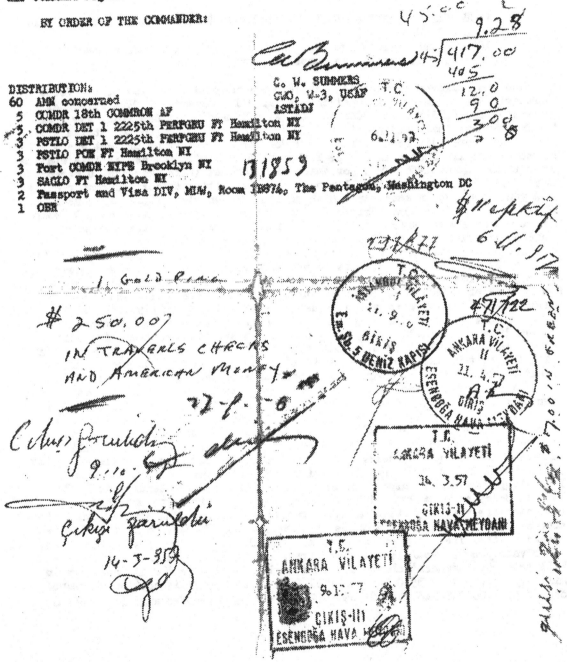

MERCURE   MAURICE #122 #214

| LAST NAME | FIRST NAME | MIDDLE INITIAL |

UPSHUR

PORT CALL DATE **SEP 9 1956** SCHEDULED TRANSPORTATION

PRE-EMBARKATION PROCESSING CHECK LIST

The Initial Reception Clerk should take your answers to the following questions:

Do you have an automobile still to be processed:

Are you taking a pet overseas?

The following five stages constitute your processing. PLEASE GO PROMPTLY TO EACH OF THESE STAGES IN THE ORDER GIVEN BELOW. (Data in boxes to be filled in by personnel completing your processing.)

1. REPORT FIRST TO **ROOM #4** (ALL MEMBERS OF FAMILY MUST ATTEND)

| Medical Processing | *MC* |

2. THEN PROCEED TO THE **BILLETING DESK** IN ROOM #.

| *Jefferson* 222 | 1600 |
| HOTEL | ROOM # |

3. THEN PROCEED TO **ROOM #5** (HUSBANDS & WIVES MUST ATTEND)

Form 8		
Postal Locator		Not Required
Passport		Not Required
UD AGO 65 or DD 720		Not Required
Military Processing	HR	Not Required

4. REPORT IMMEDIATELY TO **BUILDING #380** (ADJOINING DEPENDENTS MESS HALL)

| Hand Baggage Processing | *MC* |
| Hold Baggage Claim Checks Turned In | |

5. ONE ADULT MEMBER OF EACH FAMILY MUST ATTEND AN ORIENTATION LECTURE (IN THE BASEMENT OF THE FRANKLIN HOTEL) (AT THE POST THEATER) AT ____ HRS.

DON'T BRING CHILDREN TO THE ORIENTATION LECTURE. A Transient Nursery is available in the basement of the Franklin Hotel where for a moderate charge children under eight years of age may be accommodated.

BRING THIS PROCESSING SHEET WITH YOU TO THE ORIENTATION AND CLEARANCE.

Fort Hamilton Form 0379 (B), 4 July 56
Revised edition of 28 March 56 which is obsolete

838

BAGGAGE DEADLINE AND BAGGAGE HANDLING:

Your cabin baggage should be delivered to Building # 380 where it will be tagged and placed with all other cabin baggage to be loaded aboard your ship. In most cases, you must have your baggage delivered to Building #380 not later than 1630 hours (4:30 P.M.) of the day Before your ship sails. Any piece of baggage of suitcase size not delivered by this time, must be taken to Building #380 not later than 0700 hours (7:00 A. M.) on the morning of your sailing date. This cabin baggage will be taken to your cabin aboard ship sometime before or shortly after your arrival at the cabin.

*NOTE: Hold baggage shipped to either the Transportation Officer, Fort Hamilton, or the Transportation Officer, Brooklyn Army Terminal (New York Port of Embarkation) will be shipped to your destination overseas without your taking any action on this station. Please do not ask to have a check made on the handling of your hold Baggage.

WHERE AND WHEN TO STANDBY FOR MOVEMENT TO THE PIER:

All personnel sailing on the USNS _____**UPSHUR**_____ must assemble at the following place and time for movement via bus convoy to the pier.

    Place: AT THE REAR OF THE JEFFERSON HOTEL
    Time: **0830** HOURS   **SEP 10 1956**

All personnel must go to the pier on transportation provided by this installation. No visitors will be allowed on the pier at this time and therefore visitors cannot ride in the convoy.

HOW TO BE PREPARED AT THE STANDBY TIME AND PLACE:

Military personnel must embark and debark in a Class "A" uniform. The uniform for embarking at the present time is summer uniform with tie. Personnel debarking at Southampton, Bremerhaven, or LeHavre must go ashore in winter uniform. (Army officers must debark in pinks and greens.) Personnel debarking at Mediterranean or Caribbean ports must go ashore in summer uniform with tie. Dress for civilian personnel is informal: it is recommended, though not required, that the ladies embark in slacks and low heeled shoes.

At the Standby Time the head of each family should have readily accessible the following documents: Passports (if needed), Shot records, and at least two copies of orders. Additional orders will be issued to military personnel as they board the busses. When applicable, certificates of non-availability of quarters will also be issued at this time.

It is the responsibility of all personnel taking pets to the ship to have secured their animals from the establishment where they have been boarded and to have the animals ready at the Standby Time and Place. These persons should also have with them their pets papers.

INFORMATION REGARDING CHILDREN WHO REQUIRE DIAPERS AND/OR FORMULA:

Personnel with children who require diapers should have in their possession at the Standby Time and Place at least a ten-hour supply of disposable diapers. This supply is adequate to last until the ship's store opens. Because laundry facilities aboard MSTS Vessels are not adequate for the washing of permanent-type diapers, only disposable diapers can be used.

839a

Personnel with children who require baby formula should have in their possession at the Standby Time and Place an approximate ten-hour supply of formula. This is a generous estimate of the time it will take for the ship's formula room to prepare the several types of formula available aboard the ship. After this time formula can be drawn from the ship's formula room. This formula will be provided on the basis of the subsistence charge made for each child (see below). Baby food will also be provided on the basis of this subsistence charge.

Orientation For Surface Travel Aboard Military Sea Transportation Service Vessel:

PAYMENT OF SUBSISTENCE CHARGES:

The head of each family must be prepared to pay subsistence charges for his family sometime shortly after embarking. This charge, which covers the cost of all food served aboard the ship, is the only charge made for MSTS travel on a space-requirement basis. The charges must be paid in either cash or a combination of cash and travellers checks in as near as possible the exact amount. The amounts of these charges for each port of debarkation will be posted on the bulletin boards in the lobbies of each hotel occupied by personnel sailing on this ship.

NOTE: Two categories of personnel do not pay subsistence charges. (1) Military personnel on active duty do not pay subsistence charges for themselves. They will surrender their rations allowance for the number of days of the journey. (2) Personnel travelling on a Space Available basis will pay a space available charge prior to embarking and do not pay subsistence charges for themselves.

UNIFORMS REGULATIONS ABOARD SHIP:

MSTS Regulations require that Military Personnel on active duty wear a Class "A" uniform for the evening meal each night aboard ship. Personnel acting in a duty status should also wear a uniform when performing their official functions. The uniform requirements for all times, other than embarking, debarking, and the evening meal, will be prescribed by the Senior Unit Commander aboard ship.

REGULATIONS REGARDING FIREARMS, LIQUOR, GAMBLING, AND TIPPING ABOARD SHIP.

Firearms or weapons of any kind cannot be taken aboard MSTS Vessels. Such weapons should have been shipped from your home station under separate crate clearly marked as to contents.

Navy Regulations prohibit liquor or gambling aboard MSTS Vessels. Tipping of any personnel is also not permitted.

FACILITIES AVAILABLE TO YOU ABOARD SHIP:

Aboard ship you will find the following facilities for your convenience and recreation: A hospital and outpatient dispensary, automatic washing machines, electric irons and ironing boards, barber shop, lounges, libraries, playrooms, daily motion pictures, and the ship's newspaper.

TRANSPORTATION FROM YOUR PORT OF DEBARKATION TO YOUR ULTIMATE DESTINATION:

When you descend the gangplank at your port of debarkation, you will be met by a Transportation Corps official whose responsibility it is to arrange for transportation to your ultimate destination. Personnel travelling on a Space Available basis are not entitled to such transportation.

B39b

OBEDIENCE TO LOCAL LAWS OVERSEAS:

NOTE: All persons being transferred to oversea stations should be aware that they are subject to the local laws of the country in which they are located. Some acts or omissions, such as currency transactions, black marketeering, and motor vehicle regulations which may not be offenses in the United States, may be offenses in the local country. Specific instructions and advice will be given you overseas.

PROCEDURES FOR HAVING VISITORS SEE YOU OFF AT THE PIER ON YOUR SAILING DATE:

Direct your visitors to report to Brooklyn Army Terminal, 58th St & First Avenue Brooklyn, by their own means of transportation. Visiting hours and the number of the pier from which your ship sails will be posted in your hotel lobby.

B39c

USNS UPSHUR

Farewell Dinner

DEPARTMENT OF THE NAVY

MSTS

MILITARY SEA TRANSPORTATION SERVICE

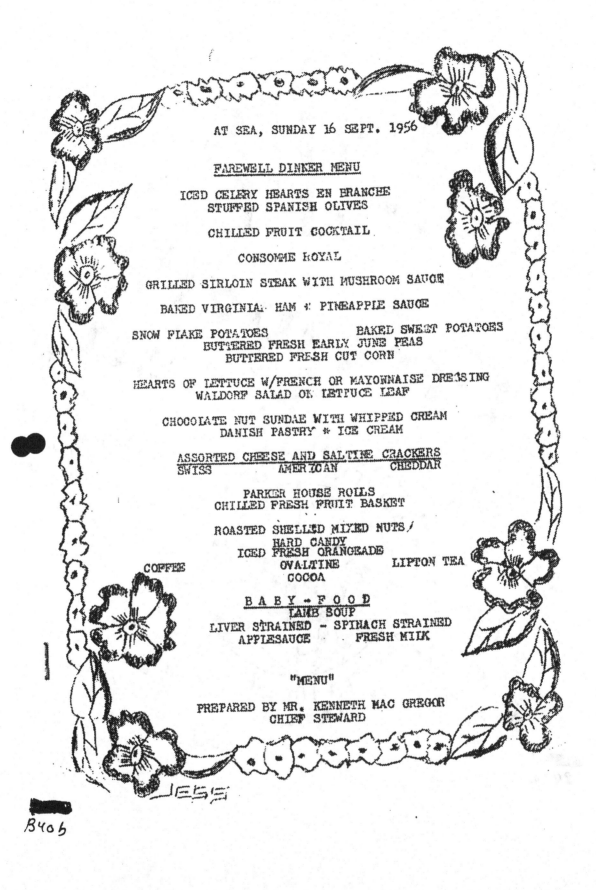

AT SEA, SUNDAY 16 SEPT. 1956

FAREWELL DINNER MENU

ICED CELERY HEARTS EN BRANCHE
STUFFED SPANISH OLIVES

CHILLED FRUIT COCKTAIL

CONSOMME ROYAL

GRILLED SIRLOIN STEAK WITH MUSHROOM SAUCE

BAKED VIRGINIA HAM & PINEAPPLE SAUCE

SNOW FLAKE POTATOES   BAKED SWEET POTATOES
BUTTERED FRESH EARLY JUNE PEAS
BUTTERED FRESH CUT CORN

HEARTS OF LETTUCE W/FRENCH OR MAYONNAISE DRESSING
WALDORF SALAD ON LETTUCE LEAF

CHOCOLATE NUT SUNDAE WITH WHIPPED CREAM
DANISH PASTRY * ICE CREAM

ASSORTED CHEESE AND SALTINE CRACKERS
SWISS   AMERICAN   CHEDDAR

PARKER HOUSE ROLLS
CHILLED FRESH FRUIT BASKET

ROASTED SHELLED MIXED NUTS /
HARD CANDY
ICED FRESH ORANGEADE
OVALTINE   LIPTON TEA
COFFEE   COCOA

B A B Y - F O O D
LAMB SOUP
LIVER STRAINED - SPINACH STRAINED
APPLESAUCE   FRESH MILK

"MENU"

PREPARED BY MR. KENNETH MAC GREGOR
CHIEF STEWARD

JESS

B40b

7250TH SUPPORT SQUADRON
7217TH SUPPORT GROUP (USAFE)
APO 254, NEW YORK, N.Y.

SPECIAL ORDERS   8 March 1957
NUMBER   30

1. Par 3, SO 21, CS, this org this sta pertaining to reassign-
ment of CAPT ROBERT L. MATHIS,  is revoked.

2. CAPT ROBERT L. MATHIS, ████████ (AFSC: 6424) having been
asgd 7217TH SUPTGRU this sta per par 27 SO 13 Hq 3345th Tech Tng
Wg, Chanute AFB, Illinois is further asgd 7217TH AEHGR, APO 380,
USAF, w/EDCSA: 9 MARCH 1957. PCA. AUTH: AFM 35-11 and Msg Hq
USAFE TPMP AC-1933.

3. T/SGT MAURICE F. MERCURE, AF ████████ this org this sta is
granted ord lv of absence for twenty-seven (27) days eff on or aft
16 Mar 57. Lv Add: 36 Shakespeare Ave, Hayes, Middlesex, England.
Amn's dependent wife (MRS MAURICE F. MERCURE) auth to accompany amn.
Air travel on a space available basis is authorized to Paris, France.
UCMR this org this sta. AUTH: USAF Msg AFCVC 42176, as amended by
USAF Msg AFCAV 32556 and USAF Msg AFCVC 40050.

BY ORDER OF THE COMMANDER:

OFFICIAL: LAURENCE M. RITNER
                                                           2nd Lt., USAF
                                                           Adjutant
LAURENCE M. RITNER
2nd Lt., USAF
Adjutant

DISTRIBUTION
    "X"

7250TH SUPPORT SQUADRON
7217TH SUPPORT GROUP (USAFE)
UNITED STATES AIR FORCE
APO 254 NEW YORK, N. Y.

SPECIAL ORDERS)   15 April 1958
NUMBER   C-32)

   1. TSGT MAURICE F. MERCURE, ▇▇▇▇▇▇, this organization, this
station is granted ordinary leave of absence for thirty (30) days
effective on or about 17 April 1958 for the purpose of visiting England.
Leave Address: Mr and Mrs. Fredrick Banks, 36 Shakespeare Avenue,
Hayes Middlesex, England. Authority: AFR 35-22.

   2. A/1C JAMES R. WILSON, ▇▇▇▇▇▇▇▇ this organization, this
station is granted ordinary leave of absence for twenty (20) days
effective on or about 2 May 1958. Leave Address: Ankara, Turkey.
Authority: AFR 35-22.

   3. A/3C FREDERICK G.C. BAILEY, ▇▇▇▇▇▇▇, this organization, this
station is granted ordinary leave of absence for thirty (30) days
effective on or about 1 May 1958 for the purpose of visiting Iran.
Leave Address: Union Pacific Hotel, Teheran, Iran. Authority: AFR 35-22.

   4. A/2C WALTER F. RAUHECKER JR, ▇▇▇▇▇▇, this organization, this
station is granted ordinary leave of absence for thirty (30) days
effective on or about 1 July 1958. Airman is authorized to
Zone of Interior. Leave Address: 6500 Martha Street, Pittsburgh, Penna.
Authority: AFR 35-22.

   5. So much of paragraph 4, SO C-29, this Hq, 14 April 1958,
relating to LEAVE of A/1C JOHN K. DIEGGEN, AF19419583 as reads:
leave of absence for twenty (20) days is amended to read: leave of
absence for twenty (20) days effective on or about 1 May 1958.

   6. SSGT EMILIO BUSTOS, ▇▇▇▇▇▇▇ this organization, this station
is authorized to ration separately effective 15 April 1958. Authority:
Part 2, Chapter 1, paragraph 20104 b(1)(b) AFM 173-20.

           FOR THE COMMANDER:

                                    ERNEST G. FREDERICK
                                    Major   USAF
                                    Executive Officer

DISTRIBUTION
10 cys EA INDIV Para 1 thru 6
1 cy A/2 Clerk
1 cy Mail Clerk
1 cy PMP
1 cy APW
1 cy TUSLOG (TPMP)
1 cy 1st Sgt

                        Polis M.
                    MEHMET ERTEKİN
                       No. 96/4162

B42a

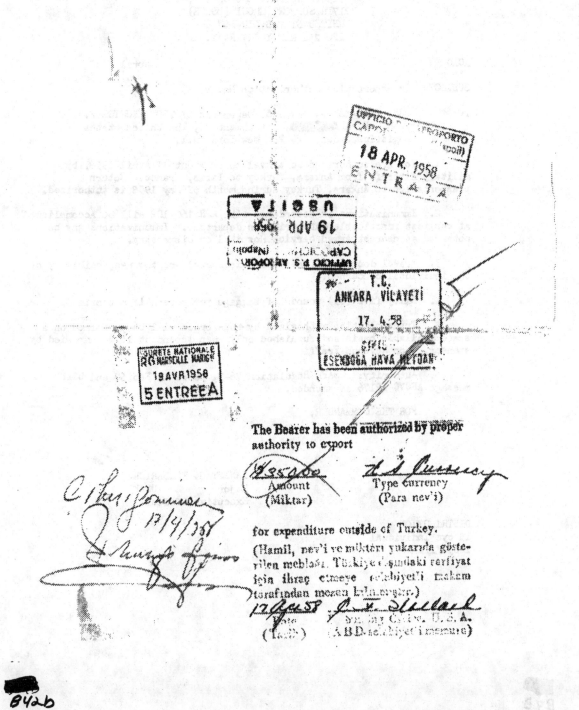

UFFICIO P.... ...ORTO
CAPPO....
18 APR. 1958
ENTRATA

USCITA
19 APR 1958
UFFICIO P.S. AEROPOR... (Napoli)

T.C.
ANKARA VİLAYETİ
17. 4. 58
ÇIKIŞ
ESENBOĞA HAVA MEYDANI

SURETE NATIONALE
RG MARSEILLE MARIGN...
19 AVR 1958
5 ENTREE A

The Bearer has been authorized by proper
authority to export

$25.00   U.S. Currency
‾‾‾‾‾‾   ‾‾‾‾‾‾‾‾‾‾‾
Amount   Type currency
(Miktar)   (Para nev'i)

for expenditure outside of Turkey.

(Hamil, nev'i ve miktarı yukarıda göste-
rilen meblağı Türkiye dışındaki sarfiyat
için ihraç etmeye selahiyet'i makam
tarafından mezun kılınmıştır.)

12 Apr 58
‾‾‾‾‾‾‾‾   ‾‾‾‾‾‾‾‾‾‾‾‾‾‾‾
Date   Sterling Officer, U.S.A.
(Tarih)   (ABD selahiyet'i memuru)

7250TH SUPPORT SQUADRON
7217TH SUPPORT GROUP (USAFE)
UNITED STATES AIR FORCE
APO 254 NEW YORK, N. Y.

ACAG   16 April 1958

SUBJECT: Transportation Authorization No. 9

TO: MRS. MARGARET D. MERCURE, Dependent of TSGT MAURICE F.
           MERCURE, AF██████, Detachment 30, The United States
           Logistics Group, APO 254 New York, N.Y.

        1. You are authorized to travel on or about 17 April 1958, by
military aircraft from Ankara, Turkey to Paris, France. Return
transportation to Ankara, Turkey during month of May 1958 is authorized.

        2. Immunizations in accordance with AFR 160-102 will be accomplished
at earliest practicable date prior to departure. Immunizations may be
obtained at nearest Armed Service Hospital or Dispensary.

        3. Travel documents (Passport, visas etc) are the responsibility of
the individual concerned.

        4. Sixty-five (65) pounds of baggage per person is authorized.

        5. Transportation authorized by this order will be performed on a
space available basis and furnished only when dependent is accompanied by
sponsor. Non Revenue Traffic.

        6. Authority: USAFE Regulation 76-3, dated 15 Feb 57 and USAF
message AFCVC 42176 as amended.

            FOR THE COMMANDER:

                                        ERNEST G. FREDERICK
                                        Major   USAF
                                        Executive Officer

DISTRIBUTION
15 cys Individual
1 cy File

B43

APPLICATION FOR IDENTIFICATION CARD		DATE OF APPLICATION 14 August 1958

I. APPLICATION

APPLICATION IS HEREBY MADE FOR AN IDENTIFICATION CARD:

FIRST APPLICATION		TO REPLACE LOST CARD (Explain on reverse side)	X	TO REPLACE DAMAGED OR ERRONEOUS CARD

PERSONNEL DATA

LAST NAME - FIRST NAME - MIDDLE NAME (Print or type)	POSITION TITLE OR STATUS	COUNTRY AND SERVICE (If other than USAF)
MERCURE, Maurice Frank	AFSC 29270	

GRADE	SERVICE NO. (If any)	EXPIRATION DATE OF ENL OR APMT	I CERTIFY THAT THIS INFORMATION IS CORRECT (Signature)
T/Sgt.	AF ███████	4 Oct 1961	*Maurice F. Mercure*

DATE OF BIRTH	WEIGHT	HEIGHT	COLOR HAIR	COLOR EYES	
14 Aug ██	190	5 8½	Brown	Blue	

BLOOD TYPE	RELIGION	OTHER IDENTIFYING FEATURES
B Pos	Pro	NONE

II. INDORSEMENT

I CERTIFY THAT THE ABOVE INFORMATION HAS BEEN VERIFIED AND IS CORRECT (Except as follows:)	TYPED NAME, GRADE (If military) AND POSITION TITLE
	E. E. PERSONEUS, Capt, Personnel Officer
	SIGNATURE *E E Perseus*

III. ACKNOWLEDGMENT OF RECEIPT

FORM ISSUED (Check one)		EXPIRATION DATE	DATE	SIGNATURE OF APPLICANT
X	DD FORM 2AF	4 OcT 61	11 Sept 58	*Maurice F. Mercure*
	DD FORM 2AF (RES)	CARD NUMBER		
	DD FORM 109	1581145		
	AF FORM 1277			

AF FORM 279 (1 APR 55)   PREVIOUS EDITIONS OF THIS FORM ARE OBSOLETE.

Air Force—USAFE, Webs, Ger

B44

TUSLOG DETACHMENT 30
APO 254 NEW YORK, NEW YORK

SPECIAL ORDERS)   22 August 1958
NUMBER   A-217)

1.   TSGT MAURICE F. MERCURE, AF ████████, (Control AFSC: 29270).
ASSIGNMENT: Relieved from assignment TUSLOG DETACHMENT 30, APO 254, NEW
YORK, NY, assigned to Special Weapons Center, Kirkland AFB, NMex (ARDC).
REPORTING DATA: 10 DALVP in the ZI. Leave Address: 293 Chestnut St,
Holyoke, Mass. 20 DALVP in Europe. Leave Address: 36 Shakespeare Ave,
Hayes Middlesex, England. Airman will proceed on or about 28 October 1958,
reporting to Comdr, Special Weapons Center, Kirkland AFB, NMex (ARDC), not
later than 19 days after departure from the continental United States Port
of Debarkation. EDCSA: 1 November 1958. October 58 Returnee.
GENERAL INSTRUCTIONS: Airman will advise all concerned of change of
address by use of AF Form 305 (Notice of change of address). AFM 35-6
will be complied with. All mail will be addressed to show grade, name,
AFSN (ZI unit). Authority: Letter AFPMP-2P, Hq USAF, 30 Jul 58, Subject:
Assignments for World-Wide Oct Returnees.
TRANSPORTATIONS: PCS. TDN: 5793500 948-132 P531.9 5503725 0100, 0231,
0398 0798 (CIC 45 948 5319 503725) Expense 531. (Authorized dislocation
allowance other). Shipment of POV authorized. Shipment of household goods
authorized. Shipment of hold baggage in accordance with paragraphs 18 and
25, AFR 75-33 authorized. 100 pound baggage allowance authorized each
individual including excess. Travel by privately owned conveyance
authorized with 9 days travel time authorized. If POV is not used, travel
time will be the time of common carrier used. Transportation of dependent
MARGARET D. MERCURE (WIFE) (Passport Nr. 227182), is authorized concurrentl
with sponsor. Travel by aircraft of foreign registry authorized. Travel
by commercial air authorized. Travel by military aircraft authorized.

FOR THE COMMANDER:

JOE R. COLLINS
Major   USAF
Administrative Officer

DISTRIBUTION
75 cys INDIV para 1
1 cy M/R Clerk
1 cy Mail Clerk
1 cy 1st Sgt
1 cy LP
1 cy Postal Officer
5 cys SWC, Kirkland AFB
2 cys ACAF
2 cys AMTR
2 cys AIMP

TUSLOG DETACHMENT 30
AFO 254, New York, N. Y.

AACM   10 October 1958

SUBJECT: Commendation

TO: Whom it May Concern

    1. This is to acknowledge the outstanding knowledge of crypto-graphic operations and the contribution made by Technical Sergeant Maurice F. Mercure, AF ████████, a member of this organization, to-wards support of the United States Air Force mission in Turkey, during his twenty-five (25) months assignment to this organization.

    2. Sergeant Mercure has performed the duty of Cryptographic Supervisor in the cryptocenters of the Joint United States Military Mission for Aid to Turkey (JUSMMAT) and TUSLOG Detachment 30. This NCO assisted to establish and to organize the TUSLOG Detachment 30 Cryptographic Account. During his twelve (12) years in the Cryptographic Operations Career Field he has developed a superior job knowledge. I have never encountered an individual more highly qualified in this speciality. He possesses a keen sense of responsibility and has dis-charged his duties in a superior manner.

    3. Sergeant Mercure is a graduate of the Strategic Air Command NCO Academy. He has constantly applied his technical training and experience to the best interest of his organization and the United States Air Force. He has excellent growth potential and is fully qualified for advancement and assumption of the responsibilities of the next higher NCO grade.

    4. It has been my pleasure to have served in Detachment 30, TUSLOG with Sergeant Mercure. His ability, devotion to duty, and loyalty to his country in the profession of arms, is commended.

FRANK O. HINCKLEY
Lt. Col.,   USAF
Commander

DETACHMENT 18, TUSLOG
APO 254, New York, New York

14 October 1958

SUBJECT: Letter of Appreciation

TO: OIC, Communication Center
        Detachment 30, TUSLOG
        APO 254, New York, New York

1. I would like to take this opportunity to express my appreciation for the services rendered this unit by your communication section; NCOIC TSgt Maurice F. Mercure.

2. On occasions he has taken time from his busy schedule to conduct training classes for this unit although there was no requirement on him to do so. He has seen to it that we have received the best possible and most expeditious maintenance on our Cryptographic Equipment which has reduced our outages considerably. In general his help to this unit has been very beneficial not only to our mission but to the air force as well.

3. Request that a copy of this letter be given to TSgt Mercure and a copy made a permanent record in his 201 file.

DONALD F. GRANAHAN
Major,   USAF
Commander

PCS

TUSLOG DETACHMENT 30
APO 254 NEW YORK, NEW YORK

SPECIAL ORDERS)   22 August 1958
NUMBER   A-217)

1. TSGT MAURICE F. MERCURE, AF ▮▮▮▮▮▮▮ (Control AFSC: 29270).
ASSIGNMENT: Relieved from assignment TUSLOG DETACHMENT 30, APO 254, NEW
YORK, NY, assigned to Special Weapons Center, Kirkland AFB, NMex (ARDC).
REPORTING DATA: 10 DALVP in the ZI. Leave Address: 293 Chestnut St,
Holyoke, Mass. 20 DALVP in Europe. Leave Address: 36 Shakespeare Ave,
Hayes Middlesex, England. Airman will proceed on or about 28 October 1958,
reporting to Comdr, Special Weapons Center, Kirkland AFB, NMex (ARDC), not
later than 19 days after departure from the continental United States Port
of Debarkation. EDCSA: 1 November 1958. October 58 Returnee.
GENERAL INSTRUCTIONS: Airman will advise all concerned of change of
address by use of AF Form 305 (Notice of Change of address). AFM 35-6
will be complied with. All mail will be addressed to show grade, name,
AFSN (ZI unit). Authority: Letter AFPMP-2F, Hq USAF, 30 Jul 58, Subject:
Assignments for World-Wide Oct Returnees.
TRANSPORTATIONS: PCS. TDN: 5793500 948-132 P531.9 S503725 0100, 0231,
0398 0798 (CIC 45 948 5319 503725) Expense 531. (Authorized dislocation
allowance other). Shipment of POV authorized. Shipment of household goods
authorized. Shipment of hold baggage in accordance with paragraphs 18 and
23, AFR 75-33 authorized. 100 pound baggage allowance authorized each
individual including excess. Travel by privately owned conveyance
authorized with 9 days travel time authorized. If POV is not used, travel
time will be the time of common carrier used. Transportation of dependent
MARGARET D. MERCURE (WIFE) (Passport Nr. 227182), is authorized concurrently
with sponsor. Travel by aircraft of foreign registry authorized. Travel
by commercial air authorized. Travel by military aircraft authorized.

            FOR THE COMMANDER:

                                        JOE R. COLLINS
DISTRIBUTION   Major   USAF
75 cys INDIV para 1   Administrative Officer
1 cy M/R Clerk
1 cy Mail Clerk
1 cy 1st Sgt
1 cy LP
1 cy Postal Officer
5 cys SWC, Kirkland AFB
2 cys ACAF
2 cys AKTR
2 cys AMP

PCS

TUSLOG DETACHMENT 30
APO 254 NEW YORK, NEW YORK

SPECIAL ORDERS)   22 August 1958
NUMBER   A-217)

    1. TSGT MAURICE E. MERCURE, AF▬▬▬▬ (Control AFSC: 29270).
ASSIGNMENT: Relieved from assignment TUSLOG DETACHMENT 30, APO 254, NEW
YORK, NY, assigned to Special Weapons Center, Kirkland AFB, NMex (ARDC).
REPORTING DATA: 10 DALVP in the ZI. Leave Address: 293 Chestnut St,
Holyoke, Mass. 20 DALVP in Europe. Leave Address: 36 Shakespeare Ave,
Hayes Middlesex, England. Airman will proceed on or about 28 October 1958,
reporting to Comdr, Special Weapons Center, Kirkland AFB, NMex (ARDC), not
later than 19 days after departure from the continental United States Port
of Debarkation. EDCSA: 1 November 1958. October 58 Returnee.
GENERAL INSTRUCTIONS: Airman will advise all concerned of change of
address by use of AF Form 305 (Notice of change of address). AFM 35-6
will be complied with. All mail will be addressed to show grade, name,
AFSN (ZI unit). Authority: Letter AFPMP-2F, Hq USAF, 30 Jul 58, Subject:
Assignments for World-Wide Oct Returnees.
TRANSPORTATIONS: ICS. TDN: 5793500 948-132 P531.9 S503725 0100, 0231,
0398 0798 (CIC 45 948 5319 503725) Expense 531. (Authorized dislocation
allowance other). Shipment of POV authorized. Shipment of household goods
authorized. Shipment of hold baggage in accordance with paragraphs 18 and
25, AFR 75-33 authorized. 100 pound baggage allowance authorized each
individual including excess. Travel by privately owned conveyance
authorized with 9 days travel time authorized. If POV is not used, travel
time will be the time of common carrier used. Transportation of dependent
MARGARET D. MERCURE (WIFE) (Passport Nr. 227182), is authorized concurrently
with sponsor. Travel by aircraft of foreign registry authorized. Travel
by commercial air authorized. Travel by military aircraft authorized.

        FOR THE COMMANDER:

                                        JOE R. COLLINS
                                        Major   USAF
                                        Administrative Officer

DISTRIBUTION
75 cys INDIV para 1
1 cy M/R Clerk
1 cy Mail Clerk
1 cy 1st Sgt
1 cy Li
1 cy Postal Officer
5 cys SWC, Kirkland AFB
2 cys AGAP
2 cys AMTR
2 cys AFMP

CERTIFICATE OF SECURITY CLEARANCE BRIEFING

NAME OF INDIVIDUAL

Mercure, Maurice F.   T/Sgt.   AF███████

I certify that I have read and understand the contents of Air Force Regulation 205-15, dated 24 April 1958.

DATE	SIGNATURE OF INDIVIDUAL
28 November 1958	*Maurice F. Mercure*
	SIGNATURE OF WITNESS
	Paul F. Pettyjohn

ARDC FORM 104 1 Jun 1956 LOCAL REPRODUCTION AUTHORIZED

SWBCOC   DEC 1 1958

SUBJECT: Verification of Security Clearance

TO: Commander
           Air Force Special Weapons Center
           ATTN: SWIM
           Kirtland Air Force Base, New Mexico

        Request that all clearances for T/Sgt Maurice F. Mercure,
AF ▓▓▓▓▓▓ be listed by indorsement hereon.

        FOR THE COMMANDER:

                                        Edward S. Richard

                        EDWARD S. RICHARD
                        MAJOR   USAF
                        Administrative Services Officer

SWIM   1st Ind

Headquarters, Air Force Special Weapons Center, United States Air
Force, Kirtland Air Force Base, New Mexico   4 December 1958

TO: Commander, 4900th Air Base Group, ATTN: SWBCOC, Kirtland Air
Force Base, New Mexico

        Reference basic communication, T/Sgt Maurice F. Mercure has
been granted a final Top Secret Clearance 4 December 1958 based
on a background investigation 17 August 1950 by the 8th District
OSI-IG. Cryptographic clearance granted 6 May 1954 based on this
background investigation has been honored by this headquarters.

        FOR THE COMMANDER:

                                    Neil R. Farley
                        NEIL R. FARLEY
                        Assistant Provost Marshal
                        Office of the Inspector General

Blue Communications

CERTIFICATE OF CLEARANCE AND RECORD OF PERSONNEL SECURITY INVESTIGATION

INSTRUCTIONS

1. A new form will be accomplished for each specific action (that is, interim clearance, final clearance, etc.)
2. Sections not used will be lined out in ink.
3. Not to be used for cryptographic clearances.

SECTION I.   BASIC INFORMATION

LAST NAME - FIRST NAME - MIDDLE INITIAL	MILITARY OR CIVILIAN GRADE	BRANCH OF SERVICE		
		AIR FORCE	ARMY	NAVY
MERCURE, Maurice F.	T/Sgt	X		

DATE OF BIRTH (Day, month, year)	PLACE OF BIRTH (City, county, state, country)	SERVICE OR SOCIAL SECURITY NO. (if any)
14 Aug ████	RFD Fairview Hampton Co. Mass.	AF ████

SECTION II.   PERSONNEL SECURITY CLEARANCE

BASIS FOR CLEARANCE (Check one)		DATE OF REPORT (Day, month, year)1
X	BACKGROUND INVESTIGATION	17 Aug 59
	NATIONAL AGENCY CHECK	AGENCY WHICH CONDUCTED INVESTIGATION1
	NAC PLUS TEN CONSECUTIVE YEARS SERVICE	OSI 59
	FIVE CONSECUTIVE YEARS SERVICE	LOCATION OF INVESTIGATIVE REPORT (Show specific OSI District or other location when appropriate)1
	NAC PLUS WRITTEN INQUIRIES	
	CHECK OF PERSONNEL RECORDS	8th Dist

HIGHEST CLASSIFICATION FOR WHICH CLEARANCE IS GRANTED	(CHECK APPROPRIATE BOX)		INVESTIGATION OF THE TYPE REQUIRED TO SATISFY FINAL CLEARANCE REQUIREMENTS REQUESTED (Day, month, year)2
	INTERIM	FINAL	
TOP SECRET		X	

THIS IS TO CERTIFY THAT THE ABOVE NAMED INDIVIDUAL IS CLEARED UNDER THE PROVISIONS OF AFR 205-6 AND MAY BE AUTHORIZED ACCESS TO CLASSIFIED DEFENSE INFORMATION, AS INDICATED ABOVE, BY PROPER AUTHORITY IN THE PERFORMANCE OF OFFICIALLY ASSIGNED DUTIES.

SECTION III.   ACCESS PENDING COMPLETION OF CLEARANCE REQUIREMENTS

ACCESS TO (Insert whether TOP SECRET, SECRET or CONFIDENTIAL) _____ INFORMATION PENDING COMPLETION OF CLEARANCE REQUIREMENTS IS AUTHORIZED THE ABOVE NAMED INDIVIDUAL FOR THE PURPOSE OF PERFORMING OFFICIAL DUTIES CONCERNING ONLY THE PROJECT OR OPERATION LISTED BELOW.

EXPLAIN BRIEFLY THE PROJECT OR OPERATION INVOLVED. (Do not include classified information. If additional space required, use reverse side.)

THIS IS TO CERTIFY THAT ACCESS PENDING COMPLETION OF CLEARANCE REQUIREMENTS IS NECESSARY AND THAT DELAY CAUSED BY AWAITING INTERIM CLEARANCE WOULD BE HARMFUL TO THE NATIONAL INTEREST. INVESTIGATION OF THE TYPE REQUIRED TO SATISFY CLEARANCE REQUIREMENTS WAS REQUESTED ON (date) _____

SECTION IV.   RECORD OF COMPLETION OF FAVORABLE INVESTIGATION
(This section to be used only when clearance action is not required following completion of favorable investigation)

TYPE OF INVESTIGATION CONDUCTED	DATE OF REPORT (Day, month, year)
AGENCY WHICH CONDUCTED INVESTIGATION	LOCATION OF INVESTIGATIVE REPORT (Show specific OSI District, or other location when appropriate)

SECTION V.   SIGNATURE OF CLEARING AUTHORITY

ORGANIZATION AND LOCATION	DATE (Day, month, year)
Hq AAFSWC Kirtland AFB, New Mexico	4 Dec 58

TYPED NAME, GRADE AND OFFICIAL POSITION	SIGNATURE
NEIL R. FARLEY, Assistant Provost Marshal Office of the Inspector General	*Neil R. Farley*

1. Applicable only when clearance is based on formal investigation.
2. Complete only when interim clearance is granted.

AF FORM 47
1 NOV 55

U. S. GOVERNMENT PRINTING OFFICE: 1965 O—368338

STATEMENT OF SERVICE

svm 534

LAST NAME—FIRST NAME—MIDDLE INITIAL

MERCURE   MAURICE   F

JUL 2 1959

TAFMSD

TOTAL ACTIVE DUTY

	DOE	DOS	TIME LOST	SERVICE THIS ENLMT	TOTAL ACTIVE SERVICE
REG AF 1ST ENLMT	5 Oct 46	4 Oct 49	0	03 ~ 00 ~ 00	03 ~ 00 ~ 00
REG AF 2ND ENLMT	5 Oct 49	4 Oct 55	0	06 ~ 00 ~ 00	09 ~ 00 ~ 00
3RD ENLMT					
4TH ENLMT					
5TH ENLMT					
6TH ENLMT					

DATE OF ENLISTMENT	TOTAL PRIOR ACTIVE SERVICE	TOTAL ACTIVE FED MIL SV DATE
5 Oct 55	09 ~ 00 ~ 00	5 Oct 46

TMSD

TOTAL INACTIVE DUTY

	DOE	DOS	TIME LOST	SERVICE THIS ENLMT	TOTAL ACTIVE SERVICE
1ST ENLMT					
2ND ENLMT					
3RD ENLMT					
4TH ENLMT					
5TH ENLMT					
6TH ENLMT					

PRIOR INACTIVE SERVICE	PRIOR ACTIVE SERVICE	TOTAL PRIOR SERVICE
	09 ~ 00 ~ 00	09 ~ 00 ~ 00

DATE OF ENLISTMENT	TOTAL PRIOR SERVICE	TOTAL MILITARY SERVICE DATE
5 Oct 55	09 ~ 00 ~ 00	5 Oct 46

Verified from original copies of discharge certificates in the possession of individual and/or official statement of service from higher headquarters.

DATE ACCOMPLISHED	TMSD	RECORDS CUSTODIAN
25 Jun 59	5 Oct 46	*Bert H Thomas* BERT H THOMAS 2nd Lt, USAF

SWPM FORM 0-59
APR 59

HEADQUARTERS SQUADRON SECTION
4900th Air Base Group
Kirtland Air Force Base, New Mexico

24 November 1959

STATEMENT

This is to state that I have interviewed the wife of TSgt Maurice F. Mercure, AF███████, in regard to application for Special Assignment. I believe Sergeant Mercure and his family will reflect the highest degree of credit on the USAF and the United States wherever they are assigned.

Horton W. Stickle, Jr.
HORTON W. STICKLE JR
Lt Colonel, USAF
Commander

REQUEST FOR AND AUTHORIZATION OF LEAVE OF MILITARY PERSONNEL

	1. DATE OF REQUEST
	31 March 1960

I. REQUEST FOR LEAVE

TO: Commander Headquarters Squadron Section 4900th Air Base Group	2. TYPE OF LEAVE REQUESTED Ordinary	3. NO. OF DAYS 5	4. ☒ EFFECTIVE ON ☐ EFFECTIVE O/A 4 April 1960

5. ACCRUED LEAVE CREDIT (Days) 82½	6. LEAVE TAKEN THIS FY (Days) None	7. DETAIL TO WHICH ASSIGNED (Complete when assigned to detail requiring replacement)

REQUESTING INDIVIDUAL

8. NAME Maurice F. Mercure	9. GRADE T/Sgt.	10. AFSN AF ███████

11. ORGANIZATION OR OFFICE Base Comm, Hq Sq Sec, 4900th Air Base Group	12. PHONE 2700

ADDRESS WHILE ABSENT

13. IN CARE OF Mrs. Margaret B. Mercure	14. STREET ADDRESS 7315 Bradshaw Ave. S. E.

15. CITY Albuquerque	16. STATE New Mexico	17. PHONE AL 6-1537

REMARKS   For Health and rest. I am on separate rations.

I CERTIFY THAT THE ABOVE STATEMENTS ARE TRUE AND THAT I HAVE COMPLIED WITH THE PROVISIONS OF CURRENT DIRECTIVES ON LEAVE.

18. SIGNATURE OF REQUESTING INDIVIDUAL   *Maurice F Mercure*

II. APPROVALS

19. SIGNATURE AND TYPED NAME, GRADE AND TITLE OF APPROVING OFFICIAL	20. SIGNATURE AND TYPED NAME, GRADE AND TITLE OF APPROVING OFFICIAL	21. SIGNATURE AND TYPED NAME, GRADE AND TITLE OF APPROVING OFFICIAL
STANLEY O. CHRIST, SMSGT	HENRY K. SCHUMACHER, MAJOR	JOSEPH F. ROSAL, MSgt, USAF First Sergeant

III. AUTHORIZATIONS

22. THE INDIVIDUAL NAMED IN SECTION I IS AUTHORIZED LEAVE AS INDICATED ABOVE (TO, AIR 85,25) AND UPON COMPLETION WILL RETURN TO HIS PROPER ORGANIZATION

23. OFFICIAL DESIGNATION AND LOCATION OF APPROVING HEADQUARTERS OR UNIT HEDRONSEC, 4900th ABGRU, KAFB, NM	24. DATE OF ORDER 1 April 60	25. ORDER NO. #222

BY ORDER OF THE COMMANDER	26. TYPED NAME, GRADE, SERVICE AND TITLE OF ORDERS ISSUING OFFICIAL SIGNATURE OR SEAL *Horton W Stickle Jr* HORTON W. STICKLE JR Lt Colonel, USAF Commander

AF FORM 1164   1 OCT. 56   PREVIOUS EDITIONS OF THIS FORM MAY BE USED.   ☆ U.S. GOVERNMENT PRINTING OFFICE: 1957 - 423041

REQUEST FOR AND AUTHORIZATION OF TEMPORARY DUTY TRAVEL ORDERS OF MILITARY PERSONNEL

(This form authorizes an expenditure of Government funds and must be prepared accurately in every detail. Continue items on reverse, if necessary)

1. TO: ADJUTANT GENERAL, OR ADJUTANT	2. DATE OF REQUEST
4900th ABG, Kirtland AFB, NMEX	12 May 1960

I. REQUEST FOR AUTHORIZATION

3. ACTIVITY REQUESTING TRAVEL ORDERS (Complete designation)

Communications Div, 4900th ABG, Kirtland AFB, NMEX

II. TEMPORARY DUTY TRAVEL ORDERS

4. GRADE	5. LAST NAME—FIRST NAME—MIDDLE INITIAL	6. SERVICE NO.	7. ORGANIZATION
MAJOR	SCHNEIDER, ROBERT L.	▉▉▉▉	4900th ABG, Kirtland AFB,
2/LT	BROWN, MERTON F.	▉▉▉▉	4900th ABG, Kirtland AFB,

8. WILL PROCEED ON:	9. FROM:	10. TO: (List itinerary)
16 May 60	KIRTLAND AFB, NMEX	NELLIS AFB, NEVADA
		INDIAN SPRINGS AFB, NEVADA

11. NUMBER OF DAYS TDY	12. RETURN TO:
2	KIRTLAND AFB, NMEX

14. PURPOSE OF TEMPORARY DUTY (State organization to visit and name of headquarters, if applicable. Explain in full)

☐ PCS ☒ TDY _____ NELLIS AFB, NEV.

To coordinate weapon handling procedures between Nellis AFB, Nev., and Indian Spri...

III. TRANSPORTATION AUTHORIZED

15. _____

16. ☐ TRAVEL BY PRIVATE CONVEYANCE AUTHORIZED, THE MODE OF TRANSPORTATION AND REIMBURSEMENT TO BE MORE ADVANTAGEOUS TO THE GOVERNMENT

17. ☐ TRAVEL BY PRIVATE CONVEYANCE AUTHORIZED, NUMBER OF DAYS TRAVEL...
IN EXCESS OF COMMON CARRIER TIME (TDY) IS _____
AUTHORIZED AS ORDINARY LEAVE (Delay en route) _____

18. SPECIAL INSTRUCTIONS

19. TYPED NAME, GRADE, SERVICE, AND TITLE OF REQUESTING OFFICER	20. OFFICE SYMBOL	21. PHONE NO.	22. SIGNATURE OF REQUESTING OFFICER
ROBERT L. SCHNEIDER, Maj, USAF Chief, Communications Division	EMX	2002	*[signature]*

IV. AUTHORIZATION

REQUEST FOR TEMPORARY DUTY IS APPROVED AND WILL BE PERFORMED, TDN	23. DATE OF ORDER	24. AUTHORITY NO.
	12 May 60	SO ▉▉▉

25. OFFICIAL, DESIGNATION AND LOCATION OF APPROVING HEADQUARTERS OR UNIT

26. APPROVED UNDER AUTHORITY DELEGATED BY
AFR 35-11

Hq 4900th ABG, Kirtland AFB, NMEX

27. _____

28. TYPED NAME, GRADE AND TITLE OF ADJUTANT GENERAL, OR ADJUTANT. SEAL OR STAMP

29. BY ☐ COMMAND ☐ ORDER OF:
FOR THE COMMANDER:

[official seal: HEADQUARTERS OFFICIAL]

Administrative Services Officer

16—68256-1 U. S. GOVERNMENT PRINTING OFFICE

REQUEST FOR AND AUTHORIZATION OF LEAVE OF MILITARY PERSONNEL

	1. DATE OF REQUEST
	31 May 1960

REQUEST FOR LEAVE

TO: Commander Hq Sq Sec 4900th Air Base Group Kirtland AFB, New Mexico	2. TYPE OF LEAVE REQUESTED Ordinary	3. NO. OF DAYS 25	4. ☒ EFFECTIVE ON ☐ EFFECTIVE O/A 6 June 1960
5. ACCRUED LEAVE CREDIT (Days) 82½	6. LEAVE TAKEN THIS FY (Days) 5	7. DETAIL TO WHICH ASSIGNED (Complete when assigned to detail requiring replacement) None	

REQUESTING INDIVIDUAL

8. NAME Maurice F. Mercure	9. GRADE T/Sgt.	10. AFSN AF█████████
11. ORGANIZATION OR OFFICE Cryptosection Communications Division		12. PHONE 2700

ADDRESS WHILE ABSENT

13. IN CARE OF Mrs. Margaret D. Mercure	14. STREET ADDRESS 7315 Bradshaw Ave S.E.
15. CITY Albuquerque	16. STATE New Mexico	17. PHONE AL 6-1537

REMARKS

Annual Leave. I am on separate rations.

I CERTIFY THAT THE ABOVE STATEMENTS ARE TRUE AND THAT I HAVE COMPLIED WITH THE PROVISIONS OF CURRENT DIRECTIVES ON LEAVE.	18. SIGNATURE OF REQUESTING INDIVIDUAL *Maurice F. Mercure*

II. APPROVALS

19. SIGNATURE AND TYPED NAME, GRADE AND TITLE OF APPROVING OFFICIAL	20. SIGNATURE AND TYPED NAME, GRADE AND TITLE OF APPROVING OFFICIAL	21. SIGNATURE AND TYPED NAME, GRADE AND TITLE OF APPROVING OFFICIAL
Wesley M. Hiner WESLEY M. HINER GS-11 CHIEF, OPERATIONS BRANCH	*Herman O Ingram Civ* ROBERT L. SCHUMACKER, MAJ USAF CHIEF, COMMUNICATIONS DIV	*J F Hogan* JOSEPH F. HOGAN, MSGT USAF FIRST SERGEANT

III. AUTHORIZATIONS

22. THE INDIVIDUAL NAMED IN SECTION I IS AUTHORIZED LEAVE AS INDICATED ABOVE (UP. AFR 35-22) AND UPON COMPLETION WILL RETURN TO HIS PROPER ORGANIZATION

23. OFFICIAL DESIGNATION AND LOCATION OF APPROVING HEADQUARTERS OR UNIT HEDRONSEC, 4900th ABGRU, KAFB, NM	24. DATE OF ORDER 1 June 1960	25. ORDER NO. #312
~~BY ORDER OF THE COMMANDER~~	26. TYPED NAME, GRADE, SERVICE AND TITLE OF ORDERS ISSUING OFFICIAL SIGNATURE OR SEAL *Horton W. Stickle Jr.* HORTON W. STICKLE, JR. LT COL USAF COMMANDER

AF FORM 1164 1 OCT. 56   PREVIOUS EDITIONS OF THIS FORM MAY BE USED.   ☆ U.S. GOVERNMENT PRINTING OFFICE: 1957 — 423041

REPLY TO
ATTN OF: MGAF

SUBJECT: Station Information   5. AUG. 1960

    TO: Technical Sergeant Maurice F. Mercure AF~~~~~~~~~
           AFSWC
           Kirtland AFB, New Mexico

    Dear Sergeant Mercure

    I have just been informed of your assignment to the Air Force Section,
    MAAG, Taiwan. I welcome you as a member of this unit.

    Attached is a station report prepared to assist newly assigned personnel.
    Your particular attention is invited to page 24 of attached station re-
    port in regard to mandatory clothing allowance. Strict compliance with
    this requirement is essential due to lack of clothing sales store fa-
    filities in this area. If you have other questions, not covered in the
    station report, please write. When you arrive in Taiwan you will be
    further briefed on your assignment.

    I expect to assign you to the MAAG Communication Center as a replacement
    for TSgt Joseph M. Hish. Sergeant Hish will write and tell you about
    the working and living conditions peculiar to this area.

    We shall be looking forward to your arrival and are sure your tour will
    be both interesting and enjoyable.

    Sincerely

    FRED M. DEAN   1 Atch
    Major General, USAF   Station Report
    Chief

1170TH USAF FOREIGN MISSION SQUADRON (MAP)
1170TH USAF FOREIGN MISSION GROUP (HQ COMD)
APO 68 SAN FRANCISCO, CALIFORNIA

REPLY TO
ATTN OF: FMS-COMDR

SUBJECT: Station Information

5. AUG. 1960

TO: Technical Sergeant Maurice F. Mercure AF▓▓▓▓▓
AFSWC
Kirtland AFB, New Mexico

Dear Sergeant Mercure

It is a pleasure to learn of your assignment to the Air Force Section,
MAAG & 1170th USAF Foreign Mission Squadron (MAP). As Commander of the
squadron I will be directly concerned with your welfare as well as your
personnel matters and the normal administration pertaining to your
assignment.

I am sure that you will find your assignment interesting. Not only will
you be stationed in a foreign country but as a member of MAAG you will
be working closely with our counterparts in the Chinese Air Force.

I wish to advise you on a few things peculiar to assignment on Taiwan.
Medical and dental facilities here are not as adequate as we would like
them to be. It is therefore imperative that you take care of any dental
work before departing the ZI.

Being so far from creditors and banking facilities financial transactions
are difficult to cope with. I suggest that you settle all bills that you
can and notify all your creditors that you will be a long time in transit
and have a long readjustment period. Creditors are usually understanding
people and will be happy to make arrangements for you to hold up on payments if necessary.

I hope that you will have a pleasant trip, we are looking forward to
your arrival.

Sincerely

WILLIAM L. CARTER
CWO (W-2), USAF
Commander

1 Atch
Brochure

ORDER NUMBER	HEADQUARTERS SANDIA BASE	DATE
225	Albuquerque, New Mexico	1 Nov 60

ASSIGNMENT OR TERMINATION OF PUBLIC QUARTERS

LAST NAME - FIRST NAME - MIDDLE INITIAL	GRADE	SERVICE NUMBER
Marcum, Maurice F.	T/Sgt	AF ███████

ORGANIZATION AND STATION

4900th ADUSU, SAFB

ACTION	TYPE	TYPE	AS OF DATE
☒ ASSIGNMENT ☐ TERMINATION	☐ OFFICER ☒ ENLISTED ☐ CIVILIAN	☐ BOQ ☒ FAMILY HOUSING	1 Nov 60

QUARTERS ASSIGNMENT

7315 Bradshaw Ave

APPROPRIATION

xx2112020.10-8020, P2703-03-07-522-014-P0211-05-522-222xx

NAME, TITLE, AND GRADE	FOR THE COMMANDER
EDWARD J. SIUTTE, Maj, CMC, Asst Adjutant	

DISTRIBUTION (2 PERS) 3 TO 1 INDIV 1 SBHO

SB FORM 27
1 OCT 60

4 November 1960

SUBJECT: Extension of Enlistment

TO: 4900th AB Gp
Kirtland AFB, N Mex.

1. Under the provisions of paragraph 33a(3), AFM 39-9, request my enlistment be extended for a period of fourteen (14) months for the purpose of meeting retainability requirements for Permanent Change of Station.

a. Date of enlistment: 5 October 1955.

b. Period of enlistment: Six (6) years.

MAURICE F. MERCURE
TSgt, AF
4900th AB Gp

1st Ind (SWBH)   4 November 1960

Hq Sq Sec, 4900th Air Base Group, Kirtland AFB, N Mex.

TO: AFSWC (SWPMR-2), Kirtland AFB, N Mex.

Recommend approval.

THOMAS P. NEARY
Lt Colonel, USAF
Commander

Ltr, Hq 4900th AB Gp, Extension of Enlistment, TSgt Maurice F. Mercure, AF██████, 4 Nov 60

2d Ind (SWPMR/MSgt Mitchmore/3136)

Hq AFSWC, Kirtland AFB, NMex

TO: Hq Sq Sec, 4900th AB Gp, Kirtland AFB, NMex

1. Approved.

2. Paragraph 33c, AFM 39-9 will be complied with.

FOR THE COMMANDER:

[signature]
FOR AND IN THE ABSENCE OF
THEO. V. PROCHAZKA
Colonel, USAF
Deputy Chief of Staff
  Personnel

B616

EXTENSION OF ENLISTMENT IN THE REGULAR AIR FORCE	DATE
	7 Nov 60

ORGANIZATION	LOCATION
Hq AFSWC(ARDC)	Kirtland AFB, N Mex

LAST NAME · FIRST NAME · MIDDLE NAME	ASSIGNED ORGANIZATION	AFSN
~~NEW~~ MERCURE, MAURICE FRANK	4900th ABGRU	AF ▮▮▮▮▮

I HAVE THIS DATE VOLUNTARILY EXTENDED MY ENLISTMENT:

TERMS OF ORIGINAL ENLISTMENT (Years)	DATE OF ORIGINAL ENLISTMENT (Day, Month, Year)	EXTENSION PERIOD (Day, Month, Year)
Six (6) years	5 October 1955	Fourteen (14) months 4 December 1962

STATE REASON FOR EXTENSION. (If applicable)

To assure sufficient retainability for completion of a normal overseas tour of duty.

TYPED NAME AND GRADE OF AIRMAN	SIGNATURE
MAURICE F. MERCURE, TSGT, USAF	Maurice F Mercure

SUBSCRIBED AND SWORN BEFORE ME THIS ___7th___ DATE OF ___November___ 19_60_.

TYPED NAME AND GRADE OF OFFICER ADMINISTERING THE OATH	SIGNATURE
BERNICE MCGHEE, 1st Lt., USAF, Hq AFSWC	Bernice Mc Ghee

AF FORM 1411
SEP 58

B42

GPO 863112

SUBJECT: Request for Reassignment Within MAAG (World Wide) and/or Transfer

TO: Commanding Officer
           1170th USAF Foreign Mission Squadron
           APO 63, San Francisco, California

THRU: Officer In Charge
           MAAG Communications Center
           APO 63, San Francisco, California

1. I, Maurice F. Mercure, TSGT, AF ▓▓▓▓▓▓▓, 1170th USAF Foreign Mission
Squadron, request that I be reassigned within MAAG World Wide and/or be
given a transfer to where I can be utilized to the best interest of the United
States Air Force.

2. The following reasons are cited for requesting this action:

    a. Since being assigned to the Crypto Section, MAAG Communications Center
I have constantly been degraded. I have been forced to work for an SFC (E6),
when I outrank by 2½ years in grade. Upon being assigned, I was not
interviewed by the OIC, MAAG Communications Center, and told where and how I
would work. But placed on shift work by the NCOIC as a Trick Chief, when I
am a Cryptographic Operations Supervisor (29171), with the indication that I
would go on days after the 1st of January. After the 1st of January I was
informed that I would continue to work shifts. I then requested to see the
OSO and ask him for a day job. Upon being interviewed by the OSO I asked for
the accounts job in the Crypto Section, which is held by a SGT (E5). The OSO
informed me that this job would be degrading for me and that as long as I was
assigned to the MAAG Crypto Section there would never be a day job for me.
Also that if I did'nt like it I could apply for a transfer. The accounts job
was previously held by an SFC (E6), who was not degraded, but has since made
E7. SP4 Reader has now been assigned to days to help SGT Coonley in the
accounts section, because he is behind in his work. A good reason he may be
behind is that he fills out Bowling League Record Cards for SFC Furgitt while
on duty.

    b. All Air Force personnel assigned and working in the Crypto Section are
being discriminated against by being refused to process or have access to
Exclusive and Personal For messages for the Chief MAAG. See attachment No. 1
for a copy of the list of personnel who are authorized to do this. Two (2) men
SGT Coonley and SP4 Reader are listed as Trick Chiefs for the purpose of
handling these messages, but are not. SGT Coonley and SP4 Reader are day
workers handling the accounting records. SP4 Reader previous to the 10th of
January was assigned to SSGT Karnes shift as an operator. I am sure that when
the MAAG Communications Centers where organized by the Joint Chiefs of Staff,
that they did not intend for any inter-service fueding or discrimination.

c. It is also very apparent that they do not need me in the MAAG Crypto Section for the following reasons.

(1). There are twenty-six (26) cryptographers assigned to the MAAG Crypto Section as follows:

(a).

RANK	NAME	AFSC OR MOS	DUTY ASSIGNMENT	DOR
SFC (E7)	Bailey	722.6	NCOIC ███████	████
SFC (E7)	*Nixon	722.6	NCOIC SUPPLY SEC	████
TSGT (E6)	Marcure	29171	TRICK CHIEF	████
SFC (E6)	Purgitt	722.6	NCOIC CRYPTO	JUN ██
SFC (E6)	Rush	722.6	OFF SHORE	MAR ██
		(Note: SFC Rush works for SFC Purgitt.)		
SGT (E5)	Coonley	722.6	ACCOUNTS	JUN ██
SGT (E5)	Dempsey	722.6	OPERATOR	MAY ██
SGT (E5)	Gray	722.6	TRICK CHIEF	JUL ██
SSGT (E5)	Karnes	29171	TRICK CHIEF	JUN ██
SSGT (E5)	VAN Dyke	29171	TRICK CHIEF	AUG ██
SP4 (E4)	Redder	722.1	ACCOUNTS	
SP4 (E4)	Stafford	722.1	OFF SHORE	
PFC (E3)	Brown	722.1	OPERATOR	
PFC (E3)	Borcher	722.1	OFF SHORE	
PFC (E3)	**Colangelo	722.1	CLERK NIGHT OFF	
PFC (E3)	Edwards	722.1	OPERATOR	
PFC (E3)	Finley	722.1	OPERATOR	
PFC (E3)	Geary	722.1	OPERATOR	
PFC (E3)	Hathaway	722.1	DOWN ISLAND COMM	
PFC (E3)	Hunt	722.1	OPERATOR	
PFC (E3)	McDowell	722.1	SUPPLY CLERK	
PFC (E3)	Pisco	722.1	OFF SHORE	
PFC (E3)	Shaur	722.1	OPERATOR	
PFC (E3)	Wolf	722.1	DOWN ISLAND COMM	
PVT *(E2)	Bailey	722.1	TERMINAL	
PVT *(E2)	Trescott	722.1	TERMINAL	

NOTE: *Working out of their MOS (AFSC).
       **Working out of his MOS (AFSC) and position not
       authorized on manning document.

(2). If, they can use so many cryptographers in jobs other than what they are here for, they do not need me. They also told me that they requested an E5, 29171 and that I was not needed.

d. There is a clique in the Communications Center. It is composed of the following personnel:

(1). SFC Bailey (Leader)
     SFC Purgitt
     SGT Coonely
     SP4 Redder
     PFC Colangelo

e. In 1956 and part of 1957, I was TDY to the MAAG Crypto Section, Ankara, Turkey. In all the time I was there, not once did any discriminatory or degrading action take place. Personnel handled all types of messages in the performance of their official duties. Everyone worked together, including Army, Navy and Air Force personnel. I considered that one of my finer experiences in the service and quite looked forward to working in the MAAG Crypto Section here.

f. Also I am now afraid that because I have spoken to them on the above subject, that I will be shanghied out to either Kinmen or Matsu Islands, as others have been, who have voiced their opinions in the past. SGT Coonley has never been OFF SHORE because he is in the clique, yet personnel who have arrived here after him, have been sent OFF SHORE.

3. I have discussed this situation with my First Sergeant, who asked me why I did not discuss it with the Air Force Duty Officer assigned to the MAAG Communications Center. I informed him, that there was not an Air Force Duty Officer in the Communications Center. He stated that a Captain Sledge was assigned as Air Force Duty Officer. I informed Sgt Biagi that Captain Sledge was working in the Starcom Relay Section (Which is not a MAAG Organization) as OIC and not in the MAAG Communications Center as a Duty Officer. He then informed me to submit a formal request for transfer and/or reassignment.

4. The CSO stated that if I didn't like it, I could transfer out. The CSO of the MAAG Crypto Section has been informed of my intentions to see my First Sergeant and requesting a transfer.

5. It is also suggested that the entire Air Force Section of the MAAG Communications Center be interviewed concerning their treatment.

6. My past records will indicate that I am not a crônic complainer and have done a good job in the performance of my duty. I am asking for this action in order for the USAF to benifit from my being reassigned and/or transferred.

MAURICE F. MERCURE
TSGT. USAF
AF ▇▇▇▇▇▇

1 ATCH:
Exclusive and Personal For
Messages Handling List.

CERTIFIED TRUE COPY:

SUBJECT: Exclusive and Personal For Messages for Chief, MAAG

TO: All Concerned

The following personnel are designated to handle incoming and outgoing
Exclusive and Personal For Messages for Chief, MAAG:

POSITION	INCUMBENT
OIC, MAAG Communications Det	Capt. R.D. Schicker
OIC, MAAG Crypto Section	1st Lt. J.S. Willis, Jr.
NCOIC, MAAG Crypto Section	SFc W.D. Purgitt
MAAG, Crypto Shift Chief	Sgt. D.G. Coonley
MAAG, Crypto Shift Chief	Sgt. F.D. Dempsey
MAAG, Crypto Shift Chief	Sgt. J.K. Gray, Jr.
MAAG, Crypto Shift Chief	SP4 G.E. Reader
MAAG, Crypto Shift OPERATOR	Pfc. R.W. Fisher
ADDED MAAG, CRYPTO SHIFT OPERATOR	PFC L.OL BROWN DC (initial in ink)

/s/Robert D. Schicker
/t/ROBERT D. SCHICKER
     Capt   SigC
     OIC, MAAG CommCen

MFM 27 Dec 60 (Initials in ink)

DEPARTMENT OF NONRESIDENT INSTRUCTION
U. S. ARMY SIGNAL SCHOOL
FORT MONMOUTH, NEW JERSEY

SIGFM/SC-DNI XXXXXXXX   MERCURE, MAURICE F.   15 February 1961 lv

SUBJECT: Certificate of Subcourse Completion

THRU:

TO: T/Sgt Maurice F. Mercure ▮▮▮▮▮▮▮
         Box 13, Hqs MAAG (Dcsc & E.)
         APO 63, San Framcisco, California

         This certifies that you have completed Subcourse _____17_____
                Signal Unit Supply
--,

an extension subcourse of the U. S. ARMY SIGNAL SCHOOL.

RATING	CREDIT HOURS	COMMENCED	COMPLETED
Superior	21	27 Sep 60	9 Feb61
	*		

H. F. Hartzell
H. F. HARTZELL
*Portion completed during   Lt Col   SigC
current retirement year.   Director

FMSC FL-205
1 May 59

REQUEST FOR AND AUTHORIZATION OF LEAVE OF MILITARY PERSONNEL

	1. DATE OF REQUEST
	18 May 1961

I. REQUEST FOR LEAVE

TO: Commanding Officer 1170th USAF Foreign Mission Squadron APO 63, U. S. FORCES	2. TYPE OF LEAVE REQUESTED Ordinary	3. NO. OF DAYS 5	4. ☐ EFFECTIVE ON ☒ EFFECTIVE O/A 22 May 1961

5. ACCRUED LEAVE CREDIT (Days) 83	6. LEAVE TAKEN THIS FY (Days) 7	7. DETAIL TO WHICH ASSIGNED (Complete when assigned to detail requiring replacement)

REQUESTING INDIVIDUAL

8. NAME Maurice F. Mercure	9. GRADE TSGT	10. AFSN AF ▓▓▓▓▓

11. ORGANIZATION OR OFFICE HQ MAAG COMMUNICATIONS CENTER (HQ MAAG DCSCOM)	12. PHONE TS 525

ADDRESS WHILE ABSENT

13. IN CARE OF Mrs. Margaret D. Mercure	14. STREET ADDRESS Lane 18, Alley 21, # 6 (Upstairs

15. CITY Taipei	16. STATE Taiwan	17. PHONE None

REMARKS

I CERTIFY THAT THE ABOVE STATEMENTS ARE TRUE AND THAT I HAVE COMPLIED WITH THE PROVISIONS OF CURRENT DIRECTIVES ON LEAVE.	18. SIGNATURE OF REQUESTING INDIVIDUAL *Maurice F. Mercure*

II. APPROVALS

19. SIGNATURE AND TYPED NAME, GRADE AND TITLE OF APPROVING OFFICIAL *William D. Purgitt* WILLIAM D. PURGITT SMS (M6) NCOIC MAAG Cryptocenter	20. SIGNATURE AND TYPED NAME, GRADE AND TITLE OF APPROVING OFFICIAL JAMES S. WILLIS, JR. 1st Lt., SigC OIC, MAAG Cryptocenter	21. SIGNATURE AND TYPED NAME, GRADE AND TITLE OF APPROVING OFFICIAL *Clyde F. Rayner* CLYDE F RAYNER MAJOR Commander, 1170FgnMsnSq(MAP)

III. AUTHORIZATIONS

22. THE INDIVIDUAL NAMED IN SECTION I IS AUTHORIZED LEAVE AS INDICATED ABOVE (UP, AFR 35-22) AND UPON COMPLETION WILL RETURN TO HIS PROPER ORGANIZATION

23. OFFICIAL DESIGNATION AND LOCATION OF APPROVING HEADQUARTERS OR UNIT 1170th USAF Foreign Mission Squadron (MAP) APO 63, San Francisco, California	24. DATE OF ORDER 22 May 1961	25. ORDER NO. TB-94

FOR BY/ORDER/OF/THE COMMANDER	26. TYPED NAME, GRADE, SERVICE AND TITLE OF ORDERS ISSUING OFFICIAL SIGNATURE OR SEAL *William L. Carter* WILLIAM L CARTER CWO (W-2), USAF Personnel Officer

REQUEST FOR AND AUTHORIZATION OF LEAVE OF MILITARY PERSONNEL

	1. DATE OF REQUEST
	8 June 1961

I.   REQUEST FOR LEAVE

TO: Commanding Officer 1170th USAF Foreign Mission Squadron	2. TYPE OF LEAVE REQUESTED	3. NUMBER OF DAYS	4. EFFECTIVE DATE
	Ordinary	18	12 June 1961

5. ACCRUED LEAVE CREDIT (Days)	6. LEAVE TAKEN THIS FY (Days)	7. DETAIL TO WHICH ASSIGNED (Complete when assigned to detail requiring replacement)
75	5	N/A

REQUESTING INDIVIDUAL

8. NAME	9. GRADE	10. AFSN
Maurice F. Mercure	TSGT	AF ████

11. ORGANIZATION OR OFFICE	12. PHONE
HQ MAAG (BGS C&E) MAAG COMMUNICATIONS CENTER	TS 525

ADDRESS WHILE ABSENT

13. IN CARE OF	14. STREET ADDRESS
Margaret D. Mercure	Lane 18, Alley 21, #6 (UP) Chung Shan N Rd. Sec 4

15. CITY	16. STATE	17. PHONE
Taipei	Taiwan	None

REMARKS

I CERTIFY that the above statements are true and that I have complied with the provisions of current directives on leave.	18. SIGNATURE OF REQUESTING INDIVIDUAL
	Maurice F Mercure

II.   APPROVALS

19. SIGNATURE OF APPROVING OFFICIAL	20. SIGNATURE OF APPROVING OFFICIAL	21. SIGNATURE OF APPROVING OFFICIAL
William B. Porsitt WILLIAM B. PORSITT SFS NCOIC	*James S. Willis* JAMES S. WILLIS 1ST LT OIC	*Clyde F. Hazner* CLYDE F. HAZNER Major, USAF

III.   AUTHORIZATIONS

22. THE INDIVIDUAL NAMED IN SECTION I IS AUTHORIZED LEAVE AS INDICATED ABOVE (UP. AFR 35-22) AND UPON COMPLETION WILL RETURN TO HIS PROPER ORGANIZATION

23. OFFICIAL DESIGNATION AND LOCATION OF APPROVING HEADQUARTERS OR UNIT	24. DATE OF ORDER	25. ORDER NO.
1170 USAF FgnMsnSq APO 63, San Francisco, Calif	12 Jun 61	TS-122

FOR ~~INDIVIDUAL~~ THE COMMANDER	26. TYPED NAME, GRADE, SERVICE AND TITLE OF ORDERS ISSUING OFFICIAL. SIGNATURE OR SEAL
	William L. Carter WILLIAM L. CARTER, CWO(W-2), USAF Personnel Officer

AF FORM 1164   1 MAY 54

Army-AG Admin Cen-Japan

REPLY TO
ATTN OF: MGAF-CHIEF

SUBJECT: Reenlistment   NOV 8 1961

TO: T/Sgt Maurice F. Mercure, AF███████
       Comm Cntr, Hq MAAG
       APO 63, U. S. Forces

1. I am delighted to learn of your reenlistment in the United States
Air Force on 31 October 1961.

2. Today, as never before, our country needs strong, competent individuals who can serve with unselfish devotion. Your record clearly
indicates you are capable of such service. Your reenlistment proves
your willingness to devote your services to your country.

3. I am proud of your decision and I wish you a continued successful
and honorable career.

KENNETH O. SANBORN
Major General, USAF
Chief

MFSC: 4111   CCL."111

	PERSONAL CLOTHING AND EQUIPMENT RECORD		NAME		PAGE NO.
	(Individual's Copy)		MERCURE, Maurice F.		1

| | | | GRADE T/S | SERIAL NO. ████████ | |

ITEM	ARTICLE	SIZE	QUANTITY			ACTIONS		TRAN.
			AUTH	O/H	O/H	(1)	(2)	
1-1	6665-526-7836 Detector		1	mfm 1				
1-2	8405-290-3566 Jacket, field	M-R	1	mfm 1		BCF OLD 538 1 ea		
1-3	8405- liner, field jacket		1					
1-4	8465-530-3692 Bag Barracks		2	mfm 2		BCF OLD 538 2 ea		

AF FORM AUG 57 538   PREVIOUS EDITIONS OF THIS FORM ARE OBSOLETE

168a

| INVENTORY | | | NONRETURNABLE ITEMS | | |

INVENTORY

I CERTIFY that transactions have been verified and quantities in the "On Hand" column are in my personal possession, in serviceable condition, as of the date appearing with my signature.

NONRETURNABLE ITEMS

The following items in the quantity listed have been issued to me as indicated by my initials.

DATE	SIGNATURE	DATE	ARTICLE	QTY.
12 Dec 61	Maurice F. Menninger	12 Dec 61	Identification tag	MFM	2
31 Dec 62	Maurice F. Menninger	12 Dec 61	Identification tag necklace	MFM	1
		1		
		1		
		2		2

REMARKS:

MAAG COMMUNICATION CENTER
ASSISTANT CHIEF OF STAFF, COMMUNICATIONS & ELECTRONICS
APO 63
SAN FRANCISCO, CALIFORNIA

11 January 1962

SUBJECT: Letter of Appreciation

THRU: Assistant Chief of Staff, Communications & Electronics

TO: TSgt Maurice F. Mercure, AF███████
2165th Comm Sqdn 095, APO 63
San Francisco, California

1. In consideration of your achievements while on duty at the MAAG Communication Center, Taipei, Republic of China, from November 1960 to December 1961, this letter of appreciation is forwarded.

2. Initially, you acted as a cryptographic shift supervisor, but in January 1961 you became NCOIC of the cryptographic accounting section. This section has as its responsibilities the accounting of all cryptographic documents of the Communication Center and the MAAG Distribution Authority, which issues cryptographic material to ten different sub-accounts on a monthly basis. The MAAG Distribution Authority handles Army, Air Force, and Navy accounts, and thus you were required not only to learn Army accounting procedures, which are completely alien to Air Force procedures, but you were also required to become familiar with documents required for operation of Army and Navy cryptocenters.

3. You quickly mastered the details of the assignment; established, maintained and improved files, and rewrote and kept up to date cryptographic SOP's and emergency plans. As a result of your efforts there were no discrepancies in the crypto account when it was inspected by the Army Security Agency during the annual ASA inspection, nor were there any discrepancies during Command Inspections conducted by Headquarters MAAG.

4. Your performance of duty reflects most favorably upon yourself and the United States Air Force.

ROBERT D. SCHICKER
Major, SigC
OIC MAAG Comcenter

MGCE (11 Jan 62)   1st Ind
SUBJECT: Letter of Appreciation

OFFICE OF THE ASSISTANT CHIEF OF STAFF, COMMUNICATIONS AND ELECTRONICS,
Military Assistance Advisory Group, Republic of China, APO 63, U. S.
Forces, 12 January 1962

THRU: Commanding Officer, 2165th Communication Squadron, APO 63, U. S.
        Forces

TO: T/Sgt Maurice F. Mercure, AF█████████, 2165th Communication Squadron
     095, APO 63, U. S. Forces

     Your outstanding contribution to the successful operation of the MAAG
Communication Center and the MAAG Cryptographic Distribution Authority is
noted and forwarded with pleasure.

                               ROBERT C. HEALD
                               Colonel, GS
                               ACSC&E

2nd Ind (CR)

2165th Communications Sq (AFCS); 18 January 1962

TO: TSgt Maurice F. Mercure, 2165th Comm Sq (AFCS), APO 63

1. It is a distinct pleasure to welcome you into our organization.

2. I am certain you will continue to make excellent operational
contributions and maintain your high standard of productivity.

JOHN B. KELLEY
Major, USAF
Commander

CR

16 August 1962

NCO of the Month (July)

TSgt Maurice F. Moreure, AF [REDACTED]
2165 Communications Squadron (AFCS)

1. As Commander of the 2165 Comm Sq., I hereby congratulate you on being selected as July NCO of the Month for the 2165 Comm Squadron (AFCS).

2. This is truly a deserving honor recognizing the many hours of extra work, the devotion to duty and the extensive knowledge of your career field exhibited by you.

3. It is a pleasure to have a man of your all around ability and willingness to work in my command.

4. This correspondence will become a part of your permanent record.

JOHN D. KELLEY
Lt Col, USAF
Commander

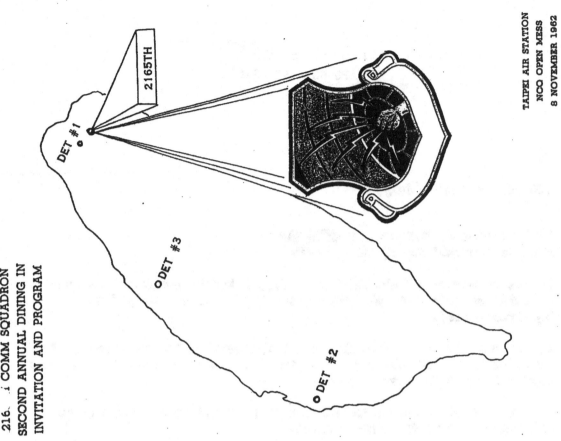

216. i COMM SQUADRON
SECOND ANNUAL DINING IN
INVITATION AND PROGRAM

2165TH

DET #1

DET #3

DET #2

TAIPEI AIR STATION
NCO OPEN MESS
8 NOVEMBER 1962

B71a

PROGRAM
8 NOV. 1962

1800 Bar Opens – Members – arrive – Members locate their respective seats.

1815 Guests arrive.

1845 Bar closes – all assemble at dining table. Remain standing – No smoking.

1850 Chairman calls for Colors.

1852 Invocation – Chairman asks for invocation.

1854 Vice-Chairman toasts the Commander-in-Chief. (Response – "To the President.")

1855 Vice-Chairman toasts the Chief of Staff, USAF. (Response – "To the Chief of Staff.")

1856 Chairman seats mess and renders opening remarks and welcome. (Vice-Chairman will toast Distinguished Guests – Response – "To the Guests.") As soon as all guests are served, begin eating.

1955 Dessert and coffee served – smoking permitted only when Chairman rises and requests permission from Commander ATF 13 that smoking be permitted. Chairman then announces, "The Afterburner is lighted."

2005 Chairman introduces Brigadier General Gladwyn E. Pinkston.

2015 Decorations presented – members remain seated – No smoking – no dining. (Vice Chairman proposes toast to achievements for award – Response – "Hear Hear.")

2017 Chairman introduces Brigadier General Gladwyn E. Pinkston, Guest Speaker. (At conclusion of speech, Chairman proposes toast to Speaker. Response – "To the Speaker.")

Return of Colors – Chairman brings Mess to attention – Honor Guard forward.

Entertainment

Chairman – Closing remarks – Brings Mess to attention, departs dining area with Guests.

Vice-Chairman announces the Mess is closed – all members may depart the dining area.

30th Air Defense Missile Squadron (BOMARC)
UNITED STATES AIR FORCE
Dow Air Force Base
Bangor, Maine

REPLY TO
ATTN OF: CCR   8 May 1963

SUBJECT: Letter of Appreciation

TO: DCOCE-1
     ATTN: Major Walter S. Reed Jr.

1. Technical Sergeant Maurice F. Mercure, AF██████ 397th Bomb Wing,
NCOIC of Communications is to be commended for exceptional aid rendered
to the 30th Air Defense Missile Squadron Communications Section. His
extensive knowledge of COMSEC procedures and Technical advice was
instrumental in the relocation of the 30th ADMS Teletype/Crypto Center,
insuring the maximum security as required by Air Force Standards.

2. In compliance with Change S, AFM 35-1, Technical Sergeant Mercure
scheduled and instructed Cross-Training Classes at Dow Air Force Base
Cryptographic Center, enabling all 30th ADMS 291X0 personnel to receive
Cryptographic Training and increase the required knowledge or tasks
necessary for Teletype/Crypto Operators to perform duties in the
Communication Operation Career Field.

3. Technical Sergeant Mercure expresses a willingness at all times to
assist 30th ADMS Communications personnel and Operations Officers in
coordinating Communications and COMSEC Matters. Assistance such as this
is appreciated at all times by this squadron.

WILLIAM C. BARNES
Lt. Colonel, USAF
Commander

Ltr, 30th ADMS (BOMARC) 8 May 63, Letter of Appreciation

1st Ind (DCO)   19 June 1963

Hq 397 Bomb Wg, Dow AFB, Maine

TO: DCOCE-1

Please extend my personal appreciation to Technical Sergeant Maurice
F. Mercure for a job well done. It is a great pleasure for me to
receive correspondence concerning an NCO under my command. It indicates the SAC desired combination of positive attitude, exceptional job
knowledge and willingness to work. Keep up the good work - this is
an example of the professionalism deserved, desired, and demanded
within SAC.

J. M. BOLAND
Colonel, USAF
Deputy Commander
for Operations

2

United States Marine Corps

This is to certify that

TECHNICAL SERGEANT MAURICE F. MERCURE AF ███████ USAF

has completed the course prescribed by the

Commandant of the Marine Corps for

BASIC MESSAGE CENTER MAN, 25.8

Given at

Marine Corps Institute, Washington, D.C.

this 19th day of September 1963

Registrar, Marine Corps Institute

Director, Marine Corps Institute

B23

Department of the Air Force

CERTIFICATE OF TRAINING

This is to certify that

TSGT MAURICE F. MERCURE, AF

has satisfactorily completed the

OJT SUPERVISOR COURSE, AJF75000 (48 Hours)

Given by

216A FIELD TRAINING DETACHMENT (ATC), DOW AIR FORCE BASE, MAINE ON 18 OCTOBER 1963

HENRY A. STORER, AFI1196568
TSgt, 216A FTD (ATC)
Detachment Commander

TSgt, OJT Advisor

AF FORM 1256 — Sept 58

IATDON

26 November 1963

SUBJECT: Completion of Subcourse

THRU:

Commanding Officer
Hqs Squadron, 397th Bomb Wing (Heavy)
Dow AFB, Maine

TO:

T/Sgt Maurice F. Mercure
AF ██████████
24 Davis Rd.
Bangor, Maine   04401

1. You have successfully completed the following subcourse of the extension course program of the U.S. ARMY SECURITY AGENCY SCHOOL.

Subcourse and Title	Date Commenced	Date Completed	Rating Attained
97-Composite I	18 Sep 63	26 Nov 63	Excellent

2. You have earned 20 credit hours for retirement and retention. Of these,   credit hours were earned during the current retirement year.

FOR THE COMMANDANT

ROBERT J. COGAN
Deputy Director
Nonresident Instr Dept

IATIN   FL 13
R 7 APR 61

SIGDNI-6 MERCURE, MAURICE F.   27 November 1963/ekc

SUBJECT: Completion of Army Extension Subcourse

THRU: Education Services Officer
         Dow AFB, Maine

TO: TSgt Maurice F. Mercure, AF ████████████
         24 Davis Road
         Bangor, Maine, 04401

Completion of Subcourse

1. You have successfully completed Subcourse Number A18

titled, Communication Center Operations

Date Commenced 28 Oct 63   Date Completed 18 Nov 63

Rating   Superior   Credit Hours   19

2. Of the total credit hours shown above,   hours were earned on
or before   and   hours were earned on or after the
beginning of your current retirement year. (Applicable only to reserve
personnel not on active duty.)

        FOR THE DIRECTOR:

                                  Mercedes M. Ormston
                                  MERCEDES M. ORMSTON
                                  Major   WAC
                                  Chief, Correspondence Study Division

REQUEST FOR TUITION ASSISTANCE—EDUCATION SERVICES PROGRAM

FROM (Name of applicant)	GRADE	SERVICE NUMBER
Mercure, Maurice F	Tsgt	AF ▚▚▚

UNIT	DUTY PHONE
397 BSC	2710

NAME OF SCHOOL	TYPE OF STUDY
Univ of Maine ☒ ON BASE ☐ OFF BASE	☐ VOCATIONAL-TECHNICAL ☒ UNDER-GRADUATE ☐ HIGH SCHOOL ☐ GRADUATE

TITLE OF COURSE(S) AND NUMBER(S)	CREDIT HOURS	DAYS OF WEEK	HOURS OF MEETING	INCLUSIVE DATES OF COMPLETE COURSE(S)
Eh 1 Freshman Composition I	3	Mon	1830 – 2100	3 Feb – 14 May 64

COST PER HOUR	COST TO GOVERNMENT	COST TO STUDENT
☒ SEMESTER 16.00 ☐ QUARTER	36.00	12.00

CERTIFICATIONS

I understand that while I am participating in the Education Services Program, the Air Force will pay not more than three-fourths of my tuition or fees in lieu of tuition, not to exceed $13.50 each semester hour, $9.00 each quarter hour, or $40.50 each Carnegie unit. I agree to pay the remainder of the tuition or fees in lieu of tuition, plus registration costs, miscellaneous fees, costs of textbooks and other equipment.

I further agree that should I, of my own volition, fail to complete the above course(s), I will reimburse the Air Force for the full amount of tuition or fees in lieu of tuition paid in my behalf. I hereby voluntarily authorize the stoppage of my pay for this amount if it is determined by the installation commander or his authorized representative that my withdrawal was not due to circumstances beyond my control. I understand that should it become necessary for me to discontinue the course(s) due to hospitalization, change of duty hours, change of station, or other requirements of the military service, I will not be required to reimburse the Government for the tuition paid. I am eligible for tuition assistance under Rule 3 of Table 1 AFR 34–52C.
My current retention or enlistment meets the applicable requirements.
APPLICABLE TO OFFICERS ONLY—If granted tuition assistance, I agree to serve on extended active duty for a minimum period of two years subsequent to termination of the above course(s) unless sooner relieved for the convenience of the Government.

DATE	SIGNATURE OF APPLICANT
28 Jan 64	Maurice F Mercure

STATEMENT OF APPROVAL

Applicants present and anticipated military assignment will permit class attendance to allow for satisfactory class completion.

☒ APPROVED ☐ DISAPPROVED	SIGNATURE OF APPROVING AUTHORITY (Commissioned officer or civilian of equivalent grade)

SIGNATURE OF EDUCATION SERVICES OFFICER (Education services branch only)

AF FORM MAY 62 1227 PREVIOUS EDITIONS OF THIS FORM ARE OBSOLETE.

U.S. GOVERNMENT PRINTING OFFICE : 1962 OF—610246—100643

I. IDENTIFICATION DATA (Complete this form in accordance with AFM 39-62.)

1. LAST NAME—FIRST NAME—MIDDLE INITIAL	2. AFSN	3. GRADE	4. DATE OF GRADE
MERCURE, MAURICE F.	AF	TSGT	1 Feb 1953

5. ORGANIZATION, COMMAND AND LOCATION	6. RESERVE WARRANT OR COMMISSION AND AFSN	7. REASON FOR REPORT
Hq Sq 397 Bomb Wing (H)(SAC) Dow AFB, Maine	none	Change of rept offl

8. PERIOD OF SUPERVISION	9. PERIOD OF REPORT
146	FROM: 9 Nov 63 TO: 5 Apr 64

II. DUTIES:

PAFSC 29170   DAFSC 29170   CAFSC 29170   NO. OF PERSONNEL SUPERVISED 6

CURRENT DUTY: Communications Center Supervisor. Responsible for the operation of the Teletype, Telephone and Cryptographic Sections of the Base Communications, including training of subordinates on the proper operation of installed equipments. Coordinates with other base activities to insure that adequate services are being provided.

III. PERFORMANCE QUALITIES (Rate each quality below by selecting the phrase most closely describing the airman's actual performance.)

1. HOW MUCH DOES HE KNOW ABOUT HIS ASSIGNED DUTIES? (Consider whether he has the technical "know-how"; knows what to do; knows the required steps.)

Not observed ☐ Knowledge is inadequate. Requires continuous assistance. ☐ Knows only the routine duties. Makes present duties difficult. ☐ Knows all routine duties. Possesses extensive knowledge of more complex duties. ☐ Has mastered all duties with knowledge of related positions. ☒ Has mastered all duties with extensive knowledge of related positions. Authority in his field.

2. HOW WELL DOES HE DO HIS ASSIGNED DUTIES? (Consider whether he is a careful worker; a thorough worker; checks his work.)

Not observed ☐ Lazy and inefficient. Produces unsatisfactory results. ☐ Needs prodding but completes most routine duties satisfactorily. ☐ Completes all assigned duties in a timely and satisfactory manner. ☐ Produces very high quantity and quality of work. Can be depended on to get the job done. ☒ Extremely efficient. Completes all duties in an outstanding manner.

3. HOW WELL DOES HE UNDERSTAND INSTRUCTIONS?

Not observed ☐ Simple instructions are usually misunderstood even though given in detail. ☐ Understands simple instructions. Hesitates to ask for clarification. ☐ Understands instructions when given in detail. Asks questions when in doubt. ☐ Correctly interprets rather difficult instructions. Needs very little assistance. ☒ Understands all instructions. Needs no help.

4. HOW WELL DOES HE GET ALONG WITH OTHERS? (Consider ability and willingness to work in harmony for and with others.)

Not observed ☐ Refuses to get along with people. A troublemaker. ☐ Has difficulty in getting along with others. Sometimes creates friction. ☐ Pleasant to work with. Promotes harmony. ☐ Consistently works in harmony with others. An excellent team worker. ☒ Develops a good "team" feeling. Outstanding ability to promote harmony.

5. HOW WELL DOES HE ACCEPT RESPONSIBILITY? (for his own actions, the actions of his subordinates and the objectives of his organization.)

Not observed ☐ Completely unreliable. Fails to accept responsibilities assigned to him. ☐ Accepts most responsibilities, but must be specifically assigned. ☐ Accepts all assigned responsibilities and assumes added responsibilities when offered to him. ☐ Assumes full responsibility for all objectives. Often seeks out added responsibilities. ☒ Assumes full responsibility for all objectives and actively seeks out added responsibilities.

6. DO HIS BEARING AND BEHAVIOR MEET AIR FORCE STANDARDS?

Not observed (B) (Bh) | A discredit to himself and the Air Force. | Usually passable. Occasionally he is lax. | Conforms to Air Force standards. | Sets an excellent example for others to follow. | Outstanding. He exemplifies top military standards.

| Bearing | Behavior | Bearing | Behavior | Bearing | Behavior | Bearing | Behavior | ☒ Bearing | ☒ Behavior |

IV. NONCOMMISSIONED OFFICER QUALITIES

1. HOW WELL DOES HE SUPERVISE? (Consider his efforts as a supervisor and leader to increase the performance of those he supervises.)

Not observed ☐ Weak and careless. A poor supervisor. ☐ Usually gets adequate results from subordinates. ☐ Obtains good results from his men. Controls unit efficiently. ☐ Succeeds under unusual or difficult circumstances. Secures high production. ☒ Outstanding ability to get the maximum out of his men and all available resources.

2. HOW WELL DOES HE UTILIZE RESOURCES? (Consider his ability to utilize effectively men, money, and materials under his control.)

Not observed ☐ Ineffective in the conservation of resources. ☐ Utilizes resources in a barely satisfactory manner. ☐ Conserves resources by implementing and maintaining routine management procedures. ☐ Is effective in accomplishing savings in resources by developing improved management procedures. ☒ Exceptionally effective in the utilization of resources.

3. HOW WELL DOES HE WRITE AND/OR SPEAK?

Not observed (W) (S) | Unable to express thoughts clearly. Lacks organization. | Expresses thoughts satisfactorily on routine matters. | Usually organizes and expresses thoughts clearly and concisely. | Consistently able to express ideas clearly. | Outstanding ability to communicate ideas to others.

| Write | Speak | Write | Speak | Write | Speak | Write | Speak | ☒ Write | ☒ Speak |

AF FORM 75 JUN 63   PREVIOUS EDITION OF THIS FORM WILL BE USED UNTIL STOCK IS EXHAUSTED.   ☐ EAD   ☐ NOT ON EAD   **USAF AIRMAN PERFORMANCE REPORT**

V. OVER-ALL EVALUATION (Compare this airman with others of the same grade and AFS. Extremes of ability are rare.)

SPECIFIC JUSTIFICATION REQUIRED FOR THESE SECTIONS					SPECIFIC JUSTIFICATION REQUIRED FOR THESE SECTIONS	
☐ An unsatisfactory airman.	☐ A marginal airman.	☐ ☐ A good airman.	☐ ☐ An excellent airman.	☐ An exceptional airman of great value to the service.	☐	☒ One of the very few outstanding airmen I know.

VI. RECOMMENDATION FOR PROMOTION

☐ DO NOT RECOMMEND FOR PROMOTION.	☐ PERFORMING WELL IN PRESENT GRADE. SHOULD BE CONSIDERED FOR PROMOTION ALONG WITH CONTEMPORARIES.
☐ CAPABLE OF INCREASED RESPONSIBILITY. CONSIDER FOR PROMOTION AHEAD OF CONTEMPORARIES.	☒ ONE OF THE VERY FEW OUTSTANDING AIRMEN BASED ON DEMONSTRATED GROWTH POTENTIAL AND PERFORMANCE. PROMOTE WELL AHEAD OF CONTEMPORARIES.

VII. COMMENTS OF REPORTING OFFICIAL (Be factual and specific. Add any comments which increase the objectivity of the rating.)

FACTS AND SPECIFIC ACHIEVEMENTS: Sgt Mercure has continued to maintain his enviable standards for producing only outstanding work. He has revised the complete filing system for Communications Center Messages thereby insuring a positive method of control and required destruction. He supervised the distribution, filing and accounting for a new Defense Communications Agency Directive requiring state wide TWX and Western Union refile procedures. He devised a new method for maintenance of required regulations and technical orders which has been copied throughout the Wing Communications Division. He planned and monitored an outstanding system for keeping current an up-to-date list of all releasing officials for messages from base to tenant units. He was primarily responsible for maintaining the enviable record of operation within his section as evidenced by the ratings given during the recent 8th Air Force Readiness Inspection STRENGTHS: Sgt Mercure is an intelligent, level headed individual with the highest moral standards. He displays a mature sense of judgement and an ability to grasp and cope with out-of-the ordinary situations. His versatility coupled with his outstanding job knowledge is a tremendous asset to any organization. OTHER COMMENTS: Sgt Mercure is fully capable to assume any duty required in his career field, regardless of the level of organization, and should be promoted to the next higher grade at the earliest opportunity.

VIII. REPORTING OFFICIAL	DUTY TITLE	SIGNATURE
NAME, GRADE, AND ORGANIZATION WALTER S. REED, JR, Major Hq 397 Bomb Wing (H)(SAC)	Chief, Ground Comm Branch	*Walter S. Reed Jr* DATE 6 April 64

IX. REVIEW BY INDORSING OFFICIAL: ☐ I CONCUR   ☐ I DO NOT CONCUR

NAME, GRADE, AND ORGANIZATION	DUTY TITLE	SIGNATURE
		DATE

X. REVIEW BY OFFICER IN CHARGE: ☒ I CONCUR   ☐ I DO NOT CONCUR

Absolutely superior type NCO. Exceptionally well qualified for more responsibility, Mercure is my first choice for promotion. He should be a MSG right now. He stands head and shoulders above his contemporaries in ability, knowledge, attitude, devotion to duty and ability to produce the best.

NAME, GRADE, AND ORGANIZATION CHARLES A. WINTERMEYER, Major Hq Sq 397 Bomb Wing (SAC)	DUTY TITLE Chief, Comm-Elect Div	SIGNATURE *Charles A. Wintermeyer* DATE 6 April 1964

75TH FIGHTER INTERCEPTOR SQUADRON (ADC)
United States Air Force
Dow Air Force Base, Maine 04401

17 April 1964

SUBJECT: Letter of Appreciation

TO: 397th Bomb Wg (C)

1. I would like to express my appreciation and that of the other members of this Squadron for the well prepared and thorough briefing on "COMSEC Material (Use and Handling)" given to us by Technical Sergeant Maurice F. Mercure, on 9 March 1964.

2. I would also like to express my appreciation for the advice and assistance Sergeant Mercure has given the Squadron Communications Officer in setting up and maintaining crypto control and security. On two occasions, he has relinquished his off-duty time to come in and solve some of the Squadron crypto problems.

3. I believe he is an asset to his unit, and, again, on behalf of myself and the Squadron, I wish to say thank you.

Mathias A. Raab, Maj USAF

WILLIAM C. DAVIS
Lt Colonel, USAF
Commander

B80a

Ltr, 75 FIS, 17 Apr 64, Letter of Appreciation

1st Ind (VC)   22 April 1964

Hq 397 Bomb Wg, Dow AFB, Maine

TO: DCO

Please convey my thanks and appreciation to TSgt Mercure for the outstanding
briefing and technical assistance he offered the 75th Fighter Interceptor
Squadron personnel in the proper use and handling of "COMSEC Material."

J L FLANAGAN
Colonel, USAF
Vice Commander

2nd Ind (DCO)   29 April 1964

Hq 397 Bomb Wg, Dow AFB, Maine

TO: DCOCE

THRU: HSC

1. Cooperation like this certainly helps in elevating the Wing's standing
with the tenant units, and I'm proud to have members like TSgt Mercure in
the command.

2. Please express my appreciation to TSgt Mercure for his efforts.

3. Request this letter be filed in TSgt Mercure's Personnel Records
Group to aid in preparation of his next performance report as authorized
by AFR 30-9.

MAXWELL V. JUDAS
Colonel, USAF
Deputy Commander
for Operations

2

Ltr, 75 FIS, 17 Apr 64, Letter of Appreciation

3d Ind (HSC)   18 May 1964

Hq Sq 397th Bomb Wg

TO: TSgt Maurice F. Mercure, AF ████████ Hq Sq 397 Bomb Wg

I am always proud to receive correspondence of this nature concerning
the performance of a member of this organization. The professional
ability and outstanding devotion to duty you displayed in briefing
personnel of the 75th Fighter Interceptor Squadron on COMSEC Material
are the qualities desired in all airmen of the present day Air Force.

William E. Griffith
WILLIAM E. GRIFFITH
Major, USAF
Commandant

4th Ind (DCOCE)   25 May 1964

TO: DCOCEO

1. This letter typifies the most important qualities required of a
professional, namely, the positive attitude to excel and the technical
skill and knowledge demanded in the USAF today.

2. Please convey to TSgt Mercure my pride and appreciation in this
performance of duty.

3. This letter is to be filed in his records and reflected in his next
APR.

Charles A. Wintermeyer
CHARLES A. WINTERMEYER
Major, USAF
Chief, C&E Division

5th IND (DCOCEO)   30 May 1964

TO: TSgt Maurice F. Mercure, AF ████████

It is a distinct pleasure to indorse testimony of this nature. It
is only through hard work, devotion to duty and the desire to excel
that correspondence like this originates. It is further a distinct
pleasure to have an NCO of your caliber working in Communications
Operations. My sincere congratulations and heartfelt pride are
extended to TSgt Mercure.

George K. Loud
GEORGE K. LOUD
1st. Lt. USAF
Chief, C&E Operations Branch

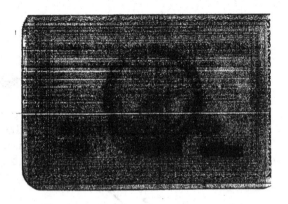

B81

HEADQUARTERS STRATEGIC AIR COMMAND
UNITED STATES AIR FORCE
OFFUTT AIR FORCE BASE, NEBRASKA 68113

REPLY TO
ATTN OF: DOCEG

SUBJECT: AIRCOMNET Communications

11 MAR 1965

TO: 8AF (DOCEOT)
Westover AFB, Mass 01022

1. Reference 2045th Communications Group Tributary Information
Letter, dated 15 February 1965.

2. We note in the referenced letter that the SAC Communications
Center at Dow AFB has been declared a member of the "TOP TEN
CLUB" for the month of January 1965.

3. Membership in this club is determined by the Andrews Air Force
Base AIRCOMNET Net Control Station after statistical analysis has
shown which of the tributaries have the lowest percentage of error
for the preceding month. Therefore, membership in this club indicates a high degree of professional performance of duty in tributary
communications operations and maintenance by the stations cited.

4. Please extend to the OIC-Captain Clement, NCOIC-TSgt Mercure
and to their operating and maintenance personnel, our congratulations
for a job well done.

FOR THE COMMANDER IN CHIEF

HAROLD K. MORRIS
Major, USAF
Directorate of Operations

Copy to:
DOCEOT

Peace . . . . is our Profession

Ltr, SAC(DOCEG), 11 March 1965, AIRCOMNET Communications

1st Ind (DOCEOT)

20 MAR 1965

Hq 8AF, Westover AFB, Mass. 01022

TO: 397 Bomb Wg (DCOCE)

1.   I note with pleasure Headquarters SAC's recognition of your communications center being named a member of the AIRCOMNET "TOP TEN CLUB" for the month of January 1965.

2.   It is gratifying to know that we have communicators of your claiber supporting elements of SAC's defense posture and practicing recognized professional skill.

3.   To Captain Clement, TSgt Mercure, and to their operating and maintenance personnel, I would like to add my own personal congratulations and urge you to continue your efforts toward maintaining a position as a member of the AIRCOMNET "TOP TEN CLUB".

FOR THE COMMANDER

HOWARD BALDWIN
Captain, USAF
Directorate of Administrative Services

2nd Ind (DCOCEO)

22 March 1965

TO: All Concerned

It is with great pleasure that I pass this letter of accomplishment on to you. I knew you could do it and am certain you will do it again. Continue the good work and show these other Tribs we can be the best regardless of our handicaps.

FREDERICK M. CLEMENT
Capt, USAF
Chief, Operations Branch

2

| MERCURE | | MAURICE | | F | AF | ~~SERVICE NUMBER~~ | | 6 | MSG | 1062 | 0865 | CC | 3008 |
| LAST NAME | | FIRST NAME | | M. | | | | COMP. | RANK. | DATE ENR. | DATE CANC. | REA. | COURSE NUMBER |

| Z0282 | | 086 | 3973 OPS SQ BOX 7107   APO NY | | | | | | | | 09282 |
| | | GR. | | | | | | | | | |

This certifies that the individual named hereon has satisfactorily completed the course indicated.

Norman E Goodwin
Major, USAF
Secretary

signature
Education Officer

ISM M39238

VOL. NR.	CR. HRS.	DATE SENT	DATE RECEIVED			GRADE	VOL. NR.	CR. HRS.	DATE SENT	DATE RECEIVED			GRADE
01	015	0963	10	02	63	085	02	015	0963	09	17	63	091
03	015	0963	11	13	63	096	04	015	0963	12	09	63	091
05	015	1063	07	24	64	096	06	015	1063	04	23	64	086
07	015	1163	04	20	64	085	08	015	1263	07	28	64	086
09	015	0564	04	23	65	076	10	021	0564	06	28	65	076
14	009	0864	08	21	64	088	16	018	0864	07	05	65	079
17	015	0964	08	30	65	085							

AIR UNIVERSITY
United States Air Force

EXTENSION COURSE INSTITUTE

Date _31 AUGUST 1965_

Be it known _MSG M F MERCURE_ _AF_ ██████ is a graduate of

COMMUNICATIONS OFFICER course _3008_

in testimony whereof and by authority vested in us, this diploma is hereby conferred. Given at Gunter Air Force Base, Alabama, this day as dated above.

★ ★ ★ ★ ★

RUSSELL V. RITCHEY
Colonel, USAF
Commandant

R. P. SWOFFORD, JR.
Lieutenant General, USAF
Commander, Air University

OFFICIAL
HEADQUARTERS AIR UNIVERSITY MAXWELL AFB ALA

██████
B84

CERTIFICATE OF MEDICAL CLEARANCE FOR DEPENDENT OVERSEA TRAVEL

I.   APPLICANT IDENTIFICATION DATA

1. NAME (LAST, FIRST AND MIDDLE INITIAL)	2. GRADE	3. SERVICE NO.	4. DATE OF MIL. TRAVEL
Mercure Maurice F.	MSGT	AF~~████~~	Sep 65

5. PRESENT UNIT AND LOCATION	6. UNIT AND LOCATION OF OVERSEA ASSIGNMENT
397 Bomb Wg, Dow AFB, Maine, 04401	3973 Strat Wg, APO New York 09282

7. DEPENDENT TRAVEL AUTHORIZED TO AREA	8. ELIGIBLE DEPENDENT WILL APPLY	9. IF AUTHORIZED, DEPENDENT TRAVEL WILL BE
☒ YES ☐ NO	☒ YES ☐ UNCERTAIN ☐ NO	☒ CONCURRENT ☐ NONCONCURRENT

II.   APPLICANTS REQUEST FOR ELIGIBLE DEPENDENTS (If more space needed, continue in "REMARKS")

I REQUEST AUTHORITY FOR MY DEPENDENTS TO TRAVEL OVERSEAS AND TO RESIDE WITH ME DURING MY OVERSEAS ASSIGNMENT. I CERTIFY THAT TO THE BEST OF MY KNOWLEDGE THEY HAVE OR DO NOT HAVE MEDICAL CONDITIONS AS CHECKED.   I HAVE READ AND UNDERSTAND THE INSTRUCTIONS.

NAME (Last, First, Middle Initial)	AGE	RELATIONSHIP	MEDICAL OR OTHER RELATED PROBLEMS	
			YES	NO
Mercure Margaret D.		Wife		XX

TYPED NAME AND GRADE	DATE	SIGNATURE
MAURICE F MERCURE, MSGT	13 Sep 65	*Maurice F. Mercure*

III.   STATEMENT OF PERSONNEL OFFICER

ONE OR MORE OF ABOVE LISTED DEPENDENTS HAS A MEDICAL OR RELATED SPECIAL PROBLEM.   FOR COMPLETION OF SECTION IV, AN APPOINTMENT HAS BEEN MADE FOR THE APPLICANT AND HIS DEPENDENTS AT:
MEDICAL FACILITY

TYPED NAME AND GRADE	DATE	SIGNATURE

IV.   MEDICAL CERTIFICATE

I CERTIFY THAT (Check applicable box)

☐ I HAVE REVIEWED THE MEDICAL RECORDS OF ABOVE LISTED DEPENDENTS AND ACCOMPLISHED SUCH VALUATION OR EXAMINATION AS IS NECESSARY.   MEDICAL CLEARANCE FOR TRAVEL TO THE ASSIGNED AREA IS GRANTED.

☐ ABOVE LISTED DEPENDENT(S) HAS (HAVE) A SIGNIFICANT PROBLEM(S), BUT I CANNOT DETERMINE AVAILABILITY OF ADEQUATE CARE IN THE ASSIGNED AREA.   I AM FORWARDING THIS APPLICATION, TOGETHER WITH A SUMMARY OF MEDICAL DATA TO THE AREA COMMAND SURGEON FOR FINAL REVIEW AND RECOMMENDATION.

TYPED NAME AND GRADE OF EVALUATING PHYSICIAN	DATE	SIGNATURE

TYPED NAME AND GRADE OF REVIEWING OFFICIAL (DBMS)	DATE	SIGNATURE

V.   CERTIFICATE OF OVERSEA COMMAND SURGEON

I CERTIFY THAT I HAVE REVIEWED MEDICAL RECORDS OF ABOVE LISTED DEPENDENTS AND	YES	NO
a. NECESSARY MEDICAL OR OTHER SPECIAL CARE IS AVAILABLE IN ASSIGNED AREA		
b. TRAVEL OF DEPENDENTS IS RECOMMENDED		

TYPED NAME	GRADE	SIGNATURE
TITLE	DATE	

AF FORM 1466   PREVIOUS EDITION IS OBSOLETE.
JUN 64

Attachment 6

VI.   CERTIFICATE OF PERSONNEL OFFICER

I CERTIFY THAT (*Check appropriate box*)

- [X] I HAVE DISCUSSED THIS APPLICATION AND THE INSTRUCTIONS WITH THE APPLICANT. BASED ON HIS STATEMENTS, SECTIONS III, IV AND V HAVE BEEN LINED OUT. I RECOMMEND THAT TRAVEL AUTHORITY BE GRANTED.

- [ ] I HAVE REVIEWED THIS APPLICATION. BASED ON CERTIFICATES IN SECTIONS IV AND/OR V, I RECOMMEND THAT TRAVEL AUTHORITY BE [ ] APPROVED [ ] DISAPPROVED.

- [ ] NOT APPLICABLE (*Based on items 7 or 8, Section I*).

TYPED NAME	GRADE	SIGNATURE
JACK E ANDERSON	CAPT	
TITLE AND UNIT Chief, Career Control Branch	**DATE** 13 Sep 65	

VII.   ACTION BY COMMANDER WITH AUTHORITY TO ISSUE ORDERS (*Check appropriate box*)

TO: (*Applicant*)

MSGT, Maurice F. Mercure   AF██████████

- [X] MEDICAL CLEARANCE FOR TRAVEL OF ABOVE LISTED DEPENDENTS IS GRANTED.

- [ ] TRAVEL FOR ABOVE LISTED DEPENDENTS IS DISAPPROVED FOR MEDICAL OR OTHER RELATED REASONS. IF YOU HAVE QUESTIONS, CONSULT WITH YOUR PERSONNEL OFFICER OR WITH THE COMMANDER OF YOUR UNIT MEDICAL FACILITY.

- [ ] TRAVEL IS DISALLOWED FOR OTHER THAN MEDICAL REASONS.

TYPED NAME	GRADE	SIGNATURE
JACK E ANDERSON	CAPT	
TITLE AND UNIT Chief, Career Control Branch	**DATE** 13 Sep 65	

REMARKS

NAME OF RATEE	LAST NAME	FIRST NAME	MIDDLE INITIAL	
	Mercure	Maurice	F	GRADE: MSGT

II. PERSONAL QUALITIES

1. WRITING ABILITY AND ORAL EXPRESSION
THE ABILITY OF THIS NCO TO COMMUNICATE HIS IDEAS IN: 1. WRITING (W) AND 2. SPEECH (S).

	LOWEST 10%	HIGHEST 10%		LOWEST 10%	HIGHEST 10%
(W) REPORTING OFFICIAL:			(W) INDORSING OFFICIAL:		
(S) REPORTING OFFICIAL:			(S) INDORSING OFFICIAL:		

2. HUMAN RELATIONS
THE DEGREE TO WHICH THE RATEE PROMOTES HARMONIOUS RELATIONSHIPS WITH BOTH SUPERIORS AND SUBORDINATES.

	LOWEST 10%	HIGHEST 10%		LOWEST 10%	HIGHEST 10%
REPORTING OFFICIAL:			INDORSING OFFICIAL:		

3. PERFORMANCE OF DUTIES
THE DEGREE OF ACCEPTABILITY OF THE WORK OF THE RATEE.

	LOWEST 10%	HIGHEST 10%		LOWEST 10%	HIGHEST 10%
REPORTING OFFICIAL:			INDORSING OFFICIAL:		

4. EVALUATION ABILITY
HOW CONSCIENTIOUS IS HE IN FULFILLING HIS DUTIES AS A REPORTING AND/OR INDORSING OFFICIAL?

☐ HAS NOT ACTED AS A RATING OFFICIAL DURING THIS REPORTING PERIOD.

	LOWEST 10%	HIGHEST 10%		LOWEST 10%	HIGHEST 10%
REPORTING OFFICIAL:			INDORSING OFFICIAL:		

5. EXECUTIVE ABILITY
THE EXTENT TO WHICH THE RATEE COMBINES LEADERSHIP, JUDGMENT, PLANNING, MANAGEMENT AND COST CONSIDERATIONS TO GET MAXIMUM EFFECTIVENESS FROM THE RESOURCES UNDER HIS CONTROL.

	LOWEST 10%	HIGHEST 10%		LOWEST 10%	HIGHEST 10%
REPORTING OFFICIAL:			INDORSING OFFICIAL:		

III. MILITARY QUALITIES

THE EXTENT TO WHICH HE MEETS STANDARDS OF BEARING, DRESS AND COURTESY, AND ENHANCES THE IMAGE OF THE AIR FORCE NCO.

	LOWEST 10%	HIGHEST 10%		LOWEST 10%	HIGHEST 10%
REPORTING OFFICIAL:			INDORSING OFFICIAL:		

IV. OVERALL EVALUATION

THE RELATIVE VALUE OF THE RATEE TO THE AIR FORCE WHEN COMPARED WITH OTHER NON-COMMISSIONED OFFICERS OF HIS GRADE AND AFS.

	LOWEST 10%	HIGHEST 10%		LOWEST 10%	HIGHEST 10%
REPORTING OFFICIAL:			INDORSING OFFICIAL:		

AF FORM 911 APR 65   PREVIOUS EDITION OF THIS FORM WILL BE USED UNTIL STOCK IS EXHAUSTED.

rcure, Maurice F.		AF████	MSgt	1 Dec 1964
ORGANIZATION, COMMAND AND LOCATION		6. RESERVE WARRANT OR COMMISSION AND AFSN none		7. REASON FOR REPORT No report one year

rcure, Maurice F.	AF████	MSgt	1 Dec 1964

ORGANIZATION, COMMAND AND LOCATION

q Sq 397 Bomb Wing (H)
ow AFB, Maine (SAC)

6. RESERVE WARRANT OR COMMISSION AND AFSN none

7. REASON FOR REPORT No report one year

8. PERIOD OF SUPERVISION 365

9. PERIOD OF REPORT
FROM: 1 Sept 64   THRU: 31 Aug 65

UTIES	DAFSC	CAFSC	NO. OF PERSONNEL SUPERVISED	UMD POSITION OCCUPIED	
				AUTHORIZED GRADE	AUTHORIZED AFSC
9170	29190	29170	7	SMSGT	29190

urrent Duty: Communications Center Operating Superintendant. Responsible for the operation
f the Communications Center and Crypto Vault. Responsible for the efficient operation of the
elephone Switchboard. Responsible to the Division Chief for the efficient operation of the
ommunications Division details and personnel problems.

I. COMMENTS OF REPORTING OFFICIAL (Be factual and specific. Add any comments which increase the objectivity of the rating.)
ACTS AND SPECIFIC ACHIEVEMENTS: MSgt Mercure is an aggressive and enthusiastic Non Commis-
ioned Officer. He constantly displays a keen interest in the welfare and morale of the
ersonnel under his supervision. He has been filling the position of Division NCOIC and
erformed the duties of a Senior Master Sergeant in a truly outstanding manner. His ability to
ork efficiently with both subordinates and superiors alike is a great asset to him. His
nowledge of communications and his ability to pass this knowledge on to others has assisted
reatly in our upgrading of airmen. He completely revised the Administrative Procedures and
eaccomplished all Operating Procedures thus increasing the efficiency of the Section and
ccomplished the same amount of work with less airmen. He constantly sets an outstanding
xample for others by his military bearing and behavior, both on and off duty. EDUCATIONAL
ND TRAINING ACCOMPLISHMENTS: Sgt Mercure continues to take ECI Courses and has completed
he Army Communications Officer Course. He continually strives to improve himself and work
or the future. SUGGESTED ASSIGNMENTS: Sgt Mercure should be assigned to a Headquarters
evel where his knowledge and experience can be put to use in the best interest of the Air
orce.

III. REPORTING OFFICIAL	DUTY TITLE	SIGNATURE
ME, GRADE, AND ORGANIZATION FREDERICK M. CLEMENT, Capp Iq Sq 397 Bomb Wing (H)(SAC)	Chief, Operations Branch	DATE 17 Sept 1965

. REVIEW BY INDORSING OFFICIAL: MSGT Mercure is one of the most outstanding NCO's that I
ave come in contact with. His aggressive attitude and devotion to duty places him in a
uperior class.

ME, GRADE, AND ORGANIZATION ROBERT SPEIRS, JR, Major Iq Sq 397 Bomb Wing (H)(SAC)	DUTY TITLE Chief, Communications-Electronics Division	SIGNATURE DATE 17 Sept 1965

. REVIEW BY OFFICER IN CHARGE: ☒ I CONCUR WITH REPORTING OFFICIAL.   ☐ I CONCUR WITH INDORSING OFFICIAL.
  ☐ I DO NOT CONCUR.

Not required, OIC is the Indorsing Official.

, GRADE, AND ORGANIZATION	DUTY TITLE	SIGNATURE
		DATE

B86 b

NO 231

OFFICER AND AIRMAN BASE CLEARANCE	PROCESSING ACTIVITY HEADQUARTERS 3973D STRATEGIC WING (SAC) APO NEW YORK 09282	DATE 23Sep65	ARRIVAL DATE 22 Sep 65
☒ IN ☐ OUT			DEPARTURE DATE

LAST NAME - FIRST NAME - MIDDLE INITIAL	SERVICE NUMBER	GRADE	EDCSA
MERCURE MAURICE F	AF~~██████~~	MSGT	25 Sep 65

ORGANIZATION FROM (Incoming) OR TO (Outgoing) FR: 397 Bomb Wg Dow AFB Maine TO: 3973 Operations Sq (SAC) this sta	AUTHORITY SO A-827, 26Jul65	DATE RCRD RCV OR FWD

I. TO BE CLEARED IN PERSON

AGENCY		CODES	SIGNATURE	AGENCY	CODES	SIGNATURE
DUTY SECTION		1, 7, 9	R Brow	ORDERLY ROOM	1	JK Schiffer
D/PERS	C&T	1	N/A	BDCL	1	Danny Christ
	ASGMTS.	1		AUTO REGISTRATION (Outgoing Only)	2	N/A
FINANCE	D/PERS (Pay)	1	MAC	BEMO	1	N Cook
	BASE	1	TR Baker	BASE TOOL ISSUE CENTER (Outgoing Only)	8	N/A
FLYING RECORDS (Rated Pers only)	AF FORMS	1	N/A	CONSOLIDATED OR UNIT MAIL ROOM	1	
	STDN DIV	1		FLIGHT SURGEON (Rated Personnel Only)	1	N/A
TRAFFIC MANAGEMENT (Incoming Only)		10	A Culver			

II. TO BE CLEARED BY THE CLEARING AGENCY OR ORDERLY ROOM

AGENCY		CODES		AGENCY	CODES	
AF AID SOCIETY		1, 2, 3		EDUCATION OFFICE	3, 5, 6	
BASE DRIVERS SCHOOL		3, 5		FAMILY SERVICES	3, 4	
BASE HOUSING		1, 3		GROUND TRAINING	1, 3, 5	
BASE LOCATOR		4		MAINT TRAINING CONTROL	3, 5, 6	
CE PROPERTY		1, 2, 3		MEDICAL SUPPLY	1, 3	
CHAPLAIN	IN	5, 6		OFF/NCO OPEN MESS	1, 2	
	OUT	3, 5				
TRAFFIC MANAGEMENT (Outgoing Only)		3		OUTPATIENT CLINIC	1, 3, 5	
CREDIT UNION		1, 2, 3		PERSONAL AFFAIRS	1, 3	
CREW PROFESSIONAL FILE (Personnel Portion Only)		5		RECREATION SERVICES SUPPLY	1, 2, 3	
DENTAL CLINIC		5, 6		BASE OJT	5	

REMARKS

RETURN CLEARANCE NLT 27Sep65

CODES

1. TDY - SACR 35-10.

2. Officers and NCOs can sign off these agencies as having settled all obligations.

3. By telephone or other means.

4. Prepare locator card (Incoming only).

5. Forward or obtain records.

6. Provide appointment slips (Incoming only).

7. Brief on classified material (Para 6-19, AFR 205-1) and separations (Para 1-5, AFR 205-1, 1 Nov 63 & SAC Sup 1, 23 Mar 64).

8. Required only if tools are issued.

9. Prior to signing this block, obtain signature of debriefing Officer(s) in Remarks section if AFR 205-53 (Admin Access) or SACR 205-15 debriefing is required.

10. Required if member has shipped or stored personal property or obtained TR.

SIGNATURE

Maurice F Mercure

SAC FORM DEC 64 460 PREVIOUS EDITION IS OBSOLETE.

UNIT PERSONNEL RECORDS CHECKLIST (Incoming and Outgoing)

INCOMING - I&OP will initially accomplish this checklist and OR/AR will double check contents. **OUTGOING** - OR/AR will initially accomplish this checklist and I&OP will double check contents. When reassignment is to another command, dispose of all SAC forms in accordance with the prescribing directive and check block NA. Each record below is identified as follows: "O" officers only, "A" airmen only, "B" officers and airmen; and will be checked (✔) as follows: "   " - inclosed, "NA" - not applicable.

FORM	RECORD TITLE	IDENT-IFIER	INCL I&OP	INCL OR/AR	NA I&OP	NA OR/AR
AF 7/11	Airman/Officer Military Record	B	✔			
47/47a	Certificate of Eligibility and record of personnel security clearance	B	✔			
75	USAF Airman Performance Report 6 Apr 64 - 30 Aug 64	A	✔			
246	Record of Emergency Data	B	✔			
617	Military Leave Record and Leave Balance Listings	B	✔			
806	Election of Options	B	✔			
1114	USAF Enlistment Agreement Certificate	A	✔			
1226	Record of Previous Convictions and Time Lost	A			✔	
1411	Extension of Enlistment in the Regular AF	A	✔			
1710	Leave Authorization-Balance Record (Bal + Auth + Adj) & Reassignment Leave Listing	B	✔			
1710-3	Leave Authorization Balance Record (Yellow copy) & Unit Leave Balance Listing	B	✔			
1711	Health - Immunization Record	B	✔			
1713f&g	Officer Suspense Control Card (Format 3) & Officer Information Roster Card (Format 4)	O			✔	
DD 4	Enlistment Record - Armed Forces U. S.	A	✔			
98	Armed Forces Security Questionnaire	B	✔			
398	Statement of Personal History	B	✔			
802	Request for and Certificate of Eligibility (and Annual Certificate AFR34-65)	B			✔	
803	Certificate of Termination	B			✔	
SAC 601, 601a & 601b	Individual Status Card, Individual Status Supplement Card No. 1, and Individual Status Supplement Card No. 2	A	✔			
333	Processing for Overseas Assignment Certificate	B	✔			

TYPED NAME AND GRADE (Custodian) | **SIGNATURE** | **DATE**

COMPONENT TITLE

For missing components, I&OP will comply with Columns B and C, Table 4, SACR 35-10. When reassignment is to another command, dispose of all SAC components in accordance with prescribing directive and check block NA. Each component is identified as follows: "O" officers only, "A" airmen only, "B" officers and airmen; and will be checked (✔) as follows: "INCL." - inclosed, "NA" - not applicable.

FORM	COMPONENT TITLE	IDENT-IFIER	INCL	NA
	Standardization Record (Rated Personnel Only)	B		✔
AF 4/10	Airman/Officer Unit Personnel Record Group	B	✔	
5/5a	Pilot and Rated Non-Pilot Individual Flight Record	B		✔
186	Individual Record - Education Services Program	B	✔	
324	Retention Interviews	A		✔
470	Personal Pay Record Group	B	✔	
480	Individual Physical Fitness Evaluation Record	B	✔	
513	Record of Career Motivational Counseling	O		✔
522	Qualification Score Card HAS NOT FIRED	B	—	
538	Personal Clothing and Equipment Record	B	✔	
623	Consolidated Training Record	A	✔	
869	Religious Interview Guide	B	✔	
	OER File (Personnel portion of Crew Professional File)	O		✔
DD722/722-1	Health Record/Dental Folder - Health Record	B	✔✔	
1360	Operator Qualifications and Record of Licensing, Examination and Performance	A		✔
SAC 156	Individual Physical Condition Certificate	B		✔
293	Individual Collateral Training Record	B	✔	

TYPED NAME AND GRADE (I&OP NCOIC)   SSGT KNUCKEY | **SIGNATURE** | **DATE** 23 Sep 65

RECEIPT FOR HANDCARRIED RECORDS

I ___ ly acknowledge receipt of the above records checked "IN". I understand that I am to turn these records over to the appropriate Processing Activity in the CBPO upon arrival at my new station; that I am responsible for safe-guarding these records enroute; and that I am not authorized to open the sealed envelope in which these records are being transmitted.

TYPED NAME AND GRADE (Indiv handcarrying records) | **SIGNATURE** | **DATE**

B875

Date <u>25 September 1965</u>

<u>STATEMENT</u>

I, <u>Maurice F. Mercure</u>, have been briefed on applicable security regulations. I fully understand and will comply with the following statement in accordance with paragraph 206, ACP 134( ):

"Switchboard operators are bound to listen in on a connection from time to time in order to supervise, but they must not listen for any other purpose. The unauthorized disclosure or other improper use of information gained in the course of his or her duties renders the operator liable to disciplinary action under security regulations."

Maurice F Mercure
_____
(Signature)

MSGT   AF ███████
_____
(Grade)   (AFSN)

Fecha _____

<u>DECLARACION</u>

Yo, _____, he sido informada sobre las reglas de Seguridad que rigen en esta organizacion, las cuales entiendo perfecta- mente. Por lo tanto me adaptare a las normas que en este respecto contiene el parrafo 206 del ACP 134 ( ):

"Las operadoras de la centralita estamos autorizadas a escuchar de vez en cuando, para supervisar las conversaciones, y no por ninguna otra razon. No estando tampoco autorizadas a divulgar ninguna noticia que escuchemos durante nuestro trabajo en la Centralita, ya que en caso contrario quebran- tariamos las leyes de seguridad a que estamos sometidas, quedando expuesto a las consecuencias que esta infraccion pudiera ocasionar."

_____
(Signature)

_____
(Grade)

DEPARTMENT OF NONRESIDENT INSTRUCTION

U. S. ARMY SIGNAL CENTER AND SCHOOL
FORT MONMOUTH, N. J. 07703

Certificate of Subcourse Completion

ENROLLMENT NO:
12247524

HROXX TO*
   MERCURE MAURICE F.   MSG-
   3973RD OPNSSODNBX7107

   APO NY 09282

0:

; is to certify that you have successfully completed subcourse: C13
JMMUNICATION CENTER FUNDAMENTALS

Date Commenced			Date Completed			Rating	Credit Hours
Day	Mo	Yr	Day	Mo	Yr		
			04	10	5	SUPERIOR	15

Credit Hours Earned
Curr Ret Yr
(USAR Only)

A

FOR THE DIRECTOR:

1100
64

B 69

UNITED STATES AIR FORCE

SMALL ARMS MARKSMANSHIP

CERTIFICATE

OF ACHIEVEMENT

is presented to

MASTER SERGEANT MAURICE F. MERCURE

IN RECOGNITION FOR QUALIFYING AS USAF EXPERT

DATE AWARDED 20 October 1965

PAUL R. HANDWERKER, Capt, USAF
Commander

AF FORM 1193 JAN 61

890

EXTENSION SCHOOL, MCEC, MARINE CORPS SCHOOLS, QUANTICO, VIRGINIA

STUDENT PROGRESS REPORT

MERCURE	MF	MSGT		4100	080685	USAF
STUDENT NAME		RANK	SERVICE NUMBER	COURSE CODE	DATE ENROLLED	UNIT CODE

THIS REPORT INCLUDES ALL SATISFACTORY LESSONS RECEIVED TO DATE FROM THE STUDENT SINCE DATE ENROLLED IN THE EXTENSION COURSE INDICATED ABOVE AND LISTS THESE LESSONS BY DATE REPORTED ON THIS OR PREVIOUS PROGRESS REPORTS. GRADED ANSWER SHEETS FOR LESSONS NOT SHOWN MAY BE RETURNED TO EXTENSION SCHOOL FOR CREDIT. UPON RECEIPT OF A DIPLOMA FOR THIS COURSE OR A SUBSEQUENT PROGRESS REPORT, THIS REPORT SHOULD BE REMOVED FROM FILE.

COURSE CODES ARE AS FOLLOWS:

3100	— OFFICERS BASIC EXTENSION COURSE
4100	— COMMUNICATION OFFICERS EXTENSION COURSE
5100, 8100	— OFFICERS JUNIOR EXTENSION COURSE
6400, 6100, 6300, 9100	— OFFICERS SENIOR EXTENSION COURSE

DATE REPORTED	SUB-COURSE	LESSON	CREDITS	SUB-COURSE	LESSON	CREDITS	SUB-COURSE	LESSON	CREDITS	SUB-COURSE	LESSON	CREDITS	SUB-COURSE	LESSON	CREDITS	SUB-COURSE	LESSON	CREDITS	SUB-COURSE	LESSON	CREDITS	TOTAL CREDITS
30NOV65	3102	6	1	3102	6	1																2
31DEC65	3104	2	1																			1
																						3

LAST FIGURE SHOWN IN THIS COLUMN IS TOTAL CREDITS EARNED

LESSON 10 INDICATED BY * IN LESSON COLUMN.

ONE CREDIT APPROXIMATES THREE HOURS OF STUDENT EFFORT.

APPLICATION FOR ACTIVE DUTY
(AR 135-210)

1. DATE 23 February 1966

2. TO: COMMANDING GENERAL, US Army Area Command, ATTN: AENAG-PA, APO, US Forces, 09184

3. FROM: (Last name - first name - middle initial) Mercure, Maurice F.

4a. PRESENT RESERVE GRADE N/A

4b. RESERVE COMPONENT N/A

4c. SERVICE NUMBER N/A

4d. BRANCH N/A

5a. MOS 721A

5b. COMPONENT USAR

6a. PERMANENT HOME ADDRESS (Number, Street or RFD No., City and State)

6b. TELEPHONE NO. None

7a. TEMPORARY ADDRESS
3973rd Operations Squadron
Box 7107
APO, US Forces, 09282

7b. DURATION Until September 1968

7c. TELEPHONE NO. Moron Air Base, Spain - 258620, Extension 2085

(Item 8 to be completed only by personnel currently serving on active duty in a warrant officer or enlisted status)

8a. PRESENT ACTIVE DUTY GRADE Master Sergeant (E-7)

8b. SERVICE NUMBER AF

8c. ORGANIZATION AND STATION ASSIGNMENT 3973rd Operations Squadron, APO, US Forces 09282

9. I HEREBY VOLUNTEER TO ENTER ON ACTIVE DUTY FOR THE PERIOD INDICATED BELOW, IN MY BRANCH OR ANY OF THE FOLLOWING OTHER BRANCHES THAT I MAY BE QUALIFIED FOR, AND, IF ACCEPTED FOR ACTIVE DUTY IN ANOTHER BRANCH, REQUEST TRANSFER TO THAT BRANCH:

a. FOR (Check appropriate box) [X] A PERIOD OF 3 YEARS   [ ] AN INDEFINITE PERIOD

b. OTHER BRANCHES (List in order of preference):

10. I UNDERSTAND THAT IF ACCEPTED FOR ACTIVE DUTY I MAY BE ASSIGNED TO ANY COMMAND (including an oversea command) TO FILL ANY ARMY WIDE VACANCY. HOWEVER, I WOULD LIKE TO BE CONSIDERED FOR ONE OF THE THREE DUTY ASSIGNMENTS AND AREA OF ASSIGNMENTS LISTED BELOW IN THE ORDER OF MY CHOICE.

	CHOICE NO. 1	CHOICE NO. 2	CHOICE NO. 3
DUTY ASSIGNMENT	Crypto Custodian	Crypto Custodian	Crypto Custodian
AREA ASSIGNMENT	England	Germany	1st Army Area

11. IF IT IS POSSIBLE, I PREFER TO ENTER ON ACTIVE DUTY DURING ONE OF THE THREE PERIODS LISTED BELOW IN THE ORDER OF MY PREFERENCE.

PREFERENCE NO. 1 (Month and Year)	PREFERENCE NO. 2 (Month and Year)	PREFERENCE NO. 3 (Month and Year)
August 1966	September 1966	October 1966

12. UPON RECEIPT OF ACTIVE DUTY ORDERS, I WILL REQUIRE THE TIME INDICATED BELOW TO SETTLE MY AFFAIRS FOR ENTRY ON ACTIVE DUTY. (Check appropriate box)

[ ] 60 DAYS   [X] 30 DAYS   [ ] 10 DAYS   [ ] AVAILABLE ON DATE OF RECEIPT OF ORDERS

13. REMARKS

14. SIGNATURE Maurice F. Mercure

DA FORM 160 1 OCT 63

REPLACES EDITION OF 1 FEB 62 WHICH WILL BE USED.

O-1023

INSTRUCTIONS

Read these instructions carefully and follow them. Reserve Component officers are normally recalled in their current Reserve grade. Grade of an individual applying for appointment and concurrent order to active duty will be determined by the approving authority.

1. Submit in duplicate. Use typewriter, if practicable; if not, print clearly in ink. If space is insufficient for a particular item, continue under Item 13, "Remarks," or on a separate sheet, indicating item number to which answer applies.

2. The following instructions for items listed should be followed. Items not listed are considered to be self-explanatory.

ITEM 2. Insert appropriate area command, such as "Sixth U.S. Army," "U.S. Army, Alaska," etc., as follows:

    a. Personnel serving on active duty in a warrant officer or enlisted status: Enter the area command in which serving on active duty.

    b. All others: Enter the area command having assignment jurisdiction over you.

ITEM 4. Items 4a through 4d will be completed by individuals currently holding appointments as Reserve officers of the Army:

a. Item 4a: Enter present grade as a Reserve officer. Warrant officers will include "Pay Grade" in this item, such as "WO, W-1," "CWO, W-2," etc.

b. Item 4b: Enter the Reserve component of the Army to which assigned, using the following abbreviations:

"ARNGUS" for members assigned to the Army National Guard of the United States.

"USAR" for members assigned to the Army Reserve.

c. Item 4c: Enter the service number assigned to you as a Reserve commissioned or warrant officer of the Army.

d. Item 4d: Commissioned officers - enter the branch to which assigned.

ITEM 5. Complete as specified below:

a. Item 5a: Enter your primary MOS.

b. Item 5b: Individuals applying for appointment as Reserve officers of the Army with concurrent active duty - enter the Reserve component for which applying. See instructions prescribed for Item 4b, above. The abbreviation "AUS" will be entered in this item by -

(1) Individuals applying for temporary appointment in the Army of the United States, without component, and concurrent active duty; and
(2) Reserve officers of the Army applying for active duty in a temporary grade that is higher or lower than their Reserve grade.

ITEM 6. In this instance the term "permanent home address" corresponds to your "Home of Record," an official term used in determining entitlement to travel allowances on separation from the service. This address will be indicated in orders placing you on active duty. NO CHANGE IN 'HOME OF RECORD' IS AUTHORIZED AFTER ENTRY ON ACTIVE DUTY.

For applicants not on active duty - Enter your permanent home address. Include "ZIP" code, telephone number at that address, and long distance area dial code.

For applicants currently on active duty as warrant officers - Enter "Home of Record" shown in your warrant officer active duty orders.

For applicants on duty as enlisted persons - Enter "Home Address" as shown on your Enlistment Record (DD Form 4) or "permanent address" shown in your Record of Induction (DD Form 47).

ITEM 7. This item to be completed if it is anticipated that you will be at this address when orders are issued. The "temporary address," if furnished, will be included in your orders and you will enter on active duty from this address.

a. Item 7b: Show maximum period you anticipate being at the temporary address, such as "Until (give month and year)."

b. Item 7c: Furnish the telephone number at your temporary address and the long distance area dial code.

ITEM 13. Include all information you consider essential from the standpoint of assignment restriction.

3. IMPORTANT - Review your application to insure accuracy and completeness. Then forward your application in accordance with the applicable following instructions:

OFFICERS OF THE ARMY NATIONAL GUARD OF THE UNITED STATES: To your unit commander.

OFFICERS OF THE ARMY RESERVE: To your unit advisor, if assigned to a TOE or TD unit; if not, to the Commanding General, United States Army Corps, to which you are assigned.

WARRANT OFFICERS OR ENLISTED PERSONNEL ON ACTIVE DUTY: To your present unit commander.

INDIVIDUALS APPLYING FOR APPOINTMENT WITH CONCURRENT ACTIVE DUTY: Submit together with your application for appointment in accordance with regulations applicable to the type of appointment requested.

ARMED FORCES SECURITY QUESTIONNAIRE

I.—EXPLANATION

1. The interests of National Security require that all persons being considered for membership or retention in the Armed Forces be reliable, trustworthy, of good character, and of complete and unswerving loyalty to the United States. Accordingly, it is necessary for you to furnish information concerning your security qualifications. The answers which you give will be used in determining whether you are eligible for membership in the Armed Forces, in selection of your duty assignment, and for such other action as may be appropriate.

2. You are advised that in accordance with the Fifth Amendment of the Constitution of the United States you cannot be compelled to furnish any statements which you may reasonably believe may lead to your prosecution for a crime. This is the only reason for which you may avail yourself of the privilege afforded by the Fifth Amendment in refusing to answer questions under Part IV below. Claiming the Fifth Amendment will not by itself constitute sufficient grounds to exempt you from military service for reasons of security. You are not required to answer any questions in this questionnaire, the answer to which might be incriminating. If you do claim the privilege granted by the Fifth Amendment in refusing to answer any question, you should make a statement to that effect after the question involved.

II.—ORGANIZATIONS OF SECURITY SIGNIFICANCE

1. There is set forth below a list of names of organizations, groups, and movements, reported by the Attorney General of the United States as having significance in connection with the National Security. Please examine the list carefully, and note those organizations, and organizations of similar names, with which you are familiar. Then answer the questions set forth in Part IV below.

2. Your statement concerning membership or other association with one or more of the organizations named may not, of itself, cause you to be ineligible for acceptance or retention in the Armed Forces. Your age at the time of such association, circumstances prompting it, and the extent and frequency of involvement, are all highly pertinent, and will be fully weighed. Set forth all such factors under "Remarks" below, and continue on separate attached sheets of paper if necessary.

3. If there is any doubt in your mind as to whether your name has been linked with one of the organizations named, or as to whether a particular association is "worth mentioning," make a full explanation under "Remarks."

Organizations designated by the Attorney General, pursuant to Executive Order 10450, are listed below:

Communist Party, U. S. A., its subdivisions, subsidiaries and affiliates.

Communist Political Association, its subdivisions, subsidiaries and affiliates, including—
Alabama People's Educational Association.
Florida Press and Educational League.
Oklahoma League for Political Education.
People's Educational and Press Association of Texas.
Virginia League for People's Education.

Young Communist League.
Abraham Lincoln Brigade.
Abraham Lincoln School, Chicago, Illinois.
Action Committee to Free Spain Now.
American Association for Reconstruction in Yugoslavia, Inc.
American Branch of the Federation of Greek Maritime Unions.
American Christian Nationalist Party.
American Committee for European Workers' Relief.
American Committee for Protection of Foreign Born.
American Committee for the Settlement of Jews in Birobidjan, Inc.
American Committee for Spanish Freedom.
American Committee for Yugoslav Relief, Inc.
American Committee to Survey Labor Conditions in Europe.
American Council for a Democratic Greece, formerly known as the Greek American Council; Greek American Committee for National Unity.
American Council on Soviet Relations.
American Croatian Congress.
American Jewish Labor Council.
American League Against War and Fascism.
American League for Peace and Democracy.
American National Labor Party.
American National Socialist League.
American National Socialist Party.
American Nationalist Party.
American Patriots, Inc.
American Peace Crusade.
American Peace Mobilization.
American Poles for Peace.
American Polish Labor Council.
American Polish League.
American Rescue Ship Mission (a project of the United American Spanish Aid Committee).
American-Russian Fraternal Society.
American-Russian Institute, New York (also known as the American Russian Institute for Cultural Relations with the Soviet Union).
American Russian Institute, Philadelphia.
American Russian Institute of San Francisco.
American Russian Institute of Southern California, Los Angeles.

American Slav Congress.
American Women for Peace.
American Youth Congress.
American Youth for Democracy.
Armenian Progressive League of America.
Associated Klans of America.
Association of Georgia Klans.
Association of German Nationals (Reichsdeutsche Vereinigung).
Ausland-Organization der NSDAP, Overseas Branch of Nazi Party.
Baltimore Forum.
Benjamin Davis Freedom Committee.
Black Dragon Society.
Boston School for Marxist Studies, Boston, Massachusetts.
Bridges-Robertson-Schmidt Defense Committee.
Bulgarian American People's League of the United States of America.
California Emergency Defense Committee.
California Labor School, Inc., 321 Divisadero Street, San Francisco, California.
Carpatho-Russian People's Society.
Central Council of American Women of Croatian Descent (also known as Central Council of American Croatian Women, National Council of Croatian Women).
Central Japanese Association (Beikoku Chuo Nipponjin Kai).
Central Japanese Association of Southern California.
Central Organization of the German-American National Alliance (Deutsche-Amerikanische Einheitsfront).
Cervantes Fraternal Society.
China Welfare Appeal, Inc.
Chopin Cultural Center.
Citizens Committee to Free Earl Browder.
Citizens Committee for Harry Bridges.
Citizens Committee of the Upper West Side (New York City).
Citizens Emergency Defense Conference.
Citizens Protective League.
Civil Liberties Sponsoring Committee of Pittsburgh.
Civil Rights Congress and its affiliated organizations, including Civil Rights Congress for Texas, Veterans Against Discrimination of Civil Rights Congress of New York.
Columbians.
Comite Coordinador Pro Republica Espanola.
Comite Pro Derechos Civiles.
Committee to Abolish Discrimination in Maryland.
Committee to Aid the Fighting South.
Committee to Defend the Rights and Freedom of Pittsburgh's Political Prisoners.

Committee for a Democratic Far Eastern Policy.
Committee for Constitutional and Political Freedom.
Committee for the Defense of the Pittsburgh Six.
Committee for Nationalist Action.
Committee for the Negro in the Arts.
Committee for Peace and Brotherhood Festival in Philadelphia.
Committee for the Protection of the Bill of Rights.
Committee for World Youth Friendship and Cultural Exchange.
Committee to Defend Marie Richardson.
Committee to Uphold the Bill of Rights.
Commonwealth College, Mena, Arkansas.
Congress Against Discrimination.
Congress of the Unemployed.
Connecticut Committee to Aid Victims of the Smith Act.
Connecticut State Youth Conference.
Congress of American Revolutionary Writers.
Congress of American Women.
Council on African Affairs.
Council of Greek Americans.
Council for Jobs, Relief, and Housing.
Council for Pan-American Democracy.
Croatian Benevolent Fraternity.
Dai Nippon Butoku Kai (Military Virtue Society of Japan or Military Art Society of Japan).
Daily Worker Press Club.
Daniels Defense Committee.
Dante Alighieri Society (Between 1935 and 1940).
Dennis Defense Committee.
Detroit Youth Assembly.
East Bay Peace Committee.
Elsinore Progressive League.
Emergency Conference to Save Spanish Refugees (founding body of the North American Spanish Aid Committee).
Everybody's Committee to Outlaw War.
Families of the Baltimore Smith Act Victims.
Families of the Smith Act Victims.
Federation of Italian War Veterans in the U. S. A., Inc. (Associazione Nazionale Combattenti Italiani, Federazione degli Stati Uniti d'America).
Finnish-American Mutual Aid Society.
Florida Press and Educational League.
Frederick Douglass Educational Center.
Freedom Stage, Inc.
Friends of the New Germany (Freunde des Neuen Deutschlands).
Friends of the Soviet Union.
Garibaldi American Fraternal Society.
George Washington Carver School, New York City.
German-American Bund (Amerikadeutscher Volksbund).

DD FORM 98
1 Jun 59
PREVIOUS EDITION OF THIS FORM WILL BE USED UNTIL STOCK IS EXHAUSTED.

Page 1

B93a

DD FORM **98**
1 Jun 59
PREVIOUS EDITION OF THIS FORM WILL
BE USED UNTIL STOCK IS EXHAUSTED.

Page 1

— — FOLD HERE — —

nan-American Republican League.
nan-American Vocational League (*Deutsche-Amerikanische Berufsge-meinschaft*).
Guardian Club.

Harlem Trade Union Council.
Hawaii Civil Liberties Committee.
Heimusha Kai, also known as Nokubei Heieki, Gimusha Kai, Zaibel Nihonjin, Heiyaku Gimusha Kai and Zaibei Heimusha Kai (*Japanese Residing in America Military Conscripts Association*).
Hellenic-American Brotherhood.
Hinode Kai (*Imperial Japanese Reservists*).
Hinomaru Kai (*Rising Sun Flag Society—a group of Japanese War Veterans*).
Hokubei Zaigo Shoke Dan (*North American Reserve Officers Association*).
Hollywood Writers Mobilization for Defense.
Hungarian-American Council for Democracy.
Hungarian Brotherhood.

Idaho Pension Union.
Independent Party (*Seattle, Washington*).
Independent People's Party.
Industrial Workers of the World.
International Labor Defense.
International Workers Order, its subdivisions, subsidiaries and affiliates.

Japanese Association of America.
Japanese Overseas Central Society (*Kaigai Dobo Chao Kai*).
Japanese Overseas Convention, Tokyo, Japan, 1940.
Japanese Protective Association (*Recruiting Organization*).
Jefferson School of Social Science, New York City.
Jewish Culture Society.
Jewish People's Committee.
Jewish People's Fraternal Order.
Jikyoku Lin Kai (*The Committee for the Crisis*).
Johnson-Forest Group.
Johnsonites.
Joint Anti-Fascist Refugee Committee.
    Council of Progressive Italian-Americans, Inc.
    h Weydemeyer School of Social Science, St.
    .is, Missouri.

Kibei Seinen Kai (*Association of U. S. citizens of Japanese ancestry who have returned to America after studying in Japan*).
Knights of the White Camelia.
Ku Klux Klan.
Kyffhaeuser, also known as Kyffhaeuser League (*Kyffhaeuser Bund*), Kyffhaeuser Fellowship (*Kyffhaeuser Kameradschaft*).
Kyffhaeuser War Relief (*Kyffhaeuser Kriegshilfswerk*).

Labor Council for Negro Rights.
Labor Research Association, Inc.
Labor Youth League.
League for Common Sense.
League of American Writers.
Lictor Society (*Italian Black Shirts*).

Macedonian-American People's League.
Mario Morganti Circle.
Maritime Labor Committee to Defend Al Lannon.
Maryland Congress Against Discrimination.
Massachusetts Committee for the Bill of Rights.
Massachusetts Minute Women for Peace (not connected with the Minute Women of the U. S. A., Inc.).
Maurice Braverman Defense Committee.
Michigan Civil Rights Federation.

Michigan Council for Peace.
Michigan School of Social Science.

Nanka Teikoku Guayudan (*Imperial Military Friends Group or Southern California War Veterans*).
National Association of Mexican Americans (*also known as Asociacion Nacional Mexico-Americana*).
National Blue Star Mothers of America (not to be confused with the Blue Star Mothers of America organized in February 1942).
National Committee for the Defense of Political Prisoners.
National Committee for Freedom of the Press.
National Committee to Win Amnesty for Smith Act Victims.
National Committee to Win the Peace.
National Conference on American Policy in China and the Far East (*a Conference called by the Committee for a Democratic Far Eastern Policy*).
National Council of Americans of Croatian Descent.
National Council of American-Soviet Friendship.
National Federation for Constitutional Liberties.
National Labor Conference for Peace.
National Negro Congress.
National Negro Labor Council.
Nationalist Action League.
Nationalist Party of Puerto Rico.
Nature Friends of America (*Since 1935*).
Negro Labor Victory Committee.
New Committee for Publications.
Nichibei Kogyo Kaisha (*The Great Fujii Theatre*).
North American Committee to Aid Spanish Democracy
North American Spanish Aid Committee.
North Philadelphia Forum.
Northwest Japanese Association.

Ohio School of Social Sciences.
Oklahoma Committee to Defend Political Prisoners.
Oklahoma League for Political Education.
Original Southern Klans, Incorporated.

Pacific Northwest Labor School, Seattle, Washington.
Palo Alto Peace Club.
Partido del Pueblo of Panama (*operating in the Canal Zone*).
Peace Information Center.
Peace Movement of Ethiopia.
People's Drama, Inc.,
People's Educational and Press Association of Texas.
People's Educational Association (*Incorporated under name Los Angeles Educational Association, Inc.*), also known as People's Educational Center, People's University, People's School.
People's Institute of Applied Religion.
Peoples Programs (*Seattle, Washington*).
People's Radio Foundation, Inc.
People's Rights Party.
Philadelphia Labor Committee for Negro Rights.
Philadelphia School of Social Science and Art.
Photo League (*New York City*).
Pittsburgh Arts Club.
Political Prisoners' Welfare Committee.
Polonia Society of the IWO.
Progressive German-Americans, also known as Progressive German-Americans of Chicago.
Proletarian Party of America.
Protestant War Veterans of the United States, Inc.
Provisional Committee of Citizens for Peace, Southwest Area.
Provisional Committee on Latin American Affairs.
Provisional Committee to Abolish Discrimination in the State of Maryland.
Puerto Rican Comite Pro Libertades Civiles (CLC).

Puertorriquenos Unidos (*Puerto Ricans United*).

Quad City Committee for Peace.
Queensbridge Tenants League.

Revolutionary Workers League.
Romanian-American Fraternal Society.
Russian American Society, Inc.

Sakura Kai (*Patriotic Society, or Cherry Association, composed of veterans of Russo-Japanese War*).
Samuel Adams School, Boston, Mass.
Santa Barbara Peace Forum.
Schappes Defense Committee.
Schneiderman-Darcy Defense Committee.
School of Jewish Studies, New York City.
Seattle Labor School, Seattle, Washington.
Serbian-American Fraternal Society.
Serbian Vidovdan Council.
Shinto Temples (Limited to State Shinto abolished in 1945).
Silver Shirt Legion of America.
Slavic Council of Southern California.
Slovak Workers Society.
Slovenian-American National Council
Socialist Workers Party, including American Committee for European Workers Relief.
Sokoku Kai (*Fatherland Society*).
Southern Negro Youth Congress.
Suiko Sha (*Reserve Officers Association, Los Angeles*).
Syracuse Women for Peace.

Tom Paine School of Social Science, Philadelphia, Pennsylvania.
Tom Paine School of Westchester, New York.
Trade Union Committee for Peace.
Trade Unionists for Peace.
Tri-State Negro Trade Union Council.

Ukranian-American Fraternal Union.
Union of American Croatians.
Union of New York Veterans.
United American Spanish Aid Committee.
United Committee of Jewish Societies and Landsmanschaft Federations, also known as Coordination Committee of Jewish Landsmanschaften and Fraternal Organizations.
United Committee of South Slavic Americans.
United Defense Council of Southern California.
United Harlem Tenants and Consumers' Organization.
United May Day Committee.
United Negro and Allied Veterans of America.

Veterans Against Discrimination of Civil Rights Congress of New York.
Veterans of the Abraham Lincoln Brigade.
Virginia League for People's Education.
Voice of Freedom Committee.

Walt Whitman School of Social Science, Newark, New Jersey.
Washington Bookshop Association.
Washington Committee to Defend the Bill of Rights.
Washington Committee for Democratic Action.
Washington Commonwealth Federation.
Washington Pension Union.
Wisconsin Conference on Social Legislation.
Workers Alliance (*since April 1936*).

Yiddisher Kultur Farband.
Yugoslav-American Cooperative Home, Inc.
Yugoslav Seamen's Club, Inc..

III.—INSTRUCTIONS

1. Set forth an explanation for each answer checked "Yes" under question 2 below under "Remarks." Attach as many extra sheets as necessary for a full explanation, signing or initialing each extra sheet.

2. Title 18, U. S. Code, Section 1001, provides, in pertinent rt: "Whoever . . . falsifies, conceals or covers up . . . a material fact, or makes any false . . . statements . . . or makes or uses any false writing . . . shall be fined not more than $10,000 or imprisoned not more than 5 years, or both." Any false, fraudulent or fictitious response to the questions under Part IV below may give rise to criminal liability under Title 18,

U. S. C., Section 1001. You are advised, however, that you will not incur such liability unless you supply inaccurate statements with knowledge of their untruthfulness. You are therefore advised that before you sign this form and turn it in to Selective Service or military authorities, you should be sure that it is truthful; that detailed explanations are given for each "Yes" answer under question 2 of Part IV below, and that details given are as full and complete as you can make them.

3. In stating details, it is permissible, if your memory is hazy on particular points, to use such expressions as, "I think," "in my opinion," "I believe," or "to the best of my recollection."

B93b

IV.—QUESTIONS

(For each answer checked "Yes" under question 2, set forth a full explanation under "Remarks" below)

	YES	NO		YES	NO
1. I have read the list of names of organizations, groups, and movements set forth under Part II of this form and the explanation which precedes it.	Yes		j. Have you ever contributed money to any of the organizations, groups, or movements listed?		No
2. Concerning the list of organizations, groups and movements set forth under Part II above:			k. Have you ever contributed services to any of the organizations, groups, or movements listed?		No
a. Are you now a member of any of the organizations, groups, or movements listed?		No	l. Have you ever subscribed to any publication of any of the organizations, groups, or movements listed?		No
b. Have you ever been a member of any of the organizations, groups, or movements listed?		No	m. Have you ever been employed by a foreign government or any agency thereof?		No
c. Are you now employed by any of the organizations, groups, or movements listed?		No	n. Are you now a member of the Communist Party of any foreign country?		No
d. Have you ever been employed by any of the organizations, groups, or movements listed?		No	o. Have you ever been a member of the Communist Party of any foreign country?		No
e. Have you ever attended any meeting of any of the organizations, groups, or movements listed?		No	p. Have you ever been the subject of a loyalty or security hearing?		No
f. Have you ever attended any social gathering of any of the organizations, groups, or movements listed?		No	q. Are you now or have you ever been a member of any organization, association, movement, group or combination of persons not on the Attorney General's list which advocates the overthrow of our constitutional form of government, or which has adopted the policy of advocating or approving the commission of acts of force or violence to deny other persons their rights under the Constitution of the United States, or which seeks to alter the form of government of the United States by unconstitutional means?		No MGM
g. Have you ever attended any gathering of any kind sponsored by any of the organizations, groups, or movements listed?		No			
h. Have you prepared material for publication by any of the organizations, groups, or movements listed?		No			
i. Have you ever corresponded with any of the organizations, groups, or movements listed or with any publication thereof?		No	r. Have you ever been known by any other last name than that used in signing this questionnaire?	MGM Yes	

REMARKS

My name was changed at age 14 by adoption, from Fraichard to Mercure.
Recorded in the U.S. Court House, Springfield, Massachusetts.

Page 3

REMARKS (Continued)

CERTIFICATION

In regard to any part of this questionnaire concerning which I have had any question as to the meaning, I have requested and have obtained a complete explanation. I certify that the statements made by me under Part IV above and on any supplemental pages hereto attached, are full, true, and correct.

TYPED FULL NAME OF PERSON MAKING CERTIFICATION	SERVICE NUMBER (if any)	SIGNATURE OF PERSON MAKING CERTIFICATION
MAURICE FRANK MERCURE	AF ~~████████~~	*Maurice Frank Mercure*
TYPED NAME OF WITNESS	DATE	SIGNATURE OF WITNESS
NELSON DONALD COURNOYER, CAPT, USAF	9 MARCH 1966	*Nelson Donald Cournoyer*

* U.S. GOVERNMENT PRINTING OFFICE : 1963 O—676651

BDCO-CE/MSgt Mercure   11 MAR 1966

Request for Waiver

Commanding General
U.S. Army Area Command
Attn: AEMAG-PA
APO, US Forces, 09184

THRU: Commanding Officer
        3973 Operations Squadron
        APO, US Forces, 09282

1. Request a waiver be granted to this application as pertains to
my Military Court Martial, June 1948.

2. The specific charge for which I was convicted is bringing
whiskey into government quarters. The sentence imposed was a fine
of $25.00. Since this unfortunate incident I have had no derogatory
information of any kind.

3. This Court Martial has not detered my military career in any
way. I have had normal progression in grade; have been cleared for
Top Secret Crypto; accepted for and performed MAAG duty from 1960
to 1961; Performance Reports, which are attached to this application
will attest to my outstanding performance of duty.

4. Because of the above and the fact that this Court Martial is
approximately eighteen years old, it should not be a determining
factor in considering my application for appointment as an Army
Warrant Officer.

                    Maurice F. Mercure
                    MAURICE F. MERCURE, AF█████████
                    MSGT, USAF

OSC/Capt Meredith   11 MAR 1966

Request for Waiver

Commanding General
U.S. Army Area Command
Attn: AENAG-PA
APO, US Forces, 09184

1.   I concur wholeheartedly that a waiver be granted to Master
Sergeant Maurice F. Mercure on his approximately eighteen year
old Court Martial. It definitely should not be a determining
factor in considering his application for appointment to Warrant
Officer. An examination of his records reveals no derogatory
information.   To the contrary, it revealed letters of appreciation,
commendation, an NCO of the Month Award and outstanding airman
performance reports.

2.   Sergeant Mercure is one of the few superior type NCO's that I
have known. In smartness of appearance, honesty, devotion to duty
and ability to do the job without unnecessary supervision; Master
Sergeant Mercure is outstanding and is truly officer material.

3.   Master Sergeant Mercure is a graduate of the Strategic Air
Command, 7th Air Division, NCO Academy. He has constantly applied
his technical training and experience to the best interest of his
organization and the United States Air Force. Sergeant Mercure
has extraordinary growth potential and is fully qualified for
advancement to and the assumption of the responsibilities of a
Army Warrant Officer.

ERNEST R. MEREDITH,
Captain, USAF

OK

DEPARTMENT OF THE AIR FORCE
HEADQUARTERS 3973D STRATEGIC WING (SAC)
APO US FORCES, 09282

REPLY TO
ATTN OF: BDPSE

MAR 15 1966

SUBJECT: Request for Educational Award

TO: 16AF (DPSE)

1. In accordance with SAC Regulation 34-2, dated 31 Dec 64, request

MSgt   Maurice   F.   Mercure   3973 Operations
GRADE   FIRST NAME   MI   LAST NAME   ORGANIZATION

be awarded SAC Educational Achievement Award

2. Award is requested based on a total of 31.8 education points earned.

3. A copy of AF Form 186 is enclosed to substantiate the following breakdown of SAC education points.

   a. 12 education points represented by semester hour credits.

   b. 0 education points represented by USAFI courses.

   c. 0 education points represented by local group study classes.

   d. 16.2 education points represented by USAF ECI courses & other.

   e. 0 education points represented by Carnegie units.

   f. 0 education points represented by Mgt-1 or Mgt-2 course.

   g. 6.6 education points earned before arrival in SAC.

4. 0 education points included above were earned in programs below the applicant's educational level, but are considered to be of such a nature as to broaden the applicant's education.

5. Individual's present duty assignment is NCOIC, Comm Center .

6. Dates of consecutive assignment with SAC /Dec 62 to present .

Sandra S. Davis

for CORNELIO de KANTER, Civilian   1 Atch
Education Services Officer   AF Form 186
Directorate of Personnel

REPORT OF MEDICAL EXAMINATION

88—109—01

1. LAST NAME—FIRST NAME—MIDDLE NAME	2. GRADE AND COMPONENT OR POSITION	3. IDENTIFICATION NO.
MERCURE MAURICE FRANK	MSgt USAF	AF ▓▓▓▓

4. HOME ADDRESS (Number, street or R.F.D., city or town, zone and State)	5. PURPOSE OF EXAMINATION	6. DATE OF EXAMINATION
43 Newton Street Holyoke, Mass	Army Warrant Officer Program	21 Mar 66

7. SEX	8. RACE	9. TOTAL YEARS GOVERNMENT SERVICE	10. AGENCY	11. ORGANIZATION UNIT ▓▓▓ Opns Sq
Male	Caucasian	MILITARY 19 5/12 CIVILIAN —	DAF	APO New York 09282

12. DATE OF BIRTH	13. PLACE OF BIRTH	14. NAME, RELATIONSHIP, AND ADDRESS OF NEXT OF KIN
(37) 14 Aug ▓	Chicopee, Mass	Margaret D Mercure(Wife) Santa Clara Chalet I-14-A Cuidad Jardin, Seville

15. EXAMINING FACILITY OR EXAMINER, AND ADDRESS	16. OTHER INFORMATION Spain
870 USAF Hospital(USAFE) APO New York 09282	Duty AFSC: 29170

17. RATING OR SPECIALTY	TIME IN THIS CAPACITY (Total)	LAST SIX MONTHS
	—	—

CLINICAL EVALUATION

NOTES. (Describe every abnormality in detail. Enter pertinent item number before each comment.. Continue in item 73 and use additional sheets if necessary.)

NOR-MAL (Check each item in appropriate column; enter "NE" if not evaluated.)		ABNOR-MAL
X	18. HEAD, FACE, NECK, AND SCALP	
X	19. NOSE	
X	20. SINUSES	
	21. MOUTH AND THROAT	X
X	22. EARS—GENERAL (Int. & ext. canals) (Auditory acuity under items 70 and 71)	
X	23. DRUMS (Perforation)	
X	24. EYES—GENERAL (Visual acuity and refraction under items 59, 60 and 67)	
X	25. OPHTHALMOSCOPIC	
X	26. PUPILS (Equality and reaction)	
X	27. OCULAR MOTILITY (Associated parallel movements, nystagmus)	
X	28. LUNGS AND CHEST (Include breasts)	
X	29. HEART (Thrust, size, rhythm, sounds)	
X	30. VASCULAR SYSTEM (Varicosities, etc.)	
X	31. ABDOMEN AND VISCERA (Include hernia)	
X	32. ANUS AND RECTUM (Hemorrhoids, fistulae) (Prostate, if indicated)	
X	33. ENDOCRINE SYSTEM	
X	34. G-U SYSTEM	
X	35. UPPER EXTREMITIES (Strength, range of motion)	
X	36. FEET	
X	37. LOWER EXTREMITIES (Except feet) (Strength, range of motion)	
X	38. SPINE, OTHER MUSCULOSKELETAL	
X	39. IDENTIFYING BODY MARKS, SCARS, TATTOOS	
X	40. SKIN, LYMPHATICS	
X	41. NEUROLOGIC (Equilibrium tests under item 72)	
X	42. PSYCHIATRIC (Specify any personality deviation)	
	43. PELVIC (Females only) (Check how done)	
	☐ VAGINAL ☐ RECTAL	

21. Tonsils enucleated.

38. There is no loss of strength or range of motion of cervical spine.

(Continue in item 73)

44. DENTAL (Place appropriate symbols above or below number of upper and lower teeth, respectively.)

O—Restorable teeth
/—Nonrestorable teeth

X—Missing teeth
XXX—Replaced by dentures

(6 X 8)—Fixed bridge, brackets to include abutments

REMARKS AND ADDITIONAL DENTAL DEFECTS AND DISEASES

Type II Exam
Class II
QUALIFIED

RIGHT	X	2	3	X	X	X	7	8	9	10	11	12	X	14	15	X	LEFT
	32	31	30	29	28	27	26	25	24	23	22	21	20	19	18	17	
	O	X	X										X	X			

LABORATORY FINDINGS

45. URINALYSIS: A. SPECIFIC GRAVITY 1.017		46. CHEST X-RAY (Place, date, film number and result)
B. ALBUMIN Negative	D. MICROSCOPIC	870 Med Gp(SAC) APO New York 09282
C. SUGAR Negative	Negative	14x17 # 66-865 Normal

47. SEROLOGY (Specify test used and result)	48. EKG	49. BLOOD TYPE AND RH FACTOR	50. OTHER TESTS
Cardiolipin Micro-flocculation Negative	Attached Normal	By Record O-Pos	Hemoglobin: 15.1 Gms/100 ml

MEASUREMENTS AND OTHER FINDINGS

51. HEIGHT	52. WEIGHT	53. COLOR HAIR	54. COLOR EYES	55. BUILD: (Check one)	SLENDER	MEDIUM	HEAVY	OBESE	56. TEMPERATURE
68½	185	Brown	Blue				XX		98.4

BLOOD PRESSURE (Arm at heart level)							58.	PULSE (Arm at heart level)				
A. SITTING	SYS. 122	B. RECUMBENT	SYS.	C. STANDING (3 min.)	SYS.	A. SITTING		B. AFTER EXERCISE	C. 2 MIN. AFTER	D. RECUMBENT	E. AFTER STANDING 3 MIN.
	DIAS. 82		DIAS.		DIAS.	80		112	84		

59. DISTANT VISION		60. Manifest REFRACTION			61. NEAR VISION		
RIGHT 20/ 25	CORR. TO 20/ 20	BY +1.00 S. Sph	CX	−	20/25 CORR. TO 20/20	BY # 60
LEFT 20/ 40	CORR. TO 20/ 30	BY +2.25 S. +1.25	CX 135	20/70 CORR. TO 20/40	BY # 60

62. HETEROPHORIA (Specify distance) VTA-ND 20'

ES°	EX°	R.H.	L.H.	PRISM DIV.	PRISM CONV.	PC	PD
8	0	0.5	0		CT Ortho		

63. ACCOMMODATION		64. COLOR VISION (Test used and result)	65. DEPTH PERCEPTION (Test used and score)	UNCORRECTED −
RIGHT	LEFT	VTS-CV: Passes		CORRECTED −

66. FIELD OF VISION	67. NIGHT VISION (Test used and score)	68. RED LENS TEST	69. INTRAOCULAR TENSION
Normal	NTBH	−	Normal

70. HEARING	71. Maico AUDIOMETER									72. PSYCHOLOGICAL AND PSYCHOMOTOR (Tests used and score)

				250 256	500 512	1000 1024	2000 2048	3000 3096	4000 4096	6000 6144	8000 8192
RIGHT WV	/15 SV	/15	RIGHT	0	0	−5	0	15	30		
LEFT WV	/15 SV	/15	LEFT	0	0	5	40	30	35		

73. NOTES (Continued) AND SIGNIFICANT OR INTERVAL HISTORY

Scarlet Fever, Mumps, Pertussis and tonsillectomy in childhood. No comp., no seq.
Pilonidal cystectomy in 1948, Eglin AFB, Fla., no mass or drainage since. Glasses worn
for reading since 1948.   Reaction to penicillin and streptomycin(rash), mild, 1961,
Formosa.   Jaundice refers to infectious hepatitis 1961, Formosa, hospitalized 4 weeks. No
resurrence.   Wore cervical collar for 4 months as treatment for cervical arthritis 1965.
(See attached consult dated 28 Apr 66.) Mother and stepsister have heart trouble. No
? is known. Examinee denies other significant medical or surgical history.

"THIS IS A TRUE COPY"

[signature]

PHIL COLLINS CAPT MC FMO USAF

(Use additional sheets if necessary)

74. SUMMARY OF DEFECTS AND DIAGNOSES (List diagnoses with item numbers)

73. History of cervical arthritis. See attached consult dated 28 Apr 66.
44. Dental caries.
59-61. Decreased visual acuity OU near and distant. Present Rx acceptable.
71. High frequency hearing loss, left, non progressive.

75. RECOMMENDATIONS—FURTHER SPECIALIST EXAMINATIONS INDICATED (Specify)

Correction of dental caries.
Refraction for decreased visual acuity.

77. EXAMINEE (Check)

A. ☐ IS QUALIFIED FOR
B. ☐ IS NOT QUALIFIED FOR   AF COMMISSION

76.	A. PHYSICAL PROFILE					
	P	U	L	H	E	S
	1	1	1	1	1	1

78. IF NOT QUALIFIED, LIST DISQUALIFYING DEFECTS BY ITEM NUMBER

B. PHYSICAL CATEGORY			
A	B	C	E

79. TYPED OR PRINTED NAME OF PHYSICIAN — SIGNATURE

PHIL COLLINS CAPT USAF MC FMO

80. TYPED OR PRINTED NAME OF PHYSICIAN — SIGNATURE

81. TYPED OR PRINTED NAME OF DENTIST OR PHYSICIAN (Indicate which) — SIGNATURE

82. TYPED OR PRINTED NAME OF REVIEWING OFFICER OR APPROVING AUTHORITY — SIGNATURE

NUMBER OF ATTACHED SHEETS

U.S. GOVERNMENT PRINTING OFFICE : 1962 O—062700

8976

STRATEGIC AIR COMMAND

EDUCATIONAL ACHIEVEMENT CERTIFICATE

MAURICE F. MERCURE

*Is Awarded This Certificate In Recognition of Self
Improvement Gained Through Participation In The
Strategic Air Command Aerospace Education Program
Given At Offutt Air Force Base,*

This 23RD *Day Of* MARCH 1966

JOHN D. RYAN
GENERAL, USAF
COMMANDED IN CHIEF

SAC FORM 133
MAY 62

B98

USAFEM 35-1

IDENTITY DOCUMENT FOR CROSSING BORDERS
DOCUMENT DE PASSAGE FRONTALIER
PERSONALAUS WEIS FÜR GRENZÜBERTRITT
AUTORIZAÇAO PARA TRAVESSIA DE FRONTEIRAS

ENGLISH
FRENCH
GERMAN
PORTUGUESE

FROM - De - Von - De	TO - Pour - An - Para	RANK - Grade - Dienstgrad - Grau
MORON AB, SPAIN	AMERICAN EMBASSY-FRANCE AMERICAN EMBASSY-GERMANY	MSGT

NAME - Nom - Name - Nome	THE BEARER'S SERVICE NUMBER - Numéro Matricule Dienstnummer - Numero de serviço militar
MERCURE, Maurice F.	AF██████████

IS A MEMBER OF THE UNITED STATES AIR FORCES EUROPE AND IS AUTHORIZED TO MOVE AND RETURN:

appartient aux Forces Aériennes des Etats - Unis d'Amérique en Europe et est autorisé(e) à voyager (aller et retour):

ist Angehöriger der Luftstreitkräfte der Vereinigten Staaten in Europa und als solcher zu folgender Reise mit Rückkehr berechtigt:

É um membro das forças aéreas dos Estados Unidos na Europa e é autorizado a viajar de ida e volta:

FROM - De - Von - De	TO - a - Nach - Para
MORON AB, SPAIN	AMERICAN EMBASSY-FRANCE AMERICAN EMBASSY-GERMANY

I HEREBY CERTIFY THAT THIS INDIVIDUAL IS A MEMBER OF THE FORCE INDICATED ABOVE AND THAT HE/SHE IS ON AUTHORIZED LEAVE OR PASS.

Je certifie que cette personne appartient aux forces militaires indiquées ci-dessus et qu'il/elle est en permission officielle.

Hiermit bestätige ich, dass die Betreffende Person der Obengenannten Militäreinheit angehört und sich auf ordnungsgemässem Urlaub befindet.

Eu certifico que o acima citado é um membro das forças aéreas dos Estados Unidos da America do Norte, e que ele/ela esta de licença autorizada.

ISSUED AT: Delivré à Ausgestellt in Emitido em	Moron Air Base, Spain	THIS le am Aos	14th	DAY OF Jour de Tag von Dia de	April 1966

UNIT STAMP - Sceau de l'organisation der Einheit - Selo da unidade	COMMANDING OFFICER OR OFFICER IN CHARGE le Commandant Kommandeur oder dienstleitender Offizier Comandante encarregado
OFFICIAL	JOHN A BURKE, Capt, USAF

IDENTIFICATION CARD MUST BE CARRIED BY BEARER	UNIT OR ESTABLISHMENT - Organisation - Dienststelle oder Einheit - Unidade
La carte d'identité des Forces Armées des Etats-Unis d'Amérique doit être en possession du porteur. Dienstkennkarte muss mitgeführt werden. A carta de identificaçao militar deve de ser trazida pelo possuidor.	Commander 3973 Operations Squadron US Forces, APO 09282

USAFE FORM 80 LRA REPLACES USAFE FORM 450, 25 OCT 54, WHICH IS OBSOLETE
OCT 62

PERSONNEL ACTION REQUEST	DATE 15 Apr 66	ORGANIZATION AND LOCATION 2188 Comm Sq Moron AB, Spain

LAST NAME - FIRST NAME - MIDDLE INITIAL
MERCURE, MAURICE F.

TO: SPANISH COMM RGN (CBPO-ASGMTS)
Torrejon AB, Spain

GRADE MSGT   AFSN AF▮▮▮▮▮▮

FROM: 2188 Comm Sq (CR)
Moron AB, Spain

PERSONNEL ACTION NR
1853

SECTION I — REQUESTED ACTION

☐ AWARD AFSC _____ AS _____ AFSC
☐ CHANGE PAFSC FROM _____ TO _____
☐ CHANGE CAFSC FROM _____ TO _____
☐ CHANGE FLYING STATUS CODE TO _____
☑ CHANGE FUNCTIONAL CATEGORY TO 20
☑ CHANGE/ANNOUNCE (ODSD) (DEROS) TO Sep 68
☐ CHANGE AD SVC COMMITMENT TO _____
☑ ASSIGN RATED POSITION IDENTIFIER _____
☑ ASSIGN FUNCTIONAL ACCOUNT CODE 3144
☐ ASSIGN PRO PAY RATING _____ AFSC _____
☑ EFFECTIVE 29170
☑ ASSIGN DAFSC 29170   DUTY TITLE NCOIC, Operations Branch

☐ WITHDRAW AFSC _____
☐ WITHDRAW PRO PAY RATING _____ AFSC _____
   EFFECTIVE _____
☐ OJT: EFFECTIVE _____
   ☐ ENTER AFSC _____ CODE _____
   ☐ CONTINUE AFSC _____ CODE _____
   ☐ WITHDRAW AFSC _____ CODE _____
   ☐ COMPLETED AFSC _____ CODE _____
☑ ASSIGN PROGRAM ELEMENT CODE 740
☐ ADJUST DOS TO _____
☐ ADJUST (TAFMSD) (PAY DATE) TO _____ EFFECTIVE 15 Apr 66

☑ RPTG OFFL IS Major Nelson D. Cournoyer AND FOR MSgt Harry D. Smith, TSgt Richard O. Burton, SSgt Wilbert L. Bailey, SSgt Herbert H. Smith, Jr., SSgt James C. Boggs

☐ OTHER _____
☑ AUTHORITY _____

TYPED NAME, GRADE AND POSITION TITLE
NELSON D. COURNOYER, MAJ, USAF, Commander

SIGNATURE OF SUPERVISOR REQUESTING OFFICIAL

SECTION II — CONCURRENCE

I ☐ DO   ☐ DO NOT   CONCUR

SIGNATURE OF INDIVIDUAL CONCERNED

SECTION III — DUTY STATUS CHANGE

CHANGE DUTY STATUS FROM _____ TO _____
EFFECTIVE _____ HOURS 19 LOCATION: _____

SECTION IV — ASSIGNMENT ACTION

EDCSA _____ ASSIGNMENT ACTION NUMBER _____ REPT NLT _____
ASSIGN FROM _____ TO _____

SECTION V — APPROVAL BY COMMANDER OR AUTHORIZED REPRESENTATIVE

DATE 27 Apr 66

COMMANDER — TYPED NAME, GRADE AND POSITION TITLE
NELSON D. COURNOYER, MAJOR, USAF

SIGNATURE

SECTION VI — ACTION BY CBPO OFFICER

DATE 2 May 66

☑ APPROVED   ☐ DISAPPROVED   ☐ BOARD ACTION REQUIRED

HEADQUARTERS
SPANISH COMM RGN
Torrejon AB, Spain
SIGNATURE

FOR THE COMMANDER — TYPED NAME, GRADE AND POSITION TITLE
EMIL A. BOKONY, CMSGT, USAF PERS SGT MAJ

THIS AUTHORIZATION REMAINS IN EFFECT AFTER AIRMAN'S DISCHARGE AND IMMEDIATE REENLISTMENT AT THE SAME STATION, PROVIDED THAT HE HAS NO BREAK IN MILITARY SERVICE.

SECTION VII — REMARKS

INDIVIDUAL COPY

SECTION VIII — CBPO COORDINATION RECORD

ADM	ASGNTS	C&T	OJT	FT	R&S	SA	PER	RP
OR	AR	I & OP	MA	MR	MP	CM	PA	

AF FORM 1098
MAY 65

PREVIOUS EDITION OF THIS FORM IS OBSOLETE.

Standard Form 513
Rev. August 1954
Bureau of the Budget
Circular A-32

C-43 - GPO - 16-77350-1

CLINICAL RECORD	CONSULTATION SHEET

REQUEST

TO: Orthopedic Clinic	FROM: (Requesting ward, unit, or activity) AFG #2	DATE OF REQUEST 21 Mar 66

REASON FOR REQUEST (Complaints and findings)

37 year old MSgt in today for Army Warrant Officer Program physical examination. History reveals cervical arthritis which is disqualifying even for enlisted service. Examinee wore a cervical collar for 4 months for this condition while stationed at Dow AFB, Maine 1965. Please evaluate and forward your opinion as to his condition.

PROVISIONAL DIAGNOSIS

Hx of cervical arthritis.

DOCTOR'S SIGNATURE s/ PHIL COLLINS s/ PHIL COLLINS CAPT USAF MC FMO	APPROVED	PLACE OF CONSULTATION ☐ BEDSIDE ☒ ON CALL	☐ EMERGENCY ☒ ROUTINE

CONSULTATION REPORT

37 year old MSgt without any symptoms whatsoever who desires to train for USA warrant officer program. Review of records reveals that he had some hyperthesia left arm and left neck following whiplash type injury several years ago. No longer present, cervical collar helped a great deal.

Physical: No motor, sensory or vascular abnormality of upper extremities.

X-ray: Cervical Spine: no evidence of foraminal compression on left side. No other evidence of osteoarthritis.

Impression: I see no reason why he should not qualify for his warrant officer program.

"THIS IS A TRUE COPY"

PHIL COLLINS CAPT MC FMO USAF

(Continued on reverse side)

SIGNATURE AND TITLE s/ J.G. BROWN CAPT MC USAF 9486	DATE 28 Apr 66	IDENTIFICATION NO. AF██████	ORGANIZATION 39773 Cpns Sq	

PATIENT'S IDENTIFICATION (For typed or written entries give: Name—last, first, middle; grade; date; hospital or medical facility)

MERCURE, Maurice F.
MSgt 21 Mar 66
870 Medical Group(SAC) APO New York 09282

REGISTER NO.	WARD NO. FMO

CONSULTATION SHEET
Standard Form 513
513-104

I. IDENTIFICATION DATA

1. NAME (SEE AFM 39-62 FOR INSTRUCTIONS)

2. MAJOR AIR COMMAND OF ASSIGNMENT

USAFE ☐ USAFSC ☐ USAFSS ☐ OTHER ☐
MATS ☐ PACAF ☐ SAC ☐ TAC ☐
AAC ☐ ATC ☐ AU ☐ CONAC ☐ NORAD ☐
AFLOG ☐ AFCS ☐ AFLC ☐ AFSC ☐
ACIC ☐ ADC ☐ AFA ☐

6. PERIOD ENDING — YR. / MONTH / DAY

5. CMSGT / SMSGT / CAFSC

3. GRADE: MSGT

4. AFSN

NAME OF RATEE	LAST NAME	FIRST NAME	MIDDLE INITIAL	
	Mercure	Maurice	F.	GRADE: MSgt

II. PERSONAL QUALITIES

1. WRITING ABILITY AND ORAL EXPRESSION — THE ABILITY OF THIS NCO TO COMMUNICATE HIS IDEAS IN: 1. WRITING (W) AND 2. SPEECH (S).

(W) REPORTING OFFICIAL: LOWEST 10% ... HIGHEST 10%
(W) INDORSING OFFICIAL: LOWEST 10% ... HIGHEST 10

(S) REPORTING OFFICIAL:
(S) INDORSING OFFICIAL:

2. HUMAN RELATIONS — THE DEGREE TO WHICH THE RATEE PROMOTES HARMONIOUS RELATIONSHIPS WITH BOTH SUPERIORS AND SUBORDINATES:

REPORTING OFFICIAL: LOWEST 10% ... HIGHEST 10%
INDORSING OFFICIAL: LOWEST 10% ... HIGHEST 10

3. PERFORMANCE OF DUTIES — THE DEGREE OF ACCEPTABILITY OF THE WORK OF THE RATEE.

REPORTING OFFICIAL: LOWEST 10% ... HIGHEST 10%
INDORSING OFFICIAL: LOWEST 10% ... HIGHEST 10

4. EVALUATION ABILITY — HOW CONSCIENTIOUS IS HE IN FULFILLING HIS DUTIES AS A REPORTING AND/OR INDORSING OFFICIAL?

☐ HAS NOT ACTED AS A RATING OFFICIAL DURING THIS REPORTING PERIOD.

REPORTING OFFICIAL: LOWEST 10% ... HIGHEST 10%
INDORSING OFFICIAL: LOWEST 10% ... HIGHEST 10

5. EXECUTIVE ABILITY — THE EXTENT TO WHICH THE RATEE COMBINES LEADERSHIP, JUDGMENT, PLANNING, MANAGEMENT AND COST CONSIDERATIONS TO GET MAXIMUM EFFECTIVENESS FROM THE RESOURCES UNDER HIS CONTROL.

REPORTING OFFICIAL: LOWEST 10% ... HIGHEST 10%
INDORSING OFFICIAL: LOWEST 10% ... HIGHEST 10

III. MILITARY QUALITIES

THE EXTENT TO WHICH HE MEETS STANDARDS OF BEARING, DRESS AND COURTESY, AND ENHANCES THE IMAGE OF THE AIR FORCE NCO.

REPORTING OFFICIAL: LOWEST 10% ... HIGHEST 10%
INDORSING OFFICIAL: LOWEST 10% ... HIGHEST 10

IV. OVERALL EVALUATION

THE RELATIVE VALUE OF THE RATEE TO THE AIR FORCE WHEN COMPARED WITH OTHER NONCOMMISSIONED OFFICERS OF HIS GRADE AND AFS.

REPORTING OFFICIAL: LOWEST 10% ... HIGHEST 10%
INDORSING OFFICIAL: LOWEST 10% ... HIGHEST 10

B762a AF FORM 911 JUN 64 REPLACES AF FORM 75, JUN 63, WHICH IS OBSOLETE.

1. LAST NAME—FIRST NAME—MIDDLE INITIAL	2. AFSN	3. GRADE	4. DATE OF GRADE
Mercure, Maurice F.	AF▄▄▄▄▄	MSgt	1 Dec 64

5. ORGANIZATION, COMMAND AND LOCATION	6. RESERVE WARRANT OR COMMISSION AND AFSN	7. REASON FOR REPORT
3973 Operations Squadron Moron Air Base, Spain (SAC)	None	Change of Reporting Offici

8. PERIOD OF SUPERVISION	9. PERIOD OF REPORT	
206	FROM: 1 Sep 65	THRU: 14 Apr 66

VI. DUTIES

				UMD POSITION OCCUPIED	
PAFSC	DAFSC	CAFSC	NO. OF PERSONNEL SUPERVISED	AUTHORIZED GRADE	AUTHORIZED AFSC
29170	29170	29170	5	TSgt	29170

Current Duty: NCOIC, Operations Branch. Responsible to the OIC for the efficient operation o teletype, crypto and telephone operations at Moron Air Base and for telephone operations at San Pablo Air Base. Responsible for supervision of the traffic analysis clerk and the chief clerk of the Comm-Elect Division.

VII. COMMENTS OF REPORTING OFFICIAL (Be factual and specific. Add any comments which increase the objectivity of the rating.)

FACTS AND SPECIFIC ACHIEVEMENTS: Sergeant Mercure is a capable individual. He has performed all duties with rigorous dispatch during this reporting period. Sergeant Mercure's backgrou in the communications operations career field has enabled him to excell at planning and coor- dinating in the various sections of communications operations; under his guidance the telety crypto, telephone and traffic analysis sections have reached peak efficiency. His ability to comprehend, retain, and apply knowledge of communications operations principles is far above average. STRENGTHS: Sergeant Mercure is completely loyal to the mission and excells in job accomplishment. His general attitude is that of a professional airman of long standing. ED- UCATIONAL AND TRAINING ACCOMPLISHMENTS: Sergeant Mercure has successfully completed the 16A Mandatory Spanish Language course and has been awarded the SAC Educational Achievement Award. He has improved his telecommunications skills by active participation in correspondence cour offered by USAFI, ECI as well as by courses offered by the US Marine Corps.

VIII. REPORTING OFFICIAL

NAME, GRADE, AND ORGANIZATION	DUTY TITLE	SIGNATURE
JOHN C. TIFFANY, Capt., USAF 3973 Operations Squadron (SAC)	CHIEF OF MAINTENANCE	DATE 6 May 66

IX. REVIEW BY INDORSING OFFICIAL:

Under Sergeant Mercure's leadership, the telecommunication branch has maintained a foremost position in competition with all the other stations in the AIRCOM relay center located at San Pablo AB. My rating in Section IV has been affirmed by hi acceptance into the U.S. Army Warrant Officer program by a board of Army officers.

NAME, GRADE, AND ORGANIZATION	DUTY TITLE	SIGNATURE
NELSON D. COURNOYER, Major, USAF 2188 Communications Sq (AFCS)	COMMANDER	Nelson D. Cournoyer DATE 11 MAY 66

X. REVIEW BY OFFICER IN CHARGE:
☐ I CONCUR WITH REPORTING OFFICIAL   ☐ I CONCUR WITH INDORSING OFFICIAL
☐ I DO NOT CONCUR.

Not required OIC is the Indorsing official.

NAME, GRADE, AND ORGANIZATION	DUTY TITLE	SIGNATURE
		DATE

B102b

PERSONNEL ACTION REQUEST	DATE 24 May 66	ORGANIZATION AND LOCATION 2188 Comm Sq Moron AB, Spain

LAST NAME - FIRST NAME - MIDDLE INITIAL	GRADE	AFSN	PERSONNEL ACTION NR
MERCIER, MAURICE F.	MSGT	AF▓▓▓	1681

TO: SPANISH COMM RGN (CBPO-ASGMT)
Torrejon AB, Spain

FROM: 2188 Comm Sq (OL)
Moron AB, Spain

SECTION I — REQUESTED ACTION

- [ ] AWARD AFSC _____ AS _____ AFSC
- [ ] CHANGE PAFSC FROM _____ TO _____
- [ ] CHANGE CAFSC FROM _____ TO _____
- [ ] CHANGE FLYING STATUS CODE TO _____
- [ ] CHANGE FUNCTIONAL CATEGORY TO _____
- [ ] CHANGE/ANNOUNCE (ODSD) (DEROS) TO _____
- [ ] CHANGE AD SVC COMMITMENT TO _____
- [ ] ASSIGN RATED POSITION IDENTIFIER _____
- [ ] ASSIGN FUNCTIONAL ACCOUNT CODE _____
- [ ] ASSIGN PRO PAY RATING _____ AFSC _____
- EFFECTIVE _____
- [ ] WITHDRAW AFSC _____
- [ ] WITHDRAW PRO PAY RATING _____ AFSC _____
- EFFECTIVE _____
- [ ] OJT: EFFECTIVE _____
  - [ ] ENTER AFSC _____ CODE _____
  - [ ] CONTINUE AFSC _____ CODE _____
  - [ ] WITHDRAW AFSC _____ CODE _____
  - [ ] COMPLETED AFSC _____ CODE _____
- [ ] ASSIGN PROGRAM ELEMENT CODE _____
- [ ] ADJUST DOS TO _____
- [ ] ADJUST (TAFMSD) (PAY DATE) TO _____

[X] ▓▓▓▓▓ DUTY TITLE Radio Telecommunications Operations Sup EFFECTIVE 28 Apr 66

[X] RPTG OFFL IS Major Nelson D. Commander AND FOR MSgt Harry D. Smith, TSgt Richard G. Barton, SSgt Wilbert L. Bailey, SSgt Herbert H. Smith, Jr., (See Remarks)

- [ ] OTHER _____
- [ ] AUTHORITY

TYPED NAME, GRADE AND POSITION TITLE	SIGNATURE OF SUPERVISOR/REQUESTING OFFICIAL
NELSON D. COMMANDER, Maj, USAF, Commander	/s/ Nelson D. Commander

SECTION II — CONCURRENCE

I [ ] DO   [ ] DO NOT   CONCUR

SIGNATURE OF INDIVIDUAL CONCERNED

SECTION III — DUTY STATUS CHANGE

CHANGE DUTY STATUS FROM _____ TO _____
EFFECTIVE _____ HOURS, 19 ___ LOCATION: _____

SECTION IV — ASSIGNMENT ACTION

EDCSA _____ ASSIGNMENT ACTION NUMBER _____ REPT NLT _____
ASSIGN FROM _____ TO _____

SECTION V — APPROVAL BY COMMANDER OR AUTHORIZED REPRESENTATIVE

DATE 2 MAY 66

	TYPED NAME, GRADE AND POSITION TITLE	SIGNATURE
FOR THE COMMANDER	NELSON D. COMMANDER, MAJOR, USAF	/s/ Nelson D. Commander

SECTION VI — ACTION BY CBPO OFFICER

DATE 3 Jul 66

[X] APPROVED   [ ] DISAPPROVED   [ ] BOARD ACTION REQUIRED

HEADQUARTERS Spain Comm Rgn

FOR THE COMMANDER	TYPED NAME, GRADE AND POSITION TITLE	SIGNATURE
	▓▓▓ A ▓▓▓▓ ▓▓▓▓ USAF Pers Sgt Major	/s/ Emil A. Bohon

THIS AUTHORIZATION REMAINS IN EFFECT AFTER AIRMAN'S DISCHARGE AND IMMEDIATE REENLISTMENT AT THE SAME STATION, PROVIDED THAT HE HAS NO BREAK IN MILITARY SERVICE.

SECTION VII — REMARKS

RPTG OFFL (cont) SSgt James C. Boggs, SSgt Rudolf J. Langheiser, SSgt James A. Miller, SSgt Charles D. Wilson, SSgt Mark L. Woods

SECTION VIII — CBPO COORDINATION RECORD

ADM	ASGMTS	C&T	OJT	FT	R&S	SA	ER/RR	RP
OR	AR	I & OP	MA	MR	MP	CM	PA	

AF FORM 1098
MAY 65

PREVIOUS EDITION OF THIS FORM IS OBSOLETE.

PERSONNEL ACTION REQUEST	DATE 20 Jul 66	ORGANIZATION AND LOCATION 2156 Comm Sq (AFCS) Moron AB, Spain

LAST NAME - FIRST NAME - MIDDLE INITIAL MERCURE, MAURICE F.	GRADE MSGT	AFSN ██████	PERSONNEL ACTION NR 2317

TO: Spanish Comm Rgn (CBPO), Torrejon AB, Spain   **FROM:** 2156 Comm Sq (AFCS), Moron AB, Spain

SECTION I — REQUESTED ACTION

- ☐ AWARD AFSC _____ AS _____ AFSC
- ☐ CHANGE PAFSC FROM _____ TO _____
- ☐ CHANGE CAFSC FROM _____ TO _____
- ☐ CHANGE FLYING STATUS CODE TO _____
- ☐ CHANGE FUNCTIONAL CATEGORY TO _____
- ☐ CHANGE/ANNOUNCE (ODSD) (DEROS) TO _____
- ☐ CHANGE AD SVC COMMITMENT TO _____
- ☐ ASSIGN RATED POSITION IDENTIFIER _____
- ☐ ASSIGN FUNCTIONAL ACCOUNT CODE _____
- ☐ ASSIGN PRO PAY RATING _____ AFSC _____
- EFFECTIVE _____
- ☐ ASSIGN DAFSC _____ DUTY TITLE _____
- ☒ RPTG OFFL IS 1stLt J.T. Baker _____ AND FOR _____
- ☒ OTHER Effective: 18 Jul 66
- ☐ AUTHORITY

- ☐ WITHDRAW AFSC _____
- ☐ WITHDRAW PRO PAY RATING _____ AFSC _____
- EFFECTIVE _____
- ☐ OJT: EFFECTIVE _____
  - ☐ ENTER AFSC _____ CODE _____
  - ☐ CONTINUE AFSC _____ CODE _____
  - ☐ WITHDRAW AFSC _____ CODE _____
  - ☐ COMPLETED AFSC _____ CODE _____
- ☐ ASSIGN PROGRAM ELEMENT CODE _____
- ☐ ADJUST DOS TO _____
- ☐ ADJUST (TAFMSD) (PAY DATE) TO _____ EFFECTIVE _____

TYPED NAME, GRADE AND POSITION TITLE JAMES T. BAKER, 1stLt, TeleComm Officer	SIGNATURE OF SUPERVISOR/REQUESTING OFFICIAL *James T. Baker*

SECTION II — CONCURRENCE

I ☐ DO   ☐ DO NOT   CONCUR

SIGNATURE OF INDIVIDUAL CONCERNED

SECTION III — DUTY STATUS CHANGE

CHANGE DUTY STATUS FROM _____ TO _____
EFFECTIVE _____ HOURS, 19 _____ LOCATION: _____

SECTION IV — ASSIGNMENT ACTION

EDCSA _____ ASSIGNMENT ACTION NUMBER _____ REPT NLT _____
ASSIGN FROM _____ TO _____

SECTION V — APPROVAL BY COMMANDER OR AUTHORIZED REPRESENTATIVE

DATE 20 Jul 66

FOR THE COMMANDER	TYPED NAME, GRADE AND POSITION TITLE NELSON D. COURMEYER, Major, USAF	SIGNATURE *Nelson D. Courmeyer*

SECTION VI — ACTION BY CBPO OFFICER

☐ APPROVED   ☐ DISAPPROVED   ☐ BOARD ACTION REQUIRED   HEADQUARTERS

DATE

FOR THE COMMANDER	TYPED NAME, GRADE AND POSITION TITLE	SIGNATURE

THIS AUTHORIZATION REMAINS IN EFFECT AFTER AIRMAN'S DISCHARGE AND IMMEDIATE REENLISTMENT AT THE SAME STATION, PROVIDED THAT HE HAS NO BREAK IN MILITARY SERVICE.

SECTION VII — REMARKS

SECTION VIII — CBPO COORDINATION RECORD

ADM	ASGMTS	C&T	OJT	FT	R&S	SA	ER/PR	RP
OR	AR	I & OP	MA	MR	MP	CM	PA	

AF FORM 1098
MAY 65

PREVIOUS EDITION OF THIS FORM IS OBSOLETE.

INDIVIDUAL CO

DATE ENTERED AF	5 Oct 46
SEX	M
AFSC-A	29172
AFSC-P	29170
AFSC-D	29120
DY PHONE	2637
ORGANIZATION	2188 Co.
	P.O.Box 7107 APO 283
AFSN	
RANK	MSgt

MERWINE, Maurice F.
LAST NAME - FIRST NAME - MIDDLE INITIAL

11. ADDRESS (Permanent mailing)	12. DATE OF BIRTH	13. DATE FORM INITIATED	14. LAST CIVILIAN SCHOOL ATTENDED	15. DATES
#26 Mayfair Trailer Ct. 211 Cordele Rd., Albany, Ga.	14 Aug	23 Feb 66	H.B.Lawrence Jr.High Holyoke, Mass.	Sep 41 - Jun 44

16. EDUCATION LEVEL (X NUMBER PRIOR TO SERVICE, CIRCLE NUMBER SERVICE ACCOMPLISHED)

8 X 9 10 11 (12) 13 14 15 16 17 18 19 20

17. AF EDUCATION SERVICES PROGRAM ACHIEVEMENT (Give dates)

PASSED HS GED TEST	HS DIPLOMA OR CERTIFICATE	PASSED USAFI COLLEGE TEST	BACCALAUREATE DEGREE	MASTER'S DEGREE	DOCTORATE DEGREE
Sep 1951 EglinAFB,Fla.	1952 Massachusetts				

18. TESTS TAKEN IN AF EDUCATION SERVICES PROGRAM

a. HS GED TESTS / b. USAFI COLLEGE TEST

DATE TAKEN	FORM	PART	STANDARD SCORE	DATE TAKEN	FORM	PART	STANDARD SCORE
Sep 51		1	41				
		2	63				
		3	59				
		4	56				
		5	40				

c. RETEST / d. RETEST

e. LANGUAGE PROFICIENCY TEST

LANGUAGE	DATE TAKEN	RAW SCORE	SPEAKING LEVEL	READING LEVEL

f. OTHER TESTS

TYPE	TITLE	FORM	DATE TAKEN	GRADE

19. COUNSELING INTERVIEWS

DATE	COUNSELOR	LOCATION (AFB)	RESULTS
23 Feb 66	S. Davis	Moron AB, Spain	Form 186 reaccomplished
May 66	C. White	Moron AB, Spain	Contacted for enrollment in U of Md. term 5
27 Jun 66	S. Davis	Moron AB, Spain	Counselled of benefits of new GI Bill.

AF FORM 186   PREVIOUS EDITION OF THIS FORM WILL   INDIVIDUAL RECORD EDUCATION SERVICES PROGRAM

20. ACADEMIC GOALS		21. IVOCATIONAL GOALS	
a. IMMEDIATE	b. FUTURE	a. PRIMARY	b. SECONDARY

22. COURSES TAKEN IN AIR FORCE EDUCATION SERVICES PROGRAM

a. COLLEGE CORE CURRICULUM - PHASE I, II, III

TYPE	NO.	TITLE OF COURSE	SCHOOL OR AFB	DATE ENROLLED	DATE COMPLETED	GRADE OR RE-SULT	SEM OR QTR HRS	INI-TIALS OF ED. OFFICER	
BRC	5	History of the US Before1865	Univ of Mary, UpperHeyford,Eng	Jun 52	Aug 52	B	3	RLO	
BRC	1	Introduction to Psychology	" " "	Nov 52	Jan 53	WX	-	RLO	
BRC	6	Hist of the US After 1865	" " "	Jan 53	Apr 53	B	3	RLO	6
BRC	31	Economics	" " "	Jan 53	Mar 53	D	3	RLO	9
BRC	1	English Composition 1	Univ of Maine,Dow	Feb 64	May 64	C	3	RLO	1
BRC	0545	Office Management	Dow AFB, Maine	Jun 64	Mar 65	Unsat	-	RLO	
BRC	1	Spanish 1	MoronAB, Spain	7 Feb 66	25 Mar 66	C	3	SD	1
BRC	Spel	Speech 1-Public Speaking	UofMd,MoronAB,Sp.	6 Jun 66	29 Jul 66	B	3	GO	1

b. OTHER COURSES

ECI	2935	Comm Center Specialist	KirtlandAFB,N.M.	Feb 60	Jul 60	Sat	47	RLO	4
ECI	0005	Leadership & Pers. Mgt	" " "	Jul 60	NA	DENR	-	RLO	
Army	5(10-1)	Basic Cryptography	" " "	Aug 60	Jul 61	Superior	3	RLO	5
Army	Sc17	Signal Unit Supply	" " "	Aug 60	Nov 61	Superior	7	RLO	5
Army	Sc 1	Tng & Methods of Instruct.	" " "	Aug 60	Aug 62	Superior	7	RLO	6
USAFI	C781	Fund of Electricity	Taipei,Formosa	Mar 62	NA	DENR	-	RLO	
ECI	3008	Comm Officer	"	Sep 62	31 Aug 65	Sat	4.6	AGM	13
MCI	25.8	Basic Message Center Man	Dow AFB, Maine	May 63	Sep 63	Sat(B)	1.0	RLO	28
Army		NCO Ldsp & Car. Dev. Crse	" " "	Aug 63	Aug 64	DENR		CW	29

23. REMARKS

Army	A 18	Comm Center Operation	" " "	Aug 63	Nov 63	Superior	4	RLO	29
Army	980	Spec Ext Crs for CommSecCk	" " "	Sep 63	Oct 64	DENR		CW	
MCI	25113	Comm Cent Inst. & Mgt	" " "	Sep 63	Feb 64	Sat(A)	.6	RLO	30
MCI	25.11	Teletype Operator	" " "	Nov 63	Apr 64	Sat(A)	.6	RLO	30
Army	MOS713	Legal Clerk	" " "	Nov 63	NA	DENR	-	CW	
MCI	25.1	Basic Wire Communications	" " "	Dec 63	Apr 64	Sat(A)	.5	RLO	31
MCI	25.3a	Bas Radio & Vis Comm Proc	# " "	Mar 64	Jun 64	SAT(B)	.4	RLO	31
USAFI	D164	Beginning Algebra 1	" " "	May 64	NA	DENR	-	CW	
MCI	25.6	Comm in the Mar Acft Wg	" " "	May 64	Jun 64	Sat	-	RLO	

Educational Achievement AWARD POINTS:_____

B105b

20. ACADEMIC GOALS		21. VOCATIONAL GOALS	
a. IMMEDIATE	b. FUTURE	a. PRIMARY	b. SECONDARY

22. COURSES TAKEN IN AIR FORCE EDUCATION SERVICES PROGRAM

a. COLLEGE CORE CURRICULUM - PHASE I, II, III

TYPE	NO.	TITLE OF COURSE	SCHOOL OR AFB	DATE ENROLLED	DATE COMPLETED	GRADE OR RESULT	SEM OR QTR HRS	INITIALS OF ED. OFFICER

b. OTHER COURSES

TYPE	NO.	TITLE OF COURSE	SCHOOL OR AFB	ENROLLED	COMPLETED	GRADE OR RESULT	SEM OR QTR HRS	INITIALS OF ED. OFFICER
MCI	25.4a	Staff Func Combat Orders	Dow AFB, Maine	Apr 64	Feb 65	Sat(A)	—	RLO
MCI	25.10	Communications Employment	" " "	Aug 64	Feb 65	Sat(B)	—	RLO
MCI	0313a	The Marine NCO	" " "	Nov 64	Mar 65	Sat(B)	—	RLO
MCI	25.14	Radio Rel.Fund & Operation	" " "	Feb 65	14 Jan 66	Sat(B)	—	CW
Army	C-13	Comm Center Fund	" " "	May 65	20 Oct 65	Superior		RLO
Army	100	Mathematics (SignalCorp)	MoronAB, Spain	Dec 65				
Army	101	Electrical Fund(SignalCorp)	" " "	Dec 65				
MCI	3100	Off.Basic Ext. Course	Dow AFB, Main	Aug 65				
ECI	0006	Mgt for AF Supv	MoronAB, Spain	21 Jan 66				

23. REMARKS

28 Mar 66 - SAC Award rec&d & issued (31.8 pts)

USAFE
Educational
Achievement AWARD POINTS: _3.0_

I. IDENTIFICATION DATA

NAME (SEE AFM 39—62 FOR INSTRUCTIONS)

2. MAJOR AIR COMMAND OF ASSIGNMENT

AAC	AFAFC
ACIC	AFLC
ADC	AFSC
AFA	

ATC	AU
MATS	PACAF
CONAC	SAC
NORAD	TAC

USAFE	USAFSO	USAFSS	OTHER

3. GRADE:
4. AFSN:
5. CAFSC
6. PERIOD ENDING

DAY	MONTH	YR.

NAME OF RATEE	LAST NAME	FIRST NAME	MIDDLE INITIAL	
	MERCURE	MAURICE	F.	GRADE: MSgt

II. PERSONAL QUALITIES

1. WRITING ABILITY AND ORAL EXPRESSION
THE ABILITY OF THIS NCO TO COMMUNICATE HIS IDEAS IN: 1. WRITING (W) AND 2. SPEECH (S).

(W) REPORTING OFFICIAL: LOWEST 10%   HIGHEST 10%

(W) INDORSING OFFICIAL: LOWEST 10%   HIGHEST 10%

(S) REPORTING OFFICIAL:

(S) INDORSING OFFICIAL:

2. HUMAN RELATIONS
THE DEGREE TO WHICH THE RATEE PROMOTES HARMONIOUS RELATIONSHIPS WITH BOTH SUPERIORS AND SUBORDINATES.

REPORTING OFFICIAL: LOWEST 10%   HIGHEST 10%

INDORSING OFFICIAL: LOWEST 10%   HIGHEST 10%

3. PERFORMANCE OF DUTIES
THE DEGREE OF ACCEPTABILITY OF THE WORK OF THE RATEE.

REPORTING OFFICIAL: LOWEST 10%   HIGHEST 10%

INDORSING OFFICIAL: LOWEST 10%   HIGHEST 10%

4. EVALUATION ABILITY
HOW CONSCIENTIOUS IS HE IN FULFILLING HIS DUTIES AS A REPORTING AND/OR INDORSING OFFICIAL?

☐ HAS NOT ACTED AS A RATING OFFICIAL DURING THIS REPORTING PERIOD.

REPORTING OFFICIAL: LOWEST 10%   HIGHEST 10%

INDORSING OFFICIAL: LOWEST 10%   HIGHEST 10%

5. EXECUTIVE ABILITY
THE EXTENT TO WHICH THE RATEE COMBINES LEADERSHIP, JUDGMENT, PLANNING, MANAGEMENT AND COST CONSIDERATIONS TO GET MAXIMUM EFFECTIVENESS FROM THE RESOURCES UNDER HIS CONTROL.

REPORTING OFFICIAL: LOWEST 10%   HIGHEST 10%

INDORSING OFFICIAL: LOWEST 10%   HIGHEST 10%

III. MILITARY QUALITIES

THE EXTENT TO WHICH HE MEETS STANDARDS OF BEARING, DRESS AND COURTESY, AND ENHANCES THE IMAGE OF THE AIR FORCE NCO.

REPORTING OFFICIAL: LOWEST 10%   HIGHEST 10%

INDORSING OFFICIAL: LOWEST 10%   HIGHEST 10%

IV. OVERALL EVALUATION

THE RELATIVE VALUE OF THE RATEE TO THE AIR FORCE WHEN COMPARED WITH OTHER NONCOMMISSIONED OFFICERS OF HIS GRADE AND AFS.

REPORTING OFFICIAL: LOWEST 10%   HIGHEST 10%

INDORSING OFFICIAL: LOWEST 10%   HIGHEST 10%

AF FORM 911 JUN 64   REPLACES AF FORM 75, JUN 63, WHICH IS OBSOLETE.

B106a

V. ADDITIONAL IDENTIFICATION DATA

1. LAST NAME—FIRST NAME—MIDDLE INITIAL		2. AFSN	3. GRADE	4. DATE OF GRADE
MERCURE, MAURICE F.		AF████	MSgt	1 Dec 64

5. ORGANIZATION, COMMAND AND LOCATION	6. RESERVE WARRANT OR COMMISSION AND AFSN		7. REASON FOR REPORT
2188 Comm Sq (AFCS) Moron AB, Spain ███████	N/A		Change of Rptg Offl

	8. PERIOD OF SUPERVISION	9. PERIOD OF REPORT	
		FROM:	THRU:
	94	15 Apr 66	17 Jul 66

VI. DUTIES

				UMD POSITION OCCUPIED	
PAFSC	DAFSC	CAFSC	NO. OF PERSONNEL SUPERVISED	AUTHORIZED GRADE	AUTHORIZED AFSC
29170	29170	29170	9	TSgt	29170

Current Duty: NCOIC, Telecom Operations. Responsible to the OIC for the efficient operation of teletype, crypto, and telephone operations at Moron Air Base and for telephone operations at San Pablo Air Base.

VII. COMMENTS OF REPORTING OFFICIAL (Be factual and specific. Add any comments which increase the objectivity of the rating.)

FACTS AND SPECIFIC ACHIEVEMENTS: MSgt Mercure performed his duties as NCOIC of Telecommunications during a period when there was no commissioned officer assigned. With minimum supervision he directed his section in an outstanding manner during a time of change of command from SAC to USAFE. He also directed the operation of a telephone central office and communications sub-office forty miles distant at San Pablo AB. He used good management principles and techniques to excellent advantage during June 1966, the month in which we see the greatest rate of personnel coming in from and returning to the CONUS. His section won the AUTODIN TRIBUTARY STATION OF THE MONTH award for the fourth consecutive quarter during this reporting period. STRENGTHS: Sergeant Mercure has an outstanding knowledge of all matters dealing in communications center operations. EDUCATIONAL AND TRAINING ACCOMPLISHMENTS: MSgt Mercure successfully completed a University of Maryland Course on public speaking. OTHER COMMENTS: MSgt Mercure's preparation of the communications portion of the base budget exemplified the application of sound management control of Air Force monies.

VIII. REPORTING OFFICIAL

	DUTY TITLE	SIGNATURE Nelson D. Cournoyer
NAME, GRADE, AND ORGANIZATION NELSON D. COURNOYER, Major, USAF 2188 Comm Sq (AFCS)	Commander	DATE 28 JULY 1966

IX. REVIEW BY INDORSING OFFICIAL:

Concur. MSgt Mercure's performance has been exceptional during a period which demanded above normal performance of duties without benefit of direct officer supervision.

	DUTY TITLE	SIGNATURE Glenn E Fleming
NAME, GRADE, AND ORGANIZATION GLENN E FLEMING, Lt Col, FR37335, Spanish Comm Rgn (AFCS)	Vice Commander	DATE 16 August 1966

X. REVIEW BY OFFICER IN CHARGE: ☐ I CONCUR WITH REPORTING OFFICIAL. ☐ I CONCUR WITH INDORSING OFFICIAL.
☐ I DO NOT CONCUR.

Not Required, OIC is the Reporting Official.

NAME, GRADE, AND ORGANIZATION	DUTY TITLE	SIGNATURE
		DATE

B106b

APPLICATION FOR SHIPMENT OF HOUSEHOLD GOODS

22-98-22
MR. RUIZ

1. SHIP OR STATION	2. DATE	3. SHIPMENT NUMBER
Moran AB Spain	11 Aug at 66	

4. FROM: (Last Name - First Name - Middle Initial)	5. GRADE, RANK OR RATING	6. SERVICE NUMBER	7. OFFICIAL HOME (City & state)
MERCURE, MAURICE F.	MSGT	▉▉▉▉	

8. TO: (Submit to nearest shipping officer)

HQ Moran AB Spain

9. IT IS REQUESTED THAT ACTION BE TAKEN TO TRANSPORT APPROXIMATELY **2600** POUNDS OR _____ ROOMS OF HOUSEHOLD GOODS.

THIS SHIPMENT INCLUDES APPROXIMATELY _____ POUNDS OF PROFESSIONAL BOOKS, PAPERS AND EQUIPMENT.

10. THIS SHIPMENT IS REQUIRED INCIDENT TO ☐ PERMANENT ☐ TEMPORARY CHANGE OF STATION ORDERS

ISSUED BY DAF HQ TWP Quick Supp Gp APO NY 09283

UNDER DATE OF 11 Aug 66 PARAGRAPH NUMBER _____ ORDER NUMBER M-752

WHICH ORDERED ME TO DUTY AT Port from Public Quarters

11. TO BE SHIPPED FROM (Street address, city and state)	12. DATE INSPECTION MAY BE MADE	13. TELEPHONE NUMBER
In Kind		

14. TO BE SHIPPED TO (Street address, city and state)	15. AGENT DESIGNATED TO RECEIVE THE PROPERTY AT DESTINATION
In Kind	

16. MODE OF SHIPMENT REQUESTED (Check)	17. DATE SHIPMENT REQUIRED AT DESTINATION
☐ DESIGNATED BY PROPERTY OWNER (Specify) ☐ DESIGNATED BY SHIPPING OFFICER	

18. REQUESTED DATE OF PICK-UP	19. SHIPMENT INCLUDES (Check)
12 August 66	☐ AIR CONDITIONER ☐ CONSOLE RADIO ☐ DEEP FREEZE ☐ PIANO ☐ REFRIGERATOR ☐ STOVE ☐ TELEVISION ☐ WASHING MACHINE ☐ OTHER (Specify)

20.
a. I CERTIFY THAT THIS SHIPMENT CONSISTS OF PROPERTY WHICH WAS IN MY POSSESSION PRIOR TO THE EFFECTIVE DATE OF MY TRAVEL ORDERS.
b. IF MY ORDERS ARE MODIFIED OR CANCELLED AND AFFECT THIS SHIPMENT, I WILL IMMEDIATELY NOTIFY THE SHIPPING OFFICER AT POINT OF ORIGIN (Or port, if any) AND DESTINATION.
c. I WILL REMIT THE PROPER AMOUNT OR PERMIT THE APPLICATION OF AS MUCH OF MY PAY AS MAY BE NECESSARY TO COVER ALL EXCESS COST OCCASIONED BY THIS SHIPMENT.
d. I HAVE NOT AND WILL NOT MAKE CLAIM FOR THE TRAILER ALLOWANCE.

21. (CHECK WHEN APPLICABLE)
☐ THE PROFESSIONAL BOOKS, PAPERS AND EQUIPMENT ARE OR WERE NECESSARY IN THE PERFORMANCE OF MY OFFICIAL DUTIES

IT IS REQUESTED THAT MY HOUSEHOLD GOODS BE PLACED IN STORAGE AT ☐ ORIGIN ☐ DESTINATION

22. PREVIOUS SHIPMENTS UNDER IDENTICAL ORDERS (If none, indicate "None")

FROM	TO	BILL OF LADING, CONTRACT OR PURCHASE ORDER NO. (If known)	POUNDS HOUSEHOLD GOODS		POUNDS PROFESSIONAL BOOKS, PAPERS AND EQUIPMENT
			UNPACKED	PACKED	
a	b	c	d	e	f

23. SIGNATURE OF APPLICANT

Maurice F. Mercure

24. CERTIFICATE IN LIEU OF SIGNATURE ON THIS FORM IS REQUIRED WHEN REGULATIONS SO AUTHORIZE:
(To be accomplished only by the Commanding Officer or his authorized representative, by signature or official seal)

THE PROPERTY IS PERSONAL BAGGAGE, HOUSEHOLD GOODS, OR PROFESSIONAL BOOKS, PAPERS, AND EQUIPMENT AUTHORIZED TO BE SHIPPED AT GOVERNMENT EXPENSE.

REASON FOR NONAVAILABILITY OF SIGNATURE	CERTIFIED BY (Signature)
NECESSITY FOR SHIPMENT	TITLE

25. CERTIFICATE OF SHIPPING OFFICER

METHOD OF SHIPMENT DESIGNATED	BILL OF LADING NUMBER
METHOD OF SHIPMENT USED	CONTRACT NUMBER
EXCESS COST OF PACKING, CRATING, AND HAULING (When required by the service concerned)	PURCHASE ORDER NUMBER
$ ☐ GOVERNMENT ☐ COMMERCIAL	

POUNDS HOUSEHOLD GOODS	POUNDS PROFESSIONAL BOOKS, PAPERS, AND EQUIPMENT	SIGNATURE OF SHIPPING OFFICER
		VICTOR A. GAINER, 1LT USAF, IDO

DD FORM 1299
1 MAR 60

DEPARTMENT OF THE ARMY
OFFICE OF PERSONNEL OPERATIONS
FORT BENJAMIN HARRISON
INDIANAPOLIS, INDIANA 46249

IN REPLY REFER TO

RCAP (Addressee shown below)   23 September 1966

SUBJECT: Appointment as a Reserve Warrant Officer of the Army under Title 10, United
States Code, Section 591 and 597

THRU: A- USAR

TO: WO (W-1) Maurice Frank Mercure, W█████   B- 721A
        2188 Communications Squadron
        APO New York 09282
        (Now serving as MSG, AF█████)

    1. You are appointed as a Reserve warrant officer of the Army effective upon
your acceptance, in the grade and with the service number shown in address above.

    2. This appointment is for an indefinite term.

    3. Execute the inclosed form for oath of office and return promptly to this
headquarters, ATTN: RCAP. Your execution and return of the oath of office constitute
acceptance of your appointment. Prompt action is requested since cancellation of this
appointment is required if acceptance is not received within 90 days. Upon receipt of
the properly executed oath of office, a warrant (DD Form 1290) will be forwarded to
you. If you do not desire to accept the appointment, return this letter with your
statement of declination thereon.

    4. The component to which you will be assigned after your appointment becomes
effective is shown after A above. Your primary MOS is shown after B.

    5. After acceptance of this appointment, any change in your permanent home ad-
dress or a temporary change of address of more than 30 days duration will be reported
by you to the custodian of your military personnel records.

    6. Failure to comply with active duty orders will result in cancellation
of this appointment.

            BY ORDER OF THE SECRETARY OF THE ARMY:

1 Incl   AARON S. SADOVE
   DA Form 71   Colonel, USA
                                        Commanding Officer
                                        U.S. Army Reserve Components Personnel Center

OPO-RCPC FL 32
   1 Aug 66
            (OPO-RCPC FL 32, 1 Dec 64, is obsolete)

DEPARTMENT OF THE ARMY
OFFICE OF PERSONNEL OPERATIONS
FORT BENJAMIN HARRISON, INDIANA 46249

/jrk

RCPAP LETTER ORDER A-09-528

29 September 1966

SUBJECT: Active Duty

TO: Officer Concerned

TC 132. Under the provisions of title 10, U.S. Code subsection 672(d), the following individual, having been appointed a Reserve warrant officer of the Army, is ordered to ACTIVE DUTY with his consent effective on EDCSA and assigned as indicated. Officer will proceed from current location to duty station shown in sufficient time to report for duty on date specified. Permanent change of station (PCS). Travel as directed is necessary in the military service (TDN). Travel by privately owned conveyance, commercial aircraft, rail and/or bus authorized. Pamphlet - "Personal Property Shipping Information," is applicable (PPSIA). Provisions of AR 612-12, AR 612-35 or AR 55-46 as appropriate are applicable.

MERCURE, MAURICE F.   WO W-1   USAR   MOS: 721A

Assigned to: Headquarters, U.S. Army, Europe APO NY 09403

Allocation: FEB-67-547
Reporting date: 16 December 1966
Estimated date of rank: 25 November 1966
Home of Record: 293 Chestmit Street, Holyoke, Hampden County, Massachusetts 01040
Current AD SN, grade org/sta: AF ████████ MSG (E-7), USAF, 2188
                              Communications Sqdn, APO NY 09282
Security clearance: Clearance for access to classified information
                    and material to include CRYPTO is required.
                    Responsible commanders will comply with AR 604-5.
Leave data: 15 DDALV
Movement designator code: PCS (MDC): 4B
Active duty commitment: OBV-3 years
Procurement program number: W3
EDCSA: 25 November 1966
Effective date of active duty: 25 November 1966

RCPAP LETTER ORDER A-09-528
SUBJECT: Active Duty

29 September 1966

Accounting classification: 2172010 01-1131-1132-1133-1134-1135-1136-1137
P1411 S99-999

Special Instructions: NA

BY ORDER OF THE SECRETARY OF THE ARMY:

G. M. DANIEL
LTC, USA
Chief, Personnel Actions Div, USARCPC

DISTRIBUTION:
  Officer Concerned (60)
  CG First US Army (5)
  CINCUSAREUR APO
    New York 09403 (10)
  7th DPU (5)
  USADATCOM (2)
  Ch Sig Br OPD (2)
  USAFMPC Randolph AFB Tex (2)
  CO 2188 Comm Sqdn, APO NY 09282 (5)

DEPARTMENT OF THE ARMY
U.S. ARMY RESERVE COMPONENTS PERSONNEL CENTER
FORT BENJAMIN HARRISON
INDIANAPOLIS, INDIANA 46216

IN REPLY REFER TO

RCPAP MERCURE, Maurice F.   1 0 OCT 1966
W2 217 441

SUBJECT: Appointment and Concurrent Call to Active Duty

THRU: USAF Military Personnel Center
           AFPMPKE Building 499C
           Randolph AFB, Texas 78148

TO: Commanding Officer
           2188 Communications Squadron
           APO New York 09282

　　　1. MSG (E-7) Maurice F. Mercure, ██████████, 2188 Communications
Squadron, APO New York 09282, has been approved for appointment and call
to active duty as a Reserve warrant officer of the Army in the grade of
Warrant Officer, W-1, USAR.

　　　2. Letter of appointment and copies of active duty orders are inclosed for transmittal to appointee. Request action be taken to discharge
MSG Mercure from his present status effective 24 November 1966 to preclude
a break in service. Oath of office accepting appointment in the Army
Reserve should be executed on 25 November 1966, notwithstanding instructions
in paragraph 3 of letter of appointment.

　　　FOR THE CHIEF OF PERSONNEL OPERATIONS:

2 Incl   G. M. DANIEL
   as   LTC, USA
                                          Chief, Personnel Actions Div, USARCPC

APO NEW YORK 09282

CR 24 Oct 66

Separation for the Convenience of the Government

Spanish Opns Rgn (CHPO-SA)

1. References

a. Ltr, USAF, 23 Sep 66, Appointment as a Reserve Warrant Officer of the Army under Title 10, U.S. Code, Sections 591 and 597 (WO W-1) Maurice Frank Navarro, [redacted]

b. DA (DCSPER) Ltr Order A-09-[illegible], dtd 29 Sep 66.

c. Department of the Army Ltr, 10 Oct 66, Appointment and Concurrent Call to Active Duty (Navarro, Maurice F., [redacted]

d. Message [illegible], 12 Oct 66, Asst [illegible], [illegible] Personnel, USAF, Randolph AFB, Texas.

e. Message, this unit, [illegible], 13 Oct 66.

f. Msg, DA, [illegible] ([illegible]), 14 Oct 66, Appointment and Concurrent Call to Active Duty.

2. MSgt Navarro will be separated from the Air Force 24 Nov 66 for the purpose of accepting an appointment as a Warrant Officer in the Army IAW para 3-14, AFM 39-10 and reference 1f, above.

3. Sergeant Navarro was due normal separation on 19 Oct 66, however, in view of the above, he will not be separated on [illegible], but will enter an extension of enlistment and separate 24 Nov 66. [illegible] advises that records previously forwarded there to effect separation on normal ETS will suffice for 24 Nov 66 separation.

4. A copy of all pertinent correspondence is forwarded for your information and action deemed necessary.

[illegible], Major, USAF
Commander

6 Attachments
1. See para 1a above.
2. See para 1b above.
3. See para 1c above.
4. See para 1d above.
5. See para 1e above.
6. See para 1f above.

APO 09282

17 Nov 1966

Professional Books

Transportation Officer

The following are my professional books:

ECI 3008 Vol-1 Errata Pamphlet
ECI 3008 Vol-1 Communications Officer
ECI 2935 Vol-4 Teletype Operating Procedures
ECI 2935 Vol-3 Message Structure
ECI 2935 Vol-2 Telephone Switchboard Operations
ECI 2935 Vol-1 Teletypewriter methods
Manual for Courtsmartial United States 1951
Alternating Current Circuits
Principles of Applied Electronics
USAFI Study Guide B781.1 Fundamentals of Electricity
USAFI Study Guide B781 Fundamentals of Electricity
MCI 25.4a Staff Functions, Combat Orders, and Communications Plans and Orders
MCI 25.3a Basic Radio and Visual Communications Procedures
MCI 25-1 Basic Wire Communications
MCI 03.3b2 The Marine Noncommissioned Officer
ECI 3008 Vol 17 Communications Planning 2
ECI 3008 Vol 16 Communications Planning 1
ECI 3008 Vol 14 Management 3 - Maintenance
ECI 3008 Vol 10 Carrier Systems and Equipment
ECI 3008 Vol 9 Teletypewriter Systems - 2
ECI 3008 Vol 8 Teletypewriter Systems - 1
ECI 3008 Vol 7 Telephone 4 - Inside Plant
ECI 3008 Vol 6 Telephone 3 - Inside Plant
ECI 3008 Vol 5 Telephone 2 - Outside Plant
ECI 3008 Vol 4 Telephone 1 - Outside Plant
ECI 3008 Vol 3 Navigational Equipment
ECI 3008 Vol 2 Appendixes
ECI 3008 Vol 2 Ground Radio 2 - Mobile and Fixed
MCS 1-18 Discipline Under the Uniform Code
MCS 1-17 Service Afloat
MCS 1-14 Marine Corps History
MCS 1-9 Organizational of the US Marine Corps
MCS 1-2 Techniques of Effective Military Instruction
MCS AP3111A Communications
MCS AP3106 Counterinsurgency Scouting and Patrolling
MCS AP3105 Infantry Weapons
MCS AP3102 Military Leadership, Training and Discipline
MCS AP3101 History and Organization of the US Marine Corps
MCS Guidelines
MCS Extension School
MCI 25.14 Radio Relay Fundamentals and Operations
MCI 25.13 Communications Center Installation and Management

MCI 25.11a Teletype Operator
MCI 25.10 Communications Employment Marine Division
MCI 25.8 Basic Message Center Man
MCI 25.6 Communications in the Marine Aircraft Wing
TM 11-660 Introduction to Electronics
TAGSUSA 368 Safeguarding Defense Information
TAGSUSA 61 TAGSUSA Composite Subcourse 1
Subcourse C13 Communications Center Fundamentals
Subcourse A18 Communications Center Operations
Subcourse 17 Signal Unit Supply
MCEC Handout History of Guerrilla Operations
MCEC SM-106 Supplement Communications Equipment Reference Data
MCEC SM-8 Military Training
MCEC SM-4 Counterguerrila Operations
MCS 3-110 Communications
MCS 2-32 Grenades and Pryotechnics Portable Flamethrower 3.5 inch and M72
          Rocket Launches 106-MM Rifle
MCS 2=31 81-MM Mortar
MCS 2-30 M60 Machinegun
MCS 2-29 Individual Weapons
MCS 1-19 Enforcement of Military Law and Order
AFM 101-8 Fundamentals of Electronics
AFM 52-8 Vol I Electronics Circuit Analysis
AFM 52-8 Vol II Electronics Circuit Analysis
AR 380-41 Control of Cryptomaterial
TM 11-5815-200-10 Operators Manual Teletypewriter Sets AN/FGC-20, AN/FGC-20X,
                  AN/FGC-21, and AN/UGC-4
TM 11-2246 Teletypewriter Sets AN/FGC-25 and AN/FGC-25X including changes 1-5
TM 11-681 Electrical Fundamentals (alternating current)
TM 11-679 Fundamentals of Carrier and Repeater
TM 11-678 Fundamentals of Telephone
TM 11-664 Theory and use of Electronic Test Equipment
TM 11-663 Electronic Power Supplies
TM 11-661 Electrical Fundamentals (Direct Current)

MAURICE F. MERCURE, MSgt, USAF

APPLICATION FOR BASIC ALLOWANCE FOR QUARTERS FOR MEMBER WITH DEPENDENTS

Use reverse for continuation of items
identifying by item numbers

SERVICE NUMBER	NAME OF SERVICE MEMBER (Last - First - Middle)	GRADE OR RANK
AF ▓▓▓▓	MERCURE, MAURICE F.	MSGT

☐ ARMY   ☐ AIR FORCE   ☐ OTHER (Specify)

STATION OR BASE
2188 Comm Sq, Moron AB, Spain

1 I HEREBY CLAIM BASIC ALLOWANCE FOR QUARTERS FOR THE DEPENDENTS LISTED BELOW, EFFECTIVE (Date)   21 Nov 66

2 FROM THE DATE INDICATED ABOVE THE FOLLOWING HAVE BEEN MY DEPENDENTS:

NAME OF DEPENDENT (Last, First, Middle Initial)	COMPLETE CURRENT ADDRESS	RELATIONSHIP	DATE OF BIRTH
Mercure, Margarette D.	N-3A, Santa Clara Housing Area	Wife	

GIVE DATE AND PLACE OF PRESENT MARRIAGE

IF ANY CHILD NAMED ABOVE HAS BEEN ADOPTED, SHOW DATE OF ADOPTION AND ADDRESS OF COURT ISSUING THE DECREE

3 IF ANY CHILDREN NAMED ABOVE ARE NOT IN LEGAL CUSTODY OF YOU OR YOUR SPOUSE, SHOW THE FOLLOWING:

NAME OF CHILD (Last, First, Middle Initial)	NAME AND ADDRESS OF PERSON HAVING CUSTODY	SHOW THE AMOUNT YOU CONTRIBUTE MONTHLY TO THE SUPPORT OF THE CHILD
RELATIONSHIP OF CUSTODIAN TO CHILD		IF SUPPORT OF ANY CHILD IS REQUIRED BY COURT ORDER OR DIVORCE DECREE SHOW AMOUNT REQUIRED

4 DEPENDENCY INFORMATION (This section must be completed for all dependents other than lawful wife and/or legitimate children under 21 years of age of male members)

NAME(S) OF DEPENDENT(S)		MONTHLY AMOUNT OF MY CONTRIBUTION	DEPENDENTS INCOME FROM OTHER SOURCES	DEPENDENTS MONTHLY LIVING EXPENSES

(For unmarried child over 21 years of age either physically incapacitated or mentally defective attach a statement from a physician showing how long the child has been under his care and the cause and degree of incapacitation. In case the child is in custody of someone other than the service member, a statement signed by the custodian showing the amount of the service member's monthly contribution, method by which the service member makes the contribution and the actual monthly living expenses of the child is also required.)

5 IF DIVORCED SHOW THE FOLLOWING:

DIVORCE DECREE GRANTED BY (Court, State, and Date)

ADDRESS OF FORMER WIFE

TYPE OF DECREE
☐ FINAL
☐ INTERLOCUTORY

NAME OF PERSON FORMER WIFE REMARRIED

DATE DECREE BECOMES FINAL

6 HAVE ANY OF THE ABOVE NAMED DEPENDENTS SERVED AS A MEMBER OF THE UNIFORMED SERVICES OR PARTICIPATED IN FULL TIME TRAINING DUTY WITH PAY AFTER THE DATE SHOWN IN ITEM 1 ABOVE?   ☐ YES ☐ NO

7 EXCLUDING OCCUPANCY OCCURRING DURING A SOCIAL VISIT OF A TEMPORARY NATURE, DID THE ABOVE NAMED DEPENDENT(S) OCCUPY GOVERNMENT QUARTERS OR HOUSING FACILITIES UNDER THE JURISDICTION OF THE UNIFORMED SERVICES WITHOUT PAYMENT OF RENTAL CHARGES AFTER THE DATE SHOWN IN ITEM 1 ABOVE?   ☐ YES ☐ NO

8 FIRST APPLICATION   ☐ YES ☒ NO   DATE LAST APPLICATION FILED   Unk

9 IMPORTANT — NOTE: PENALTY FOR PRESENTING FALSE CLAIMS OR MAKING FALSE STATEMENTS IN CONNECTION WITH CLAIMS: FINES OF NOT MORE THAN $10,000 OR IMPRISONMENT FOR NOT MORE THAN FIVE YEARS OR BOTH. ACT 25 JUNE 1948, 18, U.S.C. 287, 1001

I WILL IMMEDIATELY NOTIFY MY FINANCE OFFICER OF ANY CHANGE IN THE DEPENDENCY OF THE DEPENDENTS LISTED ABOVE. I AM AWARE OF THE FACT THAT MAKING FALSE STATEMENT ON A CLAIM AGAINST THE U.S. GOVERNMENT IS PUNISHABLE BY COURT MARTIAL. I HEREBY CERTIFY THAT I HAVE PERSONAL KNOWLEDGE THAT THE FACTS STATED HEREIN ARE TRUE AND CORRECT.

10 DATE OF CURRENT ENLISTMENT OR DATE OF REPORTING FOR ACTIVE DUTY (Whichever is later)   31 Oct 61 | CURRENT DATE   21 Nov 66 | SIGNATURE OF SERVICE MEMBER   Maurice F. Mercure

11 TO BE COMPLETED BY PERSONNEL OFFICER

I CERTIFY THAT I HAVE REVIEWED THE DOCUMENTARY EVIDENCE TO ESTABLISH RELATIONSHIP OF THE WIFE AND/OR CHILDREN AND HAVE SATISFIED MYSELF THAT THE STATEMENTS MADE BY THE SERVICE MEMBER ARE TRUE.

SIGNATURE OF PERSONNEL OFFICER

12 TO BE COMPLETED BY FINANCE OFFICER

DEPENDENCY HAS BEEN ESTABLISHED FOR ALL DEPENDENTS LISTED IN ITEM 2 EXCEPT:

BAQ $
CREDITED FROM
CL Q DED $
DEBITED FROM
CL Q DED $
DEBITED FROM

SIGNATURE OF FINANCE OFFICER

SYMBOL NUMBER

1 Indicate if step or adopted child   2 Children only   3 Include interest, dividend or rental income and contributions from others toward household or living expenses

DD FORM 137   REPLACES DD FORM 137; 1 MAY 51, WHICH IS OBSOLETE.   GPO: okj 16 - 77630 - 1

Form approved by the Comptroller General, U.S.
March 11, 1957

MERCURE, MAURICE F.

1. NAME *(Last, First, MI)* AND SERVICE NO. *(Addressograph may be used)*

2. ORGANIZATION AND MILITARY ADDRESS

HQ USAPPAR APO NEW YORK, N. Y. 09163

3. I HAVE BEEN ADVISED OF THE PROVISIONS OF PUBLIC LAW 89-214, WHICH INSURES ME FOR $10,000. I NOW HAVE THE OPPORTUNITY TO EITHER ELECT $5,000 SERVICEMEN'S GROUP LIFE INSURANCE OR TO WITHDRAW FROM THIS PROGRAM IN ITS ENTIRETY.

a. MY ELECTION IS

[X] REMAIN INSURED FOR $10,000.   [ ] TO BE INSURED FOR $5,000.   [ ] NOT TO BE INSURED.

b. BENEFICIARY DESIGNATION

THE LAW PROVIDES THAT IF I DO NOT DESIGNATE A BENEFICIARY, PAYMENT WILL DEVOLVE, IN THE FOLLOWING ORDER: TO MY WIFE, CHILDREN IN EQUAL SHARES, AND PARENTS IN EQUAL SHARES.

MY DESIRES, WITH RESPECT TO BENEFICIARES, ARE:

[X] HAVE PAYMENT MADE IN THE ORDER OF PRECEDENCE SET FORTH IN THE LAW.

[ ] I DESIGNATE THE FOLLOWING PERSON(S) AS BENEFICIARY(IES):

FIRST NAME, MIDDLE INITIAL AND LAST NAME OF EACH BENEFICIARY *(Print or Type)*	ADDRESS OF EACH BENEFICIARY	RELATIONSHIP	PERCENT EACH IS TO RECEIVE
PRINCIPAL *(First)*			
CONTINGENT *(Second)(To receive payment if principal beneficiary does not survive me.)*			

c. ELECTION OF METHOD OF PAYMENT

I UNDERSTAND THAT MY BENEFICIARY MAY ELECT PAYMENT IN A LUMP-SUM OR IN 36 EQUAL INSTALLMENTS, IF I DO NOT MAKE SUCH AN ELECTION.

MY DESIRES IN THIS RESPECT ARE:

[X] I DO NOT ELECT A SETTLEMENT OPTION.

[ ] I DESIRE TO HAVE SERVICEMEN'S GROUP LIFE INSURANCE PAID IN A LUMP-SUM.

[ ] I DESIRE TO HAVE SERVICEMEN'S GROUP LIFE INSURANCE PAID IN 36 MONTHLY INSTALLMENTS.

DATE	SIGNATURE
30Nov66	*Maurice F Mercure*

DA FORM 3054
1 OCT 65

O - 4389

THE
ARMY
OF
THE UNITED STATES OF AMERICA

To all who shall see these presents, greeting:

Know Ye, that reposing special trust and confidence in the patriotism, valor, fidelity and abilities of __Maurice Frank Mercure__

the Secretary of the Army, has appointed him *a*

Reserve Warrant Officer

in the Army of the United States

to rank as such from the __twenty-fifth__ *day of* __November__, *nineteen hundred and* __sixty-six__. *This Warrant Officer will therefore carefully and diligently discharge the duties of the office to which appointed by doing and performing all manner of things thereunto belonging. And all subordinate personnel of lesser rank are strictly charged and required to render such obedience as is due a Warrant Officer of this grade and position. And this Warrant Officer is to observe and follow such orders and directions, from time to time, as may be given by Superior Officers and Warrant Officers acting in accordance with the laws of the United States of America.*

Done at the City of Washington, this __sixth__ *day of* __December__ *in the year of our Lord one thousand nine hundred and* __sixty-six__, *and of the Independence of the United States of America, the one hundred and* __ninety-first__.

Kenneth G. Wickham
Major General
The Adjutant General

DA FORM 1290, 1 APR 55

Diese Karte wurde ausgestellt für:

WO MAURICE MERCURE
(Name)

32ND SIGNAL BN. A.P.O. 09757 NEW YORK
(Militärische Einheit oder Rechtsstellung)

Im Falle der Festnahme der vorgenannten Person wird gebeten, sofort die nächste US-Militärpolizeistelle (M.P., A.P. oder S.P.) und wenn möglich den für die festgenommene Person zuständigen kommandierenden Offizier zu benachrichtigen.

Es wird hiermit auf die Bestimmung des "Absatzes 2 (a), Artikel 22 des Zusatzabkommens zu dem Abkommen zwischen den Parteien des Nordatlantikvertrages über die Rechtsstellung ihrer Truppen hinsichtlich der in der Bundesrepublik Deutschland stationierten ausländischen Truppen" hingewiesen, welche vorschreibt:

"Haben die deutschen Behörden die Festnahme vorgenommen, so wird der Festgenommene auf Antrag den Behörden des betreffenden Entsendestaates übergeben."

Falls eine Blutprobe auf Alkohol erforderlich ist, soll der Besitzer dieser Karte der US-Militärpolizei übergeben werden, die ihn zur nächsten US-Sanitätsstation bringen soll.

AE FORM 3317   EDITION OF 1 SEP 66 MAY BE USED   O - 4012
15 JUL 66   UNTIL STOCKS ARE EXHAUSTED.

LEGAL STATUS OF US FORCES PERSONNEL
IN THE FEDERAL REPUBLIC OF GERMANY

1. Please read this card carefully and carry it always.

2. As a member of the United States Forces, civilian component or as a dependent in the Federal Republic of Germany, this card reminds you of your legal obligations and will assist you if you get involved in difficulties with German police authorities.

3. While stationed in Germany, you are subject to, and must respect and obey, the laws of the Federal Republic of Germany, as well as the laws of the United States.

4. In addition to your being subject to the jurisdiction of US military authorities, you may be arrested by the German police authorities and may be tried by the criminal courts of Germany for violation of German law.

5. Here are some DO's and DON'Ts if you are arrested by German police.

   a. DON'T resist arrest or refuse to obey instructions.

   b. DO furnish German police i m m e d i a t e l y with your name, rank and organization and show them your identification card or passport.

   c. DO request that your Commanding Officer and the nearest US Military Police (M.P., A.P., or S.P.) be immediately notified of your apprehension. The reverse of this card contains a request in German that this notification be accomplished.

   d. DO request the assistance of a qualified interpreter. Remember that any statement you make may be used against you.

   e. DON'T leave the scene of an accident in which you become involved until authorized by the police.

   f. DO request to be taken to a US medical facility if German authorities demand that you submit to a blood alcohol test.

SHOW THE REVERSE OF THIS CARD TO GERMAN POLICE IF ARRESTED

HAND RECEIPT FOR EXPENDABLE OR NON-EXPENDABLE ITEMS
(FM 10-33)

ISSUED BY:

A. CO. ARMOR
32nd Sig. Bn.

ISSUED TO: *(Name and Organization)*

MAURICE F. MERCURE
CO A. ~~████~~ (VAULT)

DATE OF ISSUE

27 DEC 66

DATE ITEMS TO BE RETURNED *(if applicable)*

ITEM (Include Stock No. if applicable and nomenclature)	QUANTITY
PISTOL, AUTOMATIC, M1911 A1, CAL .45	1 EACH
SN. #2340378, MAGAZINE, CAL 45	1 EACH

I ACKNOWLEDGE RECEIPT OF THE ABOVE ITEMS

SIGNATURE OF RECIPIENT

Maurice F. Mercure

ITEMS LISTED ABOVE WERE RETURNED THIS DATE

DATE

SIGNATURE OF ISSUER

DA FORM 10-233
1 FEB 57

O - 1777

MERCURE, MAURICE

GENERAL EDUCATIONAL DEVELOPMENT
INDIVIDUAL RECORD
(AR 621-5)

ROT DATE: 20 Sept 68

1. NAME (Last - First - Middle Initial)	2. SERVICE NUMBER	3. GRADE*	4. BRANCH
MERCURE, Maurice F. SSN:	CURRENT: FORMER:	W O	ARMY

5. MILITARY ADDRESS*

6. HOME ADDRESS*
24 Newton St
Holyoke, MASS

7. EDUCATIONAL LEVEL (Circle highest completion or equivalency attained)
4 5 6 7 8 9 10 11 (12) (13) 14 15 16 17 18 or more
INDICATE DEGREES AND FIELDS:

TELEPHONE*

8. DATE OF BIRTH	9. BPED	10. DATE AND PLACE THIS FORM INITIATED
14 Aug 46	5 Oct 46	26 January 1967 AEC McNair Kaserne, Hoechst

11. CIVILIAN SCHOOLS ATTENDED

	NAME	LOCATION	DATES ATTENDED
GRAMMAR			
HIGH SCHOOL	HB Lawrence HS	Holyoke, Mass	1941 1944
COLLEGE OR OTHER			

12. SERVICE SCHOOLS ATTENDED

COURSE	SCHOOL	LENGTH	YEAR	COM-PLETED	MOS AWARDED

13. MOS IN WHICH QUALIFIED

MOS	TITLE
PRIMARY 721A	
DUTY	
OTHER(s)	

14. TESTS TAKEN (Enter USAFI, EOC under Item 17)

a. USAFI ACHIEVEMENT TESTS

TITLE AND FORM	DATE TAKEN	RAW SCORES	GRADE LEVEL

b. GED TEST (High School)

DATE TAKEN	FORM	PART	STD SCORE
SEP 1951	1	1	41
"		2	63
"		3	59
"		4	56
"		5	40

c. GED TEST (College)

DATE TAKEN	FORM	PART	STD SCORE

APTITUDE AREA SCORES (Optional)

GT	CO-A	CO-B	EL	GM	MM	CL	RC
4				56			
5				40			

SUBJECT EXAMINATIONS

d. TITLE AND NUMBER	LEVEL	DATE TAKEN	e. RESULT	GT	CO-A	CO-B	EL	GM	MM	CL	RC
			RETEST								
f. ALAT SCORE											

15a. DATE GRANTED HIGH SCHOOL EQUIVALENCY DIPLOMA

a. BY

16a. YEAR DA EVALUATION (Date requested)

b. DATE GRANTED

17. COURSES TAKEN

DATES ENROLLED	TITLE AND NUMBER	AEC, USAFI OR SCHOOL	CREDIT EARNED	DATE COMPLETED	TESTS RESULTS OR GRADES
24 Jan 67	Conversational German AIM I	AEC McNair Kaserne, Hoechst	Dropped after 6 hours of instruction		
13 Nov 67 CC	E 485 General Psychology	USAFI CORR. COURSE AEC McNair Kaserne, Hoechst			

Continued on Reverse Side

DA FORM 1500

REPLACES EDITION OF 1 OCT 61 WHICH IS OBSOLETE

STATEMENT OF SERVICE – FOR COMPUTATION OF LENGTH OF SERVICE FOR PAY PURPOSES
(AR 37-104)

LAST NAME • FIRST NAME • MIDDLE INITIAL	COMPLETE MAILING ADDRESS OF: (Unit Personnel Officer, if member on AD) (Unit Commander, if member on ACDUTRA)
MERCURE MAURICE F	COMMANDING OFFICER CO A 32D SIG BN APO NEW YORK NY 09752
SERVICE NUMBER: W ▓▓▓▓▓	

I have held a commission; appointment as commissioned warrant officer, warrant officer, flight officer, or Army field clerk; or have been enlisted as a member of the respective service(s) shown below for the inclusive periods indicated. All National Guard service claimed hereon was federally recognized; it was not in the inactive National Guard; all officers' training camp service was in the capacity of an enlisted person and all initial appointments are shown from the date of acceptance.

SERVICE (Army, Air Force, Navy, etc.)	ENL	COM	FROM YEAR	FROM MONTH	FROM DAY	TO YEAR	TO MONTH	TO DAY	YEARS	MONTHS	DAYS
ARMY AIR CORP	✓		1946	Oct	5	1949	Oct	4	3		
US AIR FORCE	✓		1949	Oct	5	1966	Nov	24	17	1	20
U.S. ARMY		✓	1966	Nov	25	P R E S E N T					
							TOTAL CREDITABLE SERVICE (Years)			

DATE 30 NOVEMBER 1966	SIGNATURE OF OFFICER Maurice F. Mercure

SPACE BELOW FOR USE BY THE ADJUTANT GENERAL (When statement above is incorrect, correct service will be entered).

SERVICE (Army, Air Force, Navy, etc.)	ENL	COM	FROM YEAR	FROM MONTH	FROM DAY	TO YEAR	TO MONTH	TO DAY	YEARS	MONTHS	DAYS
									CERTIFIED CORRECT FOR BASIC PAY PURPOSES, DA, TAGO		
						TOTAL SERVICE CREDITABLE FOR BASIC PAY		KENNETH G. WICKHAM		

DATE 11 Apr 67 AGPF-FC/ MCD/lq	AUTHENTICATION	Major General, USA The Adjutant General

DA FORM 1506
1 MAY 61

PREVIOUS EDITION OF THIS FORM IS OBSOLETE.

TAG AUTH TO UPO   2

SEMINAR FÜR POLITIK

Mr.
Maurice Frank Mercure
6 Frankfurt/Main-Höchst
Tewtonenweg
B 6 2429

6 FRANKFURT AM MAIN, den 25.8.67
Klettenbergstraße 11
Telefon 55 44 30, 55 44 40
Bankkonto : Stadtsparkasse Frankfurt a. M.
Konto Nr. 66-12021
Postscheckkonto: Frankfurt (Main) 7 27 17

Unser Zeichen   UI/Ja.

Lieber Herr Mercure,

herzlichen Dank für alles was Sie für die Gruppe von 92 Amerikanern
aus Wilmington getan haben.

I assure you that your speach and the discussion made quite an
impresion to the kids and the teachers.

Es war nett, daß Sie Ihre Frau mitgebracht haben; es war eine Freude
Sie beide kennen zu lernen.

By the way: I didn't forget that you intended to buy me a drink.
Wir haben es just postponend, we will find an occasion very soon.
Wir mix up deutsch und englisch in diesem Brief um unser Treffen
vorzubereiten.

1. I took the invitation to come over to the NCO Club seriously!
2. I ment it, when I asked you to visit my children and my grand-
   son in their appartment.
3. Please cooperate with Mrs. Mercure to make arrangements for our
   program and call me.

Mit herzlichen Grüßen the ladies of the

SEMINAR FÜR POLITIK

(Ingrid Jaspert)   (Ulla Illing)

Thanksgiving Menu

Consolidated Mess
32d Signal Battalion
Frankfurt/Oberursel, Germany

Designed and Printed by Military Service Co.

THANKSGIVING MENU 1967

Shrimp Cocktail   Cocktail Sauce

Crackers   Lemon Wedges

Roast Turkey

Bread or Cornbread Dressing

Giblet Gravy   Cranberry Sauce

Baked Ham

Mashed Potatoes or Browned Sweet Potatoes

Buttered Peas or Buttered Corn

Assorted Salads and Dressings

Hot Rolls   Margarine

Mincemeat Pie or Pumpkin Pie with Cream Topping

Coffee   Tea   Lemon Wedges

Fresh Milk or Chocolate Milk

Apples   Bananas   Grapes   Oranges

Assorted Candy and Nuts

THANKSGIVING MESSAGE

Thanksgiving reminds us again of the deep need in human hearts to express thanks to a Divine Providence for all things that bring happiness to our daily living . . . so we join in prayerful gratitude for those many things with which, in most parts of our world today, we are so richly blessed.

Around these tables which you share here with new friends, may you pause for a moment and in your own hearts and in your own way express thanks for the food, for your place of service to our country, for health and happiness, and for the love of family and friends.

In this I join gladly with you, and pray also that we may prove worthy of the trust our country has placed in us . . . to preserve this great nation and its way of life for our children and the generations that follow them . . . a rich and proud heritage for which we can all be truly grateful.

DALE N. HOAGLAND
LTC, SigC
Commanding

TRF CARE

CLINICAL RECORD COVER SHEET (For Addressograph)
(AR 40—400) (AR 40—2 for preparation of Admitting Plate)

1. ADMISSION NOTES	2-21. PATIENT DATA	LINE	LEGEND	(2—21)

1. ADMISSION NOTES

No evid of A or N

USAD Hoechst

22. ADMITTING OFFICER

2-21. PATIENT DATA

269370 MERCURE MAURICE P   WO1 W1
M 30 CAU USA   P 21-0   1130   7JAN68
CO A 32 SIG BN   *   A-3 H
N/A   N   FEB70
7JAN68 DIR CAS P/S HOECHST
MRS MARGARET MERCURE/W
2429-B HOECHST H/A HOECHST GER
* APO 09757
O 7934   OPMR-YES   WMJ

LINE / LEGEND (2—21)

1 REGISTER NO—NAME—GRADE OR RATING
2 SEX—AGE—RACE—DEPT(USA, USAF, etc.)—RELIGION—LENGTH OF SERVICE—TIME OF ADM—DATE OF ADM
3 SERVICE NO—ORG—WARD NO—CASUALTY CODE INDICATOR
4 FLYING STATUS—AERONAUTICAL RATING OR DESIGNATION—MOS—BR OF SERVICE—NATIONALITY—PREVIOUS ADM—EXPIRATION DATE
5 DATE OF INITIAL ADM—SOURCE OF ADM
6 NAME OF SPONSOR OR PERSON TO BE NOTIFIED—RELATIONSHIP
7 ADDRESS OF SPONSOR OR PERSON TO BE NOTIFIED
8 AND 9 (For any local use desired at individual facility)
(See AR 40—2 for complete explanation)

23. DIAGNOSES (See instructions for recording as shown on reverse side. Include all required related data)

Dg 1:   7250   Herniated Nucleus Pulposus.
      LD: Yes.

24. OPERATIONS AND SPECIAL THERAPEUTIC PROCEDURES (Show date for each; show anesthetic for each operation)

NONE.

25. SELECTED ADMINISTRATIVE DATA (Show nature of and dates for board proceedings; show fact of and dates for leave, AWOL, subsisting elsewhere, detached service, etc.)

Specialized Treatment: Orthopedic Surgery.

26.

PHYSICAL PROFILE

TYPE	SERIAL						SUFFIX					PROFILE UNCHANGED
	P	U	L	H	E	S	R	T	D	O	N	
PREVIOUS												
REVISED												

27. DAYS DURATION THIS FACILITY

ALL	IN HOSPITAL OR INFIRMARY	SUBSISTING ELSEWHERE	QUARTERS OR DISPENSARY	LEAVE	OTHER
20	20				

28. NATURE OF DISPOSITION

TRFT USAGH LANDSTUHL

29. DATE OF DISPOSITION

27 Jan 68

30. SIGNATURE OF ATTENDING PHYSICIAN

SELIM V DIKMAN, MD

31. SIGNATURE OF REGISTRAR OR MEDICAL RECORDS OFFICER

KITTY N AMABILE MEDICAL RECORD LIBRARIAN

32. NAME AND LOCATION OF MEDICAL TREATMENT FACILITY

USAGH FRANKFURT, GERMANY APO 09757

33. REGISTER NUMBER

269370

DA FORM 8-275-2
1 APR 67

EDITION OF 1 JUL 62, IS OBSOLETE.

O - 11596

32ᴰ SIGNAL BATTALION

Best Wishes for a Quick
and Speedy Recovery!

The Officers of the 32d
Signal Battalion

DEPARTMENT OF THE ARMY
HEADQUARTERS V CORPS
APO 09079

Office of the Signal Officer

AETVSI   25 February 1968

CW2 Maurice F. Mercure
Company A, 32d Signal Battalion
APO 09757

Dear Chief Warrant Officer Mercure:

I note with pleasure your promotion to Chief Warrant Officer.

Promotion is not only a tangible recognition of excellence but also acknowledgement of your demonstrated ability to assume greater responsibility.

The outstanding manner in which you have discharged your duties as Assistant Crypto Officer, and as required to V Corps in performing the Annual Command Cryptographic Assistance Inspections is gratifying.

I am confident you will meet each added responsibility and wish you continued success.

Keep up the good work and sincerely hope you are on the road to good health.

                                    Sincerely,

                                    J. E. GWYNN
                                    Colonel, Sig C
                                    Signal Officer

cc. CO 32d Sig Bn

ORGANIZATIONAL CLOTHING AND EQUIPMENT RECORD
(AR 735-35)

Use pencil for authorized allowance, sizes, and balances;
ink for remaining entries. Acknowledge all transactions
with signature in appropriate numbered columns.

ARTICLES ORGANIZATIONAL CLOTHING QUARTERMASTER	AUTHORIZED ALLOWANCES	SIZE	ISSUES (Date) 27 DEC 66 / 1	24 JAN 67 / 2	31 JUL 68 / 3	4	5	6	7	8	TURN-INS (Date) 31 AUG 68 / 1	2	3	4	5	BALANCE
APRON, BAKER, BUTCHER AND COOK																
CAP, FIELD, COTTON																
CAP, FIELD, PILE	✓	1	7	1								1					1
CAP, BAKERS AND COOKS													1				
COATS, BAKERS AND COOKS																	
COAT, MAN'S, SATEEN, OG 107	1	MR			1												
DRESS, WOMEN'S, COOKS AND BAKERS																	
DRESS, WM'S CTN																	
GLOVES, LEATHER, HEAVY																	
GLOVES, WORK, COTTON																	
GLOVE-INSERTS, WOOL																	
GLOVE-SHELL, LEATHER																	
HOOD, WINTER, SATEEN, OG 107	✓	1	M	1								1					1
LINER, COAT, MANS	1	M															
OVERCOAT, MAN'S, W/REM. LINER																	
OVERSHOES	✓	1	9									1					1
PONCHO, LIGHWEIGHT W/HOOD	1				1							1					1
SCARF, MAN'S, WOOL, OD	✓	1										1					
SHIRT, FIELD, WOOL	✓	2	S	2								2					2
SHIRT, HBT, WOMEN'S SPECIAL																	
SHOES, ATHLETIC																	
SHORTS, ATHLETIC, POPLIN																	
STOCKINGS, COTTON																	
SWEATER																	
SUPPORTERS, ATHLETIC																	
SUSPENDERS, TROUSERS	✓	1		1								1					
TROUSERS, BAKERS AND COOKS																	
TROUSERS, FIELD, WOOL	✓	2	M/S	1								1					
TROUSERS, HBT, WOMEN'S SPECIAL																	
TROUSERS, WOMEN'S OUTER COVER																	
TROUSERS, SHELL, FIELD	✓	2	M/S	2								2					2
TROUSERS, WOMEN'S, WOOL, LINER																	
WAIST, WOOL, WOMEN'S																	

INDIVIDUAL MUST ACKNOWLEDGE ISSUES AND
AN OFFICER MUST ACKNOWLEDGE TURN-INS
BY SIGNING AT RIGHT IN APPROPRIATE COL-
UMNS.

SIGNATURE OF INDIVIDUAL

SIGNATURE OF OFFICER

ARTICLES ORGANIZATIONAL CLOTHING QUARTERMASTER		AUTHORIZED ALLOWANCES	ISSUES (Date)								TURN-INS (Date)					BALANCE
			27 DEC 66	24 JAN 67	30 JAN 67	31 JUL 67					31 Feb 68					
			1	2	3	4	5	6	7	8	1	2	3	4	5	
BOOT COMBAT RUBBER	7×W	1	✓		✓	✓					✓					1
LINER TROUSERS	M	1	1								1					1
LINER PARKA	MS	1	1								1					1
PARKA SHELL	M	1		1							1					
INSERTS WOOL TF	M	2	2								2					2
MITTENS SHELL TF	M	1	1								1					1
CARRIER SLEEPING BAG		1	1								1					1
POUCH AMMO		2	✓		2						2					2
MAGAZINE 7.62		15	✓													
COVER HELMET CAMOUFLAGE		1	1								1					1
ORGANIZATIONAL EQUIPMENT																
AXE, INTRCH, W/HANDLE																
BAG, BARRACK	✓	1									1					1
BAG, CLOTHING, WATERPROOF	✓	1									1					1
BAG, SLEEPING w/wp bag	✓	1									1					1
BAR, INSECT, FIELD											1					
BELT, CART, CAL 30, DISMTD																
BELT, MAGAZINE BAR																
BELT, PISTOL OR REVOLVER	✓	1									1					1
BLANKET, WOOL	✓	1	1								1					1
BRASSARD, ARM																
CANTEEN, ALUMINUM		1	1								1					
CARRIER, AXE INTRCH																
CARRIER, INTRCH TOOL, COMB	✓	1	1								1					1
CARRIER, PICK MATTOCK, INTRCH		1									1					
CASE, FIRST AID PACKET		1	1								1					
CASE, WATER REPELLENT BAG, SLEEPING	✓	1	1								1					1
COVER, CANTEEN, DISMOUNTED		1	1								1					1
CUP, CANTEEN, CRS		1	1								1					1
FORK, FIELD, MESS	✓	1	1								1					1

INDIVIDUAL MUST ACKNOWLEDGE ISSUES AND AN OFFICER MUST ACKNOWLEDGE TURN-INS BY SIGNING AT RIGHT IN APPROPRIATE COLUMNS.

SIGNATURE OF INDIVIDUAL

SIGNATURE OF OFFICER

2

ORGANIZATIONAL EQUIPMENT (Cont.)	AUTHORIZED ALLOWANCES	ISSUES (Date)								TURN-INS (Date)					BALANCE
		27 DEC 66	24 JAN 67	31 JUL 68						31 AUG 68					
		1	2	3	4	5	6	7	8	1	2	3	4	5	
GLASSES, SUN W/CASE		✓													
GOGGLES		✓													
HEADNET, MOSQUITO		✓													
HELMET, STEEL, W/DETACHABLE STRAP	1	1								1					1
INTRCH TOOL, COMBINATION															
KNIFE, FIELD, MESS ✓	1	1								1					1
LINER, STEEL, HELMET, W/STRAP ✓	1	1								1					1
PACK, FIELD, CARGO															
PACK, FIELD, COMBAT ✓	1									1					
PAD, INFLATABLE, SLEEPING ✓	1									1					
PAN, MESS, KIT, CRS ✓	1	1								1					1
PICK, MATTOCK, INTRCH W/HANDLE															
PIN, TENT	10														
POCKET, CART CAL 30 CARBINE/RIFLE															
POCKET, MAGAZINE, CARBINE 30 ROUND															
POCKET, MAGAZINE, DOUBLE WEB															
POLE, TENT, SINGLE SECTION	6														
SHOVEL, INTRCH ✓	1	1								1					1
SPOON, FIELD, MESS ✓	1	1								1					1
STRAP, CARRYING, GENERAL PURPOSE															
SUSPENDERS, PACK, FIELD, CARGO/CMBT	1														
ENT, SHELTER, HALF, NEW TYPE ✓	2	1								1					1
WHISTLE, THUNDERER															

INDIVIDUAL MUST ACKNOWLEDGE ISSUES AND AN OFFICER MUST ACKNOWLEDGE TURN-INS BY SIGNING AT RIGHT IN APPROPRIATE COLUMNS.

SIGNATURE OF INDIVIDUAL | SIGNATURE OF OFFICER

3

POST, CAMP AND STATION EQUIPMENT	AUTHORIZED ALLOWANCES	ISSUES (Date)								TURN-INS (Date)					BALANCE
		27 DEC 66	28 MAY 67							1 NOV 67					
		1	2	3	4	5	6	7	8	1	2	3	4	5	
BLANKET, WOOL		/	/							/					
COT, FOLDING															
COVER, MATTRESS															
LOCKER, BOX															
MATTRESS, COTTON															
PILLOW															
PILLOW CASE															
SHEET, COTTON															
LOCKER, CLOTHING															
BEDSTEAD															
OTHER SERVICES			/												
MASK, PROTECTIVE, FIELD M17 (chem)	/	/	/							/					
FLE m14 383792 (ord)	/	/								/					
ARBINE (ord)		/								/					
PISTOL (ord)															
BAYONET, KNIFE (ord)	/	/								/					
SCABBARD (ord)	/	/													
WATCH, WRIST (ord)															
		/								/					

INDIVIDUAL MUST ACKNOWLEDGE ISSUES AND AN OFFICER MUST ACKNOWLEDGE TURN-INS BY SIGNING AT RIGHT IN APPROPRIATE COLUMNS.

Maurice T Vonneur	Maurice T Vonneur							William F Smith				
SIGNATURE OF INDIVIDUAL								SIGNATURE OF OFFICER				

THIS IS A

☐ TRUE COPY   ☐ TRUE CERTIFIED CONSOLIDATION

☒ INITIAL ISSUE   ☐ PHYSICAL INVENTORY

ARM OR SERVICE	GRADE	OFFICER (Signature)
Sig C	2LT	Walter C. Wahlen

4

INSTALLATION CLEARANCE RECORD
(AR 210-10)

INSTALLATION
Lenzir Laserne, Kechst, Germany

Prepare in duplicate *(original to be retained in transfer activity file; duplicate to individual)*

LAST NAME - FIRST NAME - MIDDLE INITIAL	SERVICE NUMBER	GRADE
MERCURE MAURICE F	~~~~~~~	C~P

ORGANIZATION Co A, 32d Signal Battalion, APO 09757	TO DEPART *(Time and date)* 16 Oct 68

AUTHORITY FOR DEPARTURE SO 188 para 7 HQ 32d Sig Bn APO 09757	NEW DUTY STATION USARV Trans Det APO SF 96384

CHECKLIST

(Normally, officers, warrant officers, and enlisted personnel in grades E-7, E-8 and E-9 are not required to secure initials of clearing facility, their signature being official indication that all obligations are settled. Other enlisted personnel will normally have facility concerned initial applicable items. Appropriate administrative office will check items not applicable.)

FACILITY	INITIAL	FACILITY	INITIAL	FACILITY	INITIAL
1. ARMY EDUCATION CENTER		12. FIELD MILITARY 201 FILE AND ALLIED RECORDS		23. PROVOST MARSHALL (Contter)	aw
2. CHAPLAIN		13. FINANCE & ACCOUNTING OFF (Communications Account)		24. QUARTERMASTER LAUNDRY	
3. CLASSIFIED DOCUMENTS		14. FINANCIAL DATA RECORDS FOLDER (Personnel Officer)		25. QUARTERS ASSIGNMENT	
4. COMMERCIAL LAUNDRY		15. LIBRARY		26. SIGNAL OFFICER	
5. COURTS AND BOARDS¹		16. MEDICAL TREATMENT FACILITY		27. SPECIAL ORDERS FOR CHANGE OF STATION	
6. DENTAL CLINIC, DD FORM 722-1		17. ORDNANCE OFFICER		28. SPECIAL SERVICES OFFICER	
7. DEPENDENTS SCHOOL OFFICER		18. PERSONAL AFFAIRS OFFICER (A.E.R.)		29. UNIT AND REGIMENTAL SUPPLY	
8. DRY CLEANERS		19. PERSONNEL REGISTER (Sign Out)	AW BA	30. USAREUR VEHICLE REGISTRY (AE Form 3383 submitted)	
9. EFFICIENCY REPORTS		20. POSTAL OFFICER (Notice of Change of Address)		31. Orderly Room	AW
10. ENGINEER PROPERTY OFFICER		21. POST MOTOR POOL		32. Ration Cards	
11. ENLISTED OR OFFICER MESS	CM	22. POST QUARTERMASTER		33. Training NCO	

I HAVE TURNED IN OR PROPERLY TRANSFERRED ALL CLASSIFIED DOCUMENTS EXCEPT THOSE WHICH PERTAIN TO MY OFFICIAL DUTIES AND FOR WHICH I, AS AN INDIVIDUAL, HAVE BEEN DESIGNATED THE AUTHORIZED CUSTODIAN; I HAVE DISCHARGED ALL PERSONAL DEBTS ADMITTEDLY DUE AND PAYABLE AT THIS TIME IN THIS AREA OR HAVE MADE SATISFACTORY ARRANGEMENTS WITH THE PERSONS OR ORGANIZATIONS CONCERNED FOR THE PAYMENT OF SAME; AND I HAVE FURTHER NOTIFIED OF MY NEXT STATION OR POST OFFICE ADDRESS, ALL OTHER PERSONS WHO ARE KNOWN TO BE PRESENTLY ASSERTING CLAIMS OR DEMANDS AGAINST ME OR WHO HOLD INSTRUMENTS OF INDEBTEDNESS MADE OR INDORSED BY ME. I UNDERSTAND THAT THIS CLEARANCE DOES NOT RELIEVE ME OF ANY PECUNIARY CHARGE FOR GOVERNMENT PROPERTY WHICH HAS BEEN OR MAY BE RAISED ON A REPORT OF SURVEY OR REPORT OF BOARD OF OFFICERS IN LIEU OF REPORT OF SURVEY.

REMARKS Supply Room
CO Arms Room
OATC Pass
American Express
RE-UP NCO

I understand that this clearance does in no way relieve me from duty: (Initials) _____
No civilian clot as will be conn during the process of clearing post: (Initials) _____
These clearing papers will be completed and returned to the Personnel section at 2400 hrs prior rpt CONDUCT _____ ARE DENCY

DATE	SIGNATURE

ADEQUATE QUARTERS WERE FURNISHED	SIGNATURE OF COMMANDING OFFICER OR DESIGNATED REPRESENTATIVE
☐ YES ☐ NO	

DATES	TYPED NAME, GRADE, ARM AND TITLE
FROM TO	WILLIAM T. KONDIK, 1LT SigC, Commanding

¹ For pending reports of survey or disciplinary matters not referred to Company Commanders, only.

DA FORM 137 (AE) (20 AUG 65). REPLACES DA FORM 137, 1 MAR 65, WHICH WILL NOT BE USED IN USAREUR AND DA FORM 137 (AE), 1 JAN 65, WHICH WILL BE USED UNTIL STOCKS ARE EXHAUSTED.

O - 3739

STATEMENT of CHARGES
DG BILLETING FUND
TRAVIS AIR FORCE BASE, CALIF.

675 ﹡ 0004.00IL A

LAST NAME   FIRST NAME   MIDDLE INITIAL

MERCURE MAURRICE F   CW2

BLDG: 403   ROOM: 219   IN: 26 Oct 2025

OUT: 27 oct 2025

BILLETING FEE:
TELEPHONE CHARGES: TOTAL $ 4.00

      TOTAL $ _____

KITCHEN KIT
RENTAL FEE: _____
OTHER (Specify) _____

      TOTAL $ _____

TELEVISION
RENTAL FEE: _____

      TOTAL $ _____

KEY: _____   TOTAL $ _____
OTHER (Specify) _____

      TOTAL $ MFM

TOTAL AM'T. $ 4.00

147896

REQUEST FOR ISSUE			[X] ISSUE	[1]	SHEET NO.
				[1]	NO. OF SHEETS

FROM:	LAST NAME	FIRST NAME	MI	RANK	SERVICE NO.
	MERCURE MAURICE		F	CW 2	W2▮▮▮▮▮

TO:
CIF, SUP COM SGN APO 96491 (AT87FD)

NOTE:
CO. UNIT OF ASSIGNMENT: POST TO INDIVIDUAL CLOTHING AND EQUIPMENT RECORD
UPON ARRIVAL

ITEM NO.	DESCRIPTION	CODE	UNIT OF ISSUE	QUANTITY	SUPPLY ACTION
1.	BAG, CLOTHING BARRACK		ea	1	/
2.	BAG, CLOTHING WATERPROOF		ea	1	/
3.	BAND, HELMET CAMOUFLAGE		ea	1	/
4.	BELT, EQUIP. WEB SIZE		ea	1	/
5.	BLANKET, WOOL		ea	1	/
6.	BOX, MATCH		ea	1	0
7.	BOOT, COMBAT TROP. SIZE		pr	2	2
8.	CANTEEN, WATER PLASTIC		ea	1	/
9.	CANTEEN, WATER COLLAPSIBLE		ea	1	0
10.	CARRIER, INTRENCHING TOOL		ea	1	/
11.	CASE, FIELD FIRST AID DRESSING		ea	1	0
12.	COAT, TROPICAL SIZE		ea	5	5
13.	COVER, HELMET CAMOUFLAGE		ea	1	/
14.	COVER, CANTEEN COLLAPSIBLE		ea	1	0
15.	COVER, WATER CANTEEN		ea	1	/
16.	CUP, WATER CANTEEN STEEL		ea	1	/
17.	FORK, FIELD MESS		ea	1	/
18.	HELMET, STEEL		ea	1	/
19.	INTRENCHING TOOL		ea	1	/
20.	KNIFE, FIELD MESS		ea	1	/
21.	LINER, HELMET		ea	1	/
22.	PONCHO, NYLON COATING		ea	1	/
23.	SPOON, FIELD MESS		ea	1	/
24.	SUSPENDER, PACK SIZE		ea	1	0
25.	TROUSERS, TROPICAL SIZE		pr	5	5

I certify that I have received a gratuitous issue of the above listed
items in the quantities and size indicated and that upon reporting to my
unit, I will turn in one copy of this form to my unit commander. I further
certify that the above is true to the best of my knowledge.

RECEIVED BY: Maurice F Mercure   SIGNATURE: J.D.J
DATE: 30 October 1968   ISSUE BY:
    DATE: 30 oct 68

DA FORM 3161

AVCA SGH SG AD   Request for Reassignment

Commanding Officer   CW2 MAURICE F. Mercure   9 November 68
HHC, 29th General Support Gp   HHC, 29th Gen Spt Gp
APO SF 96491   APO SF 96491

1. Request that I be reassigned to the 160th Signal Group, 1st Signal Brigade,
APO SF 96491.

2. This request is for the following reasons:

   a. I am malassigned to this unit. My MOS is 721A and I am being utilized
as a 711A.

   b. A position vacancy exist in my grade and MOS in the above unit.

   c. My present unit has no TO+E position for my PMOS.

3. The following information is submitted:

   a. ETS: 25 Nov 69.
   b. DEROS: 25 Oct 69.
   c. PMOS/SMOS/TMOS: 721A/N/A/N/A.
   d. DOR: 25 Oct 68.
   e. BASD: 5 Oct 66.
   f. BPED: 5 Oct 46.
   g. SSAN: 015

                                   MAURICE F. MERCURE
                                   CW2, WO
                                   HHC, 29th Gen Spt Gp.

THRU: CO, HHC, 29th Gen Spt Gp APO SF   FROM: CO, 29th Gen Spt Gp, APO SF 96491
      96491

      CO, 29th Gen Spt Gp

TO: CO, USARYPCOM SGN,
ATTN: AVCA SGN PO
   1. Recommend approval
   2. Officers PMOS is in excess to our TO+E
   3. There is a vacancy in requested unit for this man.
   4. This action is not in contravention with AR 600-31.

DISPOSITION FORM
(AR 340-15)

REFERENCE OR OFFICE SYMBOL	SUBJECT
	Appointment

| TO Personnel Concerned | FROM OIC MACV CommCenter | DATE 7 February 1969 CMT 1 |

1. CW2 WILLIAM C. BREITHAUPT, W2, is hereby appointed Security Control Officer and Classified Documents Custodian for the MACV Communications Center, 69th Signal Battalion, in accordance with para 12 & 13, 160th Signal Group 380-5.

2. CW3 HARRY J. MARKLEY, W22____ hereby appointed Alternate Security Control Officer and Classified Documents Custodian for the MACV Communications Center, 69th Signal Battalion, in accordance with para 12 & 13, 160th Signal Group, 380-5.

3. The following named officers are hereby appointed destruction officers of classified documents and material, in accordance with para 14, USARV Reg 380-5.

> 1LT CRAMER M. GILMORE II   O5___
> CW2 MAURICE F. MERCURE   W2___
> CW2 LEOPOLD K. SALZER III   W2___

4. The following named E-5 and E-6's are hereby appointed witnessing officials for the destruction of classified documents and material, in accordance with para 15, USARV Reg 380-5.

> SSG CARLTON F. BACON   RA13
> SSG CHARLES D. BYRD   RA18
> SSG ERNEST F. CHAPMAN   RA11
> SSG CLAYTON COBB   RA53
> SSG JAMES B. GREENE JR.   RA14
> SSG JACKIE D. HAWKINS   RA14
> SSG EDWARD SANDERS   RA14
> SSG KENNETH WIBERG   RA11
> SSG JOHN T. WILKINSON   RA19
> SGT FREDDIE R. ALEXANDER   RA14
> SGT LEONARD GROVER   RA54
> SGT WILLIE L. JONES   RA18
> SGT WILLIAM McBRAYER   RA17
> SGT RICHARD D. McMASTERS   RA13
> SGT WARREN L. SCRUM   RA15
> SGT VAN DURANE STRICKLAND   RA14
> SGT JOHN TERRELL   RA14
> SGT ROBERT C. ULDRICK   RA257

BERNARD K. VOLLRATH
1LT, SigC
Acting OIC MACV CommCenter

STATEMENT BY ACCUSED OR SUSPECT PERSON
(AR 195-10)

PLACE	DATE	TIME	FILE NUMBER
Tan Son Nhut Air Base, RVN	14 Feb 69	:	

LAST NAME, FIRST NAME, MIDDLE NAME	SOCIAL SECURITY ACCOUNT NO.	GRADE
MERCURE, MAURICE FRANK	▮▮▮▮▮	CW2

ORGANIZATION OR ADDRESS

Company A, 69th Signal Battalion

PART I - WAIVER CERTIFICATE

I HAVE BEEN INFORMED BY __Major Benny L. Lockett__

OF __the 44th Signal Battalion, 160th Signal Group__

THAT HE WANTS TO QUESTION ME ABOUT __a possible Compromise of Classified Material__

OF WHICH I AM ACCUSED OR SUSPECTED. HE HAS ALSO INFORMED ME OF MY RIGHTS.

I UNDERSTAND THAT I HAVE THE RIGHT TO REMAIN SILENT AND THAT ANY STATEMENT I MAKE MAY BE USED AS EVIDENCE AGAINST ME IN A CRIMINAL TRIAL.

I UNDERSTAND THAT I HAVE THE RIGHT TO CONSULT WITH COUNSEL AND TO HAVE COUNSEL PRESENT WITH ME DURING QUESTIONING. I MAY RETAIN COUNSEL AT MY OWN EXPENSE OR COUNSEL WILL BE APPOINTED FOR ME AT NO EXPENSE TO ME. IF I AM SUBJECT TO THE UNIFORM CODE OF MILITARY JUSTICE, APPOINTED COUNSEL MAY BE MILITARY COUNSEL OF MY OWN CHOICE IF HE IS REASONABLY AVAILABLE.

I UNDERSTAND THAT EVEN IF I DECIDE TO ANSWER QUESTIONS NOW WITHOUT HAVING COUNSEL PRESENT, I MAY STOP ANSWERING QUESTION AT ANY TIME. ALSO, I MAY REQUEST COUNSEL AT ANY TIME DURING QUESTIONING.

I (XX) (DO NOT) WANT COUNSEL.

I (DO) (XXXXXX) WANT TO MAKE A STATEMENT AND ANSWER QUESTIONS. _Maurice F Mercure_
(Signature of Person To Be Questioned)

INTERROGATOR: _Benny L Lockett_ (Signature)   WITNESS: _Francis R Smith_ (Signature)

BENNY L. LOCKETT	FRANCIS R. SMITH
44th Signal Battalion, 160th Signal Group	Company A, 69th Signal Battalion
(Typed Name and Organization)	(Typed Name and Organization)

PART II - SWORN STATEMENT

I, MAURICE FRANK MERCURE, WANT TO MAKE THE FOLLOWING STATEMENT UNDER OATH:

Q. What position are you currently holding in the MACV Common User CommCenter?

A. Duty Officer Alpha Shift, nights.

Q. How long have you been in this position?

A. I became the night Duty Officer around the 30th of December 1968.

Q. What do you know about the circumstances surrounding possible-compromise of the documents that were found on the morning of 11 February 1969 that came from the MACV Common User CommCenter?

A. I knew nothing about them until I was advised that they were found. I believe that SGT Uldrick had the burning detail that night. That night I did check the barrels and the incinerator area and I found nothing.

Q. At what time did you check the area approximately?

A. About 0500 local time on the 11th of February 1969. The burn detail had already left the area. I am not exactly positive about the time.

EXHIBIT	INITIALS OF PERSON MAKING STATEMENT	
	MFM	PAGE 1 OF 6 PAGES

ADDITIONAL PAGES MUST CONTAIN THE HEADING "STATEMENT OF___TAKEN AT___DATED___CONTINUED." THE BOTTOM OF EACH ADDITIONAL PAGE MUST BEAR THE INITIALS OF THE PERSON MAKING THE STATEMENT AND BE INITIALED AS "PAGE___OF___PAGES." WHEN ADDITIONAL PAGES ARE UTILIZED, THE BACK OF PAGE 1 WILL BE LINED OUT, AND THE STATEMENT WILL BE CONCLUDED ON THE REVERSE SIDE OF ANOTHER COPY OF THIS FORM.

B1512

STATEMENT (Continued)

Q. Did you check the burn area during the night of the 9th or the 10th of February 69?

A. I believe I checked the area on the 9th but I did not check it on the 10th of February 1969.

Q. What was the extent of your search?

A. I checked the incinerator to see that it was locked and checked the immediate area inside the fence.

Q. Did you check any of the containers or bins outside of the area?

A. No Sir

Q. What does your SOP state about procedures for destruction of classified waste?

A. When I arrived here I read the SOP. I had questions on it. I was informed that the Duty Officer was no longer responsible for destroying the classified waste. However CW3 Markley suggested that we would check the area periodically.

Q. Did the OIC of MACV Common User CommCenter tell you this? LTC Huebner

A. No Sir

Q. Who did?

A. CW3 Markley and CW2 Salzer. I was not advised that there was to be any log entries or anything. To verify this you may look at the Duty Officer log. There have been no entries about this since the 14th of October. It was around that period.

COMMENT: Log entry on 12 Oct 68 was last time check of burning area was made.

Q. The SOP specificies certain actions that the Duty Officer will take in regards to destruction of classified material. Are you aware of these actions?

AFFIDAVIT

I, _____ HAVE READ OR HAVE HAD READ TO ME THIS STATE-
MENT WHICH BEGINS ON PAGE 1 AND ENDS ON PAGE _____. I FULLY UNDERSTAND THE CONTENTS OF THE ENTIRE STATEMENT MADE BY ME. THE STATEMENT IS TRUE. I HAVE INITIALED ALL CORRECTIONS AND HAVE INITIALED THE BOTTOM OF EACH PAGE CONTAINING THE STATEMENT. I HAVE MADE THIS STATEMENT FREELY WITHOUT HOPE OF BENEFIT OR REWARD, WITHOUT THREAT OF PUNISHMENT, AND WITHOUT COERCION, UNLAWFUL INFLUENCE, OR UNLAWFUL INDUCEMENT.

WITNESSES:

_____
(Signature of Person Making Statement)

Subscribed and sworn to before me, a person authorized by law
to administer oaths, this _____ day of _____, 19____
at _____

_____
ORGANIZATION OR ADDRESS

_____
(Signature of Person Administering Oath)

_____
(Typed Name of Person Administering Oath)

_____
ORGANIZATION OR ADDRESS

_____
(Authority To Administer Oaths)

INITIALS OF PERSON MAKING STATEMENT

PAGE 2 OF 6 PAGES

PPC-Japan

STATEMENT BY ACCUSED OR SUSPECT PERSON
(AR 195-10)

PLACE	DATE	TIME	FILE NUMBER

LAST NAME, FIRST NAME, MIDDLE NAME	SOCIAL SECURITY ACCOUNT NO.	GRADE

ORGANIZATION OR ADDRESS

PART I - WAIVER CERTIFICATE

I HAVE BEEN INFORMED BY _____

OF _____

THAT HE WANTS TO QUESTION ME ABOUT _____

OF WHICH I AM ACCUSED OR SUSPECTED. HE HAS ALSO INFORMED ME OF MY RIGHTS.

    I UNDERSTAND THAT I HAVE THE RIGHT TO REMAIN SILENT AND THAT ANY STATEMENT I MAKE MAY BE USED AS EVIDENCE AGAINST ME IN A CRIMINAL TRIAL.

    I UNDERSTAND THAT I HAVE THE RIGHT TO CONSULT WITH COUNSEL AND TO HAVE COUNSEL PRESENT WITH ME DURING QUESTIONING. I MAY RETAIN COUNSEL AT MY OWN EXPENSE OR COUNSEL WILL BE APPOINTED FOR ME AT NO EXPENSE TO ME. IF I AM SUBJECT TO THE UNIFORM CODE OF MILITARY JUSTICE, APPOINTED COUNSEL MAY BE MILITARY COUNSEL OF MY OWN CHOICE IF HE IS REASONABLY AVAILABLE.

    I UNDERSTAND THAT EVEN IF I DECIDE TO ANSWER QUESTIONS NOW WITHOUT HAVING COUNSEL PRESENT, I MAY STOP ANSWERING QUESTION AT ANY TIME. ALSO, I MAY REQUEST COUNSEL AT ANY TIME DURING QUESTIONING.

    I (DO) (DO NOT) WANT COUNSEL.

    I (DO) (DO NOT) WANT TO MAKE A STATEMENT AND _____
    ANSWER QUESTIONS.   (Signature of Person To Be Questioned)

INTERROGATOR: _____   WITNESS: _____
    (Signature)   (Signature)

    (Typed Name and Organization)   (Typed Name and Organization)

PART II - SWORN STATEMENT

I, MAURICE FRANK MERCURE, WANT TO MAKE THE FOLLOWING STATEMENT UNDER OATH:

STATEMENT OF MAURICE FRANK MERCURE TAKEN AT TAN SON NHUT AIR BASE DATED 14 FEB 69 CONTINUED

Reply: Which one?

Q. What do you mean which one?

A. There are several different SOP's.

Q. Will you make them available to me?

A. Yes Sir

At this time CW2 Mercure departed to obtain other copies of the CommCenter SOP. He returned and stated that a copy of the SOP with a conflicting statement would be made available.

Q. What are your duties and responsibilities as pertains to the burning of classified waste?

EXHIBIT	INITIALS OF PERSON MAKING STATEMENT	PAGE 3 OF 6 PAGES
	MFM	

ADDITIONAL PAGES MUST CONTAIN THE HEADING "STATEMENT OF__TAKEN AT__DATED__CONTINUED." THE BOTTOM OF EACH ADDITIONAL PAGE MUST BEAR THE INITIALS OF THE PERSON MAKING THE STATEMENT AND BE INITIALED AS "PAGE__OF__PAGES." WHEN ADDITIONAL PAGES ARE UTILIZED, THE BACK OF PAGE 1 WILL BE LINED OUT, AND THE STATEMENT WILL BE CONCLUDED ON THE REVERSE SIDE OF ANOTHER COPY OF THIS FORM.

DA FORM 2820, 1 OCT 67   REPLACES DA FORM 19-24, 1 SEP 62, WHICH IS OBSOLETE.

A. Selecting an E-5 and two men with one man having a TOP SECRET clearance and seeing that they complete a destruction certificate. Listing the number of bags destroyed and listing from what section the bags were received and insuring that the NCO is familiar with proper security practices.

Q. Do you have a copy of these certificates showing from what section they were received?

A. No Sir they are kept on file at M & R.

Q. What security practices are you specifically referring to above?

A. That the bags are loaded on the truck and kept under guard. Proper accounting for the number of bags, transporting to the burn area under guard, unloaded and placed in incinerator whole then properly destroyed by burning. After destruction is complete then sifting through the ashes for pieces that are unburned and inspecting the incinerator area before departing; that is inside of the fence; return to the CommCenter all scraps that have not been burned.

Q. As a supervisor what actions did you take to insure that these actions were taken?

A. Briefing the NCO and making periodic checks of the burn area and having the trick chief brief the NCO and make periodic checks.

Q. Were you aware of the SOP stating that the burn bags should be dated and numbered?

A. I was told that that part of the SOP was out. I read the SOP containing information about dating and numbering the SOP. However I was confused because there was another SOP on the Duty Officers desk containing conflicting instructions.

Q. How long had you known about these conflicting instructions?

A. Oh I had been in the station about three weeks.

AFFIDAVIT

I, _____ HAVE READ OR HAVE HAD READ TO ME THIS STATE-
MENT WHICH BEGINS ON PAGE 1 AND ENDS ON PAGE _____. I FULLY UNDERSTAND THE CONTENTS OF THE ENTIRE STATEMENT
MADE BY ME. THE STATEMENT IS TRUE. I HAVE INITIALED ALL CORRECTIONS AND HAVE INITIALED THE BOTTOM OF EACH PAGE
CONTAINING THE STATEMENT. I HAVE MADE THIS STATEMENT FREELY WITHOUT HOPE OF BENEFIT OR REWARD, WITHOUT THREAT
OF PUNISHMENT, AND WITHOUT COERCION, UNLAWFUL INFLUENCE, OR UNLAWFUL INDUCEMENT.

_____
(Signature of Person Making Statement)

WITNESSES:

Subscribed and sworn to before me, a person authorized by law
to administer oaths, this _____ day of _____, 19____

_____
_____   at _____

ORGANIZATION OR ADDRESS

_____
_____   (Signature of Person Administering Oath)

_____
_____   (Typed Name of Person Administering Oath)

ORGANIZATION OR ADDRESS

(Authority To Administer Oaths)

INITIALS OF PERSON MAKING STATEMENT   PAGE 4 OF 6 PAGES

STATEMENT BY ACCUSED OR SUSPECT PERSON
(AR 195-10)

PLACE	DATE	TIME	FILE NUMBER
LAST NAME, FIRST NAME, MIDDLE NAME		SOCIAL SECURITY ACCOUNT NO.	GRADE
ORGANIZATION OR ADDRESS			

PART I - WAIVER CERTIFICATE

I HAVE BEEN INFORMED BY _____

OF _____

THAT HE WANTS TO QUESTION ME ABOUT _____

OF WHICH I AM ACCUSED OR SUSPECTED. HE HAS ALSO INFORMED ME OF MY RIGHTS.

I UNDERSTAND THAT I HAVE THE RIGHT TO REMAIN SILENT AND THAT ANY STATEMENT I MAKE MAY BE USED AS EVIDENCE AGAINST ME IN A CRIMINAL TRIAL.

I UNDERSTAND THAT I HAVE THE RIGHT TO CONSULT WITH COUNSEL AND TO HAVE COUNSEL PRESENT WITH ME DURING QUESTIONING. I MAY RETAIN COUNSEL AT MY OWN EXPENSE OR COUNSEL WILL BE APPOINTED FOR ME AT NO EXPENSE TO ME. IF I AM SUBJECT TO THE UNIFORM CODE OF MILITARY JUSTICE, APPOINTED COUNSEL MAY BE MILITARY COUNSEL OF MY OWN CHOICE IF HE IS REASONABLY AVAILABLE.

I UNDERSTAND THAT EVEN IF I DECIDE TO ANSWER QUESTIONS NOW WITHOUT HAVING COUNSEL PRESENT, I MAY STOP ANSWERING QUESTION AT ANY TIME. ALSO, I MAY REQUEST COUNSEL AT ANYTIME DURING QUESTIONING.

I (DO) (DO NOT) WANT COUNSEL.

I (DO) (DO NOT) WANT TO MAKE A STATEMENT AND _____
ANSWER QUESTIONS.

_____
(Signature of Person To Be Questioned)

INTERROGATOR: _____   WITNESS: _____

(Signature)   (Signature)

(Typed Name and Organization)   (Typed Name and Organization)

PART II - SWORN STATEMENT

I, **MAURICE FRANK MERCURE**   WANT TO MAKE THE FOLLOWING STATEMENT UNDER OATH:

STATEMENT OF MAURICE FRANK MERCURE TAKEN AT TAN SON NHUT AIR BASE DATED 14 FEB 69 CONTINUED

Q. How long have you been here since that time?

A. Two months.

Q. Did you ask the OIC or Duty Officer about the conflicting instructions?

A. I brought this to the attention of 1Lt Vollrath and CW3 Markley that there were discrepancies in the SOP.

Q. Did they answer these questions to your satisfaction?

A. They stated the Duty Officer was not responsible for the burn detail. They said that they would take care of the other discrepancies.

Q. Did CW3 Markley have you updating the SOP?

A. He started me updating the SOP 2 to 3 weeks ago. He was doing part and he gave me

EXHIBIT	INITIALS OF PERSON MAKING STATEMENT	PAGE 5 OF 6 PAGES
	M.F.M.	

ADDITIONAL PAGES MUST CONTAIN THE HEADING "STATEMENT OF___TAKEN AT___DATED___CONTINUED." THE BOTTOM OF EACH ADDITIONAL PAGE MUST BEAR THE INITIALS OF THE PERSON MAKING THE STATEMENT AND BE INITIALED AS "PAGE__OF__PAGES." WHEN ADDITIONAL PAGES ARE UTILIZED, THE BACK OF PAGE 1 WILL BE LINED OUT, AND THE STATEMENT WILL BE CONCLUDED ON THE REVERSE SIDE OF ANOTHER COPY OF THIS FORM.

DA FORM 2820   REPLACES DA FORM 19-24, 1 SEP 62, WHICH IS OBSOLETE.

STATEMENT *(Continued)*

part to do.

Q. Did you in fact feel that you had no supervision of the personnel on the detail?

A. No, I feel that I was responsible for their supervision, but not that part of the SOP that they told me was out. This I have told you before.

Q. Have you any information as to why the three bags of classified waste were not destroyed?

A. No Sir. I can't figure it out. I have checked the area periodically and have never found anything before./ / / / / / /END OF STATEMENT/ / / / / / / / / / / /

AFFIDAVIT

I, MAURICE FRANK MERCURE, HAVE READ OR HAVE HAD READ TO ME THIS STATE-MENT WHICH BEGINS ON PAGE 1 AND ENDS ON PAGE 6 . I FULLY UNDERSTAND THE CONTENTS OF THE ENTIRE STATEMENT MADE BY ME. THE STATEMENT IS TRUE. I HAVE INITIALED ALL CORRECTIONS AND HAVE INITIALED THE BOTTOM OF EACH PAGE CONTAINING THE STATEMENT. I HAVE MADE THIS STATEMENT FREELY WITHOUT HOPE OF BENEFIT OR REWARD, WITHOUT THREAT OF PUNISHMENT, AND WITHOUT COERCION, UNLAWFUL INFLUENCE, OR UNLAWFUL INDUCEMENT.

(Signature of Person Making Statement)

WITNESSES:

FRANCIS R. SMITH
Company A, 69th Signal Battalion
APO San Francisco 96307
ORGANIZATION OR ADDRESS

Subscribed and sworn to before me, a person authorized by law to administer oaths, this 14 day of February , 1969 at TSN, RVN

(Signature of Person Administering Oath)

BENNY L. LOCKETT, MAJ
(Typed Name of Person Administering Oath)

Investigating Officer
(Authority To Administer Oaths)

ORGANIZATION OR ADDRESS

INITIALS OF PERSON MAKING STATEMENT MFM

PAGE 6 OF 6 PAGES

PPC-Japs

1 March 1969

SUBJECT: Rebuttal to Conclusion of Investigating Officer

TO: Major Benny L. Lockett

1. In rebuttal to the recommendation of the Investigating Officer for appropriate disciplinary action to be taken against me, the following is submitted.

2. In paragraph 5a, the Investigating Officer stated that SOP instructions were adequate; however, there existed two copies of a station SOP on the Duty Officer/Trick Chiefs desks. One copy in a black binder (which was frequently missing from the desk) and one in a gray hardboard cover (marked on front cover in red letters SOP). Both these SOP's had not been revised to reflect the new procedures that where verbally given to CW2 Breithaupt and CW3 Markley by LTC Hushner, OIC MACV Communications Center. No confusion or misunderstanding would have occurred if station SOP had been immediately updated by responsible persons.

3. I take exception to the statement in paragraph 5c, I have personally seen burn bags left in the poking position area for 48 hours or more.

4. Concerning paragraph 5e, I again wish to state here that all personnel were following what they thought and had every reason to believe were the right instructions. However, it was'nt clear to all personnel which was official, the verbal order, black binder SOP or gray hardboard covered SOP, i.e. Duty Officer, Trick Chief and Burn Detail NCO. As far as I am concerned, the verbal order superseded the SOP's. Upon assuming the position of Duty Officer, I discussed with CW3 Markley, which procedure was in effect concerning the burn detail. He informed me that he had received verbal instructions from LTC Hushner, OIC MACV Communications Center, that the Duty Officer was no longer responsible for the burn detail, that the burn detail NCO was; however, we should if at all possible check the burn area. At this time no mention was made of log entries. I then went on nights with CW3 Markley and he showed me what to do. At no time while we worked together, did he make any entries on the Duty Officers Log as to his checking the burn area. For that matter none of the other Duty Officers made any entries either. In fact no log entries had been made since the 15th of of October, during the night tours of duty. It must be also pointed out that during the period 20 January through 30 January 1969, I was on days, helping CW3 Markley revise that station SOP. I was informed at this time that CW2 Breithaupt was responsible as Security Officer for revising the portion on security.

SUBJECT: Rebuttal to Conclusion of Investigating Officer

5.   Since I had been told that I would have no responsibility for the activities of the burn detail, and since the pressures of supervising four Communications Centers at one time did not permit me any time to assume additional duties for which I was'nt responsible, I do not see any basis for disciplinary action against me as a result of this matter.

                                        MAURICE F. MERCURE
                                        CM2, USN

DEPARTMENT OF THE ARMY
COMPANY A, 69TH SIGNAL BATTALION (ARMY)
APO San Francisco 96307

SCCPV-UG-SN-A   9 May 1969

SUBJECT: Letter of Appreciation

TO: CW2 Maurice F. Mercure
     W2▮▮▮▮▮
     Company A, 69th Signal Battalion (A)
     APO San Francisco 96307

1. Upon my departure as Commanding Officer, Company A, 69th Signal
Battalion, I would like to express my sincere appreciation for your
outstanding performance of duty as Duty Officer, MACV Communication
Center.

2. Your attentiveness, rapid comprehension and able application of
Communication Center procedures along with your desire and willingness
to maintain the best performance standards are in the highest traditions
of the service. The acute perspective and overall understanding you
have developed concerning operational and administrative techniques has
been an asset to my command and all who have worked with you.

3. Your acceptance of responsibility, exceptional performance and
flawless conduct while assigned to this command reflect admirably
upon your abilities and brings credit to yourself, your superiors
and the United States Army. I wish you the best of good luck and
success in the future.

                                   MARK J. CHITWOOD
                                   1LT, SigC
                                   Commanding

Mr. Mercure

SGOPA-IO-OR-A   20 May 1969

SUBJECT: Pay Officers Schedule

Personnel Concerned

The following officers are scheduled to perform duties as stated on dates
indic.

COMPANY A PAY OFFICERS

1. CPT Breichampf   MAY 69
2. ...   .
3. ...   .
4. ...   .
5. ...   .
6. CPT Breichampf   ....
7. Range   ....

PLASTER COMMISSION OFFICERS

1. ... Langle   ....
   ...
   ...
   ...
   ...
2. CPT Totub   ....

Any reason for change of schedule will be coordinated with the Commanding
Officer of Company A, 69th Signal Battalion. It will be the responsibility
of the officer concerned to get a replacement if duty cannot be performed
during month scheduled.

                                          HUGH J. LANDIS JR
                                          1LT, SigC
                                          Acting Commander

ELECTION OF OPTIONS UNDER RETIRED SERVICEMAN'S FAMILY PROTECTION PLAN *(PL 87-381)* *(AR 608-30)*

DATE: 10 June 1969

1. LAST NAME - FIRST NAME - MIDDLE NAME	2. SERVICE NUMBER	3. GRADE OR RANK
MERCURE, MAURICE FRANK	[redacted]	SGM

4. PRESENT MAILING ADDRESS	5. STATUS *(Check applicable box)*	
537 Chicopee Street Willimansett, Massachusetts 01013	[X] ACTIVE DUTY [ ] NOT ON ACTIVE DUTY [ ] RETIRED	
	6. DATE OF BIRTH: 14 August [redacted]	7. NUMBER OF YEARS COMPLETED FOR PAY PURPOSES: 22 Years

OPTIONS *(Check one or more appropriate blocks)*

I UNDERSTAND THAT I MAY ELECT ONE OR MORE OF THE FOLLOWING OPTIONS, PROVIDING ANNUITIES UPON MY DEATH IN RETIRED STATUS IN AMOUNTS EQUAL TO ⅛, ¼, OR ½ OF MY REDUCED RETIRED PAY. I MAY ELECT OPTION 1 OR 2 OR 3 WITH OR WITHOUT OPTION 4, OR I MAY ELECT OPTIONS 1 AND 2 WITH OR WITHOUT OPTION 4. IF I ELECT OPTION 1 OR 2 OR 3 WITH OR WITHOUT OPTION 4 THE ANNUITY MAY NOT EXCEED 50% OF MY REDUCED RETIRED PAY. IF I ELECT OPTIONS 1 AND 2 THE AMOUNT OF EACH ANNUITY MAY NOT EXCEED 25% OF MY REDUCED RETIRED PAY. I UNDERSTAND THAT THE ANNUITY UNDER OPTION 3 WITH OR WITHOUT OPTION 4 MAY BE ALLOCATED TO MY WIDOW AND SURVIVING CHILDREN WHO ARE NOT CHILDREN OF THE WIFE NAMED AS BENEFICIARY HEREON. THEREFORE, I HEREBY ELECT THE FOLLOWING OPTION OR OPTIONS: *(Detailed options on reverse side.)*

8. ANNUITY PAYABLE TO OR ON BEHALF OF MY WIDOW

OPTION 1 WITH OPTION 4: [ ] ⅛ [ ] ¼ [ ] ½ OR OPTION 1 ONLY: [ ] ⅛ [ ] ¼ [ ] ½

9. ANNUITY PAYABLE TO OR ON BEHALF OF MY SURVIVING CHILD OR CHILDREN

OPTION 2 WITH OPTION 4: [ ] ⅛ [ ] ¼ [ ] ½ OR OPTION 2 ONLY: [ ] ⅛ [ ] ¼ [ ] ½

10. ANNUITY PAYABLE TO OR ON BEHALF OF MY WIDOW AND SURVIVING CHILD OR CHILDREN

OPTION 3 WITH OPTION 4: [ ] ⅛ [ ] ¼ [ ] ½ OR OPTION 3 ONLY: [ ] ⅛ [ ] ¼ [ ] ½

11. [X] I DO NOT DESIRE TO RECEIVE REDUCED RETIRED PAY IN ORDER TO PROVIDE AN ANNUITY FOR MY DEPENDENTS

[ ] THIS IS MY ORIGINAL ELECTION [ ] THIS IS A NEW ELECTION SUBSEQUENT TO SUBMISSION OF AN [ ] INVALID OR [ ] REVOCATION OF A PRIOR ELECTION

[ ] THIS IS A REQUEST FOR CHANGE OR MODIFICATION OF A PRIOR ELECTION* [ ] I PREVIOUSLY DECLINED TO MAKE AN ELECTION AND NOW DESIRE TO DO SO.

[ ] THIS IS A REQUEST FOR REVOCATION *(Cancellation)* OF A PRIOR ELECTION*

**The terms of the election may be modified or revoked by a member at any time prior to his retirement but any modification or revocation so made shall not be effective if he retires within three years after the date it is made. Any member who revokes an election is permitted to execute a new election after it becomes effective. The new election will become effective three years after the date made if the member is not retired.*

12. IF ANY OF THE ABOVE OPTIONS ARE ELECTED, THE FOLLOWING INFORMATION IS TO BE FURNISHED. IF NO CURRENT BENEFICIARY, SO INDICATE.

NAME OF SPOUSE *(First, middle and last)*	DATE OF BIRTH OF SPOUSE

13. IF EITHER OPTION 2 OR OPTION 3 IS ELECTED, THE FOLLOWING INFORMATION IS TO BE FURNISHED. IF NO CURRENT BENEFICIARY, SO INDICATE.

NAME OF YOUNGEST CHILD	DATE OF BIRTH OF YOUNGEST CHILD	INDICATE IF STEPCHILD OR ADOPTED CHILD

I UNDERSTAND THAT DURING ANY PERIOD OF MY RETIREMENT IN WHICH I AM NOT RECEIVING RETIRED PAY, I SHALL BE REQUIRED TO DEPOSIT WITH THE U. S. TREASURY THE AMOUNT THAT WOULD HAVE BEEN WITHHELD FROM MY RETIRED PAY UNDER THE OPTION(S) ELECTED, AND IF I FAIL TO MAKE SUCH DEPOSITS, I CONSENT TO HAVE UNDEPOSITED AMOUNTS, PLUS INTEREST, DEDUCTED FROM RETIRED PAY UPON BEING RESTORED TO A RETIRED PAY STATUS. I ALSO UNDERSTAND THAT IF I DO NOT COMBINE OPTION 4 WITH THE OPTION(S) ELECTED, DEDUCTIONS WILL CONTINUE TO BE MADE FROM MY RETIRED PAY DESPITE THE FACT THAT ALL BENEFICIARIES PREDECEASE ME OR BECOME INELIGIBLE FOR ANNUITY BENEFITS.

14. SIGNATURE OF WITNESS	15. SIGNATURE OF APPLICANT	16. DATE OF SIGNATURES
[illegible]	Maurice F. Mercure	10 June 1969

IMPORTANT: *This form must be executed in quintuplicate, all copies signed, dated, witnessed and the original and 3 copies returned to the office having custody of your personnel file. The duplicate will be receipted and returned to you. Copy No. 5 is to be retained by you pending receipt of copy No. 2 from Personnel Officer. (Legible carbon signatures acceptable on copies.)*

THIS BLOCK MUST BE COMPLETED BY PERSONNEL OFFICER

17. RECEIVED AT *(Organization and Station)*: Hq, 69th Signal Battalion (A), APO SF 96307, Tan Son Nhut, Vietnam

18. ON *(Date of receipt)*	19. ENTER POSTMARKED DATE *(If appropriate)*	20. SERVICE FOR COMPUTION OF BASIC PAY COMPLETED BY MEMBER AS OF DATE OF RECEIPT OF THIS FORM	YEARS	MONTHS	DAYS
10 June 1969			22	[illegible]	4

21. TYPED NAME AND GRADE OF PERSONNEL OFFICER	22. SIGNATURE
B. D. FARRIS, CW2, USA, Personnel Officer	B D Farris

DA FORM 1 FEB 62 1041 PREVIOUS EDITIONS OF THIS FORM ARE OBSOLETE.

SERVICE MEMBER MAKING ELECTION 2

EXPLANATION OF OPTIONS AVAILABLE UNDER THIS PLAN

OPTION 1

An annuity payable to or on behalf of the widow (or widower), the annuity to terminate on the widow's death or remarriage, whichever occurs first. The term "Widow (or widower)" refers ONLY to the spouse at the date of retirement.

OPTION 2

An annuity payable to or on behalf of surviving child or children, the annuity to terminate when there ceases to be at least one such surviving child, unmarried and under 18 years of age. However, if there is a child, unmarried and over 18 who is incapable of self-support because of being mentally defective or physically incapacitated and that condition existed prior to the child reaching 18 years of age, the annuity will terminate upon the child's marriage, death, or recovery from the disability, whichever occurs first. Payments under this option will be made in equal shares to or on behalf of the surviving children remaining eligible at the time payment is due.

OPTION 3

An annuity payable to or on behalf of his widow and surviving children, the annuity to terminate upon the death or remarriage of the widow, or, if later, the first day of the month in which there are no surviving children of the member who are under eighteen years of age and unmarried, except that if there is a child, unmarried and over eighteen years of age, incapable of self-support because of being mentally defective or physically incapacitated and that condition existed prior to his reaching eighteen years of age, the annuity to terminate upon his marriage, death, or recovery from the disability, whichever first occurs. Such annuity shall be paid to the widow until death or remarriage, and thereafter each payment under such annuity shall be paid in equal shares to or on behalf of the surviving children remaining eligible at the time payment is due. Such annuity may also be allocated so that a part may be payable to the widow and a part payable to his surviving children who are not children of the wife named as beneficiary.

OPTION 4

When combined with any of the options above, option 4 provides that no further deductions shall be made from retired pay commencing with the first day of the month following that in which there is no beneficiary eligible to receive an annuity under the option elected. If option 4 is not combined with any of the options above, deductions will continue to be made from retired pay despite the fact that all beneficiaries predecease the retired member or become ineligible to receive annuity benefits.

CW2 Maurice F. Mercure ▓▓▓▓▓▓▓
Co A, 69th Signal Bn(A)(MACV)
APO San Francisco, Ca 96307
27 June 1969

Government Employees Finance and Industrial Load Corporation▓▓▓ ▓▓
1206N. Hartford St.
Arlington, Virgina 22201

Gentlemen:

While station in Germany, in Co A, 32nd Signal Bn(Corps), I received orders assigning me to Vietnam. I wrote to your company and told you that and you ▓▓▓▓▓▓ to my letter. I told you that my car was being shipped to the states and would be stored in a garage (my ▓▓▓▓▓) at 547 Chicopee Street, Willimansett Massachusetts, and would not be used. You informed me to notify your firm when the car arrived there and to apply for necessary insurance. When my car arrived there, I ▓▓▓▓ you a letter and informed you that I wanted the necessary insurance from your company. I have not heard from you since, and seeing I am in Vietnam and time seems to go by quickly and one never seems to have time to write or remember things, it takes an incoming letter to remind one and prompt him into action. So once again I would like very much for your affiliated insurance company (Government Employees Insurance Co.) to issue me the necessary insurance required on a vehicle in storage and bill me. I would also like to have the same coverage I had before when I pick up my car in November, when I return to the states. I hope that I will hear from you on this matter as soon as possible so I can get it off my mind and concentrate on the job at hand here.

Sincerely yours

MAURICE F. MERCURE

AIR MAIL

DEPARTMENT OF THE ARMY
OFFICE OF THE ADJUTANT GENERAL
WASHINGTON, D.C. 20315

AGPO-RO Mecure, Maurice F.   18 July 1969
015-22-3017 (18 Jun 69)
SUBJECT: Receipt of Retirement Application

TO: Chief Warrant Officer W-2 Maurice F. Mercure
           69th Signal Battalion
           APO San Francisco 96307

1. Your application for voluntary retirement has been received and is
now being processed.

2. Receipt of your application does not imply that it will be approved,
or if approved, that it will be effective on the date requested. Provided
there are no restrictions which preclude your retirement on the date
requested, orders will be issued at the earliest possible date. You will
be advised of any extended delay in processing your case.

3. Movement of dependents or personal property at government expense
prior to issuance of orders is only authorized in exceptional circumstances.
Coordination should be made in advance with command personnel and transportation authorities, after complying with provisions of paragraph 2-2,
AR 55-71 and M7003-4, Joint Travel Regulations. Since retirement orders
are published at Department of the Army, statements required by the regulations that "orders will be issued" must be made by this office.

4. Should you desire to withdraw or change the date of your retirement,
your are advised to comply strictly with the provisions of paragraph 26,
AR 635-130.

BY ORDER OF THE SECRETARY OF THE ARMY:

                     Kenneth G. Wickham

                     KENNETH G. WICKHAM
                     Major General, USA
                     The Adjutant General

AGPZ FL 564
(10 Jul 68)

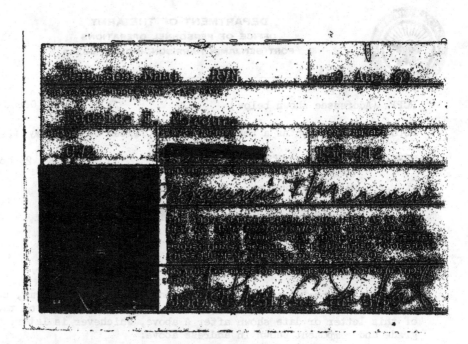

DEPARTMENT OF THE ARMY
OFFICE OF PERSONNEL OPERATIONS
FORT BENJAMIN HARRISON, INDIANA 46249

/clm

RCPP (Addressee shown below)   10 October 1969

SUBJECT: Promotion as a Reserve Warrant Officer of the Army (Para 20)

THRU: Commanding Officer   A- 25 November 1969
         69th Signal Battalion
         APO San Francisco 96307

TO: CW2 Maurice F. Mecure, 015-███████, USAR (SC)

1. You are promoted as a Reserve Warrant Officer of the Army, under
Title 10, U.S. Code, Section 598 and AR 135-158, effective on the date
of this letter or date shown after A above, whichever is later, to the
grade and component shown in address above.

2. No acceptance or oath of office is required. Unless you expressly
decline this promotion within 60 days, your assumption of office will be
effective as stated above.

3. The date shown after A above is the date you attained eligibility
for promotion to the grade to which promoted herein, and will be used in
computing time in grade for promotion to the next higher Reserve grade.

BY ORDER OF THE SECRETARY OF THE ARMY:

JOHN H. HOFFMAN
Colonel, USA
Commanding Officer
U.S. Army Reserve Components Personnel Center

CF:
SC Br, OPD
Sep Br, TAGO

RCPC FL
31 AUG 68   30   REPLACES RCPC FL 30, DATED 1 APR 68, WHICH IS OBSOLETE.

THE UNITED STATES OF AMERICA

TO ALL WHO SHALL SEE THESE PRESENTS, GREETING:

THIS IS TO CERTIFY THAT

THE PRESIDENT OF THE UNITED STATES OF AMERICA
AUTHORIZED BY EXECUTIVE ORDER, 24 AUGUST 1962
HAS AWARDED

THE BRONZE STAR MEDAL

TO

CHIEF WARRANT OFFICER TWO MAURICE F. MERCURE, ███████, U. S. ARMY

FOR

MERITORIOUS ACHIEVEMENT

IN GROUND OPERATIONS AGAINST HOSTILE FORCES

In the Republic of Vietnam during the period 30 October 1968 to 1 October 1969

GIVEN UNDER MY HAND IN THE CITY OF WASHINGTON

THIS   11th   DAY OF   October   1869

Stanley R. Resor
SECRETARY OF THE ARMY

Thomas Matthew Rienzi

THOMAS MATTHEW RIENZI
Brigadier General, USA
Commanding

MERCURE, MAURICE

W 2 ▬▬▬▬

ORGANIZATIONAL CLOTHING AND EQUIPMENT RECORD
(AR 735-35)

Use pencil for authorized allowance, sizes, and balances;
ink for remaining entries. Acknowledge all transactions
with signature in appropriate numbered columns.

ARTICLES ORGANIZATIONAL CLOTHING QUARTERMASTER	AUTHORIZED ALLOWANCES	SIZE	ISSUES (Date)								TURN-INS (Date)					BALANCE
			1	2	3	4	5	6	7	8	1	2	3	4	5	
APRON, BAKER, BUTCHER AND COOK																
CAP, FIELD, COTTON																
CAP, FIELD, PILE																
CAP, BAKERS AND COOKS																
COATS, BAKERS AND COOKS																
COAT, MAN'S, SATEEN, OG 107																
DRESS, WOMEN'S, COOKS AND BAKERS																
DRESS, WM'S CTN																
GLOVES, LEATHER, HEAVY																
GLOVES, WORK, COTTON																
GLOVE-INSERTS, WOOL																
GLOVE-SHELL, LEATHER																
HOOD, WINTER, SATEEN, OG 107																
LINER, COAT, MANS																
OVERCOAT, MAN'S, W/REM. LINER																
OVERSHOES																
PONCHO, LIGHWEIGHT W/HOOD																
SCARF, MAN'S, WOOL, OD																
SHIRT, FIELD, WOOL																
SHIRT, HBT, WOMEN'S SPECIAL																
SHOES, ATHLETIC																
SHORTS, ATHLETIC, POPLIN																
STOCKINGS, COTTON																
SWEATER																
SUPPORTERS, ATHLETIC																
SUSPENDERS, TROUSERS																
TROUSERS, BAKERS AND COOKS																
TROUSERS, FIELD, WOOL																
TROUSERS, HBT, WOMEN'S SPECIAL																
TROUSERS, WOMEN'S OUTER COVER																
TROUSERS, SHELL, FIELD					1											
TROUSERS, WOMEN'S, WOOL, LINER																
WAIST, WOOL, WOMENS																

INDIVIDUAL MUST ACKNOWLEDGE ISSUES AND AN OFFICER MUST ACKNOWLEDGE TURN-INS BY SIGNING AT RIGHT IN APPROPRIATE COLUMNS.

SIGNATURE OF INDIVIDUAL   SIGNATURE OF OFFICER

ARTICLES ORGANIZATIONAL CLOTHING QUARTERMASTER	AUTHORIZED ALLOWANCES	ISSUES (Date)							TURN-INS (Date)					BALANCE
		1	2	3	4	5	6	7	8	1	2	3	4	5	
		190069													
TROUSERS, TROP.		5	5												
COATS, TROP.		5	5												
BOOTS, TROP.		2													
UNDERSHIRTS 06		3													
DRAWERS 06		5													
ORGANIZATIONAL EQUIPMENT															
AXE, INTRCH, W/HANDLE															
BAG, BARRACK		1	1												
BAG, CLOTHING, WATERPROOF		1	1												
BAG, SLEEPING		1	1												
BAR, INSECT, FIELD															
BELT, CART, CAL 30, DISMTD															
BELT, MAGAZINE BAR															
BELT, PISTOL OR REVOLVER															
BLANKET, WOOL		1	1												
BRASSARD, ARM															
CANTEEN, ALUMINUM		1	1												
CARRIER, AXE INTRCH															
CARRIER, INTRCH TOOL, COMB			1												
CARRIER, PICK MATTOCK, INTRCH															
CASE, FIRST AID PACKET															
CASE, WATER REPELLENT BAG, SLEEPING		1													
COVER, CANTEEN, DISMOUNTED		1	1												
CUP, CANTEEN, CRS		1	1												
FORK, FIELD, MESS															

INDIVIDUAL MUST ACKNOWLEDGE ISSUES AND AN OFFICER MUST ACKNOWLEDGE TURN-INS BY SIGNING AT RIGHT IN APPROPRIATE COLUMNS.

SIGNATURE OF INDIVIDUAL   SIGNATURE OF OFFICER

2

ORGANIZATIONAL EQUIPMENT (Cont.)	AUTHORIZED ALLOWANCES	ISSUES (Date)								TURN-INS (Date)					BALANCE
		1	A	3	4	5	6	7	8	1	2	3	4	5	
GLASSES, SUN W/CASE		1	1												
GOGGLES															
HEADNET, MOSQUITO															
HELMET, STEEL, W/DETACHABLE STRAP		1	1												
INTRCH TOOL, COMBINATION		1													
KNIFE, FIELD, MESS															
LINER, STEEL, HELMET, W/STRAP		1	1												
PACK, FIELD, CARGO															
PACK, FIELD, COMBAT															
PAD, INFLATABLE, SLEEPING															
PAN, MESS, KIT, CRS		1	1												
PICK, MATTOCK, INTRCH W/HANDLE															
PIN, TENT															
POCKET, CART CAL 30 CARBINE/RIFLE		1													
POCKET, MAGAZINE, CARBINE 30 ROUND															
POCKET, MAGAZINE, DOUBLE WEB 45 CAL		1	1												
POLE, TENT, SINGLE SECTION		1													
SHOVEL, INTRCH															
SPOON, FIELD, MESS															
STRAP, CARRYING, GENERAL PURPOSE															
SUSPENDERS, PACK, FIELD, CARGO/CMBT		1	1												
TENT, SHELTER, HALF, NEW TYPE															
WHISTLE, THUNDERER															

INDIVIDUAL MUST ACKNOWLEDGE ISSUES AND AN OFFICER MUST ACKNOWLEDGE TURN-INS BY SIGNING AT RIGHT IN APPROPRIATE COLUMNS.

SIGNATURE OF INDIVIDUAL   SIGNATURE OF OFFICER

POST, CAMP AND STATION EQUIPMENT	AUTHORIZED ALLOWANCES	ISSUES (Date)								TURN-INS (Date)					BALANCE
		1	11 OCT 65	3	4	5	6	7	8	1	2	3	4	5	
BLANKET, WOOL															
COT, FOLDING															
COVER, MATTRESS															
LOCKER, BOX															
MATTRESS, COTTON															
PILLOW															
PILLOW CASE															
SHEET, COTTON															
LOCKER, CLOTHING															
BEDSTEAD															
OTHER SERVICES															
MASK, PROTECTIVE, FIELD (chem)															
FLAK VEST		1	1												
RIFLE (ord)															
CARBINE (ord)															
PISTOL (ord)															
BAYONET, KNIFE (ord)															
SCABBARD (ord)															
WATCH, WRIST (ord)															

INDIVIDUAL MUST ACKNOWLEDGE ISSUES AND AN OFFICER MUST ACKNOWLEDGE TURN-INS BY SIGNING AT RIGHT IN APPROPRIATE COLUMNS.

SIGNATURE OF INDIVIDUAL	SIGNATURE OF OFFICER

THIS IS A

☐ TRUE COPY   ☐ TRUE CERTIFIED CONSOLIDATION

☐ INITIAL ISSUE   ☐ PHYSICAL INVENTORY

ARM OR SERVICE	GRADE	OFFICER (Signature)

PPC-Japan

SECURITY TERMINATION STATEMENT AND DEBRIEFING CERTIFICATE
(AR 604)

PART I - BASIC INFORMATION

FROM (Originating Headquarters)

HHC, 69th Sig Bn (A) APO 96307

DOSSIER NO.

LAST NAME - FIRST NAME - MIDDLE INITIAL

MERCURE, MAURICE, P

GRADE (MIL or CIV)

CW2

SVC NO. AND SOCIAL SECURITY NO. (███)

DATE OF BIRTH (Day, Mo, Yr)

14 Aug ██

PLACE OF BIRTH (City, State, Country)

Chicopee; Fairview; Mass

PART II - REFERENCES

1. APPLICABLE TO ALL PERSONNEL WHO HAVE HAD ACCESS TO DEFENSE INFORMATION:
   (1) ESPIONAGE LAWS: TITLE 18, U.S. CODE, SECTIONS 793, 794 AND 798 (Temporary detention of Section 794)
   (2) INTERNAL SECURITY LAWS: TITLE 50, U.S. CODE, SECTION 783.
   (3) AR ██

2. ADDITIONALLY APPLICABLE TO PERSONNEL WHO HAVE HAD ACCESS TO RESTRICTED DATA:
   (1) ATOMIC ENERGY ACT OF 1954, TITLE 42, U.S. CODE, SECTIONS 2011-2281
   (2) AR 380-150

3. ADDITIONALLY APPLICABLE TO PERSONNEL HAVING HAD ACCESS TO CRYPTOGRAPHIC MATERIAL OR INFORMATION

4. ADDITIONALLY APPLICABLE TO PERSONNEL WHO HAVE HAD ACCESS TO INFORMATION SPECIALLY COMPARTMENTED

PART III - SECURITY TERMINATION AND DEBRIEFING

DISTRIBUTION:

FIELD 201 FILE (Military)

SIGNATURE

DA FORM 2962

B142a

OUTLINE OF GENERAL CONTENT ORAL SECURITY DEBRIEFING
(Part of Security Termination Statement)

1. PURPOSE OF DEBRIEFING. a. To establish that the individual does in fact understand the implications, to national security, and to himself, of the statutes and regulations which he has read.

b. To emphasize to the individual that he was afforded access to classified information solely because of his "need-to-know" in the performance of official duties; that this information was entrusted, as well as officially charged to him; and that his impending retirement, separation, transfer, or reassignment *(as applicable)* in no way lessens his responsibilities - and liabilities - for ensuring that the classified knowledge acquired in his most recent position is not divulged in any manner to an unauthorized person or agency.

2. SERIOUS NATURE OF THE SUBJECT MATTER WHICH REQUIRES PROTECTION. Emphasize to the individual that classified information is defined and described in the pertinent statutes and regulations which he has read. As an illustration, cite the fact that *SECRET* defense information is "information or material the unauthorized disclosure of which *COULD RESULT IN SERIOUS DAMAGE TO THE NATION"* (AR 380-5). Where the individual has had access to *TOP SECRET, RESTRICTED DATA, CRYPTOGRAPHIC* information, compartmented information, etc., cite the specific definition(s) and description(s) and emphasize that such material is even more serious in nature.

3. NEED FOR CAUTION AND DISCRETION. a. Emphasize to the individual that the responsibility is *HIS* to specifically establish that a person or agency requesting any classified information is officially authorized *(NEED-TO-KNOW)* that information; that if he is leaving the service *(includes civilian employees),* absolutely no other person or agency is authorized the classified information; that if he is being transferred or reassigned, any classified information known by the individual being debriefed cannot be divulged by that individual unless the new organization and specific person requesting the information has established the need-to-know.

b. Emphasize to the individual that the mere fact that he reads a news article which appears to contain classified information in no way authorizes him to confirm the item. Explain that good "guesses" frequently are reflected by the news media, but bad "guesses" and incorrect information also are included.

c. Caution the individual that history records a number of cases involving unauthorized disclosures in clubs and at social gatherings which have been reported and which resulted in punitive action.

4. ANY TRAVEL RESTRICTIONS IMPOSED. Cite the specific travel restrictions (e. g., as set forth in AR 380-15, AR 380-16 and AR 380-17, for NATO, CENTO, and SEATO information) AR 380-157, for restricted data.

5. SUMMARY. Specifically ask the individual if he understands what he has read and what he is about to sign. Based on his response *(and questions he may raise)* re-emphasize the content of the Security Termination Statement.

STATEMENT OF ACCESSORIAL SERVICES PERFORMED	BILL OF LADING NO.	DATE OF SHIPMENT
		22 OCTOBER 69

ORDERING ACTIVITY/INSTALLATION (Name and location)

HQ AREA COMMAND, BVN SGN

NOTE : This form is required only when accessorial services performed are chargeable to the Government. Carrier will enter complete information or "None" in column at the right and in the Storage-in-transit section.

ORIGIN OF SHIPMENT

69TH SIGNAL HQ BVN 25 SGN

DESTINATION OF SHIPMENT

MASSACHUSETTS (DOVER)

NAME OF OWNER

KROUSE, M.F.

RANK OR GRADE   **CW2**   SERVICE NO.

CERTIFICATE OF CARRIER

THIS CARRIER FURNISHED MATERIALS/PERFORMED SERVICES, AS INDICATED HEREON (Check as appropriate)

[X] AT ORIGIN   [ ] AT DESTINATION   [ ] OTHER

NAMES OF CARRIER/AGENT

COLUMBIA EXPORT PACKERS, INC.

SIGNATURE OF CARRIER REPRESENTATIVE AND DATE

TITLE   **PACKING SUPERVISOR**

STATEMENT OF OWNER/MILITARY INSPECTOR/ TRANSPORTATION OFFICER(S)

MATERIALS WERE FURNISHED/ACCESSORIAL SERVICES WERE PERFORMED BY ABOVE NAMED CARRIER AS INDICATED HEREON.

SIGNATURE(S), TITLE(S)

ORIGIN   **69TH SIGNAL HQ BVN 25 SGN**

INTERMEDIATE POINT(S) OF DELIVERY   Owner

DESTINATION

STORAGE-IN-TRANSIT

STORED AT

DATE IN   DATE OUT   NUMBER OF DAYS

NET WEIGHT   CHARGE (To be shown separately on bill)

PACKING MATERIALS	NUM-BER	UNIT PRICE	CHARGE
BARRELS (Include drums or specially designed fiber containers) NOT LESS THAN 5 CU. FT.	I		
BOXES, WOODEN NOT OVER 5 CU. FT.	4		
OVER 5, NOT OVER 8 CU. FT	3		
CRATES, WOODEN AND CONTAINERS (Glass cubic feet)	2		
CARTONS LESS THAN 1½ CU. FT.	I		
1½ LESS THAN 3 CU. FT.			
3 LESS THAN 4½ CU. FT.			
4½ LESS THAN 6 CU. FT.			
6 LESS THAN 6½ CU. FT.			
6½ OR MORE CU. FT. NOT LESS THAN 275 LBS TEST			
MATTRESS NOT EXCEEDING 44" x 75"			
MATTRESS EXCEEDING 44" x 75"			
MATTRESS, CRIB			
MATTRESS COVER (paper or plastic)			
WARDROBE CARTON NOT LESS THAN 10 CU. FT.			
HIGH SERVICES, COMPLETE EXCLUDING S-I-T			
(Check as appropriate) [ ] PICK-UP [ ] EXTRA DELIVERY			
HOISTING OR PIANO CARRY			
SERVICING OF APPLIANCES OR OTHER ARTICLES			
LABOR (Number of man-hours)			
OTHER (Specify under "Remarks")			
TOTAL ACCESORIAL SERVICES OTHER THAN S-I-T **TOTAL 8**			

REMARK (Continue on reverse side or on additional sheet bearing B/L No. and name of owner)

RESIDENCE PICK-UP WITH CONTAINERS INDICATED ABOVE FURNISHED AND PACKED BY CARRIER.

1 Explain under "Remarks."
2 Specially designed for mirrors, paintings, glass or marble top, and similar fragile articles.
3 Carton not less than 200 pounds test.
4 Specify under "Remarks" make and model of appliances and/or other articles serviced and described servicing performed.

DD FORM 619   1 OCT 66   REPLACES EDITION OF 1 MAR 63 WHICH IS OBSOLETE.

143a

REMARKS (Continued)

Following to be completed by Consignee ONLY, if goods were placed in Storage-in-Transit and carrier has already submitted original Government bill of lading for payment. Continue on additional sheet, if necessary, bearing BTL Number and name of owner.

1. Consignee's Statement of Delivery (Consignee must not pay any charges on this shipment)

I have this day _____ Received from _____
                DATE OF DELIVERY   NAME OF TRANSPORTATION COMPANY

at _____, the property described in bill of lading, number as indicated
   ACTUAL POINT OF DELIVERY

reverse hereof, in apparent good order and condition except as noted in 2 below.

_____
SIGNATURE OF CONSIGNEE OR AUTHORIZED AGENT

2. Consignee's Report of Loss and/or Damage

Notice is hereby given the carrier to whom this Statement of Accessorial Services Performed is surrendered that the shipment was received in condition shown below and that claim will be made for the value of such loss and/or damage, as indicated.

Explanation regarding loss and/or damage, to be make by consignee, who will state all the facts available concerning the nature or extent of the loss and/or damage and how it occurred.

The within shipment was received with the following loss and/or damage :

Description : _____

_____

_____

_____

_____

_____

_____

_____

_____

_____

Estimated weight of lost articles _____ pounds. Estimated weight of damaged articles _____ pounds.

SIGNATURE OF CONSIGNEE OR AUTHORIZED AGENT	DATE

COLUMBIA EXPORT PACKERS, INC.

2805 COLUMBIA STREET
TORRANCE, CALIFORNIA

NAME **CW2 MERCURE, M.F.**   BAGGAGE   B/L _____

ORIGIN **69TH SIGNAL BOQ ROOM 25**   DATE **22 OCTOBER 1969**

DEST. **MASS**   INVENTORY

EXCEPTION SYMBOLS

BE-BENT	D-BENTED	MO-MOTHEATEN	R-RUBBED	SO-SOILED
BR-BROKEN	F-FADED	PBC-PACKED BY	RU-RUSTED	T-TORN
BU-BURNED	G-GOUGED	CARRIER	SC-SCRATCHED	W-BADLY
CH-CHIPPED	L-LOOSE	PBO-PACKED BY	SH-SHORT	WORN
CU-CONTENTS &	M-MARRED	OWNER		Z-CRACKED
CONDITION UNKNOWN	MI-MILDEW			

LOCATION SYMBOLS

1. ARM	6. LEG
2. BOTTOM	7. REAR
3. CORNER	8. RIGHT
4. FRONT	9. SIDE
5. LEFT	10. TOP
	11. VENEER

NOTE: THE OMISSION OF THESE SYMBOLS INDICATES GOOD CONDITION EXCEPT FOR NORMAL WEAR.

No.	PKG. No.	ARTICLE	CONDITION AT ORIGIN	EXEPT'NS IF ANY AT DESTINATION	No.	PKG. No.	ARTICLE	CONDITION AT ORIGIN	EXEPT'NS IF ANY AT DESTINATION
1		HITACHI REFRIGERATOR			16				
2		FORK AND SPOON			17				
3		MODEL ELECT. TRAINS SHARP			18		SANYO RADIO, DOROKDER PT36 BX		
4		PANASONIC RE 6070, BOOKS, MISC			19				
4		AUTOMATIC TOASTER MODEL TH, GYROMATIC 2×2 SLIDE PROJECTOR			20				
5		2 WOODEN ELEPHANT, ROTATRAY SLIDE TRAY, BRONZE WARE			21				
6		SHARP TELEVISION 12TC 22 SPEAKER, BOARD			22				
7		2 LAMPS, BELL CLOTHES, BOOKS, MISC, SHOES			23				
9		CLOTHES, BOOKS, MISC.			24				
8		CLOTHES, MISC.			25				
11		LAST ITEM			26				
12					27				
13					28				
14					29				
15					30				

Remarks: RESIDENCE PICK-UP WITH CONTAINERS INDICATED ABOVE FURNISHED AND PACKED BY CARRIER.

8/8

"We have checked all the items listed and numbered 1 to —8/8— inclusive and acknowledge that this is a true and complete list of the goods tendered and of the state of the goods received."

	CONTRACTOR, CARRIER OR AUTHORIZED AGENT (DIRVER) (SIGNATURE)	DATE		CONTRACTOR, CARRIER OR AUTHORIZED AGENT (DIRVER) (SIGNATURE)	DATE
AT ORIGIN	T.V. HUNG	22 OCT 69	AT DESTINATION		
	OWNER OR AUTHORIZED AGENT (SIGNATURE) CW2 MERCURE M.F.	DATE		OWNER OR AUTHORIZED AGENT (SIGNATURE)	DATE

144

DEPARTMENT OF THE ARMY

CERTIFICATE OF APPRECIATION

TO

MAURICE F MERCURE
CHIEF WARRANT OFFICER W-2   UNITED STATES ARMY RESERVE

On the occasion of your retirement from active service, I wish to extend to you my personal thanks and the sincere appreciation of the United States Army for the many years of outstanding service which you have given to our country. You have helped to maintain the security of this nation during a most critical period in its history with a devotion to duty and a spirit of sacrifice in keeping with the proud traditions of the military service.

I share your pride in the contributions you have made to the Army and its ability to accomplish its mission. I trust that you will maintain an active interest in the Army and its objectives during your retirement.

You take with you my best wishes and those of your comrades for happiness and success in the years that lie ahead.

30 NOVEMBER 1969

GENERAL, UNITED STATES ARMY
CHIEF OF STAFF

CERTIFICATE OF RETIREMENT
FROM THE ARMED FORCES OF THE UNITED STATES OF AMERICA

TO ALL WHO SHALL SEE THESE PRESENTS, GREETING:
THIS IS TO CERTIFY THAT

MAURICE F MERCURE

CHIEF WARRANT OFFICER W-2   UNITED STATES ARMY RESERVE

HAVING SERVED FAITHFULLY AND HONORABLY,
WAS RETIRED FROM THE

⌐UNITED STATES ARMY

ON THE   FIRST   DAY OF   DECEMBER
ONE THOUSAND NINE HUNDRED AND SIXTY-NINE

WASHINGTON, D. C.

Kenneth G. Nickham
MAJOR GENERAL, UNITED STATES ARMY,
THE ADJUTANT GENERAL

DD FORM 363A. 1 AUG 63